MICK

PETER HART

MICK

The Real

MICHAEL COLLINS

VIKING

VIKING
Published by the Penguin Group
Penguin Group (USA) Inc., 375 Hudson Street,
New York, New York 10014, U.S.A.
Penguin Group (Canada), 90 Eglinton Avenue East, Suite 700,
Toronto, Ontario, Canada M4P 2Y3 (a division of Pearson Penguin Canada Inc.)
Penguin Books Ltd, 80 Strand, London WC2R 0RL, England
Penguin Ireland, 25 St. Stephen's Green, Dublin 2, Ireland (a division of Penguin Books Ltd)
Penguin Books Australia Ltd, 250 Camberwell Road, Camberwell,
Victoria 3124, Australia (a division of Pearson Australia Group Pty Ltd)
Penguin Books India Pvt Ltd, 11 Community Centre, Panchsheel Park, New Delhi—110 017, India
Penguin Group (NZ), Cnr Airborne and Rosedale Roads, Albany, Auckland 1310,
New Zealand (a division of Pearson New Zealand Ltd)
Penguin Books (South Africa) (Pty) Ltd, 24 Sturdee Avenue,
Rosebank, Johannesburg 2196, South Africa

Penguin Books Ltd, Registered Offices:
80 Strand, London WC2R 0RL, England

First American edition
Published in 2006 by Viking Penguin,
a member of Penguin Group (USA) Inc.

1 3 5 7 9 10 8 6 4 2

ISBN 0-670-03147-X

Printed in the United States of America
Set in Adobe Caslon

For Robin

Preface

It would be impossible for me to say how many people I have discussed Michael Collins with – the list would include several Belfast taxi drivers – but I do recall when my serious interest in him began: in my final year at Queen's University (Kingston), when Lucien Karchmar introduced me to Piaras Beaslai's *Michael Collins and the Making of a New Ireland*. My fascination continued – my first published article was about Michael Collins – and since I began teaching I have also been able to talk about him with my students, who indeed often remind me of my own reactions when I was an undergraduate.

Collins is one of those rare historical figures to whom many people feel a personal connection. I felt it myself for a long time. I am still fascinated by him – not because the mystery, mastery and charisma are so attractive anymore but because they are interesting features of a fascinating career in themselves.

The book that follows is not an exercise in debunking or revisionism for its own sake: it can hardly be gainsaid that Collins was a remarkable man with remarkable achievements. Rather, it is an attempt to move beyond fandom and the story of his life as he and his claque wanted it told and it is the first to make full use of the vast resources available to historians of the Irish revolution (perhaps the best documented revolution in world history). My aim is to place examination of Collins's life on a new factual basis and in a more critical perspective. People who amass great power should always attract great scrutiny.

This process of starting from scratch and seeking out sources has once again indebted me to a great number of archivists and librarians: Victor Laing and the Irish Military Archives; Seamus Helferty and the University College Dublin Archives; Niamh O'Sullivan and the Kilmainham Gaol Archives; and the staffs of the Trinity College Archives, Irish National Archives and National Library of Ireland. In London, the National Archives (formerly the Public Record Office), British Library,

Imperial War Museum, Liddell Hart Centre for Military Archives, House of Lords Records Office, Post Office Archives and Guildhall Library all helped me enormously in my searches. Thanks as well to Shelley Diamond at the JPMorganChase Archives. Here at Memorial University of Newfoundland I have the benefit of one of North America's best Irish collections, as well as a terrific interlibrary loan service and an enormously helpful staff.

A great many people have aided me along the way with advice, information and ideas: Paul Bew, Fergus Campbell, Marie Coleman, Vincent Comerford, Enda Delaney, Bruno Derrick, Richard English, David Fitzpatrick, Roy Foster, Brian Hanley, Sean Hanrahan, Frank Bouchier Hayes, Jim Herlihy, Michael Hopkinson, Alvin Jackson, Michael Kennedy, Jane Leonard, Deirdre McMahon, Tim Marshall, Patrick Maume, Eunan O'Halpin, Edward O'Mahony and Julian Putkowski. Carolyn Lambert carried out some very helpful research on newspapers in early 1922. Fearghal McGarry and Robin Whitaker read portions of the manuscript and told me some things I needed to hear. The British Academy and Queen's University both provided much-appreciated research funding.

I must also record my great thanks to members of the Plastic Surgery Unit at the Ulster Hospital, who restored my writing hand just when this project was beginning: Dr Amber Mozzam, Joan D'Arcy, Grainne Murray and Karen Steele.

This book would never have been written without the interest, encouragement, and enormous help of Gill Coleridge, Peter Straus and Andrew Kidd. George Morley and Caroline White were rigorous and excellent editors and Bob Davenport was a superb copy editor. Thanks also to Kate Harvey, Sam Humphreys and Lucy Luck.

Contents

PART TWO

POWER

Introduction: The Story of Michael Collins

FIRST AND ALWAYS in considering the life of Michael Collins there is the Story of Michael Collins, a story nearly fantastic in its details. Collins, the genius behind the Irish Republican Army's guerrilla campaign, the inspiration for Begin and Mao. The superspy who confounded British intelligence. The gun-runner who bought the first tommy guns right off the production line. The financial wizard who bankrolled the Irish revolution from a hundred secret accounts. The head of the clandestine Irish Republican Brotherhood, the Black Hand of republicanism stretching from New York to London. The godfather whose personal squad of hitmen always found his enemies before they found him. The statesman who could make the final deal with Winston Churchill and David Lloyd George – and make it stick. The founder and defender of the new Irish Free State, the Chairman, Commander-in-Chief and Minister of Everything, who – in seven months – assembled a new government, parliament, army and constitution. The man who strove for peace and then won the Civil War, saving Irish democracy from Irish fanaticism. The man of sweeping political vision, decades ahead of its time in its promise of economic, social and cultural progress. And then the final act: the slain hero who died fighting in his home county of Cork – two months away from his thirty-second birthday. Collins the indispensable, the irreplaceable, the Lost Leader unknown before 1917 and mourned by a nation in despair in 1922. The Big Fellow. The Man Who Won The War. What's Good Enough For Mick Is Good Enough For Me.

What takes this astonishing career into the realm of the incredible, of Monte Cristo, the Scarlet Pimpernel and Sherlock Holmes, are the innumerable tales of his miraculous feats, subterfuges and evasions of near-certain capture and death. Everywhere and nowhere, the household name without a face. The trickster who spied on the spies and hunted the hunters. The most wanted man in the British Empire, who nevertheless always kept his appointments, cycling around Dublin with a £10,000 price on his head. The escapes through skylights and hidden doors, the sheer cool bluff that carried him through a hundred roadblocks and round-ups. The buried gold in secret locations. The ring of agents so complete he could read his own file in police headquarters. Able to wipe out the cream of the British secret service in one bloody Sunday morning. And, in a life made doubly romantic, the secret affairs with famous society beauties.

The Story (the legend, the myth) of Michael Collins captivated the world, and continues to fascinate. How many figures in modern history can claim the same swift rise to greatness, command of their nation's destiny and grip on the popular imagination? In the twentieth century, perhaps only Fidel Castro. The Story has been chronicled by a dozen biographers and in numerous fictions and films – most potently in Neil Jordan's Hollywood-style epic. Recent novels have portrayed Collins as child prodigy and returning as an angel from the dead. Michael Collins was in his lifetime and is now more than ever a popular icon, his name and image a free-floating symbol, internationally recognized and randomly accessed in the manner of Guevara and Mao. His birthplace and grave are sites of political and sentimental pilgrimage, and an annual commemoration is held where he died. In January 2000 he was named in an Irish poll as the man of both the century and the millennium.

WITH FEW EXCEPTIONS, this has been the story told in every biography, of which at least thirteen have been published of book length (not including novels, web books and assorted studies and booklets). And this was no posthumous creation. All authors have been following a template laid down by Collins and his followers, largely for political reasons. As early as 1919 his men were talking him up as the real leader of the republican movement to anyone who would listen – including British intelligence agents. From 1920 onward his name and supposed exploits became regular newspaper fodder in the United States and Britain as well as Ireland.

Collins may have had little part in this, apart from telling the stories himself, and was of two minds about it. 'I would not matter very much to anybody were it not for the things the English are saying about me,' he modestly averred in a May 1921 letter. The same month, however, he described himself as 'one man and a few helpers . . . against many many men and a big Empire'. He knew his own reputation, and he was willing to use it – just as his enemies would accuse him of inflating it.

Once he began negotiating an agreement with Britain in 1921, he was a public figure and a politician dependent on party and popular opinion. He and his claque then had to project a popular persona: as a plain man of the people, a patriot above politics, a bit of a visionary, but a practical man rather than an ideologue. Some of his early life had to be hidden or adapted to fit these requirements. Fortunately for the image-makers, he had already been cast as a hero and a mystery man while waging his underground war, although the same or even superior credentials did little to help those who found themselves on the other side of the political divide. Stories of his exploits, written by supporters, appeared in newspapers to bolster this reputation, and would find their way into most biographies to come.

Collins was offered large sums (an advance of $25,000 was one such) to write his memoirs, which he was never able to undertake. He did, however, cooperate on the first book to appear: Hayden Talbot's *Michael Collins' Own Story*, published in 1922. He died before it was completed, and the resulting rushed effort is much more a manifesto for Collins's party than a real biography. The synthesis of the two is probably what Collins intended, and shows how he wanted the story of his life to be used.

Talbot, an American journalist (Collins preferred talking to reporters from the United States), was only one of several writers who sought to cash in on the story in the aftermath of Collins's death. The *World's Pictorial News* began serializing 'the Secret History of Michael Collins' by 'One of his Bodyguard' less than a month after he died, complete with a story of him escaping from Dublin Castle on a white horse. This earned the wrath of Piaras Beaslai (Pierce Beasley), a veteran nationalist writer and activist who had been one of Collins's satellites. Beaslai, like many others, had fallen under his spell and had published articles on him before he died. He now appointed himself guardian of his memory. The *Pictorial News* was banned in Ireland, and Talbot – whose work was also appearing in newspapers – was assailed as equally fictitious and scandalous.

The 'Secret History' was nonsense all right, but Talbot had interviewed Collins, and his book does contain a great deal of personal information not found elsewhere. It must be used with care, but it is particularly valuable for showing how Collins himself wanted his life to be portrayed.

Beaslai, however, intended to write the standard, definitive account. And when *Michael Collins and the Making of a New Ireland* appeared in 1926 (in two great volumes), it was a state-, party- and family-approved biography, for all three interest groups had given their assistance. The author had known Collins, and could talk to relatives and colleagues – with the significant exception of those who had fought against Collins over the Anglo-Irish Treaty – and he had access to many of Collins's own papers (some of which never resurfaced). Thus, his book too is a basic reference for later writers – very much a document of its times, and as politically driven as Talbot's in its way. Indeed, it stands as a sort of origin myth and apologia for the new Irish regime.

Beaslai continued to act as watchdog over Collins's memory for the rest of his life, and had his most notable success when he sued Sean O'Faolain, then an emerging young writer, for plagiarism in 1932 over yet another serialized 'True Story'. It would have been wonderful to have had O'Faolain's version if it had been original, given his powerful depiction of revolutionaries in his fiction but, sadly, Beaslai was right and the series was dropped. The book that did appear in the 1930s was *The Big Fellow* by O'Faolain's friend and fellow Corkman Frank O'Connor. Beaslai approved, although a franker revised edition issued in 1965 angered some old comrades. Based on interviews with former comrades of Collins, it is a masterpiece of efficient and evocative writing – the finest portrait that had appeared so far.

The next biography was not published until 1958: Rex Taylor's mysteriously researched *Michael Collins*. Like Beaslai, Taylor claimed access to previously unseen papers, and his work has been quoted ever since for that reason. Unfortunately, these documents were also never seen again, raising the question of where he got them and leaving scholars in the dark about their reliability.

Taylor's book was superseded in 1971 by Margery Forester's lengthier *Michael Collins: The Lost Leader*, which was joined by Leon O Broin's pocket 'life' in 1980. Both were overtaken by Tim Pat Coogan's *Michael Collins: A Biography* in 1990. This immediately became the standard work (although Coogan's later claim that

'Collins was virtually airbrushed out of history until my biography appeared' is hardly fair either to his predecessors or to the historians who had discussed Collins's role in the revolution). Since then James Mackay has published another account, in 1996, while T. Ryle Dwyer paired Collins with Eamon de Valera in a joint biography, *Big Fellow, Long Fellow*, in 1999.

As this book was being written, in 2003, Chrissy Osborne's *Michael Collins: Himself* appeared, as did David Fitzpatrick's monumental and essential *Harry Boland's Irish Revolution*, dealing with one of Collins's friends and colleagues. Three books have been written on Collins's death: John Feehan's *The Shooting of Michael Collins* (1981); Meda Ryan's *The Day Michael Collins was Shot* (1989) and Patrick Twohig's *The Dark Secret of Bealnablath* (1991). Ryan has also written *Michael Collins and the Women in His Life* (1996). Various biographies have also appeared on the World Wide Web, where Collins is a very popular topic for sites and discussions. The best so far is Edward O'Mahony's substantial *Michael Collins: His Life and Times*, which includes further research on how he died.

BEASLAI TOOK the Story and fleshed it out with factual detail from birth to death. His was an attempt not to understand Collins's life, nor to explain it, but rather to chronicle his revolutionary career. Only 26 of his 900 pages are devoted to the first twenty-six years of his subject's existence: half to his growing up in Cork, the other half to his life in London up to 1916. One page for every year, in other words. Another 20 per cent of the book concerns the events of 1916, 1917 and 1918, before Collins was famous or powerful. About two-thirds of the book deals with the final two and a half years of triumph and crisis. Where Beaslai has led, every other biographer has followed. Frank O'Connor goes furthest by dropping the 'early' life altogether and starting in 1916. This conflation of Michael Collins's life with the Irish revolution of 1916–23 – and particularly with the years of power and violence, 1919–22 – makes the Story a fairy tale. Collins appears on the historical stage in 1916, the preliminary mechanics of birth, parents, school and work a mere prologue to the five years that follow. From an early age he is an ardent nationalist, the natural inheritor of an organic rebel tradition. His character – charismatic, quick-witted, hard-working, decisive – is in service to the cause. His only purpose is patriotism.

His life embodies the revolution, of which he was both creator and creature.

This is the Michael Collins depicted in every biography: a man without personal ambition, who rose through the political ranks on merit alone, who based every decision on what was best for the cause – and thus always chose correctly. His dying young, at thirty-one, made the Story a tragedy as well, and embalmed his reputation as the young saviour who could have made everything so different, who was so much the superior of his power-hungry, jealous, fanatic and egotistical enemies. During his life, and for decades after, republican opponents – recognizing its propaganda value and origins – disputed this depiction. More recently, though, even their dissent has evaporated. The two historically anti-Treaty and anti-Collins parties, Sinn Fein and Fianna Fail, both speak well of him now, and even wish to claim him as their own (to the fury of Fine Gael, the party whose predecessor he helped found). It would be hard to find another historical figure who has been so little criticized in the last fifty years.

So, in essence, biographers have been writing the same book over and over again since 1922. More and more evidence has been uncovered and incorporated into the Story. New arguments have appeared over Collins's actions in particular episodes. The only real variation between these accounts actually reinforces the continuity of the myth. In Beaslai's and O'Connor's books, Michael chastely eschews the company of women – and especially loose women – in favour of manly sports, politics and camaraderie. By 1971 and Margery Forester's ground-breaking *Michael Collins: The Lost Leader* we are introduced to his correspondence with fiancée Kitty Kiernan (later published as *In Great Haste*, edited by Leon O Broin) along with Hazel Lavery and Moya Llewelyn Davies, long the subject of unpublished rumour where Collins was concerned. Forester remained faithful to Michael, however, observing, 'As always . . . Collins, while admiring beauty and temperament, remained blind to the fascination he exercised.'

It took Tim Pat Coogan in 1990 to deal frankly with Collins's romantic and sex life – and to assert believably that he did have one. He discovered an early and serious girlfriend from London days, and, with reasonable scepticism, put together evidence for what may have been affairs with several admirers (while pooh-poohing any suggestions of homosexuality or bisexuality). Coogan also included the copious evidence of Collins's smoking, drinking and swearing. He has set a new standard for biographical frankness.

But how much of a change is this really? One defining difference between the 1920s and '30s and the 1990s is what constitutes appropriate and attractive behaviour by a male hero. Collins is always seen as an archetypically Irish man, as well as charismatic and admirable to men and women, so he has gone from a virginal disregard for women to a 007esque seizing of sexual opportunities. His previously touted Catholic piety is now downplayed, while his swearing and pubbing have become a sign of a forceful and lovable personality. Whatever the definition of politically preferable Irish manliness is, there you will usually find Michael Collins.

The movies and novelizations follow this line as well, most influentially in Neil Jordan's action-movie version, *Michael Collins* (1996), featuring a superb characterization by Liam Neeson (Brendan Gleeson's in Jonathan Lewis's *The Treaty* (1991) is equally good). Jordan follows O'Connor in beginning the story in 1916. Roddy Doyle's *A Star Called Henry* (1999) provides the only really interesting fictional portrayal of the man. Louise Gherasim's theme in *Born to be Great: The Boy Michael Collins* (2001) is obvious from her title, while Dermot McEvoy's *Terrible Angel* (2002) has Collins returning to earth (or more specifically New York) as an angel. In Gerard Whelan's entertaining children's book *A Winter of Spies* (1998), his heroes assist Collins in his war against British intelligence.

My AIM IS not to debunk the Story as such, or to correct previous biographers. Instead, I would like to start from scratch and from a new, forensic, perspective. Most biographers, from Beaslai on, have done a great deal of original research with fascinating results, often locating new documents and witnesses. Unfortunately, inadequate or non-existent source notes, compounded by the fact that much of this material has been, and remains, in private hands, makes it impossible for others to review their work. Not infrequently, documents used by one writer have disappeared, so we have only their descriptions or excerpts to go on. The tendency has been for successive researchers to accept and quote all these without question, creating a creaky edifice of unsubstantiated 'fact'.

Just to be clear, I am not suggesting that any of these documents have been fabricated, but their use does raise questions. What else was written that we can't see? How does the document fit into the rest of the series or collection? Such facts inevitably alter meaning.

For this reason I have decided, with a very few exceptions, to use only publicly available documents. Anyone can check my work, and mine will be the first book to really establish a base from which future historians can work. Nor does this require losing anything in the way of detail or colour – quite the opposite. Archives and newspapers contain a vast, mostly untapped, store of information on Collins and the Irish revolution. It may be the best-documented revolution in the modern world, and I have been researching it since 1986. Where previous writers have seen the revolution through Collins, I approach him through the revolution.

I have written extensively about Cork, his home county; the London Irish, among whom he lived and worked for ten years; and the movements, organizations, communities and struggles he joined and helped to shape. This means I can place Collins in his appropriate contexts. It also means I have found things that biographers wouldn't, because they were located in collections where they didn't look. To give just one example, there are a lot of small newspaper stories one can find only by reading national and local newspapers for the whole of 1916–23. I have been able to reconstruct, for the first time, Collins's life in London between the ages of fifteen and twenty-six, including his civil-service career, his business career, his athletic endeavours, and his social and political apprenticeship. I can, I believe, give a proper account at last of his move to Dublin before the Easter uprising in 1916 and of his time in prison. I devote a chapter to his crucial tenure as secretary to the National Aid and Volunteer Dependants Fund – previously untouched by biographers – and I have put together the first full description of his burgeoning career in Sinn Fein, the paramilitary Irish Volunteers and the IRB in 1917–18.

My work is analytical and systematic rather than heroic. Forget the usual assumptions that Collins was a uniquely gifted phenomenon or a selfless patriot driven by ideals alone. These depictions, while not necessarily or wholly false, are clearly the product of propaganda and politicking. I have started from the premiss that the mature Michael Collins was a politician who sought and acquired power with unprecedented and unequalled success. The central questions of his life then become: how did he acquire it and how did he use it?

These lead us backwards into his earlier life to try to find out the sources of his ambition and drives and the background to his rise to power.

If we want to understand Collins, we must seek out and establish the patterns that structured his life. How did he organize his work? How did he solve problems? How did he win friends and allies – or make enemies? What sort of leader was he? How did he make choices and decisions? Many of these patterns can be found in London and Dublin before the Easter Rising, and reappear throughout the subsequent years right up until his death.

What I hope readers find here is not the man of legend but a dynamic and fascinating man none the less: the most gifted, ruthless and powerful Irish politician of the twentieth century.

PART ONE

RISE

1: Family

He is a young man of fair complexion, clean shaven, strong jaws and features ... He belongs to a family [of] brainy people who are disloyal and of advanced Sinn Fein sympathies. They are of the farming class.

(Police report on Michael Collins, 1916)

BEFORE HE WAS anything else, he was a Collins. Or, more properly, he was the product of the Collins and O'Brien families: born on 16 October 1890 to Michael (Mike) Collins and Marianne (or Mary Anne) O'Brien, on the farm that Michael senior had inherited from his father in the townland of Woodfield (Paulveug in Irish, he would later insist), West Cork. Michael junior's birth was recalled by sister Mary:

My mother carried the heaviest burden and at this time suffered greatly from pain in a broken ankle which I suppose was never properly set. I remember the night before Michael was born – I was then 9 – I held the strainer while she poured the milk, fresh from the cow, from very heavy pails into the pans for setting the cream. She moaned occasionally and when I asked her was she sick she said she had a toothache and would go to bed when the cakes were made for to-morrow. I was greatly troubled but said nothing as in those days children were to be seen and not heard. The next day there was the miracle of the baby. No doctor, no trained nurse and mother and baby well and comfortable!

Michael (also sometimes called Mike) was the third son and youngest of eight children. Beyond his own household lay a vast web of uncles, aunts and cousins, a long-tailed family even by the impressive standards of West Cork. His uncle Paddy – his father's older brother Patrick – lived at Woodfield, and several cousins worked on the farm. His pursuers in police intelligence would later try to chart his family tree of 'relations and supporters', but managed to record only a fraction of the O'Briens, O'Driscolls, O'Sullivans, Hurleys and McCarthys involved. They were never big people, but they got along – in both senses of the word – pretty well by all accounts. As the *Freeman's Journal* reported:

> His uncles and grand-uncles, many of whom still survive, were remarkable for what was almost a genius for getting along well with everybody. A resident of the district asserts as a positive fact that he never knew one of the Collins or O'Brien family to be either plaintiff or defendant in a law court.

High praise indeed in fractious and litigious West Cork.

It was the Collins lineage that Michael identified with, at least publicly, claiming that 'on my father's side there are records of ancestors [the O'Coileain] back 450 years, when they were chieftains of the tribes of Munster.' His father, who was born in 1815, would no doubt have heard such stories from relatives who had learned them in the eighteenth century and in the original Irish. Granny O'Brien, Marianne's mother, was a frequent visitor in the kitchen as well, and both she and her daughter spoke Irish, as was still common in the area (although only a smattering of elders remained who could not speak English). Mike spoke it too, but the children did not (their parents used Irish when they didn't want them to understand what they were saying). Certainly old (Gaelic) Ireland – shattered and almost gone by the last decade of the nineteenth century – nurtured many memories of dispossession and colonization, although the Victorian-era Collinses harboured no ancient claim to a usurped house or estate.

What did this supposed legacy mean for Michael Collins? Probably almost nothing, for he never referred to it in letters, talk or speeches. The statement quoted above is from an interview with Hayden Talbot, an American journalist, in 1922, and Collins's mention of his ancestors at this point, in the run-up to an election, sounds calculatedly political, part of his self-conscious self-presentation as one of the plain people of Ireland. Certainly just about anyone with an aboriginal Irish name could claim an equal heritage – and often did – not to mention the fact that such family histories were and are always highly selective. 'Collins' was a common name in West Cork (there were three other Collins families in Woodfield alone) and in many other parts of Ireland, where it doubtless had English roots as well. Indeed, like a great many other young rebels-to-be growing up at the same time in West Cork, Michael Collins may well have had English ancestors, even soldiers and colonists, who had assimilated over the years. Some, like the prominent and proud Hales family of Knocknacurra, even celebrated their 'Cromwellian' bloodline.

That his destiny was in his blood has nevertheless become a staple of the Story. Mike senior had a heart attack in December 1896 (at the age of eighty-one), and nearly died, although he lingered until the following March, unable to leave the house. On the night of his death, Michael's sister Helena remembered:

> Mama called us all at about 10 p.m. and we all got round the bed ... then Papa, who was quite conscious, spoke. He said, 'Mind that child [Michael junior), he'll be a great man yet, and will do great things for Ireland. Nellie (that's me, his pet name for me) will be a nun' and I never forgot it ... All else I can think of is that he had a lovely quiet holy death.

Helena, later Sister (of Mercy) Mary Celestine, wrote a letter to her brothers and sisters on her brother Michael's death reminding them that 'Oh! We have much to be grateful for, our own "Baby" has fulfilled papa's prophecy.' Her sister Mary recalled Uncle Paddy – apparently a fellow prophet – saying that Michael 'will be a great and mighty man when we are all forgotten'.

Mary and another sister, Hannie, were once looking after Michael – aged about three at the time – in the loft of the milkhouse where they both slept, when he fell through the trapdoor down the ladder to the floor below. 'Thank God he was quite happy at the drop but they got a great fright', according to Helena, 'and we talked about it for some time.' Mary: 'Our feelings may be imagined and when we got through the kitchen without being given away we took it as another proof of Michael's extra special qualities.' This story has acquired symbolic heft in recent years, and has even worked its way into Seamus Heaney's poetry. In 'The Loose Box', Michael Collins

Was to enter the hidden jaws of that hay crevasse
And get to his feet again and come unscathed . . .

That drop through the flower-floor lets him find his feet
In an underworld of understanding

Heaney here is knowing and ambiguous as usual – it's not exactly an endorsement of Collins's supernatural origins. And doesn't every babysitter or older sister have a story like this. And don't most parents think their children are special?

Even if Collins didn't know of the prophecy (there is no record of his having mentioned it, even in his doom-laden last months), the sense of being special may well have fortified his confidence and ambition – although a linear sense of mission, let alone actual success, would not be evident for many years. And if family is destiny, he was his mother's son, not his father's, as it was her prosaic plans for him that held sway.

He never really knew his father, of course, but he did tell Hayden Talbot the following story:

I was out in the fields with him one day, watching him at work – a rare privilege in my kid's eyes [we can assume some Americanization of the language here]. He was on top of a wall of bog stones, and I was on the turf below him. One of the stones, a good sized one, was dislodged under his feet and came rolling down straight at me. There was plenty of time for me to dodge it, but it never occurred to me to move. 'Twas my father's foot had done the business. Surely the stone could do me no harm. To this day I carry the mark on my instep where it crushed my foot.

The story ends with Papa declaring him a 'true Collins'. But reader beware: Collins often tinkered with his life story.

Many would later notice an over-trusting streak in him, however, as he was wont to befriend people who turned out to be cranks or spies, and sometimes naively took professed motives at face value. Perhaps this was learned from his trusting, straightforward family. In any case, one consequence of losing a father so young was that Collins's path to adulthood had many father figures to guide the way, from teachers to older friends and comrades in London and Dublin. Whether he looked for them or attracted them, they were instrumental in launching and guiding his career as a revolutionary.

Mike senior was a farmer with a sideline in carpentry or building (Michael described him as a carpenter in an early civil service application). A survivor of the Great Famine of the 1840s, which hit West Cork very hard ('Remember Skibbereen!' – a famine-stricken town not far from Woodfield – became a popular nationalist slogan), he benefited from the relative prosperity that followed it as agricultural prices rose faster than rents and credit became plentiful. This was punctuated in the late 1870s and '80s by bad weather, economic depression and, not least, political upheaval.

MICHAEL'S BIRTH in October 1890 coincided with one of the most hopeful periods in the history of Irish nationalist politics. The year before, Charles Stewart Parnell, the enigmatic and masterful chief of the Irish nationalist party in the House of Commons, had been cleared of the false charge of consorting with republican assassins, brought against him by Conservative enemies, and he was now fixed in a close alliance with William Gladstone, the Grand Old Man of the Liberal Party, who looked increasingly likely to be the next prime minister. Gladstone and the Liberals were committed to Irish self-government – Home Rule – so in a matter of a few years Parnell might be not only the 'uncrowned king of Ireland' but its actual leader at the head of a nationalist majority in the restored Irish parliament.

But November 1890 extinguished that particular dream. In that month, Captain William O'Shea won his case for divorce from his wife, Katherine, and Parnell was exposed as her lover. Gladstone severed his relationship with Parnell, and within weeks the party had divided, most of its MPs had seceded from Parnell's leadership, and he was being denounced by Catholic bishops. Over the next year the nationalist movement split into several warring parts, and the Chief himself died after growing fatally ill on the campaign trail.

This was the end to a remarkable decade in Irish politics. The 1880s had seen the creation of a great popular insurgency. It had begun in 1879 with the Land League, which was outlawed but was reborn in 1882 as the National League, and thrived on a vast membership (and American money) until it was laid low by the Parnell split. The leagues drew in priests, farmers, shopkeepers, guilds and trade unions, ambitious lawyers and journalists, and idealistic young men of all stripes in a unifying whirl of liberation and confrontation: the first true people's movements for democracy the world had seen.

The leaguers' enemies were the landlords who controlled Ireland's farmland, and the British government, which tried to suppress the leagues. Their goals were farmers' rights, the transfer of land from the few owners to the many occupiers, and the assertion of political rights against all forms of arbitrary and corrupt government (Liberal and Conservative): juryless courts, internment without trial, censorship and police brutality, all of which were employed against them. Their methods were often direct: systematic boycotts, blacklists, rent strikes, protest meetings, legal challenges, and continuous and energetic publicity. Violence was common, although only a few fringe groups took up murder and assassination.

The same democratization of electoral politics that gave the Irish Party its parliamentary power and deprived the landlord class of its influence over its tenants also created a mirror image in the northern province of Ulster: a rival mass unionist party. Here, Protestants – members of the Church of Ireland, Presbyterians and Methodists – were in a majority. Just as Parnell allied himself with Gladstone and the Liberal Party, so too did Protestant unionist MPs and peers align themselves with the Conservative Party (renamed the Conservative and Unionist Party after the first Home Rule bill was defeated in 1886). Irish unionism encompassed both aristocrats and shipyard labourers in collective anti-nationalism and opposition to Home Rule. Neither Parnell nor subsequent nationalist leaders took this other native movement seriously, seeing it as reflecting landlord-led class war in another guise, British intrigue or mere bigotry. This would prove to be a grave misunderstanding on their part.

The government of Ireland was largely in the hands of a local administration headquartered in, and symbolized by, Dublin Castle. This was headed by a Lord Lieutenant or viceroy, but usually run by a Chief Secretary – in effect, the British minister for Ireland. These men, and an under-secretary to head the bureaucracy, ran the police forces – the Royal Irish Constabulary and the Dublin Metropolitan Police – and had considerable power over the judicial system as well as over education and many other services. What made the Castle a symbol of evil in nationalist eyes was its other perceived role as the upholder of Ascendancy – Protestant and upper-class privilege. And perception was indeed reality. Government positions of all kinds were often reserved for the Liberal or unionist establishment, and much of local government was the same. The viceregal court was the centre of aristocratic, landed and official Irish society.

The Parnellite response was an endless stream of vitriol. Dublin Castle was corrupt, unrepresentative, irresponsible and inefficient (few historians would now disagree). Its denizens were bigots, tyrants, parasites, and sometimes homosexual and Masonic conspirators. Catholics who took jobs there or participated in Castle social life were 'Castle Catholics' – turncoats and Uncle Toms. Parnellite politicians would have no truck with the system, refused to take any office, and certainly wouldn't set foot in the place.

Whatever 'Parnellism' was – and the phenomenon was investigated by a parliamentary commission of inquiry – it was embodied by Parnell himself. He did not invent or build the movement – that was the job of the brilliant lieutenants who led the troops into battle. But he was its strategist, and his sense of timing and target was little short of Napoleonic. Most importantly, he was able to keep his people together in the early 1880s when their unity was threatened by the twin allures of revolution and acceptance of inadequate compromise. This meant walking a most careful line. He might withdraw his party from Westminster in 1880 as a tactical protest, but he would not stay away to start a rebellion. Rent might be withheld on disputed estates, but it should be paid to avoid ultimate eviction. Transgressors should be boycotted, but not shot. When a rent strike was finally called, in 1881, it was to save the Land League, not to overthrow landlords.

One key to Parnell's personal ascendancy was his fusion of the languages of Fenianism and constitutional home rule. Fenians – members of the secret, revolutionary Irish Republican Brotherhood – had put aside their dream of a conspiratorial *coup d'état* after a failed uprising in 1867, but maintained their long-term goal of an Irish republic. In the meantime, many had drifted into politics, where their energy and intelligence were invaluable. The Land War gave them a new cause, and the Land League gave them a vehicle to put their radicalism into direct action.

Home Rule had existed as a slogan and a modest programme since the early 1870s, but Parnell gave the idea of devolution a rhetorical blood transfusion when he demanded it as a right, not a privilege or a solution to a problem, and when he declared that the government would never simply grant it: it would have to be taken. Nor was Parliament itself a sacred institution. Nationalists should use it to get what they wanted, and if they couldn't get it there they would have to think of another way. Just as with the farmers' demands for justice, if remedial legislation wasn't forthcoming, leaguers would go out and mete out their own remedies. Fenians who wound up in jail or on a gallows were not terrorists or murderers: they were heroes who fought for a just cause. The 'young men' (code for republicans) had the right idea really, but first the parliamentary route had to be tried.

In his final desperate campaign to retain power, Parnellism was redefined by friends as the party of youth and principle and by foes as the voice of violence and extremism. Parnell died in October 1891, but the split continued for another decade and Parnellites were known as such for their 'advanced' (i.e. independent or separatist) attitude. These furious battles did much to define the political thinking of Michael Collins's generation.

THE STORY often mentions Fenian relatives and ancestors' confrontations with landlords – the standard rebel heritage of IRA autobiography. Here again the far more numerous kin who served in the army, navy (popular in West Cork), police or civil service, or who were party followers, get conveniently filtered out in the search for authenticity. Mike Collins was a much more interesting man than that. We don't know what he thought of the Land League, Home Rule or the Parnellite split, but he refused to sing rebel songs, and his one memorable encounter in the land wars was to be beaten up for breaking a boycott by lending a winnowing machine to a Protestant clergyman (presumably Church of Ireland) accused of 'grabbing' evicted land – after having been warned not to. He took the *Weekly Freeman's Journal*, the most conservative, Catholic and anti-Parnellite of popular newspapers. This could be the profile of a reactionary profiteer, but the truth would seem to be that he disliked radical politics and possessed considerable moral courage and independence of mind.

West Cork was itself a former frontier of English settlement and an occasional war zone scarred by conquistador butchery and rapparee resistance until the early 1700s. These were religious wars as well as battles for territory and survival, and their legacy remained well into the twentieth century. The nearby town of Bandon was often known as 'Orange Bandon', where 'even the pigs are Protestant'. In Mike senior's parents' memory, Catholics had been discouraged from settling within the town walls, and older Protestant residents had not so long ago still referred to themselves as a colony.

Inevitably, sectarianism persisted within all communities, and was institutionalized in many forms, in schooling, sports, marriage and politics. On the other hand, West Cork – and the county as a whole – was also receptive to William O'Brien's dissident message of 'conciliation and consent', and backed his cross-community All for Ireland League (AFIL) after 1909. O'Brien, a brilliant nationalist journalist and maverick politician, founded the latter-day land league, the United Irish League (UIL), in 1898, only to see it turned into a tool of the reunited Irish Party after 1900. This political machine swept up Catholic voters and produced a steady seventy-odd seats for its leader, John Redmond, by sticking fairly closely to the old Parnellite formula of waging at least rhetorical war on landlordism and the Castle system. O'Brien was never comfortable with this approach, as his vision of a new Ireland in the twentieth century was one of class and religious accommodation. His short-lived new party included Protestant landlords as well as Catholic farmers and land labourers.

Oddly, the AFIL was only really successful in Cork city and county, where O'Brien himself had been born and was now based. This had something to do with his appeal to Cork pride. The episode that prompted O'Brien's final break with the party was the assault on his supporters at the 1909 UIL convention when the authorities supposedly ordered that no one with a Cork accent would be allowed to speak. It was thus in a spirit of provincial defiance that O'Brien's new movement was born. He even called his new newspaper the *Cork Accent* (although the name was soon changed to the *Cork Free Press*).

Corkness even beyond the local accents was a highly identifiable quality, if not easily definable. It usually suggested some combination of ambition, slyness, self-belief and quickness to take offence at slights. Athens was said to be the Cork of Greece; the Skibbereen *Eagle* had warned the Tsar of Russia that it had its eye on him, and so on. West Cork was its own region yet again, but Collins was a Corkman and was often seen as being abundantly endowed with Corkness (although once he became a national figure this would be transmuted into Irishness). People often remarked on his accent, although he was apparently able to play it up or down as it suited him. Even a secret report written for the British cabinet in 1921 described him as 'a Cork man, therefore impetuous and rather excitable'. He did surround himself with fellow Corkmen as his career progressed, all part of an extraordinary wave of Corkmen on the make in the revolutionary movement after 1916.

Some of the Collinses and many other future republicans were O'Brienites. Many of the Collinses' neighbours in Woodfield were Church of Ireland (by far the largest Protestant denomination), with centuries-old names of their own: the Beamishes, Perrotts, Deanes, Batemans and Knowleses. Neighbourliness and friendship often trumped religion or politics within this and other townlands, as evidenced by Mike senior's helping out the local vicar. Some Protestant farmers had joined with their Catholic and nationalist fellows in fighting for lower rents and the right to buy their farms from their landlords. A few were active nationalists. The great majority were not 'active' in politics at all, but were mainly interested in getting along and getting ahead. Having neighbours who are ethnically different has never predisposed anyone to tolerance, but under his father's influence – perhaps as refracted through his sisters – Collins was absolutely devoid of sectarian prejudice.

The townland of Woodfield, in the parish of Kilkerranmore, had a population of 139 when Michael was born – down by one over the previous ten years, but about to fall quickly: only 103 people remained in 1901. There were 22 homes and families, down from 32 in the early 1850s. By 1911, three of these homes would be abandoned. This record of decline was typical of the district, West Cork, and of rural Ireland in general in these years. Seven of the eight Collins children would join the exodus, pushed out by the sheer absence of any reasonable employment on the small family farms that dominated the agricultural economy.

The family was sometimes described in potted biographies as 'poor', but poverty is relative. Woodfield was indeed a rather poor townland, but the Collinses had more – and more valuable – land than many of their neighbours. In fact there were two family farms –

Mike senior's and his brother Patrick's, both rented from Lord Carbery's estate. The two became one in 1886, when Paddy moved in with Mike and Marianne, presumably having given up the prospect of a wife and family. The result totalled 136 acres and was valued at £70, making the Collins property among the most valuable in the whole of Clonakilty district. As was typical, this was made up of a patchwork of different fields – all known by name – interspersed with their neighbours'. After his death in 1897, Mike's property was transferred to Marianne. Patrick's name disappeared from the records in 1901, suggesting he died not long after.

For the remainder of Marianne's life she controlled it all, although her will claimed only 75 acres of it (presumably not including Pat's share). In 1908, however, shortly after she died, her eldest son, Johnny, sold Mike's original holding to one Jerome Collins, a farmer with a young family, who may or may not have been a distant relative. In 1909 Johnny became the official occupier of the remaining property – along with Michael junior, interestingly enough. Was this an attempt to lure Michael back home from London or just a brotherly gesture? Either way, it didn't last long. Johnny, along with most of his neighbours, purchased his land in 1911 through a popular government scheme to transfer land from the landlords to the farmers. He was now sole owner.

By the turn of the century the farm was thriving and displayed many improvements. A horse or two and a trap to drive to town or church. A dozen or so cows, sheep and other assorted livestock. Two stables, a barn, a cow house and a calf house, a dairy, a piggery and a chicken shed, and proper machinery. There were no resident servants for the farm or the house while Michael was there, but by 1911 Johnny's own family and income had grown enough to employ both a domestic and a farm servant – one of the marks of the strong farmer.

A new house came last, as was often the case on farms. Had Mike promised one to Marianne before they married? The original house, where all their children were born, was 'very primitive' and small – it didn't even hold the entire family. Once Mike died, however, Marianne moved swiftly to replace it. She planned the new house, and got her brother, James O'Brien, to build it next to the old one with stone quarried from Collins land. When it was finished, in 1900, Michael had his own room.

Mike senior's marriage (in 1875) at the age of sixty-two to a woman of twenty-two may have reflected the same financial prudence that delayed building her a proper house, but it was but an extreme example of a general trend in Irish rural society towards late inheritance and marriage based on secured property rights. The same system usually dictated the passing of land to the first-born son upon retirement of the father. This was what made eldest brother Johnny the next – and last – Collins of Woodfield.

Equally typical were the eight children who followed the marriage in quick time: Margaret, John (Johnny to family and friends, later Sean according to revolutionary fashion), Johanna (Hannie), Mary, Helena (Lena, as she was affectionately known to her siblings – although Ellen on her birth certificate), Patrick, Katie and finally Michael – three years younger than Katie, thirteen younger than Margaret. The siblings scattered in the way of most farming families. Margaret, a teacher, married P. J. O'Driscoll and moved to Clonakilty, where they operated a short-lived newspaper, the *West Cork People*. Hannie passed the civil-service exams and went to London to work in the Post Office Savings Bank. Mary went to Edinburgh to finish school, and soon after married an excise officer in Cork city named Pat Powell. Helena took civil-service classes for a while but, mindful of her father's wish, eventually joined the Foreign Missions as a nun. She may possibly have been dreaming of Africa or Asia, but she ended up in a convent in Hull. Katie became Mrs Joe Sheridan and moved to Bohola, Co. Mayo. Pat went to Chicago and joined the police.

By local standards the Collinses were a success story – the farm safely handed on, the daughters educated and employed or respectably married off, one son in America, and one daughter in a convent. Marianne, who took over the running of the farm, proved an able manager of family and fortune. She was a remarkable woman who had had to take charge of her own family at an early age when her father was killed and her mother severely injured in an accident. She succumbed to a terrible cancer in March 1907, after seeing her last child off into the world, Michael having left for London the year before. He kept her mortuary card with him constantly – he carried it into the Easter Rising in 1916, and kept it in his office until it was found in a police raid together with family letters.

*

MICHAEL WAS KNOWN as 'Baby' to his sisters, and 'to say that we loved this baby would be an understatement – we simply adored him.' He grew up in a warm, supportive and stimulating household where accomplishment and expression were encouraged and where he was allowed to build confidence in his own judgement and abilities. Collins stayed firmly within the family circle for most of his life, following a circuit from his mother's home to Margaret's in Clonakilty while attending classes, on to Hannie's in London, and then to his O'Donovan aunt's in Dublin in 1915–16 before finally striking out on his own just before the 1916 Rising. Holidays were spent with relatives whenever possible. When he contemplated permanent emigration, it was to join Pat in Chicago.

Hannie was not the only relative in London. Jack (Sean) Hurley, whose sister Katty had married Johnny Collins, was familiar from his time in Clonakilty, and became a close friend. Three years older than Collins, he seems to have acted as a substitute older brother. Nancy O'Brien was an older cousin from his mother's side of the family who shared some of the same acquaintances. She moved to Dublin ahead of Collins, and saw him again there. After Katty died in early 1921, leaving young children behind, Nancy married Johnny and became mistress of Woodfield House in 1922.

But it was Hannie whom Michael was closest to. After Marianne died, Hannie – in Mary's words – became 'Michael's mother, sister and friend'. This was widely recognized by his friends, who rated her highly. A Mrs Hopkins – who later may have lived with her – knew them as 'the closest of chums'. John McCaffrey, a co-worker in London,

> was convinced that Michael Collins owed his success in London to the influence and cheerful companionship of his sister, Hannah [sic] ... This exceptionally clever girl passed the open competitive examination for lady clerkships in the British Civil Service and she was appointed to the permanent staff of the Post Office Savings Bank on 19th April 1899. This was a great achievement for an Irish girl in her teens ... his devoted sister kept him from feeling homesick.

According to Hannie, 'we were much more like mentally than most brothers and sisters, as we thought alike on many subjects [not politics though]. As a child he used to consult me about the things he did not know – and it pleases me to think that he never lost the idea that I knew something on most subjects.' They shared a love of reading and theatre, and for Collins's first four years in London they not only lived together but worked in the same building.

Even after leaving London, he returned as often as possible to visit, and proudly introduced Hannie to all his new acquaintances. He still sought her approval, and kept her informed about potential wives. Soon after moving out of their London home, Collins himself told an acquaintance that Hannie was 'the only one of the family who was any good'.

When Helena left to start her religious life in 1901 she was sent to a Sisters of Mercy convent in east Yorkshire. She joined the movement of Irish girls to religious lives in Britain at high tide, as one of hundreds going to jobs as teachers, nurses or social workers in industrial cities. Irish girls made up the majority of recruits to the burgeoning Catholic welfare system. Most came from farming families, and a disproportionate number of them were Corkwomen. It was a hard-working life.

Helena never saw Michael again. She could remember only 'Baby' Michael. It may be guessed that he resented her disappearance – although he could have made arrangements to visit her, he never did. In all his time in London they had no contact, and he didn't start writing to her until 1918, at Mary's request. 'Do not blame me for not writing – even to people who are not nuns I am a very bad correspondent [a white lie] – consequently I am very unwilling to submit my productions to the holy critics.' After being promoted to the rank of commandant in the Irish Volunteers, he sent her a photograph of himself in his new uniform. He wrote again a year later at much greater length, and with the same apologies about not writing earlier and the same awkwardness over her vocation. 'You know I do not often address nuns and even when I do I fear I am not as reverent as I should be.' He talked enthusiastically about the progress of the movement, hinting at his own role in making history. She was delighted to hear from him and thereafter wrote to him often, although this failed to increase the frequency of his replies. In 1920 Art O'Brien wrote from London to pass on a message from her:

My brother Miceal [the Gaelic spelling, pronounced Mee-haul] writes me that he called on some nuns at South Bank near

Middlesboro' and spoke to Sister Mary Celestine there who to his great surprise told him that she was your sister. He tells me she was most anxious about you and would like to hear a word from you occasionally.

Michael's last letter to her, in March 1921, referred to his now famous name and mentioned some of the more lurid stories making the papers. As is clear from his other letters, he wanted his sister to be proud of him – he had made it! – perhaps one reason he started writing at this late date. In 1922 he wrote to his new fiancée, Kitty Kiernan, 'People tell me she's rather nice. A convent is a queer place for one of my family.'

Little is now known of Katie, and Collins seems to have known not much more. When she visited him while he was in jail in April 1918, according to Collins's diary, she

> did not recognise me. It strikes me that I cannot have changed as much as all that. Poor thing somewhat upset. Extremely nice and kind. In the course of our interview I discover that the late P. J. Sheridan [a nationalist revolutionary] was an uncle of her husband. Her husband's father is still alive and as he has all the details . . . I hope to spend some interesting days with him yet . . . She promises to send her husband along some day during the coming week.

Katie later wrote to say his brother had died, and that's the last we hear of either of them.

Patrick, whose fond memories included walking to Bandon with young 'Mike', went to Chicago early in the new century and appears to have had little contact with Michael or the family thereafter, never returning home. His career in the police presumably started soon after arriving, and he was a sergeant by 1922. He did encourage Michael to join him in late 1915 with the idea that he could find work there. Michael came close to going, but in the end he went to Dublin and met another destiny.

When Collins's friend Harry Boland was touring the United States in 1920 he heard about Patrick and told Michael, who replied, 'I am sorry you did not meet my brother in Chicago. His address is not known to me as I have not been corresponding with him since a few months after the outbreak of war [in 1914]. Please do not go to any trouble.' This was a rather frosty and misleading response. He *had* been in touch since then, and surely could have got the address from one of his sisters. It seems downright mean of Collins therefore to tell Hayden Talbot in 1922, 'As for my brother Patrick, all I know about him – and this information reached me indirectly – is that he is a member of the police-force in Chicago. Whether he is a policeman or not I have no idea. In all the years since he went to America he has never let us hear from him.'

He may have been thinking of his reputation again. He had been publicly accused of leaving London merely to avoid being conscripted into the British army, so the fact that he had contemplated going to the United States instead would have told against him. In any case Patrick was interviewed by a *New York Times* reporter after his brother died and said he had just received a letter from Michael saying that if he was killed his brother should know that he had died fighting for Ireland.

Mary, it seems, was often the glue holding the family together after Marianne died. She kept in touch with Pat, Helena and the rest even when Michael didn't, and kept him and Hannie abreast of the latest news. Michael visited her at her home in Sunday's Well, Cork city (she later moved to Mount Nebo, Blarney Road), whenever he went back to Ireland, and they often then went home to Woodfield together. He and Jack Hurley had promised to come down on the train on Holy Thursday in 1916, but the Rising intervened, and it was she who went up to Dublin to see if he was still alive. He gave her address on his discharge papers after being released from prison in December of the same year, and it became a frequent stopover on his political travels.

After 1919 Collins mostly confined himself to Dublin, and all the news Mary got 'was from the papers and a line from a messenger . . . just to let me know he was carrying on' (once again, a bit stiff considering the outpouring of chatty letters to colleagues in the movement). She was a member of Cumann na mBan, the republican women's militia turned women's auxiliary, and her house was raided by the police. Her husband died as things were getting bad, leaving her with nine children. Always helpful, Pat wrote offering to bring her and the children to safety in Chicago, but 'I simply could not bear the idea of leaving Ireland just then or at any time and I think he misunderstood me for he never after helped me in any way.'

Perhaps it was this incident which also caused a rift between Pat and Mike, leading to the later cold shoulder.

Despite her large and young family, Mary was most active in support of her brother in 1922, when he was campaigning for the Treaty, and later in the Civil War that erupted between supporters and opponents of the compromise with Britain. She had opened one of Collins's secret bank accounts under the name 'Bridget Brown', to be used by Free State supporters when Cork was under republican control. When £8,000 worth of republican funds (extracted from customs duties or robbed from banks) was recaptured from the anti-Treaty IRA it was not returned but rather was lodged in the 'Brown' account, presumably to finance off-the-books military operations. Republicans believed Mary ran a spy ring, and later tried to burn her house down in March 1923.

Johnny was seen regularly by Collins on visits home, and they corresponded often. When Collins's correspondence files were captured in 1921, among them was an archive of letters to and from Woodfield concerning political events and – as intelligence officers described it – 'Agricultural Labour and Commercial Interests'. Still, they don't seem to have been as close as he was to some of his sisters. The brothers apparently didn't share the same winning personality: Johnny's nickname was 'Shafter', and he was after all the eldest son and, in traditional terms, the head of the family, so a certain amount of friction would have been natural. With typical (and annoying) big-brotherly authority, Johnny said of their relationship, 'I was proud of Michael and I knew he was a leader although I was more than twelve years older than he was. Yet, I remember, he would do anything I asked him to do.' That kind of thing probably didn't go over so well once Michael had embarked on his political career.

Collins was deeply fond of his eight nieces and nephews in Woodfield, however – as he was of Mary's children in the city – and worried about them during the troubles. Michael Lynch, a friend in Dublin, tells the following story:

> Peggy [Lynch's daughter, born in 1919] was a child who, for the first months of her life, never stopped crying. Big Mick would walk in, the baby squealing her head off, and say, 'Give me that baby!' He would take the child and walk up and down the diningroom, getting her to sleep. Of course we would laugh at

him, and he would say, 'You think I never nursed a baby! But I have five or six nephews of my own, and this has been my job for a long time.

Perhaps in part because of the children, Collins may have been closer to Katty, Johnny's wife. She kept in touch while he was in London, sent Christmas packages, and signed her letters with love from 'your fond sister'. Sadly, she fell ill and was 'feeble' long before she finally died in 1921. Collins told Helena: 'She is a loss not only to Johnny and all their splendid children but to the locality generally. She was a splendid type of Irish mother and many a person in South Cork will mourn her loss.' This reads a bit like a politician's press release, but a British officer who met him later that year remarked that 'when he is very much moved . . . when he spoke of the brother's wife's death, his face assumed a very fierce expression.' Collins worried a lot over the children – they were wonderful he heard, but being looked after by Aunt Nan (one of Marianne's sisters), 'well meaning but also unfriendly to us [republicans]' – and he wrote to them often during 1920 and 1921. It must have been a relief when cousin Nancy took over.

Working farmers rarely have much time to spare for politics but Johnny did have his own political career. 'He had always been an advanced Irishman,' according to Collins, and the local police thought the same. This may have been the result of Hurley influence as well, via Katty. He was the first president of the Lissavaird branch of William O'Brien's All for Ireland League, was later involved with the Clonakilty Farmers Association, and by 1921 was on the county council. Woodfield was used as an IRA safe house during the guerrilla war and, like every other Collins and O'Brien house, was raided by Crown forces. Once his pony cart was found abandoned near the site of a failed ambush in Rosscarbery (four miles away) in February 1921 reprisal was certain. The army waited until mid-April. What happened is best told in Collins's own words:

> The Enemy force came bringing with them several of the neighbouring civilians as hostages – some of the civilians were forced at the point of a bayonet to bring hay and straw into the house. The hay and straw were then sprinkled with petrol (also forced) . . . The English forces proceeded to throw them [the family] out of the house, and having done this proceeded with

the burning. The dwellinghouse itself, and every out-office (with the exception of one stable) was completely destroyed. The Hay-shed, which contained some hay, was likewise destroyed. A farm-hand was ploughing in a field near the house – the English forces went to the horses, took the harness off them and threw it into the flames. The net result was, therefore, that eight young children were left homeless and that there was no person and no thing left to carry on the ordinary work of the farm.

The children were taken in by neighbours and spent the summer in the stable (made of corrugated iron, and therefore not combust-ible). Mary quotes one of them on their experience: 'Someone told us to cry but we couldn't cry and a soldier took my little silver box – it wasn't silver, it was only Woolworths – and the smell of the corn burning in the loft was very nice – and the soldiers drank up all the cream.'

The farm their father had created, the house their mother had built, the property now fully in the Collins name, all had gone: Michael and Johnny were famously photographed in the ruins in December that year. This was just after Katty had died and the dreaded Aunt Nan had arrived. To make matters worse, Johnny was arrested on the same day as the reprisal and was interned in Spike Island camp until December. Nancy eventually took over from Aunt Nan while he was away, and that was how the marriage came about.

In the new political world after the Anglo-Irish Treaty split the IRA and Sinn Fein in 1922, the Collins name further elevated Johnny to minor celebrity status. Johnny (now Sean in newspaper stories) often represented his brother – the local MP since December 1918 – in local matters. Like Mary, in the Civil War he acted as an unofficial intelligence agent and adviser on Cork affairs, and was targeted by the anti-Treaty IRA. When Collins was killed, he was kidnapped on his way to the funeral – although then quickly released. It was he who became the administrator of Michael's estate – by default, as Collins left no will – and he and Nancy became guardians of his memory. They were instrumental in the design and erection of the much-visited memorial cross over his grave in Dublin's Glasnevin Cemetery.

*

PARTY POLITICS in independent Ireland was (and is, more than ever) surprisingly dynastic given its republican roots and rhetoric. Among Collins's revolutionary colleagues, Eamon de Valera, Cathal Brugha, Gerry Boland, Erskine Childers, William Cosgrave and Desmond Fitzgerald all produced political heirs, as did John Dillon and John Redmond among the ex-Irish Party leaders and James Larkin for Dublin socialism. Collins had no such genetic legacy, having (rumour aside) no children of his own. But he did share the same familial preference, and he made increasing use of family members for sensitive missions in 1922.

Still, the Collins name did not go to waste. Both Margaret and Mary cannily adapted their names, to Collins O'Driscoll and Collins Powell respectively. Mary's son, Sean (also Collins Powell), followed his uncle into the army as an officer, and wound up as Chief of Staff. She herself was an active member of the pro-Treaty party Cumann na nGaedheal in Cork city, and was something of a nationalist hardliner. It was Margaret, the older sister, who went further into politics, running for and winning a seat in Dublin North in 1923. Sean Collins, son of Johnny, ran on Michael's old turf, West Cork, and similarly won at his first try in 1948. Whereas Margaret's career ran its course after ten years, Sean junior kept at it until 1969.

The Collins name did not carry on past this point, but the dynasty did, as sister and nephew were succeeded by grand-nieces: Johnny's granddaughters Nora Owen (first elected in 1981) and Mary Banotti (1983), both of whom have had broadly successful careers in Fine Gael. Their roles in politics are far from symbolic, but both have used the still-potent symbolism of their grand-uncle's name to good effect. The Collins 'dynasty' has lasted three generations, spanning the life of the state.

2: Clerk

What always impressed me most about Michael Collins was his sheer unexpectedness. You never knew what he would do or say. He was brusque, nimble-minded – the kind of man who always slammed the door loudly behind him and leapt up the stairs three at a time.

(Mrs Hopkins, 'an old friend', London)

COLLINS BEGAN HIS CAREER, Horatio Alger-like, on one of the lowest possible rungs of the civil service – as a temporary boy clerk in the London Post Office. The Post Office had a special, albeit unsung, place in turn-of-the-century Ireland: as the employer of thousands of bright young men and women every year throughout the United Kingdom. It offered decent jobs and the prospect of advancement to bright boys and girls regardless of their background when other parts of government (including the Dublin Castle regime itself) and business were still closed to them. All you needed to do was to get good marks in the civil-service exams and an entry-level position was yours. Nor were jobs scarce. The volume of mail rose quickly each year in the busy late-Victorian and Edwardian era, and the telegraph and telephone services expanded along with it. For the Savings Bank, which held the accounts of over 8 million people by 1900 (20 per cent of the population: nearly double the 1890 total), worth £135 million, labour – literate, numerate labour – was in constant demand. From 200 a year in the 1880s, the number of boy clerks newly registered in the civil service each year had risen to 808 in 1906, and to 1,091 in 1907. There were nearly 3,000 employed altogether the year after that. Almost all were destined for London's great offices, the many Irish recruits being known as 'boy cops' to their local compatriots.

West Cork was one of the great breeding grounds for the service. Hannie Collins preceded her brother into the Savings Bank as a ledger clerk, cousin (later sister-in-law) Nancy O'Brien followed into a telegraph office – the Post Office was also a pioneering employer of women – and many future comrades in the revolution took the same path.

Exams were held for every grade of clerk and sorter, even for messenger boys. For boy clerks, these took place three times a year throughout the UK in designated centres. Applicants aged fifteen to seventeen, having sent in the proper form and paid their 5 shillings, demonstrated their knowledge of handwriting, arithmetic, composition and copying, along with a choice of history (English, needless to say), maths, sciences or foreign languages. The exams were competitive: usually less than half of the 2,000 or so who sat made it on to the register, and anyone declining registration or refusing a particular appointment was refused readmittance. You could put yourself on a special register for service in Ireland, but few did so as positions there were much scarcer. And, anyway, Collins 'wanted to live in the world's biggest city'.

COLLINS HAD RECEIVED the standard Irish education in the Lisavaird National School near his home. This was a boys' school with about fifty other students; a separate school housed seventy-eight girls. One in five people in Clonakilty district was illiterate, although half of them were forty or older. In his applications to the civil service Collins mysteriously gave two different dates for when he started school: it was either in September 1894 – at the precocious age of three – or in June 1895. Either way, he left Lisavaird in 1903. It was probably not a very stimulating place to be, except that the schoolmaster, Denis Lyons, was reputed at least to have possessed a powerful personality. Regardless, the national school curriculum was laid down by the Department of Education and based on a stultifying (soon-to-be-liberalized) 'passive learning' model.

Once he finished elementary school, Collins was sent to secondary school in Clonakilty, where he also could take extra classes to prepare for the big civil-service test. All over England, Scotland, Wales and Ireland thousands of other boys, with ambitious parents behind them, were being tutored as well, all to take the same exams at the same time for the same positions. In Ireland, normal intermediate schools prepared boys and girls for the Department of Education exams, quite different from those of the civil service. In fact, at that time you couldn't take the departmental intermediate exams in Clonakilty as there was no government-recognized school there. This left the ever-growing demand for civil-service instruction to be met by a host of private tutors, unregulated and living by their reputations or by the eagerness of parents to improve their children's futures. As the Board of Intermediate Education observed in 1905:

> the smaller farmers, shopkeepers, National School teachers, officials in the lower ranks of the Civil Service . . . naturally tend to send their children in the first instance to the National Schools; but they are at the same time prepared to make and . . . constantly do make the sacrifices necessary for the subsequent attendance of their children at a higher school in order to gain the advantage of a more complete education than the ordinary National School can afford.

Marianne was one such parent. It was she who decided that Michael would join the Post Office, and when she died she left a large portion of her savings to him on condition that he educated himself to be self-supporting. And it was she who sent Michael to Clonakilty to study at its No. 1 Male National School from October 1903 until early 1906. The extracurricular civil-service classes were taught by John Crowley, apparently moonlighting from his regular job as a schoolmaster. Helena had attended these as well, until she decided to join the Sisters of Mercy. It is not quite clear what sort of education Collins got here, although it must have involved hand-writing, arithmetic and essay-writing. Again, hardly an intellectual environment. He gave his own opinion of his education in 1922:

> In the matter of schooling I had the education of the ordinary farmer's son in Ireland – a kind of teaching impossible to compare with American or English systems. But at least I had the advantage of having good tutors – and of a tremendous appetite for knowledge. But it was not even a secondary-school education, as that term is understood in England.

He sat the four required and two optional boy's clerk exams at Queen's College in Cork city on 6 February 1906, along with twenty-two other boys. Compared to them, he did well – only four did better. Out of a total of 698 candidates throughout the United Kingdom, however, he came 265th: just squeezing into the top 40 per cent of the field. Even worse, his total mark was 1,371 out of 2,200 (62 per cent – a rather plebeian C) and the cut-off mark for successful candidates was 1,450 (66 per cent). There were eighty-one unsuccessful boys ahead of him. To put it bluntly, he failed.

What went wrong? His marks in handwriting, arithmetic, English composition (required) and geography (optional) were very consistent, ranging from 262 to 273 out of 400, with an average mark of 66 per cent. If these had been the only skills tested he should have just made it. Unfortunately he failed the mandatory manuscript-copying and optional mathematics tests outright, with scores of 36 and 41 per cent respectively. To be fair, he was probably handicapped by an education which did not equip him to choose Latin, French, German or Chemistry/Physics instead of maths. Such courses were much more likely to be found in better schools than good old Clonakilty No. 1. Also he was only barely fifteen – surely one of the youngest competitors. You can grow up a lot between fifteen and seventeen.

On the other hand, biographers and admirers have often lauded Collins's mathematical abilities. Here is evidence of posthumous grade inflation. Did he fall prey to exam-day jitters? After all, familial expectations and his future were in play. It will undoubtedly cheer up a few students to know that Michael Collins may simply have been one of those people who isn't good at exams. On the other hand, he would later be renowned for completing his revolutionary work on time despite far worse stress and the fate of a nation purportedly in the balance.

In any case, after what must have been a disappointing few months, he was informed in May that he had been moved on to the list of successful candidates and that a position had become available – presumably people ahead of him had turned down their offers and more jobs had opened up. His references were checked: John Crowley and a Clonakilty shopkeeper and Justice of the Peace attested to his good character. He had a satisfactory medical exam and he was told to come to London in July, where a job awaited in the Post Office Savings Bank. This was not a matter of preference but of demand, as the bank was one of the most eager employers of boy clerks.

Opened in 1903, the Savings Bank – a magnificent temple of modern bureaucracy on Blythe Road in West Kensington (still standing, forgotten) – housed the great human machine required to process all those millions of accounts and tens of millions of pounds in deposits. Here, 1,600 or so women and 500 boy clerks kept track of every single deposit and withdrawal in the United Kingdom. The daily flow of paper was astonishing and intricate. Notices of withdrawal and deposits arrived from account-holders and postmasters all over the country, by post and telegram. Every change had to be individually checked and noted in the ledgers (Hannie's job for many years), which were themselves checked every quarter against the Postmaster Returns. Deposit books – all 8 million of them – were sent in once a year for double-checking. Withdrawals were sorted and counted in the Sorting Branch, where they were then divided into sixty warrant divisions and divided again into large and small amounts. The senior sorters would enter them on lists and pass them on to the Warrant Branch. Here declarations corresponding to the notices would be taken out from lockers, and the two together would be forwarded on in batches of sixty in special pouches. Deposit dockets hit the Sorting Branch just after the withdrawals departed, to be stamped with the date, passed to the Daily Balance Branch, noted, and passed back to the sorters, who sorted them to Book Office order and rerouted them to the Paying Office, which gave them back to the sorters, who stamped each docket with its division number before handing them on to the Acknowledgement Inquiry section, which would write them up and, of course, ship them all back to the beleaguered Sorting Branch, where they were released again into the world. Every move was timed, and everything had to move on time or the whole machine would fail. The pressure was intense: to begin with, withdrawal notices had to be out of the Sorting Branch by 9.47 a.m.

Collins worked in the Writing Room, where scores of women and boys wrote (or 'mopped') acknowledgements of deposits and warrants for withdrawals, and addressed envelopes, seven hours a day, five and a half days a week, with Saturday afternoons and Sundays off. An 'average' work rate was set demanding seventy completed envelopes an hour. As hours of copying practice had taught them, mistakes, alterations or illegibility were unacceptable, and they were paid at piece rates for acceptable work only. The job paid 14 shillings a week (rising to 19 by the time Collins left). If a clerk didn't keep up, he might work seven hours but get paid for only four or five.

Eventually he would be fired. The work discipline was fierce. All clerks had to sign the attendance book by 9 a.m. At one minute after, a red line was drawn below the last name and those who came later had to explain why. Collins, it was said, had never been late.

He had also got the reputation of being a hard and fast worker, and one who knew the angles. John McCaffrey, appointed in 1910 (just before Collins left), struggled through his first week in the Writing Room until

> one day a tall, good-looking Irishman with a pleasing and cultured Cork accent showed me how to beat the 'average'. I followed his advice and a week later I was called before the Controller and congratulated on my success in achieving a record in such a short time. My mentor was Michael Collins who had the reputation of being the speediest young clerk in the Savings Bank.

He was also known for being rather earnest, being 'remembered by his colleagues as a quiet young man of striking appearance who was generally rather reserved and contemplative' except with Irish co-workers. Even then:

> his marked characteristics were great buoyancy of spirits, a pronounced capacity for seeing the humorous aspect of things, and withal, a most noticeable ability to become suddenly serious. But his seriousness was always accepted without question by his youthful compatriots and his staccato mention of their names was sufficient to put an immediate ending to a step dance or any of the similar ebulliations of spirits in which they delighted to indulge – not infrequently within the sacred precincts of 'the bank' itself, where the concreted floor of the cloakroom made an admirable platform.

Aided no doubt by his own inclinations and ambitions, Collins showed early his remarkable capacity to make the discipline of work his own. He was, in civil-service terms, a respectable and responsible boy, rated 'good' (for conduct) and 'satisfactory' (for efficiency) by his superiors.

So – a model employee on the way up? No. The temporary boy clerkships were a dead end. Billed as an entryway into the permanent establishment, they merely lured the cheapest possible educated labour, to be discarded after four years or after reaching their twentieth birthday. There was no such thing as promotion when Collins joined. The only way out was by passing another, even more competitive, exam to be a Copyist (by 1910 reclassified as Assistant Clerk) or, much better, a Second Division Clerk or Customs Assistant. If you could reach the latter heights, you had made it, as P. S. (Patrick Sarsfield) O'Hegarty, a fellow Corkman in the Post Office, remembers:

> Most of the chaps I knew were minor Civil Servants – boy clerks, assistant clerks, Post Office Sorting Clerks and Telegraphists, and so on. Second Division Clerks, Customs and Excise Officers, and so on, kept away from us, as being members of what was then 'the major establishment'.

The best bet was Assistant Clerk, but getting there wasn't getting very far: 'The work Assistant Clerks perform is the minor clerical work of the various Departments, work which is too important to be entrusted to Boy Clerks, and not of sufficient value or intricacy to warrant the employment of Clerks of the Second Division.' The starting salary went all the way up from 15 to 18 or 19 shillings a week – which was what Collins was making anyway by the time he left. The main advantage was that you could stay and aim higher, but there were still more exams standing between you and promotion, and the dismal fact was that only twenty Assistant Clerks were promoted a year in the whole civil service.

Even then, you could only sit the exams at age nineteen or after two years' service – and the required evening classes at King's College, London, usually took three years to complete. No wonder, then, that in 1907 Collins helped organize a deputation of junior clerks to see Jeremiah MacVeagh, the crusading nationalist MP for South Down, to thank him for complaining in Parliament about their conditions and prospects. The boys were also a target for the ever-larger and more forceful unions, who wanted the work given over to proper employees with proper jobs. Of course that was the whole point – boys and women could be paid less and were more malleable. Eventually the temporary clerkships were phased out: by the end of the Great War they were gone. But by then so was Collins.

Collins, along with 1,400 other young men and women in 1906 – many of them fellow Post Office boys and girls and compatriots –

enrolled in the famous civil-service evening classes run out of King's College by William Braginton since 1875 (the classes had nothing to do with King's as such so this should not be confused with any kind of university education). The work day ended for Collins at 4 p.m.; classes ran from 5.40 to 9, one night a week – usually Monday – for ten weeks. If you did well in the in-class tests and essays, you advanced to higher courses in the same subject. Braginton's methods worked, and his school was one of the building blocks of the Edwardian state, supplying thousands of successful applicants over the years: 400 in the year Collins came to London. This success rate was what attracted Collins (and fellow revolutionaries J. J. Walsh and P. S. O'Hegarty before him). Indeed, he had already competed against Braginton's day boys for his temporary clerkship – in any given competition, they typically won half.

If you can't beat them, join them. At the end of the working day, Michael travelled by bus or underground to the Strand to sit for hours in halls with hundreds of other tired teenagers, to study arithmetic ('a cyclist leaves London at noon . . .'), composition ('ours was a capital school'), orthography, and digesting returns into summaries ('Summary of Returns – Holdings of Land in New South Wales'), as well as geography, mathematics and sciences. It has been reported that Collins studied accountancy here, but the only course available was a part-time one in bookkeeping.

Collins appears to have been contemplating a career in customs or excise, and was fairly studious. He kept a Savings Bank notebook with alphabetical lists of words and their definitions. How long he kept at it we don't know, but among his surviving compositions is one dated January 1908 (some are marked 'Upper IK', suggesting he may have progressed to a higher level). These were written under exam rules, in one to two hours, presumably weekly. Their subjects are banal: 'Contentment is better than riches'; 'The Metric system'; 'Nothing Venture nothing have'. The most interesting is 'Letter to a friend who thinks that the British Empire is expanding too rapidly – His reply', in which Collins has the imperialist write from 14 Idiots Row. They seem competent and intelligent (not to mention clearly written and properly spelled – key criteria for junior clerks), but, significantly, the lecturers did not always think so. The last-named essay received a mark of 335 out of 400; another got 325, and others received between 160 and 210. The first two figures might even have been aggregate marks for two papers. Most are riddled with querulous comments from the markers of the 'must do better' sort. The reader of 'Our Insular Position', for example, complains, 'You do not show sufficient connection between your sentences & ideas, & you are not always explicit. Try to express yourself clearly, & avoid clashing of words that have a similar sound.' Collins was frequently charged with being too vague. All in all, his record doesn't seem too impressive.

We don't know if Collins ever finished the full course at King's, but there is a letter from a London friend, J. L. O'Sullivan (with whom he was soon to fall very far out), dated 28 August 1909, which includes the following: 'I must congratulate you on your success at the exam – I am very glad you got through.' It isn't clear what this refers to, but it definitely wasn't a civil-service exam. Perhaps it had something to do with King's. Alternatively, his sister Mary remembered that

> he thought he would like to go in for agriculture in Ireland and sat for an examination and actually got a scholarship, which, I think, was one of his most amazing achievements as his knowledge was founded on a small book on agriculture which was one of the text books for boys at National Schools.

She dates this to 1913, but perhaps she was mistaken. If this did happen, he obviously wanted to stay in London and clerkdom, because he never took up any such offer.

In the end, he waited nearly the full four years to sit his next exam – on 8 February 1910 – perhaps a sign of nerves or distraction. Also unpromising was his choice of Assistant Clerk, the safest bet but the smallest step up the ladder. If he was nervous, he was right to be – the results weren't flattering. He and 375 others (most or all fellow boy clerks) were in the running for 150 situations. He was quite good at geography and digesting returns, and not a bad writer. However, with 61 per cent needed to pass, his marks averaged 54 per cent. Two-thirds of the class did better than him, 89 of whom were ahead of him on the 'unsuccessfuls' list. Most embarrassing of all, he again failed two subjects – and again it was his adding and subtracting skills that let him down: he scored 145 out of 400 in both arithmetic and bookkeeping. This from the future banker, self-styled accountant and minister of finance! I think we can safely say that Michael Collins didn't test well and had little mathematical ability. It raises a question about the supposed agricultural scholarship won with only the quickest cram – perhaps, like his maths abilities, an example of his exaggerating his achievements. If so, it would not be the last time he did it.

So Collins served out his time in the Writing Room. Five hundred thousand envelopes later, he finally left in April 1910, three months before his four years was up (and six months before his twentieth birthday). In a later job application he wrote that he left 'finding the work and prospects not much to my liking' (adding wryly that the job had 'served chiefly to make one a very quick writer'), but few others lasted this long – most boys had moved on one way or another before they turned nineteen. All those months of sweated labour with next to no money and no advancement – not even to one of the better jobs given to senior boys in the correspondence branches. The reason was not discrimination and not poor work, we can be fairly sure – it's just that there were always brighter boys around. Later in life, Collins would tell people he stayed only two years, and indeed the memory must have galled. He didn't give up on the dream of a civil-service career, however, whatever he told Hayden Talbot.

THESE FIRST YEARS in London were also unsettled ones at home. That is, he and Hannie didn't really have one yet. Instead they had a landlord, a Mr A. Lawrence, whom they followed from boarding house to boarding house, and who later recalled:

> He [Collins] was a very nice fellow, but always had politics in his heart. Michael's sister rented a room from me in Minford Gardens, Shepherd's Bush. One day she said: 'I've got a young brother coming over from Ireland, father' – she and Michael always called me father – 'can you find room for him?' I took to young Collins at once, for he was always jolly and sincere . . . I moved to start a baker's shop in Coleherne Terrace, South Kensington. 'Don't think we are going to leave you, father,' said Collins. And he and his sister moved with me.

Minford Gardens was a largely residential street; Coleherne Terrace was a busy row of shops where Mr Lawrence's bakery was kept company by a stationer's, a gilder's, a dressmaker's, a draper's, a cheesemonger's, a chemist's and a dairy. Lawrence had at least three other men boarding with him at the time, so the Collinses didn't have much room to themselves.

By August 1909, however, Michael and Hannie had moved to what became their permanent address: 5 Netherwood Road, West Kensington. Collins lived here until 1915, and Hannie stayed on at least until 1922. This was definitely a step up, although they were still above a shop – Willison Brothers Dairy, long established at that location. They had a flat to themselves on a respectable street full of other flats and shops, including a pharmacy and a post office next door. It was an easy walk to work as well – the Savings Bank was only ten minutes away.

The siblings' travels never took them very far afield: Netherwood Road was only two streets south of Minford Gardens, off Shepherd's Bush Road. These were relatively new suburbs, home to much of the expanding new white-collar workforce, connected to the rest of the city by new trains and roads. Hammersmith, Shepherd's Bush and West Kensington were also popular with all the other young Michaels and Johannas over from Ireland to work in London's endless offices. Many of the Collinses' friends and co-workers lived nearby. To some extent this was probably an outgrowth of the traditional settlement of immigrants near Paddington station, but more recent arrivals were also shifting Irish London away from its miserable association with east-London slums to a new world of clubs, societies, sports, sodalities and confraternities.

This was the world the Collinses inhabited. When not at work they would be found at debates or lectures, at sports, in meetings, or talking politics and perhaps literature with each other and their peers. Mr Lawrence recalled 'some fine political arguments in my house. I had an Englishman and a Scotsman, as well as another Irishman, staying with me, and they used to talk politics 19 to the dozen.' Mrs Hopkins, a friend of Hannie's, said of the Netherwood Road flat in 1910, 'Lots of young people in London used to congregate there then, and there was much good comradeship and vivid talk in those evenings. Collins was fond of reading Irish history, and fonder still of talking of his country.'

Collins reportedly did not attend his parish church, but he was apparently a familiar figure at the Brompton Oratory on Sundays – if only because it was such a good spot to collect donations for his leagues and causes (see chapters 3 and 4). Missing from his life in

London, therefore, was a fatherly parish priest, and Collins did not lead the intensive spiritual life that so many of his future comrades in the revolution (often educated by the Christian Brothers) were experiencing as they devoted themselves to Mary and the Sacred Heart.

His intellectual life was far more active. 'He was well-read in modern literature and drama and keen to talk about them, and in the great years of the Court Theatre, and in the weeks when the Manchester Repertory Company came to the Coronet, you would find him constantly in the gallery.' 'How we discussed literature together', Hannie recalled:

> and how often we sat up long after midnight discussing the merits and demerits of the English and Irish and French writers who happened to be our own idols at the time. He was strongly modern and liked realism and the plays of the younger dramatists who wrote for the Abbey Theatre. How many a little brown-covered book of those plays he bought in those days, when he had very little money to throw away. And how generous he was with the little he had if he took you out, and how cheerfully he went short until next pay-day!

Politics could still win out over aesthetics at times, however, as Collins reportedly 'hooted' the London production of Lennox Robinson's Abbey play *Patriots* for its cynical depiction of Irish political realities. Such theatrical 'riots' were a rite of passage for young nationalists.

Thoroughly modern Michael was devoted to Shaw and to contemporary writers like Yeats, Hardy, Wells, Conrad, Bennett and Meredith (really?). He had already read much nineteenth-century fiction and poetry at home with his sisters – Dickens and the romantics – and Irish history remained a constant interest. He frequented libraries and bookshops as well as the theatre, and built up his own collection. Every collector has their white whale, the book they can't find, and Collins's was the American edition of *Tynan's Invincibles*: P. J. Tynan's 1894 memoir of the Irish Invincibles, the Fenian splinter group that assassinated the Chief Secretary and Under-Secretary of Ireland in Phoenix Park, Dublin, in 1882. When his friend Harry Boland sent him the wrong (English) edition from New York in 1920, Collins noted that 'I must be worrying you about such things,' but kept on reminding him to keep looking.

It would not be patriotic John Mitchel or W. B. Yeats he would recommend to others in later life, however. His personal gospel was the frothy and romantic *Rubáiyát of Omar Khayyám*, which he quoted and pressed on friends ('Have you been reading Omar?'). He himself owned a volume containing four editions in one.

Collins was not one to stay home reading and debating every night, however. He frequented a house in 'the Bush' kept by a former Scotland Yard detective who used to hold dances and socials on Saturday nights. Conspiracy theorists suspected these were part of a police plot to ensnare virtuous young Irishmen, and warned Collins and others away – to little effect. Probably just as troubling to puritanical elders was the even darker suspicion of drink taken and kisses exchanged. There were other dances and entertainments held under the auspices of groups such as the Gaelic League and the Gaelic Athletic Association – which Collins himself would help organize – although these were probably well chaperoned.

Collins certainly liked pubs, and was fond of both whiskey ('a ball of malt' was his usual) and cigarettes. P. S. O'Hegarty lamented that

> when he came to London as a mere boy, he fell into spasmodic association with a hard-drinking, hard-living crowd from his own place [presumably meaning West Cork, perhaps including cousin Jack Hurley], and their influence was not good. During most of his years in London he was in the 'blast and bloody' stage of adolescent evolution, and was regarded as a wild youth.

Collins was also a great swearer, a master of 'bad grammar' – not just 'blast and bloody', but 'fuck' and 'whore'. He was ranked high by fellow adepts and connoisseurs, a master of the anatomical, the blasphemous and the inventive juxtaposition. He was a natural at it – swearing was a constant part of his speech, on automatic when he was angry or drinking or with the right crowd. Warm, friendly and cheerful, or explosive and violent, he had a phrase for every occasion. So bad was it that he would be asked to leave a boarding house in Dublin by an outraged landlady.

Peadar Kearney, the author of 'The Soldier's Song' (now the Irish national anthem), was in London in 1911 and met Collins in the Shamrock Bar, Fetter Lane (off Fleet Street), a haven for Cork exiles.

Kearney became an after-midnight regular: 'There were many who came and went, just looking in for a moment or two and disappearing again. Amongst these I met Michael Collins for the first time, a tall, good-humoured boy, who gave no indication of the road before him.' The tone of such evenings was nostalgic and patriotic: 'the couple of hours were passed in song and story, recalling old times at home, and discussing the possibilities of the future.'

Collins's own party piece was a poem, 'The Fighting Race', a product of the Spanish–American War and the sinking of the *Maine* – also known as 'Kelly and Burke and Shea'. Piaras Beaslai wrote, 'In after life it was our delight, on the occasion of any festivity, to induce "Mick" to give us this recitation. He was not exactly a good reciter, but he repeated the poem with a whole-hearted appreciation of its force, its pathos, its humour, that was very pleasant to listen to.' Humphry Murphy, one of the regulars at the Shamrock Bar, later tried to capture those times in his own poem, which began:

> Old London lit its millions of lights
> For the boys were having a night of nights
> And Mick was among the boys.

3: Athlete

He was gruff but he was genial. One might have a row with him and might pitch him to kingdom come, and he might do the same, but one could never really fall out with him. All his old London comrades will remember this particular trait.

(Patrick Brennan, fellow member of the
London Gaelic Athletic Association)

COLLINS ALWAYS DELIGHTED in physical contact and competition, as a spectator, on the playing field or among friends. His interest in sport went back to his upbringing in West Cork, where athletic contests, hurling, coursing, bowls and horse racing were all popular. We don't know anything about his participation in any of these in either Woodfield or Clonakilty, however (his sisters don't mention it), except for the suggestion that he wrote reports of sporting events for his brother-in-law's paper, the *West Cork People*.

Immediately upon arrival in London, he threw himself into the Irish sporting scene there, mostly run by the Gaelic Athletic Association (GAA). This organization, founded in 1884, was dedicated to the survival and revival of Irish sports such as hurling and Gaelic football, and to the exclusion from Ireland of British sports such as cricket and rugby. Its members were not allowed to play these last, on pain of expulsion. Within a year he was a member of the Geraldine Athletic Club in West London – 'the Gers' – which included several other Savings Bank boys and 'his particular chums' Jack Hurley, Jack Gallagher, Dan Murphy and Mick Donoghue: 'they were always together at Sports and Meetings and Dances, and seemed always to be in good accord.' As so often with such teams,

Collins's bonds with other 'old Geraldines' would last the rest of his life.

The Geraldines were one of ten or so clubs affiliated with the London County Board of the Association, among them the Brian Borus, the Milesians, the Hibernians, the Cusacks, the Kickhams, the Rapparees, the Rooneys, the Davis and the Irish Athletic Club. Each had at most a few dozen members, with a smaller cadre of regulars, who often had trouble fielding a full team for football and hurling matches. These were typically held on Sundays at rented playing fields around town. Perhaps two or three hundred people might turn out to watch on a good day. The clubs also staged occasional athletic contests, either for club members only or open to all, with regular meets held on bank holidays at Easter, on Whit Monday and in August. In these, competitors raced (100 and 400 yards, half a mile), hopped, stepped and jumped, put the shot, and hit hurling balls for certificates, medals and prizes (books, pipes, tobacco). Medals and cups were also awarded to the annual winners of the hurling and Gaelic football campaigns, although, as the players often had to pay for them themselves, they did not always materialize. Money was always a problem. Dues were rarely paid in full or on time, so clubs would organize several dances a year to raise money – of course these were probably as much of an attraction as the games.

In Ireland the GAA was, by 1906, successful, popular, lucrative and politically powerful. In the émigré communities of London and other British cities it led a somewhat meagre existence in the shadow of its main foe, the Amateur Athletic Association, and the world-conquering and media-dominating sports of rugby, soccer and cricket. Above all, it depended on the work of a few dedicated and unpaid volunteers to organize, fund-raise, fulminate and cajole.

Chief among the organizers were three men who would become mentors and patrons of the teenage Collins: P. S. O'Hegarty, Sam Maguire and Patrick Belton. All were active sportsmen and leaders of teams, and all three were senior officers of the Irish Republican Brotherhood – Fenians, as they were known in songs; Organization men, as they were known to each other. The IRB – at this point a small band of activists – worked largely through other groups, encouraging them to nationalism and republicanism while awaiting the next opportunity for revolution. The GAA, with its anti-British ethos, was its heartland in both regards, as it was Parnellite in sympathy and happy to promote IRB men to positions of power. One of their duties was to keep a lookout for suitable new recruits. Collins – young, keen to join the GAA and fascinated by politics – was just what they had in mind.

P. S. O'Hegarty, a fellow Corkman, was something of a high-flyer in the Post Office (he would end up running it in independent Ireland) and a prolific journalist who chronicled Gaelic London in two successive newspapers (which he also edited), *Inis Fail* and the *Irishman*, until he returned to Cork in 1913. Too much of a contrarian to be a leader (he wasn't known as 'Pagan' just for his atheism), he was intellectually influential and helped Collins progress in both the GAA and the IRB, where he himself sat on the Supreme Council, its governing body.

Sam Maguire, who worked in the Mount Pleasant central sorting office ('Mount Misery'), was the best hurler in London by far and a frequent president of the London County Board of the GAA. His name lives on, as every Irish person knows, with 'the Sam Maguire', the silver cup awarded every year to the winner of the all-Ireland football championship – one of the world's great sporting trophies. Peadar Kearney met him and his brother Dick in the Shamrock Bar in 1911:

> It was evident that Sam Maguire was the ruling spirit. Quiet to the verge of silence, he breathed earnestness and fixity of purpose. Far from being puritanical, he had a real sense of humour and could enter into a prank with all the abandon of a schoolboy. If any of the boys had an inclination to cut loose, Sam's was the real steadying influence that compelled the delinquent to think twice. All this was done firmly but quietly, with a smile that would 'coax the birds off the bushes'.

Maguire is often portrayed as Collins's *éminence verte*, but there is no evidence to suggest his role was greater than others'. Collins and Maguire were good friends, but not so close that Hannie mentions him as a visitor to Netherwood Road. Maguire was notoriously shy and ill at ease with women (he disapproved of Gaelic sportswomen), and in this connection Dinny (Denis) Daly's assertion that 'it was Michael Collins who made a man of Sam Maguire' suggests that the influence (and help?) went both ways.

Pat Belton was president of the Geraldines and the man who brought Collins into the Brotherhood. According to O'Hegarty, he

> exercised a sort of fatherly supervision and control over the West Londoners, their national manners as well as their personal manners and contacts. Belton was one of the best fellows in the world, gruff and a bit cantankerous, but with a heart of gold. Genuine and generous-minded Collins was full of life and youth and effervescence. His whole nature was exuberant and he loved company and practical jokes and movement. Belton himself was serious-minded and puritanical ... we were all striving to be amongst the righteous men [Thomas] Davis had asked for – and Collins was sometimes a bother to him. He used to look at him sometimes with the sort of affectionate anxiety with which a duck will regard her breed of young adventuring upon a pond.

Belton left London in 1910, but would later help Collins in Dublin. Collins gave his opinion of him to fellow republican Austin Stack in 1918:

> He means very well but is a very difficult man to get on with and as you say there is some strain of the clown in him ... He is obstinate and headstrong and I have never yet known him to have any respect for any point of view but his own.

Even before starting work in July 1906, Collins was on the scene, playing as a reserve on the London Gaelic football team against Lancashire – at this point listed as a Milesian. He did not become a Ger until 1907. The Gers were a much weaker team, in need of new blood after a mass exodus of rugby players and subsequent 'steady deterioration'. Sam Maguire may have suggested the move, and Patrick Belton recruited him, but Collins was probably also attracted by the opportunity to play more regularly. It also enabled him to switch from football to hurling, a fast, rough game (think field hockey played by ice-hockey rules). Gaelic football was often seen as a townie game by the countrymen of West Cork – Collins never liked it much. He wasn't guaranteed selection until at least 1908, however.

Collins was at best a 'useful' hurler: such was the highest praise he received (unless 'strenuous' counts), although he was rarely singled out at all. He was a character player, a heart-and-soul type who could be counted on for maximum effort. He didn't score, and he couldn't play with much finesse: he was a classic second-team or reserve player, which is what he usually was when London teams were assembled. In the memorable 1913 inter-county match against Lancashire played in Liverpool, he was the lone reserve and did play – but only because 'the five best hurlers here [were] out of the team.' The Lancastrians won by an overwhelming 7 goals and 1 point to 1 goal and 1 point.

On the other hand, he was something of a leader on the field (although never *the* leader), as in the 1913 local hurling final against the Davis. After a first half which saw the teams level at one goal apiece:

> On resuming, the South London lads sent over for a minor, and shortly after Tim Collins [no relation] put them further ahead with a nice point from a free. For a short time after this it looked as if the Gers. were beaten, but Mick Collins kept urging his men on and Dan Murphy called on them to 'do something desperate'. I don't think Dan meant it. Seven minutes before the final whistle Murphy was appeased, Jack Hurley sending through for a major. The Davis tried hard to pull the game out of the fire, but the 'Gers' backs were not giving any more away, and the Southerners had to accept defeat by 2 goals to 1 goal 2 points.

Collins's most striking quality was his sheer competitiveness. Perhaps thinking of the 1913 hurling final, Pat Brennan (later an elected member of the revolutionary assembly, Dail Eireann) recalled:

> It is as a hurler that I have the most vivid recollections of him. Our respective clubs – Geraldines and Davis – were deadly enemies as far as hurling was concerned. They played many a rough match in Lea Bridge Grounds, North East London. He was not a polished hurler – more like a Clareman, in this respect, than a Corkman – but whenever arose real necessity for a spurt on the side of his team he became a kind of small cyclone which nothing could withstand. Somehow he used to impart his wild dashing spirit to the remainder of his team, with the result that often they converted almost certain defeat into sudden victory.

Joe Good, a fellow London Irishman, tells another illustrative story:

Mick was running a race and was finishing neck and neck with Joe Reilly [later his personal courier and dogsbody]; at one moment Joe would be in front, and then Mick. Suddenly Mick put on a spurt and, as he passed Joe, deliberately dug his elbow into the soft part of Joe's bent arm. The race finished; Joe was second, but there was no doubt who had fairly won the race. It struck me that day that Mick was the epitome of the individual who *must* win ... What Mick had done in that race was unpremeditated, but still as plain as a pikestaff – so much so that many people were laughing. Meanwhile Joe and Mick were face to face shouting at each other with that Clonakilty mellowness [Joe was actually from Bantry], that County Cork accent which is so mellifluous, even when belligerent.

Dinny Daly mentioned another of Collins's familiar sporting traits: 'I met Michael Collins but he wasn't any good at either hurley or football and when I was playing against him I'd play for his toes and that would make him mad. It was always easy to vex Collins ... Collins would be inclined to lose his temper at anything, talk or not.' Pat Brennan said (just after Collins's death) that 'it was all mock-serious', meaning that his good humour would soon reassert itself – and many others agreed. But the drive to compete and win was no less real for that. Seamus Kavanagh (an accountant and later a Sinn Fein and Dail functionary), who met Collins in Stafford jail in 1916, observed:

> You see, the sort he was, he wanted to be best at everything, and the fellows would combine to make it appear that one of them had beaten him. At football they would oftener than not miss the ball and let Mick take the kick instead. At 'filly-folks tail' when Mick's side was down they would all pile on Mick's back and count 24 very slowly to force Mick to give way under their weight, and if one of them slipped down and touched the ground with his foot they would all swear it was 'weak horses', meaning Mick had been unable to bear their weight. Even his own side would be against him, and so it was in all the games they played, Mick being entirely unconscious of the fact that they were all ganging up on him. He was serious about the games himself and thought others were serious too.

A further telling scene was witnessed by Joe Good:

Once at Frongoch [prison camp in 1916] I watched Mick for a long time without his being aware of it. It was during the late dusk of evening and long into the night. Mick was trying his best to put a fifty-six pound shot-weight over a high bar, a height over which that same shot had been thrown very easily by a strong Galwayman earlier that day. Mick tried and tried – thinking himself alone – and at last he got it over. Then, seeing me there watching him, he said, 'And what do *you* think of that?

Not just an urge to beat his peers, then, but an inner compulsion to prove himself and measure up.

Collins was certainly proud of his prowess and accomplishments in London: the four straight hurling championships won by the Geraldines, and the medals and cups he won in track and field, which were prominently displayed at his Netherwood Road home. The Gers won their first cup in October 1911, although this was followed in November by a bad beating at the hands of the Rooneys under P. S. O'Hegarty ('In a word the "Gers" fell to pieces'). The following March they trounced Davis on a bad pitch ('Tim Collins of "Davis" and Mick Collins, "Gers", seemed to thoroughly enjoy themselves in the mud. What's in a name?'). On 21 April 1912 they met the Hibs, and played their soon-to-be-characteristic strong second half: 'Collins and Dunne were now playing a great game for the Geraldines, and their efforts were rewarded by their colleagues notching another goal and a point, thus running out winners.' On Whit Monday they beat the Rooneys, and in September they beat Hibernians again; but the following weekend they were upset by Davis, whom they had taken for granted. It was said that the Gers were weakened by the absence of their best players – this remark did not include Michael Collins. In October they resumed their march to the cup with a convincing victory over (yet again) the Hibs, which they followed up in November with an honour-restoring rout of Davis. December brought triumph over the Rooneys but – a bad habit emerging – a loss to the underdog Hibs. Still, they had won the championship on points. Deciding the cup had to wait until June 1913, when they were beaten by the Rooneys, who lost in turn to Davis. A turn-up for the books!

The Gers went on to win the 1914 championship as well, which allowed them to represent London against Lancashire for the All-

Ireland championship. The game was played the day before the Great War broke out: according to Sam Maguire, 'that was the proudest day in Michael Collins' life.'

Collins's first reported individual triumph came at the Geraldine annual sports in August 1911, where he won the 100 yards, the mile, and the hop, step and jump, and his team beat four others in the relay race. The only contest he entered without placing first was the half-mile. This was just a club day, however (he was constantly urging they be held and be restricted to members only). At the traditional London Irish Whit Monday sports, Collins was first in the mile and the long jump, and second in the 100 yards and the 16 lb shot, while the Gers once again won the team race. The August bank holiday brought the now familiar reports of M. J. Collins winning many of his usual prizes, and adding a surprising victory in the 56 lb throw. He failed at the long jump, however, and was forced to retire from the mile, allowing his arch-rival, Charley Lynch, to win. A month later, however, Lynch and others conspired to keep him in second or third place in everything, and out of the 100 yards final altogether. Whit Sunday 1913 saw a similarly hard-fought duel, with Lynch beating Collins into second place in the 100 yards championship (by 2 feet, the two men staying even until the last 5 yards), while Collins reduced Lynch to third in the 16 lb shot, albeit losing himself by 8 inches. They tied in the long jump. Collins didn't enter the August event, but Lynch didn't win anything anyway – perhaps they needed each other for inspiration. Whatever the case, we cannot follow the struggle any further after this, as the paper of record, the *Irishman*, was no more (P. S. O'Hegarty having gone back to Ireland).

COLLINS LOVED the sport, but he also very early on showed an interest in and aptitude for organization. In 1907 he was brought on to the GAA's County Board as registrar, to handle memberships; in 1908 he became the Geraldines' auditor (the entry-level office), and in January 1909 he was elected secretary – a normally uncoveted position, owing to its thankless burden of paperwork. To a veteran of the Writing Room, however, words like 'thankless' and 'burden' had a whole other meaning, and he happily retained the job until he left London in 1915 – by far the longest holder of the post in the club's history.

Collins was a dedicated secretary, keeping minutes, writing letters and organizing dances – for which he was often on the door, and once master of ceremonies. His minutes and reports were vigorous denunciations of team-mates' shortcomings: slackness and half-heartedness were not to be tolerated. Here we find the first examples of the Collins touch: the direct, acerbic and morally superior critique of those who don't live up to his standards. His revolutionary colleagues would come to know it well. His December 1909 report, for instance, sifted 'an eventful half year' and found it 'saddening', 'heartbreaking', 'disgraceful', 'ridiculous', 'discreditable' and 'detrimental'. 'Great hopes instead of having been fulfilled have been rudely shattered,' he began, and he concluded that

> I can only say that our record for the past half year leaves no scope for self-congratulation. Signs of decay are unmistakable, and if members are not prepared in the future to act more harmoniously together and more self-sacrificingly generally – the club will soon have faded into an inglorious and well-deserved oblivion. But this is the season of good resolutions. Perhaps the Geraldines will act up to theirs – You never can tell.

The January 1910 minutes record drily that 'the secretary's report which was extremely pessimistic – not to say cynical – was adopted with practically no comment.' His July report was worse: 'It was not flattering to the members, & advocated disbanding as the club had been unable to field a team for more than six months. This suggestion was of course repudiated & the report, after the exhibition of marked enthusiasm by a few members, was adopted.' January 1911 brought a 'cheerful' report, but a year later his January 1912 report was challenged for his extraordinary statement that their 1911 sports meeting 'showed the lack of sportsmanship on the part of the majority of the Geraldines'. The motion to excise the phrase was lost. In 1913 the *Irishman* chimed in and chided the Gers for failing to field a team for a football match, urging them to 'fall in and follow Mick Collins and Paddy Dunn – to the field I mean' (as opposed to the pub, presumably).

And so it went, Collins's mood swinging back and forth. In January 1914 he was 'very gloomy', but a year later he decided that 'on the whole the position of the club was satisfactory.' Either way he constantly attacked both committee and membership for poor attendance. He himself kept a nearly spotless record – a fact he did not fail to point out.

He also often acted as treasurer (as with drummers in rock bands, this position constantly changed hands as successive holders fell ill, fled the city, or were charged with mischief), and guarded the funds, sold tickets, and collected dues with grim fervour. When his friend J. L. O'Sullivan was caught out financially, Collins publicized his 'brazen falsehoods' and pursued him like an angry wasp until the last shilling was repaid. The friendship did not survive.

MICHAEL COLLINS's time in the London GAA could be told as a story of athletic success and organizational good works. But good works are in the eye of the beholder, and success is relative. If we go back to July 1906 and look at his record in the years preceding August 1911, we find a striking fact: the Geraldines were either mired in last place or unable to take the field, and there is not one mention of Collins winning or being placed in – or entering – any athletic contest at all! Where were his remarkable ambition and compulsion then?

The same drives were present, we can assume – but insufficient. What changed was the competition. The GAA in London at that time attracted some gifted athletes capable of matching the best in Britain, whether in soccer, rugby (the London Irish) or track and field events. Yet the Association had been founded in large part in opposition to the Amateur Athletic Association, and its Rule 13 stated that members could not play 'foreign' – i.e. British – sports without being punished or expelled. Men who sought glory or fame or who simply wanted to play at the highest level possible found this very difficult to accept, and apolitical enthusiasts who wanted Gaelic games to retain the best athletes for the sake of the sport were on their side. Facing them were the purists who insisted on unyielding resistance to English influence, among them the IRB militants, with their own political agenda.

The result was repeated crises as the two sides battled for supremacy, with Collins – whether by native conviction or instinct, or led by O'Hegarty, Maguire and Belton – entirely on the side of the purists. The first of these battles came in 1907, described by P. S. O'Hegarty as the 'most disastrous year in the history of the Association in London'. This saw the Brian Borus defect and attempt to establish their own county board under AAA rules. This move was proclaimed illegal by the existing GAA board (chair S. Maguire; treasurer P. S. O'Hegarty; registrar M. J. Collins) and the leak was temporarily staunched: 'No Irish boy can exist half seonin [shoneen, i.e. more British than Irish] and half Irishman.' The following year saw four GAA members (including a different M. Collins) defy board warnings by joining the 'English' Olympic team, only to be readmitted the following year by a new slate of officers, specially elected for that purpose.

This reversal may have prompted Collins to run for secretary of the Geraldines in the first place, or else this was suggested by club president Belton. He was opposed – by pro-Olympians presumably – but got in with support from his pals and Belton. One of his first acts was to write a public letter on behalf of the club – divided though it was – protesting against readmittance. The Geraldines also voted in July 1909 never to allow such traitors into the club (hardly likely anyway). Like other clubs, however, they were divided on both motions and the dispute carried over to the election of the president. This resulted in a tie, which was resolved by Belton using his casting vote to remain president. Collins's minutes of the occasion record that 'a scene of excitement followed' – as did another vote to remove Belton from the chair, another tie, and another victory for rejectionists.

What was left was a hard-core group of Geraldines who had retained their virtue but lost both members and money: a foretaste of what was to come for the GAA as a whole in 1911. The annual convention was held in January of that year, and it appears that the liberals had instituted a system of passes to control entry, at which Collins protested, 'I think that the new departure about passes is highly ridiculous and very unnecessary . . . Of course a duly accredited delegate of a club can attend the Convention whether he has a pass or not.' He listed seven Geraldine delegates, including himself and Jack Hurley, but it seems unlikely that all were allowed to vote as their opponents managed to outnumber the militants again and to suspend Rule 13 in London by 25 votes to 20. Letters flew back and forth in the *Irishman*, rival factions staked their claim to clubs, and the hardliners (O'Hegarty's Rooneys, Belton's Geraldines and Maguire's Hibernians) finally withdrew to form their own board, which won official recognition from the central council in Dublin.

The new board was cleansed of deviants once and for all – and of nearly all the best athletes, notably those of the reformed Brian Borus, the Cusacks, the Milesians, the recently affiliated Young Irelands and the ('so-called') Irish Athletic Club. O'Hegarty would later admit that 'when the Brians and Cusacks left the Association three years ago, they took with them 80% of the good hurlers here.' Even Sam Maguire's Hibernians were hard put 'after the defection of all the good-looking chaps'.

Thus was won the Gers' first cup, and it was in the first sports under the new board that Collins won his first medals – all thanks to his very first split. 'The Split' was something every nationalist group was familiar with: as much an institution as financial irregularities, endless meetings (twenty a year in the Geraldines, if Collins had anything to say about it) and top-heavy committees (did a tiny athletic club really need a vice-president, vice-captains and auditors?).

Winning a split requires sympathetic newspapers (to declare the victory yours), superior group solidarity (it's no good being in the majority if your side just drifts away), an uncompromising devotion to principle (or at least the perception that the other side is both compromised and self-interested), a source of legitimating authority (if you can't control the organization, start a rival one and say it's the real thing – and get someone important in Dublin to agree) and a convincing (or loud) claim that you are more Irish than the other fellows (the shoneens!). In this case IRB connections provided both legitimacy and authority, and aided in the central council (itself packed with Fenians) anointing the purists as the one true board.

It all mattered very much to Collins. But did Collins matter? He wrote the appropriate letter of outrage; he helped keep the Gers watertight by backing Belton for president and supporting the militant motions, and he and his co-delegates withdrew *en bloc* from the old board and joined the new, which he served as registrar and later treasurer. Loyalty and industry brought him that far. But he was never president or vice-president of anything, never team captain either, and only briefly vice-captain. He was a valuable foot soldier, but still not officer material.

COLLINS'S POLITICAL CAREER was launched in the GAA – as were so many other people's – but he was stuck in orbit around other

people, as secretary, treasurer, the one who did the paperwork. Nor
was he the saviour of the Geraldines, as is sometimes depicted. His
tenure as vice-captain of the hurling team was disastrous in terms of
results, and it was years after his first election as secretary that club
fortunes were reversed. His numerous motions at meetings were more
often defeated than accepted. As in his clerical work, he was no
failure, but neither was he a success.

There was another pattern – one which will recur throughout his
life. An opportunity was created out of political conflict, partly by
Collins himself. He seized that opportunity to make his name as an
athlete: it would not have been possible otherwise. He was also able
to acquire positions – if not of power, then of responsibility. Was
this opportunism conscious and deliberate? He did love sport (he
often acted as referee when he wasn't playing), and he did believe in
the GAA's ideals. Even if he backed the split for this reason, however,
it is worth noting that the stories of Collins making sure his team
got to matches and chivvying them on the field all date from 1911
and after. His absence from the lists of firsts, seconds, thirds and
fourths in track and field before then might be due to his not doing
well – or he might not even have entered. We know that on one
occasion at least he chose to judge rather than compete.

Could it be that the withdrawal of better athletes in 1911 not
only allowed him (and the team) to win, but was also what encouraged him to try to win for the first time, to give it maximum effort?
After all, Michael Collins, the man who wanted to be the best at
everything, might well have refused to enter race after race, throw
after throw, jump after jump, knowing he was going to lose badly.
When things changed, on the other hand, he entered nearly every
event every time, and entered to win, as Joe Good observed. And on
the hurling field, with a cup nearly always in prospect, he pushed
hard to get it. If we are too cynical, however, we are probably getting
away from the truth of the matter: after all, it would be natural if
winning once inspired him to try harder to win again, and his innate
will-power was obvious even then.

Nevertheless, it was on the playing fields and in the committee
rooms of the Gaelic Athletic Association that Collins was able to
seize his first political opportunity. He got his start, found his place,
made his mark, and learned some lessons which would be powerfully

applied later in life: do the work no one else is willing to do; work harder than everyone else – and make sure they know it; attend every meeting – if other people don't, you have an advantage; make yourself indispensable; by sheer effort you will impose yourself; seize every opportunity for all its worth.

4: Young Republican

Collins instinctively impressed. His personality dominated all with whom he came into contact. His face repelled while it attracted. It reflected the essence of bitterness and hatred. Determination was written all over it, no trace of human kindness, not a glimmer of humour softened its harsh contour. The lines seemed to be cut out of marble – cold, harsh and cruel. The eyes were the most remarkable of an extraordinary face. Deeply set, they glowed instinctively from under shaggy brows, heightening the pallor of his cheeks, and adding the last repulsive touch to a countenance that inspired fear.

(The *Daily Sketch* on 'Mike Collins, the Super-Hater')

OUTSIDE WORK AND night classes, the GAA was Collins's major preoccupation in his first four years in London. He did not stop at that, however. The same values and principles that motivated the GAA animated a whole mini-movement in Ireland and Britain, a community within a community dedicated politically and culturally to an Irish Ireland (variously defined) and personally to living as Irish a life as possible. This meant playing only Irish games, of course (or at least ones that weren't specifically British), but also wearing Irish-made clothes (true believers wore their version of a distinctive national costume) and generally buying Irish goods wherever possible, reading Irish literature (occasionally even exclusively), and, perhaps most important and most challenging, learning and speaking Irish, or Gaelic. Gaels, as such Irish-Irelanders usually referred to themselves, varied in their commitment to this cultural and consumer separatism, but what they had in common was a world-view and the camaraderie of the siege, for besieged is how they generally thought of Irish identity, with themselves as the last defence between it and the great tide of Anglicization.

In London the Gaels were not just a minority within the Irish community and among nationalists (a few hundreds among many thousands), they were also living at the heart of the British Empire. Here the GAA was joined by the Gaelic League (founded in Dublin in 1893 to preserve and promote the Irish language), the Irish National Club, the Irish Literary Society and the Irish National Society, which merged with other political and cultural groups to form Sinn Fein in 1905. Sinn Fein – usually translated as 'Ourselves Alone' – thus started out as an umbrella group for Irish-Irelanders: those people who thought that Ireland must separate from England linguistically, culturally, economically and politically – although the question as to which of these was most important was a matter of great debate. The Irish Volunteers would arise out of the same milieu in 1914.

As with the GAA, this Gaelic clubland was driven by a small band of hard-working organizers, who had a hand in everything and kept everyone else busy. P. S. O'Hegarty called it 'this welter of meetings and discussions and lectures':

> they had local committees, and central executives, and special committees, and masses of minute books and account books to be kept, and everybody who was willing to work at all worked to the pin of his collar. There was a period during which I was secretary to one club, treasurer of a second, chairman of a third and a member of the committee of a fourth.

Overlapping memberships and leaderships meant that the whole of this little world also shared the same officious and disputatious organizational culture as the GAA. Squabbles and splits were commonplace, a product of its subculture of self-righteousness and cultural puritanism. This strain of nationalism was always a minority tendency, attracting the bright and unorthodox as well as the zealot and xenophobe – good material for a debating society, but a poor recipe for harmonious action. Disagreements and condemnations regularly filled the columns of the Irish-Ireland press, from the leading Dublin papers such as Arthur Griffith's *United Irishman* (later *Sinn Fein*), D. P. Moran's *The Leader* and the *Gaelic Athlete*, to the London monthlies *Inis Fail* and, its successor, the *Irishman*.

Mainstream Irish nationalism, as practised or supported by the great majority of Catholics in Ireland and Britain, was monopolized by the Irish parliamentary party and its various grass-roots auxiliaries – after 1900, the United Irish League and the Ancient Order of Hibernians. These were the descendants of Parnell's great army of liberation, led by the reunited factions who had divided over his leadership in 1890. They had come together again in 1900 under the compromise leadership of John Redmond, a former Parnellite who was nevertheless a consensual and gentlemanly figure. The Irish Party – known to nationalists simply as 'the Party', just as the Catholic Church was 'the Church' – still relied on the old watchwords of Home Rule and the land for the people, although the latter was now directed at both landlords and graziers – farmers who controlled hundreds or thousands of acres of land to raise cattle on, at the expense of land-hungry small farmers.

The Party's power had also been greatly increased by the democratization of local government in Ireland in 1898, which allowed the mass-membership United Irish League to take control of most municipal and rural councils and boards in subsequent elections. Now, for the first time, the Party had actual patronage to dispense to its clients, in the form of jobs and contracts. This was greatly augmented after 1905 when the Liberals were returned to power in Parliament after a ten-year hiatus. Nominally dedicated to reform and Home Rule, their appointees to Dublin Castle shifted the burden of their considerable patronage from the unionists and Protestants favoured by the Conservative regime to their nationalist and Catholic allies, and they were quite willing to listen to the Party's advice on who should get what.

Within Irish nationalism, at home or in Britain, the main opposition to this machine came from within – from those at the fringes who wanted a more conciliatory and constructive relationship with other parties, or who, as radicals, feared Liberal entanglements or wanted to wage more of a class war on behalf of small farmers. Some of these dissidents were finally extruded into William O'Brien's All for Ireland League in 1909 and 1910, but this failed to make much impact outside the contrary constituencies of Cork.

The Irish-Ireland movement disliked the Party and its much larger and wealthier organizations for their monopoly on power and for not being separatist enough, but offered at best only intellectual competition. Younger and often more radical Gaels like Michael Collins often felt a personal and generational grievance, as the machine represented not only collaboration and corruption but also an establishment that blocked their own ambitions and dreams. The republican revolution espoused by the IRB therefore meant not only the overthrow of Dublin Castle but the removal as well of the Party and its creatures. A free, Gaelic Ireland would naturally be run by Gaels, including those who had been forced into exile (as the IRB saw it) by discrimination and lack of opportunity. The movement was also distinguished by the fact that (apart from the men's club that was the IRB) men and women joined and ran its organizations together. This openness was unique, as both the Church and the Party segregated the sexes, to the great disadvantage of women. For educated women, and feminists in particular, this progressivism was a major attraction, and they in turn gave the movement much of its extraordinary vitality.

In London, local Irish Party organs had little power or patronage as such, given their minority population base, but when Parliament was in session they did have the Party MPs on hand to throw their weight and status behind their local followers. Here the Irish-Irelanders were in even more of a minority, as the logic of preserving Irish culture outside Ireland was much less obvious or urgent than at home. In any case, most migrants and their descendants weren't political at all, and if they had a collective life it was to be found in the parishes of the Catholic Church, whose nuns and priests were often imported from Ireland and whose confraternities and sodalities absorbed many Irish-Irelanders as well.

Gaeldom was by no means religiously exclusive, however. A few priests were language enthusiasts, and the majority of members and activists were Catholic, but the overall ethos was non-sectarian. This may have had something to do with the IRB, as the Fenians had always been opposed to the Church's interference (as they saw it) in politics, just as the Church was opposed to secret societies and revolution. But Irish Ireland had its own reasons to be wary. Priests sometimes caused a lot of trouble by opposing the mixing of sexes in Irish classes, and much of the Catholic hierarchy was also against making the language compulsory for students in the new National University, founded in 1908. Tensions over politics and religion inevitably arose at times, but Protestants such as Sam Maguire or

Alice Stopford Green (a popular Irish-Ireland historian living in London at the time) were generally considered as good Irish people or separatists as anyone.

The social distance between Maguire, a postal sorter, and Green, a literary salon-keeper and friend to cabinet ministers, illustrates the unusual egalitarianism of this world. A clear hierarchy remained, however – this was Edwardian London after all. The overall tone was set by white- and pink-collar workers, junior civil servants in the main, with the Post Office to the fore. At the top of the social ladder was the Irish Literary Society, of which Hannie Collins was a member. Gaelic games was the most proletarian pursuit, skill on the playing field being a trump card over collars and ties. The Gaelic League, which revolved around books, classes and tests, was a different matter. In January 1910 a 'novice at the central branch' (in London) complained in *Inis Fail* of a lack of democracy there:

> Why do those who cling to the hurling clubs and other Irish organizations hold aloof from the League . . . plenty of the 'cold shoulder' is in evidence . . . The idea, which is unfortunately so widespread [is] that the Gaelic League of London is a kind of 'House of Lords' mainly composed of civil servants, and well dressed – not shabby genteels.

P. S. O'Hegarty, the career bureaucrat, replied in even clearer class terms:

> The average Irish working man who comes to London would not come into the Gaelic class on any conditions, and you cannot force him. His ideas about things are totally different, his bent is totally different, and he works for Ireland in other ways, in the GAA, or the UIL, perhaps or he does not work for Ireland at all. But you will not find the working men in force in the Gaelic League anywhere, either in Ireland or outside it. The gulf . . . is caused more by the workingman's instinctive contempt for the clerk, and avoidance of his class than anything else.

According to Sam Maguire, Collins joined the Gaelic League 'almost on the first day of his arrival in London. He attended all the dances, concerts and outings held under its auspices.' This may well be so, but he didn't give money to the language fund – used to support the classes – or do much to learn Gaelic until years later, a fact Hannie ascribes to his concentration on his King's College classes (although their landlord believed the opposite: that Collins's extracurricular politics held him back at work). He sounds like one of those slackers whom dedicated leaguers always complained about, absent from class and then 'traipsing surreptitiously in just after 9.30 p.m. for a dance or two'. His name first appeared in connection with the League in March 1911, when he wrote the monthly note for the Kensington branch's language class. As always he reported setbacks, but sounded a hopeful note:

> Indeed the prospects have brightened considerably since Christmas. The session was not opened until as late as December, and we have to labour under the loss created by the departure to Ireland of Messrs M. O'Donoghue and P. Belton. January was dull – amazingly dull. But February has been distinctly hopeful. We have now two good classes and brilliant teachers. If only those who turn up their noses at our humble rooms in Prince's Road, would come to us for even a few Thursdays we should soon be prosperous enough to go back to Ladbroke Hall again.

The King's College classes ended before Christmas 1909; Collins left the Post Office in April 1910; he may well have taken up the language class in December, perhaps as the token militant now that Pat Belton was gone. We can only guess how much persuasion had been required to get him in, but once in he took it seriously enough in his usual way: he passed annual exams in 1912 and 1913, began subscribing to 'the fund', and wangled money for it out of the somewhat reluctant Gers. After the tenuous Kensington committee finally collapsed, he joined the school committee in Fulham – where cousin and team-mate Jack Hurley was a prominent member – and even took a part in the annual play in 1913. Reviews were mixed:

> Tomas O Donncada as the cow-doctor and MacSuibne as the shoneen postmaster being great; Miceal O Coileain as the doctor and Maire Ni Aoda as his house-keeper were also capital, though their voices were rather weak.

This was the last time anyone ever complained of Collins being inaudible!

By the time of the London League's annual convention of 1913 he was entering the lists on matters of policy, suggesting that classes should pay for themselves rather than be subsidized out of general funds (he was a great believer in self-help), and speaking in support of P. S. O'Hegarty and against rising star Art O'Brien's motion to shut down the *Irishman*. He failed to get elected to the governing council – it was later said that he wanted to be treasurer, but here his militancy and manners may have told against him. Whether he got further in later years we don't know.

The pattern of his involvement looks similar to his career in the GAA. The cast is familiar, Patrick Belton being much involved – perhaps as recruiter again – as were P. S. O'Hegarty and his pals Donoghue and Hurley. His timing was also about the same, with 1911 marking the start of his athletic successes as well. In the League, as in the Association, a larger dynamic may have been at work. After 1893 the League had grown slowly until the turn of the century, then took off on both sides of the Irish Sea. By 1902 it had 1,000 members in London; by 1906 it claimed 3,000. This was its high-water mark. As with the GAA, numbers then began falling and clubs began closing, Collins's Kensington branch being one of many. By 1908 membership was down to 534; by 1916 it was 390. The Fulham 'school' attracted 35 a week in this later period – about the same number as went in for language exams every year in the whole city. The same decline was occurring in Ireland, although there the League remained ideologically influential. The novelty had worn off. Also, many national (i.e. state) schools had taken up the teaching, so the language movement was becoming institutionalized – a victim of its own success.

Within the movement, people blamed the problems on party politics, which had come to life with the advent of a Liberal government and the return of Home Rule to the agenda – a near prospect after the closely fought elections of 1910 gave the Irish Party the parliamentary leverage to make it happen. For many Leaguers this would mean nationalist control of education and the power to revive the language. Political triumph would make further voluntary efforts redundant.

Republicans like Collins and his friends thought otherwise, but, this aside, the circumstances once again favoured him. His dedication to the cause after 1910 can't be faulted and was never merely tactical, but, once again, he surfaced as the organization declined. A falling membership meant more individual opportunity to hold office, to exert personal influence and be noticed, even if at the time the League and the wider movement appeared to be losing momentum and even their reason for being.

COLLINS JOINED SINN FEIN as well, apparently at the height of its own early popularity in 1908. It was at this point (and for a long time to come) an uneasy coalition of radicals, reformers and politicians, united by a common dissatisfaction with the Irish Party and British rule. Arthur Griffith, a veteran journalist and the editor of the standard-bearing newspaper *Sinn Fein*, was this quasi-party's guiding spirit. His blueprint for a new Ireland was the dissolution of the Act of Union of 1800 so that Ireland could regain its lost national sovereignty and self-government. He was not a republican revolutionary like his friends in the IRB, however, as he disapproved of violence – usually referred to as 'physical force' – on practical if not moral grounds. Instead, he thought Ireland should retain the monarchy as a constitutional link with Britain. Equal status, as opposed to the subordinate parliament promised by Home Rule, would give its government enough power to build up a national, as opposed to a colonial, society and economy, and to reverse the damage the Union had done.

Achieving equality would require nationalist MPs to abstain from attending the House of Commons, where they were at the mercy of the British majority. With or without them, the more democratic local councils would form a national assembly, claim sovereignty and, with presumed popular support, gradually render Dublin Castle irrelevant. Sinn Fein did little to actually bring about this miracle of people power, apart from endlessly debating rather abstract points of principle and strategy, but its members were usually active in other Irish-Ireland causes.

In London, as in Dublin, consciousness-raising meetings were held, committees were struck, dues were paid, and passionate debates blew up over physical force, republicanism and electoral participation. Little trace remains of Collins's role. In Margaret Gavan Duffy's fond reminiscence, 'into our Sinn Fein meetings on Sunday evenings . . . Mick came, and brought us his youth and enthusiasm – a breath of fresh Irish air.' Other memories were less gentle. In 1920 the *Daily*

Sketch published a profile of 'Mike Collins, the Super-Hater' ('a gorgeous thing' Collins thought):

> twelve years ago 'Mike' Collins ... was one of the leading speakers on behalf of the Sinn Fein movement ... Collins believed in his cause, and espoused it with all the fiery eloquence of the fanatic. He hated England and all things English, and while the power and fire of his eloquence drew hundreds of hot-headed Irishmen to his banner, it hampered to a great extent the progress of the movement at that time ... Collins attacked the party, denouncing its members as traitors to the cause of Ireland, the dupes of British statesmen. Collins argued that there was only one course open to Irishmen to obtain her freedom. England must be brought to her knees.

While the 'power and fire of his eloquence' may be doubted – P. S. O'Hegarty and others remember that Collins 'would get up and say what he had to say in two or three short, sharp sentences, and then resume his seat' – it was not all made up. Collins wrote immediately to Art O'Brien that 'quite possibly the article is by someone who knew him [himself] in those days – somebody who might have attended the lectures in the Bijou theatre'.

It is unknown who organized talks in the Bijou theatre, but Collins was never listed as a speaker in *Sinn Fein*. We do have two draft talks he wrote. One outlined the British government's responsibility for the Great Famine ('a manufactured famine'), and the other compared Finland and Ireland and incidentally praised the 1882 assassination of leading British officials in Dublin: 'I do not defend the murder simply as such. I merely applaud it on the ground of expediency.' It is unknown if he ever gave this talk, but, if he had, it would indeed have caused the sort of frisson described in the *Daily Sketch*. The Central Branch of Sinn Fein was the largest in the UK and hosted regular Sunday-night lectures and discussions on Irish themes. A few others spoke in the same incendiary vein as Collins's reported speech, notably Roddy Connolly (son of James, the socialist labour leader) in 1910, who dismissed democracy altogether and believed in 'the absolute necessity for the establishment of a military dictatorship ere Ireland's freedom can be achieved.' Most of the talks were on constructive subjects, however, along the lines of Cormac O Ceallachain's 'The Beetroot Industry' or P. Callinan's discourse on poultry-keeping ('the audience was not quite as large as it usually is'). Similar articles filled the Irish-Ireland press as Ireland's perceived golden future depended very much on native industries harnessing her vast natural potential. Firebrand though he was, Collins took these to heart along with Ireland's historical wrongs, and all of these schemes would come flooding out again in his later years.

Collins's passion for the cause is clear from an undated draft letter written in 1909 to Tom Kettle, a recently elected young Irish Party MP:

> Do you remember your words at Eel Brook Common two days after the North Leitrim election [in 1908]. You said that the Liberal Party would go to the country at the next Gen Elect on the distinct understanding that Home Rule would be granted to I[reland].
>
> Now Mr Kettle is this fair dealing with the Irish people who place their faith in you and your colleagues?
>
> Do you not think it would be better for you to tell the Irish People about overtaxation plaguing officialdom and a decreased population
>
> Your comment on the Black Present is wasted on Englishmen [originally 'Irishmen']. It is only in Ireland that these things are important. If some of the money spent on the party to which you belong had been invested in Irish industries how much more prosperous would Ireland be today.
>
> You are right that there is one force which can save Ireland – but it is not Liberalism – Young or old – It is the power of will of the Irish nation working through Sinn Fein
>
> In the name of love of Ireland abandon the useless farce and let yourself go with the tide of Sinn Fein.

He ended the letter by eagerly referring Kettle to a pamphlet by Arthur Griffith on overtaxation.

Collins was entirely wrong about what the immediate future held. In fact 1909 marked the high tide of Griffith's party, and 1911 did bring the concrete prospect of Home Rule. Sinn Fein had fought a by-election against the Party (and lost) and did get a few members elected on to Dublin city council, but its popularity waned after 1910, like the rest of the Irish-Ireland movement: another victim of Home Rule fever. Of course, this may only have increased the sense among the Gaelic elect that they were the last sparks of true nationality, struggling courageously against the tide, holding back the darkness. Every nationalist politician liked to claim they had adhered to principle when 'twas neither profitable nor popular, and Collins would be quick to say the same about this period (and to have it said about him). He would also feel occasional nostalgia for the good old days when the small band of righteous men fought the good fight.

But what the 'good fight' meant with Irish self-government now in sight was not so clear. Should Home Rule be opposed as an inadequate compromise, or should it be embraced as a vehicle for the advancement of the Sinn Fein agenda? Griffith, and therefore Sinn Fein, adopted a passive wait-and-see policy about it. In fact Griffith was far more exercised by a new bugbear, the tax-raising People's Budget of 1909, which had prompted a constitutional crisis and two elections before being passed into law. Griffith condemned this and associated progressive measures furiously and even obsessively as a further obstacle to Irish business.

This combination of nationalist moderation and economic conservatism caused more-radical Sinn Feiners to drift away, and the Irish Republican Brotherhood to found an alternative newspaper, *Irish Freedom*. Collins shared in the left-wing unease at Griffith's apparent change of direction and drafted a letter to his paper in 1910 headed 'A Wail of Regret': 'the trend is downward. The old *militant* attitude of the UI [United Irishman, the former title of the paper] and the earlier issues of S[inn]. F[ein]. has disappeared . . . the journal SF – the organ of the national movement – seems to be no longer independent.' The distance between the two letters, the first defending Griffith, the second attacking him, shows us Collins the patriot becoming Collins the radical.

IT WAS AT ABOUT the same time that Collins left the Savings Bank. He had done poorly in the exam for Assistant Clerk in February 1910, but – as would become habit – he was able to turn his lack of success there into opportunity elsewhere by taking a job with a firm of stockbrokers in April 1910. Horne & Co. brokerage needed a bookkeeper and correspondence clerk at its offices (now torn down) at 23 Moorgate Street, deep in the City, London's – and the world's – booming financial centre. Collins left the Savings Bank on 18 April, but he had barely begun his new job when the Civil Service

Commission informed him that, once again, he had made it to the list of successful candidates – no doubt, as in 1906, a testament to the basic unattractiveness and rapid turnover of the position. At first Collins accepted the offer to be wait-listed, and once again his references were solicited and his health was checked. His new doctor reported him vaccinated and 'free from all physical defect or disease' with the exception of his teeth. These had deteriorated badly, leaving '5 stumps in upper and one or two cavities that require attention. Also one or two in lower jaw.' Such poor dentition was possibly not uncommon in 1910, but Collins had to undertake to see a dentist to get a certificate of approval (which he did receive). That may have meant a lot of teeth being pulled and filled, and some who met him would later notice the gaps.

Despite the rigmarole, when a definite post was made available in June he had changed his mind. 'I have spoken to my employers on the subject, [and] have decided not to accept the position.' They wanted him to stay it would seem. Did they offer him more money, perhaps the prospect of advancement, with no exams required? He was definitely paid better in the end, earning £95 a year by 1914 (the average junior commercial clerk in Britain was making about £80 in 1909, so this was an acceptable amount).

Horne & Co. were Edmund Horne, H. J. S. Browne and Wilfred Lamaison, who were lucky enough to be members of the Stock Exchange in a time of general expansion and prosperity. The number of brokerage firms had nearly doubled since the 1880s, the value of securities quoted had nearly tripled, and the number of serious investors had quadrupled to reach a million: the middle-class equivalent to the working-class holders of Post Office savings accounts. The 'Kaffir boom' of the 1890s over South African mining (at which time Horne & Co. came into existence) and the Asian rubber boom of the 1900s had passed by 1910, but there were new foreign issues aplenty.

Brokers were, in effect, retailers who took orders for shares from members of the public and farmed them out to wholesalers – jobbers – who would then place the order on the floor of the Exchange at Capel Court. The broker's office would communicate by means of the telephone (Horne & Co. had three phones – the Exchange sent or received a call every second) or by messenger. This is where Collins came in. As office clerk, he later reported, 'I took charge of part of the staff [the messengers], was responsible for the preparation of the fortnightly Trial Balances, the Quarterly Balance Sheets and the daily correspondence.'

Being a broker was not a very intellectual exercise on the whole, according to one clerk at the time:

> Most members were merely passers on of information and gossip, there was little or no attempt to sift information, to analyse prospects of equities, or indeed to justify the recommendation of the many and various tips toddled out by the market and the many outsiders who frequented clubs and other convivial places where people with more money than sense assemble . . . Too many doubtful financiers were getting away with the swag owing to the fact that there were far too many so-called brokers attempting to cope with a job that called for at least a smattering of financial knowledge, and this the bulk did not possess.

Membership of the Stock Exchange had no requirements other than money and three friendly members who would vouch for you. In practice, the Exchange was a club for upper-class amateurs, who also set the tone, the politics and the social rules. The public-school code was followed rigorously. Everyone had a nickname, paper-ball fights and mischievous fires often broke out, and sports were a collective obsession: the Drones Club writ large.

If Collins's inner bookkeeper was affronted by the spendthrift culture, his nationalism must have been outraged (even stimulated?) by the politics. The City was thoroughly Tory, patriotic, imperialist and very very anti-Home Rule. In 1893, at the time of Gladstone's second Irish Home Rule bill, the Exchange clerks ritually burned a copy of the bill and led the members to a City-wide protest meeting. In 1900 the relief of Mafeking in the Boer War stopped trading for a day as a carnival of celebration broke out. After the new Home Rule crisis taking shape in 1912, with Conservatives and Unionists threatening outright rebellion, the City was entirely on the unionist side and very depressed at the prospect of the third Government of Ireland Bill going through.

Nor did the world of the small City office reflect the glory that was the Exchange. Firms were lodged down every alleyway, with clerks crammed into every nook and cranny. Horne's had two floors above a shop at 23 Moorgate Street; a detective agency (never a good sign) had the third floor. Windows were scarce and so was space, with only two 20-by-30-foot rooms to work with to fit the partners, Snelgrove and Jones, the senior clerks, the messengers and (along with who knows who else) Collins. Some observers saw bustle and life; others felt oppressed:

> Wherever one looked the scene was colourless. The buildings had a tone peculiar to the City, for which there is no name. It wasn't black or brown or dun and drab. It was not so definite as the tone of mud or the tone of cobwebs or manure. It was such a tone as you might get from wet smoke mixed with Army-blanket fluff and engine smuts. Every street was riddled with courts and alleys, where this tone was thicker, and each of the courts and alleys was a rabbit warren.

Whether this or politics had anything to do with it, it was while working at Horne's that Collins reportedly sought the scholarship to study agriculture in Ireland, and he also applied to the Board of Trade to be a labour-exchange clerk in the spring of 1914. In his application letter he described himself as follows:

> The trade I know best is the financial trade, but from study and observation I have acquired a wide knowledge of social and economic conditions and have specially studied the building trade [when?] and unskilled labour. Proficient in typewriting, but have never tested speed. Thorough knowledge of double-entry system and well used to making trial balances and balance sheets.

Labour exchanges were being set up for the first time under new progressive legislation, so hundreds of new clerks were being hired. To get the job, you still had to pass an exam, however – unless prior results would be accepted as a substitute. This Collins applied for, submitting his Assistant Clerk certificate (only half marks were needed, luckily for him). This was accepted in May, but here his file reveals no more and the trail runs cold. His name does not appear on any list of successful candidates, and he never did work for the Board of Trade. The likeliest explanation is that candidates with better results got all the jobs and no offer was made. Strike three and he was finally out of the civil service for good.

*

THE PERIOD 1909–10 emerges as a watershed in Michael Collins's life generally: a coming of age. He was no longer the country boy in his first job. He turned twenty. He and Hannie moved to Nether-wood Road, where he would remain until 1916. He became secretary of the Geraldines, and joined the Gaelic League. And he became an oath-bound revolutionary. In November 1909 Pat Belton swore him into the Irish Republican Brotherhood, still in theory a kind of army-in-waiting dedicated to overthrowing British rule in Ireland by force. Belton had vetted him, and Jack Hurley, already a member, had vouched for him. He may have passed the test when he backed them in their fight for control of the Geraldines that year, and, obviously, his greater prominence generally followed soon after this.

As we move behind the scenes to the secret world of the IRB, the parallels between Collins's work life, athletic career and politics are evident. As in all his endeavours at this time, promotion in the Organization was slow. There were about a hundred members in London, where the basic unit was the section (a local variant on the standard IRB 'circle', usually numbering about a dozen men). The city was run by an executive made up of section masters ('centres' in Ireland), which answered in turn to the Supreme Council in Dublin, drawn from regional executives all over the United Kingdom.

Pat Belton was Collins's section master, and when he left in 1910 an opening was created. Collins was suggested, but 'the Executive ruled that his name should not be admitted because of his youth and irresponsibility.' More mature than in 1906 perhaps; not mature enough yet in 1910. As in the GAA, he was not seen as a leader. Tomas O'Donoghue (later a leading revolutionary) got the post, and when the section was divided Jack Hurley got the second chiefdom. It was not until October 1913 that Collins became a master. Joe Furlong, another Geraldine, joined the Organization – and Collins's section – along with his brother Matt when they arrived in Shepherd's Bush from Wexford. He recalls meeting under cover of Gaelic League dances and the like, and smuggling a few guns to Ireland. Another member was Dan Sheehan, who later drowned trying to meet a German arms ship on the eve of the 1916 Rising. In 1914 Collins reputedly was made treasurer for the South of England division (meaning London). Hurley was already secretary, paving the way as always.

Collins later described the years before he joined the IRB as 'the very worst period in our history'. The Organization had gone through several splits, and had become moribund and riddled with informers. These 'whiskey-drinking Fenians' weren't trusted by other radicals, and had to be forcibly retired by a new and much younger vanguard – O'Hegarty, Maguire and Belton among them. The informers disappeared at the same time, a fact attributed to the moral superiority of these 'new men', who were Gaels as well as republicans. In fact the Irish police had simply stopped paying or recruiting spies, as Dublin Castle had decided that the IRB no longer posed a threat. Here was one group that was on the rise when Collins joined, although his being treated so cautiously probably reflects poorly on his progress towards new-man-hood.

The IRB's big break came with the formation of the Irish Volunteers in Dublin in November 1913. The Brotherhood's dedication to fighting for a republic had become a formality. There were no guns, and no plans to do anything with them even if they existed. The very idea of an armed uprising was met with ridicule by every other sector of nationalism, from the MPs of the Irish Party to dissidents like D. P. Moran and Arthur Griffith. The righteous new cohort were certainly more active – publishing their own newspaper, *Irish Freedom*, for one thing – and more militant than their predecessors, but they had no more scope for direct action.

The prospect of a Home Rule bill after 1910 seemed to make revolution even more unlikely – until the unionist Ulster Volunteer Force was formed in January 1913 to stop it. The UVF was a paramilitary army based entirely in the northern province of Ulster but with strong support from the Protestant majority there, giving it both money and numbers. Led by ex-army officers and backed by the Conservative Party in Britain, it became a formidable force once German guns and ammunition were smuggled into Ulster in 1914. If Home Rule was passed – which seemed inevitable now, given the combined Liberal and Irish Party majority in the House of Commons – this force would oppose any attempt to impose Dublin rule on their province by seizing power under a unionist provisional government.

The appearance of a unionist army led more or less inevitably to a nationalist armed response. And, since the Party chose to rely on its allies in the Liberal government to deal with the UVF, the response came, by default, from an anti-Party coalition of Gaelic

Leaguers, Sinn Feiners and other Irish-Irelanders. The Irish Volunteers were founded in Dublin in November 1913 with the intention
of training and arming nationalist manhood to uphold Irish national
rights. Here was the republican ideal of a self-reliant citizenry, and
here was the ideal – if improbable and unforeseeable – vehicle for
rebellion: a paramilitary mass movement whose leadership the IRB
secretly dominated from the start.

The Gaels of London followed Dublin's lead in 1914. Hundreds
of Irish Londoners enrolled in the Volunteers as the Home Rule
crisis got worse and the Liberal government dithered over what to
do. Party supporters began joining too in the spring of 1914. Popular
support reached its height when British troops tried to stop nationalist gun-runners in July 1914 and then opened fire on an unarmed
crowd in Dublin. Nationalist Ireland was horrified at the loss of life
(as was the Liberal government, to be fair) and enraged at the double
standard whereby unionist gun runners were left alone but nationalists
were killed. Three days later Collins's sister Mary wrote, rather oddly,
'Nice work that in Dublin what! I hope you are feeling more cheerful.'
What she may have meant was that the massacre promised to rally
popular opinion behind a more radical leadership and against the
Liberal government. Republicans may well have wondered: is it time
for rebellion?

The date of the violence in Dublin, however, was 26 July. A week
later the United Kingdom was at war, and the question of how the
Irish Volunteers should respond took precedence over all else. John
Redmond and the Irish Party ultimately chose to back the government and encouraged Irish Volunteers to join the British armed
forces in much the same way that unionist politicians did. In the
absence of Home Rule, none of the dissident founders of the
Volunteers agreed to this and – what else? – the movement split.
After September there were two nationalist militias (three if you
count the socialist Citizen Army in Dublin), as the great majority of
members withdrew to form the Redmondite National Volunteers.
The residual Irish Volunteers were forcibly returned to their roots as
the military wing of the counter-culture, as marginal as ever.

Collins joined the Irish Volunteers, of course, as did his fraternity
brothers in the IRB. Initially there were two companies formed in
London, north and south. Collins was among the northerners, who
met and drilled with wooden rifles in the German gymnasium at

King's Cross. The building was commandeered by the government after war broke out in August 1914 – an anti-German rather than an anti-nationalist move, as the police never bothered the London Volunteers. The British call to arms and the split drained most of their manpower away, leaving about fifty members behind. These soldiered on, eventually in one amalgamated unit, meeting and drilling more or less weekly. On 30 January 1915 a dance was held at their unofficial headquarters, St George's Hall in south London, including as entertainment 'bayonet exercises, rifle and physical drill, evolutions etc.'. This was repeated about a year later. In October, Director of Organization Patrick Pearse (whom Collins would succeed in the post) visited from Dublin and 'found an active Company of Irish Volunteers . . . The difficulties of Irish Volunteering in London under war conditions can be imagined, but this hardy group is able to keep up training in all the essentials.' Pearse, a leading Gaelic Leaguer and master of St Enda's, an Irish-Ireland school for boys, had been to London before on behalf of the Gaelic League, so Collins very likely met the man who would become the great republican visionary of his generation.

Technically (and typically), there were five company offices to fill – not only officers and NCOs, but a committee (without which no nationalist organization could exist) including a secretary and treasurer. Despite the military trappings, elections were supposed to decide the matter. Both north and south London were represented at the first Volunteer convention in Dublin in December 1914, so presumably there were two sets of officers before they amalgamated. Whatever the case, Jack Hurley was the unified treasurer (he had sworn Collins in), and one Joe Cassidy was apparently the captain. The north-London convention delegate was Maurice Sheahan, another hurler and a Gaelic teacher.

What was Collins's role? Joe Good joined at the same time:

> When I joined the only person I saw that I knew really well was Michael Collins. He was in the ranks with men the first night I joined up and the following week he was section leader. He meant to be in command. I had, and he knew it, military training [in the Catholic Boy's Brigade], and he rather ridiculed my methods of drilling, although he knew his own lack of knowledge in that matter at the time.

In a more detailed account he described how 'Mick promptly choked me off for the way I marched to attention – he had not yet learnt the necessity of the word 'halt' and I continued marching to attention until I got that order.

Sam Maguire called Collins a 'leading light' in the Volunteers because of his work in keeping members on side during the split. He certainly did work at it. 'A Friend' recalled that, at the time of the split, amid 'the interminable arguments which took place at the Council meetings in John Street, the drill grounds at Lea Bridge, and in the German Gymnasium in Camden' what stood out was 'Collins and the little band who stood fast'. 'And', says Pat Brennan, 'Micheal O'Coileain was amongst that few, working, working, working. Always working, and always the gayest of the gay.' This sounds a lot like his role in hurling: always determined, always bucking up his team-mates, always helping out. But, as on the playing field, he lacked a certain something on the parade ground. Sean McGrath, later his chief arms smuggler, recalled being put in the 'awkward squad' with him and Paddy O Conaire, the extremely unsoldierly writer. And as far as we know he didn't rise above section leader – still not quite officer material in the eyes of his peers.

MEMBERSHIPS DO NOT necessarily define beliefs or ideas. But Collins was not just an activist: he was a political junkie. He devoured newspapers and journals, reading several regularly throughout his life, even if he always found them wanting. He was even an angry letter-to-the-editor writer in his youth (a classic symptom of addiction), a practice he resumed during the revolution. He had opinions on everything from military strategy in the Great War to Bulgarian politics, and he loved to argue literature, politics, even economics. He was fascinated by big ideas – Einstein's theories, socialism, free thought, new world orders and new Irelands – and deeply attracted to novelty and modernity in politics as in literature.

His personal politics were always nationalist, although not unvarying or unalloyed. The bedrock certainties were that Ireland was one of the great nations of Europe, its ancient glories suppressed by invasion and dispossession. Scourged by landlordism and tyranny, it had never surrendered its birthright (as demonstrated by a history of heroic rebellion), and was capable of renewed greatness and prosperity if given its freedom. Any domestic opposition to sovereignty from unionists was the product of minority Orange bigotry and British manipulation, not a legitimate or genuinely Irish movement.

These beliefs were inherited in youth along with his Church. Collins himself referred to

> the never-ceasing talk of Ireland's destiny, the injustices from which she had suffered in the past, and was still suffering ... When an Irish boy in those days feasted on real bacon – to the accompaniment of his father's reminiscent comments – the spirit of nationalism was breathed into him. For the father was saying that in his youth the pigs were raised exclusively for the landlords!

Nevertheless, Collins's were not merely received opinions. He read a great deal of Irish history, and built up quite a personal library, including the works of eighteenth- and nineteenth-century patriots like Wolfe Tone and John Mitchel, and much prose and verse chronicling various rebellions and nationalist movements, particularly the United Irishmen of the 1790s, the Young Ireland of the 1840s, the Fenians of the 1850s and '60s, and the Parnellites of the 1880s. His collection included all twenty-two volumes of Duffy's Library of Ireland, once described as 'treason made easy'.

There was nothing unusual about reading Mitchel's *Jail Journal* or *Speeches from the Dock*: all this material was mass-produced for a popular audience and was read widely by future rebels and their enemies alike. However, the vivid depictions of the exemplary lives and deaths of sacred heroes like Robert Emmet, the martyred leader of an 1803 rebellion, and the constant evocation of patriotic ideals and duty, all couched in fervent romantic and mystical or religious language, armed the imaginations of Collins and his comrades in Gaeldom and the IRB with a potent self-image and a guiding narrative of direct action and sacrifice. The very fact that this pantheon and its accompanying sense of heroic nationhood were so widely shared by Catholic Ireland would make later revolutionary actions all the more resonant and powerful on a symbolic level.

What set Collins apart was his secularism. He had never been taught by brothers or nuns; he was never an altar boy; he did not belong to any sodalities or confraternities, and seems not to have read religious literature – as ubiquitous in turn-of-the-century households as Duffy's Library. In this he was different from perhaps the majority of his fellow future revolutionaries, who were deeply immersed in a new wave of highly organized piety evident in Dublin and throughout Ireland in the early 1900s, much of it devoted to the Virgin Mary and the Sacred Heart of Jesus. A large number of participants in the 1916 Easter Rising had been taught by the Christian Brothers or some other order, and belonged to religious societies, particularly the highly influential Sacred Heart Sodality. Many were total abstainers from alcohol. Collins seems to have been completely uninterested in this kind of spirituality or lifestyle, and almost never used the vocabulary of blood, souls, resurrection, sin and redemption that preoccupied so many other republicans. His letters are also generally free of the standard evocations of God and his will. Towards the end of the Easter Rising, when many rebels were resorting to their rosaries, Collins ran into Joe Good in a house on Moore Street: 'I was resting on the stairs at one period with my head in my hands and Mick said angrily to me: "Are you [fucking] praying too?"'

Nor was Collins merely indifferent to the Church. He was actively anti-clerical for much of his life, and blamed the Catholic Church for many of Ireland's problems. His oft-described maiden speech to a London audience was made memorable by what Beaslai calls its 'violent attack upon the influence of the Catholic Hierarchy and clergy' (usually dated as delivered in 1908 to Sinn Feiners, although the only reference in the party newspaper was to a talk by Sean O Siothchain entitled 'Church and the Nation'). Such attitudes – which pre-dated his becoming a Fenian – alarmed his more conventional sisters. Mary recalled travelling with Michael and Hannie (on holidays) to Skibbereen to hear him give a speech in 1917: 'before the meeting Michael told us he would attack Doctor Kelly, Bishop of Ross, who was bitterly opposed to the new policy [Sinn Fein]. We tried to dissuade him but I guessed by the gleam of mischief in his eye that he was doing a bit of leg-pulling.' To attack a bishop would hardly have been politic, and Collins never did – in fact he would be willing to invoke the Pope when it seemed useful.

Biographers usually describe his anti-clericalism as 'a passing phase', part of his slightly wild youth. However, it was more than that. Collins owned many of the writings of the American freethinker Colonel Robert Ingersoll (known as 'the Great Agnostic'), so he was obviously at least interested in atheism. This might have been a result of P. S. ('Pagan') O'Hegarty's influence, but it also fits with his interest in socialism. Any intellectually open young man living in the London of the period could not help but be affected by the great movements of the time. Militant trade unionism was on the rise in Britain and Ireland, and Collins himself no doubt encountered it in the civil service. The Labour Party emerged as an electoral force in Britain in 1906, although it didn't do well in London while Collins was there. Evidence of Collins's thinking in this period can be found in his 'Wail of Regret' letter to *Sinn Fein* in 1910:

> For the past few years as a very interested observer of Sinn Fein generally I have noticed a very marked change in policy . . . It has become the defender of the landlords – the exponent of the Capitalists . . . 'Sinn Fein' in its articles on the Patents and Designs Act flaunted before the greedy capitalists the prospect of cheap Irish land and cheap Irish labour.

In a draft talk presumably prepared for a Sinn Fein audience around the same time, he lauded Finnish revolutionaries, Russian socialists and their alliance, and added, 'May not we find it beneficial to allow ourselves to be helped by the English revolutionists?' Of course this hardly makes Collins a socialist, but it does suggest sympathy and interest – a radical enough stance for pro-business Sinn Fein.

Was this too a passing fancy, a youthful fling with the left? So it might appear, given his career choices and organizational allegiances, But it was sincere, based on a deep dislike of exploitation and poverty. Geraldine Plunkett, who met him in Dublin in 1915, recalled that some people found his politics coarse and materialist and even doubted his genuine nationalism, which might have had something to do with anti-capitalist sentiments. Collins told another person after 1916 that

> as far as he, Collins, was concerned, he would do his damnedest to see that we had no miserable copy of the English social system with all the evils that he had seen associated with it [he apparently was much exercised by prostitution] when he was working in London.

He would express much the same opinions when he came to power, although what they meant in terms of policy and action would be something else, however.

We can be sure of Collins's visceral convictions and his gradual turn to revolutionary republicanism but it must be noted that he was in no way radicalized by circumstance or experience – by oppression or by the frustration of legitimate nationalist aspirations. The opposite was true. His great leap forward into the IRB, the Gaelic League and a more militant GAA took place at exactly the moment when Irish self-government seemed on the verge of realization. He joined the Volunteers when its rationale was to support Home Rule, and he joined the anti-Party splitters after the bill was finally passed in September 1914, amid the widespread expectation that self-government would come into being at the end of a short war. Nor were the Volunteers ever prevented from meeting or drilling. Such decisions were made as part of a group, with his friends and comrades, but Collins undoubtedly thought them through – and argued them out for himself. Before 1915, however, his politics carried few risks and were quite compatible with his business career and all the rest of the life he had built up in London over the years. He was about to have to choose between them.

5: Rising

When I first met him in the yard at Larkfield in November
1915 he was twenty-six but looked younger. He was not
tall, medium height and colour, quiet and with a sense of
humour. He had lost his Cork accent but could produce it
at a moment's notice . . . He could present a perfectly blank
appearance and could not be picked out of a crowd unless
you knew him. Until I looked at his eyes he was not
remarkable.

(Geraldine Plunkett)

WAR BROUGHT MORE THAN political changes for Michael Collins:
it also brought a change of jobs. On 1 September 1914 he took up a
new position with the Guaranty Trust Company of New York. He
probably did not leave Horne's of his own accord, however. The
Exchange had closed as soon as war broke out, and, true to their
patriotic credo, many of his fellow clerks and their employers
decamped en masse into the army – where many were to die,
including Horne's partner Wilfred Lamaison. Trading continued in a
hole-and-corner way, but the Exchange proper did not reopen until
January of the following year. Contrary to the usual biographical
gloss, Collins had very likely simply been laid off. Fortunately for
him there were suddenly a lot of vacancies in other offices for
replacements for the departed warriors.

Guaranty Trust had its offices at 33, 34 and 35 Lombard Street
(destroyed in the 1940 blitz), on the other side of the Bank of
England from Horne's and down a typical City alleyway, Plough
Court. The bank had been in London only since 1896, but business
had grown steadily with the rise in international trade. Its main
business was in the discount market, buying bills of exchange and

settling or selling them. As such, it acted as both a lender and an exchange dealer, buying sterling and paying out dollars, francs or marks: very profitable and very competitive. The London office played a crucial role, as its ability to process bills more quickly than its rivals gave the New York office its edge in the marketplace. Guaranty Trust seems to have had something of a reputation in London as a dodgy Yankee upstart, but it was successful.

According to Collins, he was hired to be manager of its bill department: 'my duties there brought me into contact with banks and commercial houses all over Great Britain and Ireland, besides affording me a wide knowledge of American business methods and the processes of Exchange between America and these countries.' After his death, *his* manager described him simply as a clerk, so he may have inflated his title. The office was actually run by several Scotsmen, who managed a staff of twenty (all men), including a cashier and two bookkeepers. The latter perched on stools, the rest worked at small desks. The days were a bit longer than in other places, starting at 9.30, with no tea breaks. Employees were well paid, however, got annual Christmas bonuses, and were encouraged to set their sights high: it being an American bank, anyone could dream about rising to the top. Also imported were the US morale-building techniques of staff outings and sports, and a cheery and informative company newsletter (although that and the staff club didn't arrive until after the war). Still, employees were barred from marrying until their salary was at least £250 a year, and clerks had to wear the company uniform of black or grey suit, white shirt, starched collar, and bowler hat.

Much of the staff was British rather than American, and no doubt as jingoistic as the rest of the City. Collins didn't like the London management, and later denounced them as being 'very hostile to us'. He was also sensitive to this quality in his co-workers, as witnessed by his supervisor, Robert MacVey:

> Only on very rare occasions did his sunny smile disappear, and this was usually the result of one of his fellow clerks making some disparaging, and probably unthinking, remark about his beloved Ireland. Then he would look as though he might prove a dangerous enemy.

Collins would later refer several times to such attitudes in public speeches:

I know very well that the people of England had very little
regard for the people of Ireland, and that when you lived among
them you had to be defending yourself constantly from insults
... Every man who has lived amongst them knows that they are
always making jokes about Paddy and the pig, and that sort of
thing.

He subsequently remarked: 'I often hit one of them on the nose for
it.'

On the other hand he was at least convinced of the company's
competence. He would later insist on using Guaranty Trust for much
of the Dail government's banking both in London and in New York,
where the republican movement also used other of their services. The
company seems also to have had a good opinion of him. After his
death, the president, Charles Sabin, said Collins was 'a very good
clerk, a man of strong character ... a high-class fellow who would
have gone far. He was coming along very fast when he was called
back to Ireland.' This statement was no doubt highly coloured by the
cirumstances, but it still has a ring of truth to it.

So COLLINS ended up with a good job: responsible, reasonably
well paid, probably safe, and with genuine prospects. Like Horatio
Alger's heroes, and as his mother and sisters must have hoped, he
had reached respectability. Can we say his was a success story?
He failed to establish himself in the civil service, and his attempts
at self-improvement through education were inadequate, keeping
his income for the first four years at an abysmally low level for
high-priced London and eventually forcing him into the job market.
This was a piece of inadvertent good luck, however, as if he had
gone back into the civil service as an Assistant Clerk he would
probably have been held up there for a very long time. He found
a private-sector post easily enough, but still ended up in another
junior position for another four years until he lost that job as well
(albeit through no fault of his own). Once again he didn't stay
unemployed for long, and he managed to achieve quite a good
position at last in 1914. This meant he was able to stay in the
black-coated ranks of the lower middle class – by no means an
assured outcome. We don't know his salary at Guaranty Trust, but
banking clerks were the aristocracy of their kind and typically earned

more than their civil-service counterparts and twice as much as commercial clerks.

But Collins obviously wanted more, his ambition still unfulfilled. In Hayden Talbot's account, Collins says of his post-Post Office jobs that

> none . . . satisfied my ideas of opportunity . . . with each passing year I felt more and more convinced that London for me held as little real opportunity as did Ireland . . . there was every chance, if I remained in England, to continue to be a clerk the rest of my life . . . the one thing I had been looking for [was] a fair chance to get ahead.

Ultimately his big break would come in politics, not business. His success in one was dependent on his abilities in the other, however, and he would never really leave the office, suit and collar behind.

AFTER THE Irish Volunteers split, the anti-war wing to which Collins belonged was left with the original name and purpose, the eponymous newspaper, and the moral high ground. Its other assets were few: a few thousand disorganized members, a scattering of modern arms, and no real military expertise, money or public credibility – the Londoners being a typical unit in these respects. Its backers – the IRB in secret, Sinn Fein in public – had little clout themselves, and the GAA had refused to endorse the Volunteers even before the split. The organization could easily have faded into irrelevance.

That it did not is a tribute to the talent and dedication of the Volunteer leadership, headed by President Eoin (John) MacNeill, a Gaelic League pioneer and history professor at the new University College in Dublin. He chaired the central Executive, which in December 1914 appointed a General Headquarters Staff (referred to simply as 'Headquarters' and eventually just 'GHQ') who worked at offices in Kildare Street. MacNeill was named Chief of the eight-man staff, which included Patrick Pearse, another prominent Gaelic Leaguer and the founder of a nationalist boys' school, St Enda's, as Director of Organization; Joseph Plunkett, a writer and editor, as Director of Military Operations; Thomas MacDonagh, another writer, Gaelic Leaguer and lecturer at UCD, as Director of Training and Commandant of the Dublin Brigade; Bulmer Hobson, the founder of Fianna Eireann, a nationalist boy-scout organization, and a professional activist, as Quartermaster General; and (from August 1915) Eamonn Ceannt, a clerk for the Dublin Corporation, as Director of Communications.

Apart from MacNeill, a well-established academic in his forties, these were men in their thirties, little known outside their immediate circles and the target of W. B. Yeats's mocking tales and gibes in his club. Unbeknown to MacNeill or Yeats, however, they were also members of the IRB, along with Volunteer executives Sean Mac-Dermott, a tram conductor and barman-turned-organizational-mastermind, and Liam Mellows, a young Dublin clerk. And behind them was Tom Clarke, a veteran of the Fenian bombing campaign in England in the 1880s, which had got him imprisoned for sixteen years. Unbowed, he had returned to Dublin in 1907, set up as a newsagent, and became the godfather of the revived Brotherhood.

The official policy of the Irish Volunteers was to resist if attacked, but otherwise to stand guard over Ireland's national rights – a role they accused the Irish Party of abdicating. As laid out at their first convention, in October 1914, this meant resisting the partition of Ulster by the unionist majority there, resisting the conscription of Irish men into the British armed forces, working to replace Dublin Castle rule with a 'National Government', and maintaining the right to national self-defence embodied in the Volunteers themselves. In practice, the Volunteers would act as a deterrent to repression or conscription by the British government, and this meant playing a waiting game while recruiting, organizing, training and arming as many men as possible to present as formidable a threat as possible. By 1916 the membership numbered 15,000 – with functioning brigade and battalion staffs in Dublin, Cork and Limerick – and MacNeill boasted they were too strong for the police to handle.

Clarke, MacDermott, Plunkett, Pearse, Ceannt and MacDonagh, on the other hand, saw time as their enemy, not their ally. They were all members of an ultra-secret Military Council within the Brotherhood, and they were determined to use the Volunteers to launch a republican insurrection before the organization was suppressed or the war ended. This would be their only chance to fulfil the IRB's dream of revolution – an opportunity elevated into a spiritual necessity by Pearse and others, who believed that Ireland's soul could be saved only by an act of Christ-like sacrifice. With German and Irish-American aid, a rising was set for Easter Sunday 1916.

Volunteer leaders and activists – most of whom had no idea any such plan existed – increasingly expected to have to fight to keep their arms or to oppose conscription, and it was the British membership who had to face this threat first. The war in Europe did not yet require compulsory service, but popular and political demands for it were growing as casualties soared and recruits became scarcer through 1915. The still-Liberal government temporized by asking men to attest their willingness to enlist. This only brought the spectre of coercion nearer – and indeed it was finally introduced with the Military Service Act of January 1916.

These events provoked much discussion in Collins's circle, and set the stage for his first major decision in life. Before this, his work and home life had been closely determined by family and circumstances and his politics had developed almost organically, with membership in one group leading naturally on to others. In late 1915 all three were at stake. Should he stay with Hannie and the bank with the draft hanging over his head? He had just turned twenty-six, and nothing much was happening in his life; nor were there any promising opportunities on the horizon.

What were the options? There was always Ireland, exempt from conscription because of popular and Irish Party opposition, although nationalists feared that it was coming sooner or later. Moreover, in a few months' time a rebellion would be launched. The question is, what did Collins know and when did he know it? This would become a matter of public controversy in 1922, when opponents attacked his war record. Seamus Robinson, head of the IRA's South Tipperary Brigade, said in the Dail that 'so far as I know, Michael Collins came over from London as I came from Glasgow to avoid conscription.' To which Ernest Blythe, a Volunteer and IRB organizer in 1915–16, replied, 'That's not true.' Pat Brennan, his comrade in London, soon joined the debate: 'I knew him twelve years ago . . . when he was an unknown, a silent worker; I knew him up to the day when he came back to avoid conscription; but he came back to take a man's part in the Rising.'

Collins apparently told Hayden Talbot that he was summoned personally by Tom Clarke to help with preparations for the Rising; others refer to a message sent by Sean MacDermott to come home.

The latter does seem to have existed, but was sent to the IRB membership as a whole, and may not have arrived until after Collins had left London. Sean McGrath remembers a key meeting of the Londoners in November or December 1915: 'Mick Collins was present and we were debating what steps we could take to combat conscription. Mick in his blunt way said "Go home to Ireland, that is the only place to fight. I am going there tonight."' This sounds more like a blanket statement of intent than a revelation of secret knowledge: after all, many Volunteers expected a government crack-down sooner rather than later. Sam Maguire, the best authority (who may not have had advance warning either), states categorically that Collins did not know about the rebellion plans while he was in England.

Another possibility was to go to the United States. It has often been suggested either that his American employers, Guaranty Trust, offered Collins a place in New York or that the opportunity existed if he had wanted to apply for it. In reality, this seems a remote possibility. Why would the bank bother shipping even a talented clerk to New York in wartime when he was useful in London and when New York was presumably teeming with the like? It certainly had no intention of acting as a haven for draft dodgers: in fact it encouraged enlistment. When Collins told his boss he was leaving to join up in 1916 (not revealing that it was the Irish front he was going to), he was given a substantial bonus – a fact he was at first ashamed of, but which he would later boast about.

In 1915 the offer we do know existed – such as it was – came from his long-departed brother Patrick (a policeman):

> Now Michael regarding your coming to Chicago I have no doubt but you will be able to land something here even if it comes slow you will be sure to have a place to sleep and eat besides business is getting good all through the country now, and the prospects are pointing to a prosperous future of course you will have to use your own discretion and not do anything you may regret . . . P.S. If you don't take a chance you will never get anywhere. A little nerve is all that's necessary.

That Michael thought seriously about this is suggested by his December request for his birth certificate from the Civil Service

Commission – presumably to get a passport. Hannie was certainly privy to his thoughts:

> At the end of 1915, urged by Pat, his brother in Chicago, he seriously contemplated leaving for America, as he foresaw that conscription was forthcoming ... and he considered that by emigrating he might best be able to serve his own country ... We discussed the idea of emigration in its various bearings for several evenings. I was strongly in favour of it but about the 23rd December he said – 'There is going to be trouble in Ireland in the spring and I could not endure the thought of not being there and in it.'

This sounds about right, but the question is further complicated by the question of when he actually left London. Some accounts say about 15 January 1916; others say sometime in November 1915. The answer may be that both are right, and that this explains many of the apparent contradictions in the story.

It was in November 1915 that Geraldine Plunkett asked her brother Joseph for a reliable man to help with the bookkeeping for the family's Larkfield property in Kimmage, south Dublin, where they were both living. Joe, of course, was the Volunteers' Director of Military Operations and a leading republican conspirator. In fact he had recently returned from a Buchanesque journey to the Continent to make contact with their German allies.

Larkfield – then still in the country beyond Harold's Cross – was a disused stone mill, built on 8 acres of farmland on the river Poddle. There were also a manager's house, a cottage, a bakery, a large barn and a cottage, and a herd of Kerry cows grazed the fields. Josephine Plunkett – Joe and Geraldine's eccentric mother – had bought it years before at an auction, apparently on a whim and without telling her family. She had long neglected and bewildered her children, even to the point of living in a separate house from them while they were growing up. Joe had terrible respiratory problems and had spent much time in North Africa as a result. When he and his sister discovered Larkfield's existence – 'none of us knew when or how Ma got possession' – they moved out there by themselves for the better air, along with a 'mad maid'.

Life was further simplified when, in 1914, Ma declared that 'it was time she lived her own life' and left for the United States, taking the maid with her. Joe and Geraldine could lead a nearly self-sufficient life at Larkfield, with milk, bread, vegetables from the garden and rent to provide an income. However, Geraldine, the self-appointed manager, found that the place was in a state of disrepair and the records were a mess:

> I told Joe that I could not manage the repairs and book work any more and he would have to get someone. He agreed and told me that two men would come and I would have to choose the right one. The next day one came and he was obviously right because he was Mick Collins.

Collins had just arrived from London. He had told his firm that he was going to look after a sick relative, and this may even have been true as he was staying with his aunt, Mrs O'Donovan. However, he was obviously also pondering his future. He had met up again with the still-avuncular Patrick Belton, who presumably put him in touch with the Dublin IRB, and thus he found his way to Joe Plunkett, who took him under his wing. Like any good fraternity, the Brotherhood looked after its own.

The work was part-time and paid only £1 a week, but Geraldine was certainly impressed. 'Mick helped me for a couple of hours a day, it was wonderful to see the property being put in order and although mother threw most of his books out as soon as she got home [later in 1916], the houses were repaired and the rents collected.' 'No one ever had a better clerk, he was far too good for the work I wanted done, quick and intelligent, a splendid organizer and took very little time to do much work.' One imagines he would make quite a good rent-collector. He even tried to collect from Cathal Brugha (Charles [William St John] Burgess) – a militant Volunteer and future political antagonist – on a barn the Plunketts didn't own: an omen of financial disputes to come.

With characteristic embroidery, Collins would subsequently say of this work that 'I was accepted as Secretary to Count Plunkett's family, looking after the affairs of his property, attending to correspondence, rents etc.' Geraldine and Joe's father, George Noble Plunkett – a papal count – was director of the National Museum. They were very fond of him, but he was 'too quiet and never interfered' with Josephine. As Plunkett senior had just been elected MP for North Roscommon when Collins wrote this, in February 1917, the name-dropping is understandable. The Count did move out to Larkfield eventually, so Collins probably did meet him, but he wasn't his secretary.

Joe, the military mastermind of the conspiracy (unfortunately for his co-conspirators), must have imparted some hints at least as to coming events. In any case, no one could hang around Larkfield every day without realizing that something was in the air. It had become a kind of republican commune for drop-ins and drop-outs, and a refuge from assorted realities and oppressions, personal and political. At the heart of things were Joe and Geraldine, very attached to one another and sharing an idyllic sense of political and spiritual idealism.

By the time Collins came on the scene, the countdown to the Easter Rising had begun and Kimmage had become an unofficial headquarters for those in the know, including Rory (Roderick) O'Connor, an engineer who had returned from Canada when war broke out and was now working for Dublin Corporation; Tom Dillon, a chemistry lecturer at University College Dublin (and Geraldine's fiancé); Fergus Kelly, one of Dillon's students; and Joe and Geraldine's younger brother, George. Guests, including Collins, took pot luck for meals: Grace Gifford, Joe's flaky fiancée (and a later bane of Collins's existence), described going to Larkfield as 'like a picnic'. This is an apt description for what was clearly a very happy place. Collins must have been delighted to be so quickly part of such a friendly group of insiders.

Collins took his newly acquired knowledge back to London for Christmas, mulled it over, thrashed it out with Hannie, possibly discussed his options with pals (several of whom claimed they talked him out of an American trip), and finally decided to return to Dublin in January – only then telling his employers he wouldn't be back.

In some ways the decision may have been made for him (as had happened before). He couldn't stay in London after January 1916, as he would then fall prey to the Military Service Act. At this point, many of his comrades were leaving, as were those in Liverpool, Glasgow and elsewhere – to end up in many cases at Larkfield – so he was part of the crowd, perhaps even following it. It was late December when he asked for his birth certificate, so he may still have been trying to keep the American option open. He may even have tried and failed. Emigration for a single young man at this point was far from easy – he may have missed the boat. That left Dublin.

On the other hand, the prospect of rebellion was a positive attraction. Plunkett, a charming fantasist only a bit older than Collins, no doubt portrayed it as a glorious enterprise with a high chance of success thanks to massive German aid. After the St Patrick's Day review in 1916, in which thousands of armed Volunteers marched through Dublin, Collins wrote to a friend back in London that 'from what I have seen of the Dublin men they will give a good account of themselves.' It was the culmination of his political apprenticeship and beliefs: action instead of stasis; the real thing not drill practice. No more wooden rifles!

Collins had found a new mentor in Joe Plunkett, and Joe had found a helpmate. According to Geraldine, 'After a week or so Mick became Joe's Aide de Camp [although that title was not bestowed until later, and then not just on Collins] and carried messages and did all the things Joe could not do, as he spent a lot of time in bed.' She added that 'Mick was fond of Joe and took great care of him, but he was not sentimental.' Collins was promoted to captain, with full uniform to match (although he had to get that made himself). Whatever doubts remained were soon put aside: if Collins knew anything it was how to work a new opportunity and focus on a common goal.

Geraldine provides us with a fascinating picture of Collins on the eve of revolution, as he presented himself to a sympathetic member of the Dublin bourgeoisie:

> He was crude socially, his business manner was his best, he had crude ideas which offended others and [a] coarse point of view which made them think he was a materialist, they even thought he was an adventurer and not a nationalist at all. He was a clever peasant with a peasant's virtues and vices, he was shrewd and plain but he drank a great deal too much . . . He was a very rough diamond.

She also thought:

> He was completely honest and direct, there was no doubt about it. He was at this time, Nov. 1915, too trusting and he found it hard to suspect anyone, somewhat childlike . . . Mick was a good actor and could be a silly countryman with a strong Cork accent . . . Joe spent a lot of time talking to him and getting him to

have standards with which to judge people . . . He was unsophis-
ticated except financially, but he was really intelligent.

His acting seems to have fooled Geraldine as well, as she recalled
that 'he had no experience of culture and had never read any fiction,'
which was far from true. It may be that Collins, seeking a new
sponsor in this new world, was willing to play the neophyte. The
overtrusting nature – or gullibility – we have seen before, on the
playing field, and it would appear again.

Collins continued to do the books and help out in the early
months of 1916. Kimmage was filling up with refugees from Britain
– fellow Volunteers dodging the draft and willing to fight in Ireland.
These were dubbed the 'Liverpool lambs' for their extremely un-
lamb-like qualities, although some were from London as well. They
were a rough crowd, but they caused no trouble, and once they had
settled into the mill 'you would not know that a large number of men
were in the building.' Collins spent most of his time there for another
month, but, preferring not to bunk in with the other reverse exiles,
lodged instead on faraway North Circular Road. He may already
have decided he was something more than one of the boys.

Larkfield was now more of a garrison than a commune although,
even with swearing Liverpudlians everywhere, it retained its innocent
atmosphere of harmonious comradeship. However cosy and well-
connected the Kimmage job was, however, it did not pay very much
and did not require much attention. After a month or so at it, Collins
took a job with Craig, Gardner, an accountancy firm on Dame Street
in the heart of Dublin. Indeed, this was *the* establishment firm, the
oldest and by far the largest in Ireland. 'In that place I gained some
useful experience of Dublin [business] houses and the people connected with them,' Collins later reported. When Frank O'Connor
inquired about his time there, the company sent the following:

I have looked up our past records and all that I can find in
regard to Michael Collins is that he came into our office in a
temporary capacity on the 23rd February 1916, and that he left
some time in the month of April. The date is not mentioned,
but he appears to have only received about one week's salary in
that month. My own impression is that he was sent to the
country (I think Co. Wexford) on a liquidation matter, and that
we never saw or heard of him after Easter Week.

In effect, he was an apprentice accountant: 'After a little training in the office I was sent out in the usual way to audit accounts.' This was standard practice in the profession at that time. 'Office juniors' were thrown almost immediately into audits, travelling the circuit of client firms accompanied by a senior man. Sink or swim. The work was usually intensely dull: detailed and repetitive. Accounts had to be checked, often from start to finish, or even assembled from scratch – the grim 'brown paper parcel jobs'. Sometimes accountancy firms carried out the year-end stocktaking, but mostly the jobs were a matter of adding up long triple columns of figures, then double-checking, over and over again:

> It was 99.9% audits you know – ticking. Most of the clients didn't really keep books to the final stage, so a large element of the audit was bookkeeping, and bringing the books up to date. You were bookkeepers/auditors. You started off just ticking, ticking, ticking, ticking, and then after a while you were allowed to use your intelligence in simple things like, say, balancing the bought ledgers, the purchase ledgers and trial balances, and getting a set of accounts out. It was basically drudgery.

Was Collins contemplating making a new career in accountancy? The prospects were not necessarily that attractive. Accountancy firms were run by a few partners, who might employ a few other qualified accountants and several senior but unqualified clerks who knew the trade inside out but hadn't been articled. Below them were the semi-seniors, and then the junior drudges. The latter fell into two categories – those who were articled and those who weren't. It was possible to qualify without being articled and passing the accountancy exams, by getting an incorporated qualification, but it took nine years. Most would-be accountants paid hundreds of pounds to be taken on as articled clerks, making the profession overwhelmingly middle class in background. The great majority had gone to public or at least grammar schools and had parents or relatives backing them. A good junior clerk might become a good and valued senior clerk, but a young man without money didn't have much chance of going further. It would also have meant more evening classes, more cramming and more exams. One thing is certain, Collins did want to be thought of as an accountant and a professional man, as will be seen later.

Among Collins's new colleagues were the brothers George and

Joseph McGrath, who would become close allies in the revolution, although they didn't work with him or know him until after the Rising. George had started at the firm in 1910, while Joe arrived in the autumn of 1915. Craig, Gardner's business was national, so their employees spent much of their time on provincial liquidations – George in Sligo and Tuam, Joseph in Newbridge. Apart from the liquidation job in Wexford, Collins also audited Boileau & Boyd's, wholesale chemists. Another co-worker was Frank Henderson, also a Volunteer:

> [Collins] was in my office in Craig Gardiners [sic]. I used to wear a Faine badge then [showing the wearer spoke Gaelic]. He came over to me one day and he began to speak bad Irish. He used to wear a hard hat [a bowler] and carry an umbrella, which was I expect a London custom. We didn't know what side he was on. A recruiting officer came in to the firm one day. We were polite to him, but we didn't intend to join. The Unionists present wouldn't join nor were they very polite to the recruiting officer. Collins came in later and we said to him so as to try him out: there was a recruiting officer here and he wanted to see you about joining the army. Collins cursed and banged the table then we knew he was not friendly to the British army. Some time later there was a [Volunteer] parade in Fairview. We saw Collins with his hard hat and his umbrella on the way to the grounds. Then we knew that this fellow was alright.

As in London, jobs were available for the likes of Collins and Joe McGrath because their former holders *had* joined the army: 82 Irish accountants and clerks had done so by 1916, the number rising to 128 in 1918. Robert Gardner – recalled fondly as a sympathetic figure in fur coat and top hat – lost his son at Gallipoli. It was a unionist firm, and its rebel clerks were not welcomed back after their stints in prison.

COLLINS WAS a staff officer now, but his exact position with Volunteer headquarters is a bit uncertain. He had stopped working at Larkfield in February and got a job that sometimes took him out of the city, so he was not yet a full-time revolutionary. He was still a regular visitor to Kimmage, however, and he joined the influential Keating branch of the Gaelic League (which doubled as an IRB sleeper cell), where he met many future friends and allies, including

Diarmuid O'Hegarty, Gearoid (George) O'Sullivan, Piaras Beaslai and Fionan (Finian) Lynch. If Kimmage was the southern pole of the coming revolution, the Keating rooms on North Frederick Street near Parnell Square were the northern equivalent – both were armed camps by the end of April.

He also got to know Sean MacDermott, another of the chief conspirators, who, like Joe Plunkett, may have seen him as a kind of protégé. 'On one occasion', reported Dr Charles MacAuley, Mac-Dermott 'brought to me a young man with an injury on his hand, whose name was Collins . . . He brought him very secretly and he said he was a very valuable man.' This was our Michael, who had injured himself working with explosives in Kimmage with Tom Dillon and Rory O'Connor (later head of IRA engineering and assorted special effects). MacDermott also inducted him into his own Fintan Lalor IRB circle (named after a nineteenth-century forerunner of the Fenians, James Fintan Lalor), and Collins would later be seen by some as his political heir.

Collins resigned his accounting job in April, and at this point – along with several other eager young men – became a full-time aide to Joe Plunkett. As Plunkett was ill and then recuperating from surgery in a nursing home in Mountjoy Square, much of Collins's work was once again simply to help him physically and run errands while he was bedridden. Dr MacAuley described Plunkett, whom he also attended, as 'very thin and highly strung', not to mention paranoid. He was attended by a constant flow of young men taking notes. MacAuley 'frankly, did not take this at all seriously and remarked: "Napoleon dictating to his marshals" – a remark which was not well received'.

In no sense was Collins a leader, or seen as such. When he tried to act as one, things did not go well. 'He was throwing his weight about a bit,' grumbled one of the Kimmage garrison. Joe Good from London was also there now:

> Michael Collins sometimes visited the place where the munitions were being made, to speak to [George] Plunkett. He aggressively tried to hurry us and even to instruct us, but he displayed a lack of the most elementary knowledge of mechanics [Good was an electrician] and made himself unpopular by his aggressiveness. I was impressed by the sense of hurry and earnestness in Michael

Collins, although I had little sympathy with his drastic methods for getting the work done, since he was abusive to us.

Once, 'when a good deal of fun was going on', Mick came in a bullying mood but was laughed off. 'Mick, swearing at us, went up the stairs to George Plunkett, followed by a gibing chorus of "The birds of the air fell a sighing and a sobbing when they heard of the death of poor Michael Collins . . ." Someone remarked that Mick, as usual, had been treading in someone else's reserves.'

His demeanour was 'hurried and unusually discourteous' as he buzzed about the city. Piaras Beaslai, a journalist and Keating habitué (and Collins's future biographer), remembers that 'during the last few days before the "Rising", the rooms in North Frederick Street were an important centre of our activities. Mick was in and out continually, but was not consulted about any important matters.'

The Volunteer staff had ordered a full mobilization and exercises for Easter Sunday, 23 April – not unusual in itself, but it would provide the cover for launching the Rising. At that point a German freighter was supposed to land thousands of rifles in Kerry; these would then be distributed to Volunteer units in the south and west of Ireland, allowing them to overpower their local police forces and wage a commando war as the much-admired Boers had done in the South African War at the turn of the century.

As it turned out, the freighter arrived early and was intercepted by the Royal Navy and scuttled by her captain. Dublin Castle now knew that something was up, as did Eoin MacNeill and others on the staff who were not part of the conspiracy. In fact Plunkett had forged a purported government plan to round up the Volunteer leadership, and other lies had been told in order to fool the non-republican Volunteers into joining a revolt. These more cautious souls might have been willing to fight if the German guns and ammunition had been available, but without such equipment, and with no real provocation, they moved to stop the operation before it started. MacNeill sent out a countermanding order cancelling the Sunday manoeuvres, which did succeed in paralysing most provincial units.

The Military Council and the republican vanguard in Larkfield, the Keating branch and the Dublin Brigade were not so easily put off. Emergency meetings were held that weekend, couriers (Collins included no doubt) criss-crossed the city, more lies were told to get

MacNeill off their backs, and the end result was a twenty-four-hour postponement. At noon on Easter Monday the four Dublin battalions would occupy a ring of buildings around central Dublin, and the Provisional Government of the Irish Republic (P. H. Pearse, Pres.) would declare its existence. The night before was an anxious one, as troops or police could start raiding at any time now they had evidence of a conspiracy involving Germany. Liam Archer was on duty all day at the Keating branch:

> That night we were passing the time playing cards in the small 'guard' room and were joined by Michael Collins. I had not met him before but he was apparently well known to the others of the party. His entrance was characteristic of him as I later knew him. He forced his way to a seat at the table, produced two revolvers and announced he would ensure there would be nothing crooked about this game. Not to be outdone we all produced our weapons.

Whatever their original hopes and intentions, the rebels now had no chance of success. They had nearly succeeded in manoeuvring the Volunteers as a whole into action through forgery and promises of German guns, but this had fallen through. Fighting in self-defence to protect their right to bear arms was one thing; attacking post offices and biscuit factories for use as fortresses on a bank holiday was another. Even some in the IRB were dubious, believing Mac-Neill's strategy of deterrence made more sense militarily and politically. The conspirators had allied themselves with the even more belligerent James Connolly and the Citizen Army, gaining perhaps 200 men and women but losing the trust of many more Volunteers, suspicious of the Connollyites' socialism and connection to past labour unrest. The Proclamation of the Republic claimed to have been endorsed by both the Brotherhood and the Volunteers, but neither had done so (Sinn Fein was not involved at all). The constitutions of both were violated, and the memberships and officers of both were bitterly divided or badly confused as a result of the conspiracy.

This, then, was Collins's third great split, and once again he found himself on the side of the militant tendency. On each previous occasion – in the GAA and in the Irish Volunteers – his side had lost the battle for the majority, but had taken the higher ground of moral and patriotic superiority and had gained possession of the battlefield – the organization itself. In each case Collins had been able to make himself an insider as a result: someone in the know, in touch with the people at the top and privy to their decisions (although not a party to them). In a way, this was a split by default, as those opposed to the Rising going ahead just stayed at home – but the result would be much the same. No national credentials would ever beat fighting for your country beneath a rebel flag, and no organizational battlefield could beat the real thing.

Everyone involved in the plans for the Rising believed it to be an epochal event for their movement, their generation and their nation. It would break with a shameful past, clarify the future, and save Ireland's soul. Here was the ultimate 'in', the biggest secret, the stage on which long-nurtured political and emotional fantasies would be made real. And Collins was there, he had made it, a party to history.

ON EASTER SATURDAY Plunkett was moved to the Metropole Hotel on Sackville (popularly – and later officially – known as O'Connell) Street, despite his open wound. 'He was in a state of great excitement and talked continuously. He was wearing a striking sombrero hat,' MacAuley recalled. One of Collins's tasks that day was to visit Joe's fiancée, Grace Gifford: 'On Holy Saturday morning Mick Collins came to my house ... He had with him £20 and a revolver, and I don't know which frightened me more. He said that Joe sent the revolver for me to defend myself, and the money, in case I had to bribe the military.' Neither Gifford's nor Plunkett's grasp on reality was all that firm.

On Easter Monday, 24 April 1916, Collins – in full uniform – was at the nursing home to assist Plunkett (who had been moved back once the Sunday attack had been called off). Here William Brennan-Whitmore first met him, 'a tall, pale-faced man hovering about somewhat restlessly':

> The chief shook hands and introduced the young man as Michael Collins, his aide-de-camp. It was easy to see why this young man was chosen as Plunkett's ADC – his obvious vigour and youthful energy were assets to a man already weakened not only by great mental strain but also by grievous ill-health. I can't say that, at the time, I was much impressed with

Collins. He appeared to be silent to the point of surliness, and he gave my hand a bone-creaking squeeze without saying a single word.

Collins helped Plunkett dress – the sombrero was exchanged for full staff regalia, including riding boots, spurs and a pince-nez – and the two aides helped the chief into a cab to go back to the Metropole to pick up his guns and plans. There they encountered a lobby full of holidaying British officers, who amazedly but politely gave way to the resplendent but obviously invalid figure and his green-uniformed helpers. Plunkett lived in fear of spies, but the truth was that there were none: the authorities did not take the Volunteers seriously enough and had not bothered to alert the army or cancel leave. Back to the cab then, and on to Liberty Hall, the headquarters of the Citizen Army (another of the city's incongruous republican fortresses), also the rendezvous point for the Kimmage boys, who arrived peacefully by tram.

From here the newly minted Provisional Government – having outmanoeuvred Pearse's distraught mother – marched to declare its intentions at the General Post Office, back around the corner in O'Connell Street (next to the Metropole). Collins grabbed an unsuspecting British officer writing a telegram and told him he was a prisoner of war. He then helped Plunkett upstairs to rest, although, despite his fancy-dress costume, he would prove to be a commanding presence in the midst of crisis. The lambs were elevated in rank to 'a Company of the Headquarters Battalion of the High Command Staff', and Collins was appointed to the government bodyguard. Presumably this meant he had a ringside view as Patrick Pearse, the Commandant-General of the Army of the Irish Republic, read the proclamation outside the Post Office to a group of Volunteers and bewildered onlookers. The Post Office garrison then set about preparing their defences for the inevitable British attack.

The rebel rank and file were told that 'allies' were on the way, and this vision of German troops, artillery and machine guns routing a war-weakened British army was allowed to persist – presumably to keep up morale. This was probably unnecessary, as the rebels were driven by conviction not illusion, and were bound tightly together by blood, friendship and long comradeship. Fewer than 1,000 men and women mobilized in Dublin – not enough to hold the planned defensive ring around the city centre, but a determined force none the less.

Despite the advance warning, the insurgents caught the government – who thought the danger was over with the capture of the German guns and MacNeill's countermanding order – by surprise. This allowed them to take their positions and prepare defences unmolested, north and south of the river Liffey, forming a rough perimeter around the city centre. However, they decided not to attack Dublin Castle or key sites such as the telephone exchange or port facilities, so government officials and the British army's Irish Command were free to meet, communicate and bring in reinforcements. By Thursday there were nearly 20,000 troops in Dublin, with machine guns and artillery, preparing to isolate and overwhelm the republican defences. Quickly besieged and bombarded in their makeshift fortresses scattered about the city, the rebels did not break or panic. They stuck to their guns and inflicted heavy losses on their opponents – most of whom were as new to fighting as they were.

Inside the GPO 'there appeared to be a superabundance of officers hanging around with nothing particular to do', one bemused visitor noted. 'There seemed to be one officer to every three men.' As many as 400 Volunteers were posted there, and many more passed through. Collins was not the only one who wanted to be in the picture, but he was not seen with the provisional governors after the building was secured, and he was not on the firing line, as his damaged hand apparently prevented him from using a gun (although no one saw bandages or any sign of a disability during or after Easter week). Instead he popped up here and there, making himself useful, helping out on odd jobs or busybodying others, just as he had before the Rising.

According to Collins, he was assigned to attend (guard?) James Connolly, the Commandant-General of the Dublin Division, that Monday and they spent time on the roof of the GPO. If so, it wasn't for long. Desmond Fitzgerald was in charge of the basement kitchen:

> A great many of the men for a large part of the day and the night would have no particular duty assigned to them, and for want of anything better to do would stroll along to the restaurant to pass the time eating and talking together . . . Mick

Collins, whom I knew by sight, without knowing his name . . . strode in one evening with some of his men who were covered with dust and had been demolishing walls or building barricades, and announced that those men were to be fed if they took the last food in the place. I did not attempt to argue with him, and the men sat down, openly rejoicing that I had been crushed.

Fitzgerald describes Collins as 'the most active and efficient officer in the place', although it doesn't sound as though the competition was too fierce.

On Thursday, Dinny Daly and Joe Good came across him relegated to a windowless room on the top floor, where he had been told to guard the ladder to the roof – fellow Corkman and veteran of the London Post Office, J. J. Walsh, was in the same room minding the trunk switchboards. 'It was a post of little honour or danger. He looked bad-tempered: a case of Achilles sulking in his tent.'

He returned to action on Friday, when a fire broke out on the roof – the building was now coming under artillery fire. John 'Blimey' O'Connor, a fellow fifth wheel from Plunkett's enormous staff, was told off to fight it along with Collins: 'We held the fire at bay, floor by floor, by placing barriers of sand across the doorways and flooding the floors with a lake of water.' This wrecked Collins's uniform, destroyed his breeches, and put him in an even worse mood. On Friday he spent some time across the street in the *Freeman's Journal* offices, according to the then managing director, W. J. Flynn, who phoned from home to see what was going on. Collins answered. Flynn repeatedly demanded that he identify himself, and Collins repeatedly refused, cheekily replying 'Never mind. Who are you?' Collins, who loved telling such stories, identified himself years later.

By Friday evening the GPO was ablaze and the rebels were forced to flee, exposing themselves directly to British fire. Collins helped assemble a barricade to provide cover. After a long night huddled in nearby houses, it was clear to many that it was time to surrender. Dozens of Volunteers had been killed or wounded, O'Connell Street had been ravaged by artillery shells and fires, and the poor people who inhabited nearby tenements had suffered worst of all. If the

Military Council's point had been to make a grand gesture, it had now been sufficiently made.

Other rebels, including many of the Kimmagers, were for holding out. Steeped in the hothouse atmosphere of Larkfield, they did not want to give up and they worried that they might be treated badly on account of their British residency and if they refused military service. Collins argued strenuously that surrender did not mean that the fight would be over for good, but he carried no weight. It was Sean MacDermott who convinced the diehards, and so on Saturday 29 April the six-day drama that would become known as the Easter Rising was at an end.

Collins quickly lost his weekend cheer while holed up in the GPO, but never his nerve or his sense of duty. When he was in danger he remained cool, working with a will as always. Such was the spirit of the rebellion by and large, but it is to his personal credit as well, revealing a depth of commitment far beyond mere ambition or self-importance. As one of the many uniformed spare parts at headquarters, it could not be said that he demonstrated much in the way of initiative or ability, but he was not given the chance. He would not have been given a command, as he was still a stranger in the Dublin Brigade. He was never reckless or daring – he failed to make a name for himself as did Cathal Brugha (who was shot many times and refused to leave his post), Eamon de Valera (who commanded the most successful battalion), and Thomas Ashe and Richard Mulcahy (who led a clever ambush of a force of policemen just outside the city). But he had taken his place among the fighting men, and that would make all the difference.

6: Prisoner

A frenzied mass of swearing, struggling, perspiring men
rolled and fought over the ball in the middle of the yard.
From the din a tall, wiry, dark-haired young man emerged
and his Cork accent dominated the battle for a moment.
He was under and rose and whooped and swore with
tremendous vibrations of his accent and then disappeared
again. 'That's Mick Collins,' I was told, but the name
meant nothing.

(Desmond Ryan, on Stafford Prison yard)

COLLINS'S JOURNEY THROUGH the post-rebellion penal system
began on O'Connell Street, where the GPO garrison lined up to
surrender their weapons, herded by soldiers with fixed bayonets.
Other parties arrived from other battlefields, including one which cut
a holiday-outing dash with lit cigarettes and cigars. All were marshalled at the top of the wrecked avenue, in the grounds of the
Rotunda Hospital. Jammed together for the night with no cover, the
tired, hungry and dirty Volunteers also had to face the post-traumatic
rage of British officers who had lost comrades and men to what they
saw as a gang of traitors, and of ordinary Dubliners, who had suffered
even greater losses from fire and stray bullets.

Next stop, Richmond Barracks, in Inchicore, south Dublin, one
of a series of ancient army bases dotted around the city. Now the
mood had changed, and their captors were in high spirits from their
victory. The gymnasium had been turned into a holding pen for
suspected rebels from all over the country, which was now being
scoured for 'Sinn Feiners'. (Although the party had nothing to do
with the Rising, officials and newspapers used the name as a label.)
More than 3,000 suspects would pass through army custody in the

coming days. Some were cleared; many were quickly sent on to prisons and camps in Britain. Two weeks later, Prime Minister Herbert Asquith visited and found 'there were a lot who had much better been left at home.'

Those picked out as ringleaders by detectives were sent to nearby Kilmainham prison to be court-martialled under martial law. Over the next few days, most of the commanders in the GPO – including Pearse, Connolly, MacDermott, Clarke and Plunkett – were convicted, executed and buried in quicklime behind the prison walls. This quickly raised a storm of protest from nationalists, including those who were appalled at the Rising in the first place. A great many other prisoners, including future leaders such as Eamon de Valera and Constance Markievicz, were sentenced to death but reprieved. They too were transferred to English jails.

The last of his family to see Joe Plunkett was his father, George, who had also been arrested. As Geraldine Plunkett told it:

> When [George] was jailed in the Richmond barrack he heard a noise on the ground outside and he looked out the window and saw Joe and another prisoner and a guard of soldiers standing in the rain outside. Joe looked up and they stayed looking at each other for about twenty minutes till Joe was moved on.

The Rising put an end to their happy private world at Larkfield: 'Nothing would be the same again, it never was.'

Collins also mourned the death of his cousin Jack Hurley, in whose footsteps he had been following since 1906. Jack had fought as part of the Four Courts garrison further west along the Liffey, and had been badly wounded in the head in some of the fiercest fighting of the Rising, at a barricade in Church Street. There are two versions of his death. Father Augustine, a priest who attended many of the rebels, wrote to the dead man's mother in West Cork that Hurley 'asked the man who bore him away to tell his mother he had died for Ireland', and that 'he made his confession and said aspirations with me in a quiet and truly beautiful way . . . there seemed to be a smile on his lips.' This understandably gentle letter was quickly published among other pious profiles of rebel martyrs in the *Catholic Bulletin*, but the reality was unfortunately much grimmer – as might be expected when someone with a fatal wound dies slowly.

Who knows how far Hurley could have gone if he had lived? He had always been more popular than Collins, and a step ahead on various organizational ladders — it might have been him, rather than his cousin, who scaled the heights of the revolution. Of course the same could be said of others who died in Easter Week.

Collins, unknown to the police and never considered for exemplary trial or execution, was one of about 600 men to be shipped out in a cattle boat on the night of 1 May, 'heaped together in the darkened and stuffy hold with life-belts for pillows'. Better that than travelling with the cows, as one later batch had to do. On arrival in Holyhead, Wales, they were separated into two groups, Collins and 288 others being sent by train to Stafford Detention Barracks. Once again the prisoners were packed into confined spaces with no water or access to toilets. By the time they arrived, on 1 May, total exhaustion had set in.

Stafford was an old jail converted into a wartime military prison and guarded by soldiers. Here the rebels were kept one to a cell, stacked row on row, floor on floor, around a central atrium: solitary confinement behind an iron door with a plank bed, a table, a stool and a bucket. They were given a slate and a pencil, but were ordered to remain totally silent, not to look out the window, and to keep their rooms army-clean with creased blankets and scrubbed floors. Their daily turns under the high brick walls of the exercise yard (reminding many of Oscar Wilde's *The Ballad of Reading Gaol*) were also undertaken in utter silence. Collins, restless and active, found confinement loathsome.

This regime lasted about a month, until the prisoners were granted de facto prisoner-of-war status. Then the cell doors were allowed to stay open, and they could talk as much as they wanted and use the yard freely. Now Collins could make an impression and make friends. 'In Stafford he often dominated the exercise ground with his voice in protest or in jest,' recalled Desmond Ryan, a former student of Pearse's at St Enda's. Collins was on F landing, along with Seamus Kavanagh, who found that

> Mick Collins was a very good natured type. He always appeared to have a stock of cigarettes and other things in his cell and would never see any fellow short of anything that he could give him. If anyone was short of a smoke without telling him he

would be mad and give the fellow a good telling off. In spite of that he was the butt of a lot of fellows there.

A photograph survives of this period, showing prisoners gathered on a Stafford landing with Collins standing unsmiling and obscure at the back.

At the end of June they were moved again, this time to the Welsh countryside. The place was Frongoch, near Bala in North Wales: not so much a town as an abandoned whisky distillery. It had its own railway siding, however, and was surrounded by moors rather than farms, making it both convenient and isolated enough to prevent trouble or escape – an ideal location for prisoners of war. Its previous German inhabitants were shipped to France to make way for the Irish.

The Frongoch camp opened in the second week of June to bring together most of the Irish prisoners scattered throughout the English prison system, in Wandsworth, Wakefield and Knutsford as well as Stafford. Once concentrated, they would be brought in smaller batches before a London tribunal to assess their level of responsibility. The least guilty – the many who were caught in the post-Rising dragnet or were deemed to be simply gullible – were quickly let go. A few others, thought to be leaders or troublemakers, were shipped off to prison cells. The rest – the minor-leaguers – were brought back to Frongoch for an indefinite stay.

Yet this was not a defeated army. None of the rebel units had broken, there had been no rout, and no sense of a cause having been lost. It is striking how few attempts there had been to escape from British capture in Dublin. Far more important to the rebels was sticking with their comrades and surrendering as soldiers. There was a perverse kind of pride in it, military captivity being proof that they were indeed an army. Morale recovered after the first few exhausted days of captivity, and there was a strongly shared belief that not only had they preserved their honour, they had saved their country from shame as well. Everyone had said they wouldn't fight, that they were all talk. No one could say that now.

So prison did not mean defeat, nor even disgrace. When local politicians and priests made public pleas for the release of local boys (as happened in West Cork, although Collins's name was not mentioned), their attempts were usually indignantly rebuffed by the boys themselves as undignified and unworthy of the cause. In the heroic narrative that these men had dreamed and were now living, imprisonment was affirmation – anointment – as rebels in succession to republican heroes Wolfe Tone, Robert Emmet, John Mitchel, James Stephens, O'Donovan Rossa and Tom Clarke.

Prison was another stage on which to act out their parts to a mass Irish audience equally well versed in their roles as outraged compatriots. The script had been well rehearsed and perfected by the previous generation of heroes and politicians. Even gentleman John Redmond, the leader of the Irish Party, had spent time in jail. Internment meant near-instant public sympathy and anger at the brutal regime, editorials and resolutions calling for leniency, money to assist the relatives, and campaigns for amnesty and an early release. For the prisoners it meant ennoblement as the men who had risked all for their country: name recognition, ideological authenticity, and instant political credibility.

In short, Frongoch was *the* place to be seen for the ambitious young nationalist that summer. In a sign of personal liberation, many grew beards. Collins grew a moustache – although in typical big-brother fashion Johnny Collins made him shave it off when he got out. Scores of autograph books preserve the moment in cartoons, familiar quotations and hearty exclamations, savouring the experience and already anticipating the nostalgia: the graduation yearbooks of the class of '16. This seemingly perverse sense of accomplishment was summed up by Collins's own trite but typical contribution to the literary movement: 'Let us be judged by what we have attempted rather than what we achieved.'

FRONGOCH WAS NOT one camp but two, facing each other across a road through barbed-wire fences. The north camp was composed of two rows of wooden huts with peaked roofs: the classic POW setting. An old factory, its five floors converted into dormitories, was known as the south camp.

The dormitories were hot, airless and crowded. Rats were everywhere, including the beds. The prisoners were locked up every evening – despite the length of summer days – and by morning the stench from their own waste was excruciating. Many grew weak or ill, and the small amounts of degraded food didn't help. The tiny potato rations in particular caused outrage. The thin-walled huts of the north camp were equally crowded but cold once autumn arrived. Built on lower ground, they were also subject to flooding, and the ground turned to mud until proper walkways were built.

The first prisoners to arrive went to the distillery, until it had reached its limit (nearly a thousand), whereupon the huts began to fill up. At its peak the whole complex housed nearly 2,000 men, and about 3,000 passed through it in all. For most of its Irish history, however, the number of inmates was far lower than this: after July only 650 remained. This prompted the commandant to close up the huts and move everyone to the dorms – until October, when the distillery was emptied and they were all shifted north again.

Frongoch has been celebrated many times over as the birthplace of a resurrected revolutionary movement, the 'Sinn Fein university' ironically assembled by an unthinking British government. Here, it is said, mild-mannered dissidents were radicalized by the militants and together they forged new nationwide bonds and worked out new strategies for the greater rebellion on the horizon. There is some truth to that. Many friendships were born there, and the experience of solidarity and resistance was paradoxically empowering – but what too often gets left out is the politics and the jockeying for power. These as well as the good vibrations of camaraderie and self-educated enlightment would affect the future of the separatist movement.

Politics in Frongoch were an extension of the conflicts within separatism before the Rising: pro-rebellion vs. anti-rebellion; IRB men vs. those outside the Organization; insiders vs. outsiders. The dominant force at first was those who were mere civilians in the eyes of the fighting men: 'Sinn Feiners' swept up in the British dragnet. Their first act, by sheer Irish-Ireland reflex, was to call a meeting, form a council, elect officers, select an executive, and man a phalanx of committees and subcommittees, complete with minute books and agenda books, motions and resolutions. Once this pre-emptive coup had been arranged, the new executive requested that Volunteer and Citizen Army officers 'submit recommendations to the council for the better working of the military side of the camp'.

A parallel military staff was then set up by an elected committee. J. J. O'Connell, the former Volunteer Director of Training, was made camp commandant, and a cast of dozens was appointed below him, including a quartermaster, deputy quartermaster, aide-de-camp, provost marshal and dormitory and company commanders. William Brennan-Whitmore, one of Joe Plunkett's gaggle of aides, was made camp adjutant, and later became the unofficial camp historian when he published the still-authoritative *With the Irish in Frongoch.* Collins was said to be enraged at the book's revelation of names and details, but (possibly even more annoying) his own name was barely mentioned.

The civilian council sought to be treated as political prisoners. The military staff wanted to be recognized as belligerent soldiers and demanded prisoner-of-war status. Tension between the two waxed and waned as the council contested staff authority over the camp, but it soon drained away as the civilians were released or transferred in July. The council maintained a nominal existence, but the final entry in the minute book is dated 4 July. In any case, it was the staff officers who won recognition by the British authorities, who at first left the prisoners largely to their own devices.

The staff instituted a strict discipline and a routine to match, with daily camp order sheets, drill, fatigues, and classes on tactics and strategy. Certain of the leaders, namely Brennan-Whitmore and O'Connell (both self-taught and self-styled military thinkers), wanted to run the camp as a 'military academy': 'What Sandhurst was doing for the British Army, Frongoch Camp was bidding fair to do for the Irish Republican Army.' The Battle of the Somme was about to demonstrate that the general staff of the former could be far more inept than that of the latter, but there is no evidence that the campers paid much attention to such details (although they did revel in the British defeat).

This overenthusiastic new regime helped precipitate a second crisis of authority. The Volunteers who had arrived in the first batches of prisoners, and had thus been given commands, were often non-combatants. O'Connell had actually opposed the Rising, while sensible Tomas MacCurtain and sensitive Terence MacSwiney, the leaders of the Cork Volunteers, had even surrendered their weapons rather than fight the British army. This, coupled with widespread resentment of the officious regulations, led to mutiny. As MacCurtain recorded in his diary on 3 July:

> About eight men put on trial – playing cards for high stakes . . .
> Dickeen [Fitzgerald] said we had no power to do certain things

and they would not obey us – the rest agreed with him. Mac Ui Riann [? Ryan] said that people were saying we should not be there – that the men who fought in Dublin should be in our places.

A large number of officers resigned from their posts – joining the mess committee, who had gone a week before. The next day Brennan-Whitmore and O'Connell joined them, completing the purge. On 6 July further trouble broke out over who was to be in charge of Room 2 in the distillery. Before anything further could arise, most of the south-camp leadership (thirty men in all) were removed to Reading jail, including O'Connell and the Corkmen. Michael Staines, a GPO veteran, took over and stayed in charge, even while many other leaders were taken away.

Collins was one of the last to arrive, three weeks after the camps opened, which meant staying in the overflow camp for the first month while the first political struggles were being waged in the dormitories. Life went much easier in the north camp, under the command of M. W. (Michael) O'Reilly (yet another of Plunkett's former aides). But if anything O'Reilly was a bit too easy-going in agreeing to British demands for prisoner labour, and when his men refused he was punished and shipped off as well, to be replaced by Eamon Dorkan, who was himself later sent away.

Each hut of twenty or so men had an elected leader, also recognized by the camp guards, but the leaders' actual authority varied from hut to hut and depended on personality. Moreover, as in the south camp, the early birds got the jobs whatever their status among their comrades. So, when Collins (Prisoner 1320) arrived in Hut No. 7 at the end of June, he was one of the low men on the totem pole. As William O'Brien, a hut-mate (and a trade-union official), records his arrival, 'he looked around and did not seem impressed by the other internees . . . When Collins came in quite a number of intimate associates were with him and he and they did not relish the idea of a hut leader having got elected before they took up occupation in it.'

At the end of the month there was another big release of several hundred prisoners and the grievance was eliminated by closing the huts down and moving everyone into the distillery. Here Collins came under the remnants of the old regime and took his usual place with the awkward squad, as he wrote to Jim Ryan, the GPO garrison's medical officer (already released):

> Possibly you have heard from one or other of the 'returns' that we were all transferred from the huts to the lower station where they used to make whiskey. Most of us do not appreciate the change so much as we ought to. But there are many consolations all the same. The officers down here take themselves very seriously and insist on trying to do things on a strictly military basis. Honestly its most amusing at times but I cannot mention the incidents. They wouldn't be good for the Censor & then I couldn't do them justice by reason of the restriction writing places on one's language.

FRICTION OF this kind was surely inevitable, but it was overshadowed after August by the growing battle over prisoners' rights. This had become a constant quarrel. Officially the rebels were not prisoners of war but civilian internees, and were therefore obliged to work and liable to be punished for disobeying orders to do so. Solitary confinement, bread-and-water diets, the withholding of cigarettes or post were all meted out – and were met by evasion, hunger strikes and protest. As before, ringleaders and perceived troublemakers were deported to Reading jail. The prisoners often won, but the constantly infuriated camp commandant, Colonel Heygate-Lambert – nicknamed 'Buckshot', because of his lurid threats – never gave up. Victory, for the Irish, lay not in ultimate triumph but in the steady assertion of principle.

The greatest of these contests of will was fought over the British attempts to seize the several dozen 'refugees' – former residents of Britain – in order to make them liable to the Military Service Act. Collins, Joe Good and the others were now faced with a potential choice of conscription or court martial, just as many had feared might happen if they surrendered. To this there was mass (although by no means universal) resistance, chiefly by refusing to answer names at roll call – the only means the British had to identify many of the prisoners. Mass punishment ensued. In late October the prisoners were shifted back across the road to the huts and the distillery was used for the recalcitrant – up to 300 in the end. This culminated in a mass trial of fifteen hut leaders before a

military court in late November. Twelve were convicted but the
stalemate continued, with half the prisoners in one camp and half
in the other.

Batt O'Connor, a Dublin builder and later a TD (an MP in Dail
Eireann, the Irish revolutionary assembly) and staunch Collins ally,
'first got to know Michael Collins in Frongoch where he was always
up to horseplay, chasing and being chased around the grounds etc.',
although that was all he really knew of him at the time. Seamus
Kavanagh and Desmond Ryan had formed much the same first
impression in Stafford – of a friendly and boisterous figure who was
liable to throw his weight around, figuratively and literally. William
O'Brien made the same assessment: friendly but quick to assert
himself and his opinions. Big Man in Camp; a Big Fellow; the Big
Fellow.

The nickname stuck – a snide reference to Collins's competitive
and obtrusive attitude. He did well in camp sports, winning more
races (his final athletic victories) and taking part in football matches
(presumably hurleys were not available or permitted). But, for many
fellow inmates, that was it. Richard Mulcahy, one of the camp
leaders, recalls a (rather unlikely) 'quiet and unobtrusive' fellow, others
don't mention him at all. He was never elected to any position,
including hut leader. Brennan-Whitmore's book mentions him only
once, at the very end, and his name is surprisingly absent from most
of the autograph books (hardly a sign of popularity). Nor did the
British pay him any mind – he was never singled out for punishment,
tried, targeted for conscription, or sent to an outside prison.

Yet biographers have created an image of Collins as the genius of
the resistance, the man in charge. This reputation comes mainly from
his fellow 'refugees' (he made no claims in this regard) and from
another division in camp opinion. If Volunteers who hadn't taken
part in the Rising were sometimes looked down on, similar talk was
directed at the Kimmage veterans, who were erroneously blamed for
the surrender in Dublin by some and as the source of trouble in the
camp by others. When the conscription question first arose they met
to consider giving themselves up, but 'Michael Collins burst in on
the meeting and sat down. When he heard their proposition he told
them to do nothing of any kind but sit tight, not to mind the
cowards.' This was a crucial intervention. There is no evidence that
Collins himself organized the campaign of non-cooperation over

identities (the authorities didn't blame him for it), but he undoubtedly supported it. There remained some advocates of cooperation – who argued that military honour required it – and others who simply disliked the bother and its instigators. Not a split exactly, but Collins had once again taken the fighting side in an internal dispute, winning both friends and enemies and emerging as a leader within a group that had previously scorned his pretensions.

Collins wanted his say in how the camp was run, and he finally got it when the camp secretary, J. J. Neeson, was lost on 2 November in another British purge of leaders. He immediately wrote that 'as Neeson is gone it is very likely that I shall have to take on the job of secretary to the Camp as I've often wanted to.' He never saw paperwork without thinking he could do it better. Advanced once more because of division and the opportune disappearance of rivals, and once again a secretary, he now had real work to do – the kind at which he could excel. It was behind the scenes and at a desk that Collins made his name at Frongoch.

In fact the most impressive side to the resistance happened not on the inside but on the outside, where an effective and persistent propaganda campaign was mounted to attack British treatment of the prisoners. Irish MPs were inveigled into it, as were the Irish and English press (especially the *Manchester Guardian*), but most of the work was done by the National Aid and Volunteer Dependants Fund (the National Aid for short), an amalgamation of groups formed to help victims of the Rising. The National Aid's London office was run by Art O'Brien and fronted by George Gavan Duffy, a prominent London Gael and lawyer, and husband of Margaret. Collins, who knew both men, became their chief contact in the camp, sending them long letters giving the latest news and offering advice as to how things should be done.

These letters began in mid-October, with Collins apparently acting on his own to alert O'Brien to the attempts to arrest the former exiles. ('For some time I have been seeking an opportunity of writing to you on a matter which seems to me to transcend in importance any disabilities which we suffer here . . .') We can guess that he wrote on account of the stand that he and they had taken within the camp over conscription. He wanted the issue raised in Parliament (although 'you know what little value I attach to the efficacy of asking questions in the House of Commons') and in newspapers, and he stressed the enormous publicity value of linking it to fears of conscription in Ireland.

It cannot be said that Collins did a notably better job than his predecessor or than his superior, Michael Staines, judging by the voluminous earlier correspondence. But he was obviously competent and energetic: precise, thorough, detailed, authoritative. The voice of command came easily to him. He subbed for Staines (in correspondence at least) while he was sick, and continued to write giving his own spin on events. ('I have written to you privately but you may regard any of my statements as being official . . .') He kept up with the newspapers and what was said in the Commons, and was always urging responses and thinking of propaganda angles. Every move in Frongoch had to be publicized as a struggle between principle and tyranny: an extension of the Rising on the one hand and the excesses of martial law that followed it on the other. He penned an appeal 'to the People of Ireland' along these lines, ending in a characteristic mix of drama and truculence: 'What is before us we do not know but if we are forced to yield up those we are trying to shield it will be due to the inactivity of the only power which could help us – the power and voice of the Irish people.' He was instrumental in bringing Gavan Duffy in to defend the fifteen hut leaders in military court. This proved to be a publicity gold mine thanks to the newspaper coverage.

Collins was among the 300-odd unidentified protesters sent back to the distillery, and thus spent his last two months in camp in straitened circumstances. This occasioned a renewed and vociferous barrage of complaints about the food, medical care, cold, clothing and petty harassment. So relentless was this campaign that it precipitated the suicide of one of the camp doctors, Dr Peters, who felt his name had been sullied. The enraged commandant addressed the prisoners and blamed them for having hounded Peters to his death, as did some newspapers. Collins was resolute in rebuttal, expressing 'sincere regrets' since 'he was only obeying orders', and stating 'our firm belief that the Commandant, to facilitate his tyrannical schemes against ourselves, consistently misled the unfortunate doctor and used him as a tool'. Gavan Duffy was again summoned, to attend the autopsy.

The constant complaints and the suicide made many men uncomfortable, and aroused great hostility in some quarters towards Collins. Frank Henderson, formerly of Craig, Gardner and later a senior IRA officer in Dublin: 'I knew him in Frongoch. Then he was not at all popular. He wanted to burn down the camp. It looked almost as if he was looking for power, for he tried to run the camp then.' No one felt more strongly than Gerry Boland, the oldest of three rebel brothers, in whom a great hate was kindled in Frongoch. Robert Brennan remembers Boland insisting that Collins 'was a braggart and a bully . . . In the camp, if he didn't win all the jumps, he'd break up the match.' He even did a wicked impression of the Big Fellow, 'heaving his shoulders and tossing his head'. Boland's first and greatest charge, which he repeated for the next fifty years, was that Collins had exaggerated how bad things were in the camp for shock effect: 'Although prison conditions were good he organized a "lying petition" on bad conditions which I denied to the Prison Aid authorities. Collins had forgotten that such a document would have caused worry to our families but he was a go-getter.'

Part of the resentment of Collins was due to his involvement in organizing an IRB circle in the camp – apparently a self-selected group of like-minded men who met and began surreptitiously contacting a chosen few among their fellows. He wasn't *the* instigator, but he was one of them. This process is usually described as a straightforward 'reorganizing', but its purpose is actually rather mysterious. The Organization had very strict rules about the setting up of circles and the recruiting of new members, all of which Collins and his collaborators broke – as was angrily pointed out by other IRB members. Eamon Dore, a more senior member of the Fintan Lalor circle in Dublin that Collins had joined earlier that year, was one of those involved in the subsequent reprimand: 'Collins was called on for an explanation of his conduct . . . Mick apologized for his action to the two men, Eamon Price and Martin Murphy, who spoke to him about the matter, and tried to explain it, and there the matter rested for the moment.' It didn't help that long-time IRB members were excluded from later meetings by the previously unknown clique (including Michael Staines after he criticized the martyred leaders of the rebellion). This sense that the freshmen were getting above themselves would persist even after Collins returned to Ireland.

Collins and his co-conspirators (chiefly Richard Mulcahy and Gearoid O'Sullivan – later his colleagues in the IRA's GHQ – and Sean O Murthuile (John Hurley), a key IRB organizer) were only following the example set by their mentors Plunkett and Mac-

Dermott, who had manipulated or ignored the IRB Supreme Council and constitution in order to get their way. But what was it supposed to achieve, this secret conclave? It may have had something to do with making sure the militants could keep the fight going, or so Boland accused Richard Mulcahy in the Dail in 1931:

> I sat with you at the same meeting in Frongoch when you reorganized it [the IRB] and when I came out of Frongoch I was invited by you and by Mick Collins and I would not go. I know you are one of the people who started the whole damn thing in Frongoch, you and the bunch around you. You started false propaganda in the place. I organized a group of truthful men who would not sign a lying statement . . . I know every one of you inside out and you know me, too.

Another story has it that the plotters were contemplating entering electoral politics – an IRB no-no, due to its supposedly corrupting influence, and another reason for other members' unease.

Prisoner-of-war stories usually mean endurance, camaraderie, resistance and escape. The scene: huts, wire, guards, boredom and discomfort, endless inspections on a makeshift parade ground. The plot: organizing committees, plans, secret messages to the outside world, fooling the guards at roll call, the battle of wills with the tyrannical commandant, solitary for the ones who break his rules. And then the breakout; the getaway; freedom. The genre belongs above all to the British officer corps, whose members were fleeing German captivity almost as soon as the war broke out (one of the most daring, Jocelyn Hardy, would become notorious as a brutal intelligence officer in Dublin). The IRA can claim its own history of Colditz-style subversion and escapology, and it is in this tradition that Frongoch is usually cast, with Collins as the hero.

The secret meetings might be seen as belonging to this world of clandestine activity, directed at their captors rather than at one another, but most important were Collins's reported smuggling enterprises, a supposed prelude to later triumphs. It was Collins, according to the standard version of his life, who bribed the guards and set up the underground post office, allowing the propaganda to flow out (and cigarettes to flow in). In fact he may have become involved in this effort but, like the publicity campaign, it was really a collective activity, begun by others. Brennan-Whitmore gives credit to 'a brilliant and daring individual from Skibbereen' whom Sean T. O'Kelly identifies as Barney O'Driscoll, 'as strong, forceful and pushful as he was big . . . Like all West Corkmen, that I have ever known, he had all his wits about him.' Was he the real big fellow? It was O'Driscoll's duty to arrange supplies with the British quartermaster, and this took him outside the camp. Here he was able to pass letters (hidden in cigarette packages) to a civilian, who posted them on. When O'Driscoll was deported, his place was taken by a Clareman whom Brennan-Whitmore says remained in charge thereafter. All this happened on the distillery side of the camp, before Collins got there.

IF COLLINS made some enemies, he probably made more – and more important – friends. It was in Frongoch that he first really displayed his marvellous talent for networking. Part of this was a particular talent for getting along with difficult people: P. S. O'Hegarty in London had been one example; Art O'Brien and Gearoid O'Sullivan were two more he cultivated while in camp, even though others disliked them. Mostly, however, as it turned out, Collins was just very good at creating friendship groups and making people feel part of something special, something intimate and welcoming.

In Frongoch, his closest pals seem to have been Sean Hales (later an IRA leader), Gearoid O'Sullivan and Sean O Murthuile. All three were West Corkmen – a preference Collins would show throughout his career. Many other fellow prisoners would become friends and colleagues. Richard Mulcahy and Dick McKee would be his leading collaborators in the Volunteers, and Sean MacMahon would emerge as another loyal Collins man on the headquarters staff. Michael Staines would work with Collins in many capacities over the next few years, as would Michael O'Reilly. The three Michaels even contemplated going into business together, along with Jim Ryan. William O'Brien would help Collins gain a foothold in Dublin politics. Mick McDonnell would be the first leader of the notorious assassination 'squad'. If Frongoch was a university, then these men would make up Collins's fraternity.

Of course, many of these people knew each other anyway, and the prison experience forged many bonds. Frongoch, like the Rising, was a collective experience understood collectively. It was as a member of this whole group, now self-consciously a vanguard, that Collins's life changed. For Collins as for others, prison meant reinforcement rather than re-evaluation – confirmation of having chosen the right path.

All the remaining internees were released on 22 and 23 December, ostensibly a gesture of seasonal good will, but one taken by the prisoners as a surrender to their protests. Flushed with a sense of victory, Collins would leave the camp on a different trajectory from when he came in. In the final days it was apparently him who led the battle over the doctor's suicide, and he was the first to confront the commandant at their last meeting. It was in Frongoch that he began to break out of his orbit as a clerk, secretary, treasurer and aide. It was here that other men began to fall into orbit around him. It was here he was first called 'Big Fellow', and we can trace his subsequent rise in the evolution of its meaning from derision to respect to, ultimately, blind loyalty.

7: Manager

Shortly after our release from prison I met him, and admired the flashing eyes, the firm, handsome mouth, the strong jaw, the wonderful head, so gracefully poised and carried on the shapely shoulders – that head which so often afterwards I used to see him swing, and toss in fun and anger. And I specially saw at that first sight of him the fine forehead with the intellectual vision centres standing out prominently over the level brow.

(R.H., Dublin)

COLLINS RETURNED STRAIGHT HOME to Cork once released, to spend Christmas and the first weeks of 1917 in Woodfield. The local police kept an eye on him, but reported that he 'lived what may be considered a retired life, and no notice was taken of his presence in this locality by anyone'. Another report mentioned that 'he boasts to his friends that he was in the rebellion fighting in Church Street Dublin for four days.' The bloody battleground of Church Street was where Jack Hurley had been fatally wounded, so Collins may have been making himself out to be more the warrior than the strict truth would allow. This (modest) recasting of his own past in a more successful and heroic mould would be repeated in his accounts of leaving the civil service, coming to Dublin and his job with the Plunketts, and would be seen again in the months to come.

Collins – as always – did not have to wait long to find new employment. After a few days in Cork city with his sister Mary, during which he attended a Sinn Fein meeting, he was back in Dublin at the end of January. He was reconnecting with his comrades and casting about for the next big thing when opportunity once again presented itself: the Irish National Aid and Volunteer Dependants

Fund was looking for a new secretary. This was an amalgamation of two competing bodies set up in May 1916 to help those who suffered for participating in the Rising. The organizers of the Volunteer Fund, led by Tom Clarke's widow, Kathleen (herself well connected through her republican family, the Dalys of Limerick), suspected the National Aid Association was a front for the Irish Party – and the NAA thought the IRB was using the Volunteer Fund in the same way. Neither suspicion was true, but it took the lure of American money to bring these groups together in August, after US donors insisted on a united front. The republicans were dubious, but as they were losing the fund-raising contest badly by this point they had little choice. They won in the end, however: a year later the new National Aid was preaching the miracle of the Rising, its Martyrs and the new Spirit abroad in the Land.

The first secretary was the soon-to-be ubiquitous Joe McGrath, formerly of Craig, Gardner and the Rising's Jacob's Factory garrison. He took the job in large part to represent the interests of the now-imprisoned rebels (he had evaded capture) and the IRB, but by late 1916 he wanted out, complaining of too much work and not enough help. Republicans wanted another of their own to replace him, naturally enough, but disgruntled Frongoch veterans also wanted someone from their ranks, and trade-union representatives were pushing their own candidate. For their part, the so-called moderates on the executive hoped to reduce the influence of the honorary secretary, Fred Allan, an ex-Fenian with considerable pull in munici-pal affairs.

The job was advertised early in the new year, whereupon Collins and seven other candidates wrote to apply. Collins's introductory letter of 20 January mentions 'experience in administrative work, proficiency in book-keeping, accountancy, a good grasp of business methods, and a wide knowledge of people and affairs in Ireland', adding the name of Count Plunkett (expelled from the Royal Dublin Society that very day for the sins of his sons), the Rising and 'a knowledge' of Irish to his credentials.

Collins was nearly the perfect candidate on paper but he almost lost the job from carelessness. The search was being run by an auditor, Donal O'Connor, who assessed the applications and carried out the initial interviews. (In 1919 Collins would appoint him as the official auditor for Dail Eireann.) On 6 February he forwarded a shortlist of John Cotter, Joseph Derhan, J. K. O'Reilly (ex-prisoner and author of the popular song 'Wrap the Green Flag Around Me Boys') and Michael Collins. Unfortunately, he added, 'Mr Collins, in his application, asks for an interview, but when subsequently written to for that purpose he does not reply. This is the more to be regretted, as his application is well put, and his experience is probably good. Further details with regard to his experience would however be desirable.' In the absence of such, he suggested that either Cotter or Derhan 'would give satisfaction' and recommended Cotter, a union man.

Didn't show up for the interview! Not very Collins-like, and very nearly his downfall. In an unapologetic letter to O'Connor, also written on the 6th, he explained, 'I was unaware that the [first] letter would go before the Executive so I made it merely a formal application to yourself for an interview, when we could go into my qualifications in detail. The appointment you made for this purpose I was unable to keep being at the time in North Roscommon [where Count Plunkett was running in a by-election] doing election work.' In fact he was not electioneering so much as politicking among his comrades, as he only went up to Roscommon for election day and did not return until three days afterwards, on the 6th.

In typically adroit fashion, however, he quickly regained his footing. Presumably tipped off by someone on the committee who had read O'Connor's report, Collins hastily arranged an interview the next day, supplied a much more detailed résumé, and was seen by the executive. Here he once again betrayed confidence in the outcome:

> Miss [Anna] O'Rahilly remarked afterwards she expected to see a great fellow and was not much impressed when she saw him. She said she 'thought he would be more friendly with us. He sat on a table, dangling his legs and listening to us without speaking.

'He was appointed anyway,' and was at work by the 16th. The reason for his apparent insouciance regarding interviews was that he had campaigned hard to get the job. His prison clique was what first gave him an in. Many Frongochers were unhappy with their initial experiences of the National Aid, and wanted a greater voice in its proceedings. After Christmas they came together again in Dublin and met regularly – Collins among them. His role in organizing and publicizing their grievances in camp was no doubt recalled, and his name was pushed forward as the man for the job.

Batt O'Connor, an ex-prisoner but not yet a Collins intimate, recalls a meeting of his fellows around this time at the National Aid offices at 10 Exchequer Street:

> The place was packed with the Frongoch crowd and there was no sitting accommodation. When I entered Joe Gleeson came to me and said Michael Collins was the right man for the job but he was not known. He suggested that when names were proposed we should distribute ourselves through the room and call 'Michael Collins'. I got standing on a chair and Joe on another. People said some man was wanted who knew who was who. Joe shouted 'Collins' and others followed and that carried the crowd. The committee of women, Mrs Tom Clarke etc., did not know Michael Collins but arranged for an interview.

Collins in fact met with Kathleen Clarke and got her backing by convincing her that he planned to follow in her late husband's footsteps. She provided a priceless laying-on of hands, as the IRB had always, in time-honoured fraternal fashion, provided jobs for the boys. Brotherhood links had already worked once for Collins, when he first arrived in Dublin and hooked up with Pat Belton, Joe Plunkett and Sean MacDermott. Plunkett and MacDermott were gone, but Belton was fortuitously on the National Aid executive along with another sympathizer, Fred Allan. He vigorously supported Collins's candidacy, and would later defend him against his critics in the organization.

Another key member of the executive was William O'Brien, secretary to the Dublin Trades Council, and former hut-mate from Frongoch:

> On the way to North Roscommon [by-election] on 2 February Michael Collins told me that he was an applicant for the position of Secretary of the National Aid Association and asked me for my support. I told him to come round to my office after the election and we would discuss the proposition. He did so and as a result of a talk I promised to get him the Labour votes. Mr Keohane, Mr John Murphy and some of the influential members of the National Aid Association were supporting Mr John Cotter for the Secretaryship and the Volunteer Organization was

understood to be backing Collins. As a result of the support I
was able to obtain, Collins was elected.

Yet another supporter was Kitty O'Doherty, one of the 'committee of women', whose husband, Seamus, was acting head of the
IRB's Supreme Council. By her account, she was asked to select
someone and chose Gearoid O'Sullivan. He took a teaching job
instead, and suggested Collins, whom he knew from the Keating
branch of the Gaelic League and from Frongoch. She then brought
his name to the committee. We know it didn't happen quite like
that, but the O'Dohertys' house was a rendezvous for like-minded
people (former Frongoch commandant Michael Staines was staying
there), and Collins was known there, so hers was another vote he
could count on.

Everyone claimed afterwards that they had got Collins the job.
The credit is actually his, for a masterful lobbying campaign pulling
all available friendly and fraternal strings. The most extraordinary
sign of his determination (or desperation) to get the job, however,
was his application letter. Submitted in a hurry after missing the first
interview, it contains the following claim regarding his work after
leaving the civil service in London:

> Finding the work and prospects not very much to my liking I
> managed to secure a position with a firm of chartered account-
> ants – Messrs Baron and Co. After a little training in the office
> I was sent out in the usual way to audit accounts, and during my
> two years there I gained experience of the manner of keeping
> books and the business methods of about 50 different firms. One
> of the houses I became connected with – Messrs Horne and Co.
> Stockbrokers – offered me a post as book-keeper and correspon-
> dence clerk in their office.

There can be no doubt about it: this is an outright lie. We know so
from his civil-service record containing many statements – written in
1910 and 1914 – that he worked that whole period at Horne & Co.

Why on earth did he bother to make this story up? He was prone
to retrospective exaggeration about himself, but this went far beyond
boasting. There was such a firm: C. G. Baron & Co., a smallish
accounting firm based at Throgmorton House, 15 Copthall Avenue,
in the City of London. This was just around the corner from Horne

& Co., so he no doubt passed it many times. Perhaps he had even applied for a job there. It may very well have done the books he worked on, and so he might have known the auditors and how they worked. He could talk the talk. But still – he had plenty of office and financial experience, including with an accounting firm. It sounded good that he had been headhunted by the stockbrokers, but it hardly seems worth lying about. It does seem bizarre. After all, what if he had been found out?

Two explanations suggest themselves. The first is that Collins was in a hurry to impress Donal O'Connor – perhaps he had been told that accountancy experience would weigh heavily in the decision. The second also concerns O'Connor, but goes further back. If the auditor checked with previous employers, it made sense that he would go first to Craig, Gardner. What if Collins had told *them* all about his time at good old Baron & Co. in order to get work there? At that point, in February 1916, he would have had no accountancy experience. To keep his story straight, he would have had to tell it again – although if this was the case, he wisely dropped the story when it came to later biographical interviews.

A third theory, more speculative again: he took pleasure in the deception, or he felt psychologically compelled to lie. This doesn't really fit with the rest of his life, however – Collins had a big ego and liked to pump up his past, but his acts were usually calculated rather than compulsive. On the other hand, consider the following vignette from Armagh in May 1921, where Collins was a candidate in that year's Northern Irish election:

> The little knot of people who had watched the posting of the earlier nominations looked at the wall to see what occupation had been ascribed to Mr Collins (that of accountant) and then dispersed.

Ascription or self-description? Maybe he just always wanted to be an accountant.

THE NATIONAL AID JOB, it must be said, was not necessarily a very attractive one: formidable in scope, with minimal pay. Joe McGrath, upon resigning, declared that three more clerks were needed besides a new secretary (or 'general office manager', as the new post was described). Instead, O'Connor the auditor proposed in January that 'the work of the Association [be] centralized in one responsible and trustworthy person to whom the committee could look for efficiency in the administration of the very large sums of money placed at his disposal and thus preclude the possibility of unfavourable criticism'. This would be a tall order for anyone: Joe McGrath was no slouch, and he had given up in the belief that it was really a job for four people.

Collins's duties were to run the office and supervise the staff, deal with all general correspondence; keep track of all the incoming and outgoing money and attendant cheques, receipts and vouchers; keep in touch with the executive committee and the fourteen subcommittees (a sure sign that Irish-Irelanders were in charge); and handle all enquiries with regard to the committees' decisions and make sure these decisions were implemented. This meant not only a huge volume of paperwork and the daily grind of office management, but also dealing personally with hundreds of applicants for jobs and money, some of whose claims he would have to investigate himself. In the year and a half he was there he wrote something in the order of 3,000 letters, attended hundreds of committee meetings, dealt with more than 2,000 cases, and handled over £100,000 of money accumulated in a series of fund-raising campaigns. And all for £2 10s. a week (more than a pound less than at Craig, Gardner) – although J. J. O'Kelly, a hostile board member, suggests that Collins insisted on a rise before he was willing to write up the minutes.

It was here that the legend of Michael Collins, Superclerk, was born. 'I suppose of all the places in the world you wouldn't expect to find me in this job,' he wrote to Art O'Brien upon starting; but he kept everything running smoothly, got things done on time, and still was able to build his career in Sinn Fein, the Volunteers and the IRB – as well as contemplate going into business for himself. The various skills he had acquired in London and Dublin all came into play. He knew how to keep the books, handle the banking and investments, audit the clients, and churn out the correspondence. Given his first chance to manage an office, his efficiency-expert persona – first developed in the Savings Bank Writing Room – was quick to emerge. In his first office report, in March, he advocated firing two of his four office workers and 'defining the status' (showing his command of early management-speak) of Liam Clarke, the original organizer, who had just emerged from lengthy hospitalization and was still

being paid. Clarke was a fellow IRB member and a republican
stalwart, but he had to go. The lay-offs would backfire personally
when one of the secretaries Collins disposed of spread a rumour that
he had his hand in the till.

There were many similar outings by Collins's inner accountant.
One early case was that of J. Sheridan, who applied for a loan to buy
a horse and cart, having lost his job at Boland's Mill. Collins
interviewed the manager at Boland's and discovered that Sheridan's
brother was now doing his job. Application refused. It reappeared,
however, after Sheridan said he had promises of work if he got the
cart. It turned out that these came from the seller of the horse, whom
Collins interviewed in turn. After a month of such sniffing about, the
necessary sum was granted, with the horse-seller and brother both
having to act as guarantors.

Michael Hayes – later a TD – recalls his fiancée, a National Aid
branch officer in Rathfarnham, getting 'hot and bothered' about a
local man who also wanted a horse:

> She went out to see Collins down to the National Aid and he
> was closing the place and was coming down the stairs at about
> 10 minutes to 6 in very bad humour. She told Collins the story
> and he said 'this place is closed; you should have been here
> before half past 5.' She said 'I had to work until half past 5.' He
> took the name of the man, they had a few words about it and he
> went away very disgruntled. She was also very disgruntled and
> [I] was between the two of them. But, Collins went to Rathfarn-
> ham that night and he gave the man the price of the horse in
> spite of anything he said. That was the kind of spirit in which
> Collins worked and he certainly wasn't always laughing.

This storyline has probably been cut to fit, like so many others –
it is doubtful that Collins would just give someone money out of his
pocket on his own authority. But he probably did check personally,
and the man probably did get what he needed. And the exasperation
was probably real: yet another twilight cycling trip to see a man about
a horse! What definitely isn't true is the legend of Collins as the man
with money which could be used to further his political agenda. The
funds were tightly controlled, and cases were carefully scrutinized.
Many rebels and their families received money and jobs, but these
weren't pensions or gratuities. Maud Gonne MacBride, the widow of

John MacBride, one of the executed martyrs of the Rising, and a nationalist icon in her own right, was turned down flat. Men like Harry Boland and Tomas MacCurtain set up their own businesses; Richard Mulcahy planned to go to medical school.

Collins does seem to have applied for help himself (possibly before he got the job), and was awarded £100. He was listed as a 'civil service' case, along with those who had lost their jobs because of their involvement in the rebellion, but of course he was no such thing. He had left the Savings Bank in 1910, and had not been a civil servant since (although not for want of trying). Did he tell them otherwise, was it what Joe McGrath told him to say, or was 'civil service' just a convenient category to place him in? No application letter can be found and, to confuse matters, it has been claimed on his behalf that he refused to accept any money. On the other hand, J. J. O'Kelly ('Sceilg') wrote that 'Michael, while in receipt of enhanced remuneration as secretary, applied for and obtained the equivalent of a year's salary in consideration of the loss of his appointment in London,' adding, with false good will, 'of course, it is not suggested, in stating this, that he may not have been otherwise very generous and very charitable according to his means.' O'Kelly was expert in spreading malicious stories, but he was also in a position to know the facts, having written National Aid's exhaustive final report in 1919.

Often there were complaints: Collins himself had been one of the malcontents before he worked his way in. Harry Boland for one was apparently never happy with the money he got. The worst trouble-maker was the former Grace Gifford, whom Joseph Plunkett had married shortly before his execution, casting a completely unwarranted heroine's halo over her. She was in genuine financial distress in 1916 and 1917, and there was no question but that the National Aid was willing to help. Unfortunately, it seems that, while she demanded 'compete control of my finances', she was unable to exercise self-control with the money. At one point she threatened to put herself in the workhouse and thereby get sympathy from American donors; at another, Collins stopped payment of one of her cheques. The solution was to put her on an allowance – £5 a month, eventually rising to £8. (In itself this would not have provided a very good life, but in 1917 she apparently came into a £500 inheritance, and she also had an employment income.) The allowance was due to run out in March 1919, but further pressure got her another year's worth of payments.

Nor did any of the funds go for political purposes – into Sinn Fein or the Volunteers. Suspicions there were, both among the police and within the executive, but the accounts were scrupulously maintained – by Collins above all. When the police investigated they found nothing, and the organization was never prosecuted or banned. In fact Collins always advised local branches to follow the law scrupulously in such matters as getting licences for auctions or concerts. Hostile clergymen and newspapers attacked the National Aid anyway, probably because it was partly a propaganda outlet. West Cork, long used to such disputes, was one hotbed of criticism. There a Father McCarthy opposed National Aid collections and was backed up by his superior in Skibbereen, Bishop Kelly. Collins responded by placing notices in a large number of papers defending the organization's record. The executive even threatened to sue the *Longford Leader*, forcing it to issue an apology. When Collins asked Kelly for one, however, he did not deign to give a reply. 'Nor do I expect one,' Collins reported drily. To counteract such views, Collins helped put together a group of investors to buy a local paper, the *Southern Star*, as a Sinn Fein mouthpiece.

Equally wrong is the assumption that Collins used his job as a travelling cover for his IRB activities. In fact, apart from sallies into various Dublin neighbourhoods, he was kept quite desk-bound by his duties. Michael Staines was the real undercover agent, as he travelled openly organizing branches of the National Aid while secretly reviving broken or lapsed circles for the IRB. Collins did make such trips on behalf of the IRB and the Volunteers, but these were in his own time – almost always on weekends or during his summer holidays.

Even sitting in the office, however, most of the rebel world came to him, looking for help for themselves or a friend via a steady stream of 'Dear Mick' or 'Dear Collins' letters. Collins couldn't just give people money but he was able to tell them how best to apply and made sure they got consideration. He was the face of the National Aid in Dublin, his name was on all the cheques, and he inevitably (and often rightly) got the credit for the jobs he found, the children's holidays he paid for and arranged, and the handsome payments that hundreds of individuals and families received, enabling education, comfort, accommodation and new lives. The list of people he helped is a who's who of the new Ireland, including many past and future friends and comrades. Almost no one aside from Eamon de Valera (the commander of the Boland's Mill garrison in 1916 and the future president of Sinn Fein and the Volunteers) turned money down. Sean McGarry, for example (a future director of the IRA and president of the IRB), wrote in June 1917 to tell him that 'we cannot thank you sufficiently for the entire absence of financial worries.'

The part of his duties that Collins felt most passionately about was aid to prisoners still in jail – either those left over from the Rising or those newly incarcerated. He kept in constant touch with them, sent them money, food, books, newspapers and morale-boosting letters, and passed on their messages. He also arranged local visitors, including priests, worked with their lawyers, and had them taken care of when they were released – important when they were in England and had to be put up in London and then got home. These networks would later be put to good use in smuggling guns and explosives and in arranging escapes, but Collins never stopped worrying about prisoners, perhaps thinking of his own experiences. There was something about their plight that touched him emotionally: his letters to friends behind the wire are among the most open and revealing of his correspondence.

Collins's performance in the National Aid job quickly earned him the reputation as the man to see in Dublin, the man to get things done – and, for the newly minted activists throughout Ireland, a man who saw things their way and could be counted on to be on their side.

The fund may not have been political in the partisan sense, but it was in reality a vast American subsidy to the separatist movement at a fragile moment, without which the movement could not have advanced so far or so rapidly in 1917 and 1918. It helped keep together a whole cadre of future leaders, and enabled many to devote themselves to political work without worrying about financial survival. It was a vital publicity engine, and the first nationwide body to come into being after the Rising. Many of the new Sinn Fein clubs that popped up in 1917 began life as National Aid branches. There can be few better examples of the right man being in the right place at the right time than when Michael Collins became the National Aid's manager.

8: Insider

The next thing was I heard that Collins was coming, so I was up in the air. The crowd came in on the train one evening and all came to the election room in the apartment over my uncle's business, and I looked around at them all and I saw this one handsome man and I heard the accent and the chuckle and I saw the twinkle in his eye and I realized that this was Collins. You'd know him the minute he was in a place.

(Brigid Lyons Thornton, Longford)

COLLINS'S ABILITY TO WIN the secretaryship of the National Aid was a measure of his new status as an insider in the post-Rising separatist movement. The same was true of his simultaneous involvement in the North Roscommon by-election. It almost cost him the post he coveted, but it was where the action was in early 1917. Moreover – and quite suddenly – separatism, with its clubs, committees and splits, was where the action was in Irish politics.

The previous year had been a momentous one for the separatist movement. The Rising itself and the arrests and executions that followed it were the catalyst that converted thousands of young men and women into revolutionaries; but even more important was the very public failure of the government and the Irish Party to recover lost ground. Not that they didn't try: Prime Minister Asquith wanted a political settlement to counteract nationalist anger, and he gave David Lloyd George, now Minister of Munitions, the job of arranging it. The idea was to find a consensual way to activate the Home Rule legislation frozen since 1914. Lloyd George, a masterful and deceitful negotiator, did get John Redmond and Edward Carson – the leaders of the Irish and Ulster Unionist parties – to agree to the immediate creation of a Dublin parliament in exchange for the exclusion of the six north-eastern counties from its jurisdiction. It cost Redmond party unity, and Edward Carson likewise had to sacrifice the Protestant minority in the three counties of Ulster coming under Home Rule, so the sacrifice was mutual.

The deal fell apart within weeks, however, when Conservative and Unionist members of Asquith's coalition cabinet revolted and it emerged that Redmond had been led to believe that partition would be temporary while Carson had been told it would effectively be permanent. In other words, it looked as if Redmond had been suckered by his own supposed Liberal allies. Lloyd George himself escaped scot-free, refused to resign, and was promoted to become Secretary of War. It was not the first or the last time Lloyd George would play this particular game with Irish politicians.

On top of this public-relations disaster, the tens of thousands of Irishmen who had volunteered for the British army continued to be slaughtered on the western and every other front, and the Battle of the Somme (a death trap for the mostly Protestant Ulster Division) foretold more years of the same. At the end of the year, Asquith was deposed by Lloyd George with Conservative backing, producing a new war cabinet much less sympathetic to Home Rule. The Irish Party, with its ageing leadership, now looked bankrupt and very far from its radical Parnellite roots. The breakaway All for Ireland League was similarly stricken: William O'Brien's newspaper, the *Cork Free Press*, closed down for good at the end of 1916. For the first time in a generation, the political arena was opening up and nationalists were seeking alternatives to parliamentary paralysis.

Who would fill the new political vacuum and claim the mantle of national leadership? What was to become of the Volunteers and the IRB, divided, shattered and leaderless after the Rising? What of Sinn Fein – erroneously linked by the government to the rebellion – whose newspaper had been silenced and many of whose activists had been jailed?

Early moves had already been made to revive and reorganize all three organizations before the end of 1916, and new leadership candidates were already emerging, if only by default. The first electoral opportunity came in West Cork in November – too soon for the traditional post-crisis testing of the waters, however, and no Volunteer or Sinn Feiner ran. Two AFIL candidates did try to align themselves as separatist sympathizers (was Johnny Collins involved?) but their squabbling helped let the Irish Party man back in. In fact there was no sign yet of an anti-Party backlash in Cork, and Collins would complain over Christmas of a lack of local radicalism.

Nevertheless, 1917 brought a new constellation of groups into play – notably the Frongochers and earlier returnees from prison, along with a growing body of Irish Party dissidents, including the newly formed Irish Nation League, who objected to Redmond's willingness to negotiate partition. The calling of another by-election on 3 February, this time in North Roscommon – helped bring them together when a local priest, Father Michael O'Flanagan (formerly of the Sinn Fein executive), invited Count George Plunkett to stand as an independent candidate. Plunkett had not been part of the Rising (although he seems to have known about it), and he wasn't a politician, but he had been jailed and had been traduced by unionists, government officials and Party hacks because of his sons' involvement. As anger replaced apathy among mainstream nationalists after the Rising and the botched Home Rule deal, this background would raise, not lower, his reputation. Joseph Plunkett was now a popularly canonized martyr, and the candidate's papal title added a useful aura of respectable sanctity. Such symbolism would be vital in North Roscommon, as the Count had no actual platform, showed up late, and didn't do much campaigning.

Father O'Flanagan, a well-known radical, led the campaign, but he was joined by a gadfly Party MP, Laurence Ginnell, and a host of other dissident groups and individuals. IRB veteran Seamus O'Doherty (acting head of the Supreme Council) was campaign manager. Sinn Feiners, Gaelic Leaguers, Volunteers and trade unionists all played a part – although most were just day or weekend trippers. Rory O'Connor, Tom Dillon and Geraldine Plunkett were there, as were Joe McGrath and Michael Staines. Many of these people would have disdained both the political process and Plunkett – an establishment figure – before the Rising. However, the collapse of the old structures of separatist organizations and the silencing, killing or imprisonment of most of Irish Ireland's ideological disciplinarians allowed people to jump in without having to seek permission, risk a split, or debate policy ad nauseam.

The campaign was successful, and Plunkett won a comfortable majority. The triumph was actually primarily local – with a remarkable upsurge of youthful enthusiasm tipping the balance in getting out the vote – but the credit was taken by the motley band of outside agitators. Such is the familiar, and no doubt universal, campaign class system: the hard-slogging faithful few who put in the day-to-day effort, the first-timers who get hooked on the buzz, the last-minute volunteers wanting an invitation to the election-night party, the publicity-seeking outsiders who claim the victory. Where did Collins fit in?

He almost didn't – in another one of those what-if? circumstances that haunt this part of his life. As before and after, he was saved by his timing and connections. As with the National Aid job, it was Kitty O'Doherty who came to the rescue:

> Mick was in our house [on 1 February]. He was very anxious to get down to help at the election but did not know how he could get there. As it happened, William O'Brien [the union leader] called, and when I found he was driving down to Roscommon, I asked if he had room for a man. He said he had and Mick Collins got the seat. William O'Brien has often said to me since that I had the responsibility of launching Mick Collins on his career.

The next day – a Friday – O'Brien picked up Collins at the O'Dohertys' house on Connaught Street and, together with two other union men, drove to Roscommon. It took all day, due to snowstorms and a flat tyre, so they arrived late and got in on the action only on election day itself. Collins was an electoral novice, so it's unclear what he contributed apart from his customary bustle and hard work. He made the usual impression anyway according to O'Brien: 'Some people thought he was a pusher – and he was resented at the time. The fellows said: "Who's this?" Nobody could say much about him, although he was well known to the planners of this election.' Still, O'Brien says, 'Michael Collins took a leading part in that election. There were a certain number of men picked out as leaders and Collins was one of them.'

The second statement might well be true – IRB talent-spotters did have their eye on him. But as for his leadership role in North Roscommon: well, he was there only on election day. Michael Staines recalls, 'The first time I saw Michael Collins during the election was in Frenchpark on the actual day of the election. He had charge of one of the booths there and I had charge of the other one – there were two in the town.'

To be an observer at a voting booth is essential work, but anyone could have done it. On the other hand, these weren't just any poll booths. Frenchpark was by far the largest polling area, and had been cut off by snow from most of the rest of the constituency. The candidate would be spending election day there, but even the mighty O'Flanagan hadn't been able to get in until the day before:

> I was, therefore, rather uneasy about Frenchpark. I made my way there early on Saturday morning, accompanied by Count Plunkett and Darrell Figgis [a prominent Sinn Fein writer]. I was afraid that we shouldn't even have a personating agent to represent the Count at the polling booth. It looked as if we might have to leave the candidate himself there all day to look after his own interests. At 8 o'clock the evening before, two men had been sent to walking [from] Boyle to make sure of their appointment as sub-agent and polling agent. In fear and trembling we motored into Frenchpark. It was about nine o'clock when we arrived there. The polling was in full swing, our men were at their posts none the worse of their 18 mile tramp of the night before.

Could these two heroes have been the two Michaels, Staines and Collins? It sounds right – they would have been able for it – but Staines doesn't mention an all-night hike through snow in his memoir. Also, William O'Brien says that he and Collins didn't arrive in Boyle until one in the morning on election day. It may be that Staines and Collins relieved the pioneers at some point later in the day. Even if so, they were occupying prime electoral real estate, and spent the day with the candidate.

Collins's role in the election may have been minor, but his place in the Count's retinue was not. He remained in Boyle for several days, waiting for the result and consulting on Plunkett's post-hoc platform. As one of the Dublin newspapers reported on his return to Dublin on the 6th, Plunkett was 'accompanied by Miss Plunkett [Geraldine], the Rev. Fr O'Flanagan, C.C., and Messrs Michael Collins, Seamus O'Doherty, John [presumably Dan] McCarthy and Joseph McGrath, of Dublin, who had been assisting him in his campaign'. This was the first mention of Collins's name in the national press. As in the election and his job-pulling, we can see Collins's networks at work here: the Kimmage contingent, the Frongochers and the Fenians, among them his latest IRB godfather, O'Doherty. Previously his career had been all about maximum effort and little recognition. Here now was the triumph of insiderdom: show up at the last minute, hang around for the celebrations, get close to the candidate, and get your name in the papers.

For anyone who could read between the lines, this was also a group with a very distinct political hue: green, white and orange, the colours of the republican tricolour. Plunkett, who had been elected out of sympathy and through protest votes, declared his political intentions only after the result had been announced and after being coached by the likes of Collins, O'Doherty and McGrath. He unveiled a startlingly radical vision for a novice MP. He would abstain from taking his seat, as the UK parliament had no right to govern in Ireland, and his only representative role outside Ireland would be at the expected post-war peace conference, to put Ireland's case for independence.

NORTH ROSCOMMON had brought together all the competing separatist factions in happy cooperation towards the common goal of attacking the Party and the government. A meeting was thus arranged for 15 February at Plunkett's house to see if they could reach a consensus on policy and on fighting future elections. A smaller group, including Collins and O'Doherty, gathered the day before, but nothing was decided in advance. The conference itself produced an ineffectual advisory committee to keep the ball rolling, but failed to reconcile the four groups present: the Nation Leaguers (who had a lot of talented political professionals and priests and their own newspaper), the trade unionists (who wanted to start a Labour party), the Sinn Feiners (who were suspicious of extremism), and the republican Plunkettites, including Collins, O'Doherty and Rory O'Connor.

The last were in a distinct minority, as none of the others were much in favour of a policy of outright abstention from Westminster, but Plunkett was now insistent on the point. He would rapidly wear out his allies' welcome over the next six months, and many considered him either delusionally egotistical or a mere figurehead for the republican agenda. Michael Staines said that 'Count Plunkett, if elected, was quite prepared to do anything we wanted him to do and he told us so.' That Plunkett – by most accounts a kindly and quiet man, if pompous – was nobody's stooge would be demonstrated throughout his long second career as a political activist. Yet the radicals who wanted to build a movement and to shift public opinion in a revolutionary direction did see him as an opportunity and a counterweight to the 'moderates' (a term of derision to Collins and his comrades) who had dominated their host organizations before the Rising.

The rebels were manoeuvring to reconstitute both the Volunteers and the Brotherhood with their old structures intact, but with themselves in full control. There were many potential obstacles to this long march through the institutions, however. The Rising might be retrospectively popular, but republicanism was not. Eoin MacNeill, whom many rebels blamed for the failure of the Rising thanks to his countermanding order on Easter Sunday, was still technically the president and Chief of Staff of the Volunteers. He still had many loyalists, and his defensive approach to the use of force still had many adherents. The Irish Nation League were just anti-Redmond Home Rulers and opposed even abstention.

Worst of all in some ways, the new buzz word in politics was 'Sinn Fein' – thanks to the newspapers and the government spin doctors, who had so dubbed the rebellion and its sympathizers. By the spring of 1917 it was evident to all that a Rising-inspired wave of youthful enthusiasm for patriotic endeavour had created a spontaneous parish-level 'Sinn Fein' movement of clubs and public demonstrations – unconnected to anyone in Dublin. But Sinn Fein itself was still controlled by Arthur Griffith and his cronies, whom Collins and most other young militants had left behind years ago. If all this new energy were ultimately channelled into pacifist and grad-ualist old Sinn Fein, it would leave republicans out in the cold once again. As Collins put it to William O'Brien, 'It was outrageous to have these people going around the country and parading and hav-ing all their feastings in the papers. It was a fraud.'

Collins was part of Plunkett's inner circle, and was one of the leading advocates of an uncompromising hard line. As congratulatory messages and resolutions from local councils unexpectedly began pouring in from all corners of (southern) Ireland after his victory, Plunkett quickly took his show on the road. In a series of speeches around the country through February and March, he laid out his plan to 'call a new Ireland into existence' by creating a new national organization – replacing the Irish Party and its former competitors. This would begin with an all-Ireland convention bringing together 'the representative men of Ireland and the organizations that had been working for nationality'. Its first task would be to prepare a case for the yet-to-be-convened peace conference. Acting quickly in the hope of seizing on Plunkett's apparent momentum and high profile – and without consulting other interested parties – on St Patrick's Day his people sent out a circular inviting local councillors and others deemed representative of national life to attend a national convention on 19 April.

This sounds a lot like Griffith's, and Sinn Fein's, idea of using local councils – like Russian soviets – to form a national assembly. Previously seen as merely cranky, the post-rebellion and wartime context rendered this old Sinn Fein scheme suddenly revolutionary, especially to officials worrying about a second German-aided revolt – and doubly so in Plunkett's case, as he coupled it with a call to fight for Irish freedom on Irish soil. It is perhaps a tribute then to Plunkett's fundamental lack of credibility that no measures were taken by the government to interfere.

The radicals arranged the 'Plunkett convention' – as it became known – to get a jump on their rivals and to impose their own terms on the new national movement. However, the grandiose manifesto was widely scorned, most people ignored Plunkett's invitation, and his growing feud with the Nation League kept its members away. Collins, Rory O'Connor and Tom Dillon were the event's main organizers – by default it would seem – but their inexperience showed. No proper agenda was prepared, no resolutions were arranged, and they had to scramble to get enough delegates to fill Dublin's voluminous Mansion House. Collins was saddled with hundreds of tickets to unload – perhaps it was thought the National Aid office would be a good place to do it from.

In the end quite a few Sinn Feiners were there, along with a great many 'young men' and 'ladies' and a large contingent of priests, perhaps attracted in part by the Count's reputed religiosity. Estimates of attendance range from 600 to 1,200 with the smaller number, given by the unsympathetic *Irish Times*, probably the more accurate. There certainly wasn't unanimous or possibly even majority support for

Plunkett's plans, which proved to be, once again, startling and divisive. The new movement was to go forward as the Liberty League, and was projected to cover the country in branches (as the Parnellite and Redmondite leagues had once done). Those not committed to abstention from the House of Commons would not be welcome – an attack on the Nation League and a direct challenge to Sinn Fein. This was the classic sectarian attack that Collins had helped carry out in the GAA and the Volunteers: the strategy of the split.

Griffith and the Sinn Feiners proposed instead that an executive council be formed to represent all the various bodies and to direct their electoral and propaganda efforts. This was more or less the old Sinn Fein idea, however, and the militants were having none of it. It and other 'moderate' proposals were disallowed by the chair (Plunkett himself), and the Liberty League was launched instead. Enraged by the dictated outcome, some of those present rushed the stage and, by one account, a mêlée nearly broke out. A split was already in the offing – a new record! – when the principals withdrew to Sinn Fein headquarters at 6 Harcourt Street to discuss matters. Michael Lennon (a friend of Griffith) was there:

Suddenly the door was thrown open and a man of splendid physique entered, followed by a frail figure. It was Michael Collins, accompanied by Rory O'Connor. This was the first time I ever saw the former. His entrance was characteristic of his manner at that period. Looking around, rather truculently, his eyes rested on Mr Griffith, and he asked, in a loud voice: 'I want to know what ticket this Longford election is being fought on.' [Another by-election was nigh.] Mr Griffith looked sphinx-like, smoking his cigarette. I forget what answer was made. But Michael Collins thundered out, 'If you don't fight the election on the Republican ticket you will alienate all the young men.'

This was likewise the first time I heard anyone urge the adoption of Republicanism in its open form as part of our political creed. Mr Griffith remained silent and composed. Mr McCrann (Lanesboro') suddenly intervened by asking, 'Isn't the most important thing to win the election?' Michael Collins denounced this notion fiercely, adding that the Roscommon election had been fought under the Republican flag and that the same must apply in the case of Longford. Father O'Flanagan strove to compose matters, and as well as I can remember, he said that although the tricolour was used at Roscommon the idea of an independent Republic was not emphasized to the electors, and that the people voted rather for the father of a son who had been executed.

The discussion waned, and Michael Collins and Rory O'Connor adjourned to a table, where they began to count the proceeds of the collection made in the Mansion House. A deal was put together (literally) in a back room by Griffith and Father O'Flanagan, establishing an executive committee to keep the principals in touch with one another. Collins was not invited.

Griffith confided to Lennon that 'the men at present urging a second rising have no ability, and if they get their way the thing is hopeless.' Collins wrote in May to Thomas Ashe, one of the surviving leaders of the Rising still in Lewes prison in England, that Griffith was 'pretty rotten, and for that reason some of us have been having fierce rows with him'. Collins seemed to relish the struggle with 'the forces of moderation'. This was, after all, how he had been schooled in politics: fighting for control of leagues and associations over separatist principle, winning votes at conventions, getting the right people on committees and the like. He certainly did very little in these months to help build a united front – in fact he was working against it.

THE NEXT BATTLEGROUND was the by-election to be held three weeks away, on 9 May, at South Longford. The insiders had already met to decide on a candidate. Joe McGuinness was suggested. Like Ashe and other rebel leaders, he had been in Lewes jail since the Rising, and his brother was well known in the district – this gave him both credibility with 'the young men' and electability. Griffith disagreed, suggesting both J. J. O'Kelly, a Nation Leaguer, and Eoin MacNeill, who was anathema to Collins and other 1916 veterans. He was overruled: McGuinness, being a prisoner, would have been a sure sell even without his local connections.

When he was contacted, however, he and the other prisoners discussed it and rejected the idea. They simply weren't sure what was going on in Ireland, and they didn't trust Plunkett's antecedents or the involvement of Sinn Fein. It all smacked of politics and parties. Only Thomas Ashe – advised by Collins as a fellow IRB member –

urged him to run. Dan McCarthy (a long-time Sinn Fein organizer) remembered that 'when I was busily engaged in organizing the constituency on his [McGuinness's] behalf, Michael Collins and Arthur Griffith arrived down to Longford one night and excitedly told me in confidence that a letter had come from Joe McGuinness in Lewes Gaol demanding the withdrawal of his name.'

In an extraordinary move, the committee nominated McGuinness anyway. At this point, especially for the Plunkettites, he may have been the only viable candidate. He would be an absolute abstentionist, he was a real revolutionary, and he had a chance to win. Collins didn't make the decision, but, as he was the contact with the prisoners thanks to his National Aid work, he took the blame and, rather cleverly, the responsibility. He told Ashe:

> You can tell Con Collins, Sean McGarry, and any other high-brows [fellow Organization men] that I've been getting all their scathing messages, and am not a little annoyed, or at least was, but one gets so used to being called bad names and being misunderstood. If they only knew of some of the long fights I've had with AG and some of his pals before I could gain the present point! . . . In view of this it is rather disgusting to be 'chalked up' as a follower of his, and the refusal, though expected by me, was certainly a bit disconcerting. The only way to save the situation was to go on and this has been done. It is possible the point may be gained and the effects will be far reaching . . . But for God's sake don't think that Master AG is going to turn us all into eight two'ites [the parliamentary reformers of 1782, whom Griffith idealized].

In spite of all this, Collins seems to have got along well enough personally with members of other factions – he travelled to meetings with Laurence Ginnell, MP, and Sean Milroy, Griffith's right-hand man, as well as Griffith himself. South Longford was another collective effort, and much better organized and funded. It had to be to match a strong Party machine and its adamantine core vote. Collins was a regular campaigner this time – but only on weekends, given his new responsibilities. Whatever work he did at South Longford – canvassing, postering, office work – it attracted no attention then or thereafter. He delivered no speeches that made the record. Every Friday he and dozens of other enthusiasts would drive or take the train up to Longford to help out, finding accommodation wherever they could get it. Thus he and others came to the Greville Arms Hotel in Granard, owned by the Kiernan family. This hotel, and Co. Longford, would become a second (or third, counting Netherwood Road in London) home for Collins: one he would return to frequently – more than West Cork – until his death.

McGuinness was put forward not as a republican or a Sinn Fein candidate, but as a Rising veteran and prisoner, which was presumably good enough for Collins. This was effective, as hoped, but would not in itself have been enough to win. What did work was the ever-increasing fear of conscription being extended to Ireland, as well as opposition to the partition of Ulster mooted in the aborted 1916 Home Rule deal between Redmond and Carson, powerfully reinforced by Catholic bishops fearful of how the Catholic minority in the excluded counties might be treated.

On 9 May, the day of the election, Collins wasn't actually there, as he had to be back at work in Dublin. The first news he received was of a miraculous McGuinness landslide, so he excitedly wired the Catholic chaplain at Lewes (his go-between with the prisoners) to report the good news. This was wrong, however – the first result announced gave the Party candidate, Patrick McKenna, victory by a nose. Collins was enraged to discover that he had been misled, and vowed to track down the person responsible. Fortunately the irreplaceable Joe McGrath, acting as a scrutineer, noticed that some votes were missing and protested – and when the recount was done McGuinness had won by 32 votes. McGrath was the hero of the day and Dan McCarthy was the architect of victory, proving himself to be a campaigning wizard. The separatists were now beating the Party bosses at their own game.

But winning did not settle the running controversy over how to define or direct the political phenomenon sweeping the country. George Gavan Duffy, who had known Collins slightly in London and had worked with him in Frongoch, observed to P. S. O'Hegarty that 'Plunkett is certainly gaining ground in Dublin and he and the young Volunteers behind him seem to have a much bigger pull than Griffith; in other words the montagne is on top and Griffith is probably being squeezed.' Outside the capital, clubs were sprouting everywhere of their own accord, however, and for the most part they were calling themselves Sinn Fein.

This didn't mean that they agreed with Griffith over Plunkett, or even knew that such a debate was going on. What it meant was that Griffith's decade-long investment in his message had paid off: this was brand-name identification by first-time consumers. Liberty League branches were being formed (especially in Cork, a contrary place politically), but not nearly at the same rate. Nor did the new group have a newspaper or a headquarters – or organizers. Collins was still involved, but he can't have devoted much time to it given his job. The Sinn Feiners might have been on the run in radical Dublin, but they were winning by a landslide in the rest of the country.

The obvious solution – and one pressed upon the various leaders by the rank and file – was a merger. A temporary one was fixed up at a series of meetings in the first two weeks of June, involving the usual suspects. The Liberty League clubs would become Sinn Fein clubs, and in return the Plunkettites would get half the seats on the party executive. The really contentious matter of policy was sensibly left aside for another day. Collins and co. couldn't have arranged it better if they had planned it all along: trading in a vaporous month-old 'league' for equal power in the movement's central institution was a terrific result. And Collins (who had not been part of the Mansion House committee set up in April) was now sitting on the executive with (whatever he now thought of him) one of his boyhood heroes, Arthur Griffith. He was growing up fast.

9: Player

I used to see Mick Collins every day. He was very young, handsome and full of personality, but still I did not think he possessed the depths which he later showed. He was full of fun and had a keen sense of humour which he exhibited in practical jokes. He had, in addition, a command of language that even a British Tommy might have envied.

(Michael Noyk)

COLLINS AND HIS FELLOW republicans and Rising veterans may have entered politics and joined (or rejoined) Sinn Fein, but that was a product more of timing and opportunity than of deliberate tactics. Sinn Fein got the benefit of the Rising, whereas the Irish Volunteers and the IRB – the Rising's vehicles – had been decapitated and dismembered by casualties and executions. It was in Frongoch and Lewes that they retained their vitality, while those members at large lay low. Once prisoners started returning with the urge to get something going again, elections, committees and leagues were the only game in town.

Neither the Brotherhood nor the Volunteers had been reanimated until well into the spring of 1917, although, under the catch-all banner of 'Sinn Fein', groups of young men had begun drilling, marching and forming their own – new – Volunteer companies. Before the Frongochers had come home, a shadowy temporary Volunteer executive had been created by Cathal Brugha – a candle merchant and Gaelic Leaguer (whom Collins had met while collecting the Larkfield rent), who had been badly wounded in 1916 and therefore not deported to Britain – but it did not issue its first order until May 1917.

The IRB was similarly slow to regain consciousness. As before the Rising, many separatists and Volunteers were suspicious of hidden agendas and felt misgivings about joining owing to the Catholic Church's ban on oath-taking secret societies. Others felt its work was done now that it had finally engineered a proper rebellion, and that republicanism now had other organizations to work through. Many who had been members dropped out at this point. Still, an old guard remained, including Kathleen Clarke (not a member as such, owing to her being a woman) and Seamus O'Doherty. They believed a clandestine vanguard party was still necessary, and many of the young militants struggling for ascendancy in the new movement agreed. A provisional council was put together in 1916, but this did little apart from fending off further German assistance and sending greetings to their more successful counterparts in Russia.

Collins was actually in a rather awkward position upon his return to Dublin in 1917. His Volunteer company had disappeared, as had his vague 'staff' position at headquarters and his temporary position in the Rising. In fact he may never have belonged to a proper Volunteer unit there, since his real links were with the Kimmagers. As in Frongoch, 'refugees' from Britain such as himself were looked down on by the Dubliners. Similarly, his IRB section in London had shut down, his adopted circle in Dublin was in limbo, and his temporary and illegal circle in Frongoch had dissipated after the camp was closed. Technically, he had the barest foothold in either organization. This meant some quick footwork to re-establish himself – and here the O'Dohertys and his work for Plunkett, McGuinness and the National Aid were invaluable.

Getting back into the Volunteers meant doing so in Dublin: not too much of a problem given his role in the Rising, but which unit would have him? If he was to be an officer, who would he displace? Collins wasn't really known in Dublin as a Volunteer, but he quickly became a familiar face with those whom the National Aid helped, and he was briefly adopted as an assistant adjutant by the 1st battalion (a position probably created just for this purpose) to give him standing. Richard Mulcahy, an ally in the prison camp, may have helped, but he was away for most of 1917 as a Gaelic League organizer in Cork. Collins never actually served in any of the Dublin companies, but, since they were dormant at the time, he probably wouldn't have had the chance to even if he had wanted to.

In any case, he was only passing through on his way to the top – the newly self-appointed Volunteer executive, to which he was soon co-opted.

He had no particular brief yet, but, if only by being resident in Dublin and being able to make all the meetings, he was privy to all the executive's decision-making. Collins was thus one of the authors of the 22 May Volunteer manifesto, which declared the new executive's existence and policies. This began by stating that the executive had been elected by an all-Ireland convention (although Collins hadn't been) in order to 'complete by force of arms the work begun by the men of Easter week'. Having said this, the writers then implicitly rebuked both Eoin MacNeill and the Easter conspirators: 'In order that we may not be hampered in our next effort by any misunderstanding such as occurred on the last occasion, as a result of conflicting orders, Volunteers are notified that the only orders they are to obey are those of their own Executive.' The infamous 'conflicting orders' of Easter Sunday had been blamed on Eoin MacNeill, but if the Volunteers had followed the new rule in 1916 they would presumably have ignored the rebel officers and stayed home in obedience to him.

Volunteers were exhorted, as always, to support other like-minded groups, but to give their first allegiance to their own. If you were a Volunteer, you were a Volunteer first. Pragmatically, companies were also told that they were on their own when it came to guns, training and contacting their fellows. Finally, in another surprising swipe at the Easter rebels, the executive guaranteed that 'they would *not* issue an order to take the field until they consider that the force is in a position to wage war on the enemy with reasonable hopes of success. Volunteers as a whole may consequently rest assured that they will not be called upon to take part in any forlorn hope.'

In other words, the Rising should never have happened? The manifesto would seem to be a retrospective condemnation of the martyrs as military leaders at least, and echoes other comments attributed to Collins about how badly planned and run the rebellion actually was. More immediately, this language may also have been designed to woo back the MacNeillites, not to mention attracting potential new recruits.

A republican revolution was now the Volunteers' official objective, replacing the 1913 manifesto's call to defend and protect Ireland's rights and liberties while contemplating neither aggression nor domination. This was the sort of 'compromise' that was to feature in the revamped Sinn Fein constitution as well, revealing the shift in the balance of power from moderates to militants.

REJOINING THE IRB was trickier than getting back to the Volunteers. The Organization was smaller, more suspicious, and more mindful of tradition and rules. The unofficial circle in Frongoch was frowned upon by many: you can't just start your own circle! There was also the matter of Collins's drinking, which was anathema to the many temperance advocates in the movement. According to what Alfie White of the hyper-radical Fianna Eireann heard, 'he [Collins] had been in London but was thought to be unreliable by the IRB for he went on bouts of drink. Joe O'Rourke said they were at Larkfield in a lodging house and the lady in charge asked the National Aid to take Collins away for they couldn't stand his bad language.' Of course such talk had dogged Collins in London as well, but his superiors did eventually come to trust him. And now, as then, he had senior people to vouch for him: Pat Belton, Seamus O'Doherty and Kathleen Clarke.

The first thing Collins did was to return to the Fintan Lalor circle when it re-formed in 1917, to put himself up for election as centre (head of the circle) – a position previously held by Sean MacDermott. Running against him, however, was Eamon (Bob) Price, who had been among the officers at Frongoch and was a member of a well-known republican family. Price beat him by a large majority. Then, once the circles had all been reorganized (in May or June), came a meeting of the Centres Board. Joseph O'Rourke was centre of Dublin Circle No. 17 – otherwise known as the Clarence Mangan Literary and Debating Society – and one of those who had objected to Collins's Frongoch irregularities:

Two or three of the men came to me before the meeting and asked if I remembered about the unauthorized recruitment in Frongoch, and I said yes. They said they had been approached on the prospects of admitting two new circles en bloc to the Dublin Centres' Board and asked me what I thought about it. I said I didn't think much of it. 'You were a Secretary the same as myself and you know the care that was taken about admitting individual members, and this proposal does not sound good policy to me.' This was before the meeting. When the meeting was called to order and the ordinary business was completed, the Chairman got up and made a speech, the sense of which was: 'As you may or may not know, among your comrades in arms in Frongoch certain individuals organized a branch of the IRB in order that the fight should be carried on, and these men were tried in the furnace of action and we now propose that these two Circles should be admitted and attached to this Centres' Board.' Two or three people got up and spoke in favour, and as it appeared that nobody was going to object to it I got up and pointed out that any infringement of the Constitution or suspension of the Standing Orders would automatically release us from our obligations to the organization, and that while I had nothing to say against these men and they would be welcome as individuals entering upon the normal recruitment procedure, that I for one could not assent to their admission en bloc. I sat down and there was another speech in favour, and then somebody took my side and pointed out that we were entitled to all the safety precautions the organization could give us, which was little enough in the circumstances. There was a third speech to the same effect. The Chairman stood up and said he was ashamed at us doubting the bona fides of these proved men, and a vote was taken (secret ballot) and the Chairman's motion was passed by 9 to 8 votes against. The Chairman then said that 'by a strange coincidence the men to whom I refer are actually in the building, and if it is the will of the meeting I will introduce them.' ... Then Collins came in and I think Frank Kelly [another Londoner] with him. We were then, of course, snowed under and the majority was against us. We then got a 'pep talk' from Collins to 'get on with it'. I had thought of approaching the Supreme Council to get the decision reversed, but as only the remains of the Supreme Council was left I believed it would be of no use.

No use at all, given that Collins – now officially a centre again, as he had been in London – was soon on the council himself. This was presumably the reason for the Tammany Hall tactics, to give him the appropriate status – he wasn't interested in being an ordinary member or Volunteer any more. Splitting the Frongoch circle in two added more clout on the Dublin board. He did take his duties seriously, however, and he remained a conscientious attender of meetings throughout the revolution.

A permanent IRB Supreme Council was re-established once the remaining Rising convicts were released in June 1917. Collins' pen pal Thomas Ashe became the new president – and a new mentor – and among his colleagues were Diarmuid O'Hegarty, a pal from his days in the Keating rooms, and Sean O Murthuile, one of his Frongoch irregulars. Collins himself was the representative for southern England – his old Division – and was given his usual job of secretary. The IRB constitution was revised in line with new circumstances, and Collins, again, was one of the drafters. As with the Volunteer manifesto, an attempt was made to correct the faults revealed by the Rising. In this case provision was made for a Military Council where previously this had been an ad-hoc body set up to plan the Rising. More importantly, it was placed under the complete control of the Supreme Council. Once again, if such had been the case in 1916 the rebellion might well have been aborted.

COLLINS DID NOT just attend meetings: he lived his motto and 'got on with the work'. One vital task was to rearm the Volunteers. An arms committee (perhaps the Military Council itself) was formed with Collins in his other accustomed role of treasurer. His job was to handle the American money used to purchase guns – at this point typically bought off soldiers in pubs or home on leave. He tried a few grand schemes (as he would in later years too), but a 1918 attempt to buy old Ulster Volunteer Force arms went wrong when the whole shipment was captured. He was staying with Michael Lynch (a Dublin Volunteer officer) at the time, and this setback so depressed him that he refused to leave his room: Michael Staines, Nancy O'Brien and others had to be brought in to coax him down to eat. He didn't sulk for too long, but soon thereafter a failed explosives delivery put him off his Belfast connection altogether. On the other hand, it was not hard to build up a small but steady supply using his contacts in Britain.

Weapons were a very touchy subject in 1917. A shadow hung over many Volunteer units outside Dublin because their officers had given up their rifles without a fight after the Rising was over – thereby betraying the whole ethos of the organization. This set off an informal purge of the guilty parties. Those who had done prison time, like Cork's Terry MacSwiney and Tom MacCurtain, were let off, but these men still felt ashamed of their actions. The new wave of republican leaders were determined that these units would fight next time, and one way they made sure of this was to channel the weapons to their own people – fellow militants, if not IRB men. Fenian money for Fenian guns. Thus, within MacCurtain's 1st Cork Brigade there was a secret (self-styled) 'IRB unit' dedicated to making sure no such surrender happened again. It may be presumed that Collins knew about it, but MacCurtain didn't find out about it until the unit's bomb factory blew up, killing two Volunteers. What Collins and his comrades were doing was building a movement within a movement.

Another way the Brotherhood had of ensuring the Volunteers were politically correct was to make sure the officers were 'one of us' (as Organization men put it in their Mafia-like way). This meant either putting IRB men in place or swearing existing officers into the Organization. Collins was an active promoter and recruiter in this regard. Sean MacEoin (John McKeown) of Co. Longford, later a renowned guerrilla leader ('the Blacksmith of Ballinalee') and eventually head of the Irish army, recalls one now-famous instance:

> I had eighteen hoops in the fire when Collins arrived. He said he wanted to talk to me for a minute so I said alright what is it? I want you to take over, he gave the signal to me and the password, he said I want you to take over Longford . . . I said I can't do it, for several reasons. First of all I was not fitted and secondly I am the oldest of a family, they are all very young and my mother is a widow and I promised my dying father that I'd look after them and support them, therefore I can't do it, and he said 'You must.' Well I said the man that says 'Must' to me must be a damn sight better man than I am. Well, he said I am a better man, well I said even [though] I'm busy come out to the wood for a minute and we will see whether you are or not. We went out, there was a wood at the end of the forge and it was a wrestling match and of course I was in my shirt and trousers, he was in his city suit, so I thought I could handle him without any great difficulty. I found extreme difficulty but I got him down without much hardship, and to my holy horror he caught my ear in his mouth and started roaring into it, he broke my hold and

pinned me down and he said, 'Now ar'nt I a better man.' Yes I said by a trick. Now from that moment the friendship [between] himself and myself remained till his death.

Of course not everyone found Collins's arguments so convincing. One question faced by the new Supreme Council was what to do with the survivors of the previous council who had opposed the Rising. One such was Bulmer Hobson, a once influential republican who had sided with MacNeill against the Rising's planners. When his case came up for debate in the Dublin circles, Valentine Jackson remembers:

Collins who, at the time was standing near the window, spoke at once and said sharply, that surely I should know that Hobson could only be tried by his peers who were now all dead. I told him that I considered that he was already being judged and condemned without trial by many of his former colleagues and that surely there were still enough people left who could examine into and prove or disprove these charges. Collins now shifted his ground and said that was all very well, but that the Organization had much more important work in hand than the trial and not to be talking nonsense, or words to that effect [scatological words one assumes]. In face of this attitude I could say no more.

Collins was rarely interested in pursuing vendettas, and he probably wanted to avoid an acrimonious show trial which would do nothing to further the cause. While his aim was sensible enough, once again we have a picture of a pushy and domineering man determined to have his own way and dismissive of procedure and debate. Michael Lynch remembers meeting Dick McKee, a leading Dublin Volunteer, one night in Drumcondra Road:

We walked along, wheeling our bicycles. He asked me what did I think of Collins. I told him that Collins was a tremendous personality; he was forging his way to the front, and he did not mind who he trampled on; he had come over from London to represent the exiles on the IRB, of which he would be in control eventually. Dick said, 'We will see about that!

McKee would end up a close comrade and admirer, but not everyone came to the same conclusion.

This widespread impression of an ambitious man in a hurry,

already established in Kimmage and Frongoch, was further soured by persistent rumours of financial delinquencies. Was Collins on the take as well as on the make? Some of these stories had followed him from London, where he was said to have been IRB treasurer and where, it was said, he had tried to fill the same position in the Gaelic League in order to control its funds. Of course this may have been true – but with the intent of bringing IRB influence to bear rather than filling his own pockets.

This same charge was made within the Dublin IRB in 1917 over Collins's stewardship of the National Aid funds. Barney Mellows of Fianna Eireann and the IRB worked there, and told people 'about fellows being entertained at the Deer's Head [pub]' with much drink taken and money spent: equal crimes to the teenage zealots. When the charge reached Leo Henderson a Rising and Frongoch veteran, he tried to bring it up in an IRB meeting:

> I was that ignorant but I meant well, for I thought the matter would be dealt with through the IRB. The next thing was that Eamon Bulfin [a member of the illicit Frongoch circle] called to see me and he wanted to know who it was had given me the information and what did I mean by making such a charge against Mick Collins ... I couldn't give my source, so I had to withdraw the charge, and ever afterwards there was always a strained relationship between myself and Collins.

The reports persisted, however, and Eamon Martin, a senior Fianna officer, did make an accusation to Collins's face:

> I was centre of the IRB circle and when the question of Collins drinking and abusing funds [came up], I had to make the accusation, and the only evidence that could be produced was that of a girl whom Collins had sacked. Collins went for me over that and Garry [?] was very hot about it. Garry made the accusation. I got the brunt of it for Collins' gang was very hot about me.

Part of the problem, again, was Collins's fondness for pubs, which had already told against him in London – he would soon cut down on his drinking. Part was his combination of roles. The National Aid had to be seen to be transparently honest, while the IRB arms committee was necessarily run on a much looser basis, with a lot of risk and the only bottom line being results. This would explain the attempts to silence the whistle-blowers. There is certainly no evidence at all that Collins did anything actually fraudulent at the Aid office – if he had, accountants and enemies would probably have spotted it.

What these episodes show is not actual guilt but the assumption of guilt based on his (to some) obnoxious ambition and power-seeking. Leo Henderson, who worked against him in the IRB, and who seems to have believed the rumours about misspent funds, thought that 'Collins was a bully ... All the refugees from London who were avoiding Conscription came over here, but some of them were not much good, even when they fought. After 1916, these lads who had no jobs were hanging around, and Collins kept them as hangers on.' For the same reasons, scandal would dog Collins for the rest of his career.

10: Politician

Now when the meeting was over we brought Collins and
[Thomas] Ashe into tea and that was the first time I met
him in a social way and I must say without hesitation that
while Ashe had great qualities he struck me as too much of
the School Master as compared to Collins. Collins was
more natural in his conduct and approach. Collins was
more natural and had no dandified appearance about
him . . .

(Sean MacEoin, Longford)

WHILE COLLINS'S REPUTATION – both good and bad – was rising
behind closed doors, the revolutionary movement was rising along
with it. After the successes in Roscommon in February and Longford
in May, it got another boost in June, when the remaining Rising
prisoners were released from English prisons. Collins and his comrades again spun this as a British surrender. He wrote to Austin
Stack's brother in Co. Kerry that 'it was the men themselves who
were responsible for the release. Surely the Government is in a most
humiliated position.'

The prisoners' return to Ireland in 1917 witnessed the first wave
of violence since the Rising – a police inspector was killed in Dublin
during the celebrations, and bloody riots took place there and in
Cork city. In letters, Collins referred to the 'wonderful scenes' of the
demonstrations and the mass reappearance of the revolutionary tricolour: 'Republican flags still fly from the ruins of our Easter Week
headquarters,' he told Alec McCabe in Sligo four days after the great
homecoming (which centred on the National Aid offices). As it
happens, Collins was one of the chief dealers in these illegal flags
(not to mention photographs of Pearse and other paraphernalia)

which he peddled to his National Aid contacts, to his troops at the Plunkett convention, and to audiences on the republican-speakers circuit.

Sinn Fein chose not to contest the two by-elections after Longford's, as the leafy suburbs and unionist enclaves of Belfast South and Dublin South were not favourable battlegrounds. The next target was Clare East, on 10 July, which would mark the political debut of Eamon de Valera. This formerly obscure Gaelic Leaguer and academic – eight years older than Collins – happened to be the last surviving battalion commander from the old Dublin Volunteers, and the man behind the only successful battle in the city – at Mount Street bridge – and had thereby acquired a heroic reputation while in prison. As one of the returning prisoners, he was greeted as a national saviour returned from exile, his Spanish name (his mother was Irish and he grew up in Ireland, but he was born in New York) adding a touch of exotic mystique. Fortunately for the revolution, he also proved to be a superb politician.

Clare brought everyone together again in what was now an efficient and well-financed machine run by Dan McCarthy. Collins took part in the campaign as before, and again as a worker rather than a leader. He told Thomas Ashe that 'I quite agree with you that the fight in East Clare will be stiff – quite as stiff as South Longford,' and the Irish Party did mount a serious effort to retain one of its banner seats. It had been held by Willie Redmond (brother of John), who had died in battle in France. Clare had also been the site of Daniel O'Connell's great fight for Catholic emancipation in 1828, and so was doubly significant. De Valera still won an overwhelming victory, cementing Sinn Fein's position as a national force.

Four days later the Kilkenny City seat also became vacant (after yet another sitting Irish Party MP had expired), and the *Irish Times* commented that, if Sinn Fein won, the Party 'must receive their death blow' at the next general election. William Cosgrave did duly win – the third veteran of the Rising and the fourth republican to be elected. This time, as befitted a newly appointed member of the party executive, Collins was organizing speakers as a member of the election committee.

He also made his debut as one of Sinn Fein's growing pool of spokespeople. As the movement took off, requests poured into party headquarters for speakers to draw a crowd and spread the new gospel.

Typically, local clubs asked for the big names: Arthur Griffith, the party's founder, Eamon de Valera, the military hero and victor in Clare, or Constance Markievicz, the only woman officer in the Rising. No one ever asked for the unknown Collins, but someone had to get the touring company. His assigned beat was the northern midlands: counties Longford, Leitrim, Sligo and Roscommon – two of which he already knew from by-elections. Thus we find him in the company of Thomas Ashe (and once with Arthur Griffith) travelling around Longford and Sligo on successive weekends in July to establish new clubs. In their version of a bad-cop-good-cop routine, Ashe declared that 'if he saw his chance again and that England was overpowered he would call out his men again as he did in Easter Week,' while Collins mildly added that 'when an opportunity occurred they would be able to put England's representatives out of Ireland.'

In August Collins was in Carrick-on-Shannon town hall (in County Leitrim) to urge the formation of Sinn Fein clubs to fight every election at every level, to deny the movement was pro-German, and to reassure the audience that the Pope 'had not forgotten so Catholic a country'. 'The speech was very moderate,' the local police report noted approvingly. While there, he travelled to Roscommon on a similar errand. In September he was in Ballymahon in Longford to say that 'We are not pro-Germans or pro-English, but any nation good enough to strike a blow at England is good enough to be a friend of Ireland.' On such trips he doubled as an emissary of the Supreme Council and practised his rough wooing of Sean MacEoin (and assorted innkeepers' daughters).

He also travelled home to West Cork regularly, and was a regular fixture at local events. He was in Clonakilty in the last week of June to welcome Con O'Donovan back from prison, accompanied by the usual crowd and band. (He was identified in the *Cork Examiner* as 'M. J. Collens of Woodfield', although this would be the last time his name was misspelled.) He later addressed meetings in Skibbereen and Bantry. On the latter occasion he was accompanied by Gearoid O'Sullivan and Ernest Blythe, an old IRB hand, who later recalled:

> The first time I ever heard Collins deliver a public speech was at the Aeridheacht [a Gaelic League festival]. He spoke very vigorously, but the time had not yet come when he could grip

the crowd. Although his reputation was growing, it was by no means made, and he did not reckon as any more important than an ordinary local speaker.

THE CLARE ELECTION had brought out the Volunteers in numbers and in uniform for the first time since the Rising, which, together with the riots and flags – not to mention Sinn Fein's successes – shocked the Irish administration into one of its periodic clamp-downs. Collins wrote to Madge Daly (sister of Kathleen Clarke) in Limerick on 31 July that 'It is, I think, quite likely that the arrests will start again on a big scale,' but added, 'of course, that will only do good.'

He was right about the first part. Dozens were arrested for sedition or illegal drilling in late July and August, one of whom was Tom Ashe, wanted for one of his Longford speeches. Ashe had gone into hiding in Batt O'Connor's house when the arrests began, but after six weeks, according to his sister Nora, 'At last he could bear the confinement no longer and he went into town one night. He was arrested immediately at the [Nelson's] Pillar.' Collins wasn't arrested, as he wasn't seen as significant or immoderate enough to warrant it.

Ashe was a gentle, devout and much-loved man, cut from the same idealistic cloth as Patrick Pearse and Joseph Plunkett. Mrs Batt O'Connor thought him 'a beautiful man with his tall noble figure and lovely wavy hair'. His poem 'Let me carry your cross for Ireland, Lord!', written in prison, captured better than anything this generation's evangelical republicanism. Collins attended his court-martial in early September, and sent an account to Nora:

> The whole business was extremely entertaining, almost as good as 'Gilbert and Sullivan's skit trial by jury'. The President of the court is obviously biased against Tom and, although the charge is very trivial, and the witnesses contradicted each other, it is quite likely that Tom will be sentenced. However, let us hope that it will be light.

Ashe was found guilty and was sentenced to one year's hard labour. He was sent to Mountjoy prison in north Dublin along with other Sinn Feiners, and together they began a campaign to be treated as prisoners of war rather than as common criminals. This led to a hunger strike (the first of the revolution), which was met in turn by force-feeding – both techniques developed in the pre-war suffragist struggle in Britain. Collins, a veteran of such protests in Frongoch (although the hunger strike there wasn't nearly so serious), was then a firm believer in their efficacy and believed that they had worked both there and in Lewes. He also knew well the propaganda dividends that such struggles paid. It was time for passions to be roused and for the enemy to be humiliated again.

Tragically and vilely, however, the force-feeding went wrong, and Ashe was fatally injured. Joe Good was present at the prison that day:

> A huge mob was milling outside Mountjoy; they had worked themselves up almost into a state of hysteria, by praying, singing, etc. Collins and [Cathal] Brugha at that critical moment arrived on a common sidecar, addressed the large crowd and precipitated something of a riot.

Some Volunteers attacked the police cordon, but were beaten off. On 25 September Ashe was removed to the Mater hospital, where he soon died.

The strikers' demands were, as Collins would have predicted, immediately granted by an aghast administration. Nationalist public opinion was outraged and Sinn Fein recruitment soared. Volunteers saw Ashe's death as little less than an act of war. Along with this went the sense that the pious Ashe was a genuine martyr for his faith. All these emotions came together at his funeral on 30 September, attended by tens of thousands of mourners and organized by the IRB (using a cover name, the Wolfe Tone Memorial Society) and the Dublin Brigade of the Volunteers, which was effectively reorganized by the occasion. The whole event was put together by Richard Mulcahy and Dick McKee, who made their names in doing so: Mulcahy was appointed brigade commandant immediately afterwards, and McKee replaced him when he was promoted to the Volunteer executive (where McKee soon followed).

As movement activists flooded into Dublin, Collins's letters were an odd mixture of mournful and vengeful, calculating and exultant. On the one hand, 'The death of poor Tom Ashe has filled everybody, even political opponents, with horror and indignation, but a day of reckoning will come.' On the other:

Dublin is in the hands of the Volunteers again this week. No
living person ever witnessed such a crowd as thronged the streets
from Phibsboro' to O'Connell Bridge, when the remains were
being removed last night. His death has done more good than
his life would in some ways but, on the whole, he is the greatest
loss we could have sustained. The end is not yet . . . Whatever
happens let the people hear the true aspect of the case on
Sunday.

Spoken like a true revolutionary! We may mourn, but our lives are
merely means to the greater end. To be fair, Collins talked about
himself this way as well – at least until he came to believe he was
indispensable.

What Collins meant by letting the people know 'the true aspect
of the case' became clear when the time came on Sunday for the
graveside oration. Such funerals were central to nationalist culture,
and their most important aspect was the speech over the grave. The
last such occasion had been old Fenian O'Donovan Rossa's funeral in
1915, when Pearse had ended his speech with the electrifying call to
arms: 'The fools! They have left us our Fenian dead, and while
Ireland holds these graves, Ireland unfree shall never be at peace.'
Now Ashe was to be buried in the same place, Glasnevin Cemetery,
with only John O'Leary's grave between his and Rossa's.

On this occasion, after the funeral and the procession, after
Ashe's body had been interred, twelve uniformed men fired three
volleys over the grave. Then, according to the *Irish Times*:

Mr Michael Collins, after the firing, stepped forward and said
there would be no oration. Nothing remained to be said, for the
volley which had been fired was the only speech which it would
be proper to make above the grave of a dead Fenian.

That the speaker would be Collins and that there would be no
oration had been kept a secret, apparently even from Mulcahy. It was
surely intended to make a great impact on the crowd as a declaration
of defiance and intent akin to Pearse's prophecy (although did this
mean Pearse's speech was improper?): a purely symbolic display,
uncluttered by rhetoric. Translation: we mean business. As Mulcahy
– who can't have been amused, as he had done all the work and was
worried about disbanding the Volunteers peacefully after the funeral

– would admit much later, however, it wasn't necessarily taken that way:

> As a matter of fact great surprise was expressed at the name of the person who spoke over Ashe's grave (if one could call it speaking). Whereas you had an oration over O'Donovan Rossa's grave, what happened over Ashe's grave was that there were three volleys fired and some young man whom a lot of people had never heard of before, just said 'that was the only thing worth saying over a Fenian's grave.'

As J. J. O'Kelly recalled it:

> How Mr Collins – up to then practically unknown in Ireland – was being pushed into prominence by a hidden force, some of us first detected on the occasion of the Ashe funeral. At the last moment it was casually mentioned to the Funeral Committee that he should deliver an oration at the graveside. The announcement elicited expressions of surprise and a question [no doubt from O'Kelly] as to whether it was to be in Irish, the upshot being that the oration, as such, was abandoned . . .

Those who did know Collins may not have been all that surprised. As Mulcahy also observed, with unusual candour, 'At any rate, Collins came on the political horizon when he stood at Ashe's grave.' It was a rare opportunity that he let slip by.

Not that Collins was planning to eschew oration altogether. He was soon on the road again to make Ashe's death do some more good. On 7 October he was back in Ballinalee, where Sean MacEoin was blacksmith and where Ashe had made the supposedly seditious speech. He was fourth out of six speakers, so funereal fame hadn't yet made him the headline act. When his turn came, he quickly established the fact that he had accompanied Ashe on that fateful day and afterwards added that:

> Thomas Ashe is not dead – his Spirit is with us if he could only speak and appear. What Ashe died for should be carried out, and organizing ourselves will allow us to put our case before the peace conference.

Actually it was Collins who had talked about peace conferences and Ashe who had talked about rebellions, but Collins did say finally,

'As someone had said nothing would be got from England unless you approach them with the head of a Landlord in one hand and the tail of a Bullock in the other.' Not quite up to Pearse's standard: perhaps another reason why he chose to let the guns speak for themselves.

BY THE AUTUMN of 1917 the Liberty League had come and gone, the Volunteers and the IRB were in republican hands, the by-elections had been fought and won, the new mass movement had its first post-Rising martyr, and Collins had played a leading part in each drama. One battle remained: the constitution and leadership of Sinn Fein. Amalgamation had not resolved basic conflicts over policy, but the advent of de Valera as a putative national leader changed the dynamics of the argument. His great goal from the very beginning was to create and maintain a united national movement, and his great achievement was to bring this about under the banner of Sinn Fein.

Collins had already formed a mixed opinion of 'Dev' – '*distant, strange, stand offish*' – but he was one of the first to suggest him as a replacement for Plunkett as the 'advanced' (i.e. republican) candidate for president of Sinn Fein at the forthcoming Ard Fheis (convention) set for 25 October. Until then, Griffith was still nominally head, and the party's official ideology remained non-republican. It was widely expected that Griffith would fight to retain his hold on the movement he had created, so both sets of partisans (although not everyone chose sides) spent much of October mobilizing support among the 1,700-odd delegates.

Broadly speaking, Volunteers saw de Valera as 'their' man and, backed by the Brotherhood, tried to ensure he would have a majority. In Cork city, for example, Liam de Roiste found that 'the Volunteer organization is working quite independently, and is capturing, or endeavouring to capture and completely control Sinn Fein as such ... Every man who is not a Volunteer or in the good graces of the chiefs of the Volunteers is to be pushed aside.' A Volunteer convention had been called for the 27th, the day after the Sinn Fein one ended, so hundreds of men were planning to attend both. When they arrived in Dublin, many were directed to the offices of the Keating branch of the Gaelic League, now at 46 Parnell Square, where they were met by members of the Supreme Council of the IRB including Collins, Diarmuid (Jeremiah) Lynch, Diarmuid O'Hegarty and Sean O Murthuile (three Corkmen and a Limerick man – the Munster mafia), who handed them a list of who to vote for in the Sinn Fein executive elections.

In fact Griffith had already secretly agreed to make way for de Valera (whom he admired) as president of the party, and the new constitution had already been hammered out by the provisional executive during three nights of hard bargaining. Collins, Cathal Brugha and others had almost walked out over the Griffithites' resistance to an outright declaration of republicanism, but de Valera had kept them in the room and suggested a workable compromise formula: that Sinn Fein would aim at gaining international recognition for an Irish republic (the peace conference again), and once this was achieved a referendum would be held to determine the form of government. Both sides could claim they had got what they wanted. Ideologies were further reconciled by the simple expedient of tacking a republican preamble praising the Rising on to a Griffithite agenda for national reconstruction, to be carried out by a sovereign national assembly. It was one of de Valera's finest achievements.

Why, then, did the IRB proceed with its planned takeover? According to Diarmuid Lynch, because it was 'still doubtful as to what may happen at the Convention'. Paranoia aside, essentially it still wanted the power. De Valera was now only a nominal Volunteer and was no longer even a nominal Brother – and moderates could still dominate the new executive. After all, the former Liberty Leaguers got half the seats on the provisional executive only because of Griffith's generosity. They would have to make sure that those in charge would interpret the ambiguous clauses of the constitution in the right way.

The plan failed abysmally – and publicly, after it was outed and condemned on the convention floor. So was a rival list of anti-republicans organized by the much-loathed Darrell Figgis, but, when it came time to vote in a new leadership, it was the militants whom the delegates decided to punish. Count Plunkett dropped his challenge for the presidency and ran instead against Griffith and Father O'Flanagan to be one of the two vice-presidents, only to be mauled, getting only one-sixth of the total votes cast. Republicanism was fairly well represented but only three active IRB men – Collins, Diarmuid Lynch and Harry Boland – were elected on to the twenty-four-person executive, and there were none among the party officers. Only Collins, Cathal Brugha, Austin Stack from Kerry and Diarmuid

Lynch could claim to be active Volunteers. Embarrassingly, Collins just squeezed into last place. He got 340 votes and Plunkett got 386 – which sounds as if the IRB machine controlled fewer than 400 votes. Its minority status seems to have stayed about the same as it had been before the Rising, when it had also needed to conspire to acquire power.

The conspirators also failed in their aim of keeping particular people out of power. Heading this list was republican bugbear Eoin MacNeill. De Valera was intent on bringing him into the movement – a canny move designed to appeal to the great majority of Volunteers who hadn't taken part in the Rising, as well as to the Gaelic Leaguers and others who still saw him as a trusted leader. The 'advanced' men wanted no part of this gesture of unity: if the new movement was to be built on the foundation of the Rising, MacNeill must be excommunicated.

Collins had worked against MacNeill's rehabilitation for months, writing in June that 'at all costs it seems to me that he must after this contest [the East Clare election where de Valera invited MacNeill to share a platform] make a statement saying that he intends devoting himself solely to literature or some such think [sic].' MacNeill was not willing to go away so easily, so he was targeted for defeat at the Ard Fheis. In the event, Constance Markievicz – never one to shirk from condemnation – and several others attacked him openly and abusively, de Valera came to his defence, and MacNeill ended up topping the poll thanks to a sympathetic backlash. Markievicz was backed up by other senior women present – including Kathleen Clarke – in a show of female solidarity. In contrast, the IRB frat boys kept studiously silent, unwilling to go public even after their secret schemes had failed. The women made their opinions of male valour clear afterwards, but it was probably not cowardice so much as better judgement that had kept the men silent.

Collins didn't say much at all at the Ard Fheis – his only intervention (if it was from him and not another Mr Collins) came in a discussion about British firms taking over Irish banks, which led to an amendment being proposed calling for such banks to be boycotted. This would have been meat and drink to old Sinn Fein, but 'Mr Collins' briskly suggested it be referred to the executive committee and no more was heard about it. He also backed Cathal Brugha's proposed organization scheme against de Valera's more complicated one, but it went down in flames, attracting only two votes – presumably Collins's and Brugha's. Not one other person out of more than a thousand present voted with them. Some sort of record, surely.

The one clear militant victory was to uphold the sovereignty of the Volunteers. The new Sinn Fein constitution included a subclause authorizing the organization to 'make use of any and all means available to render impotent the power of England to hold Ireland in subjection by military force or otherwise' – quite possibly inserted at the behest of the Volunteer and IRB negotiators. Several priests wanted to amend this to read 'legitimate means' or the like, and to require the approval of the proposed national assembly. De Valera and Brugha scoffed at the idea that the Irish people would ever do anything immoral or illegitimate, while Brugha said that no assassinations were intended (though some would soon take place). This led to some enthusiastic amendments to turn Sinn Fein into a paramilitary body – and a stern lecture from Michael Lennon that 'the Volunteers have so far been able to get along very well without much help from Sinn Fein and we can get arms enough from drunken soldiers without Sinn Fein assistance.'

The Ard Fheis ran two days and, factional grumbling aside, was a huge success in presenting a genuinely united front. The provincial vanguard returned to their homes with renewed energy and optimism. But on the third day, after the Sinn Feiners had gone, it was the turn of the Volunteers to meet – this time in secret, at a much smaller gathering at the GAA grounds at Croke Park. Almost all of those few hundred present had been at the public meeting at the Ard Fheis, but this time there were no real debates or obvious factions. De Valera presided again, and was once again elected president by acclamation. The IRB was present in strength, but did not need to exert itself to dictate policy or personnel. It was taken for granted that the Volunteers were now a republican organization. Eoin MacNeill was raised again, and it was agreed that he would be accepted into the movement – no hard feelings – but not back into the army. And there the matter rested.

The only other real item on the agenda was the election of a national executive, which would technically be the organization's seat of authority – although subject to the will of annual conventions. Despite being very serious about being an army, the Volunteers were also determined to be a democracy: ultimate sovereignty rested with the membership. Its representatives on the national executive met once a month until 1920, but on a day-to-day basis power was devolved to a resident executive made up almost entirely of Dublin-based men. Cathal Brugha was chair, and Sean McGarry (uncoincidentally the new head of the IRB Supreme Council) was secretary. The convention also appointed directors, just as had been done before the Rising. Michael Staines got Supply; Richard Mulcahy, Training; Rory O'Connor, Engineering; Diarmuid Lynch, Communications. Staines, O'Connor and Lynch were already Collins's friends and close collaborators. Mulcahy would soon join them. Collins himself was given the Organization portfolio – Patrick Pearse's old job. He also worked part of the time out of Cullenswood House, home to St Enda's, the school that Pearse had founded. Did he feel the hand of recent history upon him?

COLLINS'S RAPID elevation from clerk (or its military equivalent) to various executives reflected his demonstrated abilities and also his perceived importance as a leader among the 'young men' of militant republicanism. By the end of 1917 he held an extraordinary collection of positions: treasurer of the IRB (and centre for his own Mac-Dermott Circle); Director of Organization for the Irish Volunteers; executive member of Sinn Fein. And these were in addition to his full-time job as manager of the National Aid. The only other person to achieve national power in all three groups was Diarmuid Lynch (aged forty – an old man by revolutionary standards), who was deported to the United States in 1918 for his pains. Collins's accomplishment was extraordinary considering where he had started from in January. And he was only just getting started.

Not so extraordinary, however, if we look at the rise of the movement as a whole. The seismic shift in political possibilities brought about by the war, the Rising and the collapse of the Irish Party not only radicalized a new cohort of young activists: it also provided an unprecedented opportunity for bright and ambitious men and women to change their lives, make their mark, and do something for their country. They, like Collins, had been apprenticed in the Gaelic League, the GAA, the Volunteers or Sinn Fein, and had known the frustration of minority irrelevance. The new movement changed that to optimism and empowerment.

If you had actually taken part in the rebellion you had an additional advantage: hero status, a key friendship network, and financial backing from the National Aid. Participation in the Longford and Roscommon elections had similar pioneer cachet. Simply by acquiring the right credentials, then, Collins was destined for promotion. In fact he was just one of a group of rising new national leaders who shared these experiences and qualities: Harry Boland, Richard Mulcahy, Austin Stack, Joe McGrath, Gearoid O'Sullivan, Diarmuid O'Hegarty, Dan McCarthy and Michael Staines had all created dynamic new revolutionary careers for themselves as well.

Also, while Collins did more than his fair share of scratching and clawing, the explosive growth in movement numbers, combined with the leadership vacuum arising from the post-Rising executions and purges, pulled anyone with a modicum of duty or desire upward to satisfy the movement's insatiable demand for functionaries, speakers and organizers. The endless offices, committees and secretaryships still so characteristic of Irish Ireland had to be filled by someone. A willing body who could actually do the work well and come back for more must have been a godsend.

There hadn't been this kind of wholesale opportunity in Irish politics since the early 1880s, and there wouldn't be again – ever. Collins's luck and timing were impeccable: not just for being in Dublin in 1916 and 1917, but on a number of specific occasions. What if he hadn't been able to get a ride to Roscommon for the election? What if he had lost the National Aid job through missing the interview? What if he had been arrested along with Tom Ashe? His awareness and excitement at finding himself in this epochal position can be read in his letters of the period. He was having fun in the big time, on the inside. He and his friends were making history: a bunch of teachers and clerks and tradesmen taking on the politicians, the employers, the civil service and the police – and winning.

11: A Day in Court
with Michael Collins

Offender – Michael Collins
Offence – Inciting to raid for arms etc.
His description is as follows – Clean shaven – Youthful
appearance – Dresses well – dark brown eyes, regular
nose, fresh complexion, oval face, active make,
5 ft 11 in high – About 30 years of age – Dark hair –
Generally wears trilby hat and fawn coat.

(Arrest warrant, April 1919)

BY 1918 MICHAEL COLLINS had performed many of the great roles
in Irish revolutionary theatre. He had conspired to overthrow Dublin
Castle, worn the uniform of a rebel army in battle against the British
army, fought for his rights in an English prison, and delivered a
graveside tribute to a slain comrade. But one scene he had never
played was the courtroom speech from the dock, defying his per-
secutors and declaring fealty to the undying cause. His chance came
on the morning of 2 April of that year, when he was arrested on
O'Connell Bridge by detectives for an offence under the Defence of
the Realm Act.

The charge was inciting people to steal guns. The crime had been
committed at an after-mass rally on Sunday 3 March, in the village
of Legga, Co. Longford, not far from where Tom Ashe had given
his fateful speech the summer before. Like a good salesman, Collins
was still working his territory, now on behalf of the revived Volunteers as well as Sinn Fein and the IRB. The *Longford Leader* – not a
fan of Collins or Sinn Fein – described the rally as 'a big blow-out
. . . 300 men, women and gossoons [young boys] assembled to hear
the new gospel preached'.

His speech was a conventional mixture of rebel poses and hot-button issues:

I don't know much about speech making but I do know a little about the working of the GPO in Easter week ... In South Armagh [a recent by-election] though we were defeated we claim it as a victory for us. The Orangemen voted to a man for Donnelly, the follower of the Allies. I was in a place in Armagh at the election and I heard that there were 150 Ulster Volunteers there and that during Easter week when wild rumours were abroad that the South and West had joined the rebellion those 150 Ulster Volunteers went by night and gave in their arms and ammunition at the hall fearing they might have to fight the rebels.

Sheridanism [a reference to the brutal American Civil War general] is now ripe in County Clare and other places in Ireland. The old set [the unionist ascendancy] are at work again trying to discredit our organization. I wish Longford and every county in Ireland was like Clare today, that every little village in it was occupied by military with artillery, armoured cars and machine guns. Captain Murray of the Irish Volunteers was shot down by the police and they ordered the people to stand aside till they would finish him ...

The British government is at its wit's end now about the manpower question of the Empire. Ireland too is thinking about her manpower. Emigration has ceased for the past few years and it [manpower] has increased considerably. The Irish Party claims to have defeated conscription but I claim it was the men of Easter week who defeated it. The cabinet might attempt to do it again but it will take five soldiers to take one man and 50,000 with fixed bayonets to enforce it on Ireland. I will say to the Irish Volunteers if such is attempted, stand together and remember Thomas Ashe.

He then read out a Volunteer general order warning members not to raid houses for arms or to drive cattle belonging to big ranchers (a way of forcing them to hand over their grazing land to small farmers). At this point, however, he departed from his script and added, 'When Volunteers do raid for arms they will go where they will find ones that will be of some use to them.' Finally, he drilled the eighty-eight Volunteers present, telling them to 'click their heels like Prussians'.

He had at last committed an 'outrage' deemed worthy of arrest, as the note-taking policemen on the scene interpreted his off-the-cuff remark to mean that Volunteers should attack the police to get their guns. An outrage report was filed with the Longford County Inspector, the Competent Military Authority was consulted, the Resident Magistrate was informed, a warrant was obtained under the Defence of the Realm Act and sent to the Dublin Metropolitan Police and, a month later, on the first Tuesday in April, Detectives Bruton and O'Brien of 'G' Division easily found Michael Collins leaving the National Aid's new office on Bachelor's Walk at 11.30.

Here accounts begin to differ as, thanks to the diary he kept of the whole episode, we have Collins's version of what happened, the newspaper reports, and his comments on their reporting after he had read his reviews. Once in court, we also have Collins's and the police observers' versions of what happened in Legga and at the arrest. It is a revealing sequence of rival storytelling.

The *Irish Times* records that Collins protested when the detectives arrested him and this 'brought a crowd around, and the sympathy of some found vent in their cries'. Several uniformed constables came to the detectives' aid, and they brought him across the bridge to the south side of the Liffey. 'The more daring of the accompanying crowd seemed about to release the arrested man,' and the constables drew their batons. They turned into D'Olier Street, where 'the demeanour of the followers again grew menacing.' The police fought off the most insistent, and were able to lead Collins into the Great Brunswick Street police station, whereupon the crowd dispersed.

The *Freeman's Journal*'s story is almost identical. Collins's protest is noted, as are the gathering crowd's objections and the arrival of police reinforcements. While still on the bridge, 'a number of men made as if to effect a rescue.' Batons were drawn, and on D'Olier Street the 'attitude of the crowd (which by this time had swelled to over a thousand) became threatening'. The constables drove them back and brought the prisoner 'who continued to resist' all the way to the police station. 'During the excitement some members of the crowd jeered at passing soldiers and cheered for the Kaiser as well as shouting "Up the rebels!"' They milled about the station for a time and then dispersed, although one man was detained.

Crowds had managed to rescue prisoners on several recent occasions, so the police had a reason to take precautions. The nearby location of the newspaper offices make the reports plausibly first-hand and accurate.

Collins's story is similar in detail, but – not surprisingly – distinctly different in tone:

> The detectives who seized me were O'Brien and Bruton. Refused to proceed until they produced warrant. Of course this was for the purpose of annoying them. Crowd quickly gathered and like every other right minded crowd in Ireland were hostile to the police. Poor O'Brien especially in a blue funk. Bruton endeavoured to act the bully but I soon stopped that. Of course the moral support of the crowd was an acquisition. The miserable hound knew that a word from me meant a mauling for him. At this particular point what amused me most was the way O'Brien and Bruton cursed Smith – another member of the detective force who apparently had the warrant for my apprehension. The detectives aided by uniformed policemen were gradually moving me towards Great Brunswick St. Both police (uniformed) and police detectives were very rough towards young boys and girls. Saw one member of the 'B' Division particularly brutally fling a slender girl of about 15 on the pavement at a point about 10 yards past the Red Bank Restaurant. I shouted out this man's number and hope some of the crowd took note. There was no attempt at rescue at any time – even no interference on the part of the crowd whose activities were entirely confined to vocal performances. In spite of this I have seen in the press since that poor Fred Shelly was charged with an attempt to rescue me. The unfortunate boy made no such attempt and I am sure afflicted as he is never even thought of it. Eventually I was conveyed into Great Brunswick St Police Station and Fred Shelly and [blank] were brought in under arrest (I suppose) also. I at once asked them to release Shelly as I knew he'd have a fit if detained. Notwithstanding my protest and explanation he was kept in custody and did have the fit.

Here Collins is the master of the situation. He puts a stop to 'the miserable hound' Bruton's bullying, and his word – manfully withheld – would have condemned the detectives to a beating. He finds them merely amusing until they get rough. He recognizes Shelly as a harmless scapegoat and urges compassion. The police are incompetent, cowardly and nasty. The right-minded crowd offer only moral protest.

He spent the rest of the day and evening in a succession of inevitably filthy, cold and badly ventilated cells. The next morning he was woken by an obnoxious RIC sergeant (Gallagher), whom he proceeded to enrage by dressing leisurely. He was then handcuffed:

> My first acquaintance with the bracelets. Didn't like them ... although I offered no resistance I did not willingly submit to being pinioned but let my hands fall as if lifeless. When the clasp of the handcuff nipped my skin I jerked my hand away and uttered a very emphatic threat to the policeman responsible. That unfortunate was very crestfallen the more so as the sergeant muttered something about awkwardness and pushed the offender aside. Be disdainful with members of the force and then patronize them, in this way you'll command respect from them and your wants will, generally speaking, have attention.

No doubt the police present would recall a quite different scene – one that didn't involve them being overawed by their prisoner.

The journey back to Longford to be tried then began, and was charged with drama for Collins, who recalled it all with emotion-saturated vividness. The Black Maria taking him to the railway station was 'an atrocious thing', and he was guarded by a 'formidable array' of policemen – only to be met by a 'further large force' at Broadstone railway station. 'Although not one of my friends knew of my departure the authorities were quite plainly taking no risks.' In fact the escort was doubled in size to six only because he was being taken outside Dublin, thus requiring separate escorts for the train and the city. And all railway stations had police details at this time – it was a matter of routine security and surveillance.

At the station, two young boys recognized him and brought him a newspaper – the *Irish Independent* ('Hair Grown in a Flower Pot! Big German Thrusts Foiled Again!'). This made an intense impression:

> I did not get time to thank the urchin so rapidly was he hustled away by the police. Assuredly though if ever by any good chance I come across those boys again they will not be sorry for having done me so kind a turn. It may seem a small thing to an ordinary

member of the public who has never been within the pinions of British Law. In reality it is a princely thing, aye and for mere children a courageous thing.

In contrast I have but to mention that in the same carriage were two laymen whom I discovered later on were 'Sinn Feiners' but they had not the stamina to speak to me.

Courage and cowardice, friendship and betrayal echo through his account.

The journey was free of incident and the escorts were innocuous – although Collins was 'not quite satisfied' that their solicitous draping of a rug over him was not actually intended to hide his handcuffs, so as to save them any trouble.

And so to familiar Longford town, where he was met by friends and, at the courthouse, his nemesis and namesake, District Inspector Collins from Granard: 'He shifted his eyes in an uneasy manner under my gaze – no character in that man. Every inch a coward.' Collins wondered if the inspector had had anything to do with the case against Thomas Ashe: 'I make a resolution to hold converse with him some day on the matter.' Local friend Alice Lyons appeared in the courtroom with some breakfast, but the magistrate (Jephson) 'in ponderous tones' ordered her away. 'Resolve inwardly that the R[esident].M[agistrate]. will some day do a similar hunger strike.' He'd be back.

In fact, according to the *Longford Leader*, Collins was smoking a cigarette and talking to some friends until the judge appeared and told him to put it out. The breakfast arrived as soon as the trial was over, and Collins was allowed to eat then.

This was a special juryless court designed to hear political cases, although it did not have final jurisdiction as military courts did. At worst, Collins would be sent to trial at the next assizes. A Mr Delaney was the prosecutor. Both sides knew the script and their roles well. When asked to acknowledge his identity, Collins replied (according to the *Freeman's Journal* account): 'What my name is has nothing to do with you. I am a citizen of the Irish Republic, and I am here against my will.' The first witness was Sergeant Gallagher, who reported taking Collins into custody in Dublin that morning and reading the charge to him.

In his diary Collins merely observes that 'he hadn't but had told me of it.' In court he said a great deal more, according to the published accounts, starting with 'that is a lie.' The judge asked him if he wished to question the witness, and Collins responded:

> I have no questions to ask, why should I ask questions? I don't know who you are, or who any of you here are, and I have been brought here and am kept here by force. This man has stated lies; he said he read something, which is a lie, but that does not matter. Let the farce go on; 'let Joy be unconfined'.

The second witness was Sergeant McNabola, who had been present when Collins spoke at Legga. He read from his notes regarding Collins's comments on raiding for arms, which the prisoner admitted were accurate enough, although conveying 'some very misleading impressions of course'. McNabola emphasized the comments that (in the words of the *Freeman's Journal* reporter) 'what they wanted were rifles and they knew where to get them.' The diary says, 'I interjected a few remarks for the sake of keeping my spirits up,' but, if so, these went unreported. Collins also decided that McNabola was put up to the prosecution by his wife, who had once confronted Collins over his politics. 'The poor devil looks the type that would fall an easy victim to domestic discipline.' Another spineless coward, then. (Some months later, in the same courthouse, McNabola was hit from behind by a Volunteer and had to be hospitalized for two months.)

The last witness was the second policeman on the scene, whose report was 'fairly accurate too – I think I said in court remarkably accurate for a police witness, which means to anyone who knows the RIC that he didn't tell as many lies as he was wanted to tell'.

It was now Collins's turn to make a statement. The short version, as published nationally, was as follows:

> As I protested when arrested in the streets of Dublin yesterday, I claim that no man has any right to lay hands on me or deprive me of my liberty. I address my remarks to the gentlemen of the Press, and through them to the larger public outside. I am brought here by force, by an unlawful, immoral Government in this country, with the object of preventing me doing the work I have been doing for Ireland. Gentlemen of the Press, that is all I have got to say.

According to Collins he said a great deal more than this – denying that the court or the police had any authority over him, but also, 'for the sake of preventing inaccuracies', rereading what he had read out at Legga: the Volunteer general order prohibiting the raiding of private houses and cattle-driving. Of course, this was not the problem – it was what he had said afterwards that had got him arrested. Finally, 'I know the intention is to keep me in jail indefinitely so that I may be prevented carrying on the work I have been doing for Ireland.'

In fact there is no evidence that this was anything other than a routine prosecution for a minor offence. Collins seems to have been trying to have it both ways: denouncing the court, but defending his innocence. In this regard it is interesting to note that he referred to himself as a 'citizen' rather than a 'soldier' of the Irish republic, as was standard practice at the time. He may not have thought about this much, but it is also possible that he still hoped to get off.

In the end he was bound over for trial at the Co. Longford assizes in July, while bail was set at £40 along with sureties of £20 apiece from two members of the community. Collins replied that 'I don't enter into bail with blackguards and tyrants,' and was sent to Sligo jail to await his day in court. Just sitting in jail was anticlimactic, however, and he quickly grew impatient and depressed alone in his cell. He was correspondingly delighted when his principles were overturned and he was ordered to get out on bail a week later.

For all his protestations of suffering and tyranny, the episode surely shows a remarkably lenient regime in operation, considering that Collins had recently taken up arms against the British army and was more or less openly organizing another rebellion – while the country was at war. He was arrested on a legal warrant without any brutality, and was moved as quickly as possible to his public hearing, where the police and prosecution were reasonably fair and he could say what he wanted. He was then offered immediate freedom in return for a very affordable bail: he could have been out in less than a day! He claimed he hadn't incited anyone to raid for arms – quite the reverse – but the police had caught his off-the-cuff remark about rifles and where to find them. He may not have meant to, but he had incriminated himself. Anyway, he would have the opportunity to challenge that interpretation again at a trial where he could have a lawyer and would face a jury. It's hard to find any human rights being violated here.

But of course that would hardly have fit the Sinn Fein storyline or Collins's own internal heroic narrative. The nationalist narrative demanded victimhood and oppression, and Sinn Fein propaganda brilliantly delivered. But the events may well have seemed like that to the embattled republican activists at the time – their spin was their reality.

So how do we rate Collins's performance? That's certainly what it was, recorded word for word in a diary and aimed at the 'gentlemen of the press' in hopes of good publicity. (He hadn't forgotten what he had learned at Frongoch or over Tom Ashe's death.) He had delivered his lines well enough: the right-on vocabulary of young republicanism, the tough humour, the manly defiance, the moral ascendency over the cowardly tormentors. At least that's how he rated his scenes. When the reviews came in it was another story. The *Independent*'s report was 'perfectly awful' and 'badly mutilated', he moaned, but this may have been a reaction to the fact that it was brief and not headlined. He didn't see the *Freeman*'s rather lavish notice, apparently, but the *Longford Leader* (which he misremembered as the *Roscommon Herald*) was another farrago, perpetrated by a reporter he thought 'probably had his knife in me since we made him bite the dust over the National Aid business last year' (a reference to a story about National Aid money being misused which had been the subject of legal action). Inaccuracies apart, the reporter also wrote that this was 'an additional halo for my martyr's crown. If he only knew what little anxiety I had either for the crown or the halo he wouldn't trouble himself.'

The snide remark was probably a reference to the fact that refusing defence or bail and going to jail had become a fad among provincial Volunteers. Many had been or would be in and out of prison four or five times following the Rising, and they almost always won early release after riots, hunger strikes and public pressure – to the disgust of the policemen who had sent them there. It was a badge of honour, a passport to local celebrity, and a rite of passage for would-be guerrillas. So much so that ambitious or anxious Volunteers courted arrest and worried if they were ignored.

Whether Collins was so motivated is unlikely, but that he revelled in the public arrest and trial – imagining himself a hero – seems clear from the language and detail in his diary. There was nothing unusual about that, however: it was the common mentality of the new-wave republicans, living the dream of youthful and righteous rebellion. Prison was one of the vital transformative experiences that made clerks and farmers' sons into new men: soldiers and martyrs. The revolution had to be imagined before it could be enacted, and the revolutionaries had to imagine themselves into history to give themselves the power to change it. To stand in the dock and defy the Crown, to be cast into prison for being a patriot – these were clichéd but immensely powerful roles, endlessly rehearsed in nationalist songs, histories and literature. By re-enacting them you could become your heroes. What seemed immature or naive to observers at the time, or to sceptical historians since, could have the force of a religious conversion to the people who were living it. Of course Collins wanted the halo and the martyr's crown, and he wanted the world to see them – even if a true patriot could never admit such a thing. Playing the role of the defiant rebel was far more than mere theatricality. It was a source of power and energy and solidarity – part of the basic chemistry of the revolution.

PART TWO

POWER

1. *Right.*
Charles Stewart Parnell
(1846–1891), the lost leader
of Michael Collins' youth
and the politician he
most resembled.

2. *Below.*
The Collins family at
Woodfield, early 1900s.
From left to right:
Mary Anne Collins
(Michael's mother),
Mary Powell (his sister)
and her daughter Nora,
and Johanna O'Brien
(his maternal grandmother).

3. The Dublin General Post Office after the Easter Rising, looking northwards up O'Connell (Sackville) Street. Collins spent much of his time on the top floor and the roof, far away from the decision-making and bustle of the lower floors.

4. Republican prisoners in Stafford Jail, June 1916. Collins is standing at rear right, with an 'x' marked over his head.

5. *Right.*
Collins, having his portrait taken after being released from Frongoch prison camp, c. 1917.

6. *Below.*
Eamon de Valera speaking during the East Clare by-election in July 1917.

7. *Left*. Thomas Ashe (1885–1917), the first head of the reorganized IRB Supreme Council after the Rising and the first IRA hunger-strike martyr. Collins famously gave his funeral oration in September 1917.

8. *Below, left*. Collins in his new commandant's uniform in 1918. This may have been taken for the general election of that year, as it was used on his campaign posters.

9. Sinn Fein MPs (TDs) at a meeting of Dail Eireann, most likely in April 1919.

1. Philip Shanahan
2. Sean Etchingham
3. Emmet Dalton
4. Peter Paul Galligan
5. Dr Richard Hayes
6. Piaras Beaslai
7. Joseph McDonagh
8. Sean McEntee
9. Peter Ward
10. Alex McCabe
11. Desmond Fitzgerald
12. Joe Sweeney
13. James Dolan
14. Con Collins
15. Padraic O'Maille
16. James O'Mara
17. Brian O'Higgins
18. Seamus Burke
19. Kevin O'Higgins

20. Patrick Moloney
21. Terence MacSwiney
22. Richard Mulcahy
23. Joe O'Doherty
24. Sean O'Mahony
25. Joe McGuinness
26. Patrick O'Keefe
27. Michael Staines
28. Joe McGrath
29. Dr Bryan Cusack
30. Liam de Roiste

31. Michael Collivet
32. Rev. Michael O'Flanagan
33. Laurence Ginnell
34. Michael Collins
35. Cathal Brugha
36. Arthur Griffith
37. Eamon de Valera
38. Count George Plunkett
39. Eoin MacNeill (?)
40. William Cosgrave
41. Ernest Blythe.

10. *Left*. Austin Stack (1879–1929), one of Collins' confidants in 1918 and 1919, and one of his foes in 1921 and 1922.

11. *Below, left*. Sean MacEoin (1893–1973), IRA leader in Longford – 'the Blacksmith of Ballinalee' – and one of Collins' key IRB recruits.

12. *Below*. Arthur Griffith (1871–1922) and Eamon de Valera (1882–1975), after the former was released from prison in July 1921.

13. Tom Barry's wedding party gathers at Vaughn's Hotel in August 1921.
This was the highlight of the republican social season, although it was more
high politics than high fashion. Barry (1897–1980) and his bride, Leslie Price
(1893–1984), are seated in the first row, on either side of de Valera.
Gearoid O'Sullivan (1891–1948) is seated on the ground in front of Barry;
Harry Boland (1887–1922) is seated in the first row, second from left; and Collins
is standing in back, towards the left, with head lowered to avoid identification.
He appears to be one of the few people actually smiling.

14. Collins throwing in the ball to start a hurling match at Croke Park,
Dublin in September 1921.

15. The Irish negotiating team arrives in London in October 1921 – minus Michael Collins. From right to left: Arthur Griffith, Robert Barton (1881–1975), George Gavan Duffy (1882–1951) and, standing behind and to the left of Duffy, Erskine Childers (1870–1922).

16. The Irish plenipotentiaries in London. Seated from left to right: Arthur Griffith, Eamon Duggan, Collins (typically, the only one in motion and at work) and Robert Barton. Standing, left to right: Erskine Childers, George Gavan Duffy and John Chartres (1862–1927).

12: Director

Collins, [Tomas] MacCurtain and I . . . slept three of us in a double bed and talked into the small hours. I liked Collins. He had a mobile, expressive face, quick wit and a quick temper. He was gay, boisterous, optimistic, bubbling with dynamic energy. That would not have made a man of him, of course, but behind the dashing exterior there was keen intelligence, great strength of character, steadiness, determination and vision. He had the qualities I then thought we needed most in our leaders.

(Florence O'Donoghue, Cork)

THE REASON WHY COLLINS was bailed out in April 1918 – despite the principles he had been trumpeting in court – was that the government had finally declared that conscription would be introduced in Ireland. The nationalist response was immediate and united. The leaders of Sinn Fein, the Irish Party and the All for Ireland League joined with trade unionists to launch a resistance campaign, backed by a meeting of Catholic bishops. The politicians and trade unionists spoke of using 'the most effective means at their disposal'; the bishops endorsed 'every means consonant with the law of God'. Irish Party MPs withdrew from Parliament while the threat lasted, and unions called a general strike, which took place on 23 April.

The Irish police admitted to being helpless in the face of mass opposition. It was not even clear that policemen would be willing to enforce a press gang. Nor did the Irish civil service support the cabinet's sudden lurch into confrontation. In fact the decision had nothing to do with any real prospect of gaining Irish soldiers, and everything to do with British politics. The German spring offensive had caused a military crisis requiring more men in France, but to send them would cause a domestic crisis without at least the appearance of sharing the pain with Ireland.

Thus followed the appointment as Lord Lieutenant of Field Marshal Lord French, an Irishman himself and the previous commander of the British Expeditionary Force, as well as a new Chief Secretary and army commander. One of their tasks (using a briefly enlarged secret service fund) was to look for evidence of German plots. Unsurprisingly, they found one – that, after all, is what 'intelligence' is for – and on the strength of a threadbare accusation of collusion between Sinn Fein and Germany, dozens of Sinn Fein leaders were arrested on 17 May and deported to English prisons. Among those taken were Eamon de Valera, Arthur Griffith, Count Plunkett and Kathleen Clarke. Collins was on the list, but in his case all the authorities had to do was to revoke his bail and bring him back to Sligo, as happened to many former hunger-strikers around this time. He evaded capture and went 'on the run' – although the intensity of the hunt can be gauged by the fact that he barely varied his working and sleeping habits after the first panic had passed.

Even before conscription was introduced, the Volunteer executive had decided to put the organization on a quasi-war footing and establish a general staff. This was set up in March 1918. The top post would be that of Chief of Staff. Collins had been in the running, but lost out to Richard Mulcahy, who was backed by the dominant Dublin Brigade – still the only unit to have fought the British army. They wanted one of their own rather than an impetuous blow-in. Collins was made Adjutant General instead, which seems to have suited him fine, as it was both a continuation of his directorship and allowed him to be the nascent army's head fixer and troubleshooter. He held both posts at once, being described in print as the D/O but signing his letters as Adjutant General. Both were theoretically ranks in themselves, but he seems to have also been promoted from captain to commandant-general, Plunkett's and Pearse's rank in 1916. However, unlike most other Volunteer officers, Collins never held an elected command.

These events, along with his arrest, more or less ended Collins's work with the National Aid – which was itself winding down in any case. The victims and veterans of the Rising had been taken care of, the last great funding appeal had gone out, and both income and expenditure were falling. As tension escalated, Collins's political work intruded more and more into the organization's offices, bringing police attention and executive disapproval. He had always laced his correspondence with politics, but once he began running the Volunteer organization in late 1917 he sometimes used the National Aid office for this purpose. In fact it was at this point that the office was moved to Bachelor's Walk near O'Connell Bridge – 'somewhat incomprehensibly' according to J. J. O'Kelly.

It was moved again in April 1918 – to Collins's great irritation, as he was in jail at the time and wasn't consulted. According to Patrick Belton, O'Kelly and other enemies on the committee 'rushed the change without awaiting a meeting. It was this action which decided Collins to finish with the Association for he felt the executive had 'left him in the lurch' while a prisoner in Sligo in April. Soon after, the now-vacant Bachelor's Walk premises (outside of which he had been arrested) were raided and his correspondence with Volunteer units all over Ireland was captured, along with organizers' reports, affiliation forms and other incriminating documents. It was a major breach of Volunteer security, although it doesn't seem to have harmed his reputation.

Another problem was the fact that Collins was now on the movement's board of directors, so to speak, while still taking orders from those on the National Aid executive. Many of these were his opponents in the struggle for political power, and the Association itself was no longer a significant operation. This situation can only have caused trouble on both sides, and no doubt he felt it was time he stepped into management with both feet.

By this time the rest of the paid staff had been laid off. There appears to have been a confrontation between Collins and the board at the first executive meeting in May, and after the 'German Plot' arrests he seems to have simply stopped coming to work. A running debate followed as to his position, ending in an extraordinary meeting on 1 July at which he was unanimously dismissed with one month's salary in lieu of notice – an inglorious end to a great beginning. Collins was quite good at leaving things (and people) behind and not looking back.

Ernie O'Malley, a medical student and Volunteer staff officer, met Collins at work just before his arrest in April 1918:

I found Michael Collins in his office on Bachelor's Walk, Dublin. He was pacing up and down. We shook hands . . . He jerked his head to a chair to indicate that I should sit; he took a chair which he tilted back against the wall. On shelves were green membership cards, heaps of *The Irish Volunteer Handbook*, and stacks of white copies of the organization scheme. Behind his desk was a large map of Ireland marked with broad red streaks radiating from Dublin.

O'Malley was to organize a brigade in King's County (Offaly). He was given the standard package to pass on: copies of the organization scheme and how-to guides on field rations, making explosives, and wrecking railways. Organizers had gone out before, including Collins, but only on an ad-hoc basis. Most of the hundreds of Volunteer companies formed across Ireland in 1917 and 1918 were formed by self-appointed enthusiasts. The 1917 convention brought many of them together for the first time, and only then did anything like an army begin to emerge, if only on paper.

Collins's first job was to get the paper flowing and to make everything official. Every company had to be duly accredited, elect its officers, and pay its affiliation dues. Problems frequently emerged even at this stage, as parishes produced rival companies, men refused to accept officers, and dues were not always forthcoming. There was also the perennial matter of sorting out the companies from the Sinn Fein clubs – the two often went hand in hand, but headquarters wanted them firmly separate. Once companies were established, they had to be grouped into battalions with new staffs to be elected and new boundary, authority and discipline problems to be sorted out. The 1918 reorganization that brought the headquarters staff (referred to as the GHQ) into being also created a brigade system – usually one brigade to a county to begin with, although the now-pervasive factional disputes (especially in Munster) meant frequent subdivisions and endless angry letters back and forth between a perpetually annoyed Collins and the aggrieved local chiefs.

A few months after their first meeting, O'Malley saw him again at another office: 'Collins was working at a big wooden table, his back to a bare white-washed wall; a pile of addressed envelopes in front of him . . . He continued to write; the pile of envelopes increased.' Who would have guessed that four years in the Writing Room would have prepared him for his life as a revolutionary?

Collins was also instrumental in reviving the Volunteers' in-house journal, *An tOglach* (*The Volunteer*), as a vehicle for instructions, advice and militant republicanism. As such, it was something of a counterbalance to Arthur Griffith's writings. Piaras Beaslai, a friend since before the Rising, was put in charge, but Collins played an active role in guiding editorial policy and finding writers. He did the same with an IRB-funded newspaper, the *Irish World*, established about the same time. He brought in his former superior from London, P. S. O'Hegarty – who had left the Post Office and opened a bookstore in Dublin – as editor, but annoyed him mightily by rewriting some of his leaders to fit the Supreme Council's party line.

He also contributed *An tOglach*'s 'Organization Notes' until May 1919. In these he laid out the official formula for unit organization and the duties of officers: elaborate and unrealistic, both were essentially unchanged from before the Rising, and would prove to be largely irrelevant in the coming struggle. Laced between the instructions to section commanders and adjutants and insistence on detailed paperwork, however, were sensible admonitions to adapt them to local realities. Early on he told his readers that

> We are not establishing or attempting to establish a regular force on the lines of the standing armies of even the small independent countries of Europe. If we undertake any such thing we shall fail. Our object is to bring into existence, train and equip as riflemen scouts a body of men, and to secure that these are capable of acting as a self-contained unit.

After becoming official Volunteers, men were supposed to find (or make) weapons and teach themselves how to be soldiers. Mostly this meant drill practice – forming fours and marching up and down a back road once a week. Ideally, an organizer would visit at least once to show the flag, demonstrate to the locals how things were done, and oversee an officers' meeting or two. Collins went on several such excursions.

On the first weekend in March 1918, for example, he travelled up to Longford on one of his regular trips to organize and socialize. On this occasion he had a busy schedule. First off on the Saturday he addressed an eleven o'clock meeting of about 200 people coming from mass at Ballinamuck church. He was third on the bill after a county councillor and the secretary of the Sinn Fein club, who informed the crowd that independence was only a peace conference away and that the blasphemous Redmondites of South Armagh – the victors over Sinn Fein in a recent by-election – had cursed the Pope.

'Captain Collins' was then introduced, and proceeded to give a dead-on-message speech. He greeted the 'fine crowd of young people', and advised all men over eighteen to join the Volunteers, to get ready for 'self independence', and to be prepared to assert their rights when the time came. In the meantime, Ireland should not export food so as to avoid another famine (a fear then being drummed up by Sinn Fein propagandists). His political message was that the government-sponsored Irish constitutional convention (boycotted by Sinn Fein) had failed, and that the choice was now between independence and remaining a vassal state of John Bull. Freedom could be gained at the post-war peace conference. The benefits of independence were manifold: lower taxes, and an army and navy. Defying the obvious contradiction between a military build-up and decreased revenue, he waxed eloquent on the future triumph of the Irish navy: 'I say that in three years her revenue could build ten submarines then they would make England keep her Dreadnoughts, Super Dreadnoughts in their own ports where the Quadruple Alliance's were keeping them at present.' He had a thing about submarines, as he would demonstrate again in later negotiations with British officials.

Two more speakers followed, friends from Granard. Afterwards, Collins and the others drilled the forty men who had enrolled in the handball alley, instructing them on forming fours, right and left march, and how to keep step while marching. Before leaving, the amused police reported, Collins warned them 'to get those moves right and not have these gentlemen laughing at you'.

The next stop was Tullyvrane's Sinn Fein hall, to preside over a court martial. In a typical internal dispute, the Rathcline Volunteer company had split after the captain had hit his lieutenant for calling him a '[land] grabber'. While the police peered in through the windows, Collins delivered his verdict: both men were reduced to the ranks, and a new slate of officers was appointed. Another company joined them for exercises, including fencing practice with hurleys, after which Collins gave them a pep talk, 'there being great clapping of hands at intervals'. Eventually, in a show of defiance, the fifty-six men were marched to the police barracks at eleven that night, and dismissed, after which Collins set off for Longford.

The next day, Sunday, it was nearby Legga's turn. Once again the tricolour was planted in a field near the church to signal a Sinn Fein meeting, and Captain Collins gave another of his after-mass barnstormers, in which, as we have seen, his departure from the careful script would get him arrested.

Such fieldwork grew much rarer once conscription was in the offing, however. Mostly, Collins's official Volunteer work meant sitting in some makeshift office or other with no secretary, badgering captains and commandants up and down the country for their dues and reports while arbitrating their disputes and fielding their requests and complaints. When the police arrested Volunteer officers in this period, they frequently found letters from Collins in this vein.

To take one two-month period, November–December 1919, the Armagh Brigade wanted to court-martial an officer for going on holiday, battalions in the Offaly Brigade were feuding over another court-martialled officer seeking re-election and an independent company refusing to follow orders, Carlow was refusing to pay its subscription to *An tOglach* ('As I have personal knowledge of the sense of justice, honour, integrity etc. of the Brigade Staff of Carlow, I accept your statement with a pleasure only equalled by that with which I shall accept payment of your amount'), North Cork, South Tipperary and East Limerick were competing for control of the formerly independent Galtee Regiment ('This will, I think, be a simple matter . . .'), while East Limerick itself was riven by feuds ('Quite clearly the officers are not doing their work') and the commandant of the recently reorganized Leitrim Brigade was still not in touch with the northern half of the county.

Much of this work seems remarkably similar to what he was doing in the National Aid. He kept track of names and accounts, investigated applications and complaints, and depended on travelling organizers and local activists to do the work on the ground.

His power was limited by distance and lack of resources. Sacking local officers often caused more problems than it purported to solve – parochial and personal loyalties being typically paramount. He didn't have much in the way of money or guns to offer or withhold. There were no prisons or other instruments of discipline. He had to bluster, cajole, embarrass, harass, persuade, mollify, encourage and flatter to get his way – a careful balancing act requiring shrewd judgement and a fair measure of personal empathy and authority. He constantly told provincial units to stand on their own feet. To Cavan's request for an organizer, Collins replied that 'this is quite out of the question. An Organizer spent a considerable time in your Area last year, and when he completed there, we were of the opinion that the organization could be developed by the existing Brigade, and you are accordingly directed to see that this is done.' Another source of friction was arms, which brigades demanded in order to get under way, but which Collins insisted could be given only to those who had already proven themselves. Favoured men might come away with a few revolvers.

On the other hand, provincial leaders, who had all the same problems within their own brigades as Collins did with them, were often on the verge of despair. One such, Seamus McGuill of Dundalk, wrote in August 1919, 'You know Mick there is absolutely no use in my holding on to this job, it's only a farce in this damn city.' One way of countering such sentiments was to convince complainers that he understood, was on their side, was in their corner. When he went to visit, he would make time to be friendly, informal, enthusiastic, to listen to complaints and ideas, to build relationships. When the country boys came up to Dublin, he would make them welcome, introduce them to his friends and his favourite pubs and hotels, even take them to the seaside or the races (horses and dogs). He tried to take care of them – the men who counted anyway – like he took care of the men in prison. When Liam Deasy of the favoured West Cork Brigade went up for a meeting in October 1919, he met with the Collins crowd in the friendly back rooms of Vaughan's Hotel: 'The ready comradeship which they so warmly extended to me was the source of great encouragement.' No one felt the same way about Dick Mulcahy (more formal, less sociable), and hardly anyone went to see Cathal Brugha, the chairman of the resident executive and later Minister of Defence.

In mid-1918, with little organization beyond the company level, and very few modern rifles, the GHQ planned to meet the imposition of conscription with a parish-by-parish, street-by-street uprising. Each unit would barricade its own roads, cut all available railway lines, and besiege its local police barracks, while all labourers would leave their jobs. Only Protestant Ulster would have failed to join in. The British government would have needed tens of thousands of troops to arrest the resisting recruits, who would have been useless as soldiers. Since Prime Minister Lloyd George and his cabinet weren't all that serious about carrying out conscription in Ireland in the first place, it is not surprising that they opted to try for more voluntary recruits first. As the summer wore on, and the German army was pushed back, the threat of conscription receded (although not in Sinn Fein propaganda, needless to say). Sinn Fein and the Volunteers had won without firing a shot – a lesson totally lost on Collins and his fellow militants.

ONE OF COLLINS'S least recognized but most important accomplishments was to arrange a system of communications, an internal post office of sorts, to carry messages and reports between Dublin and the great beyond. This involved effectively taking over a third directorship – that of Communications. Diarmuid Lynch was the original holder of this post, but he had been arrested for seizing some pigs bound for export (in his capacity as Sinn Fein Food Controller) and deported in early 1918.

Volunteer messages were transmitted in two ways – by couriers or via a network of postal drops, using the regular mail. The hand-delivery method, first instituted in 1918 during the conscription crisis, was a marvel of theoretical efficiency, complete with forms to fill out: a system worthy of a Savings Bank graduate. Each message or package was to have a time sheet attached, so that each Volunteer who handled it could record the date and hour of its receipt and dispatch. This would allow Collins to identify and punish 'slackness', as had been done in the Savings Bank and as no doubt he had done to the messengers in Horne & Co. The map Ernie O'Malley had seen on Collins's office wall probably showed these courier routes.

Inevitably, many units failed to meet Collins's standards. One such was the Limerick Brigade, whose Commandant de Lacy received many black marks over the summer of 1918. The long-simmering Mount Collins finally erupted on 18 August, when a dispatch dated the 4th arrived: 'There was no time sheet. May I take it that it was sent by you along the ordinary communications route? It's simply appalling to think of all that time being lost.' On the 29th came a report dated the 10th: 'That's about the limit. Of course there was no time nor was there any indication of what hands it came through. When it has been considered I'll write you fully.' De Lacy was soon to disappear from the scene – along with the precious time sheets, which do not seem to have survived into 1919.

The stress of guerrilla war would have undone the intricate system in any case. Messengers were still used of, course – especially in Dublin, where Collins relied especially on Joe O'Reilly, once considered by the police to be more important than Collins but now merely his faithful sidekick. He would also tap any and all travellers he trusted to act as couriers on an ad-hoc basis, while maintaining a few regular routes for important matters. Intelligence and other material passed frequently between Dublin and Cork, for example, as Edward O'Neill explained:

> A man named Jack Good, whom I never met, had charge of the Cork end of things. A similar arrangement existed at both ends. The system was that the dispatches were brought from either end on a goods train on the Great Southern Railway, each of us knowing a man on the train who would deliver them to us. When I got the dispatches I brought them to Michael Collins at No. 6 Harcourt Street [Sinn Fein headquarters].

The default option – also complicated, but more flexible – was to use the double-envelope system. Thus, letters to Volunteer headquarters would be sent within a second envelope to an innocuous street address, sometimes under a fictitious cover name, where they would be collected by a messenger or secretary. The same system would be used in reverse for letters to Galway, Limerick or Longford – or to Manchester or London. Letters from the United States often went to Liverpool before being readdressed to Dublin. Lists of names and addresses were occasionally captured and covers blown, causing Collins vast anxiety, but British intelligence never managed to shut things down. There was no mass censorship of the mails after the Great War, and Collins constantly set up new routes to new addresses. Anyone could be chosen – sympathizers, relatives, relatives of sympathizers, friends, even former girlfriends in the case of Susan Killeen whose home address was used for a time.

It wasn't Collins's pipeline alone – as always, much of the work was done by other people at all points of the compass. But he and his people held it together, and he was its self-appointed plumber. Moreover, while Sinn Fein was supposed to have its own lines of communication, little of any use was done for years, since they just used the Volunteer system instead. In fact the whole apparatus of revolution came to depend on it in later years.

COLLINS'S OTHER directorship was with Sinn Fein. Membership of the executive entitled him to take part in the quarterly meetings of the governing body, the Ard Chomhairle. He declared this to be 'a not very impressive gathering', and in any case real power was largely in the hands of the standing committee, which met weekly. Collins was not originally part of this body, but once conscription appeared imminent in 1918 he and Harry Boland, his then best friend, were named as substitutes in case the government moved against the incumbents. This occurred as expected with the 'German Plot' arrests in May, and Boland became one of the secretaries – a key position leading up to the general election in 1918.

Collins, on the other hand, was distracted by Volunteer duties, sceptical of Sinn Fein's value to any active resistance, and dismissive of what he took to be its excessive moderation. He rarely went to meetings, and played little part in politics as such until the eve of the post-war general election in December. His main preoccupation was, as always, to argue for an aggressive and uncompromising policy – no backsliding from the positions staked out at the Ard Fheis – and no interference with the Volunteers.

In effect, Collins and Boland acted as a team, Collins working the paramilitary side of the street while Boland looked after politics. This partnership came from being close pals who loved to hang out with each other. Boland, a Dubliner from a devoted republican family, was a fellow GAA hurler – they practised together for a while in Dublin – whose outgoing cheerfulness complemented Collins's drive and hair-trigger temper. So close were they, they would eventually end up pursuing the same girl's hand in marriage.

They also shared a secret: they were both new arrivals on the IRB Supreme Council. With Diarmuid Lynch deported and Sean McGarry taken by the May dragnet, Boland was elevated to the presidency, with Collins still in charge of the treasury and Sean O Murthuile, a Gaelic League organizer from West Cork (and a Friend of Mick), as secretary. As such they were equally interested in promoting fellow Fenians to positions of power and in promoting the ideals of 1916.

On the eve of an Ard Chomhairle meeting on 20 August 1918,

Collins wrote to fellow vanguardist Austin Stack (another of the party's secretaries, then in prison in Belfast) that 'there are certain resolutions being proposed with a view to unearth and destroy any attempt at compromise. The SF organization lacks direction at the present moment.' The threat was a rumoured British offer of Dominion Home Rule (self-government along Canadian lines) that might split the movement. The rumour was false, but the threat was scotched anyway with an endorsement of the republican ideal and an instruction that there would be no negotiations held on this subject.

The second 'new Sinn Fein' Ard Fheis was held at the end of October, with war drawing to a close and the prospect of conscription dissipating. This time Collins was somewhat more prominent, despite being one of the 'men whom warrants have for months hidden away from public places' according to an admiring reporter from *New Ireland* (a pro-Sinn Fein journal). He offered no resolutions himself, but spoke several times in support of the very first one, put forward by friend Piaras Beaslai ('the frail man'): a demand for absolute independence. Collins, speaking 'with an almost Prussian intensity, made a brave fight for an amendment' demanding 'restitution for wrongs inflicted on Ireland by oppressive taxation and the destruction of Irish trade and credit'. The amendment was carried, but left to the discretion of the standing committee and forgotten – except by Collins, who was very attached to the idea of reparations and who would bring it up again at the Anglo-Irish talks of 1921.

Collins did better in executive voting than a year previously, coming eleventh out of twenty-four rather than last – a rise due possibly as much to a dwindling of resentment as to any positive increase in popularity. Overall, however, although it is a commonplace to suggest that the arrests of de Valera, Griffith and all the rest allowed the 'advanced' men to take the place of the moderate majority, there is little evidence of it in the executive itself. De Valera, Griffith and O'Flanagan were (*in absentia*) returned to their former places at the top, the treasurers were anodyne, and the committee contained only two more IRB men and one more Volunteer than before, with Dick Mulcahy, Michael Staines and Piaras Beaslai replacing Diarmuid Lynch and Austin Stack alongside Collins and Harry Boland. There were just as many priests elected, and Eoin MacNeill still topped the poll.

The one big militant gain was the confirmation of Boland's

appointment as joint party secretary. His energy and opinions domi-nated the convention, as *New Ireland* observed: 'Harry Boland rose again and again, and with that directness which Crossmaglen has cause to remember, gave the ne plus ultra on many questions.' This was no coup or stroke though. Boland was a superb organizer, and an essential rallier of the troops at Sinn Fein headquarters. He and Collins certainly pushed for the hardest possible line, but this was hardly a conspiracy: everyone knew what they thought.

Nevertheless, it was widely believed that the two friends went on to rig the selection process for candidates in the coming general election, in which it was predicted at the Ard Fheis that Sinn Fein would win 80 of Ireland's 105 seats. Some men, including the ever-petulant P. S. O'Hegarty and Darrell Figgis, blamed Collins for not giving them nominations, and this sort of talk caused trouble for him later on. But such resentments always occur when a party faces a walkover and seats are there for the taking, as was the case for Sinn Fein in 1918 thanks to the death of John Redmond and the collapse of the Irish Party: there is always a much longer list of eager would-be candidates than places to put them. And O'Hegarty and Figgis weren't anyone's idea of good colleagues or leaders. In fact, while Boland did have a great deal to do with scouting likely prospects and filtering out wrong 'uns, local constituency associations had the final say, and all candidates had to be approved by the very non-militant standing committee. Collins no doubt backed Boland up and put in his two cents' worth, but there is no real evidence of his involvement beyond this.

The proof of the pudding lay in the people put forward and elected. Boland, Beaslai, Diarmuid Lynch, Michael Staines, Dick Mulcahy, Joe McGrath and Con Collins were all Friends of Mick and either Brothers or senior Volunteers or both. Brugha was an ally; Jim Ryan an old Stafford and Frongoch pal. Ernest Blythe, although no longer an active Volunteer, had written 'Ruthless Warfare' in *An tOglach*, an attack on pacifism that Collins admired. Prominent provincial Volunteers included Terence MacSwiney and Tomas MacCurtain from Cork, and Liam Mellows of Galway. Many had taken some part in the Rising. It would be hard to say that any of these people owed their nominations to Collins or Boland. These were pretty well all experienced and familiar veterans of the separatist movement, the Brotherhood, Volunteers, Gaelic League, the GAA or Sinn Fein itself. Ryan was practising as a doctor in his constituency and had been the staff doctor in the GPO in 1916; Beaslai (despite his later recasting of himself as Collins's Boswell) was a long-time activist and writer; McGrath had fought in 1916 and was the hero of the Longford by-election; Mulcahy fought under Ashe in 1916, had been a senior officer in Frongoch and a Gaelic League organizer, and was now Chief of Staff of the Volunteers as well as being a party officer. Both MacSwiney and MacCurtain disliked the IRB, and neither knew Collins all that well – both had been active Gaels in Cork for years. The main part of the new caucus was neither warlike nor conspirators. There simply was no radical takeover.

The same rumours and accusations would surface at the next Ard Fheis, in April 1919, with equally small evidence that they were true. It was not until the Irish general election of 1921 that the Volunteers (by then known as the IRA) would emerge as a dominant political presence, and then due to the war, not to any covert manipulation.

Collins had little to do with the election campaign as such, apart from running in his home constituency of South Cork. He did not appear, but he did issue an election address:

> You are requested, by your votes, to assert before the nations of the world that Ireland's claim is to the status of an independent nation, and that we shall be satisfied with nothing less than our full claim – that in fact any scheme of government which does not confer upon the people of Ireland the supreme, absolute and final control of all this country, external as well as internal, is a mockery and will not be accepted.

This was probably directed as much to fellow Sinn Feiners as to his constituents: a reassertion of unconditional-victory terms, even if the word 'republic' was not mentioned in deference to more cautious voters. It was also probably taken from a template written up at Sinn Fein headquarters to ensure a consistent party line, rather than composed from scratch by Collins himself. It did, however, include a photo of himself in uniform, looking young and idealistic.

Still, it sits a bit oddly with his other contribution, which was to help work out an arrangement with the rival Irish Party in north-east Ulster. Here, competition between nationalist parties would allow Ulster Unionists to gain otherwise unwinnable seats: the alternative was to agree to share safe seats and keep them out of a common enemy's hands. Cardinal Michael Logue, the Catholic archbishop of Armagh, was the prime mover in this, and Eoin MacNeill (an Ulsterman) and John Dillon, leader of the Irish Party, were the main negotiators, but Collins played a leading role in devising Sinn Fein's policy and in accepting Logue's final decision to split the eight marginal seats down the middle. This made sense both tactically, as it assured Sinn Fein of a strong presence in Ulster, and strategically, as unprecedented Unionist victories would be used to bolster the Unionist Party's claim to speak for 'Ulster' and demand the partition of the island.

On the other hand, it also clearly placed Catholic and nationalist solidarity above ideological principle. To Protestant unionists, it looked like a sectarian scheme, putting the lie to the republican rhetoric of all-Ireland brotherhood. Here was an old-fashioned compromise among party bosses, a carving up of territory for mutual benefit – and Collins right in the middle of it. There was nothing in it to benefit him, of course, although he would later be elected in Co. Armagh. It made perfect sense, it was for the good of the party, and he was a party man.

The election was held on 14 December. Although the results would not be announced until the 28th, Sinn Fein was guaranteed 26 seats where its candidates ran unopposed and ended up winning 73. One of the uncontested seats was in South Cork. On 15 December 1918 Collins became the Honourable Michael Collins, MP.

13: Minister

Looking back at my first meeting with Michael Collins, I cannot say that I was impressed. As a matter of fact I was a good deal disappointed, as I had not heard of Collins before that night ... Although Collins was minister of finance at the time, he was so youthful-looking that I had taken him to be a mere official from headquarters rather than an important figure. Even my school-teacher friends knew nothing about him at that time and told me later that they were as unimpressed as I was. The way in which he asked questions and took notes were more characteristic of a civil servant than a military leader.

(Jeremiah Mee)

COLLINS'S GROWING INFLUENCE was demonstrated by his prominent place in Sinn Fein's deliberations over what to do with all its new MPs. Collins was named as a party whip (along with Beaslai), he was on the local-elections committee to plan strategy for the next round of council contests, and – in February 1919 – he was named to the party subcommittee to prepare the agenda for the next quarterly meeting and to determine the new standing committee. However, the party would soon be overshadowed by the Volunteers and their war and by Dail Eireann, the revolutionary assembly and administration.

The most important of Collins's new tasks – and the most prestigious if it came off – was the Special Foreign Affairs Committee formed in December to try to meet President Woodrow Wilson in London. Sinn Fein's official policy, and its main election promise, was to seek recognition at the forthcoming Versailles peace conference, so this might be a crucial endeavour. This semi-secret diplomatic mission (it wouldn't look good if it were rebuffed) included fellow MPs Sean T. O'Kelly, Robert Barton and George Gavan Duffy. Collins may have gone along in his usual capacity of Volunteer watchdog.

They spent Christmas in London, Collins presumably at Netherwood Road. They had no luck in their task, however: as Barton recalled, 'We never got any nearer to him [Wilson] than a Second Secretary in the American Embassy. We had no success at all.' To pass the time, they decided to call on newspaper editors. O'Kelly and Barton went to see C. P. Scott of the *Manchester Guardian*; unfortunately we don't know who Collins went to see. By 9 January they were back in Dublin.

On 21 January, Dail Eireann, made up of those Sinn Fein MPs not in jail, met for the first time, in the Dublin Mansion House. A Declaration of Independence was issued, and a government was formed to carry out Sinn Fein's election pledges. While the occasion was public and watched by policemen, it was ignored by the British government as just so much hot air. This republic was indeed imaginary – as was its ability to govern – but those concerned were very serious about making it a reality.

Cathal Brugha was made acting president in de Valera's absence. Collins was named to the Home Affairs portfolio. Eoin MacNeill, that perennial object of republican suspicion (Piaras Beaslai even voted against him), was the first finance minister, but otherwise the political complexion of the group is striking: apart from Brugha and Collins, Count Plunkett was foreign minister and Richard Mulcahy was defence minister. Three Volunteers in all, including two GHQ staff members and two IRB men. This was a caretaker cabinet, however, formed while Griffith and de Valera were still in prison in England. The posts were merely nominal, and Collins never acted in his first ministerial incarnation – the first cabinet may never even have officially met. The really interesting fact is that executive correspondence – to Diarmuid Lynch in the US anyway – was written as 'we' and co-signed by Brugha and Collins, suggesting they held equal power.

In fact Collins was not even in Ireland for his first cabinet appointment: on 21 January he was on his way to help de Valera escape from Lincoln Jail. The President-in-waiting had managed to get an impression of a key, and this had been smuggled to Dublin, where keys were made from it and sent back in (what else?) a cake.

Or, more precisely, four cakes. Files were added to the mix as well, to give it that old-fashioned touch.

With the Dail's permission, but largely using IRB resources, Collins and Harry Boland were the bakers-in-chief, headquartered in Manchester. Collins drew elaborate plans of everything, although none were needed in the event. D-Day was 3 February and, despite various mishaps – including Collins's breaking off of a key in the outer-door lock (another great turning point in history missed?) – de Valera was free, along with Sinn Feiner Sean Milroy and IRB president Sean McGarry. Even in his prison breaks, de Valera made sure he brought his left and right wings along with him. Boland and the escapees went into hiding in Manchester, while Collins was off to London once again.

De Valera returned to Dublin a couple of weeks later and the rest of the prisoners were released on 6 March (they had never been charged with a crime), thus paving the way for a full public meeting of Sinn Fein TDs at the second session of the Dail on 1 April. De Valera was elected president, and he selected a full cabinet, including Collins at Finance, Griffith now at Home Affairs, Brugha at Defence (Mulcahy was out altogether), Plunkett still at Foreign Affairs, MacNeill at Industry (a vast demotion to a token job), William Cosgrave at Local Government, and Constance Markievicz at Labour. They were joined in June by Sean Etchingham as fisheries minister and J. J. O'Kelly in charge of the Irish language, and in November by Austin Stack, who replaced Griffith when he was made acting president – de Valera having strangely decided to go to the United States in June. This was de Valera's cabinet, however, even in his absence, and a much more balanced group than the first, with only two Volunteers and one IRB member out of eleven – fairly representative of the movement as a whole.

Why Collins for Finance? We don't know what calculations or negotiations went into it, but the post was clearly right up his alley. He had the greatest financial expertise of any TD (although that wasn't saying much), and the experience of handling both National Aid money and Volunteer organization. De Valera probably also wanted an IRB man and a Volunteer in a senior post, to keep his military wing appeased, and Collins was both rolled into one. He had long been the voice of the Volunteers on the party executive, and after the Ulster election pact, the diplomatic trip to London and his brief tenure as party whip he was probably considered a safe pair of hands. Long before officially taking MacNeill's portfolio, Collins had already replaced him on Sinn Fein's committee for Dail funds and was signing himself as 'Minister of Finance'.

FINANCE BECAME Collins's main burden from mid-1919 on. As minister, he was in charge of both revenue collection and financial administration for the whole government. Fortunately he inherited some money when he assumed the post. A few loans came in in early 1919 from Sinn Fein and wealthy supporters – although Volunteer, IRB and Sinn Fein accounts remained resolutely separate. Party and government matters were not to be confused: this was no one-party state. Subscribers to the 1918 all-party Anti-Conscription Fund did re-donate £12,000 to the Dail, but this was a disappointing fraction of the original quarter of a million it had accumulated. (True to form, the Catholic Church was competing hard for the money as well.) A Self-Determination Fund was set up for direct donations, eventually reaching a very respectable £55,000. An American Victory Fund, begun in February 1919, raised $1 million within the year, but the nominally supportive Friends of Irish Freedom were loath to part with it, and only a lesser share ever reached Ireland ($115,000 in the autumn), to Collins's everlasting disgust.

But, to implement the ambitious agenda set by Sinn Fein policy and the Dail government, the movement would need not thousands or tens of thousands, but hundreds of thousands of pounds. Once the various Dail departments got properly under way in 1920, a boycott of unionist firms in Belfast and the revolutionary courts became a lucrative source of fines – but of course money was needed to get these operations going in the first place. The obvious method was to collect a republican income tax. Collins and others did try to figure out a workable tax scheme, and even promised one, but eventually had to give it up as beyond their means.

So they borrowed. A bond drive – familiar from the Great War – would provide not only cash but also propaganda. Parties or movements ask for donations; governments sell bonds. Success would give the Republic legitimacy as well as substance. Failure, of course, would be disastrous on both counts. The plan was announced by de Valera in the Dail on 10 April, with the goal of £500,000 – half to be raised in Ireland and half elsewhere. He left for the United States soon thereafter, in pursuit of both money and recognition for his regime. James O'Mara, a former Irish Party MP and now a Sinn Fein TD, went with him to act as the Finance Ministry's representative and to take direct charge of the fund-raising, while Harry Boland tagged along as a general fixer and the representative of the IRB Supreme Council – thus ending his year-long partnership with Collins.

The US campaign was officially run out of New York by the American Commission on Irish Independence, sidelining the recalcitrant (and Philadelphian) Friends of Irish Freedom. Starting in August 1919, leaflets, letters, handbooks and the like were dispatched far and wide, the Irish-American press was engaged, organizers were hired, and de Valera and company toured relentlessly.

Bond sales opened in January 1920. The actual collecting was done by faithful foot soldiers – typically members of the Ancient Order of Hibernians, the Knights of Columbus and (despite their faction fighting) the rival Friends and Clan na Gael. Some 300,000 people bought certificates, 100,000 in New York alone. Massachusetts was equally outstanding. The rest of the country was a patchwork. All in all, a little over $5 million was raised by November 1920, and a second drive netted over $600,000 by the end of 1921 (the exchange rate floated between 3.5 and 4 dollars to a pound). The original target was $1.25 million. This had been raised to $5 million, although de Valera had asked the Dail to authorize a total borrowing of $25 million, to allow for a series of bond issues (a $10 million drive was being prepared in 1921). The first American loan was thus officially oversubscribed, and was recognized as an impressive accomplishment at the time.

Michael Collins had very little to do with it, and de Valera can take much – albeit rarely granted – credit for his hard work. On the other hand, Dev can probably take the – frequently bestowed – blame for the many potential sales lost because of the anger and confusion resulting from his in-fighting and poor political judgement. Nor was he able to tap many wealthy contributors or the Catholic Church, who would pour money (another $5 million) into the American Committee for Relief (for victims of British-government or loyalist violence) soon after he left in December 1920. (Collins spoke warmly in contrast of 'the power of energetic clergy here at home'.) He also drove O'Mara to resign twice – to Collins's consternation. It is not surprising that Collins resisted being sent to the United States himself to pick up where de Valera had left off.

Raising money was one thing; getting it to Ireland was another. Only £58,000 of this booty had reached Dublin by mid-1920. When little more had come by mid-August, Collins wrote Harry Boland in New York that 'You misled us very seriously in this connection. The figures which have now been sent from USA are nothing short of disastrous.' He had promised striking railwaymen American help, but it had not come through: 'There is nothing in any reply which would ease one's feelings.' Finally, in late September, Boland was able to tell him that roughly $3 million was available for transfer, although de Valera declared himself anxious that they would be able to keep it safe in Dublin. Collins replied rather tartly that 'our chief way of safeguarding it up to the present had been by spending it.'

Ultimately about half the US loan was sent to Ireland, mostly in 1921. A million and a half dollars was used in any case to fund the various American campaigns (and de Valera's and Boland's rather high lifestyles, it was often alleged). So the Republic would have to rely on the Irish, or internal, loan through most of 1919 and 1920. Initial planning for this was done by a Dail finance committee made up of sixteen TDs, but this only met twice: after that it was Michael Collins's job to keep the revolution afloat.

It was raising the loan that preoccupied and nearly broke him in late 1919 and the first half of 1920. Although there were still similarities between this effort and his previous jobs, this was a project of unprecedented scope. Recognizing this, he sought advice from Henry Mangan, an expert in municipal finance as the accountant for the Dublin Corporation. As before, he was dependent on a national network of activists – volunteers of varying competence and dedication over whom he had little real control but who bombarded him with complaints, queries and excuses. As usual he had only a few organizers he could send out to help or to chastize and once again there was the familiar flood of paperwork. Each constituency required a separate loan account, for which individual bond certificates had to be issued. Collins ran the Dublin office and its agents, cleared the correspondence, looked after accounts and the money, and kept an eye on the big picture of policy and strategy.

The basic idea was to use the Sinn Fein organization to sell the bonds and collect the money. TDs would take the lead in their constituencies, and local *cumainn* (clubs) would provide the person power. As per standard operating procedures, organizers would be employed to tour the country, act as couriers, and represent the Ministry. At the Sinn Fein convention of August 1921, Collins explained how it had gone:

> The organizers sent out had to do nearly all the work. We started out with a kind of idea that there was a Sinn Fein Organization functioning in the ordinary way, but we found that we had to do nearly all the work ourselves, and in some cases after abusing and criticizing the people we got them to work after a while. What we did was, we divided each constituency into a number of areas, we divided it so as to make three, four or five areas, and in each area we got a few good men, who did the work and handed their reports fairly regularly. The *Comhairle Ceanntair* [constituency executives] met a couple of times and they were able to say how much money was collected and sent the reports to Headquarters. In some cases, however, their reports were got by the British Government.

It was up to these few good men and women to spread the word and distribute the loan prospectuses, as the government quickly censored the initial advertising campaign and sending the hundreds of thousands of prospectuses through the mails was risky. On 15 November 1919 Collins reported to de Valera that £30,000 had been subscribed so far:

> You will understand that this is not very satisfactory, but the hindrances have been simply enormous. Indeed, at the present moment the main enemy objective is still directed to secure the failure of this enterprise . . . Advertising is impossible practically, meetings are impossible practically, movements of prominent Sinn Feiners are greatly interfered with, so that everything has to be done quietly, unassumingly, and with much labour. The combination does not appear to appeal to several people.

Or, as he told Harry Boland in January 1920, 'Unfortunately the work is uninteresting, and many people who should be busying themselves at it are not doing their share.'

The result was a remarkably varied response, ranging from an extraordinary £32,000 from East Limerick to East Wicklow's measly £819. Some northern constituencies produced even less, owing to the preponderance of unionists, but, less excusably, none of the Dublin ridings gave more than the average (£3,629). It would seem that the results were often due to the commitment and grit of the locals (and particularly the IRA, as the Volunteers were gradually renaming themselves), which Collins and his staff could realistically do little to change, however much they abused and criticized. Many TDs failed to do their duty.

The contrast was nowhere more evident than between Terence MacSwiney, future hunger-striker and martyr, and member for Mid-Cork, and Liam de Roiste, the splenetic and sanctimonious Cork city TD. MacSwiney printed his own circulars, set up sub-executives, and set them to organizing a house-to-house canvas. By December 1919 Collins was praising him as an example of 'what work and energy will do'. Comparisons, he added cattily, 'will suggest themselves at once'. This meant de Roiste, who admitted to his diary in January 1920 that progress was 'very slow'.

That same month Collins asked MacSwiney to help de Roiste, who responded by being 'deliberately "slow" ... particularly so because of the ["contemptuous"] attitude towards me'. After some months of doing de Roiste's work, MacSwiney seized control altogether. Collins declared that 'were it not for that, I should be out probably with a scalping knife.' De Roiste claimed his poor results were because he wasn't willing to threaten people. MacSwiney continued to complain of de Roiste's non-cooperation and had the party executive unanimously order him to turn over the money that he still held. De Roiste took this as evidence of jealousy and an IRA power grab, but Collins saw it as just one of numerous cases of petty, cowardly or lazy behaviour: 'There are people who have always to be complaining about something.'

In April 1920 he complained to Boland that 'after a pretty hard year every little divergence tells heavily ... This enterprise will certainly break my heart if anything ever will. I never imagined there was so much cowardice, dishonesty, hedging, insincerity and meanness in the world, as my experience in connection with this work has revealed.' By the end of the month he was feeling more sanguine: 'I am about to wind up the business here in Ireland, and we certainly have not got as much money as the people were willing to apply for.

Of course the hindrances were simply terrific, and it must be admitted that taking the thing all round the result is hopeful enough.'

Hopeful enough all right: the loan was closed in July, at the end of which £355,000 had been collected – increasing to a final total of £370,000 by September. Given that the official goal was £250,000, this was an outstanding result in the circumstances. It allowed some of the Sinn Fein dreams to become reality: consulates in Paris, Berlin, Rome and Buenos Aires; a Land Bank dedicated to the purchase and redistribution of farms; reforestation and fisheries co-ops; port and housing schemes; courts and a police force to enforce their laws. Best of all from Collins's point of view, the Volunteers could plan to buy shiploads of guns.

Secretly, Collins had his own insurance policy for permanent revolution:

> I am anxious that an appreciation of say £500,000 be made as a permanent Republican Trust Fund. The principal to be untouched and untouchable. The interest annually say £30,000 to be available for Republican Political purposes up to date of Recognition and Evacuation. Even then the Principal should not be realized and the interest should be added each year for perhaps 100 years or so. The Republic may not come in our lives and this Fund should be securely tied up against the possibility of Colonial or any other Home Rule landslide in the country for 15 or 20 years.

Clearly he was harking back to the bad old days of the IRB, tiny and dependent on American charity: never again!

In the end, none of the Dail's policies worked out too well (except in propaganda terms) and much of the programme didn't happen at all: there was not enough money. But spending was pushed upward: from about £100,000 in the eighteen months up to June 1920, to around £600,000 by December, adding £366,000 in the first six months of 1921 and another £440,000 up to the end of the year. Well over £1 million in all, according to the auditors, although hundreds of thousands remained in reserve and further bond drives were planned.

Much depended on looking after the money prudently once it had been raised. It was here, far more than in raising the loan, that success or failure rested on Collins, personally and alone. And it was here that he was able to exert the close control he desired.

The first step was to hide the money and guard against its seizure by the British authorities. They had tried hard to stop it being collected, and in the beginning they tried just as hard to find it. Collins's first line of defence was simple: deposit the funds in a large number of ordinary deposit accounts lodged in a variety of Irish banks. Some were under fictitious names, but most belonged to supporters of the cause, including some well-known names such as Erskine Childers, the British writer and former clerk of the House of Commons, now an ardent supporter of the republican cause. These accounts proliferated over time as Dail departments opened their own accounts, spending and receipts rose, and the financial machinery grew more complex. London became a second financial hub as agents of the revolution required more and more cash to travel, buy guns, rent offices, and spread propaganda. Art O'Brien, Collins's front man there, developed his own little financial empire – which Collins had to go to court to dismantle in 1922.

American money posed a special problem, as it meant handling very large sums at once. This was solved in a number of ways. Some drafts (usually in the neighbourhood of £10,000) were drawn 'in favour of certain names' directly on a Dublin or Cork bank, while others were drawn on London banks in favour of, for instance, 'John Henry, Jermyn Court Hotel, Piccadilly'. This address was used with a number of names. Another method was to use Corrigan & Corrigan, whom Collins first encountered as solicitors to the National Aid (patriotic work maybe, lucrative definitely). Cheques, disguised as the proceeds of legacies or the like, would be sent to them from US firms and then legally laundered before being moved to Finance accounts.

A second safeguard was the gold reserve which Collins painstak-ingly assembled out of sovereigns and half-sovereigns. These amounted to some £20,000 in the end (figures vary), sealed in tobacco tins and buried ('at dead of night', naturally) in the premises of the Corrigan brothers (the undertakers, not the lawyers) in Camden Street. Only they, Collins and one of his staff knew of the location. The gold was exhumed in October 1921 and counted by Donal O'Connor (the National Aid auditor) before being reinterred under Batt O'Connor's floorboards in Donnybrook – in a baby's coffin. Not surprisingly, given the macabre details, the legend of Michael Collins's buried treasure has persisted.

The last line of defence was deadly force, but this was employed only once. In late 1919 Dublin Castle brought Alan Bell, a resident magistrate in then peaceful Portadown, to Dublin to head a series of inquiries into republican doings. These included the Dail funds. Raids on Sinn Fein offices produced useful evidence as to where the money was going, and in early March 1920 Bell issued summonses to officials of the Hibernian and Munster & Leinster Banks – the latter was especially favoured by Collins and other nationalists – and began taking depositions from them. On 26 March Bell was grabbed on his way to work and shot dead in the street. The investigation stopped there.

The odd thing is that Collins had just written to James O'Mara that he had been holding off on dealing with a $200,000 draft O'Mara had sent 'owing to a certain Banking Inquiry that was going on here. I was waiting until I could satisfy myself that everything would be perfectly in order, and I am on Monday [the 22nd] sending down to His Lordship [Michael Fogarty, Bishop of Killaloe, one of the Dail's financial trustees] the necessary assurance.' Either the inquiry was going nowhere or he felt confident that Bell would soon be killed – or both. A cool customer.

In October 1920 British intelligence did track down some of Collins's money after capturing a chequebook in an office raid. This led them to a branch of the Munster & Leinster – around the corner from Dublin Castle – where staff were intimidated into giving information. In all, £4,000 was taken, although the brilliance of the heist is somewhat lessened by the fact that the money was in old Volunteer accounts lodged plainly under Collins's, Richard Mulcahy's and Gearoid O'Sullivan's names. It was all returned with interest in 1922.

The other aspect of looking after the money was keeping track of it within the Dail government: keeping the accounts. To this end, Collins installed an accountant-general in October 1920 – George McGrath – and launched the world's first (and last?) audit of a revolution. Collins held some typical treasury views on financial control (he should have as much of it as possible) and spending ('We must reduce ruthlessly'), but he also had his own grand and expensive designs (income tax, for one) and was responsible for some of the most wasteful gun-running expeditions to Germany, Italy and the United States.

Mostly what he wanted was that line departments should send in full reports and estimates on time, so he could keep his own accounts straight and manage the revolutionary budget. This entailed a second rolling barrage of correspondence with McGrath and others over accounts and payments belonging to departments, individual TDs, committees, bureaux, consulates and offices, not to mention the mysterious New Ireland Goose Club ('We must somehow get the damn thing stopped'). For accounts to balance precisely was an extraordinary aim given the circumstances, but Collins was insistent. When the police threw the loan office into chaos in November 1919, he groaned, 'I can see my reputation lost over this damned raid.'

COLLINS WAS THE most successful of the politicians and administrators elected in 1918. De Valera's record in the United States in 1919 and 1920 was chequered by his feuds with various Irish-American leaders and his failure to achieve the recognition of Irish independence he sought. Griffith did little as a minister before being kicked upstairs to the acting presidency. Home Affairs and Local Government under Austin Stack and William Cosgrave performed well at first, but suffered from police harassment. Other departments had their own achievements. But all depended on Collins and Finance to do anything: his failure would have meant total failure.

On the other hand, raising money and hiding it from the government was an old game in Irish politics: the Fenians had done it in the 1860s and '70s and later, and the Land League and National League had done it in the 1880s. Collins was simply following in their footsteps, and had little to do with the American effort. Nor did the Irish police or British intelligence ever have effective tools for tracing and seizing funds, so there was little real danger of losing money in any case. Far more worrisome was the prospect of over-spending and running out altogether. US sources could not be counted on for ever – especially once an economic recession began to bite on both sides of the Atlantic in 1921. Collins could do little about that unless he went to the US personally.

He could not do that without abandoning his other posts in the Volunteers and the IRB, however, and it is this multiplication of roles that makes his performance extraordinary. For, unlike the other

Volunteers-turned-politicians, Collins had kept one foot firmly in 'the army', as it was increasingly called. So he not only ran the most important Dail department, and ran it well, he was also waging a secret war against the men who were trying to catch him.

14: War

Collins is the son of a small farmer, and is 30 years old, 5 ft. 10 in. In height, well set up, with a slight fair moustache. Usually he carries an umbrella under his arm, and has a habit of standing to look behind him when in the street. He generally carries a neat walking-stick.

(Police description, *Weekly Summary*)

COLLINS LIKED TO PRESENT himself as a soldier when it suited him – a common conceit among volunteers even when, or especially when, they were giving a speech in an election campaign: nothing could harm a political career in the movement more than being labelled a politician.

The warrior self-image came closest to realization in 1916, in Kimmage, during the Rising, and in Frongoch, when uniforms could be worn openly, full-frontal battle was joined, and the result was de facto prisoner-of-war status. Collins posed for a uniformed portrait after being promoted to commandant, used it in his election posters in 1918, and continued to wear recognizably paramilitary gear into 1919. Thereafter the realities of an underground life – and the advice of more sensible friends – forced him back into his business suits and dust- or raincoats.

His change of costume in 1919 coincided with the IRA's decision to start shooting policemen. The resulting war between republican guerrillas and the British government goes by many names: the Anglo-Irish War, the War of Independence, the Tan War (after the Black and Tans, the British war veterans drafted into the Irish Constabulary in 1920) or the Troubles. Around 4,000 people were killed or wounded in the process, most by the IRA who emerged as a powerful and resilient force – particularly in Dublin and in the Munster brigades of the deep south.

Collins's views on violence were carefully calibrated. In his own words he had 'strong fighting ideas or I should say I suppose ideas of the utility of fighting'. This echoes his approval in a London talk of the Phoenix Park assassinations of 1882, not because they were murder, but because they were expedient. This distinction between using force in a realistic way to accomplish concrete goals and violence or self-sacrifice for its own sake had divided Volunteers and the IRB before the Rising as well as after, and would emerge again in the Treaty debate over the question of returning to war against Britain. Collins happily took part in the Easter Rising, but he criticized its conduct afterwards and worked to safeguard the IRB and Volunteers from a repeated 'blood sacrifice'. At the same time he guarded the Volunteers' freedom of action in 1917 and '18 and, as a member of the resident executive and headquarters staff, took an aggressive stance over the right and necessity to use force.

Eamon Dore was staying in Vaughan's Hotel in Parnell Square in the spring of 1918 when he ran into Collins and his mates Gearoid O'Sullivan, Diarmuid O'Hegarty and Sean O Murthuile:

> I listened to a discussion between them about the prospects of some kind of military action that would compel the British to keep a large armed force in the country and so embarrass the British war effort at that critical period. At this discussion it was remarkable that there was no reference or mention of purely political action such as elections, but on the contrary it seemed to be accepted that the only hope was in some form of physical force. There was no spirit of defeat among this party; no feeling that the Rising had been our best effort, and while others might be content to counter enemy action when it occurred, this group wanted to take the initiative and were only in doubt as to what particular shape to give their effort.

This debate was overtaken by the subsequent conscription crisis, whereupon Collins campaigned against a strategy of passive resistance. The plan devised by Dublin brigadier Dick McKee was for concerted nationwide resistance at the local level: if the government tried to press Irish men into service, Ireland would be made ungovernable. Collins's job was to get the companies that would carry out the plan organized into some semblance of a coherent army. At the same time he was coordinating the IRB smuggling effort to get at least a few guns and explosives – and to ensure that the decision to fight remained in the right hands. So far so rational and uncontentious: preparation, keeping options open.

Ironically, while the IRB's continued efforts deliberately followed in the footsteps of Thomas Clarke and Sean MacDermott, McKee's essentially defensive plan marked a return to Eoin MacNeill's pre-Rising strategy of deterrence, with successful action dependent on popular support. As had been made clear in the reorganization of 1917, the GHQ was adamantly opposed to any pre-emptive action *à la* Plunkett and Pearse.

As at Legga in March 1918, even Collins's motivational speeches were conditional: we will strike 'when [if?] an opportunity occurs'; the head of a landlord and 'tail of a Bullock' were needed to get something from England (an old Parnellite standby: you get only what you can take); defend your weapons and be prepared [if you are attacked]. His only departure from this script came on home ground, in Skibbereen, also in March 1918, when the *Irish Times* reported him as saying:

> You heard England talking of reprisals. Let me take a leaf out of England's book. Bernie O'Driscoll [a local Sinn Feiner on hunger strike] is in jail for inciting to crime. I, too, incite to crime, and if Bernie O'Driscoll suffers I trust the Volunteers of Skibbereen and elsewhere will do their duty. The time for talking is past. You must do your duty when ordered by a superior.

The two policemen present recorded a rather milder form of words, however, so even this 'Ireland expects' message haunted by the spectre of Ashe may in actuality have been milder still – a significant contrast to the less subtle Gearoid O'Sullivan, who said on the same occasion that 'if anything happened to him in jail British officers would be shot.' And even this was conditional, another kind of deterrent.

It was the 1918 crisis that brought the first real dilemma. Cathal Brugha, then head of the Volunteer executive, suggested that the British cabinet be shot en masse if they attempted to enforce conscription. So much for his pledge to the Sinn Fein Ard Fheis only months before not to engage in assassination (not that anyone commented on this earlier promise). We don't really know if this suggestion was made before or after the 'German Plot' was 'exposed' – if before, de Valera was present: a fact he later denied (although at least one member of the executive remembers him approving it). Collins was for it according to Dick Walsh and against it according to Richard Mulcahy. Or, most likely, he approved along with the rest of the executive at the meeting and then derided the idea in private. Either way, he helped Brugha – who went to London himself, along with a few other low-level volunteers – with IRB contacts, but otherwise stayed out of it. If events had gone differently, Brugha's name might now stand out luridly above all others in twentieth-century Anglo-Irish history. But nothing did happen. The German army was defeated and Irish recruits were no longer needed. After a few months the gunmen went home again.

A second revealing moment came when the Great War was finally over. Collins, like many revolutionaries, had been convinced that British propaganda was utterly false and that Britain was losing the war. This helps explain the discussion Eamon Dore heard about tying down British troops in Ireland – it might help Germany win. Nor was this belief without foundation, of course. After all, Russia had been knocked out in 1917, and Italy very nearly was. The same year brought the United States in, however, making the prospect of Allied defeat remote. Still, some republicans were counting on the Central Powers being able to at least force Britain to a peace conference at which Ireland could be represented. Collins may even have been contacted by German agents about a second rising, but prudently kept his distance, distrusting anything to do with the 1916 debacle. The eventual unconditional Allied victory in November 1918 was therefore a disappointment, even if the American agenda seemed to offer self-determination as one of the principles of Woodrow Wilson's new world order.

For this and other reasons, Armistice Day, 11 November 1918, turned into a long and bloody street fight in south Dublin. Loyal celebrants invaded the Mansion House and Sinn Fein headquarters in Harcourt Street, and were attacked in return on Grafton Street and Stephen's Green. Collins described it to Austin Stack as follows:

No soldier was shot and no Volunteer kicked to death [as had been reported]. As a result of various encounters there were 125 cases of wounded soldiers treated at the Dublin Hospitals that night. These were the actual figures taken down by L of the Ind[ependent] and a statement giving details was sent in by the Ind but absolutely struck out by the censor. Before morning 3 soldiers & 1 officer had ceased to need any attention and one other died the following day. A policeman too was in a very precarious position up to a few days ago when I ceased to take any further interest in him. He was unlikely to recover. We had a staff meeting so I wasn't in any of it but my sparring partner Moloney [Con of South Tipperary?] was. He was his own most formidable opponent by reason of his violent hitting. Cut his knuckles and that sort of thing.

A rare spurt of bloodthirstiness this, written two weeks after the event and describing the supposed (probably exaggerated) injury and death of what may well have been fellow Irishmen – especially considering the rather lame 'I was in a meeting' excuse. Collins didn't lack physical courage, but nor did he lack prudence. He was a senior officer on the run, and due for a long jail sentence if rearrested. One suspects a definite decision was made not to get involved.

COLLINS ENTERED 1919 as Director of Organization and Adjutant General, still patching together the Volunteer organization. His first act of the new year as such was, as part of a Christmas trip home to Woodfield, to preside at the first meeting of the West Cork Brigade with Frongoch buddy and IRB stalwart Tom Hales as commandant. Some time after this, however, he also assumed the directorship of Intelligence (sometimes referred to as Information). The exact date of this is uncertain – perhaps as late as July. His self-appointment reveals his fast-growing power: no one else in the GHQ or the Dail government could have simply announced such a thing. Mulcahy recalls general surprise among the staff, but no demur. As with his effective takeover of Communications and Supply, the rationale was the perceived incompetence of the incumbent – in this case Eamon Duggan, a lawyer and TD, who left willingly.

When Collins took over Intelligence, there was no department as such to go with it. Duggan kept his files hidden in his office between the pages of his legal briefs (they were later captured) and had only one assistant, who was not kept on. For a new business-like staff,

Collins turned from law to insurance – or, more specifically, to the New Ireland Assurance Company.

New Ireland was something Collins himself had helped found. While in Frongoch in 1916, he and others had discussed the long-standing nationalist idea of setting up an Irish insurance company to overthrow the English monopoly. When they got out, M. W. O'Reilly, the former camp commandant, began learning the business. Collins provided constant encouragement and partners, whom he brought together at the (in effect) founding meeting in April 1917 at the Wexford County Feis (Gaelic festival) in Enniscorthy. Michael Staines was there, and Jim Ryan (another former hut-mate and future TD), as well as Liam (William for business purposes) Tobin and Frank Thornton, two other veterans of the Rising.

They put their scheme before the National Aid executive, but apparently failed to get help. (So much for Mick the wire-puller!) Nevertheless, these were smart men who stuck to their plan, and the rising Sinn Fein tide gave them invaluable brand-name cachet and a ready-made market. On 5 January 1918 the company – New Ireland Assurance – was launched by Eamon de Valera, and within a year was well established in the market, with forty-nine agents (typically republican activists) and an income over £1 million.

By 1918 Collins had withdrawn from any direct involvement – if he had thought of going into business as a sideline, he had eventually dropped the idea. Since he was still working at the National Aid, and had added Sinn Fein and Volunteer executive duties by then, we can assume it was matter of priorities. His friends and colleagues carried on, however, and New Ireland would become another of his resources and bases of support. Joe McGrath was brought in, as was Eamon Duggan, and for a long time the Bachelor's Walk offices doubled as a secret movement headquarters. Until the police figured out what was going on, both the Dail loan and IRA Intelligence were being run under cover of New Ireland.

Liam Tobin and Frank Thornton were part of company management in 1919 when Collins tapped them to run his new department, along with Tom Cullen, a much-berated assistant Quartermaster General. Both were already working for Collins as IRA organizers, and both continued to work in the New Ireland offices and did not formally take leave of their jobs until 1920. Showing a keen appreciation of the importance of titles, Collins named Tobin his Deputy

Director of Intelligence, Cullen was Assistant Director, and Thornton was Deputy Assistant Director. In practice these three men acted as a triumvirate and effectively ran the department from their offices in Bachelor's Walk and then from Crow Street near Dublin Castle, consulting Collins on a nightly basis. Collins was the boss, but the success enjoyed by IRA Intelligence is at least as much attributable to their canniness and hard work as to his direction.

This was very much a Dublin operation, and when further staff were needed they were chosen from the Dublin Brigade – often from the Drumcondra-based 2nd Battalion on the north side of the city, which also dominated the brigade staff. The department was nominally in charge of the whole country, and sent out occasional 'how-to' circulars on intelligence, but the flow of information was generally one-way: from outer units to the centre.

The 1st Cork Brigade's Florence O'Donoghue built up a very impressive operation in Cork city, and most country units had an intelligence officer by 1920. This was often a job given to an older or married man (often a teacher) who maintained a normal life – someone who wasn't up for the guerrilla life anyway. Like their British counterparts, these people had to start from scratch with no training. As with all other aspects of the war, the local boys were pretty much on their own.

Collins carried on as Adjutant General for a few months more, but once the loan effort got under way in the late summer of 1919 he was forced to hand over this responsibility to Gearoid O'Sullivan. In any case, with the brigade system pretty well set up, this was no longer an impact role. As Collins correctly judged, intelligence would be the key to the coming struggle, and it was this that earned him his mystique as the man who triumphed over the already legendary British secret service.

The key to success was good intelligence from inside the Irish administration, which IRA intelligence acquired in bulk from 1919 onward. This was a matter not of preparing a network of republican spies to penetrate government departments, but rather – as is so often the case in such matters – of taking advantage of the information that insiders were offering. All Collins had to do to begin with was recognize the opportunity for what it was and sort out the genuine offers from the bogus. He was not so good at the latter, and had to be saved by his subordinates and agents on several occasions. Still, it was he who realized and grasped the weapon that had been placed in the movement's hands and he organized an efficient department to exploit it systematically. Without him, it would not have happened: here Collins's characteristic opportunism was joined with his administrative finesse and deployed to great purpose and effect.

INFORMATION HAD long been on offer to the movement from inside Dublin Castle and the Dublin police. Even before the Rising the Castle had sprung a few leaks, and Joseph Plunkett had had access to documents concerning possible action against the Volunteers. After the Rising, a sympathetic detective in the Dublin Metropolitan Police (DMP), Joe Kavanagh, got in touch with Thomas Gay – a librarian who had been in the fighting but had avoided capture – to pass on messages from prisoners along with copies of the banned republican journal the *Gaelic American*. 'Naturally I was at a loss to know what to do with it [secret information],' Gay later admitted, but he – somewhat suspiciously – kept in touch through 1917 and passed the material on to Eamon Duggan, who was equally clueless.

The events of 1918, with the conscription crisis and 'German Plot' arrests, destroyed government credibility for most Irish Catholics. Policemen and civil servants were typically professional and loyal to their service, but many were becoming alienated from their political masters. The GAA and the Gaelic League had attracted a large number of junior clerks and the like in Dublin just as in London. Many ended up as movement leaders, but others stayed in their jobs, potential underground collaborators. As a unionist cabal took charge in the Castle in 1918 under new viceroy Lord French, doubts grew even further. Compounding the politics was a long-term decline in police recruitment, pay and morale. If policemen turned traitor, it was sometimes because they felt they had been betrayed first.

So it was that a police clerk in the detective office, Ned Broy (who didn't know about Kavanagh), decided to contact Sinn Feiners to let them know about documents the police had captured (including the plans for resisting conscription) and to warn those who were targeted for arrest. To his intense frustration the warnings were rarely heeded, partly because they took so long to be delivered. He had to wait until he got off work to inform a friendly railway clerk, Patrick

Tracy (married to his first cousin), who would take the information to O'Hanrahan's Store, owned by a republican family (where Broy himself could not be seen), whereupon someone – usually Greg Murphy (a senior IRB man) – had to be found to take it to Volunteer headquarters, where it might then be rerouted to Eamon Duggan before the actual target would be warned. By the time the information could be acted upon, it was useless: a classic symptom of dysfunctional intelligence systems the world over.

The 'German Plot' arrests in May 1918 were what brought Collins into the intelligence effort. Collins passed on Broy's warning to the rest of the Sinn Fein leadership, but most refused to hide, preferring to take the high ground as wrongly imprisoned political prisoners. Collins himself, who had no such desire, escaped only by luck. Impressed, he arranged a meeting with Broy. As the detective recalled:

> I was filled with curiosity. Would this Michael Collins be the ideal man I had been dreaming about for a couple of years? Looking up the police record book to see what was known about him, I discovered that he was a six-footer, a Corkman, very intelligent, young and powerful. There was no photograph of him at that time in the record book. So, steeped in curiosity, I went to 5, Cabra Road, and was received in the kitchen by the Foleys, a place where every extreme nationalist visited at some time or another. I was not long there when Greg Murphy and Michael Collins arrived. I had studied for so long the type of man that I would need to act efficiently, that the moment I saw Michael at the door, before he had time to walk across and to shake hands, I knew he was the man. He was dressed in black leggings, green breeches and a trenchcoat with all the usual buttons, belts and rings. He was very handsome, obviously full of energy and with a mind quick as lightning. The Foleys went away and I had a long talk with Mick from about 8 o'clock until midnight. He thanked me for all the documents I had sent and all the information, and said it was of the utmost assistance and importance to them. We discussed why so many arrests took place and, particularly, the German Plot information – why that went wrong, especially the arrest of de Valera. He said that a few minutes before train-time de Valera looked at his watch and announced that, notwithstanding the threatened arrests, he was

going home. They had dissuaded him, but he insisted on going home and left the station . . . I asked Mick why he allowed de Valera to do that . . . Mick shrugged his shoulders and looked at Greg Murphy, and Greg Murphy looked at him, and they both smiled.

Another conquest, another soulmate: Collins's ability to make connections with people, to build personal bonds, would be a tremendous asset in this new game. At times it also led him astray, however, as his faith in new friends kept several spies and informers in business until Tobin and Thornton winkled them out.

Collins was able to cut out the middlemen and arrange for regular – sometimes daily – meetings with Broy. In a sense (exaggerated in Broy's memoirs) Broy and Collins were partners, for it was Broy who had first thought about using the information he gathered and launching a war on his co-workers.

Broy, as confidential clerk of G Division, the plain-clothes detective branch of the DMP, was the cornerstone of Collins's intelligence franchise. Joe Kavanagh died in 1919 of heart failure, but not before recruiting a third man, James MacNamara, a confidential clerk for the assistant police commissioner in Dublin Castle. He and Broy fell under suspicion in 1921, but by then Collins had been put in touch with another young policeman, David Neligan, who was not only a detective but was later transferred into the military intelligence system. Another agent in the Castle was Lily Mernin, a typist in the military garrison adjutant's office, who typed up reports on Volunteer activities and court martials and, later, the names and addresses of court-martial officers. She was a relative of Piaras Beaslai, who had passed her name on to Collins. Many postal clerks were also willing to copy police letters and telegrams.

So Collins had worked his way into the intelligence business well before he officially created his department – taking over from Duggan was probably an acknowledgement that he couldn't do it alone or with a few IRB pals any more. He dealt in all kinds of information, much of it false, of course, but the gold amid the dross mostly consisted of timely tip-offs: advance warning of raids and arrest warrants. On one occasion he was even able to sneak into the G Division offices and look at the suspect files: a moment worthy of a master spy. He was also able to eliminate many of the delays previously plaguing the system, through regular face-to-face meetings or via his retinue of messengers. In the end, the agents often had to make their own decisions about what had to be done, however – they were activists in their own right, not just puppets at the whim of their master.

IMPRESSIVE THOUGH they were, these were essentially passive accomplishments: providing secrecy and time to evade capture. As 1918 became 1919, however, the movement was moving on. The general election had been won, the Dail was founded and *An tOglach*, the voice of the headquarters militants, began to advocate a much more offensive strategy. It was time to think about a second rising. As usual, this placed the militants in a minority: the executive did not agree that the time was right for rebellion, nor did the Dail, nor the GHQ staff as a whole. Most suggestions for operations from eager provincial brigades were turned down. The ban on raiding private homes for weapons that had got Collins into trouble in Legga in 1918 remained in effect.

Militant groups within the Munster IRA were not always willing to wait. Apart from anything else, they were not protected by Collins's early-warning system. Royal Irish Constabulary barracks and patrols were attacked in 1918, and in January 1919 members of the South Tipperary Brigade ambushed the police escort of an explosives delivery to a mine at Soloheadbeg, killing both men. Further attacks and deaths followed in Tipperary, Cork and Limerick, while in March the Dublin Brigade pulled off a clever heist at Collinstown aerodrome and got away with seventy-five rifles. In June another threshold was crossed when a particularly aggressive police inspector in Thurles was gunned down on a busy street and none of the witnesses were willing to cooperate with the investigation. None of this had anything to do with Collins: the gunmen were starting their own war.

The Intelligence Department was set up in the same spirit of direct action but also more or less in tandem with another initiative, a Dublin Brigade project under the industrious Dick McKee. McKee is now mostly remembered for his murder by policemen in November 1920, but – as Collins himself said – he was one of the prime movers of the revolution and had as much to do with directing the approaching secret war as the intelligencers. Not that there was any sort of contest. As commanding officer of the most important unit in Ireland, McKee had a seat at the headquarters table, and he, Collins and Chief of Staff Mulcahy were close collaborators by mid-1918. Collins always worked in this way, whether politically, administratively or militarily. He was no Napoleon when it came to decision-making, preferring the comfort and safety of a group whenever possible and accepting their verdict even if it went against him.

Before Collins had his own organization up and running, McKee had already set some of his men to follow police detectives, even keeping track of their movements in notebooks. Nothing had yet been done with the information, but the logic of the situation was obvious: to remove the threat they posed, they would have to be eliminated. Get them before they get us. However rational this conclusion might be, it also involved a huge moral and psychological leap into new and previously shunned territory. After all, assassination had been denounced as unworthy on the floor of the Sinn Fein convention less than two years previously, and the IRB had previously prided itself on its record of purely honourable violence.

Ned Broy claims to have thought of it, and may well have done, but it was McKee and Mick McDonnell (of the 2nd Battalion yet again) who created the unit and assembled the men who were to do the shooting. According to McDonnell, 'From an early stage I advocated the execution of those who were responsible for the identity of the men executed in 1916 and who were at the same time watching us. This was at first turned down by Dick McKee who felt that the people would not stand for this action at this time.' Such was the official line as dictated from the executive. It is not clear where the change came from, but in mid-1919 McKee and McDonnell began asking men if they were willing to carry out 'special duty'. One was Jim Slattery, another 2nd Battalion and Frongoch man:

> I received instructions to proceed to a house in North Great George's Street, I think it was No. 35. On arriving there I found a fairly big number of Volunteers present. Dick McKee and Mick McDonnell were there, and they picked out a number of us and took us to an inner room. Dick McKee addressed those of us who had been selected and asked us if we had any objection to shooting enemy agents. The greater number of Volunteers

objected for one reason or another. When I was asked the question I said I was prepared to obey orders.

About six men were chosen to start with, and more were recruited in the months that followed. McDonnell was in command, with direction from Intelligence. It would become understood that Collins's was the guiding hand, but, even if this was true later on, he usually worked through intermediaries. The gunmen rarely saw him. McKee was the man on the spot. They did odd jobs at the Brigade's or GHQ's request, but their main quarry was the G Division of the Dublin Metropolitan Police.

NED BROY's depiction of Dublin Castle as 'a cold blooded serpentine organization' was and is the standard image of the forces arrayed against Collins: a surveillance system covering the island, a secret police to spy on those who opposed British rule, a secret-service fund to bribe informers, a file on every suspect. In fact, while the Great War lasted, British concerns were primarily with the war against Germany, and most of the 'political' work was carried out by ordinary policemen. County inspectors of the Royal Irish Constabulary reported to Dublin Castle on the state of affairs under their jurisdiction, and it was their uniformed subordinates who pursued political lawbreakers and the evidence needed to convict them – as was the case when Collins was arrested and then pursued for jumping bail.

Only two small groups within the Royal Irish Constabulary and the Dublin Metropolitan Police functioned as anything like a 'secret service'. In the provinces, the Crimes Special Branch, made up of part-timers – a sergeant at each county headquarters and a constable at most district headquarters – tried to gauge the strength of political organizations (very broadly defined), recorded potentially seditious speeches (like Collins's), and followed suspects. Records were kept locally and in an office in Dublin manned by a few clerks (including Collins's agent James MacNamara). In practice, the branch was often little more than the sum of its files, as much of the actual fieldwork was done by whoever was available in the relevant local barracks at the time.

Among the plain-clothes detectives of G Division of the DMP were around a dozen men (increased to twenty by 1920) whose job it was to keep an eye on dissidents and rebels. They shadowed suspects, watched meetings, and spent a lot of time at railway stations to see who got on or off trains. Far from being an invisible hand, they became very well known to their targets. A few were in touch with informers, but 'the G' had no spies or undercover agents.

These men were often quite effective in collecting information, but they made little attempt actually to infiltrate Sinn Fein, the Irish Volunteers or the IRB, as had been done in the past. 'Secret service' funding did rise somewhat after 1916, but fell again once the Great War ended.

In other words, Collins and his comrades were not facing a formidable secret police. On the contrary: their enemies were demoralized, underpaid, underfunded, undermanned and now out-numbered and outgunned.

McDONNELL's and McKee's special duty squad – soon known just as the Squad – first went into action on 30 July 1919, when they shot Detective Sergeant Patrick Smyth, one of the political 'G' men, known to those whom he pursued as 'the Dog'. James Slattery, Tom Keogh, Tom Ennis and Mick Kennedy had waited every day for a week near his house to intercept him. None of them had killed anyone before:

> We had .38 guns and they were too small. I thought that the minute we would fire at him he would fall, but after we hit him he ran. The four of us fired at him. Keogh and myself ran after him right to his own door and I think he fell at the door, but he got into the house. He lived for a fortnight afterwards [actually about a week]. I met Mick McDonnell the following morning and he said we had made a right mess of the job the night before, but I can assure you that I was more worried about it until Smith [sic] died than Mick was.

Collins immediately put out an urgent call to his contacts in the United States and in Britain for .45 calibre revolvers and bullets, so as to rearm his killers with heavier weapons.

Over a month went by before the next job. On 12 September Dail Eireann was declared illegal and Collins was almost caught in a raid on Sinn Fein headquarters in Harcourt Street. That same night Jim Slattery was visited by Mick McDonnell, who 'asked me would I mind going on a job. I told him I would not mind, and he said,

"They very nearly got the man we want to guard. They nearly got him to-day" – he was referring to Mick Collins. That was the first time I got an inkling that Collins was the heart [rest of sentence missing].' The detective in charge of the raid, Daniel Hoey, was shot dead the next day. Here we have the other motive for setting up the Squad, at least as understood by McDonnell, Tobin, Thornton and Cullen: to protect Collins personally from capture. Hence the indignantly denied rumours that he travelled with bodyguards – in a sense he did.

Shootings in Dublin continued at the rate of about one a month. On 13 October a young constable named Mick Dowling – unarmed like the rest of the uniformed force – was shot dead on his beat by a group of men with revolvers. No one ever claimed this killing, but it was very probably the work of the Squad or some other group of armed Volunteers. Dowling might have accosted them as they waited for their next victim and they were afraid he could identify them later, or someone might have got trigger-happy. His killing might also have been deliberate: a warning to the uniformed service to stay out of political work or face the fate of their colleagues in the RIC now being attacked and boycotted throughout the south and west. And indeed the men of the DMP would ultimately refuse to carry arms or to act as a counter-insurgency force – although their duties did occasionally bring them into conflict with the rebels and more would be shot.

The last of the year's tally of targets, in November, were detectives Thomas Wharton (who survived and was pensioned off) and John Barton (who didn't). In December a Detective Constable Walshe, a clerk like Broy and MacNamara, was attacked but managed to get away unscathed. In January 1920 William Redmond, a Belfast detective brought in as assistant commissioner to run 'the G', was shot dead. In February two constables, Walsh and Dunleavy, were ambushed; Walsh was killed and Dunleavy was wounded. Could Walsh be the Walshe whom the assassins had missed two months before? The policemen were armed and fought back, apparently wounding one attacker, so they were not ordinary patrolmen.

On 14 April, Detective Constable Henry Kells was murdered. Kells was a plain-clothes 'G' man, but in the crime rather than the politics division. Either his killing was a mistake or he was investigating the wrong robbery or premises and got too close. A week later, on the 20th, it was the turn of Detective Constable Laurence Dalton, who had just transferred into G Division. Another policeman with him was wounded. David Neligan, Collins's new man in the force, was a friend of Dalton's and was horrified at his death. Dalton had 'never lifted a finger against Sinn Fein', but he had reportedly angered J. J. Walsh, a Sinn Fein TD, by refusing to let him go when he was caught in a raid. To Neligan's disgust, a rumour was spread that Dalton had worn a priest's clothes to catch a suspect and had therefore only himself to blame: 'All that can be said now is that personal antagonism brought about this man's death, which I deeply regret. It was one of the tragedies of the time.'

On 8 May, Detective Sergeant Richard Revell, a clerk for G Division – now moved to the Castle for supposed safety – was shot seven times near his home, in broad daylight, but survived. This marked the end of the campaign against the DMP and its detectives. It was a clear and decisive victory for the IRA, putting not only G Division but the whole force out of the war at the cost of twelve men shot and at most only one Volunteer wounded.

WRITING IN 1922, Collins, in line with Sinn Fein propaganda (and probably genuine belief), declared the Volunteers' 'organized and bold guerrilla warfare' to be a matter of self-defence, a response to murderous oppression. 'We did not initiate the war nor did we choose the battleground.' The Rising would seem to deny both propositions, and so does the campaign against 'the G'. For, while Collins and the Volunteers had decided they were fighting a war, that's not what any police force was doing. The handful of 'political' detectives weren't trying to defeat them as an army. They were compiling evidence against individuals, arresting suspects, or hunting for fugitives like Collins: carrying out their routine duty. This was an advantage, an opportunity, a weak point as far as the revolutionaries were concerned – one Collins was instrumental in seizing. But in the second half of 1919, and especially in early 1920, it was the IRA that was doing most of the shooting and policemen who were doing most of the dying. The men of 'the G' never killed anyone. The IRA's accomplishment should be measured against the reality of the opposition that the Intelligence Department faced.

The question of timing also arises. 'Intelligence' is often presented as being merely a matter of information collection and analysis. This is partly true, of course, but it is always also another word for politics. Declaring a secret war on the police was a very political decision and, not surprisingly, a very murky one. Who exactly made it, under what authority, and when?

We know that the militant tendency in the Cork, Tipperary and Kerry IRA were already in action and that their efforts were not supported by a majority of Sinn Feiners, members of the Dail or nationalists in general. And it was this very opposition to a 'physical-force' offensive that drove some of the hard men into action. They were afraid that the whole movement was drifting into politics, in danger of becoming just another party. Their companies, battalions and brigades were growing moribund as the threat of conscription receded and as it seemed that election victories would suffice. Action was required to turn their men into an army and to achieve the republic declared in 1916.

Collins shared these views, but often found himself outnumbered in the cabinet and on the Sinn Fein standing committee. The main event in early 1919 was the return of de Valera to Dublin after his February escape. Collins and other Volunteers announced a triumphal reception in the name of Sinn Fein, but without the knowledge of the standing committee. When the meeting was banned by the government, he urged that the order be defied. The committee overruled him, as he angrily informed Austin Stack, then a prisoner:

Well your letter was I think somewhat prophetic – we are having our Clontarf Friday [nationalist leader Daniel O'Connell no-toriously cancelled a meeting at Clontarf in 1843 when faced with a similar ban, so as to avoid violence]. It may not be as bad but it is bad and very bad. The chief actor [de Valera] was very firm on the withdrawal as indeed was Cathal [Brugha] – I used my influence the other way and was in a practical minority of one. It may be that all the arguments were sound but it seems to me that they have put up to us a challenge which strikes at the fundamentals of our policy and our attitude.

The reasons for not challenging the ban were that lives could be lost and that Sinn Fein would still have its publicity coup as the government was preventing legitimate political expression. De Valera may also have been guarding his reputation. On the eve of his trip to the United States he probably didn't want his image to be blood-stained.

According to Darrell Figgis, who was present at the committee deliberations, Collins made the following case:

> He spoke with much vehemence and emphasis, saying that the sooner fighting was forced and a general state of disorder created through the country the better it would be for the country. Ireland was likely to get more out of the state of general disorder than from a continuance of the situation as it then stood. The proper people to make decisions of that kind were ready to face the British military, and were resolved to force the issue and they were not to be deterred by weaklings and cowards.

Figgis disliked Collins, so he may have made him sound more aggressive than he was, but it seems authentic, a genuine reflection of what the 'active', 'forward' and 'advanced' men were thinking. Collins was putting forward the views and frustrations of his main constituency at the time, with all the belligerence that such meetings seemed to bring out in him.

Collins complained of his colleagues' attitudes repeatedly in letters through the spring and summer of 1919. On 18 May he wrote to Austin Stack (still in prison) about the regime's increasing heavy-handedness towards the Dail (then meeting publicly in the Mansion House) and declared presciently that:

> Things that way were never better and as they pass on so to speak from the police patrol to the military lorry they positively put more and more weapons in our hands. Yet in spite of the good aspect of things in this view I am not so sure our movement or part of it at any rate is fairly alive to the developing situation. It seems to me that official SF is inclined to be ever less militant and ever more political & theoretical . . . There is I suppose the effect of [sic] tendency of all Revolutionary movements to divide themselves up into their component parts. Now the moral force department have probably been affected by English propaganda – the yarn . . . that the secret revs had got hold of Sinn Fein – you can see it working in the minds of the moderates. It comes to the surface in all sorts of rumours, whisperings, suggestions of differences between certain people – all that sort of thing. It's

rather pitiful and at times somewhat disheartening. At the moment I'm awfully fed up.

On 20 July he told Stack of de Valera's positive reception in the United States, but added, 'Yet our hope is here and must be here. The job will be to prevent eyes turning to Paris [the Versailles peace conference] or New York as a substitute for London.' In August he wrote to say that GHQ (including himself) opposed the idea of a prison hunger strike as 'after all they [the government] are in no way amenable to public opinion just now.' Here lay the basic premiss for violence: moral pressure is useless, and force is the only language the government can understand.

Not just force alone, however. As the last statement suggests, Collins was always concerned about shaping public opinion and about the political impact of violence. He saw clearly that blatant oppression meant more backing for the movement, so the more soldiers on the streets the better they could sell the revolution. At the same time he seems to have agreed with the GHQ policy that the Volunteers should not get too far ahead of what most nationalists thought acceptable – this would only produce the opposite effect.

So as not to besmirch his militant credibility, he mostly let Dick Mulcahy make this point to eager commandants who wanted to rob banks or lay siege to police barracks. His own posture was one of masterful ambiguity. He asserted Volunteer autonomy constantly, but used it only with great circumspection. He made sure his friends and allies knew he was fighting the 'forces of moderation', but maintained cabinet solidarity once the decisions were made.

A telling episode in this regard was the summoning to Dublin of the South Tipperary Brigade leadership, the men responsible for the Soloheadbeg ambush, which had been carried out to give the movement 'a push' in early 1919. Seamus Robinson, the brigade commanding officer, remembers it as a disconcerting encounter:

> Collins was waiting for us on the street with his note book out. This meeting which was in the street instead of in an office was the first indication we had that if we ('the big Four') were not exactly persona non grata, at best we were decidedly not warmly welcome in any HQ office . . . Collins seemed to be keeping his eyes peeled watching everyone in the street without moving his head. His glance would come back to us. He greeted us with

'Well, everything is fixed-up; be ready to go in a day or two.' 'To go where?' I asked. 'To the States' he said. 'Why?' 'Well, isn't it the usual thing to do after . . .' 'We don't want to go the States or anywhere else.' 'Well,' said Mick, 'a great many people seem to think it is the only thing to do.' I began to be afraid the GHQ had begun to give way to Sinn Fein pacifism, and with a little acerbity I said: 'Look here, to kill a couple of policemen for the country's sake and leave it at that by running away would be so wanton as to approximate too closely to murder.' 'Then what do you propose to do?' 'Fight it out of course.' Mick Collins, without having shown the slightest emotion during this short interview, now suddenly closed his note book with a snap saying as he strode off with the faintest of faint smiles on his lips but with a big laugh in his eyes: 'That's all right with me.'

In other words, he began by giving them the official Volunteer policy, saw which way they thought, and left it at that. Presumably if they had been willing to go he would have gone ahead with shipping them out and no more said. Later, once the Tipperarymen became revolutionary heroes, they returned to a much warmer welcome and Collins's proffered friendship. In early 1919, however, Collins was playing a very careful game.

The final factor in the timing of the attacks on the detective force was de Valera's departure for the USA in June 1919, which removed the one man who held an effective veto over movement policy. Once the shootings began he did not object, but he did push for a new oath of allegiance binding the Volunteers to the Dail and the Republic. Collins and other IRB men on the Volunteer executive opposed the idea, but were overruled. If you can't stop them, de Valera may have been thinking, at least make sure they're loyal.

The thread that connects such incidents to the eventual assault on G Division was, it may be inferred, Collins's search for the politically correct circumstances or targets to launch a physical-force campaign. Ordinary policemen, such as those killed in South Tipperary, were not yet seen as legitimate targets for cold-blooded killing. Asserting the right to free speech at de Valera's homecoming would have been seen in a very different light, however, as would the increasing police harassment of the Dail: this in particular was the opportunity he believed Sinn Fein was letting slip away. The G men were prominent in these raids, and were far from ordinary policemen.

Sinn Feiners as well as Volunteers knew them well: they were symbols of the hated Castle regime as well as its vanguard of enforcers. Here, then, was the place to strike – not just in furtherance of an extremist agenda, but as a way of protecting the Dail government and challenging unjust repression without alienating too many moderate activists or supporters.

The militants seem to have received at least the tacit or informal permission of the cabinet and Volunteer executive – although probably only retroactively, once these bodies were presented with a fait accompli. This wasn't unconditional or official support, however, as Mulcahy made clear at a meeting of 'active-service' men in Dublin in mid-1919. (This may have been the first meeting of the Squad, after the first members were recruited.) According to Seamus Robinson, who happened to be there, he insisted on low-risk operations where no IRA men would be captured or killed. This was because 'if any of us were caught or killed we would be quite possibly disowned. The meeting was horrified at this latter suggestion but no one said anything.' The Dail and GHQ were not willing to take responsibility, especially since neither was formally outlawed before September. Mulcahy even told the guerrillas that there must not even be a laundry mark on their clothing to identify them. Collins was never around when such announcements were made.

The fact that most of the Volunteers asked if they would be willing to shoot policemen said no reveals the presence of a hidden fault line even within the IRA between those who felt guerrilla warfare was a legitimate means of warfare and those who did not. This difference required time to be resolved – and remained a constant source of struggle within many units – so the official go-slow policy remained in place until January 1920.

Nor were the gunmen unleashed in 1919 until their targets in 'the G' were warned and given a chance to get out. Such was the case with Detective O'Brien, one of Collins's captors in 1918. He was captured and tied up in early 1919 and was told he would be shot if he continued in his work. He took the hint and soon resigned (the other arresting officer, Bruton, wound up as chief inspector by default).

The picking off of individuals one by one also gave the stubborn ones the chance to realize the warnings weren't a bluff. Nor were those who transferred or who left the force pursued out of revenge.

This was partly what Collins had in mind when he stressed the utility of force: the minimum necessary to achieve the objective in a politically acceptable or productive way. On the other hand, a shift is also detectable in the DMP killings: from removing those who were a direct danger to movement leaders, to killing new recruits and ordinary policemen to deter others from acting against them. Both approaches were effective, but time would show that it is much harder to control a terror campaign.

This raises the also very political question of the limits of violence. Who wasn't killed? The answer is: politicians. No Unionist, Irish Party or British politicians were assassinated in 1919–21 (1922–3 was another story). This is not to say that no such attacks were attempted or planned: plans were made in abundance. At one time or another, Prime Minister David Lloyd George, his cabinet, coalition MPs, Basil Thomson (head of Scotland Yard), Henry Wilson (Chief of the Imperial General Staff), and both Lord Lieutenants, French and Fitzalan (who replaced French in 1921), were all supposed to be kidnapped or killed, and both Buckingham Palace and the Houses of Parliament were to be assaulted in various ways (by germs and bombs, respectively). In almost every case the object was to deter or punish British reprisals in Ireland. It would have been easy too, as up until the end of November 1920 Downing Street and Westminster weren't protected with barricades or armed police and politicians didn't have bodyguards.

What was Collins's role in all this? His image as the man who gave the orders and pulled the strings notwithstanding, these were rarely his ideas. In 1919 the big idea was to get Lord French, the Lord Lieutenant and the figurehead for the whole anti-nationalist trend in Irish policy since conscription and the 'German Plot' arrests. How eliminating him would have helped the cause remains unclear, but republicans certainly felt that he deserved it. Dan Breen of Tipperary – who, like Seamus Robinson, preferred the bright lights of Dublin to Tipperary – declared that French's death 'would arouse all peoples to take notice of our fight for freedom'. Sympathy might have been more muted than they expected, given that French had commanded the British Expeditionary Force in France and Belgium and his title was Viscount French of Ypres.

Originally there was an elaborate plan to 'plug' him at a parade in College Green, probably on Armistice Day in November 1919. Plans ranged from a single Jackal-like sniper (a volunteer who 'would not come back') to an all-out attack on the soldiers present by the whole of the Dublin Brigade. Whatever the final plan, it was organized by Dick McKee and called off the night before by either Brugha or Richard Mulcahy as 'the people would not stand for it.' Other ad-hoc attempts were made (twelve in all, according to Dan Breen), and French's car and escort were eventually ambushed on 19 December – with no effect on French and one IRA fatality. 'They are bad shots,' remarked Lloyd George on hearing the news.

Seamus Robinson thought the whole thing was a bit fishy:

> The first time I found Mick Collins to be a bit of an artful dodger, was when he arranged the first, the 'phoney' attack on French ... He came personally to Mrs. Boland's [Harry's mother's house] to waken up Breen and me and Ned O'Brien and Scanlon of Galbally for, as Mick said: 'An attempt of French's life'. Mick gave Sean Treacy and me the 'They shall not pass' point to hold: the last corner French would pass before the Castle was reached. We were told that the convoy was to be attacked all the way from Dunlaoghaire; if French escaped these ambushes we two were to see to it he didn't get past us alive ... At 5 o'clock we heard the noise of a number of men walking round the corner talking loudly and laughing. We wheeled round to see what or who was coming. Round the corner from Dame Street came Mick Collins, Sean Ua Muirlihe [sic], Sean Mc-Garry, Thomas MacCurtain [then commander of the 1st Cork Brigade] and others. 'It's all right' shouted Mick 'he isn't coming' ... I learned much later that French, instead of being in Britain was in his Roscommon estate and there was no word at all of him coming that time to Dublin. However, Mick was able to give the impression to the Volunteer officers from all over the country that he not only organized the attacks on spies that had begun in Dublin but that he also led them, taking part in them!

Robinson may have been overly cynical (although he wasn't alone in his suspicions), but Collins wasn't in on any of the later attempts on French. He did later boast in the Dail of having taken part in ambushes, however.

The next grand scheme was proposed in September 1920, when Terence MacSwiney, the much-loved Lord Mayor of Cork and commander of the 1st Cork Brigade (MacCurtain having been murdered by policemen), was on hunger strike in Brixton jail. Collins didn't like hunger strikes after Ashe died, and he always felt an emotional connection to prisoners. MacSwiney's sufferings became an agonizing ordeal for many of his friends as well as for nationalist Ireland, which was gripped by a daily death watch. Collins wanted to kidnap British MPs as hostages, but as MacSwiney slowly drifted towards death this turned into a revenge operation whereby his death would trigger the assassination of the Prime Minister and his cabinet: a return to Brugha's 1918 proposal.

When MacSwiney finally died, after a mind-boggling seventy-four days, 'it was the first time I saw Michael Collins really upset,' reported Sean McGrath, the London gun-runner. 'He talked then about shooting in England.' Nothing happened in the end. Mac-Swiney's death was a huge propaganda defeat for the government: mowing down British MPs would have instantly returned the favour and condemned the movement to horrific repression. Collins was, above all, a rationalist.

When the assassination idea came up yet again, in 1921 – this time revived by Brugha on his own – it was resisted by the men he ordered to do it and countermanded by Collins and Mulcahy. In early 1921, when British patrols in Dublin began carrying Sinn Fein hostages on their lorries as a defence against ambushes, Frank Thornton and other intelligence operatives were sent to London to work with local men to kidnap MPs in retaliation. The plan was called off when the use of hostages ceased. The other, rather mad, plans (such as truck-bombing the House of Commons) were the brainchildren of Rory O'Connor. Collins, who was in constant touch with the leaders of the British IRA and IRB, was uneasy at such projects. According to Denis Kelleher, an officer in the London IRA, 'Michael Collins was more for the publicity which an undertaking would create, but Rory O'Connor more for the spectacular event and he did not care about human life.' Here again the concept of political utility in guiding violence was uppermost in Collins's mind.

The only outright political assassination carried out in this period was that of Frank Brooke, the sixty-nine-year-old chairman of the Dublin and South-Eastern Railway Company and a well-known Unionist. On 30 July 1920 he was shot dead in his office by members of the Squad: a killing which usually goes unmentioned in biographies and celebratory histories. Brooke was a friend of Lord French and sat on his Privy Council, and he had been on the advisory council two years before during the conscription crisis, so he was definitely a hostile establishment figure. Was his killing a warning to others of his ilk? Was he suspected of involvement in some sort of covert activity? The only concrete reason put forward for his being on the Squad hit list was that he had suggested bringing in army engineers to run the trains when the drivers went on strike in 1920. And, according to senior gunman Paddy Daly, while 'we had his name on the list ... there were no definite plans to shoot him' until some Squad members took it upon themselves to do so. The men who did the deed say only that they had no idea why he was fingered: they just followed orders from the Intelligence Department.

In many ways Collins and his assistants were scrupulous, especially when compared with IRA units elsewhere. GHQ intelligence normally asked questions and gave warnings first before shooting later, and Collins himself may have prevented as many killings as he ordered. He would never admit mistakes, however: they were always someone else's fault or swept under the rug. As with many many other deaths in this period, the killing of Frank Brooke remains a mystery.

15: Spy

Height about 5' 8". Broad and heavy in build. Weighs 12 or 13 stone. Must have been a powerful man a few years ago; now heavy in movement and greatly out of condition. Coarse, pale face with heavy jowl. Clean shaven. Looks like a publican. Eyes stern; and have purpose in them. Over-hanging eyebrows. Except for the eyes he is now quite unlike earlier photographs. Looks about 40. Now wears a moustache.

(Military intelligence description)

ON 2 MARCH 1920 a man's body was found in a lane in a 'quiet, secluded district' of Glasnevin, north Dublin: 'discovered with the head lying in a pool of blood on the roadway'. He had been shot at close range in the head and heart. 'The whole occurrence is involved in profound mystery,' wrote the *Freeman's Journal* reporter on the case – a mystery that Irish and English newspapers, sensing a good story, were keen to unravel. The coroner's inquest provided further tabloid-approved detail. The arms of the corpse were covered in oriental-style tattoos, including a snake, a mermaid, flowers and 'a representation of what is said to be a woman with the name "Phyllis"'. He was identified only as a Mr Jameson, staying at the Granville Hotel on O'Connell Street. To the hotel staff he was a commercial traveller known for his affable references to a former life in the Wild West (of the United States, not Ireland) and for the birds he kept in his room. The police themselves maintained a suspiciously discreet lack of interest in him. However, only two days after the man's death it was being said 'in some quarters' (of the republican movement) that 'Jameson' had been a secret agent. The next day he was claimed by Mrs John Charles Byrnes of Romford, England, as her husband.

With the departure of Mrs Byrnes, and with fresher killings to divert attention, the tattooed man receded from the public memory – only to be resurrected time and again by biographers as a foil for the genius of Michael Collins. Byrnes became one of the exemplars of British failure in Ireland. He was indeed a secret-service spy, but he was suspected from the start, failed to do any damage, and was ultimately liquidated because of his blind persistence. The Jameson affair was another successful skirmish in Collins's secret war, and an unfailingly good story to tell.

What makes it something more – and ultimately something different – is our ability to trace the story from both sides. Uniquely, we know what Collins was thinking and what Byrnes was reporting.

Byrnes and his killing could have been invented by Buchan or 'Sapper', but in fact he was head of a suburban family at semi-detached 34 Laurel Bank, Romford. The real Bulldog Drummond in this case was Ralph Isham, a Yale man who made adventure, sleuthing and intrigue his life. A self-described 'financier', a big-game hunter and later the discoverer of the James Boswell's long-hidden Papers, Isham was (like many Yalies) an Anglophile. He volunteered for the British army in the Great War, joining as a private in the Royal Engineers and being promoted to temporary lieutenant in 1917. His big break came in March 1919, when he was advanced all the way to the rank of temporary lieutenant-colonel 'whilst specially employed'. He ended up as a full colonel with a CBE, the beneficiary of a peculiar opportunity.

At the end of 1918, once the war was over, British soldiers wanted badly to go home. Dissatisfaction over the pace of demobilization became open unrest: the spectre of Bolshevism haunted the officer corps. Enter Lieutenant Ralph Isham, whose 'wonderful gift of influencing his fellow men' at one camp gave him an instant reputation as a troubleshooter with the General Staff. In March 1919 he was given his own branch – A2 – to organize anti-Bolshevik and morale-boosting lectures for the men encamped in Britain and on the Continent.

Isham's efforts did not end with rot-stopping. He was after bigger game: the Soviet agents so obviously behind the trouble. For Isham was a pioneer in the great twentieth-century crusade against

Communism, and A2 was his fledgling empire. Credited with a flair for detection work, he soon had his own agents, chief among them John Charles Byrnes.

Byrnes remains an uncertain, insubstantial figure. Born in London, his only Irish connection was a soldier grandfather, although he was able to convince his targets that his blood ran greener than that. He was born in 1885, the son of a china-shop manager. He spent some time in the artillery, became a gas fitter, and was called up as a reservist in 1914. His war was spent in dreadful Salonika and then in a Malta hospital before being discharged in the summer of 1918 on medical grounds with the rank of sergeant-major. No doubt these miserable experiences helped convince him of the necessity of political change, for he was immediately active in ex-servicemen's groups and the (not exactly revolutionary) Romford Labour Party.

How exactly Byrnes met Isham is unknown. Basil Thomson, the head of Scotland Yard, described him as 'a certain Irish soldier at one time concerned with fomenting unrest among the troops'. It may be guessed that Byrnes began as a sincere union man whom Isham turned into a government mole, possibly by persuasion, certainly with money. On the other hand, Byrnes may have already been working for Scotland House – Basil Thomson's Directorate of Intelligence. Thomson claimed Byrnes as 'my man', although his scatty memoirs also refer to him as Isham's informant. Such confusion was typical of Thomson, but is also indicative of the overlapping muddle in British intelligence agencies, multiplying and turning inward upon a whole constellation of domestic threats, Irish and otherwise. Isham and Thomson shared information and agents and considered radicals of any sort to be partners in a common revolutionary front menacing the Empire.

Isham had other agents, but Byrnes was his ticket to the big leagues. It was Byrnes who had the confidence and credibility to maintain a double life (his wife, like the IRA, thought he was a travelling salesman) and a convincing political cover. Others cracked or were blown, but Byrnes sailed through, a natural spy: 'the best secret service man we had' according to one cabinet minister.

His main target was the Soldiers', Sailors' and Airmen's Union (SSAU), formed in early 1919 after a series of camp mutinies. Believed to be plotting Russian-style soldiers' councils, the union was in fact small, weak and doomed by demobilization. It would probably have died much sooner without the influx of agents from A2 and Special Branch: at least five found their way on to the executive committee. Byrnes himself became an energetic general secretary. This all-too familiar scenario of intelligence agencies propping up the organizations they supposedly seek to destroy (the FBI and the US Communist Party being another notorious example) did have one justification: it gave the agents access to the whole radical scene, and allowed a military agency to spy on civilians.

Thus A2's mission rapidly morphed from adult education (boring) to surveillance of industrial unions, the Independent Labour Party, the *Daily Herald* and anyone else who crossed its path (exciting and career-enhancing). And, since actual revolutionaries were hard to come by, agents soon became provocateurs. Who wants guns? Who thinks we should shoot people? Not many British socialists in 1919, as it turned out. Irish republicans, however: they were another story. And Collins, trying to start his own revolution, bought it all – hook, line and sinker.

The route to Michael Collins lay through Art O'Brien, the movement's go-to guy in London. Money, organization work, speech making, safe houses, anything Gaelic – all were in O'Brien's domain. Collins and he were in daily contact. Guns were different, and were usually handled by Sean McGrath, the smuggler-in-chief in London. But in the spring and summer of 1919 McGrath was in jail, having been caught red-handed. Meanwhile Collins was pressing hard for revolvers and automatics to wage his new war. In the summer of 1919 word came through of an answer to his problem.

THE FIRST SUMMER of peace was one of promise for London's radical underground. The class war had been taken up afresh, its foot soldiers buoyed by the example of Russia's revolution. Unions, leagues, strikes, rallies, writings and meetings abounded, all organized in a feverish haze of committees. Everybody belonged to everything. Irish republicanism was part of this world, its enemies the enemies of all, its activists often just as prominent in left-wing politics. In London, some branches of the newly formed Irish Self-Determination League (Sinn Fein's English front) were little more than Labour Party branches under another name.

It is not surprising, therefore, that Byrnes quickly encountered republicans. At first these came in the form of Misses Mooney, Rose, Copperweat, Sullivan and O'Neill. Was it the tattoos? All responded eagerly to Byrnes's hints. His line – now familiar from a thousand undercover book or movie scenarios – was that he could deal only with the principals, no third parties. Miss O'Neill was one of Art O'Brien's secretaries, and the connection was duly made. Although he would later deny it, on 28 July O'Brien tendered his order for .45 revolvers and .38 automatics: Collins's wish list. Discussion led to a second meeting, and Art O'Brien was hooked. Here was the perfect mark: the kind who wants to believe the con so badly he convinces himself and his friends it's true.

Further meetings followed through August, September and October, during which O'Brien and Byrnes happily discussed various grand schemes. It was November when Byrnes got what he and his masters wanted. The middleman finally introduced him to Mr Big. Michael Collins was in town (possibly after a trip to Manchester to visit some recently escaped prisoners), and O'Brien was eager to show off his man.

So Isham's star spy became Art O'Brien's star contact, and used him to penetrate to the heart of the Irish revolution. All for a handful of handguns. In fact Byrnes was able to change targets at the perfect time. The threat of Communism was receding, especially within the army, and senior officers were preparing to end their distasteful experiment in espionage. Even worse, Special Branch was sniffing about disapprovingly, and other A2 men were being openly denounced, sacked or jailed. Despite the odour of betrayal now surrounding the SSAU, O'Brien ignored whatever warnings came his way and failed to check up on Byrnes's bona fides, determined that so promising a source of guns must not be lost. Isham had finally, if inadvertently, hit gold. He was seconded to the Home Office to work under Basil Thomson, and got ready to move to Ireland.

Meanwhile the Irish administration, on Thomson's advice, was overhauling its own intelligence apparatus (such as it was) to repair the losses in G Division. By far the best information collected in early 1920 came from the army, which launched a very successful counter-insurgency campaign in Munster until it was called off for political reasons in April. The Dublin IRA and GHQ were a lot more elusive, and here Dublin Castle was still in charge; so, with advice from Basil Thomson, a Special Branch solution was adopted.

Informers were to be recruited, and special agents and investigators –
including the ill-fated Alan Bell – were brought in. Byrnes and Isham
were to be key players in the new effort.

COLLINS THOUGHT well enough of Byrnes after meeting him that
he agreed to host the next session in Dublin. This was delayed when
a police raid there took (as Byrnes reported) 'practically the whole of
the leading lights [in Sinn Fein] together with all papers'. Byrnes
wrote to Dublin on 13 November 1919 to keep things on track, but
Collins wrote back (via O'Brien) on the 15th to say that 'he should
not expect to hear from one for at least a week, owing to the rush
of work here arising out of the seizure of all the Staff.' Punctual
as always, on the 22nd he wrote to the equally eager O'Brien, 'Will
you kindly convey to this gentleman that we are perfectly willing
that he should come over here – and if possible stay a fortnight.
When he does come it is suggested that he should stay at the
"Granville Hotel" in O'Connell Street.' There followed a familiar
battle between Collins-the-accountant and O'Brien over who would
pay the travelling expenses.

His British handlers wanted Byrnes to make a good impression. The first item on the agenda was guns, of course, but he also
claimed to have sources in the army who could tell him about troop
movements and the like. Even further, Art O'Brien reported enthusiastically on 3 December, 'In addition to the other matters I understand that he will also be able to give you a copy of the ABC code
from the same party. This will be useful to you; He may also have
other documents which he will take with him.' These 'other documents' were encoded telegrams gleefully composed by Basil Thomson
himself. Collins replied, 'I shall be sending to him on Monday
evening at about 7.30. This will give him time to have had a meal
after arriving.' Byrnes arrived at the Granville as 'John Jameson', a
traveller for Keith Prowse & Co., a music company. What follows is
an excerpt of his report, the only account in existence of a British
agent's meeting with Michael Collins:

He was met at the time appointed by a Runner who blindfolded
him for the last five or six hundred yards of the journey to the
meeting place. The house in which the meeting took place was
near Redmonds Hill and, as far as can be judged, was the house

of a Confectioner and Baker in an Alley off St Georges Street south of the Fruit and Poultry Market.

Upon the bandages being removed from his eyes No 8 [Byrnes] found himself in a small room barely furnished and confronted by Michael Collins and McCabe [Liam Tobin?] and another man who was not introduced.

Collins at once spoke to 8 of their recent meeting in London and asked him whether he understood the situation in Ireland, stating that the Military were trying to suppress them and that they were being closely watched. He warned 8 that he must on no account recognize any of them in the street or in public places, and that he should not be seen in any place which was known to be connected with the Sinn Fein movement. He might even go so far as to display antipathy to the cause in any public demonstration. [Collins. gave the same advice to his other agents.]

No 8 suggested that the Sinn Feiners should fraternize with the troops stationed in the country and that the Dances and Social Functions should be encouraged for this purpose. Collins immediately agreed with this suggestion and handed to No 8 a list of troops and their stations indicating that those underlined in red were most antagonistic to the cause. No 8 indicated that it was impossible to visit these troops in order to test their feeling in the matter unless he had a few pounds with which to treat them – this was agreed and later in the week No 8 received a sum of money for this purpose which was sent to him by a Runner.

No 8 is convinced that this man COLLINS is the Chief Director of all active movement amongst the Sinn Feiners and that he has now taken the place of De Valera owing to the long absence of the latter.

Although Collins does not take any active part in the shooting affairs there seems to be no doubt that he is the organizer.

Byrnes also met with various socialists and one McCallam (unknown), who:

expressed great surprise that 8 had had an interview with Collins and said that 8 must have come on a very important mission. He further stated that Collins would be a very difficult man to take as so many people were prepared to assist him in eluding the Police ... He stated that if Collins were taken his followers were prepared to put Dublin flat. We rely on Collins more than on any man in Ireland – he plans everything including the shooting ... It is a wonderful organization ... He stated that Collins was still in Dublin and was very much upset by the recent raids, but was not frightened and he was being well looked after.

Collins himself reported to O'Brien simply that Byrnes 'has duly arrived and has been interviewed by three of us – I shall report developments later on'. Still, he was hooked as well, and British intelligence now had their man on the inside.

Byrnes returned to England with his report, but went back to Ireland two days later on a fresh urgent invitation. This time he reported having 'twice seen the leader, the second time in his own house [probably Batt O'Connors), after the most meticulous precautions'.

In fact the second rendezvous did not go that smoothly, to Art O'Brien's proprietorial dismay. On 17 December he complained to Collins that 'You kept him waiting four days and never showed; I advised him to return tomorrow – and I advise *you* to meet him as he has important information.' To which Collins replied, 'There has been a slight misunderstanding over last week-end arrangements ... However, he is being looked up at once.'

Jackpot! Regular meetings with Collins, a tour of his haunts, and introductions to the IRA headquarters staff. Number 8 was kept busy, and Isham spent a celebratory New Year's Eve in the Shelbourne Hotel – Dublin's finest. Meanwhile, Collins's and O'Brien's messages vibrated with the happy hum of satisfied customers:

Collins to O'Brien, 2 January 1920:

He has paid another visit since bringing with him a very useful document and so far as we are concerned here we are satisfied with the results ...

6 January:

You might inform him that I have received the communications that were sent for him to the Granville Hotel. You might ask him, when you see him, if he could get the concluding portion of the Poem [coded document?] he sent me. Two lines I think must be missing.

12 January:

I should certainly have mentioned in my former memo to you that I had taken up with him the very point that you deal with, and his answer was that the trip for his firm would be a business trip and that he had every reason to think that it would be successful from a business point of view. His firm also takes the same view and are rather pressing him to make the trip for this reason. In these circumstances you would not of course incur any financial liability, except for the ordinary out of pocket expenses which you mention.

13 January:

Jameson – in town this morn. I shall see him during the day.

O'Brien to Collins, 15 January:

Jameson – reported his interview with you was very satisfactory. It transpired that Jameson himself is a Rep. of the Soviet Govt here. [This was a new one: was it the spy or his masters inflating his importance?]

Then came fateful doubting words:

Collins to O'Brien, 16 January:

Jameson I had been trying to fix him definitely in my own mind and had concluded that he had some such position as you tell me of.

Some of the letters are missing, but it seems that Collins was having second thoughts about Byrnes and that O'Brien had tried to reassure him as to his man's bona fides. It didn't work. On the 20th, as 'Jameson' was due for his next – fifth? – visit, Collins sent O'Brien the following:

Jameson It is rather a pity that the arrangement to come over has been made for so early a date. Unfortunately I shall not be available for at least three weeks and my call away has been so sudden that I have not been able to make the necessary arrangements with anybody else for dealing with such a subject. It is possible that within a week I shall be able to make the necessary arrangements by means of correspondence, but if possible at all, hold back J. as I fear it would be a waste of time to come at the moment.

This was actually a lie: he wasn't going anywhere, but he needed a quick excuse to fob off Byrnes. What had tipped him off? There are many different versions of how Byrnes got caught. They are contradictory and unreliable, but all mention police raids on the houses and offices he had just visited. These raids may well have aroused suspicion, but it is just as likely – given the continued faith in him over at least four previous trips to Dublin – that these became significant only *after* he became an object of suspicion.

In fact Collins was trying to 'fix him definitely' in his mind because an intelligence source in the Dublin police had informed him that there was a man from London who was an active British spy. He went through the likely candidates in a message to O'Brien marked 'special' and 'private', and concluded:

What I have to say with regard to him [Jameson] will probably be somewhat of a thunderbolt to you. I believe we have the man or one of them. I have absolutely certain information that the man who came from London met and spoke to me, and reported that I was growing a moustache to Basil Thompson [*sic*].

That Collins was growing a moustache (something he would, oddly, later deny) did indeed make it into military intelligence files. Here was a rare moment of rushed anxiety, of near-panic: 'I am not quite certain. My note [presumably from his police informant] is not very clear.' How much does 'Jameson' know? Whom did he talk to? What did I tell him? Where did he go? What people and which addresses are compromised – in Dublin and London? Meanwhile, suspicion was rapidly blossoming into certainty:

Collins to O'Brien, 22 January:

James. My opinion is stronger and stronger ever since.

The next day, however, an 'astonished' and infuriated Collins was told that, contrary to his instructions to O'Brien, Byrnes had arrived back in Dublin. In fact Art O'Brien had been hit by a car on his way to address a rally in London. He made the speech, trouper that he was, but collapsed afterwards and did not receive the message to stop Byrnes. Sean McGrath, fresh out of jail, replied for him:

> Unfortunately I did not get your memo in time to delay his movements ... The information is somewhat disconcerting. I shall be glad if you keep me informed.

Collins wrote back the next day:

> I am most awfully sorry to hear of Art's accident, and do hope most sincerely that it is not more serious than you think. Even though his absence is a great inconvenience he should not return to the office too soon.

Nevertheless: 'I would ask that this matter be referred to Art at once and that I be informed.' Art, now bedridden at home, replied, declaring himself 'disappointed' and 'anxious':

> The incident (or rather the incidents) in connection with *J.* were most unfortunate, i.e. the delays, mishaps, etc. Had it not been for my accident I should have gone over at the weekend to consult you as to a plan of action. However as this is not possible, and as *J.* is now over there you will, I take it, deal with the matter.

Byrnes was told that Collins was away on holiday. He met repeatedly with Liam Tobin in lieu of the suddenly absent mastermind, and discussed at length his fantastical offers to subvert the British garrison. He was finally fobbed off with the promise of £1,000 to lubricate his efforts: 'The idea was agreed to and that I better leave by boat that night.' Tobin's relief at good riddance seems to waft from the page, and Byrnes's dimness was further emphasized by Tobin's other promises: 'I thought it was better to go on their Council as a Propaganda Minister so that no doubt when I am next in Wales [Ireland] I shall be formally initiated on to the Central Council...'

Meanwhile the special inquiry into the man the IRA's Intelligence Department now code-named 'Corry' was going slowly. All they really knew, it turned out, was his declared employment with Keith Prowse & Co. as a salesman of mechanical pianos to cinemas. The company itself would tell them nothing. The day before Byrnes left Dublin, an anxious Collins – no doubt looking over his shoulder

– demanded that London provide a conclusive report: *'Jameson* – reply favourably or unfavourably.' But on 2 February he informed McGrath and O'Brien (presumably on the basis of his own sources) that

> There is little doubt now that my estimate of this man was entirely correct. Of course there is just a lingering hope, but I shall report more fully as things develop.

With Byrnes returned to England, he regained his composure:

> I shall only have to retain my soul in patience until I get the details verbally. I shall be glad to hear the result of the inquiries from K.P and Co. Shall be glad as well to know whether or not there is any report of him these days.

Needless to say, Byrnes did not get his £1,000, was not named Minister of Propaganda – and did not take the hint. Or rather Isham and Thomson didn't. What is more pathetic than a spy whose cover is blown but refuses to accept it? On 9 February Byrnes reappeared in London, as Sean McGrath immediately and breathlessly reported:

> *Corry.* This man rang up office [of the Irish Self-Determination League] this afternoon, and made appointment at 5 pm at Restaurant. We had a chat for 5 minutes. He said he met Tobin in Dublin, and was informed you would not be back until the end of Feb, and that Tobin agreed with him that he could do more useful work this side. He said he arrived in London Saturday morning. He has asked me to tell A[rt]. that information of the moving of *80* thousand men to Ireland and that Martial Law is contemplated, that he was anxious to do propaganda work among them, and it would mean visiting Yorkshire, Salisbury and Edinburgh. He mentioned a code which requires to be safely sent over. He gave me a similar card to one shown to our people.
>   He is not known by *Keith Prowse and Co..* He also mentioned he had friends in War Office. I pretended ignorance of all matters in connection with his visit to Ireland.

A week later Byrnes was back to see McGrath, insisting that O'Brien delegate some of his duties to him and complaining that his letters to Dublin got no reply. McGrath again refused 'to allow him to tell me anything'. A few days after that Byrnes tried to see O'Brien, but was refused admittance on the grounds of ill health. Collins approved, and told McGrath, 'Total ignorance is your position, but keep closely in touch with Art.' Presumably Byrnes and his handlers thought that re-establishing his connection with O'Brien was the key to resuming his mission.

On the 20th Collins was still not sure what to do:

> I may have something to say later regarding this man, but not until the end of the month as it is as well to leave him under the impression that I am away. He may get a line from someone who is acting for me. His communications have been received, but if he asks you again your position will be of course that you know nothing of whether they have or not.

Collins wanted to consult with Sam Maguire, still the senior IRB man in London, but by this point he was no longer in a hurry. After all, 'if Sam can work on his holidays it would save expense.' In any case, whatever was to be done, 'he [Byrnes/Jameson/Corry] certainly should be kept away.'

Despite this sudden and obvious cold shoulder, Byrnes returned to the Granville Hotel for what would be the last time on 28 February. Republicans were ordered to avoid him, but by simply wandering about central Dublin and looking in likely places he ran into them anyway – including Joe O'Reilly, Collins's chief errand boy. In the meantime, bizarrely, he took to buying pet birds, which he kept in a cage in his room. Boredom? Loneliness? Nerves?

On 2 March several men called to take him to Collins, so they said. They were members of the Squad. They took a tram north to Glasnevin, walked him to a lane near a farm, and told him they were going to kill him. Depending on who tells the story, he either insisted on his innocence or confessed and said he would die for the King. Either way, they shot him at least twice and left his body to be found by the next passer-by.

THE JAMESON CASE was the single most serious breach of IRA security, and the most embarrassing. Blame circulated widely and freely, with no one to accept it. This explains why there are so many – and such contradictory – stories about Byrnes/Jameson: those involved wanted to get their version on the record. Many of the principals claimed afterwards to have seen through him at once, and to have thought up elaborate tricks to prove his guilt. One thing is certain: it wasn't Collins who found him out – Collins had to be convinced to see sense, and didn't until it was almost too late. Collins's own verdict? 'Yes indeed the mishaps were very unfortunate. Of course they cannot be helped now.'

Before moving on, however, he couldn't help letting O'Brien know who was ultimately at fault:

> By the way, with regard to the original introduction my recollection is that he was sent along to you by some of our friends in London, and after some communication with him you mentioned the matter to me.

Oddly enough, O'Brien was thinking the same thing about Collins:

> I wonder if you can carry your mind back to the channel of introduction through which J. came to me. You made some inquiries at the time and were satisfied that we could go ahead.

In the end, no heads rolled and the verdict of history is simple: IRA 1, Brits 0. British intelligence had almost nothing to show for their efforts. But Byrnes and Isham had played it perfectly in setting Collins and company up. It is conceivable that Collins, Tobin, O'Brien, Mulcahy and others could all have been caught and convicted with a bit more cunning and effort on Byrnes's part, or better planning from his handlers. Combined with the army's successful offensive in Munster in early 1920, this would have been a huge blow to the IRA. Richard Mulcahy, for one, was amazed that they'd escaped: 'What he was delaying about that prevented him getting us caught with him . . . I don't know.'

What made Collins's continued freedom even more remarkable is the fact that Byrnes was not alone. Almost the same story was re-enacted twice more in the early months of 1920. The first such instance involved H. H. Quinlisk, an ex-soldier who had been captured by the Germans in France and joined Roger Casement's Irish Brigade, which recruited prisoners of war to fight against Britain. A civil servant before the war, he was the son of a senior officer in the RIC. Quinlisk fetched up in the Munster Hotel on Mountjoy Street at the end of 1918 – by coincidence (it would seem) a boarding house favoured by Collins and many of his movement pals. He and

Collins became friends, and Collins helped him with some National Aid money and introduced him around – presumably on the strength of his association with Casement. He even got him a job at New Ireland Assurance.

Unfortunately this helpfulness set the tone for their relationship, as the parasitic Quinlisk always wanted more. According to Dick Walsh, a member of the Volunteer executive, by May 1919 Collins was getting tired of him 'and said that he would like to get rid of him'. He gave him £100 to leave the country, but Quinlisk apparently blew it at the Galway Races and came back again. At this point he 'was told by Collins very blunt that he was finished as far as Collins was concerned, and would receive no further assistance from him'.

Quinlisk then turned to blackmail, and when that didn't work he tried to sell what he knew to the police. In November he wrote to Dublin Castle complaining that 'the scoundrel Michael Collins has treated me scurvily and I now am going to wash my hands of the whole business.' He was interviewed by G Division, and as usual it was Ned Broy who typed up the results and, of course, passed them on to Collins. Confronted, Quinlisk claimed he was a double agent for the IRA and continued to plead for money. He got nothing from either side, and Collins left Mountjoy Street so as not to be found. Like 'Jameson', Quinlisk searched high and low for him but was told he was out of town. Finally Collins's lieutenants decided to find out what he was really up to. He was told that Collins was in a particular hotel in Cork city, and immediately passed the information on to the police. The Cork IRA kidnapped the terminally stupid informer and shot him dead outside the city. He was buried in a pauper's grave in the workhouse grounds, his funeral unattended.

Another close shave, and another wasted opportunity for 'the G'. The value of having agents like Broy inside the police was confirmed by this episode alone, but once again Collins on his own had been fantastically reluctant to act decisively against his former friend. It doesn't say much for his reputation for ruthlessness or street smarts, but it does reflect his abiding reluctance to have someone killed without having absolute proof and giving them a second or third chance to stop. Such attitudes were notably absent in the rest of the IRA once a nationwide war on informers was launched a year later.

The third dead spy was one Patrick Molloy, 'tracked down and shot' in broad daylight on a crowded street by three men on 24

March 1920 (three weeks after Byrnes) according to the aghast *Irish Times* report. A clerk at army headquarters, he was dressed in civilian clothes and carried documents identifying himself as 'Private Smith'. According to IRA memoirs, he was working for military intelligence, was outed by Lily Mernin, and was killed by the hard-working Squaddies. In the meantime he had pretended to be a double agent and offered to get arms – a combination of Byrnes's and Quinlisk's appeals that worked well enough for him to get to know Liam Tobin and to set up the now-familiar meeting with Collins at Batt O'Connor's house (where Collins had also met Byrnes). When the ever-trusting Collins was confronted by evidence of Molloy's guilt, he angrily ('Sold again!') agreed to his assassination. Alan Bell was killed two days later for good measure, and the first British spy network was no more.

THE SECOND ROUND would be fought by a more formidable team. In April 1920 both the army and the police were shaken up. General Nevil Macready was appointed to head Irish Command, and General Hugh Tudor was hired as Police Adviser and then made Chief of Police. Macready was an old hand at interventions in domestic crises – Belfast in the Home Rule Crisis, Welsh mining strikes, in 1910, the London police strike in 1919 – but Tudor was an artillery man with no experience of Ireland, politics or policing. A general was wanted to lead the British ex-soldiers now being recruited into the RIC (the 'Black and Tans'), and he got the job because he was good friends with Winston Churchill, the Secretary of State for War.

In an attempt at imposing a political solution, the Lloyd George government had also introduced a new Home Rule bill (the fourth), which spent most of 1920 passing through the House of Commons. The resulting Government of Ireland Act offered the usual limited self-government by a local parliament, only this time there would be two such parliaments: one in Dublin and one in Belfast. The northern Irish MPs would run the six north-eastern counties with Protestant majorities or large Protestant minorities – the same territory that Redmond and Carson had agreed on in the failed deal of 1916. This partition would keep the Ulster Unionist Party (and the Conservative members of Lloyd George's cabinet) happy and would satisfy the nationalist objection to Ireland being ruled from London. The bill was also intended to show that the government had an Irish policy. Less realistically, it was also supposed to undermine support for Sinn Fein and the IRA. In fact, the proposal was dismissed as worthless by every shade of nationalist opinion, so the Government of Ireland Act had no effect on the guerrilla war.

As part of the revamped counter-insurgency effort, it had been decided to unify the various intelligence services under police control. One of the problems in early 1920 had been a lack of coordination between different groups. Byrnes, Quinlisk and Molloy had reported to Scotland Yard, G Division and military intelligence respectively. Perhaps if each had known what the other was doing, and if information had been shared between handlers, events might have gone differently. Numerous veterans of Great War espionage were available for the job of Director of Intelligence: perhaps someone who had run agents in occupied Belgium or France. Nevertheless, the man hired to carry out this most critical task was Colonel Ormonde Winter, another artillery man, whose only distinction was being friends with Tudor. He cut a rather ludicrous monocled figure, and was considered a failure by Macready and his colleagues, but he did institute an aggressive new system in Dublin using British ex-officers as agents.

These 'hush-hush men' (as they called themselves) were mostly brought over from England and based themselves in hotels and houses around the city centre under civilian cover – often living with their wives. They acted in small groups, devoting themselves to ambushes and raids. Several were killed on the job, but, apart from Sean Treacy's death in a gun battle in October (he was one of South Tipperary's 'big Four', along with Robinson and Breen), there is no record of them killing anyone before November 1920, either in the movement or outside it. They have been lumped together with the Black and Tans and the Auxiliaries – a special force of ex-officers attached to the regular police – as perpetrators of bloody reprisals, and this reputation has been given as a moral justification for their murder. It is false. The only specific killing usually attributed to the 'hush-hush men' was that of John Lynch, a Co. Limerick Sinn Feiner, in a hotel on 23 September 1920, by anonymous men in well-covered uniforms. Lynch had reportedly brought Loan money to deliver to Collins, and he had been much sought after by his local constabulary. It was speculated that he had been mistaken for Liam Lynch, the commander of the North Cork IRA Brigade, but the truth seems to be (insofar as David Neligan reported it) that among the murder party were RIC men – perhaps up from Limerick to identify him – and a regular-army officer on court-martial duty. Another man present may well have been an intelligence officer. It is unknown who did the shooting, but official claims that Lynch had fired on them were obvious lies.

Michael Collins is often quoted (perhaps apocryphally) as saying that he had to get them before they got him. In fact it was the other way around. The Dublin Special Branch was indeed responsible for murder and torture, but the hush-hush men did not begin murdering and torturing until *after* a dozen of them were killed in their homes by the IRA on the morning of 21 November 1920 – a day that would become known as Bloody Sunday.

Bloody Sunday was meant to be part of a cross-channel 'spectacular' involving both the crippling of British intelligence in Dublin and the simultaneous sabotage of Liverpool docks and warehouses, Manchester power plants, and London timber yards. The idea was to meet British reprisals in Ireland with a massive counter-reprisal. Collins was part of the planning, but it was a joint GHQ operation, not the Napoleonic master stroke depicted in Neil Jordan's film or in biographies. Rory O'Connor, still Director of Engineering, ran the show in England, while Dick McKee did most of the organizing in Dublin. The Intelligence Department supplied some of the names and addresses, but the information was easy to get – the mysterious Englishmen who lived in groups and went out at night were hardly inconspicuous. Other targets were added to the list by the Dublin Brigade. Frank Thornton claims to have proved that each one was 'secret service' to a joint meeting of the Dail cabinet and the GHQ, but some were not intelligence officers as such but court-martial officers charged with prosecuting suspects rather than finding or capturing them. At least one man was wrongly identified as a secret agent: an Irish vet who had come to Dublin to buy horses. Never one to take responsibility for errors, Collins blamed it on faulty brigade intelligence.

In the event, the plans for England were captured when Mulcahy's office was raided, and only the Liverpool arson attacks went ahead. The Bloody Sunday operation took place as planned, involving the Squad and scores of regular Volunteers. Neither the 'hush-hush men' nor their superiors had ever contemplated such attacks – no 'G' man or spy had ever been killed at home – and so they had taken no precautions. Eight separate houses were targeted by the IRA hit men, and twelve men were killed, while several others were wounded. Two Auxiliaries ran into one of the assassination teams and were also shot dead. No guerrillas were injured.

The day earned the title of Bloody Sunday not from this episode, however, but from another massacre – of civilian spectators at a GAA match, by enraged Auxiliaries. And, at the end of the day, British intelligence had its own revenge when it captured Dick McKee and Peadar Clancy, the brigade quartermaster, who were promptly shot 'while trying to escape' from Dublin Castle. These murders threw a terrible shadow over the day for Collins and the Dublin IRA, who had lost their leader and chief strategist. As Liam Tobin put it, 'The arrest of Dick and Peadar knocked all the good out of it . . . we had no sense of jubilation as the enemy had evened up on us.'

Nor did the killings end the intelligence threat. While the Dublin Special Branch was eviscerated, Bloody Sunday prompted a backlash that sent the IRA reeling. Detention without trial was introduced, and, freed from their legal leashes, intelligence officers were able to round up hundreds of IRA officers in a matter of weeks. Soon martial law was declared in Munster, and informers were coming forward to reveal the location of hideouts and arms dumps. Many units were hard-pressed just to survive, and many of the Dail cabinet were driven underground. Arthur Griffith was caught. Bloody Sunday temporarily eased some pressure on the top echelons of the IRA by wiping out many of their immediate pursuers, but it had the opposite effect everywhere else. And within a few months the British intelligence effort in Dublin was back on track and on Collins's scent once again.

THANKS TO BLOODY SUNDAY and the Intelligence Department, contemporary legend and British vilification would crown Collins 'Commander-in-Chief' of the IRA, and supporters and admirers lauded him as 'the man who won the war' (a phrase coined by Arthur Griffith, of all people). Political opponents scoffed at the stories and inflated titles, but biographical convention would eagerly dub him a military genius, 'the founder of modern guerrilla warfare, the first freedom fighter'.

In reality, Michael Collins did not plan, start, direct or control the war. No one did – no one person or headquarters that is. Most

Volunteer units outside Dublin had been formed locally, elected their own leaders, funded, armed, motivated and trained themselves, planned and mounted their own operations, and succeeded or failed, with very little input from headquarters beyond demands for dues and reports. There were no front lines or rear areas. Each brigade operated in its own territory almost exclusively, requiring little coordination with neighbours. If some busybody organizer showed up, bristling with manuals and notebooks, he might well be sent packing if he tried to tell the local boys what to do or how to do it. Senior staff, including Collins, almost never went outside Dublin after mid-1919, so country commandants had to come to them – not surprisingly, they often arrived in Dublin with a chip on their shoulders. They fought their wars all on their own.

The IRA's only decisive military advantage in its war against British rule lay in the narrow realm of 'secret service': the covert competition to penetrate opposing organizations and prevent the enemy doing the same. In this game of spy vs. spy, Collins and his men scored a hat-trick. Not only did they develop well-placed agents throughout the government, they were able to turn some of the opposing players against their own side. And, by intimidating or killing detectives, intelligence officers and their agents, they protected themselves, and the movement, from being penetrated in turn. Despite repeated attempts right up to the July 1921 truce, British intelligence agencies never succeeded in infiltrating the underground.

Once again, however, we must keep politics in mind, as Collins certainly did. What set Collins apart from his fellow guerrilla commandants at this point was that he was thinking not just of war but also of peace and how to achieve it as quickly and advantageously as possible. Bloody Sunday might be only a bloody nose rather than a death blow, but, if it bought some time and delivered a temporary shock to the system, that might be good enough to open up a political way forward. As his anxious queries to 'Jameson' demonstrated, in late 1919 he was already worried about what would happen if the British army was reinforced and given a free hand, and in mid-1920 he was contemplating the possibility that public opinion might, under pressure, accept Home Rule after all, forcing republicans back into the wilderness. Their revolutionary momentum would not last for ever; their opportunity, if lost, might not come again.

16: A Day at the Office with Michael Collins

I remember one morning about a quarter past nine ... I was casually watching the traffic coming from the direction of Butt Bridge ... when who should I see but Michael Collins cycling in the stream of traffic ... He did not notice me and passed on. He wore a high quality soft hat, dark grey suit, as usual, neatly shaved and with immaculate collar and tie, as always, seeming to be ready for the photographer. His bicycle was of first-class quality and fitted with a lamp and many other accessories. He looked like a bank clerk or stockbroker or 'something in the city' and cycled on as if he owned the street.

(Ned Broy)

COLLINS'S WORK DAYS – Monday through Saturday, and often part of Sunday – began early and ended late. 'The office' was more a state of mind than a location: 'business-like' was his highest term of praise, and he lived up to his ideal. He had been obsessed with tidiness and punctuality since childhood – his desk and his person were always neat and tidy, and he was always on time. Those who weren't got lectured, sworn at and swiftly fired if they didn't shape up.

He worked wherever he went, and he moved about constantly between offices and meeting places in every quadrant of the city, on foot, on his bicycle or by taxi. His vast and volatile energy was the quality most remarked upon by those who knew or met him, and all his colleagues would pay awed tribute to the unmatchable quantity of work he was able to produce or transact. As Kevin O'Higgins put it, he 'crowded into every day 17 or 18 hours of grim, intensive work' – an attribute that became part of his public image, much lauded in the Dail and in the press in 1922. And, despite a growing tendency to badger and micromanage, this work was carried out efficiently and effectively, thanks to years of training and practice in London and in the movement. If Collins was a genius, files and memos were his medium.

Since his record of sociability is also remarkable, with sessions in pubs or hotel rooms a nightly occurrence, almost invariably followed by practical jokes and horseplay, and visitors unfailingly entertained, the obvious corollary is that Collins got very little sleep – as his anxious hostesses could attest. When he did sleep, he slept badly – a problem that may have begun in prison in 1918, and which he often complained of in years after. In a letter written in August of the same year, he told Austin Stack that he 'read practically all night as sleep deserted me', and by September 1921 he admitted to Kitty Kiernan that 'to prove my scorn of a night without sleep I remained out of bed last night until 4 this morning . . . But it's useless, I'm getting too old!'

Collins often didn't go to bed until well after midnight, and he was usually up before anyone else as well. As Sean MacEoin (and many others) attested, 'He slept from about one o'clock in the morning until four, and then while the rest of us were trying to pull ourselves together he insisted that there was too much time lost in sleep.' His weary subordinates had to put up with him whether they liked it or not. Ned Broy, who was with Collins in London for the Treaty negotiations, describes the frankly bullying routine:

> He duly pulled us all out of bed in the morning whether we complained of fatigue or not, and repeated the process when going to bed in the small hours, unless one had taken the precaution of locking the bedroom door when retiring. He discovered that the feet of some of our beds were hinged and the legs could be bent back leaving the bed sloping towards the foot. I remember looking into Emmet Dalton's bedroom one night and seeing him in his bed with the bed making an angle of thirty degrees with the floor. As Collins had not yet come in I asked Emmet what happened to his bed. He said Collins would come in to bend his legs later on, and to save him the bother, Emmet had bent them up himself.

Collins was one of those rare people known as 'short sleepers'. That is to say, he simply did not need to sleep seven or eight hours a night to function well. Many politicians and businesspeople have claimed the same as the basis for their success – Margaret Thatcher and Winston Churchill, for example – thanks to their resulting enormous advantage in productivity. In some cases such people napped during the day to maintain their energy, but there is no record of Collins ever doing this (unless his secretaries and sidekicks were covering for him). He did complain of overwork and exhaustion at times ('My work is increasing every day . . . when I have got rid of one routine thing another claims my attention, so that no matter what additional help I get, I am always more and more busy'), but he was able to maintain his work rate almost ceaselessly up until his death.

Here, then, was the secret of his success: he worked harder, longer, on more tasks than anyone else. However, being a short sleeper is not just an arbitrary gift of time: it also appears alongside certain familiar personality traits – busyness, ambition and confidence. This dual pattern of sleep and activity can be further linked to aggression, competitiveness, impatience and irritability: so far, so Collins. Furthermore, and most interesting of all, there is a tendency for such personalities to place themselves under time pressure, to be driven by a sense of urgency, of time running out, and to solve problems by sheer effort rather than reflection.

In other words, it may be that Collins not only felt a political commitment to his work and a furious desire for success: he may also have felt an inherent compulsion – compounded by circumstance – to drive himself and others as hard as possible, and a blinding intolerance for those who challenged him or seemed not to measure up and therefore got in his way. This can be detected as far back as his London GAA days. His work was his life in more ways than one.

AFTER LEAVING THE National Aid premises on Bachelor's Walk during the conscription crisis, Collins set up shop in Cullenswood House – formerly the home of St Enda's, Patrick Pearse's private school – in much more upmarket surroundings in leafy south Dublin. The 'republican hut', a disused building next door, effectively became Volunteer headquarters. Dick Mulcahy lived and worked there as well, and it became a hang-out for Collins's crowd.

In mid-1919 he began working regularly in the Dail offices on Harcourt Street, first at No. 6 – Sinn Fein headquarters – and then at No. 76, both of which were raided in late 1919 (he was just missed). The Department of Finance was moved to Mary Street, where it shared space for a while with the IRA's also relocated GHQ. A raid in 1921 forced Finance further up the street, with a spin-off office being set up in St Andrew Street. George McGrath's counting house found space above Corrigans' the undertakers (literally watching over its buried gold). Another of Collins's secretaries, Evelyn Lawless, worked alone in Camden Street until she gave it up in the summer of 1920 to enter a convent. The Intelligence Department began life in the New Ireland Assurance offices, but in 1920 it set itself up in Crow Street. Collins himself established a private office at a house on Mespil Road later that year. Here he was helped by Jenny Mason, formerly de Valera's secretary, but now his own indispensable assistant and confidante. This too was lost to a raid in 1921, along with many of his files, whereupon he took refuge with Finance on Mary Street until a new den was prepared for him at Harcourt Terrace.

Most of these offices were above or behind shops, the idea being that people going in and out would blend in with the traffic on the street. Collins's personal cubbyholes – where visitors weren't encouraged – were private homes complete with residents to provide cover. Most had secret rooms, closets or other hiding spaces for people or files: even British investigators who uncovered some of them were impressed by their ingenuity. None was defended as such. Escape was the only option in case of being found, and nearly every office had its share of near misses or else experienced the final, dreaded moment when the lorries pulled up outside and heavy boots could be heard on the stairs.

Collins's day at the office was largely taken up with correspondence. Letters, memos and messages poured in constantly, brought by couriers (especially Joe O'Reilly), by Jenny Mason or Alice Lyons (his secretary in Finance at Mary Street), from Dail departments (or the Dail office itself, run by that vital cog Diarmuid O'Hegarty), from George McGrath in accounting, from de Valera in the US or from agents in Britain, arriving via other offices or from the various postal drops around the city. Collins prided himself on turning things around quickly, so output matched input. He had no trouble keeping three secretaries very busy. He was a great dictator – able to rattle off whole sentences in rapid succession on a long list of disparate topics, one letter after another. The shorthand versions would then be typed up for his signature before being sent on their way, no later than the next day if at all possible.

Collins would thus spend his time going through batches of paperwork as they arrived, digesting them, discharging a salvo of replies, and turning to another secretary or office while he waited for them to be processed, often switching back and forth between them over the course of a day. He would start work officially at nine o'clock (although he was up much earlier), usually in his private office on Camden Street/Mespil Road/Harcourt Terrace, deal first with whatever happened overnight, and then enter into that day's operations with Jenny Mason. Alice Lyons would drop by to deliver mail and pick up work, and would often spend an hour or two taking dictation or typing before returning to Mary Street. Later in the day Collins might visit the Finance office himself, do a few hours' work there, and ride off again on his bicycle.

There were also the inevitable meetings to attend. His own departments had regular internal meetings, and the GHQ met once a week, as did the Dail cabinet. The Volunteer executive met about once a month until mid-1920. Finance questions dominated the cabinet agenda and required particularly time-consuming preparations. Sinn Fein's leadership also met weekly and more or less openly until mid-1919, when police surveillance – and increasing irrelevance – closed them down. The IRB Supreme Council had its own schedule to keep, and Collins also managed to chair most of his MacDermott Circle meetings. On top of all that, he saw some of his police and prison guard agents on an almost daily basis.

Collins liked crisp, quick meetings that started on time, ended on time, and lasted an hour at most. Anything over that and he was liable to get up and leave. In the chair or out, he stuck to the agenda and the main issues: he wanted decisions, not discussion. No small talk or digressions, let alone inconclusive debate. In a statement that could stand as a personal motto, he told de Valera that 'it is practical work that counts, not speaking,' and his correspondence is littered with snide remarks about those who talked big but achieved little.

Headquarters and Executive meetings were most often held in the Dublin Typographical Society rooms on Gardiner Street, at least until Bloody Sunday (November 1920). The back rooms of cheap hotels in the Parnell Square area were also regular resorts. Other secret meetings were typically held in the homes of sympathizers who it was hoped were unknown to the police. IRB gatherings

generally seem to have been held on the north side of the city; Dail
and cabinet sessions most often on the more prosperous south side.
One frequent hostess was Julia O'Donovan, whose house was in
Rathgar:

> One night in the autumn of 1920 – my daughter thinks it was
> the night Sean Tracy [*sic*] was killed, 14th October – I came
> home and was told by her that a messenger – probably Joe
> O'Reilly – called to ask my permission for a meeting to be held
> that evening in the house. She gave permission and placed the
> usual refreshments in the drawing-room. She was rather indig-
> nant to find that one of those at the meeting – Frank Thornton
> or Tom Cullen – sent out for more refreshments. She had not
> expected so many visitors to come. She does not remember
> whether Gearoid [O'Sullivan] or Mick were there or how many
> visitors came as she only let in about the first half-dozen, some
> of whom were strangers to her. Frank Thornton or Tom Cullen
> let in all the others. We heard afterwards that Broy of the
> Detective Branch was there and that he brought a lot of others.
> The meeting, which lasted a couple of hours, was over when I
> returned from the Opera. We never knew what the meeting was
> about. We always refrained from showing any curiosity in such
> matters.

A similar conclave took place in the home of Alice Wordsworth
(one of the well-connected Stopford sisters) in Foxrock, one Thursday afternoon in June 1921:

> First to arrive was Dick Mulcahy who examined the house for
> any means of escape if the necessity arose. But the front and
> back doors were the only exits. There was not even a skylight.
> Then came Ginger O'Connell [Assistant Chief of Staff] and two
> or three others. They all came singly on bicycles and I opened
> the hall door to each in turn, mentioning my name to indicate
> that they had come to the right house. I saw an active figure
> dump his bicycle in the garden and run energetically up the
> steps, and when I opened the door saying 'Good afternoon, I am
> Mrs Wordsworth', the reply was, 'Pleased to meet you Mrs
> Wordsworth, I am Michael Collins.' I was much interested to
> see for myself that all the stories I had heard of the various
> disguises adopted by Michael Collins were completely without

foundation and that he never took any precautions of that sort, or indeed of any other as far as I could learn. Presently I glanced out the window and there were five bicycles stacked up in the front garden. I went to the door of the room where they were all sitting, put my head in and said, 'Are you all quite mad?' They looked up in surprise and I said, 'All those bicycles standing in the garden. They are just asking for trouble.' Michael Collins sprang up exclaiming, 'A brain wave!' and dashed down the steps and up again carrying a bicycle in each hand and depositing them in the hall. The rest followed suit. This is just an illustration of how careless of danger they had grown. When they were going Dick Mulcahy said they would like to come again the next day but one at the same time. This was arranged and they said good-bye and went off one by one.

In fact her house was raided by Auxiliaries the next day, just missing the IRA Director of Purchases, Liam Mellows.

When the office staff went home in the evening, Collins's second work day began, stretching from early evening to midnight and beyond. Wherever he had been that day, he usually ended up in Parnell Square (still officially known as Rutland Square), at the top of O'Connell Street. This and adjoining Parnell Street and North Frederick Street had been colonized by nationalist organizations for years, perhaps because of the cheap office and hotel space available as compared to the other side of the river. Here could be found the headquarters of the National Foresters, the National Volunteers (now under republican control), the Gaelic League and its radical Keating branch, and others. Around the corner at 36 Lower Gardiner Street was the Dublin Typographical Society. After 1916 this was radical territory: IRA and IRB territory. By mid-1920 it was also known to outsiders as 'Michael Collins territory', with Vaughan's Hotel on the square his clubhouse (referred to by insiders as 'the joint'). Kevin O'Shiel recaptures the scene in the back room on the hall floor:

When you opened the door of the Collins room, you would make out, through a fog of cigarette smoke, a considerable number of vigorous young men, sometimes as many as twenty, standing around; few seemed to sit in Vaughan's. On a large table in the centre of the room were tumblers and glasses containing the beverages of the company. You were not many minutes there before a certain thing became obvious to you – that one young man amongst them completely dominated the scene. That young man was Michael Collins ... Yes: Mick certainly dominated, quite naturally and unconsciously, all present in that room ... he successfully combined business with pleasure in a most remarkable way. Only a man of genius could have done that, particularly in his difficult conditions; and that, of course, was what he was. One moment you would see him talking rapidly and seriously to one of his men, or with bent head, listening intently to what he was saying, or, perhaps, skimming through a document or letter, handed to him. Having finished what he was talking about, or reading, he would abruptly dismiss his man, and call over to him someone else from the company that he wanted to talk to. Sometimes you would see him shaking his head energetically and arguing with a fellow, when suddenly the firm mouth would snap down and the man would move off – he had made his decision on the point. I have seen him occasionally in one of his tremendous rages, and tremendous and mighty they were, but they never lasted long ... The amount of highly important business he transacted in that smoky room must have been fabulous. Every now and then he would relax for a bit, joke, laugh and exchange stories with the fellows and you would think he had given over the business side of things; but presently he would be back in his job again, as some newcomer came along, perhaps a Volunteer or IRA leader up from some field of war in the country.

Here Collins met informally with intelligence men and agents, headquarters staffers, and IRB men and visitors from the provinces, Britain or abroad. Here too parties would be held – to see Harry Boland off to the United States, for example. These were all stag nights: no women entered this inner circle. It became so well known that he was to be found at Vaughan's Hotel that it is astonishing that his British pursuers never managed to do it. However, he did vary his watering holes once pursuit became more vigorous, with the nearby Kirwan's and Devlin's pubs becoming Joints Nos. 2 and 3, but his first loyalty remained with Vaughan's. Tom Barry's wedding reception – the social event of the republican season in the summer of 1921 – was held there, and Collins continued to drop in up until the outbreak of the Civil War in 1922, nearly getting himself killed in the process.

WHAT WAS MICHAEL COLLINS like to work for? Often intimidating, at least to begin with; brusque and demanding. Molly Ryan, Diarmuid O'Hegarty's secretary, recalled, 'I found him frightening at first. I thought him cross. He made some remark, such as: "I hope you will behave yourself."' Maire Comerford, whose memoirs provide an invaluable secretary's-eye view of the revolution, remembers him as

> a kind natured man, but foul mouthed, and on occasion very bad tempered. Mary Nelson once arrived from Glasgow with money for the Loan. In his office she found a girl all smeared with ink and tears. She was sitting before a very old typewriter. When Mary offered to help in correcting the obvious trouble the girl could only moan 'Oh, he is so angry' over and over again. Mary, now an indignant feminist, told her to wash her face and get ready to be on top of her job. When Mick stamped back into the room Mary had the machine and the work going. He asked her who the hell she was, and what she was doing there. She gave him back as good as she got, and he calmed down. He liked people with spunk, and his anger passed quickly.

She added, 'That was what made him a leader of volunteers,' and Molly Ryan herself declared, 'In a short time I changed my opinion about him and thought him a grand type of man.'

Collins made sure his people were paid quite well – they got rises at least once, and were fully compensated for overtime work, for example. He also ordered Christmas bonuses of an extra week's pay in 1920. Perhaps he hadn't forgotten his own years of desk drudgery with little to show for it. He was also dutifully protective of his female staffers, and made sure they got home safely at night.

The revolutionary typing pool was composed of young women, often just graduated from training colleges, whose families were usually deep in the movement or were well known to those who were. Joe O'Reilly knew Molly Ryan; everyone in Dublin knew Evelyn Lawless's father and brothers. Still, they would often be screened by one of the lieutenants before seeing Collins himself. Ever-increasing work meant he was usually on the lookout for new people, but he was particular – in July 1921 he wrote to Joe MacDonagh that 'I have been looking for a good assistant . . . for the past two or three months, but I haven't come across just the right person.' When Constance Markievicz recommended Mrs Eamonn Ceannt (widow of a Rising martyr) the response was '*Sorry No*. She is not adaptable enough for our service.'

When just the right person did appear, he or she was sometimes in another department – in which case it was time to mount a headhunting expedition. By mid-1921 Finance had six staff who had been transferred from other offices. In October 1921 George Mc-Grath talent-spotted one Tomas McCanna, who knew shorthand, typing and Irish (the holy trinity, and two better than Collins) and was of 'good appearance' to boot. The problem was, he worked in the Local Government Department, run by William Cosgrave. When Kevin O'Higgins, the assistant minister, objected to the attempted clerknapping, Collins wrote to Cosgrave that

> I shall eternally be grateful to you if you arrange a transfer – even a temporary one . . . Will you, therefore, use your persuasive powers with the assistant Minister. If it doesn't do, I shall only have to go and use my influence with his incoming Partner! [O'Higgins was about to be married.]

Here was yet another habit guaranteed to infuriate his fellow ministers. He had already tried to recruit O'Higgins as a secretary to the Treaty negotiation team, but O'Higgins had turned the job down in order to get married.

WHEN COLLINS finally finished his day's and night's work, 'home' could be almost anywhere in the city: any hotel room or private home where he could find a bed and a meal. Most times, however, he knew where he was going that night, and in fact he had a series of movement 'houses' where he was taken care of by a host of substitute sisters, mothers and uncles. These were a peculiar institution, vital to the revolution but as much organic as organized. Maire Comerford described the phenomenon best:

> 'Houses' were all-important, and the word had a different meaning from the usual one. A hunted man's house was not his home. It was the place where he could count on a bed and food,

and perhaps the news and some stimulating conversation. A man's 'house' or houses changed according as the enemy found them out, and he had to move on. Much more often than not a man and his houses were complete strangers when first they met . . . This business of houses . . . this was women's work.

Collins didn't have to go permanently on the run until 1920, however, and before he had to rely on 'houses' he did have a kind of home. After Christmas 1916 – and apparently after he had been thrown out of another house for using bad language – he moved to a boarding house at 44 Mountjoy Street, known as the Munster Hotel, or 'Grianan na nGaedheal' to the initiated. It was run by Miss McCarthy, a den mother to a whole generation of revolutionaries. Fionan Lynch, her nephew, had joined Gearoid O'Sullivan there in 1912, whereupon both joined the Keating branch of the Gaelic League, around the corner in Parnell Square. Like the Keatings, the denizens of '44', as it was known, tended to be Munstermen – half a dozen or so of them. Sean MacDermott stayed there to avoid arrest, and arms were cached in the ceiling. Once Collins got to know O'Sullivan in 1916, he hung out there too; he was lodging close by, on the North Circular Road. The night before the Rising '44' was raided, as the address was found on the body of Con Keating, one of the men who died in a car accident on the way to meet the German arms ship off Cahirciveen, Co. Kerry.

In 1917 O'Sullivan was away teaching, and 'Fin' Lynch was in Lewes prison with Ashe and de Valera, but the same atmosphere of sedition and high jinks prevailed, with Collins now the star boarder. The police were well aware of where he was, however, and in the 1918 crisis he moved to the Cullenswood House 'hut'. He was back in '44' after the election, but, once the double agent Quinlisk had moved in and turned against him, Mountjoy Street got too hot again. After this, one of the first places he stayed was Julia O'Donovan's house, along with Gearoid O'Sullivan (her cousin). They left in February 1920, but Collins continued to use her house for meetings and as a clearing house for guns. He and O'Sullivan came back for Sunday lunch every week up to the July 1921 truce.

Collins often ate with good friends Batt and Mrs O'Connor (who fed a great many people in these years), but he rarely slept there as it was too well known. Far better was a house that was completely unsuspected, which Batt set up in 1921 when he arranged for Mary Woods to rent a house on St Mary's Road for Collins to use. As cover, Mrs Woods and her husband (who also looked after Liam Mellows when he came back from the United States in 1920) would go there at night: 'I used to stay there to get Mick's breakfast and my husband used to stay there with me. Mick did not come there every night ... For Mick he [Mr Woods] had the highest regard and during 1921 breakfasted with him on many mornings.'

The Woodses never knew if Collins was coming or not, or how late, or whether he might be preceded by a police raid:

> One night my husband and I were in the hall on our way to bed when we heard a shuffling and noise outside. We opened the door. The night was very dark. We dared not put the hall light on [because of a British-imposed curfew]. Some one or two men were at the gate. There was a muttering or whispering. My husband was in his slippers, I in my stockinged feet. We went quickly to the gate, Collins was picking himself up swearing softly as he picked up the bike.

When a replacement housekeeper was needed for Mrs Woods, Collins was very picky and turned down several candidates. Eventually, Mrs Comerford, mother of Maire, was suggested, Collins came to tea to look her over and 'it was settled'. According to Maire:

> Mother was impressed by Mick's indifference to the curfew law. He was out at all hours of the night. The strong likelihood that he might be caught abroad in some volley racked street made no difference. His escort used to leave him at the door, and then go their dangerous way, certainly not to homes of their own.

Looking after Collins (and Liam Mellows, Austin Stack, Desmond Fitzgerald etc.) certainly brought out maternal instincts. Mother Comerford 'was distressed because he was a bad feeder, and hardly seemed to sleep at all. She used to make up two beds in his room and both would be tossed in the morning.' Mrs Woods 'could not help loving Michael, for despite malignant rumours to the contrary, Michael was a selfless man. Once I said to Mrs Batt O'Connor "Michael is neglected by himself. His meals, if you can call them meals, are irregular. Often he has only a bowl of soup late in the day when he runs into us and I get it for him."' Collins could take care of himself in other respects, however. Mrs O'Connor had Collins and Harry Boland overnight once, and when she looked in on them 'Mick had his arm resting on the little table by the bed, with his revolver lying beside it.'

Nor was Collins always the ideal guest. Mrs O'Connor again:

> Mick Collins was one of these four [with Harry Boland, Austin Stack and Cathal Brugha] that I knew the least because he was always too engrossed in his important occupations to take part in small talk. But the women who worked for him and with him overlooked that characteristic in him and did not expect anything different from him because they knew how much he had on his mind.

The men who knew him don't recall an absence of small talk, but Phyllis Ryan – Dick Mulcahy's sister-in-law, and a republican activist in her own right – had the same experience: 'He was a rough type and more or less ignored the women.' Mulcahy's wife, Mary (Min), thought the same, and Maud Griffith, wife of Arthur, didn't like him either. De Valera once wrote that Collins (and Arthur Griffith) had a problem working with women. Collins may have seen female activists as the servant class of the revolution, rarely as colleagues or comrades, more often as landladies, maids or cooks.

Collins lived under constant pressure of duty and danger after November 1919, but in other ways his existence was the stuff of bachelor fantasies. He was looked after by doting women (and sometimes men). He never had to cook or clean or sew – or even watch his own bank balance. He could spend hours and days with his pals, who just happened to be his comrades. 'Work' meant meeting in pubs and bars on a nightly basis, drinking and smoking. As he himself said several times, he was not someone to seek comforts in the ordinary sense, but his extended work days were mixed with a great deal more pleasure and fun than was available to most ordinary clerks and working men. Here was the life of patriotic and purposeful endeavour dreamed of by revolutionary ascetics. As lived by Collins, it at times looked more like a revolutionary frat house.

OFFICE WORK also inevitably means office politics. Perhaps equally inevitable in anyone's upward career in any organization are competitors, rivals and detractors. How much more so is this the case among politicians, and most of all around a cabinet table? So we must take some measure of tension and conflict within the republican leadership as a given. When Eamon de Valera left Ireland in early June 1919 he left behind a band of brothers, buoyed by the defeat of conscription, the 1918 election victory and the freeing of the prisoners in England, with old disagreements swallowed by the grand enterprise of the revolution. When he returned a year and a half later, at Christmas 1920, after Arthur Griffith's arrest, he found factions, squabbles and resentments – with Collins at the root of almost all of them.

Biographers and historians have sided with Collins in his feuds with fellow ministers and directors, accepting his claim that he was only promoting efficiency and attacking error and sloth, if perhaps a little too zealously. Those who disliked or opposed him were carpers or else motivated by jealousy of his power and growing reputation. The evidence suggests otherwise. More than anyone else, Collins was to blame. He was a good boss and a fine comrade, but he could be a truly awful colleague. It was one of his greatest failings as a politician.

His problems originated with his manner and mindset. He was consistently interfering and insulting, dismissive, critical and undermining of anyone who didn't do what he wanted, wouldn't let him do what he wanted, or didn't meet his standards. This demanding and bossy attitude was familiar from the Geraldine Athletic Club, the Kimmage garrison, the GPO and Frongoch, and to brigade commanders who didn't follow his orders correctly (i.e. fill out the forms). In the first months of the Dail regime he did not apply the lash of his personality, but 1920 saw it again in action once everyone was on the run, departments were set up, and the bullets were flying: only now there was often a distinctly whining or bullying tone to his comments.

One of his first targets was the Department of Propaganda (or Publicity) under Desmond Fitzgerald. Generally speaking, the British government had a very high opinion of the Dail's spin machine – an opinion endorsed by historians. Collins saw only lax security, inefficiency and missed opportunities, and often made his opinions clear. (In fact he welcomed Erskine Childers's replacement of Fitzgerald after his arrest in 1921 as a guarantee of improvement.) A typical letter from January 1921 (to de Valera) stormed that Fitzgerald's reply to a query from Art O'Brien was 'disgraceful' and 'simply an indication of their ordinary slip-shod carelessness'. A few months earlier, after Bloody Sunday, Collins had even questioned his courage. Fitzgerald had gone to ground for a few days to avoid reprisals, until Collins winkled him out. Maureen McGavock, who was sheltering him, later commented, 'I still remember his humiliation at the reproach – entirely undeserved – in a note from Mick Collins, "What is all this digging in about?"'

William Cosgrave, the Minister for Local Government, received the same treatment. Like Propaganda, his was a well-run, well-staffed department that achieved a lot. But, like Fitzgerald, Cosgrave was shocked by Bloody Sunday. He fled Dublin for a while, telling his staff (according to James Kavanagh), 'Things were getting too hot, that he was going into hiding and he advised us . . . to go and do likewise. We continued working as usual.' Collins was not impressed, and thereafter ostentatiously treated the assistant minister, Kevin O'Higgins (who stayed), with greater respect – although this did not stop O'Higgins attempting to resign after a fight with him. He also famously denounced Cosgrave in cabinet for his incompetence, and the familiar letters of complaint to Dev followed ('I don't want to be bothering you with these things but . . .).

Both Cosgrave and Fitzgerald were veterans of the Rising, had seen prison time, and had lived on the run while attending to their duties, just the same as Collins, so they had a right to feel aggrieved. His harshness over their flinching from danger may well have had a larger intent to it, however, as the British counter-offensive that followed the events of late November 1920 rocked the whole move-ment, including many IRA units. Collins and others had to scramble to steady the troops, while at the same time presenting a determined face to the government. If the movement showed signs of panic the enemy would smell blood, so it was imperative that leaders be leaders – and Collins was the acting president after Griffith was arrested.

But this doesn't explain the ongoing persecution of Cosgrave's and Fitzgerald's departments, or everyone else's. Regarding the Department of Labour under Joe McDonagh (another supposed weak link in late 1920): 'I am not at all satisfied with the way this department is being worked.' Austin Stack, formerly a close friend whom Collins helped obtain high office, was estranged by Collins's badgering. His Home Affairs Department was in charge of the highly successful Dail courts and the not-so-successful police force – a mixed but by no means a bad record given the obstacles. Yet Collins was unrelenting in his criticism and interference, culminating in an exchange over a boycotting case in Cork city in which a former High Sheriff, W. J. O'Sullivan, was punished for a letter he wrote to the Lord Lieutenant in 1920. Eventually an inquiry was ordered. Collins, who saw Cork as his home turf, and believing he was 'aware of the inner and outer circumstances', intervened with the local Sinn Fein executive in what he saw as a miscarriage of justice. By doing so he bypassed the responsible ministry, Home Affairs, and word of this was sent to Stack in May 1921.

How much they actually disagreed on the merits of the case is unclear, but Stack wrote to Collins immediately to see if what he had heard was true. Stack's letter was formal but correct. Collins's reply explained that he had been misunderstood, but then introduced a personal note:

> May I however, as a Member of the Government, take this opportunity of protesting against the carriage of this case . . . I would be lacking in my duty if I did not make the protest – No amount of special pleading or connection should alter us in our plain, definite, straightforward stand on a matter of public justice . . . As usual, I have no doubt that my protest will be unavailing, but, at any rate, I make it.

Stack's reply was restrained and began by accepting that Collins had been misrepresented and assured him, with presumably intentional irony, 'I know you would not interfere with the work of another Department by giving directions or anything which might be regarded as such. I think you will agree with me that it would be better if Ministers refrained from expressing their views in cases like this except to their colleagues at Ministry meetings.' He ended by doing a minister's duty and defending the reputation of his staff: 'I do not know what you mean by referring to the carriage of this case. Everything was above-board – as is usual in all matters concerning this Department I am proud to say.'

At this, Collins had a mini-meltdown:

> I am afraid you misunderstood my attitude altogether – It appears to be a question of a different outlook, and if this is so

really, there is very little good in talking or writing further on the matter ... This is my own opinion and it is as clear to me as it would be to me that £2 added to £2 makes £4 ... As to interfering in the work of another department I am truly surprised and sorry ['you think' crossed out] that anybody could think of me in such terms ... As to Ministers expressing their views, I am expressing my views in half a dozen or a dozen or two dozen letters every day of the week – until the Enemy is successful I shall continue doing so, because I say nothing that I cannot fully stand over.

Apart from anything else, this series of letters surely gives the lie to the standard image of the hapless Stack being put down by a masterly Collins and storing up resentment as a consequence. If anything, Stack had touched a sore spot of Collins's, and the latter reacted with juvenile petulance. And, needless to say, it all ended up in de Valera's lap again. It should also be noted that the Intelligence Department was responsible for several miscarriages of 'justice' (they being judges, jury and executioners) that attracted other people's ire, and Collins acted just as Stack had done.

Collins did not usually find this sort of carry-on necessary in the GHQ, as Dick Mulcahy as Chief of Staff was entirely amenable to his plans and ideas and many of the other directors were part of his circle of friends. Gearoid O'Sullivan as Adjutant General was a pal and an acolyte; Rory O'Connor, head of Engineering, had long looked up to Collins; Eoin (Owen) O'Duffy was a protégé handpicked to be Deputy Chief of Staff; and so on down the list. The exception was Liam Mellows, who was appointed Director of Purchases in November 1920, after a long hiatus in the United States. Previously, while Joe Vize, an IRB and Collins man, had done much of the work in Britain, Collins, with his unmatched contacts there, had run the arms-smuggling show. Tiny, jolly, hard-working and already experienced in covert operations, Mellows – already a friend of Harry Boland's and a TD to boot – would seem the perfect fit for Collins to hand off some of his work to but – he was not anyone's man. Collins saw his appointment as an invasion of his territory and IRB territory as well: a powerplay engineered by Cathal Brugha, the Minister of Defence, with whom Mellows was, quite correctly, in close touch.

And so followed the full Collins treatment, including talking behind Mellows's back with British IRA men. Mellows was referred to as the 'little man' in correspondence, and when the locals complained they hadn't enough money Collins replied huffily that 'I could forward you some money for your own use, but *in the way things are going here at present*, I don't like doing this. *It is up to those people who are making so much fuss to attend to things. Nothing like it happened when I was in charge of a certain number of details.*'

The reality was that the unhappy Mellows found himself caught between the two combatants. Brugha was indeed trying to use him to get at Collins, and was obsessive about economizing: 'Cathal would sit all night with his mouth like a rat trap over half a crown.' At the same time, Mellows came to distrust Collins so much that he refused to stay in the same house as him – to Mary Woods's distress, as she was very fond of both men:

> He said he [Collins] was interfering with his job as Director of Purchases by buying arms across the water and paying more for them than he was [a complaint Collins endlessly made of others]. He was buying them, he said, not to use them but to prevent him (Liam) from getting them. This shocked me . . . he was aware that I adored Mick as a little God.

It seems most doubtful that Collins was actually keeping arms out of circulation, but he may well have been doing what he had always done – funnelling them into IRB hands and keeping them under his control.

POWER SEEMS TO BE the underlying theme in all these squabbles, not politics or personality. Cosgrave and Fitzgerald, whatever they felt, would become key collaborators with Collins in later political struggles. Brugha and Boland didn't get along, but they ended up together on the opposite side. Stack had been a very close friend and militant ally, but Collins still attacked him. Arthur Griffith and Eoin MacNeill, with whom he worked well in cabinet, had been ideological foes before the general election. What drove Collins into these conflicts was his desire to acquire or exercise power, or else his fear that someone was trying to take it away.

The only case where personalities actually seem to have been at the heart of the problem was the greatest feud of them all: between

Collins and Brugha. When and how this originated is unclear, but it seems to have been long in the making. Other people seem to have liked Brugha as a straightforward and decent man, but somehow he rubbed Collins the wrong way and, eventually, vice versa. He wrote to Collins in September 1919 to say, 'I am just as sorry I was the cause of your losing your temper . . . I hope we will be none the worse friends.' The quarrel is unknown, but another came along in May 1920: 'With great respect and without wishing to offend you, I would suggest that things would run much more smoothly between us in future if you would weigh your facts before you make statements . . .'

What may have begun as personal friction would become a struggle for power. As chair of the Volunteer executive, Brugha was privy to all the important decisions and wielded considerable author-ity, as his 1918 cabinet-killing scheme showed. Once the GHQ was up and running, a shooting war broke out, and intelligence became central, the executive became a security liability, faded into insignifi-cance, and stopped meeting in mid-1920. To add insult to injury, acting-President Arthur Griffith replaced Brugha with Collins as his successor in case of arrest, and Collins duly assumed the role in December.

Brugha had been made Minister of Defence in de Valera's 1919 ministry, but this post turned out to be quite disconnected with headquarters and operations. Like Collins, he could no longer keep in touch by visiting units himself, but, unlike Collins, provincial officers didn't bother visiting him when they went to Dublin. Even there he was out of the decision-making loop, as the headquarters staff met without him and Collins, Mulcahy and the rest mostly ignored him.

Brugha tried to ensure ministry oversight by tying the Volunteers to the Dail with an oath of allegiance, but this made little difference. To a great extent, this was his own fault. He placed none of his own men at headquarters until after the 1921 truce, he never established a staff or office, and he was only a part-time minister, continuing to work at his business. Tellingly, British intelligence paid no attention to him either, as his name almost never figured in captured corres-pondence. However, he was quite right that Collins was amassing power and dominating the central institutions of the revolution, that he had a large personal following, and that he was also an active leader and promoter of the IRB within the IRA. And, as events would soon prove, an independent and ideological army was a very dangerous thing regardless of who was in control.

By Christmas 1920 the relationship was poisonous, and it wasn't long before Brugha's discovery of what he saw as IRB-inspired financial impropriety gave him the ammunition to set off a war. In January 1921 Brugha discovered that some money intended to buy arms had gone missing in Glasgow, and raised the issue at a cabinet meeting. Collins rushed to his typewriter as soon as the meeting was over to tell George McGrath off: 'I was taken entirely by surprise this afternoon. If there are any matters of this kind arising, you should take care that I am informed.' A hectic search followed, and turned up some embarrassingly sloppy procedures with £1,000 cheques flying about with no one paying much attention. 'The thing is a heartscald to me and I am awfully anxious to get it settled up,' Collins wrote a month later.

On 10 February 1921 Collins began a personal letter to the President with 'Now as a specimen of what I have to submit to and contend with Id like you to look at the enclosed note [about the missing money] from M/D [Brugha] to Chief of Staff [Mulcahy].' He went on to complain that 'It is not gentlemanly + it is not dignified + above all it is not organization', and that Brugha was just 'raking up petty technicalities'. He ended, 'God knows I am sick of it and no wonder + I don't want to be adding to your worries [a constant refrain] and my own but there it is.' De Valera did try to patch things up, but the intended reconciliation meeting (aided by a well-meaning Stack) reportedly ended with Collins in tears and Brugha walking out, refusing to shake hands.

As a financial scandal it wasn't up to much, but Collins was always very touchy about such matters, and had been since his days as the Geraldines' treasurer. An accusation that something similar had occurred during his National Aid tenure probably didn't help either. Much worse happened elsewhere when money disappeared into the pockets of fascist, Communist or merely commercial fraudsters on the Continent. Buying guns was a tricky business in which normal rules were often abandoned, and Glasgow was a sinkhole for all republican efforts. Nevertheless, Brugha would continue his Javert-like pursuit almost until his death, dragging in de Valera, the GHQ, the cabinet and eventually, and in public, the Dail.

It was this feud, and the worsening atmosphere in cabinet, that most probably prompted de Valera's attempted removal of Collins to the United States in January 1921. This made sense in several ways, as it would get him out of harm's way, provide a publicity boost there, accelerate the arms-smuggling effort, and provide the leadership for a second loan. In fact de Valera had already suggested Collins come over in 1920, but Collins had vetoed the idea. Now, however, thanks to his assembling good staff under excellent middle managers, his ministry could run without him (both loans were fully collected), as could the Intelligence Department.

In personal terms, Collins was overstretched and often ill, as betrayed by his appearance. A British intelligence report from late 1920, around Collins's thirtieth birthday, gave the following description: 'Must have been a powerful man a few years ago; now heavy in movement and greatly out of condition. Coarse, pale face with heavy jowl . . . Except for the eyes he is now quite unlike earlier photographs. Looks about 40.' He was prone to bouts of flu, and he seems also to have developed chronic stomach and kidney problems that could leave him bedridden or functioning in great discomfort. In political terms, he had become such a symbol of defiance that his capture or death would surely be a terrible blow to movement morale, so he was – by some calculations – worth more alive in the States than dead or imprisoned in Dublin.

The most telling thing about the proposal was that it wasn't discussed at full cabinet (in Collins's presence), but all the ministers individually agreed to it. In effect, the decision was made behind his back. Hardly surprising, given his record of colleague abuse, and not a flattering comment on his recent tenure as acting president. He was in an isolated position in the cabinet but he didn't end up going. Either he refused outright, as before, or the passage was too risky. Either way, this episode did nothing to improve his relations with his fellow ministers.

Interestingly, the proposed American exile didn't impair Collins's good working relationship with de Valera himself. This was at least partly due to the President's skilled handling of him, involving many soothing words of sympathy and much personal attention. De Valera invested a great deal of time in this effort, with many an invitation to come and talk about things. ('Are you free Saturday night? If you are try to come over.') To Collins's first barrage of complaints in January 1921 – after being asked to leave the country – Dev replied, 'I would be sorry to think that your feeling discontented and dissatisfied and fed up was due to anything more than natural physical re-action after the terrible strain you have been subjected to.' A few weeks later he was writing again of how 'it is damnable when the grit of little personal animosities enters in to rasp up all the bearings.' In the same letter, on 10 February, he agreed with Collins that 'it really is not fair to throw every task that comes along ultimately upon your shoulders, and it must stop . . . You have got enough of things, God knows, to attend to.'

Along with these friendly sentiments, de Valera tried to gently steer him away from confrontation: 'The Almighty did not give every body the ordered mind he gave you. If you think of that now and again you will not expect etc.' And when Collins brought up some of his charges against Cosgrave, de Valera agreed that 'your fundamental is unquestionable', but found 'your judgement too harsh'. Harsh words were never exchanged between them. They could address each other as 'Dev' and 'Mick' (in 1917 it had been 'Eamon' and 'Michael'), and Collins continued to feel free to let his president know what he was thinking and feeling, as he otherwise did only within his circle of intimates. The overall impression given by their correspondence is one of genuine partnership, with de Valera projecting a supportive and tolerant presence. This was undoubtedly the most important, and perhaps the most complicated, of Collins's relationships in 1921. He would spend the rest of his life trying to deal with it.

What doesn't appear true in all this is the oft-repeated accusation that de Valera, Stack, Brugha, Mellows and others had formed a cabal against Collins out of jealousy and resentment of his position and popularity. Mellows did not like Collins or Brugha, and, like de Valera, he tried to steer a course between them. Similarly, Stack tried to end the fight between Brugha and Collins. These men would cooperate against Collins in 1922, but that happened under different circumstances, when they were joined by many people who liked and admired Collins, so it cannot be read back into earlier events.

Collins was the only revolutionary leader to have assembled a kind of court – or at least to have one form about him. While people certainly attached themselves to de Valera – Boland for one – this was nothing compared to the following that Collins attracted. Not only did he have friends and admirers surrounding him at Vaughan's

– where he practically held court to visiting IRA chieftains up from the country – he had his own retinue of drivers and couriers, led by Joe O'Reilly, formerly a notable character, who seems to have submerged his personality in Collins's. He had a steady stream of flattering letters telling him how important and indispensable he was, and he was perceived (by no means always accurately) as doling out guns, money and Sinn Fein seats to his favourites – notably fellow Corkmen – and withholding them from enemies.

J. J. O'Kelly, an ally of Brugha, was one who crossed swords with the 'Collins' or 'West Cork' group ('for at no time was Dublin second to Cork in the quest for office'): 'Gearoid O'Sullivan was particularly active in that matter ... He was very sharp that way...' They objected to O'Kelly becoming first Minister for Irish and then, in 1921, Minister of Education, and they nearly succeeded in manoeuvring him out of it. He in turn saw intrigue behind Joe McGrath becoming Minister of Labour: 'That was another appointment about which much could be said.'

It is not clear to what extent Collins himself was responsible for such wheeling and dealing. For example, when Collins became acting president, in late 1920, O'Kelly recalled that 'he was hardly twenty-four hours in harness when the New York *Gaelic-American* had a full-page photograph of Ireland's new fighting chief.' In fact the picture had appeared earlier in the year, and Collins had been horrified rather than pleased. John Devoy, the American godfather of Irish republicanism, whose paper this was, had actually published it without his knowledge as a way of annoying de Valera, with whom he was feuding.

Collins may have served as a figurehead or stalking-horse for other groups and interests – jobbing IRB men, ambitious politicians, the Cork mafia – as well as a focus for genuine loyalty and admiration. The bottom line is that many people promoted and defended him against supposed critics and rivals, and talked him up as the real leader of the revolution – and many of the same people rose with him as he gained prominence and power. It is not surprising that a good many others saw Collins as a man consumed by personal ambition.

17: Peace

'There's a man over there who should interest you as a psychological study.'

The speaker, a Dublin doctor, addressed these words to me last Saturday in a well-known Dublin hotel. The man to whom he referred was seated at a table close by taking lunch with a dozen friends, men and women. The face was pale, with a conspicuous pallor, made more pronounced by a crown of thick, wavy brown hair carelessly brushed back from a good forehead. The nose was well chiselled. At first glance it appeared a handsome and a weak face. A second glance showed that it was neither handsome nor weak. The lower part destroyed the classic lines promised in the nose and forehead, and simultaneously dispelled the idea of weakness. This was, in reality, a plain man and a strong man.

('Harley Street specialist')

If it had been up to Collins, a truce between the IRA and the British government would have been declared in December 1920. The new British policies of 1920 had all failed to destroy the guerrillas or to shift nationalist public opinion away from Sinn Fein. A new Home Rule bill had been introduced, providing elections and self-governing parliaments for both northern and southern Ireland, but neither Irish nationalists nor British Liberals thought this limited measure was a serious political solution any more.

The government's attempt to avoid martial law by waging a 'police war' with ex-soldier Black and Tans and ex-officer Auxiliaries might possibly have made sense, but in practice it was astoundingly counter-productive. Instead of targeting IRA activists as the earlier army campaign had done, the now militarized police formed their own death squads (the so-called anti-Sinn Fein societies) and regularly engaged in reprisals against civilians. IRA violence only increased. Lloyd George himself may have colluded in this counter-terror (in case anyone dismisses more recent accusations of a similar conspiracy in Northern Ireland out of hand) and applauded it in public. 'We have murder by the throat,' he declared on 9 November, with Bloody Sunday only days away. 'We struck the terrorists and now the terrorists are complaining of terror.' It was this attitude, and reprisals in general, that the 21 November killings were directed against, more than the specific actions of the men killed.

If Lloyd George were willing to discuss other alternatives, this would present a new problem to the Dail cabinet, which had never formulated a negotiating policy. According to Sinn Fein's 1917 constitution and its 1918 election manifesto, the goal was recognition as a sovereign republic. Unofficially, by the autumn of 1920 it was reasonably clear to many British policy-makers in Dublin and London that many republican leaders would accept a ceasefire followed by negotiations without preconditions, and that an offer of Dominion status – roughly equivalent to that of Canada or South Africa – would be acceptable to a great many nationalists, even in Sinn Fein.

Such were the signals being sent from October onward in response to informal British feelers. Patrick Moylett, a republican businessman, was the first go-between. He got in touch with officials in the Foreign Office in London and with Herbert Fisher, the Minister of Education and the only real liberal on the British cabinet's Irish committee. To them, Moylett passed on a proposal from Arthur Griffith in November that the Dail be allowed to meet and that a conference be held to settle the Irish question. Concessions were offered on Ulster and British security concerns. When Griffith was arrested on 25 November in the post-Bloody Sunday backlash, however, Moylett blew his cover by telling his story to the *Irish Independent* and this avenue was closed off.

Other, parallel, lines of communication were opening up as well, but were equally threatened by Bloody Sunday, the Liverpool burnings, and the wiping out of an Auxiliary patrol in West Cork, all within ten days. Nevertheless, it was in December that the best opportunity appeared. On the 1st, Joe Devlin, one of the few remaining Irish Party MPs, arranged for Lloyd George to meet Catholic Archbishop Patrick Clune from Australia. The Prime Minister gave Clune safe passage to meet Griffith and other leaders in Dublin to test the waters for a deal. Clune met with Griffith in jail and with Collins in secret, as well as with British officials in Ireland. Negotiations focused on the earlier idea of a truce and the resumption of the Dail, but ill-timed statements by Father O'Flanagan, acting president of Sinn Fein, and by a Sinn Fein TD, local councillors in Galway and a Catholic bishop in favour of immediate peace, convinced Lloyd George and others that the movement was crumbling and that the strategy of counter-terror and the new military offensive were working after all. In December and January reports poured in that the IRA was demoralized and that public opinion was turning against it. Lloyd George now added a condition to the agreement: that IRA arms be surrendered. This was instantly refused, and the talks foundered.

Lloyd George had to consider his own position as head of a minority-Liberal–majority-Conservative coalition. If he lost back-bench support or if his cabinet split he would probably be replaced by a Conservative prime minister who would be far less inclined to compromise. He also wondered about timing: if British forces were winning, how could he justify calling a truce and, in effect, recognizing the rebels? What if the offer of Dominion self-government was rejected: where would they go from there? Besides, according to his military and police advisers and his Irish committee, the government might defeat the guerrillas outright in a matter of months, allowing the new Home Rule act to work. He was unwilling to take these risks.

Lloyd George himself told Clune that his hands were tied by his hardline colleagues, and Griffith for one accepted that he 'apparently wants peace but is afraid of his Militarists'. Interestingly, this was the mirror image of how many British officials saw the republicans, with Griffith and de Valera wanting peace but being held hostage by the extremist gunmen, led by Collins red in tooth and claw. Scotland Yard's agents reported throughout 1921 that de Valera wanted to negotiate and make a deal but that Collins had a veto and the IRA was holding out for a republic. So strong was this belief that, when it was Collins who made the running as a peace negotiator in London, a rumour spread among Conservative politicians that the real Collins had been kidnapped and replaced by an impostor.

Collins himself thought 'There is far too much of a tendency to believe that LG is wishful for Peace, and it is only his own wild men prevent him from accomplishing his desires . . . I am not convinced that he is the peace-maker.' In a double inversion of perceptions, it may have been Collins who was most enthusiastic about the abortive peace process. He encouraged both Moylett and Clune, and was disgusted at the former's leaks to the press: 'Nobody can tell him anything.' About the Clune initiative, he wrote to Griffith that 'a truce on the terms specified cannot possibly do us any harm.' Julia O'Donovan saw Collins at this time:

> I have a distinct recollection of Mick Collins's excitement at the time Archbishop Clune was over . . . He did not usually talk about his business to us – in fact he was very close; but that time he was bubbling over with the excitement which he could not keep altogether to himself. He was making a lot of jokes about the matter such as, 'I must be in the state of grace now that I am going to see his Grace', but at the same time I could see that he was very serious about it . . . He was very wroth with Father O'Flanagan . . . He said, 'That ruins things for us,' and he was not surprised when the negotiations broke down.

Wroth he certainly was, enraged at what he saw as the stupidity and interference of O'Flanagan and the other peaceniks. Sean MacEntee had it 'upon *Mick C's* authority that a truce was on the point of being concluded', and Collins's report to de Valera and the cabinet in January 1921 'pointed out particularly how the rushing in torpedoed the efforts'. However, Collins's own reputation was put in jeopardy when Moylett's leak suggested that it was his safety that was the sticking point in negotiations. He immediately wrote angrily to the *Independent* that 'No person in Ireland, or anywhere else, had any authority to use my name. My personal safety does not count as a factor in the question of Ireland's rights. I thank no one for refraining from murdering me.' The paper wouldn't publish his next, longer, letter on 'Irish peace', fearing reprisals, but it appeared in the Dail's *Irish Bulletin*. In it he repeatedly told the republican rank and file to 'get on with the work' and once again denounced 'foolish talk' and 'gross misrepresentation', concluding that 'we were not asking a truce – that if one were offered we would not reject it, but we did not ask for it. That is the position.'

A week later he explained his analysis of the situation to Griffith:

You will understand that I am looking at it from an entirely utilitarian point of view. We have clearly demonstrated our willingness to have peace on honourable terms. Lloyd George insists on capitulation. Between them there is no mean; and it is only a waste of time continuing. It may make it appear that we are more anxious than they, while of course Dr Clune is Ll G's envoy, not ours . . . It is entirely in their favour to continue this position – *to allow a feeling of the continuance of negotiations to exist* while they continue their attacks unabated . . . Yet in emphasizing Ireland's wish for peace . . . we need not fear to stand on the firm simplicity of our steadfast position. Hence I agree with you, that re-stating our willingness in the terms mentioned cannot do us any harm . . . Let Lloyd George make no mistake – the IRA is not broken. The events of the week & these days are more eloquent on that question than all his military advisors.

Collins was flexible about the details of a truce, short of surrendering arms. This became clear when the process was briefly revived in mid-December ('Events of the past two days have again done somewhat of a somersault,' he told an anxious Joe McDonagh on the 16th) and the question arose of whether the Dail and Sinn Fein would be allowed to function peacefully. 'Personally I am rather strong on insuring that our peaceful activities will not be interfered with,' he wrote to Griffith, 'but I incline to your view that it would be better to take this for granted . . .'

Collins was, by Griffith's wishes, acting president while all this was happening (until de Valera returned a month after Griffith's arrest), and he consulted first Cathal Brugha and Austin Stack and then the whole cabinet. Collins reported Stack as saying 'He agrees with the entire thing if I do' – an attitude that would change dramatically before another year had passed. They agreed the acceptable terms of a truce: 'If the English government calls off its present aggressive campaign, we can respond by urging the cessation of the present acts of Self-defence.' A nice phrase that last one, but the key word here is 'urging'. This preserved IRA independence and distanced the Dail from its acts. In reality, Collins and Cathal Brugha were both ministers and IRA leaders, so no urging would be necessary. Despite this consensus, Collins's secret dealings as well as his intelligence contacts within Dublin Castle would soon lead to talk that he was conducting his own negotiations, and cutting his own deal. The first time Collins heard of these rumours he joked about them, but later he took them much more seriously.

Unfortunately, the British cabinet continued to insist on arms being given up, and 'of course nobody would dream of entertaining such a proposition.' So the opportunity slipped away, taking with it the limited-war strategy that Collins and McKee had followed in Dublin. With McKee dead, British forces on the attack, and the government doubting republican resolve, the Dublin Brigade as a whole went on the offensive – not just assassinating selected targets, but ambushing and killing Crown forces whenever and wherever they could.

THE IRA IN GENERAL adapted and survived in the winter and spring of 1921, and violence continued to escalate throughout Ireland. The pressure on the movement was most intense in Dublin now. British intelligence may never have penetrated the revolutionary leadership, but its cumulative operational success became impressive, in both accuracy and ruthlessness. Major arms dumps were uncovered, as were Dail and GHQ offices – including several of Collins's. IRA arrests and deaths mounted.

As they did so, the guerrillas launched a war on suspected spies and informers. With doubters, Collins argued the evergreen paramilitary party line that these were 'acts of self-defence' required by British aggression, and that, without the IRA, things would go far worse for the nationalist population; he also believed that police riots and murders were deliberate tactics and could be shut down whenever the government wanted. This assumed both rationality and intentionality, as Collins was wont to do; but he was mistaken. In Ulster (six counties of which were about to become self-governing Northern Ireland under the Government of Ireland Act), and Belfast in particular, Protestant vigilantes had attacked Catholic neighbourhoods and a sectarian civil war was brewing between the communities. Everywhere violence was increasingly aimed at civilians and was getting out of any central control – and further and further away from Collins's professed precision killing.

The strain was reflected in Collins's correspondence. His letters never stopped coming, and continued to display as much energy and attention to detail as always, but they also reflected a growing sense of strain. He had always alternated long periods of optimism – his natural state – with bouts of brooding brought on by overwork, ill health or the loss of a close comrade. December and January were bad but by February he was able to write that 'Notwithstanding everything, [things] ... have improved, and the people are better than ever.' His tone soon swung back to an emphasis on personal risk (although not fear) and the lonely burden of his many offices:

[8 March] The work seems to be increasing every day, and with this damn nine o'clock curfew it gets worse and worse ... They don't spare little brutalities. It is ghastly.

[19 April] We have been having many losses here recently, and I have just learned that one of our pivotal men in this regard [couriers] is gone, but I'll do my best.

[21 April] They ran me close a couple of times and they have been doing any amount of harrying.

[4 May] Myself: things have been v. hard. In fact, too hard. I am sorry to say that the risks have to be taken. Some of the tales are a good deal truer than people think, and there are others that people don't know of truer still – if you follow my meaning.

[28 May] I am somewhat late in replying as the enemy brushed shoulders with me Thursday with my staff. They didn't get really very much ... They just walked into the office where they expected to find me working ... it was the most providential escape yet.

[31 May] they have kept up a v. raging offensive during the week-end for me. They are continuing to-day. It is a pretty close tug of war this time.

The stress never turned into despair. On 28 May Collins declared, 'I believe the present moment to be a critical one, & I am convinced that by boldness we shall win through,' while on 29 June he wrote, 'Some times the pressure is overpowering, but all the same the heart keeps good.' As on the hurling pitch, he was still the gamer, the scourge of flagging team-mates, the mounter of last-minute rallies, the character player. He never altered his routines (except to change addresses when one was blown), never went into hiding, never adopted a disguise (except by carrying false papers) or voluntarily missed a day's work – unlike many of his cabinet colleagues.

Nor did Collins alter his basic view of the way forward. A mutual and equal ceasefire was required, including full political freedom for Sinn Fein and the Dail. To get there, the British government must be convinced that it could not win and that the revolutionaries could not be intimidated and were the only potential negotiating partners. Above all, this meant no show of weakness or disunity and a constant eye on the presentation of the movement's case to the general public in Ireland, Britain and the United States. As Collins reiterated to George Gavan Duffy, now a Dail envoy in Rome, on 18 June, as another peace process was getting under way

> Real progress is much more to be estimated by what is thought abroad than by what is thought at home. But, of course, real progress depends upon the action at home . . . There are always those who want to insist on shaking hands before the combat is over, and in my opinion, we are not so near the end yet that we can afford to start the hand-shaking.

When, in early July, Lloyd George issued a public invitation to de Valera to discuss a settlement, Barry Egan – a Cork Sinn Feiner – publically welcomed it and said he was sure it would be accepted. Collins feared a repeat of the December fiasco: 'A statement like Egan's anticipating things – correctly or incorrectly – is, as you know, always inclined to interfere with the freedom of decision, which is so important in cases like this.' Nevertheless, with the intervention of various southern unionists, King George V, Prime Minister Smuts of South Africa (a hero to Irish nationalists, including Collins, since the Boer War) and James Craig, the new premier of Northern Ireland – and with the obvious approval of Irish and British public opinion – a truce was arranged to begin on 11 July.

Why a ceasefire now, when it had been impossible to arrange one seven months before? For the government's part, the summer of 1921 had brought the final failure of the patchwork policy stitched together in 1920. The Tans hadn't terrorized the terrorists, the early gains of December and January had faded as the IRA raised its game and the body count, and the May election of members for the new southern parliament had been a disaster: a total and unopposed sweep for Sinn Fein. Among the new MPs was a large contingent of prisoners and guerrilla commandants, signalling a long war yet to come. Collins himself was elected in Cork, and in Armagh in the parallel Northern Ireland election.

As a result, and with the main body of Ulster Unionists now apparently secure within their own borders, Lloyd George and his Conservative colleagues were willing to talk to the terrorists and decided to offer the south Dominion Home Rule. If that didn't work, the army was preparing contingency plans to wage an unrestrained war against the guerrillas and their supporters. Martial law would be declared everywhere outside Northern Ireland, including Dublin; colonial government would be imposed on southern Ireland; military reinforcements would pour in (a process that had already begun); and the whole country would be put in a state of siege, stopping all transport.

Collins received accurate information about government contingency plans in mid-June. He passed this on to de Valera, noting that his source (apparently well connected in Dublin Castle) was 'in a veritable panic to avert the awful times', and coolly added that 'I regard it as being of interest generally.' It might be a bluff to push them into accepting British terms, or it might be genuine: 'A measure of Martial Law for the whole of the 26 counties is not unlikely.'

He prudently – and typically – refused to commit himself either way, but it would soon be apparent that martial law was exactly the alternative they faced if peace were not secured. Collins's own counter-proposal if this happened suggested a massive escalation in return, to match executions of rebels with the killing of loyalist hostages and to wipe out the whole administration. 'My chief desire is not to single out any particular institution, but to get at them all.' He laid out his conclusions in August in a private Dail debate after objections were raised to a proposed decree along these lines:

> They [the critics] were basing all their remarks on a wrong conception of the situation as it existed now and as it would exist after the termination of the Truce ... Any official who was acting for the English government whom they [the republican government] did not exempt was guilty of treason to the Irish side and that should be the basis of anything they did with regard to any of those officials. It was not a question of preventing those officials from functioning, but a question of not allowing the British government to carry on any functions at all in this state ... If hostilities were resumed he believed they would be on a much more definitely military scale than before the Truce and that they would be forced to have a standing

army. Under such circumstances he thought the English government would not allow any civil functioning to go on save any
useful to themselves. It would be the Republic's interest to stop
all these people.

If war were resumed, then, Collins's previous restraints would be
dropped altogether. His aim was to give the resistance an approved
free hand, but his speech had another purpose as well: to maintain
his position as a hard man and, most importantly, to make sure the
Dail realized the real alternative to a negotiated peace.

18: Negotiator

Collins turned up in immense force ... turned everybody, including an unhappy typist, out of the room with a sweep of his arms and settled down to talk for an hour and a quarter. The telephone rang at intervals when he sprang upon it fiercely as an enemy and yelled a challenge that might have split the instrument ... In spite of these mannerisms I found him a straightforward and quite agreeable savage.

(C. P. Scott, London)

AT NOON ON 11 JULY 1921 both the IRA and the British forces stopped their operations, although many guerrilla units had made a point of killing as many enemies as possible up until the last minute (twenty people in the last thirty-six hours). The details of the Truce had been worked out in a conference between de Valera and General Macready, leaving the IRA more or less free to train, to recruit, and even to act as a police force. As far as is known, Collins had no part in these negotiations, although he was quick to accuse the British of breaking the spirit of the agreement.

Once the ceasefire was in place, everything depended on positioning. For the republican leadership, the key was to position themselves to best advantage whether the Truce lasted or not, whether they got what they wanted from the negotiations or not. It would be vital that they not be seen as responsible for the Truce failing, or for rejecting what might appear as a reasonable offer. If Lloyd George were seen as having made such an offer and the rebels, in turning it down, looked like extremists unwilling to compromise for peace, he would be politically empowered – and forced – to declare all-out war and crush the IRA. They would lose public support, earn the outright opposition of the Catholic Church, and split Sinn Fein and the Dail.

Of course, if republican negotiators compromised too early or too much, they would lose their militant wing, and most of the active IRA. This meant evading any British preconditions – on Northern Ireland or Ireland's position in the British Empire, for example – before entering any substantive discussions. Ideally they should impose their own. Collins worried about this as soon as Lloyd George sent his initial invitation to talks to both de Valera and James Craig, the leader of the Ulster Unionist Party: 'His letter is only an effort to put us in the wrong'; '. . . to get us to accept by implication the partition of Ireland.'

Within the movement, another battle for position was going on, along the old fault lines of militancy vs. moderation. The Truce met the conditions laid down in December by Collins and Griffith, but, in cabinet, Cathal Brugha was still dubious as 'the country had been brought up to a high pitch of resolution and . . . if the fighting were stopped it might not be easy to get things going again.' J. J. O'Kelly, the Minister for Irish, agreed, but no one took him seriously and Brugha didn't push his objections. Collins favoured acceptance, and, according to Ernest Blythe, 'The truth was that at that time when Collins and de Valera were in agreement on any point, there was practically no possibility that the majority of the Cabinet would go against them.'

Nevertheless, disagreement followed immediately over who would go to London to meet Lloyd George. De Valera would lead, and decided to take Arthur Griffith, Count Plunkett, Austin Stack, Robert Barton (the Minister of Agriculture) and Erskine Childers. No Collins. This caused a furious row on the evening of the Truce, as reported by de Valera's secretary, Kathleen O'Connell, in her diary for Monday 11 July:

> Truce signed at 12 noon. Very busy all day at M.H. [Mansion House, where the Dail re-established itself] M.C. called out this evening and spent several hours with the President. Hot discussion. President rather upset. Great excitement getting ready for London. Up until all hours.

De Valera would later say that he didn't want Collins being photographed in case they returned to war, and it seems reasonable to have left at least one senior politician behind to keep an eye on things. The Truce could easily have been broken after all, and a sudden crisis would need a safe pair of hands on the spot. On the other hand, however, as far as anyone knew this might be it – either a deal could be made in London or possibly they could be back at war. It might be a pivotal moment in Irish history, and Collins wanted to be there. The all-Sinn Fein delegation also violated the unwritten rule that a Volunteer must be present at all times.

Once in London, de Valera had several meetings on his own with Lloyd George, while the others waited in their hotel to hear what had happened. Collins was in regular contact by letter and telephone. His irritation did not impair his collegiality, and he remained supportive and cheerful in his letters to the President, asking whether 'apart from the little unpleasant things on Monday evening [the night of their argument], have you got some value from the talk?' His one known piece of advice, written on the 11th, was to delay the meeting for as long as possible, presumably to maximize the IRA's respite from pursuit and to get past the most dangerous time of year for guerrillas – the long days of high summer.

Collins maintained a no-nonsense tone in his letters, showing no inclination towards conciliation. On 17 July he reported that 'their [the British] civilian and military heads have said that it would not be wise for Michael Collins to appear too publicly – my answer to them was that I hadn't the slightest doubt that no street members of their forces would touch me.' He explained that 'the whole thing is an effort on their part to make us believe they have irresponsible forces,' while 'my effort of course is the very contrary'; but talking about himself in the third person and suggesting his own importance sounds like a reminder to de Valera not to forget the Big Fellow. His final thought – 'It will be seen later how I mean to make them responsible' – strikes a note of defiant independence.

His next letter, written after a two-day trip to Cork to reassure IRA and IRB leaders (and visit Woodfield), contained similarly tough sentiments:

> The car in which I was travelling was held up in Clonakilty by regular troops although they have no power whatever to under-take such action. I was not in it at the time. The situation was very funny. Of course everybody knew I was in the town. Captain

Blest and some companion paraded the street for half an hour or so evidently hoping to see me. I had it conveyed to them that if they were on the streets when I went out they would be regarded as breaking the truce. I don't know whether this intimation had any relation to the fact that they were not on the streets when I did go out a few minutes afterward.

He also warned that intelligence indicated that the army planned 'to attack us the moment they decide to finish their offers', and advised that de Valera stipulate that 'no matter how bad the terms are they would be submitted to a full meeting.' This would buy them some time – and, of course, ensure Collins was included in the discussion. He seemed to be positioning himself to be able to say 'I knew it all along' if the worst happened, so as not to be hostage to the peace process (as had threatened to happen in December).

After the first meeting, de Valera wrote that Lloyd George was preparing a proposal and that 'I am not dissatisfied with the general situation . . . we will be free to consider [it] without prejudice.' Collins replied that 'You confirm exactly what I was thinking about the thing' and reported that all was well – although, typically, 'there was a little more relaxation than I should have liked.'

The talks quickly stalled once de Valera insisted on prior recognition of Irish sovereignty and Lloyd George refused, and on the 20th Collins observed that 'things "smelt" like an ending.' Lloyd George offered a limited form of Dominion status that day, without military or fiscal autonomy and with Northern Ireland staying as was, under a Home Rule government as part of the United Kingdom. This would give southern Ireland far less independence than Canada, and de Valera dismissed it as inadequate, as did most of the delegation. They quickly returned home to formulate a response.

On 24 July the Dail cabinet and a few extra invitees such as Dick Mulcahy met at de Valera's house in Blackrock to begin the process of defining their own terms for a settlement. According to Austin Stack:

Whilst everyone except Cathal Brugha and myself appeared to be cautious, I got the impression strongly forced upon me that Griffith and Collins and Mulcahy were inclined to view the proposal favourably – that is, that they were in the main acceptable. Cathal was bluntly opposed to anything less than the recognition of the Republic, and I supported him as well as I was able.

A second meeting was held of the full ministry, where, again, caution was the order of the day. No one liked partition, and most were 'dead against' it, but Griffith's response was generally favourable and Stack recalls Collins saying the offer was 'a great "step forward"'. Later, however, when Griffith and Collins were nominated as plenipotentiaries, Stack (in his words)

> entered a weak kind of objection and said that my reason was that both gentlemen had been in favour of the July proposals. Griffith first challenged this statement, and I repeated it and said I understood from him he only wanted some modifications. 'Yes,' he said, 'some modifications.' Collins then took up my objections to himself, and denied that he would accept the proposals. I reminded him of what he had said at Blackrock. He protested he said nothing of the kind. Cathal and the President then assured me I had misunderstood Mick at Blackrock. I accepted this and said no more.

Stack's memoirs are not entirely reliable, but this does seem like honest confusion on his part as to what Collins had said, which was shared by J. J. O'Kelly (another ardent republican). All O'Kelly could divine from what Collins said was, in essence, 'You all know my opinion.'

What did Collins say, exactly? The only record is de Valera's rough notes from the meeting of the 24th, which summarize Collins as follows:

> *Mick* Step on road – not important – Free Dominion a step – document will set country against us(?)
>
> Fighting men would prevent return of troops
>
> Criticize document as document – wean people away from it –

This is indeed rather obscure (although that might be de Valera's fault), but the best guess is that Collins was offering a practical assessment of the costs and benefits of the British offer. It might provide an opportunity for future freedom, and once British troops had left Ireland an Irish army could stop them from returning. On the other hand, if they turned it down flat they would lose public support, so it would be necessary to 'wean' moderates away from settling for Dominion status and partition.

Collins was the epitome of caution, and it seems likely he did not want to stake out any clear position as yet. He was leaving his options open. Everyone knew Griffith was in favour of negotiating on the basis of the British offer, and de Valera later said that he also thought that Collins 'from my own weighing up of him . . . was contemplating accepting the Crown'. The question was, under what conditions? One thing was for sure, he saw the opportunity to make a deal, and wanted the cabinet to be open to it, but he hadn't made his mind up yet and was determined to stick to the consensus. He would wait as long as possible before he took a clear stand.

COLLINS SEEMS TO have had nothing memorable to contribute to the discussion on how to proceed – unlike Brugha, Griffith and Erskine Childers. De Valera was accepted as the strategist and spokesman. His alternative to Dominion status, which he called 'external association', was not quite so well accepted – or understood – but the cabinet did agree to it, with modifications. The official reply to Lloyd George, dispatched on 10 August, insisted on the recognition of Irish self-determination – i.e. sovereignty (for the island as a single unit) – as a basis for a conference, and suggested a 'treaty of free association' whereby Ireland's relationship to Britain and the Empire would be determined by choice and mutual benefit rather than imperial right. Britain's interests – trade and security – would still be protected, but Ireland would be constitutionally external to the Empire rather than an internal member under the Crown like Canada or South Africa. Hence 'external association'.

This third way forward constitutionally was a brilliant concept, and indeed presaged the successful evolution of the Commonwealth to include future republics like India. De Valera did not care about the future of the Empire, of course: his ultimate concern was shaping an agreement that would satisfy both the movement as a whole and the British government. In particular, he was worried about dogmatic republicans, now a major voting bloc in Sinn Fein and the Dail and the dominant element within the IRA. Without their consent, there would be no permanent peace, the revolutionary movement would split, and disaster would follow.

Unity had been the President's watchword since bringing the various factions of Sinn Fein together around his similarly finessed constitution of 1917. He had helped build the nationalist alliance against conscription in 1918, led Sinn Fein to victory in the general election, and he had kept his cabinet together and the IRA under control in 1921. A deal that split the cabinet, the Dail and the party, and turned the IRA loose, would not be worth making in his opinion. He was willing to compromise on association with the Empire, on national security, on sharing the imperial debt, and on Northern Ireland's right to self-government but, to keep Brugha, Stack, J. J. O'Kelly and others on side, he could not agree to the new state deriving its authority from the Crown. Even external association would be going too far for many in the movement, but it would get enough support, de Valera calculated, to prevent a serious rift – if the cabinet stuck together.

Thus began a lengthy exchange of proposals and rebuttals between de Valera in Dublin and Lloyd George in London (and on holiday in Scotland), with each seeking to force the other to negotiate on his chosen ground: self-determination or Empire. Fifteen messages in all were exchanged through July, August and September, while the IRA recruited, trained, paraded, raised money, and brought in more munitions, and the Dail and its departments re-emerged, free for the first time to establish their parallel government. The republican claim to rightful authority was made concrete, and nationalist opinion was clearly behind the Sinn Fein leadership. However, it was also clear – as Collins pointed out – that there would be no support outside the movement (and much opposition within it) if a generous British offer was rejected and renewed war was the result.

Fortunately, the British cabinet, meeting on 7 September in Inverness, decided against issuing an ultimatum to negotiate on their terms or else and instead offered a conference 'to ascertain how the association of Ireland with the community of nations known as the British Empire could best be reconciled with Irish national aspirations'. The clever inclusion of the key word 'association' proved to be the winning formula. De Valera made sure to restate his principle of sovereignty, Lloyd George refused to recognize it, and de Valera replied opaquely that 'we can only recognize ourselves for what we are' before finally accepting. Both men complained that they had to take their 'wild men' into account. The conference would be held at 10 Downing Street, starting on 11 October.

ALMOST AS SOON AS the Truce came into effect, Collins moved his main office and residence to the Gresham Hotel on O'Connell Street, one of his regular stopping places while on the run and still close to the various 'joints' around Parnell Square. Here he could hold court and conduct all his one-on-one business in a hotel room, or over lunch or dinner. He continued to use other, more private, offices, but stayed headquartered here well into 1922.

The Intelligence Department stayed active, as did its British equivalents. Most of Collins's time seems to have been spent, as before, on the Finance portfolio. Once the Dail resumed sitting in August, he attended, gave reports, defended his department, and sparred with various critics in the private sessions. He stayed silent during the debate on negotiations – although, intentionally or not, he and de Valera were something of a tag team, with Collins offering his apocalyptic vision of the next war to force any fantasists to recognize the alternative to negotiation, while the President (who, in contrast to Collins, spoke incessantly) insisted that some sort of compromise would be required, 'seeing that we are not in the position that we can dictate the terms'.

It was de Valera who personally chose the plenipotentiaries who would go to London to negotiate the Treaty. His hand-picked team, announced on 14 September was Arthur Griffith as chairman, assisted by Collins, Robert Barton, Eamon Duggan and George Gavan Duffy. Their secretaries would be Erskine Childers and Harry Boland – although Boland was instead sent back to the United States (once again leaving the stage at a crucial moment) and was replaced by Diarmuid O'Hegarty. Other advisers, mostly chosen by Collins as it turned out, would come and go as needed. The big question: Why wasn't de Valera going?

The fact that de Valera stayed in Ireland remains one of the great talking points of Irish history, and became one of Collins's main defences for his ultimate decision: If you wanted a better deal and thought it was possible to get it, why didn't you go? However, it was no surprise, as de Valera had made his mind up and announced his intentions well before the delegation was chosen. In the same speech in which he laid out the reality of their negotiating position, he equally firmly announced that 'I do not want and will not be' a delegate. He had given this a lot of thought, and gave part of his argument then: he would be more valuable at home, running the government, and there might well be divisions in the Dail and the cabinet, in which case he wanted to be in a position to assess the best way forward. When the matter came before cabinet, he still met with strong opposition – including from Collins – and won a tie vote only by casting his own. Defending his decision before the Dail afterwards, he elaborated on his earlier rationale:

> I know fairly well from my experience over in London how far it was possible to get the British government to go and when they came to that point they would have to deal with the matter in a very practical manner. To be in the very best position for the possibilities of a break down and to be in the best position to deal with those questions as they would arise and not to be involved in anything that might take place in those negotiations – to be perfectly free – I ask the cabinet not to insist on my going.

He added that 'I really believe it is vital at this stage that the symbol of the Republic should be kept untouched' by compromise, however necessary that compromise might be (although it must be pointed out that he had changed the constitution to make himself that symbol, as before 1921 he had merely been the president of the Dail), and he reminded his listeners once again of their far-from-strong position: 'to win for them what a mighty army and navy might not be able to win for them' would be too much to ask of any nego   d to act as they saw
fit, (l be referred home
befoi

I   )lic, would stand for
the r   iations failed to get
that   veryone else) would
have   and objective must
not l   under way, or else
move   : struggle would be
impei   dership had already
abanc

W   :n to do the talking for him? On 21 December, after the negotiations were over, he explained his thinking to Joe McGarrity, the leading republican in the United States:

> Having decided that I should remain at home, it was necessary that Collins and Griffith should go. That Griffith would accept the Crown under pressure I had no doubt. From the preliminary work which M.C. was doing with the IRB, of which I had heard something, and from my own weighing up of him, I felt certain that he too was contemplating accepting the Crown, but I had hoped that all this would simply make them better bait for Lloyd George – leading him on and on, further in our direction. I felt convinced on the other hand that as matters came to a close we would be able to hold them from this side from crossing the line.

After that, Brugha and Stack were too doctrinaire and unimaginative, and 'A.G. and M.C. wouldn't work with them' – or with Mary MacSwiney, TD, the implacable sister of the martyred hunger striker Terence MacSwiney '– women in general I suppose,' de Valera added, probably accurately. 'The only thing left was to send [Robert] Barton' as a republican counterbalance, supported by his cousin Erskine Childers. 'I felt that with these in touch with the delegation, and the Cabinet at home hanging on to their coat-tails everything was safe for the tug-of-war.' Duggan and Gavan Duffy, both lawyers, 'were mere legal padding'.

This is very much a hindsight-assisted account, but it seems obvious that de Valera was trying to achieve the usual representative balance be͏   t: old and new
Sinn Fein   s, with Barton
and Child   ːposes. On the
other han   he made out.
Griffith w   ster of Foreign
Affairs he   ɡation. Among
other miı   ;grave thought
Dominioı   ꓒ be unlikely to
push the   ꞵe to include at
least one   who had a lot
of Londo   ꞁa and Stack in
fact had :   ꞁly other senior

minister available – and the only one who had the confidence of the IRA. De Valera told the Dail that 'he felt it was absolutely necessary that the Minister of Finance should be a member. It was from the personal touch and contact he had with his mind that he felt and he knew the Minister for Finance was a man for that team. He was absolutely vital to the delegation.'

Neither this nor his letter to McGarrity fully explains his thinking, just his conviction that Collins was essential. This is often presented as a Machiavellian plot to set Collins up as the fall guy for either compromise or failure, but many other people agreed with his going, both inside the cabinet and out. Robert Barton, at that time still a good friend of his, felt 'it would be hard to overawe Collins' and urged him to go. So did at least some of his fellow IRB Supreme Councillors, including Harry Boland.

Collins, on the other hand, did not want to go. In a neat and rather surprising reversal of the situation in July, he was being urged to go and resisted all the way. He, like other ministers and TDs, wanted de Valera to go. They discussed it face to face, with Harry Boland present, on the night of 30 August. Collins wrote to Longford girl Kitty Kiernan (whom both he and Harry were pursuing at the time) that 'I had to talk very very high politics from 10.30 until 2.30, and high politics are very tiresome unless one is in very good form.' Boland's diary describes it as a 'long sitting to decide as between Chief [de Valera] and Collins as plenipotentiaries'. Interesting. Why not both? Perhaps for the same reason that de Valera had wanted Collins at home for the first trip: he didn't want both of them and Griffith in London – somebody with personal authority had to remain in charge.

As always with these big decisions, Collins agonized over the choice and did not agree until the final cabinet meeting on 9 September. Batt O'Connor recalls that

> I will never forget his agony of mind. He would not sit down, but kept pacing up and down the floor, saying that he should not be put in that position. It was an unheard-of thing that a soldier who had fought in the field should be elected to carry out negotiations. It was de Valera's job, not his.

This idea of Collins as the simple soldier unprepared for the much more wicked cut and thrust of international diplomacy is often accepted by biographers. It must have been someone else, then, who had attended all those political meetings, gave all those speeches, sat on all those committees, got elected in two constituencies in three separate elections, sat on the executive of his party, wrote those memos on electoral strategy, belonged to the Dail cabinet as Minister of Finance, and had briefly been acting president of his government. And why had he wanted to go in July, then? In any case, the twentieth century is full of cases where fighting men represented their movements politically. We needn't take Collins's protestations seriously: he was simply positioning himself politically, just like de Valera.

If we go back to Boland's diary entry and to Collins's contrary behaviour in July, an alternative suggests itself: it wasn't that Collins didn't want to go – he just didn't want to go without de Valera. He hadn't wanted the President to go to London in July without him, and, according to Patrick O'Keefe, his view now was that 'I'll never go to London without Dev.' So at the September meeting it may be that what Collins was saying was: Either you go or I won't.

Why was Collins so reluctant to go, at least without de Valera? Most probably because he felt it might be a can't-win proposition. If the negotiations failed, either others – de Valera – would have to take over or else they would be faced with a war they could not win. But for Collins, success would mean that he had compromised, and therefore that he had been compromised, potentially alienating him from his natural power base in the army and among republican militants. He already had a taste of this when he presided over an IRB meeting in Cork on his post-Truce tour in July. Most of those present were not happy about the talks, and Collins 'became somewhat annoyed, and in assuring the meeting that nothing out of accordance with the desire of the IRB would be agreed by him, he said "I expected to find a different spirit in Cork," meaning, of course, that he was surprised to find his friends in Cork should suspect him.' De Valera's whole case for staying revolved around his acknowledgement of this suspicion. But why should Dev stay pure while Collins was tainted by association with Downing Street?

Collins's political anxieties were exacerbated by his enemies in cabinet. Brugha, as Minister of Defence, was now feuding with Mulcahy as well as with Collins, and accused them both of insubordination and incompetence. In July he declared his intention of 'putting our Department of Information [Intelligence] on such a footing that things of this kind cannot occur in future' after another mix-up by Collins's men, and he demanded that Austin Stack activate his nominal position as Deputy Chief of Staff to represent him within the GHQ. To Mulcahy's objections he hissed, 'Before you are very much older, my friend, I shall show you that I have as little intention of taking dictation from you as to how I should reprove inefficiency or negligence on the part of yourself or the D/I [Collins], as I have of allowing you to appoint a deputy chief of staff of your own choosing.'

Collins was not the principal this time, but he did back Mulcahy, as did everyone else on the GHQ staff and in the country units. De Valera, as always, took neither side but worked to keep Mulcahy from resigning and came up with his usual creative solution, whereby the Chief of Staff could have the deputy he wanted while Stack would get an unspecified staff role in recompense. Dev had no problem with GHQ himself, but he was intent on keeping Collins's enemies on side for a political settlement. Some Friends of Mick assumed this meant he was conspiring with them against Collins, but there is no evidence that this was the case. The only conspiracy around was the one that everyone knew about but only Brugha dared mention: the IRB that Collins now controlled as head of the Supreme Council.

This cabinet controversy segued into another over the recommissioning of the IRA officer corps under the full control of the Dail. Here de Valera and Brugha were clearly on the same side, although with different motives. Brugha wanted more control over the army at the expense of the GHQ and the IRB, while de Valera was probably thinking ahead to a possible peace settlement, when it would be absolutely vital to maintain control of the 'young men'. The last thing he wanted was another split like that in 1914, which had allowed the republicans (including himself, of course) to gain control of the Volunteers. He may also have been thinking of Parnell's famous argument after his party split in 1890: that his leadership was necessary to keep the 'hillside men' (Fenians) from turning to violence. The 'new army' would be more or less identical to the old model, but the cabinet would assume the authority of the now dormant Volunteer executive and the GHQ would be subordinated to it. In other words, the IRA would finally lose its long-protected autonomy.

There were other, operational, reasons to assert political control over the IRA. The cabinet had become concerned with mounting ill-discipline and breaches of the Truce, and if war was in the future, rather than peace, then Collins's view that they would have to fight as a standing army would have to be taken into account. Brugha wanted 'to put the Army in an unequivocal position as the legal defence force of the Nation under the control of the Civil Government', which would (hopefully) force the British army to treat IRA men as regular soldiers and prisoners of war.

However sensible the reasoning behind them, the upshot of the proposed changes would be more power for Brugha and less for Mulcahy and Collins. In the end, the 'new army' programme changed things only on paper and was rendered irrelevant by subsequent political events. When it was proposed in cabinet on 15 September, however, it coincided with Collins being named a plenipotentiary. As it was obvious that Brugha and Stack would be the main cabinet opponents of any deal that Griffith and Collins might bring back, it can only have added to the latter's sense of foreboding about his own reputation and future.

So why go? Presumably he could have said no like Brugha and Stack, or as he did when the same people told him to go to the United States. As it was, he made sure everyone knew he was reluctant and unhappy – his scribbled comment to 'Dev' from London the day after talks started – 'this place bloody limit. I wish to God I were back home' – was repeated many times to friends and colleagues. He would also threaten to quit at least once, although this was the usual politician's trick to get his way rather than a serious threat – once he was there he was there till the end.

The bottom line was that duty called, and so did many of his friends. To refuse would be to publicly place his personal preferences above the wishes of his President and the cabinet – and perhaps the IRB Supreme Council – and, by implication, above his country. Not going to the US was different, as it meant staying in danger: no one would accuse him of shirking on that count. He had no such defence in this case. Nor did he have a clear rationale for staying, as de Valera did.

In the end, however, Collins must have felt drawn to the main stage. He had spent the last six years putting himself at the centre of the action: alongside Joe Plunkett, in the GPO, at the Roscommon election, in the Sinn Fein executive, on the IRB Supreme Council, with the delegation to meet Woodrow Wilson, rescuing de Valera from jail, in the Dail cabinet, at the head of Intelligence. This was why he had refused the American job. How could he resist being on the spot for the biggest job of all, where history would be made? Surely he must have sensed opportunity.

IF HE WAS GOING, it would be on his own terms. The delegation rented two houses in London, one for Collins at 15 Cadogan Gardens and one for everyone else at 22 Hans Place. Both were highly respectable addresses on private squares just off Sloane Street in South Kensington – a far cry socially from West Kensington, where Collins had lived. He didn't travel over with the other delegates, and once there he didn't socialize with them either. According to Robert Barton, 'The whole set-up at Hans Place was distasteful to him.' Erskine Childers was in charge of the secretariat and the arrangements, but, in his own personal campaign for external association, Collins insisted on controlling every detail of his own household. One housekeeper did not meet with his approval. Childers noted in his diary on 6 October, 'M.C. furious and countermanded her.' The next day: 'Ordered Housekeeper to go. M.C. explained but did not apologize.' He brought his own staff, including couriers and bodyguards – the now ex-detective Ned Broy among them. Eamon Duggan, while officially a full-powered delegate, was seen more or less as a Collins staff member by all sides.

Collins's intention was to carry on the day-to-day running of his various operations, with the minimum of delegation. The monster work days continued as before. He kept a close eye on his departments, and worked his cross-channel messengers hard. Having his own house kept things secure, particularly where intelligence and army affairs were concerned. It also allowed him to revive his preferred boarding-house environment, with endless practical jokes and reported heavy drinking (the bill for damages was the subject of scandalous rumour). These did not go down too well among the more elderly and female inhabitants of Hans Place, who looked upon Cadogan Gardens as Animal House. When Childers invented a mock menu for a dinner party there, the last item was 'Liqs Miceal's Mixture', presumably a snide reference to the reputed heavy drinking at the other place.

The drinking seems to have got out of hand one night in October, when Collins and two minders (using false names) went to visit his old friend Neil Kerr in Wormwood Scrubs prison. According to the indignant governor, 'He had evidently been drinking heavily and reeking of whiskey ... He said his two companions would also be present ... I replied that I had only instructions to admit him, Michael Collins. He then assumed a bullying demeanour saying "Mr Lloyd George won't thank you for being discourteous to me" ... By this time he had become trulucent and announced his intention of seeing all the prisoners.' Once he got to see Kerr, he was caught trying to slip him some tobacco, whereupon he told the warder, 'You go and sit down, you did not ought to be here at all.' The warder reported that 'I consider Mr Michael Collins was not in a fit condition to visit prisoners, as in my opinion he appeared to be under the influence of drink.' In the end, he spent over three hours in the prison, 'boasting about all the loyal people he has shot', until the chief warder 'persuaded him to go'. This episode was hushed up by the government, but it may show his anxiety at being in London and under such pressure.

Childers and Barton, with whom Collins had previously been friendly and comradely, found his suddenly aloof attitude puzzling. They had done nothing – he just cut them off. In this he may have been following Griffith's lead, as the chairman had not wanted Childers on the team, disliking him both personally and for being 'English' (as indeed he was, as well as being a devoted republican). Both Collins and Griffith may also have made the same calculation as de Valera: that the two cousins were there to keep them on the path to external association. It has been suggested that Childers was actually a spy, but his much-speculated-upon secret letters to de Valera were actually straightforward reports on the negotiations, with only approving comments about Collins. Nevertheless, Collins's actions and suspicions and Griffith's hostility soon created two cliques within the delegation. In some ways this replicated the atmosphere in cabinet, for which Collins was also largely responsible.

*

DID COLLINS go into negotiations with clear ideas about what his bottom line would be? Despite his warlike image, he had never attached himself publicly to the full republican demand. In his speeches, his election addresses, his correspondence, even his interviews with the press, the word 'republic' was almost completely absent. He had pushed for it to be included in the Sinn Fein constitution in 1917, and he had taken various oaths to the Irish Republic as a Volunteer, an IRB man and a TD, but he was not naturally inclined to ideological thinking.

Two interviews with the American journalist (and British spy) Carl Ackerman are revealing in this regard. In August 1920 he was quoted as saying that 'the same effort that would get us Dominion Home Rule will get us a Republic', but off the record (according to Ackerman's report to Basil Thomson of Scotland Yard) 'he was much more accommodating. When told by the interviewer that an Irish Republic was impossible he said "No-one has ever defined a Republic."' In a second, later, interview he repeated his line about effort and what it would get – but on both occasions he used this to avoid ruling anything in or out. Collins supported de Valera when he made an ill-informed suggestion in the United States in 1920 that Cuba's subordinate position under the Monroe Doctrine might provide a model for Ireland's relationship with Britain; he agreed with him that Unionist Northern Ireland could not be forced under a Dublin government, and also that they would not be able to get a republic at the negotiating table.

Collins was a de Valeraist, then, in every important respect. In fact the whole delegation adhered to the President's ideas for almost the whole period of negotiations. The two key issues were the constitutional status of the Irish state and the status of Northern Ireland. On the first, de Valera would be willing to make concessions on British naval bases, Irish armaments and the imperial debt, and acknowledge the Crown as the head of the Commonwealth (as the self-governing parts of the Empire were now being rebranded), if Britain acknowledged Ireland's national sovereignty: 'external association'. On the northern problem, de Valera was willing to accept the continued existence of the northern Irish Home Rule government so long as Ireland was given legal sovereignty over the whole island: 'essential unity'.

De Valera's strategy was to use the northern Irish question as leverage to extract British agreement on the imperial question. Northern self-government could be conceded in a final trade-off, but before then it must be used as a bargaining chip. De Valera calculated that the British government would be on shaky political ground if the negotiations broke off over Ulster Unionist intransigence. Northern Protestants refusing to accept any compromise were no longer a popular cause in Britain as they had been before the Great War.

On the other hand, if republicans refused to yield on a narrow question of constitutional law, particularly if it had to do with the Crown, it would be the revolutionaries who would be at a disadvantage with Irish and world public opinion. What, risk a terrible war over some abstract legal point of sovereignty? Who would support that?

The soundness of de Valera's thinking was demonstrated by Lloyd George's identical reasoning: he knew that if he could settle the potentially embarrassing issue of Northern Ireland first – or at least get it off the table – he would have the advantage in the final round of negotiations over the Crown and Empire. Positioning would be more important than ever, and everything would come down to how well the individual negotiators were able to impose their priorities on their opponents.

As it turned out, Collins was a mediocre negotiator, and Griffith and the others were not much better. Lloyd George, on the other hand, had an extraordinary genius for manipulation and manoeuvre. Downing Street was his home turf, he seized control of the agenda by submitting the first detailed proposal, he set the necessary emollient tone of the meetings, and he was also able to orchestrate a grand finale to close the deal.

He had able helpers of course – notably his secretary, Tom Jones, go-between Andy Cope (who had been involved in all the secret talks leading up to the Truce) and his cabinet colleagues, particularly Austen Chamberlain, the Conservative leader and Lord Privy Seal, and Lord Birkenhead, the Lord Chancellor. Winston Churchill, now Colonial Secretary, was present, but did not play a major role – his main contribution being to keep most of his counterproductive (to put it politely) ideas and opinions to himself. He and Collins would come to loathe each other, Churchill's posthumous compliments notwithstanding. At the time, however, all the principals got along, at least in private.

What did the British ministers and civil servants make of Collins? They were certainly curious, just as were the press and the public. We don't know what intelligence reports they would have read, but an analysis prepared especially for the talks (possibly by Andy Cope) called him a 'quick thinker . . . the strongest personality of the party; claims influence which at this juncture will be exercised on the side of moderation'. The last comment is surprising given his reputation, and probably premature, although prophetic none the less.

Still, after the first round of plenary talks, he seems to have made a favourable impression. Robert Sanders, a Conservative politician in close touch with Secretary of War Lamar Worthington Evans ('Worthy Evans'), reported that 'Collins seems to have attracted everybody.' Chamberlain thought, 'He had his own code of honour, and to it he was true; but it was not mine, and between him and me there could be no real sympathy, and perhaps only partial understanding.' In October, Lloyd George was heard to say that 'Collins was undoubtedly a considerable person,' although he also confided to C. P. Scott (editor of the *Manchester Guardian*) that he was 'an uneducated rather stupid man but he liked him'. Lionel Curtis, co-secretary with Tom Jones, wrote to Cope after Collins's death that 'he was such a loveable creature', but a few months later rated him more coolly: 'the cornerboy in excelsis. The trouble about poor Mike was that he literally carried the Napoleon of Notting Hill [a novel by G. K. Chesterton erroneously rumoured to have influenced Collins] in his pocket. He never could quite see the picture through his own reflection in the glass.'

The general attitude was that, while Collins had an impressive personality, Griffith had brains and integrity (and a great poker face), and their colleagues were not worth talking about. Art O'Brien, the republican representative in London, who buzzed about like a housefly, was dismissed by the Prime Minister as 'that swine'. Of Robert Barton Lloyd George remarked, 'Why did they bring that pip-squeak of a man Barton with them? I would not make him a private secretary to an under secretary.'

Collins would later dismiss talk of how the 'atmosphere of London' had influenced him, but any such occasions have their own centripetal dynamic. Call it the summit syndrome. Mutually hostile and suspicious antagonists, stuck in small rooms together for week after week, often bond in the superheated atmosphere. They develop unlikely friendships and trust, sympathize with each other over their respective extremist colleagues and their unachievable expectations, and end up feeling like allies with each other against outsiders. That's how Collins and Griffith felt, and that's what Lloyd George played upon, as other master politicians have done in similar circumstances. And that's what de Valera's plan was designed to guard against: he would stay out of the ring so as not to be influenced, and the cabinet would act as a check on whatever the plenipotentiaries came up with.

Apart from this susceptibility – Griffith for one bought Lloyd George's claims about a right-wing threat to his position – the whole Irish team focused too narrowly on the two central issues of the Crown and national unity, to the neglect of other crucial aspects of sovereignty – over the Irish economy and the right to self-defence. Financial considerations such as sharing the imperial debt (greatly inflated by the costs of war) and reparations for British misdeeds (a Collins hobbyhorse) were similarly sidelined when they might have been used for bargaining purposes. Finally, when Collins would later complain in populist vein that he understood things only in 'the plain Irish way' and was 'befogged by constitutional and legal arguments', he was inadvertently stating a very real weakness. In the end, checking the fine print on the final draft of the Treaty and getting it properly lawyer-proofed would be crucial.

All of these problems were magnified by the division of labour among the Irish team whereby most of the actual negotiating was done by Collins and Griffith in private sessions with senior British ministers, leaving Barton, Duffy, Duggan and Childers out of the loop. The others were kept informed, but their advice usually went unheeded as it was almost always seen as mere obstructionism. Barton was astounded at the way trade issues were ignored, and Childers, while not actually a lawyer, possessed easily the best critical intelligence of any of them as well as a very keen eye for potential problems. However, the process rolled right over them.

THE TALKS OPENED with full plenary sessions at which all the delegates were present – seven in all between 11 and 24 October, held on various mornings and afternoons in Downing Street. The negotiators sat around the cabinet table, the Irish on one side and the British on the other, with their secretaries behind them. Collins and Griffith were in the centre, facing Lloyd George, Chamberlain and Birkenhead. No one sat directly opposite anyone, however, and Lloyd George solved the always awkward handshake dilemma (not with terrorists/murderers!) by meeting the Irish at the door as they entered and offering his hand. Only when they were seated did the rest of the British participants enter.

This first round of talks ranged over nearly every aspect of Anglo-Irish relations, and produced principled and practical disagreement in every case. There was also a great deal of sparring over violations of truce terms. Collins's performance was mixed, with insight and sharp reasoning marred by habitual bluster. For example, his protest at the third session over policemen searching passengers arriving in Ireland for arms (which were still being imported, at a greater rate than ever) concluded by declaring, 'I would certainly never allow myself to be searched in this way.' In the fourth session's discussion of Northern Ireland he stated that there was no intention of using force – although 'not because Ulster would not be defeated in a fight'. In the fifth, Griffith brought up a leaked British army circular outlining plans in the event of the Truce breaking down. When Worthington Evans replied that 'we don't even know that it was issued', Collins boasted, '*We* know. You can't issue these documents without my knowledge,' and went on to reveal that it was 'no accident' he was being followed by English agents. Finally he complained that 'I have asked what you thought of the honour of a soldier who during the truce circulated a photograph of myself, and the question was treated as a joke.' Lloyd George described Collins's attitude as 'a little uplifted. He fancied he had met and defeated the whole might of the Empire ... If the necessity came he would find out his mistake.'

In the general meetings Griffith got most of the lines, with Collins – followed by Gavan Duffy, Barton and Duggan in descending order – acting in a supporting role. Collins's main original contribution may have been inadvertent, as he seems to have been the first to use the term 'boundary commission' in discussing possible solutions of the northern question. His exact words were 'There will be a plan for a boundary commission, or for local option, or whatever you may call it,' showing a disregard for vital distinctions that would come back to haunt him.

There were also side meetings on finance and defence held around

Whitehall. Collins was the only delegate on either side to attend them all, and he took the lead in these discussions, accompanied by Childers and backed up by hand-picked experts. For the committee on defence, he brought over Eoin O'Duffy, the controversial Deputy Chief of Staff, along with Emmet Dalton, the chief liaison officer, and J. J. O'Connell, Director of Training – all of whom had supported Mulcahy in the struggle with Brugha and Stack – much to Brugha's fury, as he was not consulted.

Surrounded by these familiars (Diarmuid O'Hegarty was also present), Collins tried to turn the discussions into a debating society, pressing his arguments again and again, seeking to score points off his opponents. He spent a lot of time arguing over the details of naval policy and technology with the bemused likes of Air Marshal Hugh Trenchard and Admiral David Beatty (the heads respectively of the air force and navy), in a well-briefed but futile attempt to convince them that controlling Ireland in a naval war wasn't so important really. For the final defence committee meeting Collins submitted a 'technical document' along these lines which Churchill praised as 'very able and considered' and 'logically sound from the point of view from which it is written'. Lloyd George called it 'formidable'. Childers, a former naval person and author of the maritime thriller *The Riddle of the Sands* (1903), was the brains behind this, as he was behind many of the Irish documents.

More important was Collins's argument for security cooperation, premised on Irish neutrality rather than automatic subordination to imperial requirements. He stated and restated this in many different ways, but eventually summed it up in a sentence: 'Good feelings are better than good clauses,' thus proving himself an early master of the sound bite. As the meetings ground on, he fell back on his stock of business analogies. In the final defence committee meeting, on 18 October, he put the following to the British: 'You know something about Company promoting. When you set up subsidiary companies you give the shareholders certain options. You would be in quite a different position if you said to the shareholders "you must do these things whether you like it or not."' This made sense, even if his opponents refused to accept the comparison, but at the end of the meeting he went an analogy too far: 'Excuse me, you must not exclude any avenue. For instance: if you put a man in charge of a rubber plantation you do not restrict him from making certain experiments.' To this Worthy Evans replied, 'I am sorry, Mr Collins, I generally understand you, but I must confess beaten in this case; I cannot follow you.'

Essentially, Collins's point was that British acknowledgement of Irish freedom and equality would create good will and an effective basis for agreement, and it would then be in Ireland's own interest to help protect its neighbour. If Britain were fighting a just war, Ireland would of course be happy to help. If necessary – harking back to de Valera's American analogy – Ireland would accept a Cuban-style proviso that it would do nothing to injure its own liberty or the liberty of Britain (by, for example, signing a treaty with another power).

Of course, as Churchill pointed out, the whole argument over neutrality was just another way of pursuing de Valera's basic strategy of association based on sovereignty, and did nothing to develop any specific solutions. Collins may have deliberately avoided making any side deals at this point in order to put pressure on the British to compromise on the big issue – with the implied quid pro quo of security guarantees to follow. In fact he spent much of his time challenging Churchill and Worthington Evans to tell him what exactly was wrong with neutrality and equality in principle, perhaps hoping to draw them into some embarrassing or revealing statement that could be turned against them. Collins even said as much when he baited Churchill that 'it would look very bad for you in the eyes of outside nations if this conference broke, not on the question of freedom of Ireland but on the question of the amount of freedom which Ireland was to possess,' and that 'it would look very bad for you if other countries thought that you were endeavouring to secure places in Ireland as a jumping-off ground for an offensive war.' Churchill merely replied, 'No: I think we can deal with that.'

We should not be too cynical. Collins may have seen the tactical possibilities, but he also championed the arguments for their own sake, and he seems genuinely to have believed that he had a good chance of convincing the British of them. After the discussion of the Collins naval memo, Childers wrote to de Valera, described the 'two hours warm discussion', and added that 'MC thinks we can get neutrality yet. I am more doubtful.' Yet it is usually Collins who is portrayed as the realist.

The final committee meeting concerned financial relations. This

discussion, as usual, centred on a British proposal, this time suggesting that, as its share of the imperial debt, Ireland pay the British
exchequer £18 million a year for two years, after which the amount
would be subject to revision. And once again, while the Irish had no
detailed counter-proposals (an absence which explains much of the
waffle), Collins took off on another tack altogether and suggested
starting with a clean slate: 'Let us treat the past as the past.' After all,
if all past accounts were still due, Irish nationalist demands included
reparations for over-taxation and 'arrested development'. Collins's
example – the destruction of the Irish tobacco industry – was drawn
straight from the Sinn Fein playbook. 'I will put some arguments
that may surprise you,' Collins challenged, and a weary Worthington
Evans replied that 'Mr Collins will never surprise me again.' Collins
still managed to confound him: 'According to my figures our counter-
claim works out at £3,940,000,000.' Laughter all round: 'I suppose
that dates from the time of Brian Boru. How much did we owe you
then?' The meeting ended soon after, and financial issues were also
relegated to the back burner.

The last session with everyone present took place on 24 October,
after the Irish delivered their first proposals – not far removed from
de Valera's July statements, and couched in strident assertions. Lloyd
George opened by saying that 'the stage is critical and we cannot
much longer prolong discussion on these questions.' Ireland's neutrality or place in the Empire was the central issue, and when Griffith
finally allowed that 'we accept the principle that your security should
be looked after' Lloyd George immediately adjourned so as to end on
a positive note. This also ended the plenary sessions, as Collins,
Griffith, Lloyd George and Chamberlain met in private afterwards
and agreed to continue in this manner, without secretaries present, as
an ongoing subcommittee.

Lloyd George's ostensible reason for this was to leave out the
more troublesome members of his own team, but all the principals
thought they could talk more freely and make much better progress
this way. There was no desire on either side to seriously mislead their
colleagues about what was going on, but Lloyd George was surely
also aware that his bag of arm-twisting and leg-pulling tricks would
work much better in a more intimate context.

*

NOW BEGAN A month-long series of subcommittee meetings, usually confined to Collins, Griffith and one, two or three British ministers. No Irish secretaries were present, but Tom Jones often was, and Lloyd George met Griffith alone on several fateful occasions. From the start these meetings were constructive and reasonable, with the main setbacks coming from the less flexible memos and proposals produced by the Irish delegation as a whole, as approved by de Valera. There were times when people on both sides thought the end might be near, and Collins threatened to resign at least once while Lloyd George did it at least twice. Austen Chamberlain (who would go on to win a Nobel peace prize) comes out well, as a calm and sensible presence, and Tom Jones did more than anyone to keep the two sides talking. At the end of November, however, though both sides had come to fully understand each other's concerns and had made significant advances, the rival final offers were still not close enough.

In the first of these meetings a new, streamlined agenda was set. Lloyd George and Chamberlain said Ireland would have to accept the Crown as head of state, and Griffith countered that he might be able to recommend some sort of association with it if the British would concede essential unity. It was then agreed to bracket the issue of ultimate authority and return to it once other matters were settled.

As before, the British controlled the agenda. A parliamentary debate on Ireland was looming on 31 October and the annual Conservative conference was not far behind on 17 November, both of which would force Conservative cabinet ministers to defend their actions and reassure their followers. This was a real concern for Chamberlain and Birkenhead, but Lloyd George was able to turn the threat to great tactical advantage. On 30 October, the night before the Commons debate, Griffith and Collins were summoned to Churchill's house, where they met with him, Birkenhead and the Prime Minister. Or rather for forty-five minutes Lloyd George met with Griffith alone, while his ministers and Collins entertained each other with a jolly exchange of war stories, endlessly repeated later as proof of their camaraderie.

What Lloyd George wanted was for Griffith to offer some guarantees of Irish concessions on the Crown, Empire and security so he could fight the Tories over Northern Ireland, where he would push for essential unity and for the Northern Irish government to be placed under Dublin's jurisdiction. If this proved impossible through Ulster Unionist intransigence, the alternative would be some sort of boundary revision to place Catholic-majority areas under southern control. This would be the cabinet's peace platform. If the Northern Irish could not be moved, Lloyd George and at least some of his colleagues would resign rather than go to war. Griffith refused to give any promises himself, except to write a letter agreeing to recognize the Crown if they got unity and the other things they wanted.

Griffith's letter went through many revisions as first Gavan Duffy, then Barton and Childers, objected to any deviation from the official line and then the British delegates wanted changes in the new version that took these objections into account. In the end, the letter sent on 2 November stated that ultimate agreement was 'conditional on the recognition of the essential unity of Ireland'. Gavan Duffy was disturbed enough to protest to de Valera personally about the direction the negotiations were taking, with private meetings leaving himself and Barton in particular on the bench. As far as de Valera was concerned, however, it was so far so good. Griffith was sticking to external association (which was compatible with a recognition of the Crown as head of the Commonwealth) and to the strategy of making the north the breaking point.

He should have been more worried. Lloyd George had extracted concessions on naval bases, and was able to keep the definition of acceptable north–south unity usefully vague. This would later prove to be a vital chink in the Irish negotiating position. More importantly, he had managed to build an alliance between himself and Griffith – and by extension Collins and Duggan – against not only his Conservative enemies but also the other members of the Irish delegation. This would be the foundation on which he would build the final agreement.

Unfortunately for the Prime Minister, not only did Northern Ireland Prime Minister James Craig dismiss all his proposals, he received powerful backing from Andrew Bonar Law, the once and future Conservative leader. On the face of it, Lloyd George was placed in a no-win situation: either keep his pledge and resign, or break his promise to Griffith and kill the negotiations. Either way war would be the result.

His solution was to repeat the trick that had worked the first time. Tom Jones went to Griffith and Collins to present the nightmare scenario of a Conservative takeover and to suggest an alternative: a boundary commission would determine the border between the two Irelands. The Irish negotiators had previously insisted on a constituency-by-constituency plebiscite to solve this problem. Collins was afraid accepting a commission would mean giving up national unity, but Griffith saw an opportunity to claw back all the Catholic-majority areas of the six counties while in the meantime improving the nationalists' political position if the talks failed. After all, Craig and his British backers could hardly claim support for a war based on keeping Catholic people in Northern Ireland against their will. Either the Unionist government would be forced to come under an Irish government or the commission would strip away that half of Northern Irish territory where Catholics were in the majority, making the rump state financially unviable. The crucial point here was that the commission would have to work in the way Griffith wanted in order to put Craig in such a position.

On 9 November, Griffith told Jones the commission was not his proposal and he wouldn't take responsibility for it, but he also wouldn't 'queer his [Lloyd George's] position' by saying so. Lloyd George, encouraged by this opening, quickly got a follow-up agreement that the commission would take in the whole of Ulster (thus raising the prospect of Northern Ireland gaining, as well as losing, ground). On the 12th, in a second private interview with Griffith, he pressed harder. He laid out his new plan of forcing Craig to agree to either an all-Ireland state or boundary revision, and renewed Griffith's promise not to reject the idea in public and swore him to secrecy about the meeting itself (surely another bonding technique). On the 13th Griffith was shown this proposal in writing, said it looked fine – and told no one about it. The Conservative conference – and Bonar Law – backed the peace process fully: so long as the Empire and Ulster were secure, full self-government for southern Ireland was acceptable, along with an altered Northern Irish border if necessary.

BOTH SIDES NOW FELT they were moving into the endgame. New British proposals – although not yet in the form of a draft treaty – were forthcoming: much the same as before, but with the addition of a boundary commission should Northern Ireland decide to opt out of an all-Ireland state. Childers prepared a counter-proposal on 22 November, outlining external association based on Irish popular sovereignty with the only link to the Crown appearing in Ireland's association with the Commonwealth. The details were the subject of bitter debate, as the proposal was written in some ways as if Griffith's and Collins's recent discussions had not taken place, and still hewed closely to de Valera's line. Griffith and Childers fought bitterly over it – or rather Griffith attacked Childers bitterly for the most part. Collins and Duggan sided with the former, and Barton and Gavan Duffy with the latter.

This document did show significant movement from the original Irish position – it did accept an indirect link to the Crown – but the British cabinet, optimistic the week before, were still very disappointed. Lloyd George had Tom Jones tell Griffith that if this was their final offer the talks were over. At this point neither Collins nor Griffith was willing to budge, but Jones convinced them to meet with Lloyd George the following day in case there had been a misunderstanding. Barton went along as well. This led to a second clarification session the next day, this time with Gavan Duffy and John Chartres, a legal adviser, in tow. Griffith extolled the virtues of external association, but the British weren't buying it and wanted detailed proposals on the Crown.

Collins, as usual, played no great role in these constitutional discussions. His most interesting contribution was a memo he submitted at a meeting on the 24th, focusing not on the principles of freedom or free association, but on the actual and future nature of the Empire/Commonwealth itself. The undated, unsigned document makes a case for restructuring the organization as a voluntary league of fully independent nations laying the foundation for a 'new world order' (!) in which 'war would become impossible'. How? By offering the United States – and Irish Americans – an attractive alternative to the League of Nations. This dream could never be realized, however, unless Britain recognized the equality of the other nations first – as the Dominions themselves were demanding. It would eventually become a reality anyway as the former colonies matured, but if it were embraced and used as a model for international affairs it would increase Britain's security, not threaten it.

When Austen Chamberlain sent the memo on to Birkenhead he wrote, 'This is extraordinarily interesting though sometimes perverse and Utopian. Who (outside our six) would guess the name of the writer?' Collins claimed authorship, but to Barton and other delegates the authorship was very much in question, owing to the – for Collins – unusual subject matter and style. He certainly hadn't written anything like it before. Collins's administrative and policy memos were usually clear and to the point, but his more speculative thoughts on politics tended towards incoherence. In fact Collins admitted to de Valera that the memo 'was sketched roughly by myself, and developed by a friend from my notes. It is very rough but it may interest you as it expresses, perhaps not very perfectly, my own ideas, and it may, I think, form the basis of some kind of constructive proposal regarding association.'

His ghost writer was almost certainly John Chartres, the so-called mystery man of the delegation. Chartres, a lawyer, had been a long-time agent of Collins's in the Ministry of Labour in London. (His itinerant Italian wife, Annie Vivanti, also impressed Collins greatly.) He subsequently joined the Dail's pseudo-diplomatic service, and was stationed as a republican envoy in Germany until called to London as part of the delegation secretariat. It was he who drafted many of the detailed legal proposals for external association, including the idea of recognizing the Crown as head of the association (i.e. of the Empire/Commonwealth) rather than as head of the Irish state.

In any case, Collins certainly liked and believed in his 'new world order', and he once again proved his cleverness in adapting such concepts for his own use. This one would become a key weapon in his political armoury, only aimed at an Irish rather than a British audience. The prospect of a progressively freer Commonwealth of Dominions became one of the main justifications for accepting a place in it, even under the Crown. Ireland would gain independence alongside the other countries, who would be strong allies and guarantors in the push for equal status. It was not only an effective argument, it was correct, as the subsequent evolution of the association would demonstrate.

At the end of November the delegates convened with their colleagues in Dublin to discuss the state of play. The Dail cabinet approved recognition of the Crown as head of 'the Association' of Commonwealth states, and, in a symbolic gesture, agreed to contribute to the king's Civil List (or personal revenue). When the next Irish proposal was submitted to the British, on the 28th, the extent of the association was also laid out: 'Ireland will be associated with the British Commonwealth for all purposes of common concern, including defence, peace and war, and political treaties.'

A furious Lloyd George told Jones 'this means war', but of course what it really meant was another meeting, that night. Collins wasn't present, as he had stayed on in Ireland. The British countered with two major concessions. First, they were willing to agree to any limitation of the Crown's actual power, reducing it to the purely symbolic role it had in Canada. Second, they suggested a modified oath of allegiance to the Crown to be taken by Ireland's elected representatives to demonstrate that symbolic authority – one more compatible with nationalist scruples.

Discussions continued the next day, this time with Collins present along with Griffith and Duggan. Lloyd George delivered a revised offer and set 6 December as his deadline for sending the final British terms to Northern Ireland, to get Craig's decision on whether his government would accept Dublin's authority or not. The Irish delegates unaccountably accepted this arbitrary deadline, and arranged for a final cabinet meeting in Dublin on 3 December to decide yea or nay.

19: Treaty

No one could mistake his nationality. He was Irish through and through, in every respect a contrast to his taciturn neighbour [Arthur Griffith]. Vivacious, buoyant, highly strung, gay, impulsive, but passing readily from gaiety to grimness and back again to gaiety, full of fascination and charm – but also of dangerous fire.

(David Lloyd George)

THE MOST INTERESTING THINGS about Michael Collins are the decisions he made, and his biggest decision by far was to sign the Articles of Agreement (known ever after as 'the Treaty') with the British government on 6 December 1921, proposing the creation of an independent Irish Free State. This was the defining moment of his life and career, and the first really surprising thing he had ever done.

Why did he do it? There is no mystery about his rationale, which he repeated many times. The Treaty offered peace with honour and real sovereignty as a Commonwealth Dominion, and, although it accepted the existence of a partitionist regime in Northern Ireland, it included a mechanism to resolve that situation without further violence. Immediate unity and total independence were preferable, but were not attainable by negotiation. The only realistic alternative was another war with Britain: this time a total war, which would be far more destructive and which the IRA was bound to lose.

Collins seems to have come to most of these conclusions – or justifications – well before he agreed to sign at the dramatic last-chance session in 10 Downing Street. Once it was done, he threw himself behind the Treaty and never seriously wavered in his commitment to it. But – and this is the most interesting aspect of the whole process – he did not agree to sign until his hand was forced by both British and Irish negotiators, and he might well have refused under a host of other circumstances. It was his most agonized decision by far, and one he almost did not make.

THE IRISH DELEGATES got the supposedly final British offer on 30 November. Ireland would be a Dominion, its relationship with Britain and the Crown identical to that of Canada. It would provide naval bases, and Britain could have more in time of war. With a few exceptions, it would not be able to regulate trade between itself and Britain. If Northern Ireland chose not to be ruled by the new state, a boundary commission would be set up to act according to the wishes of the inhabitants, but also taking into account 'economic and geographic considerations'.

No one got much sleep the night before the Dail cabinet meeting on 3 December. De Valera and Griffith – who arrived in Dublin ahead of the other delegates – stayed up late to argue, while the ferry Collins was on collided with a fishing boat, killing several men and forcing a long delay (and giving the Irish press a chance to portray Collins as a potential life-saver rather than a life-taker). To begin with, the cabinet and the delegation met as one, and the delegates spoke first. Each had something different to say. Griffith was in favour of the deal as it stood, refused to break on the Crown, and thought rejection would 'hand to Ulster the position from which she had been driven'. Robert Barton believed 'England would not be willing to go to war over allegiance to the Crown' and that the offer would give Ireland neither Dominion status proper nor essential unity. George Gavan Duffy also thought Lloyd George was bluffing and that he would eventually give them what they wanted. Eamon Duggan agreed with Griffith and refused to take responsibility for saying no, given the horror of what might follow.

This left Collins – who had typically waited to speak last – to break the tie among the delegates. He gave the most interesting answer of all:

> Mr Collins was in substantial agreement with Messrs Griffith and Duggan. The non-acceptance of Treaty would be a gamble as England could arrange a war in Ireland within a week. Sacrifices to NE Ulster made for sake of essential unity and

justified. With pressure further concessions could be obtained on Trade and Defence. Oath Allegiance [to the Crown, sworn by members of the Irish parliament] would not come into force for 12 months – question was, therefore, would it be worth while taking that 12 months and seeing how it would work. Would recommend that Dail go to the country on Treaty, but would recommend non-acceptance of Oath.

Childers' diary records things somewhat differently:

AG said he wanted to prevent fresh war. MC difficult to understand, repeatedly pressed by Dev, but really I don't know what his answer amounted to. RCB said he would not. G.D. ditto. EJD same as M.C.

The first set of notes was written up – apparently after the fact – by Colm O Murchadha, a Collins loyalist who worked with Diarmuid O'Hegarty, so they may not be strictly accurate or unbiased. They are certainly incomplete. Collins had played his cards very close throughout the process, and his answer can be interpreted as either nuanced or uncertain. The tone of the remarks was fairly consistent with some of the things he had said in the 24 July discussion, but they were still rather confusing. He agreed with Griffith that non-acceptance would risk a rapid return to war, and defended their agreement to a boundary commission – although how this was done for the sake of essential unity is unclear. Surely it was recognition of the Crown that could be justified this way, not recognition of Northern Ireland. Perhaps the note-taker got his arguments mixed up. Was Collins for or against the oath? He seems to suggest provisionally accepting it, while using the time before it would have to be invoked to see if the rest of the agreement worked out all right. Or did he mean to renegotiate it? To get themselves into a stronger military position? And then he seems to contradict himself twice: first by saying the oath was unacceptable, then by saying the Treaty should be put to the Dail – when rejecting the oath would mean rejecting the Treaty, and thus risking war. The reference to the Dail may have also signified agreement with Griffith's position that he would neither break on the Crown nor sign the Treaty, but would instead put it to the TDs for a vote.

No wonder Childers and de Valera found him impossible to pin down. Austin Stack recalled only that 'Collins did not speak strongly in favour of the document at all.' Collins could see the arguments on both sides, and wasn't sure what he thought. He felt torn between Griffith and de Valera, and didn't want to definitively take sides. After all, he had been following de Valera's plan and Griffith's lead throughout: who would he side against? Neither, he was probably hoping. Always the careful politician, he wanted to keep his options open until the last minute.

Further clues as to what Collins thought can be found in his annotated copy of the proposed Articles of Agreement. He made detailed notes, most of which are concerned with minor matters such as his beloved submarine chasers. Others are suggestive. He seems to have wanted to clarify whether Britain could declare war for Ireland (neutrality again). He preferred that the oath be altered and be hidden away in an appendix rather than have it appear in the main body of the agreement, thinking no doubt of making it easier to sell. Similarly, 'Empire' was changed to 'C'wealth of Nations', just as Ireland was to be a Free State rather than a Dominion. Beside clause 9, stating that protective duties on trade would not be imposed, he wrote '? helping our infant industries'. Most intriguingly he wrote, 'No re. Commission', presumably referring to the boundary commission: did this mean he didn't like the scheme? All in all, he seems to have been thinking of making improvements, not wholesale changes, marking him as being more of a 'yes' than a 'no' man, but also one who thought changes necessary and possible.

Once the delegates had had their say the cabinet alone continued the meeting. De Valera was still working towards his model of external association, and the question now really came down to the wording of the oath, which would define the Free State's relationship with Britain and the Crown. This in itself marked a major step outside the box for the putative republicans, but only Brugha now balked at the mention of the Crown, and de Valera managed to talk even him around.

While proponents of the Treaty would soon ridicule the very idea of going to war over the wording of a few sentences, this was not a purely symbolic issue. At stake were the fundamental nature of the Irish constitution, the source of governmental authority (the people or the king), the relationship with Britain (equal or subordinate) and, in concrete political terms, the survival of the republican movement and the prospect of civil war. Only de Valera seems to have thought deeply about this last aspect of the problem. Anyone in the IRA, the Dail or the IRB had already taken oaths of allegiance to the republic which the proposed settlement would seem to betray. Again, only de Valera had addressed this problem when he stated explicitly in the Dail (albeit in a private session) that his oath bound him only to do the best he could for the 'people of Ireland'.

According to the cabinet minutes, it was unanimously agreed that the oath would have to be changed. De Valera suggested a revised oath pledging allegiance to the constitution of the Free State and the Treaty and recognizing the king only as head of the associated states. That way there would be an oath and the Crown would be in it – hopefully satisfying the British government's minimal requirements – without actually making the monarch the head of the Irish state. It was a typically clever dodge from the master of linguistic compromise. However, this proposal was to be presented as their own bottom line: 'Delegation to return and say that Cabinet won't accept Oath of Allegiance if not amended and to face the consequences, assuming that England will declare war.' If the talks broke down, 'Mr Griffith to inform Mr Lloyd George that the document could not be signed, to state that it is now a matter for the Dail, and to try to put the blame on Ulster.'

De Valera was thus sticking to his original strategy to the bitter end, and this included staying in Ireland himself. This was perhaps his most important decision, which he kept to despite the urging of Barton and some others. In the face of potential crisis and war, preserving movement unity and political freedom of manoeuvre was more important than ever, as was keeping a consistent party line in propaganda terms. And so far he had accomplished his goal, keeping his cabinet together through the decision to negotiate, the policy of external association, concessions on Northern Ireland, and the acceptance of an oath. He had also, not incidentally, kept the delegation intact despite various upheavals and threats to resign.

More immediately, he also thought Griffith's pledge to neither break nor sign, but rather to present the terms to the Dail, meant that nothing would be decided in London. However, his final oral instructions to the delegates were fatally ambiguous with regard to demanding a better oath, and different people came away with different conclusions as to what might be acceptable or what had been agreed or promised. If de Valera had been more specific or had put detailed wording in writing – or if he had gone himself – Irish history might well have taken a very different turn in the days that followed.

Not going was a failure of leadership and an abdication of responsibility at the most critical moment of the movement's history. Very definitely it helped tip the scales in Collins's (and therefore Duggan's) ultimate decision on whether to sign or not, and it later gave those in favour of the Treaty an invaluable debating point: who was de Valera to say that more could or should have been done when, over and over, he had refused to go?

Collins had his own ideas about revising the oath, and he consulted the IRB Supreme Council on the subject while he was in town. In fact he had kept it informed throughout. His usual tone over the weeks of negotiations was pessimistic but, according to Sean O Murthuile:

> When our meeting would end he would stand up and stretch his restless bones, and assume the buoyant attitude that was one of his characteristics, and gather his most intimate colleagues around him while he related to us the humours which had arisen in the case of recent Downing St Meetings – telling us how he scored or how Griffith scored, and never placing the honours on one side; he was always willing to give Birkenhead or Lloyd George marks in wit and argument.

On 3 December, however, he was stuck in the cabinet and could not make the council meeting. The councillors agreed that the oath would have to be changed, and suggested a new version – similar to de Valera's – which was passed on to Collins by O Murthuile over a hurried lunch at the Wicklow Hotel before Collins returned to London for the final round.

Back in Hans Place on 4 December the delegates fell into bickering again over the redrafting of the Irish proposal, based on conflicting interpretations of the meeting. Childers resignedly noted what he saw as 'Mick's' obstructionism, attempts to make the document useless, sneers, and finally 'more sneers and bluster'. In the end it was pretty much the same offer of external association as before. As a result neither Griffith nor Collins – and therefore Duggan – wanted to go to the meeting with the British ministers, as they expected the offer would be rejected as before, marking the end of the peace process. Griffith changed his mind at the last minute, and led Gavan Duffy and Barton to meet Lloyd George and several others that evening. He gamely tried to follow cabinet instructions by concentrating on Ulster, to force the British to break there, but the less wary and experienced Gavan Duffy let the side down by saying the Empire (i.e. the Crown) was the problem. This gave British ministers the opening they were looking for, and they walked out at that point with the upper hand. There was no way they were going to agree to the Irish terms anyway, but this would give them an invaluable edge in being able to put the blame on the Irish and justifying whatever they did next.

Why did Collins stay away? Not that he would probably have made any difference, but it seems bizarre, even childish, to sulk with your country and cause hanging in the balance. It surely was an indication of his emotional state in facing the most terrible dilemma of his career. In a memo written the next day to explain himself he said, 'I had, in my own estimation, argued fully all points', but at the cabinet meeting he had argued that 'further concessions were available.' He also said he wanted Barton and Gavan Duffy to see for themselves that the British weren't bluffing; but even if so, why couldn't he go along as well? It seems most irresponsible, and a repeat of what de Valera had just done – and this indeed was probably the point: he was trying to avoid the blame for failure, just as he saw de Valera doing. He was trying to salvage his political reputation. It is worth noting, however, that if the talks had ended there – as they might well have done – both Collins and de Valera would have gone down in history as having refused to attend the final meeting.

Fortunately for him, he got a second chance: a morning meeting alone with Lloyd George, as requested by Griffith in a subsequent meeting with the relentless Tom Jones. The always responsible Griffith – a rare ego kept fully in control – was no doubt desperate not to leave things as they were, as it would be a disaster for Ireland. He cajoled Collins into going at the last minute. Lloyd George was ready for him with his one-man good-cop–bad-cop routine.

The Prime Minister began by saying he was planning to tell his cabinet at noon that the conference was over and that the blame would fall on the Irish for refusing to stay in the Empire, even as a fully independent country. Once the threat was in play, he became sympathetic and encouraging, saying that he was willing to consider any alternative oath. Collins, responding to the cues, 'said I wished to express what my view was on their document', and proceeded to go down his list. He was 'perfectly dissatisfied' with the position of Northern Ireland, whereupon Lloyd George cleverly pointed out that he [Collins] had already said it would be economically unviable. Collins agreed, and added that it would lose two of its six counties and parts of three others (where Catholics were in the majority) if it stayed out, so it was all the same to him what James Craig's government decided so long as it decided soon.

Next came the all-important oath. Collins gave Lloyd George a copy of the IRB-approved version, but Lloyd George refused to discuss it, saying he would do so only once Dominion status was accepted. Inevitably, Collins returned to his favourite topic, but 'Mr Lloyd George said that if I had the idea of building submarines they could not allow that.' He also brought up trade and fiscal autonomy, where the Prime Minister was also amenable to further discussion. In the end, a hopeful Lloyd George suggested an afternoon meeting and also promised that, if the delegates agreed to Dominion status, he would wait upon the decision of the Dail (and the voters) before taking further action.

Now on offer were a better deal on trade and defence and an improved oath – not to mention an end to the immediate threat of war – in exchange for agreeing to accept the Crown as a member of the Commonwealth. The stage was set for the final series of meetings, which stretched from three in the afternoon of the 5th to two o'clock the next morning, with a break from about seven to eleven. This is perhaps the single most controversial day in modern Irish history, and one of the most dramatic – rivalled only by the confrontations between Charles Stewart Parnell and his foes over his leadership in Committee Room 15 in 1890.

Griffith would write the next day that 'things were so strenuous and exhausting that the sequence of conversation is not in many cases clear in my mind', and added that on four separate occasions the meeting 'was on the point of bursting to fragments.' As with the talks as a whole, the final hours were dominated by Lloyd George, who exercised a mesmerizing influence over the exhausted and disunited Irishmen. So much is evident from a variety of sources, but his personal mastery was captured in Robert Barton's embarrassingly frank account of proceedings to the Dail, where he spoke of 'the power of conviction that he alone, of all men I met, can impart by word and gesture – the vehicles by which the mind of one man oppresses and impresses the mind of another'.

The Irish delegates had accepted 6 December as the deadline for giving a firm answer to the British proposals, and so, it would appear, had the Dail cabinet. As Collins later put it (without any contradiction), 'It was well understood at that Cabinet Meeting [on the 3rd] that Sir James Craig was receiving a reply from the British Premier on Tuesday morning. Some conclusion as between the British Delegation and ourselves had, therefore, to be come to and handed in to the British Delegation on the Monday night.' As intended, this did much to focus the minds of all present and put more pressure on the Irish delegates as each hour passed.

At the start, Collins, Griffith and Barton lined up against Lloyd George, Chamberlain, Birkenhead and Churchill – who, Griffith noted in his final letter to de Valera, was 'in a bad mood'. Childers waited outside the door reading Abraham Lincoln (although he failed to profit by his hero's example of flexible statesmanship). Griffith, with Collins in support, tried to counter Lloyd George's demand to know about Dominion status before going on by withholding their response on constitutional status until the British could give them an answer on unity. The hope was that they would either make progress on the north or be granted their fall-back excuse for a refusal to sign.

Lloyd George had a trump card to play, however. He accused Griffith of going back on his word not to repudiate his (Lloyd George's) Northern Ireland solution, devised to avoid a breakdown in the talks, which was itself predicated on Ireland being a Dominion. In a theatrical gesture, he retrieved the secret memo resulting from their private 13 November agreement, to Collins's amazement. Griffith hadn't actually agreed to Dominion status at that meeting, or even to the boundary commission, and he hadn't signed the document, but such was the shock of the memo's reappearance and the weight of the occasion that Griffith said simply, 'I said I would not let you down and I won't.'

With the north taken care of – and the Irish strategy checkmated – the British cannily made a series of concessions. The new oath supplied by Collins was adopted with minor changes, the Irish Free

State was given more power over its security, and full control over trade was conceded, allowing Ireland to do as it pleased to protect its industries and restrict British imports. Collins had also wanted the time allowed for James Craig's government to make its decision to be shortened to six months – the British went further and agreed to one month, to allay Collins's concerns about forcing the issue as soon as possible.

The negotiators took a break then and reassembled at seven o'clock. Lloyd George asked if the Irish would now sign, and Griffith said he would but he couldn't speak for the others. After more toing and froing, the Prime Minister, eager to close the deal, resorted once again to bogus yet mesmerizing stagecraft. With a letter in each hand, he announced that one contained articles of agreement, the other a declaration of failure. The former meant peace, the other war – and 'war within three days'. He had to send one to James Craig in Belfast that night, to meet his self-imposed 6 December deadline. Which would it be? Griffith replied that he would sign, even if he did so alone. That was not good enough, Lloyd George declared – all would have to sign to avert a war. Griffith said they would have an answer by ten o'clock, and the Irish left to return to Hans Place.

THIS LAST ACT was played out in front of the world's press (a 'cold and dreamy vigil' for the doorstep men at Hans Place and No. 10), with each new newspaper edition reporting the latest developments. Back in Ireland, de Valera – expecting an unhappy ending like everyone else – was on the warpath. He had gone west on the 4th, to Ennis in Co. Clare and to Galway (with Brugha and Mulcahy in tow), to warn publicly that the country had to stand firmly behind Sinn Fein and that there were some things the Irish negotiators 'could never give up – no matter what the alternative'. The next day, in Limerick, he declared that 'Never – not till the end of time will they get from this nation allegiance to their rulers.'

This rather undermined the delegates' efforts to make partition the key issue. Lloyd George's politicos were New Labour-like masters of spin, leak and rumour – men against boys compared to the previously effective Dail publicity machine. The suppliers of quotes to news reporters were telling all and sundry that the Irish were intransigent, that the talks were failing despite Lloyd George's best efforts, that the Empire was the issue. The press was buying it.

The *New York Times* painted a rather unflattering portrait of the delegates as being out of their depth. They had started out in October driving to meetings in luxurious private cars; by December they were showing up all stuffed in one taxi. At Hans Place 'there was much coming and going, much banging of doors and telephoning galore'; no one knew what was going on, or if they would have to flee the city at a moment's notice. On that last night, one of the secretaries, Kathleen Napoli McKenna, recalled being surrounded by shadowy figures whom she took to be British agents, but most, if not all, of these besiegers were probably reporters lurking about for something to happen. All in all, it was a tense and rather chaotic atmosphere in which Collins had to decide his own and his country's future.

Collins had been silent throughout the final discussion in Downing Street, looking – in Churchill's description – 'as if he was going to shoot someone, preferably himself'. Asked by reporters if they would come back, he said only, 'I don't know.' Had the conference broken down? 'I don't know.' The British thought they had only got Griffith, that the others had got away. So did Barton. He was thus amazed when Collins announced on the crowded taxi ride home that he would sign too. Erskine Childers picks up the story:

> Home to drama. Meeting of delegates 9 p.m. Final discussion. AG spoke almost passionately for signing. It seems other side insist *all delegates* shall sign and recommend treaty to Dail. Monstrous demand. MC said nothing. Bob [Barton] refused to sign and GD then long and hot argument – all about war and committing our young men to die for nothing. What could GD get better? Etc etc. GD answered quietly Bob shaken. Asked me out. I said it was principle and I felt Molly [Erskine's American wife] was with us. Suddenly he said 'well I suppose I must sign' . . . RCB went in and said he would sign under duress and solely because, if he didn't, country would get no opportunity to decide. AG then said he would say they signed under duress and if they refused tell them go to the devil. EJD strongly contested this (weakest of all, all team). [MC] supported EJD and it was dropped. [GD] couldn't hold out if 4 signed. MC AG and RCB to go. We left at 11 pm (an hour late). My chief recollection of these inexplicably miserable hours was that of Churchill in evening dress moving up and down the lobby with his loping

stoop and long strides & a huge cigar like a bowsprit. His coarse
heavy jowls making him a very type of brutal militarism.

The next day Childers rehashed the event with cousin Bob: 'We
agreed that Duggan's behaviour and speeches were miserably ignom-
inious and hypocritical. AG jarred too with his perpetual harping on
men who had died. MC said too little, but it was he who prevented
a break, several times suggesting delay when it had practically been
decided to break – coats on etc.'

Barton, the most honest and reliable observer, has provided his
own account:

> First of all, Collins and Griffith and Duggan were going to sign
> whether Gavan Duffy or I did, or not, and Lloyd George had
> said all five must sign, or war would follow. Gavan Duffy and I
> were in this position. Neither of us knew what de Valera or the
> Dail would do if Collins, Griffith and Duggan signed. If we
> refused to sign and war was resumed immediately, the Dail
> would have no option of accepting. If war was made on the
> country, we should have to carry the responsibility; and neither
> of us knew whether we would have de Valera, or anyone behind
> us. We might well be asked, 'Why did you commit us to war
> without consulting us?' Three leaders had committed themselves;
> that was a new situation, one never at any time considered in
> Dublin. In Dublin Griffith had stated to de Valera that he would
> not sign without referring the term[s] back ... You must
> remember that for three hours we had a most frightful battle in
> the delegation, among ourselves, at which the most terrific things
> were said to Gavan Duffy and to me by Collins and Griffith and
> Duggan. They called us murderers, stated that we would be
> hanged from lamp-posts, that we would destroy all they had
> fought for. The most terrible prospect was held out by Collins
> and Griffith to us.

It was the normally dormant Duggan who made the 'lamp-posts'
remark and added 'that he would feel that he betrayed his comrades
who died with him at the barricades if he refused these terms'. As for
Griffith, according to Barton, 'he stood in front of the fireplace, held
up his hand and said "If they [the Ulster Unionists] don't agree to
join us there will be a Boundary Commission. They will lose half of
their territory and they can't stay out." Griffith said the same thing

over and over again. Griffith was highly optimistic about the results of a proposed plebiscite.' Collins made the pessimist's case about their prospects in a second war: 'He stated that only 2,000 active Volunteers were operating and asked me [Barton] whether I wanted to send them back to be slaughtered.' He also remarked, 'If it goes back to war, make no mistake about it, I'm going down to the trenches. I'm going down to Cork to lead [a threat he had uttered many times before].'

Collins and the other two willing signatories got up to leave several times, but returned to the fray until, according to Barton, 'our opposition was finally broken down.' Veteran backroom boy Dan McCarthy was at Hans Place that night, fielding increasingly anxious calls from Tom Jones, and he backs up Childers's description of Collins holding things together until all agreed to sign.

They returned as a body to Downing Street, arriving late, after eleven. Two hours were spent on last-minute details to remove a few more aspects that the Irish found objectionable (the status of Ireland's defence forces was raised to that of a national army, for one), and at last the final draft was agreed. Two copies were signed by both delegations at 2 a.m., and then they shook hands for the first time.

WHY DID COLLINS SIGN? Why did any of them? Barton and Gavan Duffy signed under pressure from the other three. Duggan signed because Collins did. And Collins followed Griffith. Griffith had been happy with the idea of the Dominion of Ireland since it was first mooted in July, and was convinced that the boundary commission would solve the Ulster Unionist problem in short order. Once the British conceded full economic independence, he had few remaining substantive objections. He was also persuaded that the British were willing to fight, and that the result would be disastrous. Moreover, Lloyd George was their only hope for a reasonable interlocutor, so if he and they failed to reach an agreement it would be a victory for the reactionary forces Griffith thought were waiting in the wings.

Nevertheless, Griffith did follow de Valera's strategy faithfully until the moment when he felt he had no other honourable choice – which is to say, the very last minute. Not only had he lost the ability to break on Northern Ireland (thanks in part to de Valera and Gavan Duffy), but he had also come to the conclusion that it was his duty to put the Treaty to the Irish public, that it would be wrong to risk war without them knowing what was being turned down. Anyway, the oath had been amended, as per de Valera's rather vague instructions at the last cabinet meeting. As for signing before bringing the agreement back to the cabinet, de Valera had refused to come himself, and it was he who had insisted that his oath of office meant he had to do what was best for the people.

Griffith impressed his British counterparts as a man of tremendous moral courage. Collins did not. Here is the test: if Griffith had not precipitated the agreement, would Collins have been willing to go it alone (or alone except for Duggan)? Collins spent the rest of his life saying that the alternative to the Treaty was war to the death, and that the agreement was a good deal that was worth signing on its own merits anyway, so he would presumably have had a clear conscience. But the answer is, almost certainly, no. Griffith had to act first for Collins to follow.

No one had known what Collins really thought before he made his declaration in the back of the taxi – except that he didn't want to have to make the decision and that he felt he was being used to do the dirty work that others in the cabinet could not face, and that he was being stabbed in the back. His personal history of siding with the militants in splits and of earlier quarrels with Griffith, his power base among conspirators and gunmen, and his fear of being blamed for compromise or failure should have predisposed him to say no. His indecisiveness, keeping options open and waiting until the last minute were all classic Collins behaviour, all directed at giving him the opportunity to make the best choice: to make *a* choice when it came right down to it. He had done the same thing before his decision to go back to Ireland in 1916, and in his decision to join the delegation in the first place. But once Griffith had cast the die it only took him minutes to go along – between leaving the conference room and arriving back home.

Collins was apparently as surprised by Griffith's sudden announcement, and by the secret pledge to Lloyd George, as Barton was at his decision to go along with it. He knew Griffith's opinions – public and private – and he had sided with him (and vice versa) in the various squabbles with the cabinet and the other delegates. He knew of Griffith's refusal to break on the Crown, and also of his promise to consult the cabinet before doing anything else. However, Collins had not gone with him to the meeting on 4 December and

Griffith had had to work hard to convince him to see the Prime Minister the next morning. Both men thought the talks were more or less over at that point, and neither had any apparent intention of splitting with the rest of the delegates and signing on his own. Griffith was probably mostly concerned with trying to break on the north. All the evidence points to Griffith deciding to sign only at the second-last meeting on the 5th, with Collins making up his mind shortly afterwards.

Why did Arthur Griffith's decision matter so much? The political logic of the situation suggests the following. Griffith was Collins's guide through the negotiations as well as his key ally and comrade in the delegation and in cabinet. Not following him would leave Collins isolated, and might lose his respect and friendship. Nor was it likely to reconcile him with his cabinet enemies or with hardliners at home who were already accusing him of selling out.

But what finally made Griffith the key was de Valera's removing himself from the decision-making process. Collins clearly felt let down by the President's repeated refusals to join them, and he was now probably convinced he was being set up to take the fall, as his entourage had been telling him for months. Collins's decision was predicated on Dev's decision to stay at home and Griffith's decision to sign.

On the other hand, while acting on his own would probably mean failure and political suicide, joining with Griffith and Duggan, and dragging the whole delegation along with them, offered a huge political opportunity. He had the IRB Supreme Council's blessing, as well as the backing of powerful IRA friends (he assumed), and the certainty (both he and Griffith seem to have believed) of public backing for peace and self-government. Griffith had his own connections, cronies and influence. Together they could lead a powerful pro-Treaty coalition. They may also have thought that de Valera might agree with the new and improved terms.

Nor was Collins jumping into the dark. In utilitarian terms, he had firmly concluded that this was as good a deal as they could get, and that further military action could only harm the movement's position. He had thought a great deal about the possibilities inherent in the Treaty, and in fact had alluded to them at the last cabinet meeting when he had said that they had twelve months before they had to take the new oath of allegiance, to see how it would work. To dubious republican friends he explained what 'seeing how it would work' meant. First, to IRA comrades he argued it would give them the chance to build up an army and establish a proper government, from which vantage point they could defy Britain or, if necessary, fight a second war for full independence. Second, as he wrote to a disappointed Art O'Brien the day after signing the Treaty – and as he suggested to many other republicans – they would get a second chance to define Ireland's status when they wrote the actual constitution of the Free State. Once the British were committed to the transfer of power and had withdrawn their armed forces and disbanded the police, republicans could renegotiate the oath from a much better vantage point. Collins said nothing of this in public, but from the outset he was calculating alternatives and planning future moves.

Not that he wasn't deeply troubled by the prospect of making a decision, or anxious once he had made it. Not that it didn't take courage to break with so much of his past, even if he didn't quite realize yet that that was what he would have to do. But almost from the moment he signed, as on similar occasions in the past, his indecisiveness vanished and he was looking ahead and repositioning himself to work the new opportunities.

20: The Speech

Michael Collins' appearance upset all the preconceived ideas of one who had known him only through the newspapers. He is tall, with a slight leaning towards *embonpoint*, and with a great mass of jet black hair, giving the impression of an almost Falstaffian geniality. Unless his look belie him, Mr Collins has an abundant sense of humour.

(*Irish Times*, 1921)

HAVING SIGNED THE TREATY, Collins – along with Griffith – now had to sell it to enough of his fellow ministers and TDs to have it accepted by the cabinet and the Dail. The full cabinet met on 8 December, and here the delegates had to face the fury of a de Valera scorned. He felt the delegation had caved in under pressure, had exceeded their authority by acting without consulting the cabinet again, and (in the case of Arthur Griffith) had broken a clear promise to that effect. They had not got either essential unity or external association, and they had destroyed his whole carefully arranged bargaining position. Moreover, he felt personally betrayed, as he had clearly understood that nothing would be signed without his being consulted first, and had been publicly positioning himself for the threat of war. Even before the cabinet met, he declared he could not recommend the agreement and would oppose it, and other republicans in the United States and Ireland said much the same. Collins's response to the *New York Times* (he always preferred talking to American reporters) was 'I expect trouble but have had trouble before and expect to overcome this one.'

De Valera's first instinct, and his whole aim throughout the subsequent debate, was to reverse what had happened at 10 Downing

Street, and to return to the position held in early December, with a movement united behind the demand for full sovereignty. He did not want to split Sinn Fein or the Dail, and most certainly not the IRA, which he was trying to keep out of politics. He had long been aware of the danger of a split – had based his whole strategy around keeping most of the gunmen and republicans on side – and he continued to work to avoid this outcome (contrary to the partisan allegation that he courted civil war in pursuit of power). However laudable, this proved to be a disastrous guiding principle in the weeks ahead as Collins, Griffith and their allies outmanoeuvred, out-argued and outspun him on the way to a decisive political victory.

This process was well under way by the time the cabinet met. Newspapers in Ireland, Britain and around the world had been telling the story of the talks as a narrative of hopeful reconciliation, with breakdown being a disastrous failure. An agreement was the approved happy ending, representing not just a compromise between politicians but an end to centuries of strife. Once Lloyd George set his deadline, suspense had built up to the preset climax, accelerated by the crisis atmosphere engineered by Downing Street in the final days. War or peace was the time-honoured media mantra.

Thus the news of the final breakthrough on the 6th was greeted with elation and congratulation, which were what also greeted the delegates when they arrived at Euston station to take the boat train home. Editorials in Britain and Ireland welcomed the news joyously, and telegrams began flooding in to republican leaders from governments and leaders in the United States and the Commonwealth. Collins and Griffith gave interviews to the press talking the Treaty up. Rather like the British government dictating the agenda to the Irish negotiators by making Dominion status the focus of the talks, the advocates of the Treaty had a huge head start by the time the struggle within the movement began, as they had already won the battle to frame the debate in their terms. War or peace. Who wouldn't be in favour of peace?

The official minutes of the six-hour cabinet meeting are sparse, but we once again have Erskine Childers's diary to give us the details. As he walked into the meeting, the first thing he saw was 'Dev head on hands reproaching MC with having signed'. De Valera started things off, and, in his Castro-like way, did most of the talking throughout. 'Dev said delegation had broken its instructions not to make a serious decision without consulting Cabinet & to send to it our draft to be signed.' Griffith answered by pointing out that de Valera had refused to go himself – the soon-to-be standard rebuttal to almost anything the President said. 'Dev said this was because he trusted our undertaking.' A good quick reply. Collins then came in to point out that they *had* only recommended it to the Dail. This was quite true – the cabinet and parliament could reject it. However, this was not how it had been announced to the public, and de Valera knew it. The world thought it was essentially a done deal. 'Dev said really much more. He would have to oppose Treaty.' 'Strangely enough,' according to Austin Stack, 'we were not unfriendly towards one another.' Finally, the delegates unanimously agreed that none of them had thought of consulting the cabinet. De Valera grumbled that 'it was not team work.'

The discussion then turned to the text itself, although not in any great detail. Curiously, neither side sought to prove the other wrong on the merits of the agreement. Griffith said he stood by it all, and then the issue of duress emerged. Barton declared he would not go back on his signature, but said he had been 'intimidated' by the threat that he would be responsible for war otherwise. Childers was then astonished to hear Collins say *'he did the same (!)'* In fact what he said was that 'if there was duress, it was only the "duress of the facts"' ('whatever he meant by that' the unsubtle Stack complained). What Collins meant was that he did not feel compelled to sign by Lloyd George's three-day warning, but he had to acknowledge the situation as it was: war and defeat would be the inevitable, unacceptable, alternative. He would return to this fine but (to him) vital distinction again and again in the following months.

Kevin O'Higgins, who was not able to vote as he was only an assistant minister, argued that the Treaty should never have been signed, but, given the fait accompli, they should make the best of it. This was a curiously unenthusiastic position considering his later hard line against anti-Treaty republicanism, but it may have been designed to get de Valera on side. At this point, however, Barton 'strongly reproached President said it was due to his "vacillation" from beginning. At last moment had chance of going to London and refused. Said the disaster was because we were not a fighting delegation.'

De Valera refused "to come into line" and summed up his

position. 'He had worked from the beginning for an "association" which the Cahal [Cathal Brugha] party could justly [just] accept + which would not give up his [the?] Republic. Now all thrown away without an effort.' Still, he did not despair of getting the terms he wanted, by overturning the Treaty and starting again, based on the fact that it was signed under duress and was therefore non-binding.

Collins (and Griffith and Duggan) denied the accusation that they had been compelled to sign. Griffith had signed on the Treaty's merits, and Collins explained what he had said earlier: 'In a contest between a great Empire & a small nation this was as far as the small nation could get. Until the British Empire was destroyed Ireland could get no more. On that [basis?] only was intimidated.' He had already seemingly contradicted this position when he suggested working the Treaty for a year to see what they could get out of it, and that (as he was telling his army buddies) once the Irish army and state were built up they would be in a better position to renegotiate. He would continue to use both lines, depending on his audience, along with a full-out defence of the Treaty as not just the best terms possible but a good deal in itself.

Eventually a vote was called. With Collins and Griffith was Barton – angry, opposed in principle, but feeling honour-bound to stick to his signature. Against were Stack, Brugha and de Valera. William Cosgrave broke the tie by voting for the Treaty. This may have come as something of a shock (particularly to the Treaty's opponents), as Cosgrave had objected to the oath to the Crown at the previous meeting. If he had once wavered, however, he was now committed. There is no evidence that Collins or anyone else had anything to do with his change of heart. Both sides agreed that they could not serve under the other if they lost in the Dail. They would continue in their posts until the matter was decided, but this would be their last meeting in the same cabinet.

ON THE 14TH the scene shifted to the Dail, meeting for the first time as a complete body, as the thousands of Sinn Fein and IRA internees had immediately been released once the Treaty was signed (a huge boost to its popularity). The location, as usual, was the Mansion House, familiar from Sinn Fein conventions, previous meetings of the Dail and the Truce talks. The voting body of the Dail comprised 119 men and 6 women, elected that summer in the northern and southern elections. Few had faced any competition; a great many were IRA commandants (unknown to the general public), representing brigades and divisions as much as constituencies. They often stayed in groups in small hotels whose owners were known to be sympathetic, including Vaughan's, and gathered together in rooms and bars at the end of the day to talk things over and complain about politicians. Pro- and anti-Treaty operators, who had their own back rooms, would circulate among them, rallying supporters and keeping running tallies of how people were planning to vote. Journalists – British, Irish and American – also joined the fray, looking for their own inside information. Meanwhile, crowds outside the Mansion House cheered everyone they recognized and hoped for the best.

There followed what has gone down in history as 'the Treaty debate' – often derided as hysterical and intellectually unimpressive, but unfairly so. This was one of the very few occasions in modern history in which Irish nationalists sought (or were forced) to define and defend themselves and their politics in open debate, and they did so often with great skill and insight, as well as with passionate intensity. They discussed Irish history, the state of the post-war world, and the principles of nationality, democracy and citizenship. There were many personal testaments of belief alongside the abstracted logic of constitutions and practical assessments of what the movement had achieved. Out of this sprang most of modern Irish politics, its parties and ideologies. Few other countries can claim such an honest and profound starting point.

De Valera dominated the debate from start to finish, imposing his agenda on the proceedings and speaking to every point at great length. Collins had never been much of a parliamentarian, speaking rarely in the Dail, and then to little effect, but he proved his ability here. He marshalled and led his backbench followers, and took on Dev in the head-to-head battle of the speeches.

Of course he did not do this alone. The supporters of the Treaty clearly had the superior team, composed of savvy journalists and propagandists, lawyers, war heroes and the majority of the cabinet, all deployed to good effect by Collins, Griffith and the irreplaceable Dan McCarthy. Griffith had his old circle of committee men to fall back on, including Sean Milroy, William Cosgrave and Patrick O'Keefe. Collins employed his troops well – Sean MacEoin, Richard Mulcahy, Gearoid O'Sullivan, Sean Hales and Eoin O'Duffy – while

McCarthy, Sinn Fein's electoral mastermind, appointed himself chief whip of the embryo pro-Treaty party. 'I think nobody will deny the fact I know something about elections, and I regret to say I am responsible for having some of the members here to-day,' he remarked in his speech.

De Valera had no such coherent group, as many of those opposed to the Treaty were guerrillas who didn't know him very well, didn't agree with his preferred solutions, and would not follow his lead in parliament or in making public statements. Unfortunately for the soon-to-be ex-President, he would not have a party he could call his own again until 1926.

The first round of battle occurred almost entirely in secret, as on the 14th de Valera moved that the Dail meet in private session. There he launched his first major bid to refocus the movement around external association, arguing that the plenipotentiaries had not been empowered to sign any agreement, that they had violated the cabinet's instructions given ten days earlier, and that, in any case, as Gavan Duffy and Barton testified, they had signed only under the threat of immediate war. Moreover, the final Irish proposal – the draft treaty last rejected by the British – was a far superior alternative to what had been agreed to. 'The question we have to decide is one which ought to be decided on its merits, and it would be very unfortunate if . . . what I might call an accidental division of opinion of the Cabinet . . . should cut across these deliberations.'

His proposal might embody the risk of war with Britain, but the 6 December Treaty certainly meant the destruction of the movement and civil war, leaving them at the mercy of the British government once again. De Valera was not looking merely for a vote in his own favour: he wanted essentially unanimous agreement to give him a strong negotiating position to achieve his final goal – and confidentiality was necessary to make the case properly. It was an ambitious scheme, consistent with his perennial concern for unity as the only basis for effective action.

To this end, he gave the TDs his alternative treaty, very similar to the signed Articles of Agreement, but with a somewhat different oath and an explicit statement that sovereignty belonged to the people, not the Crown. This was his first great error. His intention was to show that his demands were vital yet not radical or impossible to achieve. The effect was to paint him as a legalistic quibbler, willing to risk war for trivial changes in the wording of a document. Nor did it reassure ardent republicans about the soundness of his leadership, as this was far from the separatist ideal as set out in the 1916 proclamation – now the touchstone of the republican faith.

De Valera realized his mistake, and requested that 'Document No. 2', as it became known, not be released to the public. This meant only that Treaty supporters could ask him over and over again in public what his alternative was if he didn't want the Treaty, confident he could not give a satisfactory answer. And inevitably it was published in the end, to general public derision.

De Valera's preferred secrecy also reinforced the Treatyites' most basic argument: that the majority of people (that is to say, of southern nationalists) wanted the Treaty, so any democratic vote would almost certainly be in their favour. Their opponents even conceded as much. Collins cleverly made this his main point of attack, and even more cleverly withheld most of his arguments for the Treaty until they could be made in public, thus forcing de Valera on to disadvantageous ground. 'I as a public representative cannot consent, if I am in a minority of one, in withholding from the Irish people my knowledge of what the alternative is,' Collins thundered.

Instead of expending all his ammunition when 'it is only a waste of time making speeches that can be made in public session', Collins sent his IRA lieutenants out to shore up his military front. Mulcahy, MacEoin, O'Sullivan, O'Duffy and Pat Brennan of Clare could all speak credibly as 'plain soldiers' that if the Dail could give them the means to fight on they would do so, and – in MacEoin's hair-raising words – 'the man or number of men who attempt to flinch my bullet crashes through his brain on the spot.' In its present state, however, the IRA could not win another war, MacEoin insisted. 'Whatever has been done, was done by bluff' (Michael Collins's bluff to be precise), and the Treaty would actually give them the rifles to finish the job.

These men were carefully prepped with some of the best pro-Treaty lines. Collins would become famous as the author of the image of the Treaty being a 'stepping stone' to the republic but it was actually an old phrase of Griffith's, first used in the debate by Eoin O'Duffy, who declared that he recognized the Treaty 'as a stepping stone only. I regard it as not being final, otherwise I would be false to my oath and my country.' Sean Hales of West Cork had earlier spoken of the agreement as 'a jumping off point . . . the best rock to jump off for the final accomplishment of Irish freedom', suggesting an agreed party line was in use, even if Hales had mangled the wording.

By eleven at night on Saturday the 17th, de Valera had had enough. He closed the session by telling them all off: 'The whole object for which I put this paper before you has evidently been lost sight of . . . If you had imagination to see it you would, tomorrow, reject that Treaty and accept the other.'

IN THE FIRST four days of the debate, Collins and his allies demonstrated superior political wit and self-control while de Valera seemed to say whatever entered his mind, repeatedly interrupting other speakers to no good effect. Their ascendency over de Valera was further demonstrated on Monday the 19th, the first full day of public discussion. Griffith opened with a cogent and succinct defence of the negotiators' conduct and of the agreement as the best deal possible under the circumstances. It would allow Ireland to rebuild 'the Gaelic civilization broken down at the battle of Kinsale [1601]'. This counsel of moderation was deliberately followed by Sean MacEoin, figurative rifle in hand, who proclaimed 'to the world and to Ireland I say I am an extremist' but (paraphrasing) that meant he was extremely sure the Treaty was the right way to go.

Then came de Valera, with his first public statement of where he stood. He started well with a strong statement that 'I am against this Treaty, not because I am a man of war, but a man of peace,' because an agreement that failed to reconcile 'Irish national aspirations' would not end the conflict. And this one didn't, because it satisfied neither 'the party in Ireland which typifies national aspirations for centuries' nor 'the test of whether the people were satisfied or not'. The former was a coded reference to militant republicans, and to the IRA in particular, who would have to accept any deal for it to mean genuine peace. His definition of the 'people' and their preferences was also obscure, as he did not mean to suggest holding an election to find out what they wanted. The Treaty might well win a 'snatch election', thanks to war-weariness, but it would not bring peace, only division.

Rather than spell out what he meant in concrete terms, however, de Valera became enmeshed in a lengthy comparison of Ireland to a prisoner who still aspired to freedom – one might accept the reality

17. Collins, emerging in characteristic style from 10 Downing Street during the Treaty negotiations in 1921.

18. Lloyd George, F. E. Smith (Lord Birkenhead) and Winston Churchill leaving 10 Downing Street at a more sedate pace.

19. Collins in London, showing off his latest moustache.

20. *Above.*
Dail Eireann
in session in the
Mansion House,
1921.

21. *Left.*
As Collins would
have seen it: the
crowd outside
the Mansion
House.

22. *Above.* Kitty Kiernan (1891?–1945), date unknown (but possibly taken after 1922).

23. *Right.* Hazel Lavery (1880–1935), waving a cat in the air at a St James' Palace Garden Party in London, 1919.

24. Anti-Treaty TDs pose for a photograph in 1922. Cathal Brugha (1874–1922), with coat and hat in hand, is at centre. The bearded man behind him is Count George Plunkett (1851–1948). On the right, Eamon de Valera is partially obscured by the cameraman.

25. Collins greets Sean MacEoin on his wedding day in June 1922. This was originally supposed to be a double wedding with Collins and Kitty Kiernan but events forced a postponement.

26. Rory O'Connor (1883–1922) addressing a Dublin crowd, 1922.

27. Richard Mulcahy speaking in 1922.

28. Collins, with Joe McGrath (1888–1966) on the left and Sean McGarry (1886–1924) on the right, in 1922.

29. *Left*. Collins, de Valera and Harry Boland at the Sinn Fein Ard Fheis in February 1922. Their good humour coincided with one of their periodic bouts of deal-making.

30. *Below*. After the deals fell through: the Four Courts at the time of the siege in June 1922.

31. The Provisional Government cabinet minus Collins. At the head of the table is William Cosgrave (1880–1965). To his left are Ernest Blythe (1889–1975) and Kevin O'Higgins (1892–1927). Closest to him on his right is Desmond Fitzgerald (1888–1947) and closest to the camera is Diarmid O'Hegarty (1892–1958).

32. Collins, as Commander-in-Chief of the National Army, marching in Arthur Griffith's funeral procession in August 1922 with Richard Mulcahy beside him and staff officers behind him.

33. People queuing to see Collins' body at Saint Vincent's Hospital in Dublin, August 1922.

34. Johnny and Hannie Collins praying at Michael's graveside in Glasnevin Cemetery.

of the cell, but one never gave up the right to escape. The Treaty would give up this right, and would entomb the Irish nation for ever. It would be a betrayal not just of the republic, but of Parnell's great dictum that no man can set the boundaries to the march of a nation. Showing a far-from-keen insight into the hearts of Irish farmers and shopkeepers, he asserted that 'the Irish people would not want me to save them materially at the expense of their national honour.'

However, in a particularly convoluted passage, he went even further:

> Criticism of the Treaty is scarcely necessary from this point of view, that it could not be ratified because it would not be legal for this assembly to ratify it, because it would be inconsistent with our position ... and the very fact that it is inconsistent shows that it could not be reconciled with Irish aspirations.

The significance of this logic seems to have passed many listeners by, but it was fateful indeed: according to its President, the Dail simply could not – morally, legally, legitimately – surrender its existence, as the old Irish parliament had done in 1800. The Dail's authority was derived from the Republic declared in 1916 and ratified by the 1918 and 1921 elections, and that authority could not be asserted and denied in the same breath. The Republic was the fundamental law, and could not be subverted.

The *New York Times* thought it 'a good speech in its way, but it was a tragic speech'. On paper, it is rambling and ineffectual, showing little preparation or consultation, and gives the air of something sketched out late the night before. The most important messages were wrapped in metaphor or code, there was little concrete detail, and no real discussion of alternatives – either war or external association. De Valera was careful to point out that his was not 'an uncompromising stand for the republic', but without Document No. 2 (and a blackboard to explain external association) that is what people took him to mean. Why would the Treaty settlement, so obviously superior to Home Rule, be such a terrible fate? How many Irish people really did want to sacrifice their material well-being and security – or lives – to uphold national honour as defined by de Valera? Were there no better arguments for risking British reconquest? It is hard to imagine any undecided listeners or readers being convinced by his argument, let alone following it from start to finish.

De Valera had given better speeches a few days before, and would do so again. At this point he seems to have been worn out. The *Freeman's Journal* thought 'he looked ... a little tired,' and the *New York Times* reported that 'he finished as pale as a sheet, and thoroughly exhausted.' He had talked at breakneck speed – 'a torrent' – as if everyone at large had already heard the more elaborate and forceful arguments he had made in private. At one point he even wearily said, 'I have spoken generally, and if you wish we can take these documents up, article by article, but they have been discussed in Private Session, and I do not think there is any necessity for doing so.' But he wasn't just talking to the deputies any more. This was still the great age of parliamentary debate, where whole speeches were printed in newspapers, and the whole country had been waiting since 6 December to hear what their leaders had to say. This was the President's best and probably his only chance to change minds or instil doubt. His speech was another terrible mistake, and it created a huge opportunity that Collins was not going to let slip.

After de Valera came Austin Stack and Count Plunkett, who invoked, respectively, a Fenian father and a martyred son to damn the proposed oath of allegiance. Then Joe McBride spoke for the Treaty, to make it three speakers apiece, and the House adjourned at one o'clock.

When the deputies reconvened at 3.45 it was Collins's turn. According to the *Independent*, 'A dark December evening had begun. Michael Collins (clean-shaven again now that his on-again, off-again moustache had gone again) was on his feet in an instant and plunged right ahead.' He began slowly, by defending the signing of the agreement – a defence that culminated in the following:

> The answer which I gave and that signature which I put on that document would be the same in Dublin or in Berlin, or in New York or in Paris ... There has been talk about 'the atmosphere of London' and there has been talk about 'slippery slopes' ... If the members knew so much about 'slippery slopes' before we went there why did they not speak then? The slopes were surely slippery, but it is easy to be wise afterwards. I submit that such observations are entirely beside the point. And if my signature has been given in error, I stand by it whether it has or not, and I am not going to take refuge behind any kind of subterfuge. I

stand up over that signature and I give that same decision at this moment in this assembly (applause). It has also been suggested that the Delegation broke down before the first bit of English bluff. I would remind the Deputy who used that expression that England put up quite a good bluff for the last five years here and I did not break down before that bluff (applause, and a voice, 'That is the stuff'). And does anybody think that the respect I compelled from them in a few years was in any way lowered during two months of negotiations? That also is beside the point. The results of our labour are before the Dail. Reject or accept. The President has suggested that a greater result could have been obtained by more skilful handling. Perhaps so. But there again the fault is not the delegation's; it rests with the Dail. It is not afterwards the Dail should have found out our limitations. Surely the Dail knew it when they selected us, and our abilities could not have been expected to increase because we were chosen as plenipotentiaries by the Dail. The delegates have been blamed for various things. It is scarcely too much to say that they have been blamed for not returning with recognition of the Irish Republic. They are blamed, at any rate, for not having done much better. A Deputy when speaking the other day with reference to Canada suggested that what may apply with safety to Canada would not at all apply to Ireland because of the difference in distance from Great Britain. It seemed to me that he did not regard the delegation as being wholly without responsibility for the geographical propinquity of Ireland to Great Britain.

All this was to pound home the message that de Valera (not to mention Stack) could have gone but didn't – and that sending him now, as his alternative entailed, would not change anything. Which brought Collins to his second point: the 'vexed question' of whether they were sent to get the Republic and nothing less. He quoted Lloyd George's 29 September invitation to the conference and de Valera's acceptance as evidence that (in the first of several immortal phrases) 'it was the acceptance of the invitation that formed the compromise.' 'If we all stood on the recognition of the Irish Republic as a prelude to any conference we could very easily have said so, and there would be no conference.' Of course it was de Valera himself who had bravely made this point before the negotiations began, while Collins remained silent. But that had been in private session as well, and now Collins could use it to make his opponent look the extremist in public.

So what was it they had brought back, then, if the Republic wasn't on the table? Here again the punchy lines rolled out to take their place alongside Parnell's in the pantheon of Irish political quotations. 'I do not recommend it for more than it is. Equally, I do not recommend it for less than it is. In my opinion it gives us freedom, not the ultimate freedom that all nations desire and develop to, but the freedom to achieve it.'

Collins then touched briefly on the fact that 'we had not beaten the enemy out of our country by force of arms,' and asserted that he had not been intimidated into signing; but he wisely did not dwell on the negative reasons for signing or agreeing. Instead he went on to echo Griffith's (and Irish Ireland's) constructive vision of a renewed Gaelic civilization. This would now be possible because of 'the immense powers and liberties' the Treaty would give the Free State to reverse the 750 years of 'peaceful penetration' and 'exploitation' that was the real legacy of British rule. Colonization had been enforced by force of arms, it was agreed, so did not 'the disappearance of that military strength give us the chief proof that our national liberties were established'?

Here Collins turned two of de Valera's arguments inside out. Where the President stressed the centuries of struggle and how they must not be betrayed, Collins argued that 'it has been much more a history of peaceful penetration over 750 years', and this would not be reversed by 'for ever keeping on an impossible fight.' This was the real – economic and cultural – surrender and matter of honour, which the Free State could immediately begin to redress. De Valera might contrast the material and the 'national', but in fact the two were interwined. Yes, this peaceful penetration had been enforced by British military strength, and here was the real test of whether Ireland had achieved freedom or not: the Treaty would 'rid the country of the enemy strength'.

The obvious rebuttal to this had been that the British armed forces could come back whenever they liked – and would still possess bases in Ireland. In another brilliant display of rhetorical judo, Collins turned the argument on its head. Ireland would be weak no matter what happened, because of its geography, but the Treaty actually protected them by association with Canada and the other Dominions. Ireland would acquire allies in any confrontation with an overweening Britain. 'They are, in effect, introduced as guarantors of our freedom, which makes us stronger than if we stood alone.' And, through Ireland's constitutional status being linked to that of the larger Dominions, Ireland would rise to full equality alongside them. In other words, the wording of the Treaty itself guaranteed that the nation would not be trapped in de Valera's imagined prison. Here Collins was rather selectively scavenging his memo on the future of the Commonwealth to support Dominion status rather than external association.

De Valera had argued that the status granted to Ireland was ambiguous, and that 'if there are differences of interpretation we know who will get the best of them.' But Collins had an answer to that one as well. Definitions don't count: it is 'our power to take it and to keep it [full Canadian status]' that matters – and 'I believe in our power to take it and to keep it. I believe in our future civilization ... As a plain Irishman I believe in my own interpretation against the interpretation of any Englishman.' And a final thrust: thinking that British politicians will automatically triumph 'is what marks the slave mind'.

Collins then turned to the question of what rejection might mean. It would mean war – and war 'until you have beaten the British empire'. That was fine with him if that was the national policy, but 'I would not be one of those to commit the Irish people to war without the Irish people committing themselves to war.' His opponents talked of principles, so 'I can state for you a principle which everybody will understand, the principle of "government by consent of the governed" ... the only firm principle in the whole thing.'

After a very quick mention of Ulster (a sore spot, but then almost no one else even brought it up) he drew to a close. 'There was never such an Irishman placed in such a position as I was by reason of these negotiations,' he declared, and he restated his fighting credo and credentials to show that he stood by everything he had done. He was still the same man. Others said the Treaty was a betrayal of 'the dead men' – those who had died in the struggle – but the bottom line was this:

I think the decision ought to be a clear decision on the documents as they are before us . . . On that we shall be judged, as to whether we have done the right thing in our own conscience or not. Don't let us put the responsibility, the individual responsibility, upon anybody else. Let us take that responsibility ourselves and let us in God's name abide by that decision.

MUCH OF IT HAD BEEN said before, but not all at once and not so well. The sentences and the logic were carefully honed, and it had structure and rhythm. Collins no doubt had the final say on the speech, and may have been the principal author, but he obviously had collaborators as well. As with his memo on the Commonwealth, many of the ideas and themes and some of the language were his, but the construction and packaging were probably the work of better writers. If it is compared to his many later speeches in 1922, the differences in form are striking.

Erskine Childers, who followed directly after Collins, praised it with his usual self-defeating decency as 'a most able and eloquent speech . . . All of us agree, I think, that we have listened to a manly, eloquent, and worthy speech.' Unfortunately for him, his own well-reasoned arguments were submerged in its wake, as, once Collins had finished, much of the audience got up and left.

The speech may have been practised as well as prepared: it was delivered well and with great feeling, impressing its audience. The *Independent*'s parliamentary sketch writer described the scene:

He spoke passionately, eagerly, pervadingly. He had his manuscript before him. He rarely consulted it. He preferred to rely on his intuition – on the unfailing native power of the Irishman to move, rouse and convince his hearers. Now and again he felt his smooth chin. He tossed his thick black hair in his hands. He rummaged among his documents. Like Mr de Valera, he stands now bent, now calm, and now quivering with emotion. On a previous occasion I said Michael Collins spoke slowly. He does – until he is aroused. Then the words come in a ceaseless stream.

Under the headline 'Collins Dominates Session', the starstruck *New York Times* man gushed:

Michael Collins is beyond question the outstanding figure in the Dail. His youth, his confidence, his resonant voice, his emphasis, his scorn, his sheer robustness, can work wonders inside the Dail as well as out. He has only to say definitely 'I stand by my decision' to raise ringing cheers ... but his argument was continuous as well and well-presented.

It was easily the best speech of Collins's life, and one of the great statements of political rationality in Irish history.

THE DEBATE CONTINUED, long after the principals had finished that day and much longer than anyone had expected. Collins and de Valera spoke again, of course – de Valera incessantly, until he broke down in tears while trying to get the last word in after the final vote on 7 January. Few speakers after Griffith, de Valera, Collins and Childers had much impact.

The vote was always going to be close, thanks to the presence of dozens of IRA officers and the overall republican bias in the House after the wartime election in 1921. One TD, Frank Drohan, resigned as he was unwilling to vote for the Treaty but did not want to flout the will of his constituents by voting against it. One up for the Treatyites. But Eoin MacNeill, who was pro-Treaty, did not vote so they lost on that account, and again when Pat McCartan abstained. Even worse, Tom Kelly was too ill to attend and two undecideds voted 'No'.

In the end, 64 approved and 57 opposed, with Gavan Duffy and Barton honour-bound to vote for the Treaty despite their reservations or outright disapproval. Once freed of his duty to uphold his signature, Barton would get his revenge by becoming one of Collins's most persistent and troublesome critics, poking holes in Collins's often adulterated accounts of the negotiations. Still, the role of honour in the debate has often been disparaged as destructive and irrational, but without it the Treaty would have an even more close-run thing.

One of the most striking features of the whole debate is the extent to which Collins himself became an issue. In the public sessions, pro-Treaty speakers contradicted the charge that the Treaty was forced upon them by appealing to Collins's war record. Arthur Griffith coined the label that stuck when he called him 'the man who won the war' in his speech proposing the Treaty, although Sean Moylan, the anti-Treaty commander of the North Cork Brigade, had already referred to him as 'the man who made the army'. Fin Lynch,

Collins's old house-mate from '44', continued this theme on the 20th by asking if the opposition were 'trying to tell the people of Ireland that Lloyd George shaking a paper in front of the face of Michael Collins was able to put the wind up Michael Collins. Let the people of Ireland judge whether it is so easy to put the wind up Michael Collins.'

This position was summed up in the popular phrase 'What is good enough for Mick is good enough for me' – a line invented or quoted later the same day by Patrick McCartan, who added, 'Personally I have more respect for Michael Collins and Arthur Griffith than for the quibblers here.' Eamon Duggan brought it up again the next day, by which time Mary MacSwiney had had enough:

> Michael Collins – his name alone will make that thing acceptable to many people in this country, as he made it acceptable to many of the young men of this Dail – 'What is good enough for Michael Collins is good enough for me' (applause). If Mick Collins went to hell in the morning, would you follow him there? (Cries of 'Yes' and 'No'.) Well, of course, I frankly have no answer to the Deputies who declare that they would transfer their allegiance from God to the devil at Michael Collins' behest.

After the Christmas break, opposition deputies went from decrying Collins's influence to slighting the man himself. On 6 January, Seamus Robinson of the South Tipperary Brigade muttered:

> But suppose you know that such a man was not really such a great man; and that his reputation and great deeds of daring were in existence only on paper and in the imagination of people who read stories about him ... If the Michael Collins who signed the Treaty ever did the wonderful things reported of him then I'm another fool.

The next day Cathal Brugha, infuriated by the Collins claque, pointed out that, technically, 'he is merely a subordinate in the Department of Defence.' Facing furious barracking from Dan McCarthy, Fionan Lynch, Eamon Duggan, Sean McGarry and Joe MacGrath – all Friends of Mick – he soldiered on to suggest that Collins sought 'notoriety', spread flattering stories about himself, and had never fired a shot. While memorable, this merely looked petty and jealous to most observers.

What should give Collins admirers pause is the treatment meted out to the anti-Treaty side. Brugha had been sneered at several times, as when William Cosgrave said of him that 'except for war he is not worth a damn for anything else,' and de Valera and Childers were smeared as un-Irish (the former was half-Spanish, the latter English by birth but brought up in Ireland). The legitimacy of de Valera's birth was even questioned. Childers was a gentleman, a patriot and the best mind on the anti-Treaty side, but many of the Treatyite deputies ostentatiously shunned him and they told the *New York Times* reporter that it wasn't right for him to take such a prominent role in the proceedings. (It was widely assumed that he was de Valera's chief adviser.) Griffith disliked him before the negotiations, and hated him afterwards, while Collins did nothing to hold his ally back. When there were complaints in the Dail about insulting comments made by the *Freeman's Journal*, Collins defended its right to free speech and spoke piously about his own eschewing of personal remarks – an implicit reference to the attentions paid to him. Turnabout is fair play?

On 9 January de Valera resigned as president of the Republic. He had been comprehensively beaten – out-argued, outprocedured and outvoted – but he had one last trick to play: he offered himself for re-election as president on the condition that he be given dictatorial powers. If only a few pro-Treaty voters changed sides or abstained, he might win. In the event it very nearly worked. He gained one vote, the other side lost four, and he was defeated by 60 votes to 58.

With Griffith due to be chosen in his stead, the next day the anti-Treatyites – now in effect an opposition party – walked out in protest. As they did so the following outburst was recorded by the official Dail reporters:

Mr. M. Collins: Deserters all! We will now call on the Irish people to rally to us. Deserters all!

Mr. Ceannt [Kent]: Up the Republic!

Mr. M. Collins: Deserters all to the Irish nation in her hour of trial. We will stand by her.

Madame Markievicz: Oath breakers and cowards.

Mr. M. Collins: Foreigners – Americans – English.

Madame Markievicz: Lloyd Georgeites.

Controversy immediately swirled around Collins's exact words. The *Freeman's Journal* had Markievicz screaming 'Traitors and cowards!' with Collins hitting back ('fiercely and decisively'). 'Foreigners! English!' The *Independent* agreed, while the omnipresent *New York Times* described Collins as 'redoubtable', and recorded his words as: 'Foreigners, traitors, English.' Collins weighed in, as he so often did (he had a sure grasp of the news cycle), with a letter to the editor of the *Freeman's Journal*: 'I am reported as having used the expression at to-day's Dail meeting – 'Foreigners, Traitors, English.' I did not use the word "traitors" . . .' So he did call them foreigners and English, and perhaps Americans as well. These comments were directed at Childers, the 'Englishman', and de Valera, the 'foreigner' and 'American', who was born in New York and had a non-Irish father.

Later that day, now-President Griffith flew into a rage when questioned by Childers and refused to listen to a 'damned Englishman', to the apparent general approval of the government benches ('It is nearly time we had that'). Griffith's comments are rightly infamous, but Collins's have been forgotten. Both were of a piece – not just fighting words but killing words, as Childers became a hate figure. If we admire Collins's parliamentary performance, we should also keep in mind the lengths he was willing to go – and tolerate – to gain his victory.

21: Loving Michael Collins

A delightful dinner Hazel Lavery gave with Winston [Churchill], Michael Collins, Mr [Eamon] Duggan and [Kevin] O'Higgins. Three nicer men I have never met and Michael Collins is quite irresistible. No wonder he was never caught: all the women must have been so glad to hide him! He is a real 'Playboy' with a tremendous twinkle and sudden quick impulsive gestures, and was worshipped by Duggan.

(Juliet Duff)

THE STRANGEST MOMENT of the Treaty debate came on 3 January 1922, when Constance Markievicz reported that 'there is a suggestion that Princess Mary's wedding is to be broken off, and that the Princess Mary is to be married to Michael Collins who will be appointed first Governor of our Saorstat na hEireann [Irish Free State].'

Needless to say, the accusation had no basis in fact, and it is difficult to imagine where Markievicz had got such an idea. Collins was not present at the time, but he returned to the Dail that afternoon to respond, adroitly deploying the ghost of the Parnell scandal, the reverse class put-down (in part a rebuttal of Markievicz's accusation that the Free State would be a haven for privilege), and the dual roles of gentleman and plain man:

Some time in our history as a nation a girl went through Ireland and was not insulted by the people of Ireland. I do not come from the class the Deputy for the Dublin Division [Markievicz, whose maiden name was Gore-Booth] comes from [Protestant landed gentry]; I come from the plain people of Ireland. The lady whose name was mentioned is, I understand, betrothed to

some man. I know nothing of her in any way whatever, but the
statement may cause her pain, and may cause pain to the lady
who is betrothed to me (hear, hear). I just stand in that plain
way, and I will not allow without challenge any Deputy in the
assembly of my nation to insult any lady either of this nation or
other nation (applause).

This bizarre episode brought together many of the threads of
Collins's new life since the Truce. It marked his public announcement
of his engagement to Kitty Kiernan, which was itself a long and
tangled story. It brought to the surface just one of the many rumours
swirling around him and a number of (to republicans) politically
suspect women. And it reflected the extraordinary phenomenon that
was his Irish and international celebrity.

WHAT WE KNOW for sure of Collins's romantic relationships with
women is quite conventional. Of course, as with the rest of humanity,
what we know is dwarfed by what we do not and never will. Did he
ever visit prostitutes in London or Dublin? Did he sleep with
admirers or employees – or with his fiancée? Did he ever share any
sexual experiences with male friends? Since opportunities and urges
to do at least some of these things undoubtedly existed, as did vast
amounts of hypocrisy on the part of respectable people in general
(pious republicans included), it would hardly be surprising if one or
more of these things happened. On the other hand, he might also
have been as clean living as his first biographer, Piaras Beaslai,
insisted.

As his response to Markievicz suggests, Collins's attitudes
towards women were firmly Edwardian, reinforced perhaps by his
closeness to his eminently respectable sisters. According to a story
passed on by Elizabeth, Countess of Fingall, Collins was at a dinner
party at John and Hazel Lavery's house in London in 1922 with Lord
Birkenhead:

Hazel had a small Peke who was pawing at Lord Birkenhead
under the table. Hazel looked down and called the little dog.
'Oh, I am sorry, I thought you were making advances,' said Lord
Birkenhead. Up rose the big IRA leader, towering over him in
wrath: 'D'ye mean to insult her?' Hazel threw oil on the troubled

water quickly: 'Lord Birkenhead was only joking. 'I don't understand such jokes,' said Collins.

In June 1920 he wrote primly to Art O'Brien about some
underground doings that had been delegated to a woman: 'I don't
think a great deal of the people who give these commissions to
ladies.' This did not stop him from employing women as secretaries,
couriers and covers for his safe houses, but he was certainly protective
of them, making sure they didn't walk home alone at night and so
on. He apparently thought little of women as political leaders, and
there is almost no extant correspondence with any in Sinn Fein or
Cumann na mBan.

Particularly elevated were nice Irish girls – with true Irishness and
purity being synonymous – as he suggested in a letter to O'Brien in
February 1921: 'I note what you say with regard to lady spies. The
number you give is an understatement altogether. I think there are
probably ten times as many, and of course they would be Irish, but
they would be Irish of a type that is not Irish. They will not and
cannot get Irish girls to do this class of work for them.' When Eileen
McGrane, a journalist whose house hid one of his secret offices, was
arrested in June 1921, he was infuriated at the thought of her going
to an English prison – 'the abominations who inhabit such places' –
and by her caddish captors: 'The whole action against her is typical
of England ... at her first examination they made all sorts of
villainous suggestions, and the gallant English officers bandied her
name around with every possible low suggestion.'

Such sentiments were obviously genuine, and just as commonplace. So were double standards, especially where not-so-nice girls
were concerned. We have very little to speculate with on the subject
of Collins and what he might or might not have got up to on the
streets of London or Dublin, but we should not dismiss the possibilities out of hand. Republicanism was not the opposite of sex,
despite its hyper-respectable self-image. It had its secret liaisons and
its bohemian fringes – as in the Plunketts' Larkfield commune. His
pals in London weren't choirboys either, and nor was he. Frank
O'Connor felt that Collins was too 'shrewd' (whatever that means) to
pay for sex, but it may have been pretty difficult to get otherwise.
Nor would it have been out of character for swearin', drinkin' and
smokin' Mick Collins to try another temptation.

Collins was definitely interested in girls (even British army commander General Macready described him as 'an admirer of the opposite sex'). A few surviving letters speak of the usual boyish emotions. An invitation to a party from a G. Coffey in the summer of 1914 promised 'no restrictions on anything so you'll be quite free to get some of those "Holy Words" off your chest – !' and added a PS: 'I have a very nice little girl for you but the only fault, I'm afraid, she will be too slim – her name is Miss Cox. Don't forget.' More daintily, an undated draft letter reports a holiday away: 'Met Miss C in C[lonakility?] as I was about to start my return journey so am all alone now and feeling very lonely – hope it doesn't last long.' This may well have been the same Miss Cox: perhaps she wasn't too slim after all. Whatever the truth about her, Collins does seem to have had a steady girlfriend for a time (1914–15 at least): Susan Killeen, another postal employee in London (and later Dublin), and a friend of cousin Nancy. This relationship may not have lasted much, if at all, beyond 1916.

After Susan, the next woman we know he was interested in was Helen Kiernan of Granard, in Co. Longford. She was one of four sisters who lived and worked with their brother in the family hotel, the Greville Arms. This was one of the lodging places used by Sinn Feiners in the South Longford by-election in the spring of 1917, and by Collins and others in later campaigning stops. Due to the presence of the attractive young sisters, it became a popular destination in its own right, and a home away from home for Collins until travel became too dangerous as the war heated up in 1920.

When Collins was jailed in Sligo in April 1918, Helen wrote and then came to visit. He wrote in his diary, 'I succeeded in prevailing on Miss Kiernan to remain over in Sligo tonight and come to see me again in the morning.' This she did, so 'I had the pleasure of seeing her again today. Promises to come again later on.' It sounds fairly serious – unless it was just her sense of duty – but hardly passionate, to judge by his referring to her as 'Miss Kiernan'.

In September 1918, however, Collins made cryptic reference in a letter to Austin Stack to someone named Grace (surely not Grace Plunkett?), about whom he 'had great hopes which is all at the moment'. He also referred to 'Ana – she has money which is her only recommendation. No.' In October he wrote of 'the lady of my affections', presumably Grace again. Was he shifting targets or just hedging his bets? In May 1919 Harry Boland asked, in a letter to James Flood of Granard, 'Is Mickel [*sic*] still engaged to Helen Kiernan or was he ever? Talk things over with him.' Whether things did progress that far seems doubtful, as there is no mention of it elsewhere, and Helen was soon engaged to the man she would marry: solicitor and non-revolutionary Paul McGovern. A letter from Helen of about this time informed Collins of her decision and rather wistfully reflected, 'I often think of all the good nights we had together.' He may have been too busy or unwilling to commit, or his charms may have faded.

Harry himself was courting Helen's sister Kitty, and with greater success. Another sister, Maud, had apparently attracted Thomas Ashe's attentions before he died, and eventually married Gearoid O'Sullivan, another of Collins's close companions. It was not so unusual for sisters to marry comrades within the movement in this way, given the size and intimacy of the republican marriage market, but the Kiernans were not Cumann na mBan or Sinn Fein activists, just sympathizers. Perhaps that was part of the attraction.

Collins naturally knew Kitty as well, and when Boland went away to the US for – as it turned out – most of 1919, 1920 and 1921 he stayed in touch with her and they would see each other in Dublin. Somewhere along the way they became romantically inclined. This hardly seems up to his high standard of chivalry, but when Boland came back for a visit in August 1921 Collins wanted (he wrote Kitty) to 'give you that chance to which he is entitled? Do you remember what I said to you about this?' Boland took the chance and ran with it, proposing marriage:

> I told M. how matters stood atween us, [he told Kitty]; and he, I fear, was most upset . . . I told him as well as I could that you and I are engaged, and further that if he (M.) had not entered into yr Life that I w'd now have you as my very own Wife. Of course, he was upset and assured me that 'it did not follow if you did not marry me that you would marry him.'

Kitty's short romantic attention span is indicated by her previous promise to marry some poor sap named Lionel, but, after weighing her choices, she ultimately chose Collins – on the day Boland left to return to the United States in October. 'Why not marry the one I really love, and what a cowardly thing of me to be afraid to marry the one I really love, and who loves me just as well as any of the others I had thought of marrying,' she told Collins afterwards. 'Just as well' doesn't say much for Collins as a man of towering passion either. They apparently cemented their engagement at New Year's, just before Boland returned home for the last time (this may not have been a coincidence). Markievicz's ridiculous outburst made it public. So Collins won the vote in the Dail and Kitty's hand in marriage at the same time – to the double dismay of Boland (who opposed the Treaty).

THE NEW COUPLE'S relationship was carried on through letters and occasional visits by one to the other. The correspondence reveals a lot of awkward misunderstandings and friction to begin with. Quarrels were frequent. But they were probably just getting used to one another and to the idea of spending their lives together. There was little enough time for relaxation, and no chance for escape given Collins's profile and responsibilities.

Kitty worried over the state of Collins's health and soul. Collins earnestly explained himself and his faults, and sprinkled his letters with the principles he professed to live by: early rising, hard work, confidence, responsibility, honesty, sticking to your word. He was who he was, bad temper and all, and he wasn't going to change or soften:

> I am not demonstrative (except in showing my temper some-times) and I hate demonstrative indications of feeling – I mean before people. They stand somehow in my mind for a kind of insincerity. That always makes me say that m'yes of mine when I hear people at it. It may not be a pleasant way and it may not appeal to people but there you are. It's there and I'm afraid there it will remain.

It definitely did not appeal to Kitty, who was quite wounded at times by Collins's reticence. After a February 1922 visit to Dublin she complained:

> At times you made me feel almost uncomfortable. I didn't know where I stood with you. I found myself wondering . . . All the days seemed empty until I had you. Then I was disappointed . . . On the *other* hand, I almost shudder at the thought of the

strength of my love, what I do believe I am capable of feeling and that, without you, life held nothing for me.

After many such letters, Collins's brief, matter-of-fact and only dimly affectionate responses ('fondest love'; 'may God bless you anyway') seem rather heartless, even considering his busyness and fear of having his mail intercepted. '"Why is he afraid to write his love all through the letter as I do, and then end up with just an M?". The first and best goes to Ireland, I am only a good second, at least at the present time.'

Did they ever consummate their relationship? From Kitty's intimate letters one might well think so; from Collins's distracted notes it is unclear. They certainly spent weekends together, but that means little on its own. Much depends on this passage from one of Kitty's letters, received by Collins on 26 June 1922, after he had made a quick trip to Longford:

> Well, lovie, I was anxious to go with you last night, but I also had another feeling, a desperate ... If I had gone with you, it might have been for good. (I can't exactly describe it, but perhaps you understand.) I'd have stayed with you, I'd have wanted you. Last night was a real wedding night for you and me. Didn't you feel that way too, but couldn't put it into words? I wanted to run away with you. That must be the feeling with people who do run away like that. We had it last night. That was our night. Glad today, for *both you and me*, that I did not go. Isn't this right? *Tell* me. Do – am I not right? Heaps of kisses that you should have got yesterday, and heaps and heaps of hugs and love and love and hugs and kisses.
> Your own little pet,
> Kit.

The reference to 'a real wedding night' has been taken to mean that they slept together, but this misses the crucial fact that the letter was written after Sean MacEoin's wedding day, which they presumably attended as a couple. Even more to the point, it had originally been scheduled as the date for *their* marriage, as he and Sean had planned to marry together. The press of events had forced a postponement.

Choosing not to 'run away with you' could mean that they restrained themselves, and, if they did have sex, why would she send him kisses 'you should have got yesterday'? Collins's reply throws further cold water over the notion (and her), as he ignored her urgent command to '*tell* me' and simply said her letters were 'all very nice and I was delighted with them'.

COLLINS IS OFTEN described as a romantic figure, but Kitty probably didn't think so after they were engaged for a while. It was very definitely part of his public image, however: the mysterious guerrilla general; the good-looking rebel who played by his own rules. Mass curiosity and anticipation were the inevitable accompaniment, and as soon as he began appearing in public he was sought out and mobbed by admirers, who wanted to see and touch him. The same was true of other republican leaders, but it was Collins who was the centre of attention wherever he went and whomever he was with. He was the revolution's Princess Diana, its star and sex symbol – and the first example of that twentieth-century phenomenon: the guerrilla celebrity.

His new status in the mass media and the public imagination was evident when the republican negotiating team first went over to England in October 1921. They were met at Euston station in London by a huge crowd of well-wishers, but when it turned out that Collins was not with them 'there was keen disappointment' – not least among the legion of photographers lying in wait. Pictures of stout Arthur Griffith with his glasses and moustache were not going to sell many newspapers.

Celebrity was being redefined by gossip journalism, photography and the cinema in these post-war years, led by the first Hollywood stars and scandals (the Fatty Arbuckle trial had been big news in Ireland and Britain). In his pioneering way, Collins was one of the first to do battle with that new enemy, the paparazzi, and he quickly became notorious among the press for his running entrances and exits, glowering head down and protected by bodyguards.

When the plenipotentiaries arrived at 10 Downing Street on 11 October a crowd was waiting; well to the fore were excited young women who 'shouted out the names of the prominent Irishmen' as they arrived, 'the most conspicuous being that of Mr Collins'. Despite his best efforts, photos of him appeared throughout the press and he became instantly recognizable. After that, if he went out and was spotted, 'girls . . . pursued him for favours' (as Tom Jones put it), meaning they would run up and kiss him on the street – surely a first for a politician in London.

This mass fandom culminated in the great send-off of the delegates from Euston station on 7 December, after the Treaty was signed. In a rock-star-style near-riot, the crowd's frenzied attentions grew so insistent that people had to be lifted out of the way to let Collins and the others through:

> The Irish leaders had to be half dragged half carried to the carriage door ... Michael Collins was the first of his party to break through the rough crowd. He disappeared through the carriage door nearly on all fours ... Collins was a particular favourite of the women. The police were powerless to check the wild stampede made toward him during his fight to his carriage and one young woman succeeded in embracing him and kissing him heartily on both cheeks. 'God bless you Michael!' were the last shouts of a few hundred of his women admirers [one of whom stole his hat]. As the train steamed slowly out of the platform Collins ... stood at the window and smiled his farewell.

When the station master apologized for the scenes, Collins replied, 'Oh that's all right, I quite enjoyed it.'

This Collinsmania was a London phenomenon, which resurfaced every time he returned – a kind of media-aided craze that was about sheer celebrity as much as anything else. Nothing like it had ever happened before in the movement, where Collins had never been considered God's gift to republican women. Handsome, dedicated and dangerous young men were a dime a dozen in Ireland, and his frequently dismissive treatment of women didn't help. Still, he was now also famous among the general public in Ireland, where photos, autographs and handshakes were in constant demand, and where he was liable to be mobbed on occasion. At the first big pro-Treaty rally in Dublin on 5 March:

> When the speakers moved away to enter a motor-car in waiting for them, Mr Collins was surrounded by a large section of the crowd, who cheered him almost frantically, some endeavouring to carry him on their shoulders. The big throng moved slowly across College Green, while Mr Collins made several attempts to reach his car, but so persistent were the people that he was unable to do so ... Finally he managed to enter a tramcar, to

which the crowd immediately clung, cheering as vociferously as ever ... Mr Collins, making another effort to get away, was again surrounded, and retired to the interior of the car, which did not again stop until it had crossed O'Connell Bridge [where] Mr Collins was at length able to get into his motor-car which had been following in the rear, and so finally escaped from his admirers, among whom were quite a number of women.

It may be that this kind of visceral excitement wore off as Collins was increasingly identified with party politics and then civil war, but his premature death would embalm his reputation and keep his youthful romantic image intact and almost inviolable. His glamour and mystique remain as potent now as they were at their height in 1921.

IF CELEBRITY STATUS and hero worship attracted crowds, they also opened previously closed doors to new social worlds and provided unprecedented sexual opportunities and dangers, in the form of groupies and stalkers. And sometimes it was hard to tell the opportunities and the dangers apart.

Collins's arrival in London in late 1921 brought an endless stream of invitations and meetings with other celebrities, from J. M. Barrie and George Bernard Shaw to T. E. Lawrence. Mutual admiration was usually the order of the day – Collins had seen Shaw's and Barrie's plays, and Barrie was impressed by Collins: 'obviously a leader of men and with a boyishness at times almost as gay as ... [Siegfried] Sassoon's'. But Collins could also be a fish out of water, as when he did the rounds of curious socialites and intellectuals. When the Countess of Fingall met him at the house of Horace Plunkett (the great prophet of co-operation) outside Dublin, she found him 'not at all an eloquent man' and the party 'dull'. Kevin O'Shiel tells of another such occasion at the Dublin house of surgeon and writer Oliver St John Gogarty, with W. B. Yeats, George Russell ('Æ') and other literary types in attendance:

The 'Mahatma' [Russell] was in excellent form that evening. Reclining in the armchair in his comfortable loose-fitting suit of rough Irish tweed, he pontificated with great verve, realizing that he had a most important and attentive listener in Collins ... He appeared to be propounding some of his more mystical theories

– the tranquil might of moral and spiritual power as against the angry forces of evil in the contemporary 'cosmos'. Mick, with head bent towards him, listened intently and eagerly to 'AE' for quite a while; then, pulling out his famous note-book that he was never without, and his fountain-pen, he asked, 'But what is your point, Mr Russell?' 'AE' was wholly nonplussed, almost staggered at the question, and an uncomfortable feeling of embarrassment fell on the company at the enormity of putting such a query, of all queries, to the prophet.

In this case the reader's sympathies may lie with Collins, who probably knew very well what he was doing.

The social spider who snared Collins first was Hazel Lavery, American wife of John Lavery, a famous London (but Belfast-born) painter. She was a daring, cunning and charming society hostess who also kept a home in Ireland. Once the Treaty negotiations were under way, she wanted the social triumph of having the famous and exciting Irishmen to dinner, and her husband wanted to paint portraits of them. Once Collins showed up at the studio he was hooked.

After that he became friends with them both, and went to their dinner parties both in London and in Ireland. Hazel Lavery was also apparently a regular correspondent – though whether he wrote as often to her is unknown. From this came persistent rumours that they were having an affair and that she was a major influence on his signing the Treaty. Much prurient controversy exists on these points, and, as always, it is very difficult to prove they did nothing. What all these rumours have in common, however – apart from republican paranoia – is Hazel Lavery's strenuous self-promotion.

The idea that the Laverys had a serious political role is based only on their say-so, which is hardly reliable or credible. As for an affair, she constantly publicized their friendship and surreptitiously pushed the idea that it was intimate. In this she was aided by Shane Leslie and other professional gossips. Since she flirted with everyone and undoubtedly had a seductive personality, Collins was probably attracted to her. Did they ever have sex? She reported that they did, but, as always, who knows? We certainly shouldn't just take her word for it. She got much of what she wanted from publicity and rumour, so an actual physical relationship may have been unnecessary – unless she wanted the thrill of adding to her collection of conquests.

Kitty was naturally worried about Hazel, so Collins was at pains to reassure her – to the extent of passing on Hazel's letters to him. He also remained friends with John Lavery, and saw him almost as often as he saw his wife. To fool him in this way as well as Kitty would have been gross duplicity indeed.

If Hazel Lavery was a kind of super-groupie, then Moya Llewelyn Davies emerges as something of a stalker. Collins first met her and her husband, Crompton, when he and other newly elected Sinn Feiners went to London at Christmas 1918 to try to see Woodrow Wilson. Moya was Irish, and the daughter of a former nationalist MP. Her mother and all her siblings had been wiped out when she was a child, in a case of shellfish poisoning. She was a cultured, upper-middle-class woman and a Liberal Party activist, but she did not move in the same elevated social circles as Hazel Lavery. Interestingly, given Collins's own history, she was apparently an atheist.

Crompton was an uncle of the Llewelyn Davies boys who had inspired J. M. Barrie to write *Peter Pan*, that favourite of Irish nationalists ('to die will be an awfully big adventure'). He was a close friend of Bertrand Russell, whom he greatly influenced, and knew many senior Liberal politicians well on account of his lifelong work for land reform. He was an independent thinker and with the Liberals in power he became a senior civil servant. Margaret Gavan Duffy, who knew them in London, thought him and his wife 'the most devoted couple I ever saw', and very retiring.

Moya's first impressions of Collins were of a loud-mouthed chain-smoker. Aided perhaps by his rapid acquisition of glamour and power, dismissal soon turned to interest. According to Robert Brennan, who knew both her and Collins well, when de Valera escaped from Lincoln jail in 1919 Collins went to see her in London:

> As she was not well and was in bed she asked Mick to come up and see her, which he did, and he showed her the key which had opened the jail gates for de Valera. It was quite clear that she was much affected by this incident and I came to the conclusion that, though ... she was passionately devoted to Ireland, the culminating point in determining her to come to live here [Dublin] was her infatuation for Collins; an infatuation which, however, he seemed to be quite unaware of, and more or less indifferent to.

They became regular correspondents – she was also in touch with Art O'Brien in London – and around late 1920 she took a house in north Dublin to be at the heart of the action, and closer to Collins. Collins visited her there – and here reports differ sharply. He may have stayed overnight at times – as in a safe house – and this started the rumours about them having an affair. Robert Brennan says no: 'He never stayed overnight. She told me that she had the greatest difficulty in talking to him and she did not know what to talk to him about.' In 1921 their letters to each other were captured, Crompton lost his job, and Moya was briefly jailed before being deported to Britain. Collins was very worried while she was in Mountjoy prison, sending flowers to her and daily reports to O'Brien.

Once the Truce was declared Moya returned to Dublin and took a room in the Gresham, where Collins now had his headquarters. When Margaret Gavan Duffy encountered her again, 'Her talk was fantastic. She had an absurd opinion of her own importance. She thought she was the centre of the movement. She was, in fact, quite silly in her new found idea of her own importance and when I expressed my opinion of her she did not like it at all.' She seems to have claimed to have been a spy, which everyone in the movement dismissed as nonsense. People also said she was a close adviser of Collins – another of her claims? – but this was more likely to have been true of Crompton, whom Collins guiltily put on the revolutionary payroll.

Nancy Wyse-Power (daughter of Jenny, a senior Sinn Feiner) recalls, 'She had lived in England and her ways were not ours. I think her ambition was to play the part of the power behind the throne and while she had some influence on Collins, the extent of that influence was in my opinion overrated, no doubt by herself too. Collins's intimate male associates disliked her, as can easily be explained.' Brennan concurred: 'The lieutenants of Michael Collins resented Mrs Davies' attentions to Mick, as they would have done in the case of any other woman, particularly a married woman, and they feared that his personal reputation would suffer.' Plans to publish her memoirs were apparently scotched by them as well. At this point, in late 1921, with Kitty Kiernan in the picture and photographers and reporters about, there is definitely a sad whiff of unwanted presence, of Moya refusing to let go. Finally Batt O'Connor was detailed to get rid of her.

Later in life Moya claimed that she and Collins had been lovers. Was this a fantasy? It wouldn't be all that implausible for such a relationship to have occurred in early 1921, when he was unattached and she was alone and very available. If so, he didn't take it seriously and edged away pretty quickly within a few months. He had the gift of making people believe he was a close friend, that they were special to him, but he was also capable of moving on again just as quickly if the friendship became inconvenient. That may have been the case here, but whatever his feelings were she mistook them for love. Unlike Lavery, she seems a lonely and vulnerable figure. Whatever happened, it is a sad story.

22: CEO

Among the various Sinn Feiners with whom from time to time I came in touch, Michael Collins struck me as being the easiest to deal with. Of a type common in Ireland, his like can be seen by the score on any Irish racecourse but he had, what few of his countrymen possess, a sense of humour, and above all, the gift during a conversation of sticking to essentials.

(General Nevil Macready)

THE HIGH POINT OF Michael Collins's career came on 16 January 1922, in a place he had often feared it would end: Dublin Castle. In the event, his entrance was a triumphal one. The occasion was the formal handover of power by the Lord Lieutenant (Viceroy) of Ireland, Viscount Fitzalan, to the Provisional Government that would oversee the establishment of an Irish Free State. Collins was its chairman, and the star of the show. Crowds cheered as he drove into the fortified Castle Yard, nodding 'broadly and agreeably as he passed along', civil servants hung out of windows to catch a glimpse of him, and reporters peering through windows at the reception observed him 'smiling and looking absolutely self-possessed as he met the Viceroy'. It was the first and last time he would appear in the Irish court circular, otherwise devoted to the lunch partners of the decorated, titled and ennobled.

The first ever Provisional Government press statement, signed by Collins, described the event as the 'surrender' of Dublin Castle, and the nationalist press eagerly followed suit, ensuring a smashing propaganda victory. They gleefully reported the resentful presence of Auxiliaries and various other counter-insurgents, as well as the flight of lorries bearing the remains of the old regime. The reality was much trickier, and required these lashings of patriotic treacle to make it palatable. The papers may have crooned about the Castle capitulating in 'abject humiliation' to a sworn rebel, but, according to the terms of the Treaty, Collins owed his new position to a vote of the southern parliament established under the Government of Ireland Act (the pro-Treaty Dail members acting as such for the purpose) and to the devolution of authority by the Crown, as represented by the viceroy. In legal fact, he was not taking power in any revolutionary way: it was being granted to him by the government he had sworn to overthrow.

The Republic, the Dail and its ministries did not vanish with the creation of this new centre of authority. Keeping them in being was good politics, as it added nationalist and democratic legitimacy to the new government, so the Dail ministry continued in much the same shadowy way as before, with its cabinet meetings – under the presidency of Arthur Griffith – continuing until April. Griffith reappointed Collins to the Department of Finance, which continued to administer funds and to issue its accounts – and to take up considerable portions of its minister's increasingly scarce time. His dual role – as the first nationalist head of an Irish government (an achievement that eluded Parnell, Redmond and de Valera) and as (in effect) an appointee of the British government – would challenge Collins's political and dramaturgical skills to the utmost.

Collins was now the most powerful man in Ireland. Griffith, while still a key player in post-Treaty politics, had no particular desire to lead or rule, so the two regimes functioned as one. Collins was its figurehead and its main spokesman. He was the only person to hold positions in both the Dail and the Provisional administrations, and he was able to choose much of the latter's cabinet from among his friends and loyalists, including Joe McGrath, Fionan Lynch and Eamon Duggan. Diarmuid O'Hegarty was made Cabinet Secretary. In the Dail, long-time ally Dick Mulcahy replaced Cathal Brugha as Minister of Defence, and he in turn was replaced as Chief of Staff by Eoin O'Duffy, a Collins protégé. Many of these men were also IRB members, and therefore doubly attached to Collins as the still-reigning president of the Supreme Council of the IRB.

Collins set the tone of his administration at its first meeting: 'Mr Collins indicated that he would take charge of the Finance arrangements.' Not only did he want to keep his hands on all the purse strings, thereby ensuring a 'businesslike' government, he wanted to let his colleagues know he would be the one to decide what role he would play and how much power he would have (just as he had over Intelligence in 1919). It was 'my government', responsible to no parliament. He was Chief Executive Officer, Chief Financial Officer, Chairman of the Board and a major shareholder all in one.

The Dail Department of Finance was still in Mary Street, and Collins still had a lot of work to do there. He also retained his Harcourt Terrace office for a time, and continued to use the Gresham Hotel – although he would later move his private office to the new Government Buildings on Merrion Street. He spent a lot of time in the Mansion House, where the Dail government stayed on, but his first Provisional Government office was in the City Hall – next to Dublin Castle, to give easy access to his new and vastly greater bureaucracy but untainted by its politics. It had formerly been occupied by the British army, so its new occupants were another sign of liberation. Collins and his personal staff were accommodated in what used to be the town clerk's office, while the other ministers displaced other municipal departments. An armed garrison was installed, although it took a while to find it uniforms.

Collins could easily have been overwhelmed by the flood of detail demanding his attention in these early weeks, but he maintained his focus throughout. He had a plan and an agenda: the most rapid possible transfer of power. To this end, he and others travelled almost immediately to London to arrange the transitional timetable with the British government, dealing largely with Winston Churchill and the Colonial Office. What he wanted was the quick passage of a one-clause British act ratifying the Treaty. This would trigger everything else: the Dail would dissolve; an election to ratify the Treaty would be held (Collins hoped there would have to be one in the north as well); the new parliament would pass the yet-to-be-drafted constitution, which would then be approved in London, establishing a Free State and allowing the boundary-commission clock to start ticking. If the Northern Irish cabinet did not agree to inclusion, a month later the commission would begin its deliberations. As Collins imagined it, the entire situation should resolve itself well before the end of the year.

*

WHAT WOULD THE IDEAL new Ireland look like? Collins (possibly aided by others) wrote a series of newspaper articles in 1922 to defend the Treaty, explain how it fulfilled historic nationalist dreams, and outline his vision of the modest paradise that would follow. This echoed his boyhood thoughts with impressive consistency and extended them into a semblance of an economic programme:

> We want such widely diffused prosperity that the Irish people will not be crushed by destitution into living practically 'the lives of the beasts' . . . We must not have the destitution of poverty at one end, and at the other an excess of riches in the possession of a few individuals, beyond what they can spend with satisfaction and justification . . . The development of industry in the new Ireland should be on lines which exclude monopoly profits. The product of industry would thus be left sufficiently free to supply good wages to those employed in it. The system should be on co-operative lines rather than on the old commercial capitalistic lines of the huge joint stock companies. At the same time I think we shall safely avoid State Socialism, which has nothing to commend it in a country like Ireland.

The way to achieve such an economy, compatible with an unmaterialistic but well-fed Gaelic Ireland, was to get the banked or exported capital of Ireland to work in Irish industry, thereby keeping out rapacious foreign investors and their attendant 'evils'. Strikes could be avoided by sharing ownership with workers. If grazing ranches were divided up into family farms, they could hold a much larger and more productive population. The resources of an independent Ireland were allegedly vast (or so nationalists dreamed), including untapped mineral deposits, so energy and raw materials could underpin continued prosperity. All that was needed was sovereignty, and the elevation of national interest above sectional concerns.

This sounds all very nice, not to mention familiar: Parnellist economics by way of Arthur Griffith and Sinn Fein, mixed with the collectivism of Horace Plunkett and the co-operative movement, and perhaps a trendy touch of social credit. Some of it – the protection of native industry, the breaking up of the ranches – was tried by de Valera's Fianna Fail governments of the 1930s and '40s, which shared the same avowed disdain of material wealth. Much of what Collins was writing was conventional wisdom among nationalist politicians of all stripes, although he did depart from Griffith in his approval of the co-operative ideal. He had obviously thoroughly digested his Irish-Ireland pamphlets and newspapers – and all those mind-numbing monthly lectures on the prospects of the beetroot industry he had heard in London had turned out to be useful after all.

It certainly wasn't socialism, however, as has sometimes been suggested by those seeking to retrospectively enlist Michael Collins in their cause. Unions had little place in his thinking, nationalization was out, and individual firms were to be the driving force of the new economy – albeit cosy co-ops rather than possibly alien entrepreneurs. Collins continued to use terms such as 'proletariat' and 'the masses', and seems to have sympathized with Bolshevism when it first appeared, but he was never a fan of the British Labour Party, whom he derided for 'the absence of putting their theories into practice. There does not seem to be any reality to these people.' Seen through Irish nationalist eyes, their hand-wringing was not much help.

Articles written with an election around the corner are one thing; private memos and discussions are another. In July 1922 Collins drafted a memo on the 'general situation' in which he declared that

> we shall be friendly with the Labour people and will accept their help if they give it, but our National aim will be one which will embrace theirs and in which theirs must take its place as an element. There is not going to be another revolution, there is going to be a revival of the Nation. In our new State each element will have scope. Humanity and reason will have opportunities they never had before. [Re-establishing order is] not a repressive or reactionary step. It is a step forward ... the liberative movement for allowing Irish ideals to be realized.

He also wrote that 'the important thing is that the National Forces – which is [the] expression of our Nationhood – must keep the lead and must retain the direction of the national movement towards a new Ireland.' Here he may have been referring to the IRB and the army in which it still survived. He also expressed strong pronatalist sentiments, and returned to his earlier concern with babies and their care: 'Our third and perhaps greatest inspiration is not merely to extend the franchise to women, but to endow motherhood and to establish a modern system of national clinic[s].' Women weren't to be demeaned by work outside the home, presumably.

All of which sounds rather corporatist, possibly even quasi-fascist in some ways – echoing ideas which were gaining currency throughout Europe at the time (Mussolini came to power in Italy in 1922) and which Collins certainly knew about and may well have been attracted to. After all, socialists weren't the only ones to distrust international capital (although Collins, unlike many colleagues, never showed a hint of anti-Semitism). We mustn't get too carried away here, however: this is Collins in big-idea mode, not a generalissimo planning to establish himself as Father of the Nation. The idea of the army as embodying the nation was a commonplace within the IRA, going back to the foundation of the Volunteers in 1913, while protecting motherhood was (and is) hardly an unusual political slogan.

In private sessions of the Dail and during the Anglo-Irish Treaty negotiations Collins also revealed much harsher views, more compatible with the parsimoniously conservative ethos of William Cosgrave's Cumann na nGaedhal governments of 1923–32. He seems to have objected almost instinctively to government spending. On the subject of poor relief – 'the dole' – he could be scathing. When the matter had come up in the Treaty negotiations, Collins had scoffed at Liberal progressivism: 'If we were in charge we would make these fellows work, and deduct their Pensions from their wages, or something like that. The system of Pensions has created a lot of demoralization.' Collins's ideas on government are more plausibly located in his actual experience as a minister of finance, and were rooted in his business career among the accountants, stockbrokers and bankers of the City. The more businesslike and less bureaucratic a government was, the happier he was.

As far as Collins was concerned, the main obstacle to realizing this vision was the anti-Treaty opposition, still led in the Dail and at large by the indefatigable Eamon de Valera. It was a constant theme of Collins's – ironically echoing pre-Treaty de Valera – that a united front was a necessity in dealing with the British and Northern Irish governments. Dev, however, refused to accept the legitimacy of the Dail votes or the Provisional Government, and continued his non-stop opposition campaign. He wanted the election postponed. The longer it took to hold it, the more time he would have to recover the ground lost in his botched parliamentary efforts.

The Dail may have split into two parties but Sinn Fein still remained officially whole. A pro-Treaty standing committee was elected in January, and it called an extraordinary Ard Fheis in February to discuss the Treaty. This required local clubs to select delegates – a process which revealed a bitterly divided membership as rival factions struggled for control. The republicans did well – thanks in large part to the efforts of the anti-Treaty IRA – and ultimately mustered an apparently clear majority of the 3,000 people who gathered in the Mansion House on 21 February. De Valera, who retained his party presidency, spoke at length suggesting he would lead a secession.

Collins, now a vice-president of the party (albeit one of four), followed him. In an earnest but rambling speech (no sound bites this time), he set out to 'try to put a case for no division'. As Dev had done, he admitted that the revolutionary movement had always had 'political unity only, and that there were certain currents working here and there, that would have broken up that unity'. However, its members had stuck together and should continue to do so. After all, 'When we have divided will we be stronger or weaker? I believe we will be weaker.' He admitted that the antis had a majority in the room, but countered by asserting that the Treaty was accepted by the general electorate. And herein lay the deal he was proposing: an election on the Treaty would be delayed for about three months, as de Valera wished. In return, the opposition would stay in Sinn Fein, not force a break, and allow him and his colleagues to establish a government. As he put it, 'If it is accepted that there is a majority for this and that we can avoid an election I will do my best to avoid an election ... If we can avoid an election until we can produce the Constitution we will avoid it.' In essence, the opposition must agree not to obstruct or ambush the pro-Treaty party in the Dail. After the proposed three months, 'we will see the position very much more clearly.'

Collins claimed this was 'simply my own private idea', and it may well have been: at least one of his allies – former IRB head Sean McGarry – was heard to mutter, 'I am in favour of an election.' Dependable Arthur Griffith backed him up, however, even though Collins had derailed his motion in favour of the Treaty when he brought up his proposal. The next day the principals conferred at length while the delegates sang and recited (as had happened at conventions before when the action moved behind the scenes). They emerged with an agreement along the lines Collins had suggested, with an election delayed, a loyal opposition in the Dail, and a promise that the constitution would be placed alongside the Treaty when it came time to vote. In the meantime the convention was adjourned and the pro-Treaty standing committee was replaced by the officer board, giving equal power to either side.

Here was the first big decision of Collins's premiership. He could have accepted the logic of the split, listened to the urgings of many of his colleagues and allies like McGarry and Griffith, and gone ahead with a snap election to create a new Dail more supportive of his government. As matters stood, the parliamentary parties were almost evenly balanced, as several of those who voted for the Treaty were either ambivalent like George Gavan Duffy or else supported de Valera over Collins, as did Robert Barton. It would be a disaster if de Valera managed to wangle a majority out of the situation. The Dail had not reconvened since 10 January, presumably in part because Collins and Griffith were afraid of just such an outcome.

Collins had argued for an election in the Treaty debate, and this was made cabinet policy at the first Provisional Government meeting. He also told British ministers that an election would be held in mid-April, and that 'if they did not have an election till after the Constitution was drafted, the Treaty would be beaten in Ireland.' And it was Collins himself who, long before the convention, had submitted the motion to immediately submit the Treaty to the people and to divide party funds in the event of a formal split. Moreover, the universal expectation, even among republicans, was that the Treaty party would win a large majority of seats.

So what made him change his mind? Uppermost was the fear of a violent crisis that might set back all his plans. He did not want to risk the consequences of an outright struggle for power. Moreover, he saw the situation as an opportunity to fulfil his strategic aim of keeping the republican movement together. This, after all, was part of his vision of a renewed Ireland: not just state power, but an ongoing national front to push it forward politically. As he said in his Ard Fheis speech, 'I pointed out to [de Valera] that the only reason why we were going forward with this election was in order that we might be given the power, if we had the responsibility.' If de

Valera was willing to concede the right to govern, they would not need popular backing to give them clear governmental authority.

He and others had tried before to get de Valera to accept some such compromise allowing him to retain his self-appointed role as guardian of republican aspirations. Dev had always refused. But now, with the election delayed, his power in the party intact, and the Dail to resume sitting – and with the ultimate lure of an acceptable constitution – he had accepted. In the breathing space allowed by this three-month reprieve, Collins could work on reconciling opponents and building up the new state to show what the Treaty could bring.

Collins had already used the private promise of a constitution that would reinstate republican values to sway dubious comrades such as old London hand Richard Connolly and Armagh IRA commander Frank Aiken – just as he had asked the Munster IRB leaders to trust him before the Treaty. With this in mind, a constitutional committee was struck in late January, consisting of outside experts but with Collins exercising a veto as chair. Not that he wanted to attend the legal discussions – these he left to his deputy, Darrell Figgis, a Griffith favourite but always an unfortunate choice because of his toxic personality. Collins and Griffith (who attended the first meeting) wanted a short, clear document based not upon Canadian law, as had been agreed during the London negotiations, but upon popular sovereignty. A 'true democratic constitution' – so there should be no mention of the Crown or an oath. This was de Valera's much-mocked Document No. 2 (introduced and then withdrawn in the secret sessions of the Treaty debate) returned to life. But Collins seems to have believed – you can always find a lawyer to tell you what you want to hear – it was in accord with the Treaty. The reasoning was that such details had nothing to do with Anglo-Irish relations. But it was wishful thinking, based more on his intense desire to satisfy his co-ideologists than on any realistic expectation of how the already suspicious British government would react.

For Collins's strategy to work, the transfer of power and the creation of new institutions would have to proceed at high speed. The constitutional committee was supposed to meet in absolute secrecy and report by the end of February, but within days Collins was irritated by its leaks and delays. It did report in early March, but with three drafts rather than one, requiring further modification. The final version of the constitution was not presented to the British government until the end of May.

Other projects similarly failed to match Collins's desire for rapid results, the new police force being a case in point. As a consequence of the IRA's war on the police and the arming of thousands of young men in the name of the Republic, violent robberies had become commonplace. Collins's first response was to put his intelligence men and Squaddies on the job as 'special police', headed by Liam Tobin. They were given Oriel House in Westland Row as a headquarters – several government offices being hurriedly turfed out in the process – and plenty of guns and fast cars in order to meet fire with fire. 'Special police' has an ominous ring to it, and soon so did 'Oriel House', which doubled as a bodyguard and odd-jobs service and answered only to Collins.

The RIC itself could not be saved politically – unlike the uniformed men of the Dublin police – and was quickly disbanded. The republican police, set up in 1920 as a rival force under Austin Stack's Ministry of Home Affairs, were seen as incompetent and, equally important, were too anti-Treaty to be useful to the new government. So the usual committee was struck, headed by old reliable Michael Staines, who by March was commissioner of the Civic Guard, a nascent force in training in the grounds of the Royal Dublin Society. Among the officers were some of Collins's former police agents. Time was too short and the job was too much for Staines to handle, however. The men eventually mutinied and locked him out of their new base in Co. Kildare, requiring Collins's intervention to calm the situation. It was irretrievable, however, and the government had to start again from scratch in August.

The civil service was a success story by comparison. Here, as Collins promised after the Treaty was signed, there were no purges below the most senior ranks. A few Collins men were put in place here and there – P. S. O'Hegarty was rewarded with the secretaryship of the Post Office – but otherwise the personnel worked just as well with former guerrillas as they had with their pursuers. Collins's main strategic decision was to turn Finance – a department that had not previously existed in the Castle scheme of things – into a superministry. Under his direction it swallowed all five treasury departments, two of the twenty-five local offices, and nine of the seventeen UK departments in Ireland, along with the office of the civil-service commissioners. As was his practice, Collins first hired an able departmental secretary in Joseph Brennan, a career civil servant who had secretly advised him on financial matters in the Treaty negotiations, and then delegated much of the administration to him. Although relatively smoothly accomplished, delay was inevitable and the actual transfer of power over departments was given effect only on 1 April.

COLLINS WAS WIDELY CRITICIZED for his about-face on elections, but it was typical of his risk-averse style. As always, he wanted to keep his options open and did not want to force a decision before he had to. Maybe the constitution would rescue his position; perhaps anti-Treaty fervour would fade. In the meantime an Irish government would come into being and give him a platform for national leadership.

As he stated over and over again in his Ard Fheis speech, Collins's preferred rallying point was Northern Ireland, since here he was on common ground with his opponents and could safely appeal to the higher national interest. 'If we say to the Northern representatives that we stand together on this business, it will be the greatest stick we can use against them.' It also usefully put the British government on the defensive, just as it had during the Treaty negotiations – once again Collins was borrowing from de Valera's playbook.

Crisis and civil war had already arrived in James Craig's Northern Ireland. Loyalist Protestant 'pogroms' had displaced thousands of Belfast Catholics, while law and order was now in the hands of a partisan local Home Affairs ministry. Catholic gunmen and bombers were active against Protestant targets as well, but it was the minority population that suffered the most, with thousands of men expelled from their jobs by co-workers as well as losing their homes to thugs and arsonists. The IRA had never been strong in the six partitioned counties, and the British government was reluctant to become involved. After all, the whole point of its Irish policy since 1919 had been to remove the British government from Irish politics.

Collins's views on Ulster and its unionists were no different from those of the rest of the Sinn Fein leadership, or indeed from those of almost any of his predecessors or successors in nationalist parties. According to this view, Ulster's economy was actually less successful than the south's, despite the presence of Belfast's great industries;

many Protestants were secretly nationalists and would be happy to be ruled from Dublin; the 'Protestant proletariat' were being suckered by their unionist employers, although their natural interests coincided with those of their Catholic co-workers; and interfering British interests were at the root of the problem. As he put it in a newspaper article:

> Capitalism has come, not only to serve Britain's purpose by keeping the people divided but, by setting worker against worker, it has profited by exploiting both. It works on religious prejudices ... Such a policy – the policy of divide and rule, and the opportunity it gives for private economic oppression – could bring nothing but evil and hardship to the whole of Ireland.

The whole problem, as he saw it, boiled down to a rotten elite and a gang of Orange gutties armed first by the Conservative Party and then by the British government. Collins, like de Valera and Griffith, had little experience of the north. A telling commentary on southern nationalist perceptions was the universal use by Collins and others of the term 'our people' to describe northern Catholics: an unconscious bias that had found expression in Collins's bishop-brokered deal with the Irish Party to preserve nationalist seats in the 1918 election.

Southern nationalist opinion was outraged by anti-Catholic violence in the north as well as by a partition scheme that included majority-Catholic Fermanagh, Tyrone and Derry city under an antagonistic Unionist government. After the first anti-Catholic riots had begun in 1920, the Dail had launched a very effective Belfast boycott in the rest of Ireland, aimed at unionist firms in the absurd belief – shared by a great many nationalists, including Collins – that greedy unionist businessmen would give in to avoid losing profits and property. Although popular with 'our people' and destructive to banks, distillers and other firms, it did nothing to halt the violence.

The Dail claimed authority over all thirty-two counties, and refused to recognize the northern government. With negotiations in mind, however, de Valera had adopted a policy of non-coercion: Northern Ireland would not be forced to rejoin the rest of Ireland. Collins endorsed this in a speech in Armagh in September 1921 (his only visit to the constituency that had elected him in May) and reiterated it in his Treaty speech in December. On the other hand, he had warned Lloyd George during the negotiations that 'freedom of choice must be secured in order to enable the people to say whether they would come with us.' As Arthur Griffith put it in early 1922, while they would not force unionists into a united Ireland, they also would not allow districts which wanted to be ruled from Dublin to be forced under Unionist rule.

The Provisional Government assumed the protectorate of the northern nationalist minority in 1922, intending to speak and act on their behalf to the Unionist and British governments. Collins and Griffith expected the boundary commission to carve out large chunks of Craig's jurisdiction within the year if he did not agree to joining the Free State. They hoped that this prospect would force him to negotiate, with the carrot being the same devolution of power to Belfast as now existed. Collins hoped at first not to have to summon the commission, as 'any kind of even temporary partition is distasteful to me. We may reduce the North-East area [as Sinn Feiners referred to it] to such limits that it cannot exist without us, and that it will be forced in. But there would be much rancour' – a view he restated at the 1922 Ard Fheis. He also hoped for a swift resolution to show the benefits of the Treaty – and, not incidentally, to demonstrate his leadership.

Thus came about the first Craig–Collins pact, as it was known. The two leaders met in London on 20 January, during one of Collins's many cross-channel visits to see Churchill, who brought them together over dinner. Aided perhaps by the claret, they were able to reach a number of agreements. The southern government would call off the Belfast boycott, Craig would seek to reinstate expelled Catholic workers, and they would then settle the boundary issue between them – thereby, as Collins trumpeted it, eliminating 'English interference'. As would so often be the case in 1922, this was Collins making it up as he went along and telling his colleagues later.

Craig would find it impossible (and politically uncomfortable) to return workers to shrinking industries. Collins undid his own handiwork in the following days through a series of overweening statements as to what the agreement meant. He told reporters that Craig had approached him rather than the other way around (which Craig denied), and added that, while the Provisional Government was acting 'in good will and generosity the nation had always the power to assert itself in the event of the North failing to reciprocate such patriotic action'. The spin worked, and newspapers were full of expectations of a wider agreement coming out of a second meeting, in Dublin, on 2 February. The day before, however, Collins and Griffith met publicly with nationalist delegations from South Down and South Armagh (where Catholics were in the majority as well) who were worried that they might be sold out in the negotiations. Collins assured them – to much relieved laughter – that they were forcing an open door. The government was fully prepared for the boundary commission, 'they would give way to no one who was not a democrat,' and generosity would gain them Orange converts.

Craig was not amused. He thought Collins had agreed not to convene the commission, and in any case he had been assured by British politicians that at most the border would be only slightly adjusted. Collins, of course, had been led to think otherwise, but had not got the promises in writing. The conference broke up after two hours, with Craig and his Cabinet Secretary appearing 'strained and anxious' and 'Mr Collins looking rather tired'. Collins issued his own statement to say that 'we are giving the peace policy a decent chance,' and defended his interpretation of the Treaty, arguing 'there is nothing ambiguous' about the wording. He was obviously wrong. It was not just the 'wishes of the inhabitants' that counted, but also economic and geographical circumstances. No one yet knew what this meant. And, foolishly, Collins and Griffith had not insisted on defining the area of inquiry or the method of consulting the inhabitants, even though they had discussed it in detail during the negotiations. It was entirely their fault that they were now in a position of total uncertainty about what might take place.

The Provisional Government had decided its official northern policy the day before this meeting. It would be a 'peace policy' as advertised, but, in line with previous Sinn Fein policy, 'a policy of non-recognition was emphasized.' As before, the idea was active non-recognition. Bureaucratic cooperation with the government of Northern Ireland would be refused. Any local councils who refused to recognize the Belfast regime would be supported financially, as would Catholic school managers and teachers.

This was the abstentionist platform that Collins had been elected on in Armagh in 1921, and it was also the thinking behind arranging for the Fermanagh and Tyrone county councils to declare allegiance to Dail Eireann later that year, in the hope of influencing the London negotiations. They were swiftly suppressed by the Northern Irish government, but this failure was oddly undiscouraging. In the end, the policy cost thousands of pounds a week and had to be publicly denied (the money came out of the secret-service fund), even when northern ministers rather embarrassingly pointed out that they knew what was going on. Nevertheless, it had the unanimous backing of both the Dail and the Provisional Government cabinets.

NONE OF COLLINS's policies worked to heal the split. The Dail resumed sitting after the Ard Fheis and soon after, in early March, de Valera formed a new parliamentary party – Cumann na Poblachta (the Republican Party) – making him president of two parties simultaneously. He embarked on a speaking tour, to the guerrilla heartland of Munster in particular, attacking the Treaty and warning in graphic terms of a civil war if it were ratified. Other republicans, such as Collins's erstwhile confidant Harry Boland, did the same elsewhere. It seemed to be a quasi-electoral campaign, only they were actually campaigning *against* holding an election on the great issue of the day. The once and future President denied that he and his colleagues were inciting violence, but his message was clear: the government had no right to implement the Treaty, and those who opposed them were justified in doing anything to stop it.

Collins was enraged and disappointed at what he saw as de Valera's betrayal of the 'spirit' of their agreement. Still, he and his party were doing much the same. Dan McCarthy was once again doing what he did best: organizing constituencies and raising money – now easy to come by with Dublin's business elite on side. Meanwhile, the Provisional leaders went on tours to match de Valera's, starting on 5 March with a huge pro-Treaty rally in Dublin. A week later Collins was in Cork city and county, where he was filmed in all his arm-waving and chin-jutting glory and made himself available for photo opportunities at factories and churches. Next were Waterford and Dungarvan; the week after, Athlone and Castlebar; the week after that, Wexford. McCarthy's money and the advantage of incumbency could be seen in the special trains used by Collins and in the elaborate arrangements for transporting supporters to the rallies.

De Valera and his arguments were his usual target, but by mid-

April Collins too was warning of civil war if the political divide continued to widen. Outside the republican movement, other groups and organizations were demanding – and working for – peaceful compromise. These included numerous local politicians, Catholic bishops and the labour movement. On 14 April a conference was held at the invitation of Dublin's mayor and Catholic archbishop, to bring together Collins, Griffith, de Valera and Brugha. They met from three to six in the afternoon, but Collins indicated the extent of progress when he left, giving reporters one of his typically alarming quotes: 'It is all over.' The next day he wrote to Kitty Kiernan that 'We did nothing at the Conference yesterday – except talk, talk all the time – it's simply awful. And the country! But they never think of the country at all – they only think of finding favour for their own theories, they only think of getting their own particular little scheme accepted.' On the 26th Kitty told him that Harry Boland (they were still friends) had told her in a 'burst of confidence' of 'Dev's dislike for you, because you were too anxious for power', to which Collins replied that 'I have known it all along. That's what he says of everyone who opposes him.' It did not augur well for the talks, which dragged on until finally breaking down on the 29th.

The main issue now, with the three-month deadline imposed by the Ard Fheis approaching, was the election itself. De Valera wanted it delayed for another six months; the Labour Party suggested a government of national unity; Collins and Griffith insisted on holding at least a plebiscite. De Valera scoffed at the idea of a 'stone age plebiscite' held by priests after Sunday mass. Collins continued to criss-cross the country to tell audiences it should be up to them: that, contrary to de Valera's dictum, the majority had a right to do anything it liked.

Public opinion and pragmatism kept the negotiations open, first between teams of TDs in the Dail, and then again between the two champions of their respective causes, who met as the clock was running out, on 18 May and again on the 19th. Theoretically, time would be up on 21 May: at that point an election would have to be called. Fencing warily, 'We opened by exchanging expressions of being able to understand and appreciate each other's difficulties,' Collins noted. This was probably true – Collins and de Valera were both men in the middle, pressed on all sides.

Soon they were discussing how a coalition – a reunited Sinn Fein

– would work. Both had the idea of running an agreed slate of candidates and then forming a joint cabinet, but they were divided by details. First was the question of how many nominations and cabinet seats would be allotted to each side. Collins wanted an advantage of six to four in the executive and something like fifteen seats in the Dail, along with explicit recognition of the legitimacy of the Treaty. This was his old requirement of parliamentary security, guarding against a vote that might bring down the government or the Treaty. 'He asked Mr De Valera to appreciate that he and those with him had a greater responsibility' and that while 'he was not looking for scalps or for anything that could be designated surrender . . . a working majority was required.'

De Valera insisted over and over again that 'it would be safe for Mr Collins and his colleagues to depend upon the fact of the Coalition itself as the disappearance of the party spirit would bring ample security . . . If he were in Michael Collins' position he would take the risk.' More concretely, he added that Collins 'should also rely on the added strength acquired from a return of independent candidates', but this was rejected as 'problematical'. (Oddly, both men would come to reverse their views of this issue within a few weeks.) Finally, if Collins acted generously, Dev offered to 'go to some members on his side and secure they would not take a mean advantage'. This seems comically naive – or else that's what he thought of Collins.

In the end, after some seven or eight hours of talking (his forte), de Valera said he would see if he could get some guarantee from his TDs if Collins in turn would waive 'the number of nominations question'. The next morning Dev met his party, who refused to give way on any point, and he was still in the meeting when Collins called to invite him to another session. Collins could go no further either, and confessed that 'some members of his Party thought he, himself, had gone beyond the limit of concession.'

No trust, no deal. That afternoon Arthur Griffith got up in the Dail to call the scheduled election. Before the vote could be taken, however, it was derailed by Harry Boland's counter-motion (over Griffith's protests) that the negotiations be debated first. And, in a bizarre repeat of the February Ard Fheis debate, when he had pre-empted Griffith's pro-Treaty motion, Collins rose to move an adjournment on this basis, immediately seconded by Harry Boland

and carried by the House. He was not hopeful – 'We had pleasant conversations but they did not result in anything' – and more rhetoric (he spoke of 'the misery of listening to all the speeches') was 'not going to be the cause of stopping civil war'.

That night, after dining with John Chartres at the Shelbourne Hotel (a much classier joint than Vaughan's), Collins sent him as an emissary to anti-Treaty whip Sean T. O'Kelly's house, also on Stephen's Green. Perhaps they had learned a few tricks from Tom Jones in London. O'Kelly listened to Chartres relay Collins's 'deep earnestness' for peace, then met with Mulcahy and finally saw Collins himself, who gave him 'a few abusive, but nevertheless friendly salutations'. The abuse may have been more heartfelt than that, as Collins had recently accused O'Kelly of slander ('I should like to meet the man who says it or repeats it'), but the upshot was another session with de Valera at the Mansion House the next day.

The meeting, according to O'Kelly, did not start well. When he and Mulcahy looked in, Collins exclaimed, 'We haven't got past the first bloody line.' They were joined by go-between extraordinaire Boland, and the five of them spent the next three hours thrashing out an election deal. 'There was heated argument, there was abuse, which sometimes almost led to violence' [who can that have involved?] but around four o'clock, 'weary and hungry', they had agreed an electoral pact.

They now had to sell it to their respective parties. Around the corner in Earlsfort Terrace, where the Dail was now meeting, Griffith was already frustrated, but, compounding injury with insult, Collins had agreed to most of de Valera's terms. There would be no statement acknowledging the Treaty, no guaranteed pro-Treaty majority, anti-treaty TDs were effectively guaranteed renomination, insulating them from public disapproval and denying seats to pro-government candidates, and they were also promised four cabinet members to the majority's five. Collins had set the stage for retreat by once again making the first move (as at the Ard Fheis), and this was the logical result.

It wasn't just Griffith who felt that Collins had let him down. Most of Collins's cabinet colleagues were dismayed, as were some of his backbenchers, including Michael Staines, Eoin O'Duffy, Sean McGarry and Sean Milroy. But everything depended on Griffith's answer. According to Ernest Blythe:

He seemed to me to be under tremendous emotional stress. He worked nervously with his neck-tie in silence. He took off his glasses and wiped them, and I noticed that his hand was shaking so that he could hardly hold them. He put on the glasses, fiddled with his tie again; again he took off his glasses and wiped them, the whole thing occupying, it seemed to me, three or four minutes while dead silence reigned round the table. We all realized if Griffith said no, a split, the consequences of which could hardly be foreseen, would almost be upon us. On the other hand, I think the majority of us almost wished that he would say no, in the hope that Collins would be forced to reconsider his support of the Pact. Ultimately, however, Griffith said 'I agree' and made no further comment.

He never called Collins 'Mick' again.

Back in the Dail that afternoon, teeth gritted, Griffith amended his motion to include the Pact, and an election was called for 16 June – less than a month away. Collins repeated his arguments that the united front would improve their position when dealing with their foes in Belfast and London. He may also have read the mood of the Dail and of the country better than his colleagues in sacrificing principle for unity. 'Peace' was the priority now, as in December, and his decision was aimed above all at avoiding a final break followed by civil war. As recently as 5 May he had told John Chartres that 'it seems certain beyond a doubt that civil war will result,' while retaining his knee-jerk optimism that 'I am not without hope that we'll pull the situation through.' He just did not want to take that fateful step while other options remained.

On 23 May Collins returned to the stage of the reconvened Sinn Fein Ard Fheis to receive the prearranged approval of his party for his pact. As on the previous occasion, he and de Valera announced a partnership of good will (no one seems to have noticed the parallel with the two failed pacts with Craig), and for once Collins was the more verbose of the two, eventually prompting an increasingly irritated Dev to shut him up by adjourning the meeting. He spoke with apparent relief and satisfaction, and called the deal 'a triumph for the Irish nation'. In reply to criticisms that their pact threatened the Treaty, he declared:

> They had made an agreement which they thought would bring stable conditions to the country, and if those stable conditions

were not more valuable than any other conditions they must then face what those stable conditions would enable them to face (prolonged applause).

He added that 'that much was quite clear'(!), and this has often been taken as an implied reversal of his previous strategy of sacrificing movement unity for the Treaty. These magnificently vague words – reminiscent of his statements on the Treaty in cabinet – could conceivably mean all sorts of things. No doubt they sounded one way in the cheer-filled hall, and could be spun another way to anxious British officials and cabinet colleagues. Either way, they signalled that he had yet to make up his mind what he would do if he were again forced to choose between the Treaty and his reunited movement.

23: Promises

Meeting him for the first time there is certainly nothing impressive about him. He is just like the big young pleasant prosperous self-satisfied cattle dealer in a big way of business with which Ireland is full, and he is certainly as Macready says much too quick to make jokes of everything and often bad ones. But he is undoubtedly quick to understand and I should imagine is twice the man if he is up against you than when his obvious object is to be agreeable. Strong, brave and quite ruthless ... I certainly thought more of him at the end of the interview than the beginning.

(Mark Sturgis)

THERE WAS ANOTHER REASON why Collins's pact with de Valera was necessary – one which was discussed in cabinet on 25 May and subsequently presented to the British government: 'They were not prepared to wage war against Bolshevism [i.e. criminal violence] sheltering under the name of Republicanism, and it was essential that there should be unity of all political forces in the country to cope with disorder.' Collins blamed de Valera and his cohorts for weakening the government and for seeking advantage from the nation's difficulties, but he felt sure he could beat them in an election any day. They were no longer his main obstacle, however. The big problem now was the gunmen who held a de facto veto over the very holding of an election and who were in control of much of the country.

Collins had encountered them many times in recent months. His supporters were often held up on their way to hear him speak; rail lines and signals were wrecked to block his and their trains, and shots rang out whenever he spoke. In Dungarvan, Co. Waterford, the lorry that Collins was speaking from was hijacked and driven off until one of Collins's men held a gun to the driver's head to make him stop. In Castlebar, Co. Mayo, a firefight broke out under similar circumstances, a woman was wounded, and Collins himself was briefly held at gunpoint. In Killarney, Co. Kerry, his platform was burned down and he was banned from speaking in the marketplace. On 16 April he and his escort engaged in a headline-grabbing shoot-out outside Vaughan's Hotel, which ended with Collins disarming one of his astounded opponents. 'Asked whether the man knew whom he was attacking Mr Collins replied, "He didn't, and when I told him my name he looked a bit serious."'

This was the work of the IRA that Collins had done so much to create, to arm and to protect from civilian interference, and which had become the most important and radical institution of the revolution. Now the creature was loose. He didn't control it; de Valera didn't control it. Its members were a small minority even of the total Volunteer membership, but they held the future of Ireland in their hands.

IRA opinion ran heavily against the Treaty from the outset. Most of the headquarters staff stayed in place in support of the Provisional Government, and some key commanders like Sean MacEoin in Longford and Michael Brennan in Clare also remained loyal. However, very soon after the Treaty was passed, the great majority of the active army − 'the men who counted' as they liked to call themselves − repudiated the agreement, seceded from GHQ and Dail control, and effectively declared independence. Almost the whole of Munster (led by the ultra-efficient Cork brigades), most of the Dublin Brigade, and key units and commanders throughout the country formed a loose anti-Treaty front under the eventual leadership of a breakaway executive and Army Council. The rapid British evacuation of police and army barracks gave them territory, bases and more arms than ever before. In these liberated zones, the guerrillas continued to pursue their vendettas against suspected spies and informers, killing or driving out scores of Protestants, ex-soldiers and newly retired policemen. Once the government cut off their funds, they also resorted to seizing buildings, horses and vehicles, levying funds from local farmers and businesspeople, and outright robbery (banks were temptingly unprotected).

This was no simple division between Pros and Antis however.

The IRA existed in its own political world, quite detached mentally and organizationally from the Dail, governments or parties. Many splits between or within units were founded on earlier grievances and rivalries. If the Brennans of Co. Clare supported the government, it was a sure thing that the competing Barrett clan would oppose them. The same was true of the rugby-playing clerks of Limerick city's 1st Battalion and the resentfully blue-collar 2nd Battalion – and so on through Cork, Kerry, Waterford, Donegal and the rest of the country.

Apart from such local feuds, there was a large contingent of commanders who disliked the Treaty but stayed nominally loyal to Richard Mulcahy, the new Minister of Defence, and Eoin O'Duffy, the new Chief of Staff. Many others, including Cork's Sean Moylan and Liam Lynch (elected in March to head the new executive), retained their affection and respect for Collins and stayed in close touch with the pro-Treaty army, partly through a joint 'watching council' established in early January. These men shared with Collins and his friends not only the same republican ideals (whatever their views on the legitimacy of the government), but also the preference for a permanent, united and independent IRA to act as the guardian of national honour and freedom.

COLLINS WAS NO LONGER inside this paramilitary loop. Showing his true soldierly inclinations, he had left the GHQ as soon as the Treaty had passed and, as Chairman of the Provisional Government, had no official military role. The government did not even officially claim control over the IRA. That responsibility lay with the Dail ministry, although Mulcahy eventually began sitting in on Provisional cabinet meetings from time to time.

The Treaty did allow an Irish army – thanks to Collins's efforts – and one did come into existence at Portobello (also known as Beggar's Bush) barracks in Dublin, the new location of the GHQ. The first unit of the new model army was the Dublin Guards, based in part on the old Squad and the Dublin Brigade Active Service unit, and therefore led by men personally loyal to Collins. The sketchy plan was to create a professional nucleus and a larger militia, based on the IRA but properly trained and organized along British lines. (The British army's field manual had always been the guerrilla bible.)

This worked about as well as the new police force. Imposing a new culture on old IRA men was almost impossible, and importing veterans of the British army caused tremendous friction. Collins almost never visited, and Mulcahy and O'Duffy were more concerned with the north or with their old comrades in the anti-Treaty camp. J. J. 'Ginger' O'Connell, the Director of Training and commander of the regular troops, noted 'a mental reserve among those members of GHQ who were supporting the Government'. Liam Lynch and other anti-Treaty leaders were 'constantly calling' at Beggar's Bush, and 'Lynch had a very great influence with certain members of GHQ which was hard to understand.' He was even able to interfere with O'Connell's orders at times. The pro-Treaty forces were riddled with anti-Treaty IRA men, and even between supporters of the government the antagonism was so great that various factions were brought to the brink of open mutiny on several occasions.

O'Connell's conclusion was that 'practically from the beginning . . . hidden forces were at work in the Army'. This meant the IRB, whose executive, directed by Collins, had approved the Treaty (although, contrary to republican mythology, it did not tell its members in the Dail how to vote). Collins had hoped its continued existence would prevent a split – it was his secret weapon – but in fact republican fraternalism proved almost entirely irrelevant to individual decisions about which side to take. Most of the anti-Treaty officers were IRB men, and didn't care what the Supreme Council told them. Mick's followers in the army were mostly IRB, but their loyalty was personal or professional rather than institutional. O'Connell was correct to the extent that the Brotherhood did still provide a forum for negotiations between different groups after the Treaty, but it was not able to direct events.

Despite its lack of real power, the IRB's reputation as a ruthless mafia grew spectacularly in these months. Non-members on both sides suspected it of undue influence, reducing its effectiveness and tainting those who belonged – not just Collins, but also Mulcahy, whose later political career was blighted by this part of his past. It was also seen as a vehicle for corruption. Collins used every appeal he could think of to bring men to his side, not least of which was the offer of a job or high rank in the new regime. Handouts and jobs for the boys had been part of his reputation since 1917, and many anti-Treaty men have recorded their indignant replies to such advances in 1922. Harry Boland was reportedly offered two jobs.

Collins's ambiguous position and limited influence over the various elements of the IRA were illustrated in the Limerick crisis of late February and early March – before the anti-Treaty army convention formalized the split. The local brigade repudiated GHQ's authority when it began moving into evacuated British positions, whereupon the commandant was defied in turn by some of his pro-Treaty officers. Mulcahy and O'Duffy sent a force under Michael Brennan of the 1st Western Division to reinforce their supporters, while Ernie O'Malley's 2nd Southern Division did the same on the republican side. The cabinet ordered a zero-tolerance policy and wanted the barracks recaptured. Collins agreed, albeit in a 'lukewarm way'. Once anti-Treaty Corkmen arrived on the scene, however, the government was overmatched. Griffith stood firm against any compromise, but O'Duffy and Mulcahy ignored him and (as de Valera had privately urged them) cut a deal with Liam Lynch in the Beggar's Bush mess hall on 10 March to leave the anti-Treaty units in charge of the barracks in return for peace.

Lynch later wrote to the press to say that Collins was 'present', but Collins told a furious O'Connell that 'when he entered the room it was clear to him that GHQ had made up their minds to surrender to Lynch's demands' and so he felt obliged to go along. This reversal took place shortly after the February Ard Fheis, so it was of a piece with his first agreement with de Valera to delay the election, and was no doubt prompted by the same desire to avoid a decisive break and maintain his political manoeuvring room. Griffith and others were most disturbed by this apparent surrender, but again could do little once faced with a fait accompli.

The situation grew worse, not better. Not only did the 'Irregulars', as the anti-Treaty IRA were dubbed, harass Collins and his colleagues through March and April, they also renewed their confrontations with government forces and were able to overpower several garrisons and steal large numbers of guns from them and the new police. The March army convention was banned by the Dail cabinet but was held anyway, in Dublin, in an open challenge to Provisional authority. Shortly after that, on 13 April, the 'rebel' executive, lacking a proper barracks, seized the Four Courts and a number of other prominent buildings in the capital. The phrase 'military dictatorship' was in the air and in the newspapers (although no such thing was ever seriously contemplated). 'God help them!' was Collins's comment.

IRONICALLY (or revealingly), it was pro-Treaty forces who were actually engaged in real fighting in the winter and spring of 1922 – in Northern Ireland. It is often asserted that this was part of a covert plan to subvert the northern government, masterminded by Collins – who was obsessed with the northern problem – and hidden from his cabinet colleagues. The truth is, he had no military strategy or even the ability to direct one, and Griffith and the rest of the cabinet knew about almost everything that happened (as did anyone who could read the newspapers). The strategy of non-cooperation with the north was cabinet policy, not Collins policy, and was derived from pre-Treaty decisions made under de Valera. Collins's main original contribution may have been to cancel the official Belfast boycott in January – hardly a covert master stroke.

Collins was genuinely troubled and angered by the treatment of Catholics in Northern Ireland, and, as usual with key issues, he made it his own. But his feelings and rhetoric were shared by all nationalist politicians, all factions of the IRA, and the whole of nationalist public opinion and the press. Nor do we need a high-level conspiracy to explain the violence that took place on the border in early 1922, any more than we need one to explain the violence elsewhere, north or south. The IRA was fragmented and volatile, lacking any central control even within the executive or the GHQ-led forces. The various headquarters did not have full control of their local commandants, and they in turn were vexed by the many unauthorized operations carried out by their subordinates.

What the northern situation demonstrates is the same ambivalence and lack of control over 'his' men as was the case in the south. Here again, O'Duffy, MacEoin and other IRA leaders on the border had their own ideas. These men were as independent-minded as their anti-Treaty comrades, and sometimes as willing to act on their own.

One of Collins's main aims in talking to James Craig in January had been to get some IRA prisoners released from northern jails; several of them were under sentence of death in Derry for killing a warder after the Treaty was signed. He probably felt for the imprisoned men, as always, but he was no doubt also thinking of what might happen if the locals took matters into their own hands.

Unfortunately, on 14 January an IRA squad on their way to rescue the condemned men (led by O'Duffy's friend and successor as divisional commandant, Dan Hogan) were themselves arrested, thereby doubling Collins's headache.

James Craig suggested they simply apply for bail, but this otherwise simple solution (offered before he fell out with Collins) required them to recognize the northern government. This the southern leadership would not agree to, as it would give the Unionist regime legitimacy. The prisoners' comrades back in Monaghan and elsewhere wanted to retaliate, and put increasing pressure on O'Duffy to grant them permission. O'Duffy, aware that their political allegiance was on the line (as was true for nearly all border units), agreed to the kidnapping of unionist hostages and informed Collins and Mulcahy, who apparently acquiesced, so long as 'certain details of their detention were altered' (to make it either better or more deniable). It was the next day that the Provisional Government adopted its policy of non-cooperation and Collins heightened his anti-partition rhetoric, sabotaging his talks with Craig but perhaps thinking a dynamic 'peace' policy was needed as an alternative to a border war.

Several dozen hostages were taken in raids by Sean MacEoin's men a week later, after which Mulcahy wrote to him that 'we will do the best we can to get these men [the captured guerrillas] released . . . I see that you have captured the High Sheriff.' In fact the Derry men had been reprieved that same night, as Collins had tried to tell the kidnappers before they acted, but it was too late to stop the escalation. A few days later a trainload of Ulster special constables – the hated 'Specials' – foolishly stopped in Clones, in Co. Monaghan, and a fight broke out. Four died, many others were wounded, and the survivors became hostages as well. This was a spontaneous action by the Monaghan IRA (one of whom was killed), angry over Dan Hogan's arrest and by anti-Catholic violence. More followed in the weeks after: 'They were not really official but were tolerated by GHQ,' according to one participant. Southern Protestants became targets as well – many were kidnapped in Sligo, for example, in emulation of what the Monaghan men had done.

After the Clones ambush, the British government arranged for Hogan's release, over the northern administration's protests. He immediately returned to planning cross-border raids, thereby proving the protesting northern government right. Inevitably, rather than gain any further releases, he and MacEoin just got more of their men captured – and more hostages taken in return. Getting them back became a major preoccupation for Andy Cope, still the British government's man in Ireland, and he reported that 'Collins has had great difficulty in holding in certain sections of the IRA who were out for hostages.' Collins certainly did try to get them released. MacEoin recalls him arriving ostensibly on an inspection tour (at the beginning of April) but in fact searching for prisoners: 'I had to hustle him past a tool-shed into which the hostages had been pressed.' MacEoin was not entirely successful, as Collins was eventually able to locate ten of them in Athlone, MacEoin's headquarters, while Gearoid O'Sullivan, still Adjutant General, found another seventeen in Dundalk.

Collins accepted Churchill's suggestion that a joint liaison committee be established to monitor the border, but when its members visited Hogan in his Clones stronghold on 21 February the border reaver told them that, unless all the IRA prisoners were released, 'there would be . . . further raids made either by his order or by the order of the local Commandants on the spot, without necessarily waiting for orders from the Government.' There was only so much that O'Duffy, let alone Collins, could do with these pocket warlords.

INSIDE THE SIX COUNTIES it was a different story again – particularly in Belfast, whose Catholic population bore the brunt of ethnic violence. The IRA units here were weak and demoralized by the long siege of their communities, and were largely ignored by GHQ in the early months of 1922. In February, however, O'Duffy convinced Mulcahy to pay for a permanent self-defence unit, the Belfast City Guard, with Collins's approval. This desire to protect 'our people' – after having failed to convince the British and Northern Ireland governments to do so – drove GHQ efforts thereafter. That and politics: further aid was promised after the breakaway army convention in Dublin in late March, in conjunction with a purge of anti-Treaty elements in the northern divisions. O'Duffy sent a member of his staff, Seamus Woods, to Belfast to take charge, and Mulcahy arranged to pay all the northern officers who stayed loyal to the Provisional Government. Their orders were to defend themselves if attacked, but otherwise to avoid confrontations with the enemy.

Little changed until a second Craig–Collins pact was signed on

30 March. British anxiety about where the violence was leading brought northern and southern negotiators to London, and this time it was a full cabinet effort, with Griffith and Kevin O'Higgins accompanying Collins to meet Churchill and Craig. Together they assembled an elaborate agreement covering most of both sides' grievances – with the notable exception of the boundary. Churchill inserted 'Peace is today declared' at the head of the agreement, but it was no more successful than the first back-of-the-envelope pact or Collins's peace efforts in the south. It would never have been signed without British pressure, and neither side could deliver. Within days Collins and Craig were back to disputing the meaning of what they had signed and complaining to London about each other's broken promises.

Collins and his colleagues did want to give the second pact with Craig a chance to work – or at least to avoid being cast as the wreckers – but they were also at a loss to know what else to do. At a key 11 April meeting of the recently established Northern Advisory Committee, including both cabinets, many clergymen, O'Duffy, Mulcahy and Woods – Collins was unable to suggest any reasonable alternative to the peace policy embodied in the new pact. His aims were very limited: 'It seems to us that if we can get this inquiry [into recent murders in Belfast], the prisoners released, and raiding stopped by the "Specials" we are in a very much better position from our point of view in any co-operation we undertake.' He also complained, as he often did, that his plans were being ruined by the anti-Treatyites: 'We are trying to defend the people of the North East, and our political opponents come along and call us traitors.' Taking action would prove he was still as good a nationalist as he always had been, and gain him allies against the republicans.

In general, Collins wanted the committee to give specific recommendations as to future policy while avoiding committing himself. He certainly provided no leadership, nor any militaristic arguments. The participants did openly discuss the state of the IRA, its operations and their effectiveness, and the cabinet ministers present can have had no doubt that Mulcahy, O'Duffy and Woods were responsible for at least some of the violence. Collins conveniently absented himself from this part of the debate, but he did have something to say about 'burnings' – the term used by all to describe arson attacks on unionist/Protestant houses and businesses – which had already been brought up in the Dail cabinet 'as an alternative policy' to a renewed boycott.

'Burnings' had considerable support among the Belfastmen ('There were some beautiful fires'), but were opposed by Griffith and Mulcahy – from a practical rather than an ethical standpoint. Griffith felt that this tactic had been tried and failed: 'If the people are willing to take that risk I don't say we could object,' but 'that does not save the lives of our people.' Collins's response was evasive when no consensus had been reached: 'I know for a good many months we did as much as we could to get property destroyed. I know that if a good deal more property were destroyed – I know they [the unionist leadership] think a great deal more of property than of human life. The whole thing is, what is the proposal?'

Some of those present felt that the main obstacle to a successful arson campaign – or to successful self-defence – was the lack of arms available to the northern IRA. To remedy this, Mulcahy (probably with Collins's, but not the cabinet's, knowledge) contracted with English arms dealers to secretly purchase large quantities of rifles, revolvers and chemicals necessary for making explosives, in order to place northern brigades on an equal footing with the Ulster police. The government army did not want to send British-donated guns that might be traced back to them, and for this reason Mulcahy and O'Duffy arranged with Rory O'Connor and Liam Lynch, the two principal leaders of the IRA executive, to swap guns so that the Irregulars' weapons could be shipped north.

Collins had little to do personally with any of this. O'Duffy, Lynch and others all went public with this plan, so it seems unlikely that Griffith did not know of it. In any case, a meeting of the Northern Advisory Committee in Belfast in May, of which Collins, Griffith and Mulcahy were all fully informed, did recommend 'carrying out a campaign of destruction ... with a view to making government by the Belfast parliament more expensive and difficult'. And several days later Collins, Griffith, Mulcahy and O'Duffy joined with de Valera, Brugha, Lynch and O'Connor to meet a northern deputation led by Frank Aiken, who commanded a cross-border division in Louth, Down and Armagh. They urged a reunification of the Dail and the army so as to deal the unionists 'a staggering blow', and it is inconceivable that these men talked for two hours without mentioning the war.

The northerners don't seem to have received all that many guns somehow, but they burned with enthusiasm through April, May and June, with or without authorization from Dublin. Kevin O'Shiel, one of the key intermediaries in all this, observed that 'the army for long had one policy and the civilians . . . a series of policies that changed as quickly as the circumstances.' The army, in effect, carried on as it had done before the Treaty, running its own war. The political leadership did the same, with its emphasis on propaganda and boycotting. As before, the Dail and the ministries (apart from Defence) had only a distant knowledge of what the military men were up to, and mostly didn't want to know. Collins was now somewhere in between, not pulling strings so much as being pulled in different directions by the men on the ground, the army leadership, northern lobbies, the cabinet and the British government.

IF COLLINS WAS now in the position of a negotiator rather than a commander where the IRA was concerned, at least the negotiations finally began to make progress in May. Three successive IRB conferences had been secretly summoned to Parnell Square in January, March and April, with Collins, Harry Boland and Liam Lynch all seeking a peaceful solution to the army split – but good will was not enough. Both sides sought to inveigle their brothers into their way of thinking, with Collins assuring everyone of his republican intentions while Lynch and Boland urged him to be true to his uncompromising nature (as they saw it) and return to his roots.

At the heated final meeting in April, Sean MacEoin threatened to throw someone out of the window, while Collins and Liam Lynch exchanged barbs over the promised republican constitution, with Collins asking if Lynch would know a republic if he saw one. Collins was chairing the meeting and asked for opinions on the Treaty from everyone present. Seeing that the majority were against him, he cleverly adopted Florence O'Donoghue's suggestion that a committee be struck between the two sides to review the constitution when it finally appeared.

Because the IRB 'could not announce its existence' (not that it was fooling anyone), this committee called itself an IRA officers group. Its public statement, issued on 1 May, was a major political coup for Collins, as it called for army reunification and an agreed government accepting the Treaty's popular support in order to maximize national strength. This was the essence of Collins's position, now backed not only by Mulcahy and O'Duffy, but also by Sean O'Hegarty, Florence O'Donoghue, Tom Hales, Dan Breen and Humphrey Murphy, major figures in the 1st Southern Division, the backbone of the anti-Treaty IRA. Lynch was not convinced, but he was outmanoeuvred (as usual). On 3 May, O'Hegarty – backed by many of the signatories – addressed the Dail and more or less appealed to the opposition to accept their minority position and join a government of all the talents to prevent civil war.

This had an immediate impact on party politics, and the next day a joint Dail committee was formed to discuss the so-called army proposals, beginning the process leading to the Collins–de Valera pact. On the army front, Lynch and O'Duffy agreed to a four-day truce, later extended indefinitely. Collins was only peripherally involved in these discussions, and in the army unity talks that followed. Mulcahy and O'Duffy were the lead men on the pro-Treaty side, while Lynch, O'Hegarty and other Corkmen made most of the running on the other. Little progress was made until the sudden 20 May election agreement; in fact, the week before this was signed, Collins's doubts were such that he told Winston Churchill he intended to fight and asked for 10,000 more rifles for pro-Treaty forces. Still hedging, however, he told Churchill the guns would be used to 'deal with outside areas such as Drogheda and Castlebar and to leave Republicans in Dublin undisturbed'.

The pact with de Valera meant not having to face such a decision. The IRA executive had threatened to stop an election if one were called, and some units had even seized local voting registers. Now Lynch and Mulcahy made rapid progress, encouraged by the election pact's stipulation that the Minister of Defence would 'represent the army', implicitly independent of either party. This fit with the IRA demand for autonomy in a new regime and with Collins's ideal that the 'National Forces ... must retain the direction of the national movement.' He had in fact sketched out just such an arrangement in an April memo. In it he argued that 'a case may perhaps be made from democratic principles' that soldiers should have a say in their commanders, just as citizens determined their government. Thus the army would elect the members of a Defence Council, which could veto any senior appointments, or that of the minister himself.

This agreed principle laid the basis for an army coalition agreement to match the political one – with Collins's approval, but to the horror of many cabinet members, who had swallowed the pact with de Valera but who now faced sharing power with rebel gunmen as well.

FOR A FEW DAYS in May, then, it seemed as if everything Collins had worked for was falling into place. His cabinet and party were behind him, along with the nationalist press, and he now had his united front in the south and the prospect of a better-defended minority in Belfast to give him greater leverage in Northern Ireland (or so he thought). The truce between the Provisional Government and the IRA was holding, the executive (anti-Treaty) forces in Dublin began to withdraw from the buildings they had occupied – except for their headquarters in the Four Courts – and the stolen voters lists were returned. This stitchwork of compromise, wishful thinking and delay would begin to fray almost as quickly as it had been sewn together, but while it lasted the juggling act was an impressive achievement in itself. If the entrance into Dublin Castle marked the symbolic apex and conclusion of Collins's revolutionary life, arranging a more or less free and peaceful election, with an almost guaranteed favourable outcome, showed his future as a party politician to be bright indeed.

Once the electoral pact was decided, Collins and the Provisional Government were in a hurry to make up for lost time. The Parliament of Southern Ireland was dissolved on 27 May, although the Dail made a point of meeting again on 8 June and preserved its claim to legitimacy by planning to reassemble on 30 June to formally ratify its successor. Nominations closed on 6 June, the election was on the 16th, and the new parliament was due to assemble on 1 July. This would be a purely provisional body, giving the transitional government the democratic authority to pass the constitution and establish the permanent Free State. After that, another election would be held, under a new register, to give southern Ireland its first proper government. It was also understood that the constitution would be made public before election day, although the original rationale of giving voters a chance to pass full judgement on the Treaty settlement was presumably rendered irrelevant by the Pact itself, which made peace and stability the Sinn Fein platform. It was assumed that the constitution would provide the main subject of debate in the provisional parliament, that it would be passed sometime that summer, and thus that it would bring the boundary commission into being well before the end of the year. If it all worked out, Collins's plans would still be more or less on schedule.

Electioneering began almost immediately, with the Labour Party, the Farmers' Party and the Ratepayers' Association (all pro-Treaty) also entering the race. None ran anything like a full slate of candidates, however. Seven of the twenty-seven new multi-member constituencies went uncontested, automatically giving coalition Sinn Fein 34 of 128 seats – and an almost certain majority by default. A few independent candidates and their supporters were attacked as anti-national – including Patrick Belton, Collins's erstwhile mentor, now a prosperous farmer and militant ratepayer. (P. S. O'Hegarty was backing yet another independent candidate.) By the usual standards of Irish elections, however, it was a reasonably peaceful and competitive affair.

It has often been suggested that Collins never meant to honour the Pact, and that he either planned to renege once the voting was finished or else was counting on non-Sinn Fein candidates displacing enough republicans to give him majority support without them (as de Valera had suggested in their April negotiations). However, his renewed machinations with Harry Boland (not only in the Pact negotiations but in other side deals as well) and his implied disapproval of non-coalition parties suggest otherwise.

He didn't campaign much personally, but that was because he was caught up in external crises and had to spend a lot of time in London. In his talks with de Valera he had been dubious of the benefits of having other parties run candidates, and he does seem to have been seriously contemplating the workings of a joint government after 1 July. Other people assumed he would be its head, and he probably did too – although he told Dev he wouldn't be. The draft constitution even made provision for external cabinet ministers, who, Collins would argue, would not have to take the oath to the Crown.

Collins and de Valera did not start campaigning until after the Dail stopped sitting: not until 9 June, when both attended a gala coalition rally held (where else?) at the Mansion House. Griffith was notably absent. Collins spoke of the 'spirit of the agreement' – a reference to a joint appeal to voters that he and de Valera had issued that day, disapproving of parties other than Sinn Fein:

In view of the fact that one of the most obvious aims of the Agreement was the avoidance of electoral contests, which could not fail at present to engender bitterness and promote discord and turmoil, the signatories . . . had hoped that the spirit of the Pact would have ensured that such contests would be reduced to a minimum . . . We are confident that this does not need further emphasis from us.

It was not until his famous speech in Cork on the 14th that he seemed to waver upon this point:

I am not hampered now by being on a platform where there are Coalitionists, and I can make a straight appeal to you . . . to vote for the candidates you think best of, whom the electors of Cork think will carry on best in the future the work that they want carried on. When I spoke in Dublin I put it as gravely as I could that the country was facing a very serious situation, and [for?] that situation to be met as it should be, the country must have the representatives it wants. You understand fully what you have to do and I will depend on you to do it.

These words – and the occasion as a whole – were probably unplanned, as he spoke from his hotel after arriving late from London via Dublin. His language was somewhat cloaked and was not unambiguous, echoing earlier pro-coalition statements. Anti-republican newspapers seized upon the 'vote for the candidates you think best' line (as did republicans after the election), but there were no stories interpreting it as a break with de Valera. When he spoke the next day in his home town of Clonakilty, he much more circumspectly asked his audience to 'support the agreement that has been made in the spirit in which it was made', before telling them 'their duty was to vote for the people they thought would carry out that policy.' And after the contentious Cork vote count was over on the 24th he declined the opportunity to offer 'a political manifestation of faith . . . The situation was so difficult at the present moment that anything said by him at that moment might complicate it.'

If he wasn't trying outright to subvert the Pact, however, he was troubled about what the immediate future might bring. On the 12th, just back from London, he wrote to Kitty Kiernan that 'I have a pretty bad week before me and I suppose a worse time coming.' Squaring de Valera, Cumann na Poblachta and the IRA with his own cabinet and party was one thing, but it was another challenge altogether to convince the British government – the provisional regime's not-so-silent partner – that the Pact was acceptable.

The brief post-Treaty glow had long since worn off Collins's relationship with Churchill, who was increasingly suspicious of Collins's real intentions towards Northern Ireland and the Treaty. If Collins wasn't preparing to betray the agreement, he at least seemed (to Churchill) to be losing the will to stand up to the republicans. On 16 May, Churchill briefed the cabinet to this effect, having written to Collins the day before to denounce the idea of an agreed election as an 'outrage'. The problem, he told his colleagues (with input, no doubt, from Cope) was that 'the Ministers of the Provisional Government live far too much in the narrow circle of their own associates and late associates.'

Once the Pact was announced on the 20th, Collins, Griffith and Duggan were swiftly 'invited' to London to explain themselves. That these invitations could not be turned down was made clear to Collins when he told Cope he might not be able to make it. 'Your absence would I fear be misunderstood,' wrote Churchill (with 'great apprehension'), 'and certainly it would be deeply regretted.' Collins settled for arriving defiantly late on the 26th: one bemused British official referred to him as 'the Hamlet of the piece'.

Collins hoped to return home in a day or two, but ended up staying a week in the Metropole Hotel, along with much of the Provisional Government. Here they were reunited with Lloyd George, Chamberlain, Birkenhead and Tom Jones. The Irish ministers argued that there would have been no election without a deal, and that political unity was necessary to restore order. In other words, the Pact facilitated the Treaty. The result was British acceptance of an agreed election – provided the resulting government adhered closely to the terms of the London agreement, as Churchill made plain in the House of Commons. In a strange scene, he defended his policy, chastized the Provisional Government's, and warned off a republic, all while Collins, Griffth and William Cosgrave (all three being MPs, of course) watched from the gallery – and while the curious MPs below watched them. Collins was seen to smile frequently, fidget copiously, and (breaking the rules) make notes with a pencil, guarded by Cope in the seat behind him. Griffith – morose and even more sphinx-like than usual – said and showed nothing.

Collins shrugged off Churchill's speech in public, but privately fumed over the constant British prodding and Churchill's 'insolent' remarks.

The election pact was the least of the problems as far as British ministers and officials were concerned. Much worse was the draft constitution, all seventy-eight articles of it. Delayed in committee and then passed laboriously through the Provisional cabinet, this was submitted at the same time the Pact was being discussed – and, as Collins had promised both friends and enemies in the movement, it was effectively a republican document. The provocative preamble ('an end has been made of foreign rule in Ireland') was mercifully deleted at the last minute, but the first articles asserted total state and popular sovereignty, with no mention of the Crown. The Governor General – the representative of the Crown – was not mentioned at all, nor was common citizenship with Britain, nor was the all-important oath of allegiance. Foreign affairs were a matter for the Irish government alone.

Ulster; the timing of the election; the Empire; the status of the Crown; ultimatums and deadlines and gloomy newspaper stories: it was as if the calendar had turned back seven months. Both sides dug in and bombarded each other with memoranda while the generals executed their familiar manoeuvres. Griffith was once more forced to defend a policy he didn't like, Lloyd George made dramatic speeches threatening another war, and Collins growled about going home to fight it out, had to be cajoled into staying, and muttered to reporters about how difficult and critical the position was.

'Things are serious – far more serious than anyone at home thinks,' he wrote to Kitty around 28 May. By the 30th, things were 'bad beyond words, and I am almost without hope of being able to do anything of permanent use'. The next day was 'awful', and the day after that 'ghastly'. As before, he wished 'to God someone else was in the position and not I', before adding the characteristic pragmatic coda 'but that's that.' Tom Jones found him 'pugnacious', 'belligerent' and 'militant'. Lloyd George thought him a 'wild animal', and when Jones compared negotiating with him to writing on water the Prime Minister replied, 'Shallow and agitated water.' After the final confrontation, on 2 June, the Prime Minister reported to cabinet (according to a minister present) that Collins was '"all over the shop", "jumping and hopping about", evidently in a state bordering upon hysteria, sometimes threatening, sometimes apologetic, and woolly-headed nearly all the time.' The apologetic Eamon Duggan explained to Jones that his boss was 'very highly strung, and over-wrought, and sometimes left their own meetings in a rage with his colleagues'. Nothing new there, then.

The Irish negotiators tried once again to go on the offensive over Northern Ireland, where violence was again on the rise. This was still the British political weak point but, after the suspicious election deal and the unacceptable constitution, Collins had run out of room to manoeuvre. Churchill's personal response came when a border dispute flared up on the Fermanagh–Donegal border in early June. British troops and artillery were deployed, and the village in question was shelled and then occupied, several Volunteers being killed in the process. Lloyd George had tried to stop the operation, Collins complained bitterly and demanded an inquiry, but the Provisional cabinet got the message and on 3 June ordered that 'no troops from the twenty-six counties ... should be permitted to invade the six-county area.'

The negotiations went on for weeks. Collins, however, returned to Dublin on 2 June, leaving Griffith and others to do most of the detailed bargaining. He wanted to go to Cork, but was preoccupied with the northern crisis until he finally collapsed with a bad cold. Meanwhile, in London, the Free State was forced back into line with the Treaty, although the symbolically powerful declaration that the people were sovereign was allowed to remain. On 12 June the pro-visional ministers approved the bulk of the final draft, and on the 13th Collins rejoined his colleagues in London to complete the pro-cess, then left again that night. The British cabinet signed off on 16 June, the day the constitution was made public: the day of the election. Republicans would claim this delay was deliberate, to prevent the supposedly inadequate constitution being an election issue, but Collins's and Griffith's intentions were quite the opposite.

So – to return to the infamous Cork speech – Collins took the boat train to London on the 12th, attended the crucial meeting on the 13th, arrived back in Dublin on the morning of the 14th, and got on the train to go to Cork that evening. By this point he knew that, under the rewritten constitution, all members of the Free State parliament and all ministers of its government would have to swear the oath to the constitution and the Crown, and he knew that none of his opponents was going to do so. There would be no coalition government if the constitution passed – and no peace with Britain if it didn't.

Exhausted and – as usual – blaming republican dissidents for handicapping him in the talks, he gave his speech on arrival in Cork city. He may have meant to sabotage republican candidates – perhaps just in Cork itself, where stiff competition did nearly bring down one of Collins's chief tormentors in the Dail, ultra-republican Mary MacSwiney. If so, he thought better of it the next day in Clonakilty.

The Pact held regardless. A republican myth would take hold as soon as the campaign was over that republican supporters had kept their side of the bargain while pro-Treaty voters hadn't. Betrayal is always a useful excuse for losing, but, as usual, it wasn't true. Southern Ireland was now divided into multi-member constituencies, allowing voters to transfer their votes beyond their first choice candidate, so we know who voters' second and third choices were. Both pro- and anti-Treaty voters overwhelmingly transferred their votes to each other's candidates – although they naturally preferred candidates on their own side of the party where possible.

The real problem was that Sinn Fein garnered only 60 per cent of the total votes (although this does not include the support available in the uncontested seats it won), and Labour and Farmer's voters were just as loyal to their parties as were Sinn Fein's. If they gave later transfers to Sinn Fein, it was to pro-Treaty candidates, and this made a big difference. While Provisional Government supporters elected 58 of their 65 candidates, republicans could manage only 36 out of 58. As de Valera privately conceded, 'We are hopelessly beaten, and if it weren't for the Pact it would have been much worse.'

Collins was able to celebrate the largest personal vote, from the largest electorate in the whole country (and in the constituency with the longest name: Cork Mid, North, South, South-East and West), despite opposition vote-tampering. With over 17,000 votes, he was nearly 10,000 ahead of the Labour candidate, Michael Bradley, and nearly 13,000 ahead of the closest republican, Sean Moylan. On the other hand, his transfers did help elect two republicans as well as two Free Staters, and failed to bring in old ally and Sinn Fein party hack Patrick O'Keefe, who was given the governorship of a prison in compensation. Friends of Mick had a perfect record: Gearoid O'Sullivan, Sean Hales, Michael Staines, Joe McGrath, Piaras Beaslai, Fionan Lynch, Sean MacEoin and Eoin O'Duffy were all returned. Critics did not fare so well: Seamus Robinson, Erskine Childers, Liam Mellows and Constance Markievicz all lost their seats.

FROM DECEMBER 1921 onward, Collins enmeshed himself in an ever-stickier web of promises and agreements: the Treaty with the British government which started it all; the first Craig–Collins pact in January 1922; the Ard Fheis deal with de Valera to delay the election and avoid a split in February; the second Craig–Collins agreement in March; the electoral pact in May to keep Sinn Fein united yet again, at the cost of preserving many republican seats and giving republicans nearly half the cabinet posts; and finally the agreed Free State constitution in strict conformity to the Treaty – agreed, that is, with the British cabinet rather than any other Irish party.

Essentially, just as de Valera had tried to use external association to escape the straitjacket of the republic in the last half of 1921, so Collins spent the first half of 1922 trying to escape the Treaty – or its consequences – through his endless negotiations with republicans, unionists and the British government, and his own crypto-republican constitution. He failed in each case. Churchill and others tilted in favour of James Craig because of Collins's relationships with anti-Treaty republicans, the British cabinet took a hard line in constitutional negotiations for the same reason, and republicans were ultimately alienated by the tainted result. What he was left with in the end was what he had started with: the Treaty and the government it produced.

24: Commander-in-Chief

Lady Lavery brought Michael Collins to supper. This was my first talk to the commander in chief of the army of the provisional government. He is an interesting personality. Too fat, but virile, 32 years old, forcible, direct, simple and yet cunning. A bit crude (perhaps due to shyness) in the expression of his views.

(Horace Plunkett)

WHAT NEXT? Once all the votes were counted and seats allotted – a week-long process, given the complexity of calculating transfers – all parties looked forward to the last sitting of the old Dail and the opening of its successor, only a week away. Press reports assumed the coalition was defunct and that the new Dail would be as preoccupied as before with constitutional issues. Both republicans and the Labour Party assumed that changes could be made through parliamentary debate. Despite Collins's assurances, de Valera had expected a document along the lines delivered. He emphasized that it was still just a draft constitution, subject to debate and amendment in the Dail. He still expected to be offered coalition cabinet seats, although whether he planned to turn them down or take them until the constitution was actually passed is unknown. According to Sean T. O'Kelly, Boland went to see Collins after the election to make arrangements, but was told to be patient.

Collins was spending most of his time these days in Cork, possibly to avoid just such encounters and decisions. He travelled to Longford to see Sean MacEoin married on 21 June, in company with Griffith and O'Duffy, but was back in Cork on the 22nd and 23rd to keep an eye on the vote count, which wasn't wrapped up until seven o'clock the following morning. He returned to Dublin that day, and spent the night at his regular retreat, the Grand Hotel in Greystones, south of the city ('the first real sleep I had in a week. Talk of being tired . . . it was awful.'). Still 'very tired', on Monday the 26th he attended a cabinet meeting which decided to move the new Dail to the Royal Dublin Society theatre and issue the summons for the new parliament in the names of Griffith as president of the Dail and Collins as chairman of the Provisional Government.

Within the IRA, things were not so quiet. Mulcahy and Liam Lynch reached agreement on army reunification, but the anti-Treaty army executive rejected it, demanding the right to nominate the Chief of Staff. Lynch persevered, and brought his proposals before a full army convention at the Mansion House on 18 June. Tom Barry – an aggressive new executive member from West Cork – countered with a resolution to attack the British garrison in Dublin. This was barely defeated. Rather than allow Lynch's agreement to reach the floor, Rory O'Connor defied his authority and took half the delegates to the Four Courts to brood over what to do next. None of this was made public, but the papers were aware that the army question was 'causing uneasiness' in political circles. Mulcahy and the pro-Treaty IRA would probably have known what was happening, as would Collins, although he took no part in any of these negotiations.

On the 22nd, unconnected with any of these events, two members of the now defunct London IRA shot and killed Sir Henry Wilson at his own door. Both were captured and declared they were acting on their own, on behalf of northern Irish Catholics. Wilson, formerly Chief of the Imperial General Staff and now an Ulster Unionist MP, was a bigoted anti-nationalist and the northern regime's security adviser. His intent was to instil a more military and less murderous spirit in the police forces, but nationalists believed he was the evil mastermind behind anti-Catholic violence.

One of the assassins was Reggie Dunne, the former commander of the London IRA. He had met Collins, and knew Rory O'Connor and Liam Mellows of the republican executive even better. Did one of them order the assassination? All factions in Ireland denied responsibility. The British government accused O'Connor and the Four Courts. Subsequently the lion's share of suspicion has fallen on Collins, to the point where his guilt has been widely accepted as fact. There isn't any convincing evidence to this effect, however, nor is a conspiracy needed to explain what happened. Collins did not have much control over the IRA any more and would have needed an awfully good reason to arrange such a provocative murder at such a critical time. No such reason has ever been presented. And, since he showed no other signs of madness or bloodlust to give us an irrational explanation, we can acquit him of the charge.

In any case, Collins's guilt was not at issue in June 1922. After an emergency cabinet meeting on the day of the assassination, Lloyd George sent Collins (still in Cork) a telegram demanding he take action against the Four Courts as he had evidence to prove their guilt. The Irish government never gave a formal answer. Both Lloyd George in private and Churchill in public declared they would consider the Treaty broken if nothing were done. There was still a small garrison of British troops in Dublin, and in the heat of the moment General Macready was ordered to attack the Four Courts on his own. He wisely delayed doing anything, and the orders were retracted after cooler consideration.

Within the space of a few days, then, both the executive-led IRA and the British garrison had nearly attacked each other before thinking better of it. The consequences would have been disastrous either way. It is unclear what the breakaway Four Courts group were going to do instead. They considered a unilateral attack on Macready's men, and they also wanted to intervene in Northern Ireland. One thing was certain: in such a volatile and factionalized situation, someone was bound to do something.

On the 26th, Leo Henderson, the director of the executive's unilateral Belfast boycott, led a party to a Dublin garage supposedly owned by a unionist firm, and seized four cars and a lot of petrol. This was a clear breach of the truce agreed to in early May, and when Henderson blithely returned to take the rest of the vehicles a force from Beggar's Bush barracks was waiting to arrest him and his men. A similar series of events occurred in Drogheda, close to the border, suggesting a larger IRA plan: either to aggressively enforce the boycott or to prepare for a filibustering expedition into the six counties. In Limerick, republicans seizing a new building were turfed out by government forces: along with the arrest of Henderson, this indicated a countervailing Provisional Government plan to get tough with the Irregulars. In addition to all this, an ex-soldier was murdered in his home near Bray (just outside Dublin) on the 22nd – another in a long line of unsolved murders since the Treaty, probably carried out by republican gunmen.

Collins had stated repeatedly that the Pact's goal of 'stability' and the electorate's desire for 'peace' meant that the new government would finally have to impose law and order, and he was able to argue that his party had a mandate now to do so. However successful, this new spin on the Pact and the election results conveniently ignored the majority backing for nationalist solidarity and opposition to civil war – but neither the British government nor his cabinet colleagues would allow any further tolerance of IRA activity.

So when Rory O'Connor's Four Courts men took Ginger O'Connell hostage on the 27th, in retaliation for Henderson's detention (which was the kind of thing the pro-Treaty IRA had been doing to unionists and Protestants), the cabinet – including Collins – swiftly responded with an order to leave the building and surrender all arms and property. If not, 'necessary military action will be taken at once.' A press release was issued saying the cabinet's hand had been forced 'owing to the series of criminal acts committed under cover of an illegal imposition of a boycott on Belfast goods, culminating in the kidnapping of the Assistant Chief of Staff'.

O'Connor and his comrades predictably ignored the order and stayed put. The imposing Courts buildings, squatting on the north side of the Liffey, were heavily garrisoned and surrounded by barbed wire. To avoid a bloody shoot-out, the government borrowed some British field guns. Early on the morning of 28 June the guns opened fire.

It was Griffith rather than Collins who took the lead in this decision – just as in agreeing to the Treaty. It was Griffith who wrote the press release, and when a Labour Party delegation came to appeal to the cabinet for a ceasefire to evacuate the local population it was he who met them and 'replied fiercely that "they were a Government and they were going to govern. They were not going to be drawn aside by the 'red herring' of the civilian population."' This was a reference to the March Limerick crisis in particular, when the same argument had been used to get the government to back down, over Griffith's objections. Perhaps Collins or Mulcahy had used it again in cabinet to try to prevent or delay the attack on the Four Courts, only this time Griffith and other hardliners like Ernest Blythe and Kevin O'Higgins weren't buying it.

Mulcahy and his staff handled the attack itself. Collins warned his colleagues not to sleep at home in case of reprisals, but otherwise his only documented contribution on the 28th was to write a long letter of complaint to Churchill about the Northern Irish government. This is not to say he wasn't busy, but it was as part of the beleaguered cabinet, now living as well as working day and night in government buildings. It can well be imagined that he was at this point depressed as well as exhausted, although he blamed the republicans entirely for what had happened and was convinced he had gone to the limit to prevent war.

IF COLLINS WAS dejected, however, he soon snapped out of it. As with the Treaty split, the outbreak of civil war may have dashed his highest plans and hopes but it also represented an opportunity for another sort of victory: a quick end to his internal enemies, freeing him to make progress on other fronts. As he put it to Kitty on 23 July, 'It is one of my strong points (or weak points perhaps) that when a thing has actually happened, I do not give myself to what must be vain regrets but plan for the future and learn by the experience.' Assuming a short war, the year could still see the full establishment of the Free State, complete with a proper army and police force. Public order would be restored under a new judicial system, allowing for economic development and for fully democratic politics. The boundary commission would follow, with the prospect of regaining lost territory. He could go to the polls in 1923 on a platform of achievement, with a campaign to reunite Ireland and build a Gaelic state. Thus, once he agreed to suppressing the IRA, he was determined to do it swiftly and decisively.

This sounds a lot like his endorsement of the Treaty based on his vision of a quick and easy transition to full independence. He and his cohorts were predicting a short war, on the assumption that all they had to do was to defeat Rory O'Connor's breakaway group in Dublin and mop up pockets of resistance elsewhere at will. The rest of the anti-Treaty IRA had refused to follow O'Connor's lead before 28 June, so if these men – their IRB brothers and negotiating partners in the army talks – stayed out of it, their opponents would not be able to put up much of a fight. Collins's previous tentative plan – leaving Dublin alone while putting down Irregulars elsewhere – was presumably based on the same idea of avoiding unnecessary fighting.

At the outset, Gearoid O'Sullivan – still Adjutant General – told the cabinet the Irregulars would be beaten in a week or two. Collins at first seems to have thought the Four Courts battle might see the end of it. On 2 July he wrote a memo suggesting an amnesty for IRA members who would give up their arms and 'behave decently in support of the administration'. The government had proved its point by taking action – 'a lesson has been taught' – but it would look better if it was magnanimous in victory. 'We do not want to mitigate their weakness by resolute action beyond what was required.'

In accordance with this minimalist policy, the Provisional Government troops did not try to capture the Four Courts, as that could result in many deaths. Inside the Courts, there was little food and no clear plan, apart from defiance and martyrdom. In the end, mines laid in the ammunition dump exploded, the building caught fire, and the IRA garrison, including Rory O'Connor and Liam Mellows, were forced to give themselves up.

This was nearly a perfect ending as far as Collins was concerned. Unfortunately for all concerned, however, events did not otherwise follow his preferred script. The mostly anti-Treaty Dublin Brigade rose in solidarity with their besieged comrades and, as in 1916, occupied buildings on either side of the Liffey. By the time they had been dislodged, on 5 July, a week-long battle had killed scores of fighters and civilians, including Cathal Brugha, who chose death over surrender. As in the first Rising, much of O'Connell Street was destroyed.

A few anti-Treaty officers remained neutral as Collins had hoped, but most gravitated sooner or later to Liam Lynch's reunited Army Council. What Collins's political manoeuvres had picked apart in April and May, his (or the government's) surprise attack in June had put back together. The IRA, scattered across the country, posed no offensive threat but the fledgling National Army was in little better shape itself, and was dependent on loyal IRA units in the west and midlands hanging on to their own territory. The government would have to reconquer most of the country before it could govern.

The army was now the keystone to state power. On 1 July, Collins announced that Mulcahy had assumed command of the army in Beggar's Bush barracks and that he – Collins – would take his place as Minister of Defence – in addition to being chairman and Minister of Finance. On the 12th, with republican forces pushed away from Dublin (or driven underground), Wexford captured and fighting begun in Limerick, Collins announced the creation of the post of Commander-in-Chief for himself, leaving Mulcahy to occupy the dual role of Minister of Defence and army Chief of Staff. They, along with O'Duffy – appointed to head the newly created South-Western Division, covering Cork and Kerry – would form a War Council to run the campaign.

As usual, Collins brought his posse of pals and IRB brothers with him: Fionan Lynch would assist O'Duffy, Joe McGrath became Director of Intelligence, and Diarmuid O'Hegarty would be Director of Organization. Kevin O'Higgins, more a reluctant protégé than a friend, would work with Gearoid O'Sullivan. In addition to all this, the Dublin Guards, the government's shock troops, were commanded by Patrick Daly, a former head of the Squad, while Liam Tobin and Frank Thornton ran the Oriel House gunmen. Sean O Murthuile became governor of Kilmainham jail, where the Four Courts prisoners were held. Collins and his men were in total control, and he had finally claimed the title of Commander-in-Chief awarded to him by British intelligence, and so resented by his enemies within the movement.

No one outside the army seems to have been consulted on these changes. No one even defined the duties or power of the Commander-in-Chief: it was seemingly left up to Collins to decide. It was only an afterthought when he wrote to Griffith on the 14th that 'it would be well, I think, if the Government issued a sort of Official Instruction to me nominating the War Council of Three, and appointing me to act by special order.' The cabinet had to ask him to send daily reports, and two weeks later they had yet to receive any. Collins had temporarily handed his governmental duties over to William Cosgrave (who was unlikely to do anything contrary to Collins's wishes), but he kept his place at the cabinet table. As often as not, however, he would communicate by letter, advising and instructing his colleagues on the conduct of the war.

This was the same old IRA independence in action, coupled with Collins's now habitual arrogance where his colleagues were concerned. His desire for control went both ways, however – that is, he wanted both to limit civilian interference *and* to keep his military subordinates in check. The newly minted generals might be used to having their way, but they would not be independent from him. This, indeed, may have been the main reason for his reimmersion in the army. Mulcahy's early move to active command seems to have failed, partly because he could not deal with the headstrong O'Duffy, who was resented in turn by both the intelligence men and the more conventional soldiers like Ginger O'Connell. Divisional commanders – Sean MacEoin and Michael Brennan for example – also needed reining in. Only Collins, with his personal connections and authority, could command them all. Only he could shuffle O'Duffy into the field with Fionan Lynch as a minder, using a purely nominal place on the War Council as compensation. Only he could put Joe McGrath in charge of Tobin and Thornton, before moving them to the southern front as well.

AFTER THEIR DUBLIN strongholds fell in early July, the IRA made little attempt to hold on to towns or cities, and were far too few in number to hold a defensive line in open country for any great period. The National Army was able to reinforce its Limerick garrison at will, and took the city with few casualties by 21 July. It was held up in its southward advance for a fortnight – as much by lack of transport as by the enemy – but once troops were moved by sea to land in Cork and Kerry in early August the IRA pulled back to avoid being trapped. Cork city was abandoned on 11 August at the same time as most towns in West Cork. Elsewhere, Dundalk changed hands several times and Frank Aiken's 4th Northern Division scored some notable successes against the government, but they were eventually forced back into the guerrilla life like their comrades in Munster. This was exactly the sort of quick and clean campaign that Collins had anticipated.

Collins seems to have directed the war in partnership with Mulcahy. It did not require the skills of a great captain on either of their parts, given the myriad vulnerabilities of their foes, but they distinguished themselves by providing responsible leadership, responding sensibly as events unfolded, and by doing nothing stupid – which is more than can be said for many more experienced generals in neighbouring countries.

Collins therefore spent little time drawing arrows on maps or reading up on the art of war. Nor did he – or Mulcahy – ever take command of operations. His policy, as stated in numerous memos, was to win as quickly as could be – but with the least possible nastiness. In strategic terms, this meant a rapid military build-up and taking the offensive wherever possible. His self-prescribed role was, as in the struggle against Britain, largely managerial and political: to build an efficient army and prepare for an advantageous peace.

To minimize distractions and dissent, the opening of the Dail was delayed when fighting first broke out in Dublin, and was then delayed again and again as the end of the war kept receding. The decision lay with the army, and Collins wanted to wait until resistance in Munster had been stilled. The last postponement was issued on 18 August, with the Dail now scheduled to meet on 9 September. The Labour Party was eager for a chance to debate the war, but few believed the republican party would turn up. De Valera himself had gone on the run when the war began, even more depressed than Collins. He was now nominally a soldier in the IRA, somewhere in Munster.

Nevertheless, Collins was constantly calculating the politics of the situation: hence his constant insistence on retaining public support and giving opponents a decent opportunity to end the war on honourable terms. This was evident as early as his first wartime memo, on 2 July, which spoke of keeping open 'some avenue or avenues to peace' and suggested, 'We will meet them in every way if only they will obey the people's will.' Over the following weeks he continued this train of thought as specific problems came up. On republican political activity he opined, 'Let them have their Halls and their Meeting places in public, so that everybody can see and know in a general way what is going on.' On punishing civilians living near ambush sites: 'I myself think that this will not make a great difference from a Military point of view.' On propaganda: 'Much of the criticism lately has been inclined towards abuse. This is not good from our point of view, and it is not the best way to tackle them. The men who are prepared to go to the extreme limit are misguided, but practically all of them are sincere.' On snipers: 'I may say that I am in favour of drastic action being taken but I am against shooting down unarmed men in any circumstances.'

At issue, in essence, was which side would be labelled the new Black and Tans – that is, thieves, bullies, murderers. Newspapers had long since tagged the anti-Treaty IRA as such, and now republican propagandists were trying hard to do the same to government forces. While Collins was alive, they did not succeed. The National Army rarely killed civilians or prisoners and never deliberately destroyed private property. The IRA were even more scrupulous in their fighting methods, but they did burn many buildings and seize horses, cars, food and clothing as they retreated. Partly as a result, they lacked the necessary popular support to carry on an extended guerrilla campaign – although that didn't stop them trying.

Many of Collins's admonitions were directed at the Provisional cabinet, who were, ironically, far more bloodthirsty than the fighting men. Just as most of the cabinet had wanted to attack the IRA while Collins and Mulcahy were reluctant, now they wanted the war prosecuted with much greater ferocity. On 22 July, for example, they decided in Collins's absence to order guerrillas caught operating behind the lines to be shot. When the army had failed to do this by the 27th, 'it was decided that the Commander-in-Chief should be informed that the Government are of the opinion that the time had now arrived for the issue of a proclamation regarding Sniping etc.,' and this came up again on the 30th.

This was part of a larger, if unspoken, power struggle between Collins and his political colleagues, recalling somewhat the antics in the de Valera cabinet in 1921. For months Collins had more or less got his way on every point of policy, from the north to dealing with the IRA. Some of his ministers had been running out of patience by June, such that the old spirit of deference was missing from the July and August meetings. Decisions were taken in his absence, his wishes were sometimes denied – as on appointments – and he was given orders, which were pressed in spite of his objections. No more could he just say something was an army matter, as in 1920 or 1921, and have everyone shut up: now they wanted reports and accountability.

The army had unilaterally assumed control of censorship: the cabinet ordered it be put under civilian control. The mysterious and rapidly expanding Oriel House theoretically answered to the military Director of Intelligence: it was ordered to be transferred to the Ministry of Home Affairs. By August, Collins's critics even took the daring step of striking a committee to reconsider northern policy, although when it recommended a less confrontational policy, on the 19th, a proviso was added: 'subject to . . . obtaining the approval of Commander-in-Chief'. Dissent had yet to turn into outright rebellion.

The other – and far more time-consuming – side of Collins's

new job was administrative. He treated the National Army as he had treated his previous portfolios, whether Finance, Intelligence or the Provisional Government. He built up and protected his power (or the power of his agency), delegated much of the work to trusted subordinates, and then fussed over innumerable matters of detail while badgering people constantly in the name of businesslike efficiency. Despite his familiar complaints that 'it is physically impossible to look at everything,' he gave it a good try. Notes and memos poured from the office of the Commander-in-Chief telling people *exactly* what to do about the most mundane problems. Whenever the phrase 'my opinion' appeared, someone was going to get it. As usual, Collins's solution frequently lay in a properly constructed and filled-out form.

The Minister of Home Affairs was told on 13 July that his reporting on Civic Guard numbers was inadequate: 'It should be done in tabular form and furnished in duplicate.' On the 15th the uniformed Dublin police were failing: 'My own opinion is that the higher officers are at fault, and stern action should be taken with them.' On the 19th Michael Staines – in his last days as head of the police – was given The Lecture on proper reporting (he'd heard it before) after Collins found local police reports inadequate: 'It is never sufficient to say that nothing happened ... Without details these reports will not show whether or not there is any work being done.' Spoken like a true graduate of the Savings Bank! When a minor intelligence report from Kilkenny came across his desk on 7 August he declared, 'The Intelligence Officer is wrong and the Adjutant who submits the report is wrong – and quite clearly lazy and inefficient'. On 8 August he wrote Mulcahy a long, angry and minutely specific memo about the way a traffic accident had been handled by the Chief of Staff, the Adjutant General and the Legal Adviser: 'There is undoubted neglect indicated in all the offices ... The handling of the case is unmilitary and unbusinesslike.'

After the first weeks of fighting, with the republicans in retreat, he was able to take his show on the road in a series of inspection tours, first to the midlands and then to Limerick and points south, where he was able to castigate his targets in person. He had definite opinions on everything. One of his favourite topics was mattresses – something he may have become sensitive to given his sleeping problems and the number of different beds he had used while on the run. On 1 August he wrote to the Quartermaster General (Sean MacMahon) that 'in going on inspections one of the things that has struck me most is the untidiness and uncleanliness that come from bad mattresses. The first thing that strikes one is the queer assortment that exists almost everywhere'; he then proceeded to categorize it.

Another recurring theme was the state of the army's cars and trucks. He had personal experience of how bad this could get on an epic cross-country trip from Dublin through Kerry on 12 August (as he reported to MacMahon). They started at 4 a.m. (Collins standard time) with a touring car for himself and two escorts:

> Practically speaking from the outset the Lancia Car was in difficulties and at Naas it went on fire. It was re-started and engine difficulty continued at frequent intervals until, nearing Roscrea, one of the back wheels went completely . . . A few miles further on, near Roscrea, the Crossley Tender ran out of Petrol. There was no spare Petrol in any of the cars . . . [at Roscrea the Lancia was replaced by a second tender] At a later stage in the proceedings it was found that the first Crossley Tender was punctured, and although there was a spare wheel, there were no valve parts. This was discovered at a critical part of the journey in Kerry. Also tubes were found to be frightfully defective . . . During the journey to Kerry, the Armoured Car supplied from Limerick got 'ditched'. In my own opinion this was due largely to incompetent driving.

In his comments, Collins demanded to know 'Who exactly was responsible for passing the fleet as fit in every way?'

With vengeance in his heart, he returned to Limerick:

> On Thursday 15th August at 11-40 a.m. I ordered GEN O'DUFFY to send for CAPT. O'NEILL to come to HQ, Limerick City and bring with him a list of Transport.
>
> CAPT. O'NEILL came along without a list, stating he had been told 'to come to GEN O'DUFFY with some papers'. I asked him to supply a list in 10 mins of the Transport under his control in the Command. He smiled at this requirement and seemed to regard it as being a joke. I told him I regarded his attitude as being insubordinate in the extreme and ordered him to parade with his list. After about 3/4s of an hour he did turn up, and supplied me with 2 slips, copies of which are attached.

You will observe that these particulars are really quite useless, from the point of view of value, to the Officer Commanding. I pointed this out to CAPT O'NEILL and gave him a Draft Form to supply me with proper particulars ... This Form was to have been completed and in my hands by three-o'clock. I heard, however, that CAPT. O'NEILL had taken ill and was consequently not able to prepare it.

If poor Captain O'Neill felt ill after a sudden encounter with his Commander-in-Chief, imagine how Captain McCormack felt when, one morning, Collins turned up unannounced at his post in a commandeered house in Castleconnell. There was no sentry at the gate, the grounds were littered with used cigarette packets, and the trench contained 'one tin of meat, opened, and apparently putrid, egg shells, empty match boxes, sweepings from the house. Part of the trench under water, depth of 2" or 3".' McCormack had to be woken up, and appeared half dressed and unshaven. The men's quarters were 'I should say, most unsanitary', and the men themselves had 'long, unkempt hair'. 'They were all tired from over sleep, that is evident at a glance.' Fortunately for them, 'Time did not permit me to make a detailed inspection.'

Collins's Patton-like scourging of unit after unit was obviously intended to impose proper military standards on the almost completely untrained, unskilled, inexperienced and very young men who made up his army. No doubt he wanted to see the situation for himself as well as show the troops he was with them. It can hardly have been good for morale, however, going around humiliating junior officers. The National Army had come into existence only a few weeks before, had been engaged in fighting along a moving front ever since, and lacked most of the normal military infrastructure. Weren't the line units entitled to some leeway? And didn't he have anything better to do? Wasn't this the job of the Chief of Staff, the Adjutant General, the Quartermaster General and the directors of Organization and Training, not to mention the field commanders? Mulcahy had done a circuit of the southern front only two weeks before Collins, and O'Duffy was engaged with exactly the same problems. It seems like classic staff officer behaviour of the sort that had made Mulcahy and GHQ organizers unpopular with brigade commanders in 1921 (and that Collins was supposed to disdain). Austin Stack,

William Cosgrave and Desmond Fitzgerald would have recognized the symptoms.

COLLINS COULD NEVER be accused of mere paper-pushing, however. After the first days of the war, he travelled regularly around Dublin in an ordinary car, and his ventures beyond his offices in Beggar's Bush and Government Buildings took him into dangerous territory. Athlone and Dundalk were not so bad, but he drove to Limerick and back twice in August, and into Kerry and Tipperary, where heavy fighting had recently taken place and guerrillas were still active.

Harry Boland was shot dead on 31 July, and republicans accused Collins of murder. This did much to raise the level of bitterness on the republican side. Next to go was Arthur Griffith, who died of a brain haemorrhage on 12 August. Collins walked at the head of Griffith's funeral procession to Glasnevin Cemetery, presenting an easy target for any nearby gunmen (although the solemn occasion made an attack very unlikely).

As for Collins himself, it was widely reported that the IRA were trying to ambush him, and on 16 August, the car he used in Dublin was attacked – although he was on tour elsewhere at the time. On the other hand, there is absolutely no evidence at all that there was any republican assassination plot, and the ambushes of National Army cars, trains and convoys interpreted at the time as attempts on Collins's life were probably just ordinary guerrilla operations against obvious targets. Nor is there much solid evidence of him having a death wish, as is sometimes suggested. Collins was tired and ill, as he had been during other times of stress (his illness was reported in the press and denied), but his correspondence does not register nearly the same apprehension as it did in early 1921.

There was nothing remarkable, then, about his setting off for a tour of Co. Cork on 20 August. Biographers often exclaim at the risk being run, and shroud his journey in foreboding, but he had visited other liberated areas from Dundalk to Tralee in the last few weeks in exactly the same way. He had returned from Limerick and north Munster just a few days before. On this occasion he drove along the now familiar route to Limerick, with his usual escort of troops and an armoured car, inspecting as he went, and arrived safely in Cork city at the end of the day. He was ill and in a bad mood, but that was hardly unusual either.

Collins had various political and administrative tasks to perform there: meeting with local representatives, setting up an intelligence network (Liam Tobin was with him), and recovering money seized by the IRA from banks and customs offices. He travelled through mid-Cork to Macroom and back, and he spent time in the city with his sister Mary and his nieces and nephews.

Rumours abounded that he had also come on a secret peace mission. The *New York Times* reported that 'one rumour, characterized as absurd, represented him as visiting Eamon de Valera in a remote part of Cork.' This had come up earlier in press reports, and an ad-hoc People's Rights Association in Cork had in fact attempted to broker a truce between Collins and Liam Lynch. Lynch offered to stop fighting if Provisional Government forces stopped their advance. Collins refused, saying, 'The choice is definitely between a continuance of war and the Irregulars sending in their arms to the people's Government in trust for the people.' The IRA had to decommission and go home, accepting the authority of the new regime. Captured guerrillas could already avoid imprisonment by swearing not to take up arms again, although most had refused and some of those who did went back on their promise.

Surrendering would never be acceptable to the embittered IRA leadership, but Collins may have hoped to draw off rank-and-file support, and to bring de Valera or other republican TDs back to the Dail. He may also have hoped to convince some old comrades personally on his travels through Cork. Sean O'Hegarty and Florence O'Donoghue had opposed the Treaty but had stayed neutral in the conflict, and they could get in touch with those still fighting. The People's Rights group had their own contacts. Whether anything was happening on these fronts is unknown, but Collins had no plans to meet de Valera, who was indeed in West Cork.

The rumours may have caused some anxiety in the cabinet, however. Cabinet members knew that Collins's firm rhetoric belied a heady capacity for U-turns, and they certainly would have been outraged by any unilateral conciliation, even with Griffith now no longer among them. When the *Irish Independent* reported in late July that secret peace negotiations were under way, his colleagues instantly

asked that Collins 'issue an immediate statement contradicting categorically the statements contained in the Article in question'. On past
form this might not have stopped him, of course, but we have little
evidence beyond conjecture to suggest he was secretly planning
anything. He certainly never did meet any of his enemies on the trip.
Nor would doing so have made much sense, given the rapid progress
of the military campaign and the unlikelihood of IRA officers
agreeing to surrender just because Collins – whom many of them
thought had stabbed them in the back – asked them nicely. After all,
they hadn't listened before when he had tried to get them on side.
Why would they do so now?

Early on the morning of the 22nd, Collins set out to continue his
tour of his constituency and return to Woodfield for the first time
since the June election. He stopped in at Clonakilty, Bandon and
other towns to greet the locals – including brother Johnny – and
inspect the garrisons: the Big Fellow's victory lap.

The way back to Cork lay through Bandon and Macroom. In
between the two towns lay the village and valley of Beal na Blath
(usually translated as 'the Mouth of the Flowers' but more prosaically
meaning something like 'the Passage to Pasture'). Here an IRA
ambush had been arranged: as the British army had learned in
1920–21, it was a cardinal mistake to travel the same road on
outward and return journeys. Newspaper reports suggested the convoy
of a dozen or so men was outnumbered ten or twenty to one, but in
fact the outgunned ambushers numbered either six or nine, as the
adjutant of the 1st Southern Division – who was nearby but did not
take part in the fighting – reported to the republican Chief of Staff
two days later:

1. On Tuesday 2nd inst at 8.35 a party of Free Staters about
   30 strong passed Beal na Blaith on the road to Bandon.
   They were preceded by a motor cyclist and travelled in a
   Touring Car, Lorry and armoured car. Ml. Collins was one
   of the party.

2. A picked column 32 in number was mobilized and took up
   a position about 1/4 of a mile from Beal na Blaith to await
   their return.

3. At 6 pm we got definite information from Bandon that the

party had gone to Clonakilty. At 7.45 pm we gave up hope of anything and decided to withdraw for the night.

4. Some of us had got as far as the Cross at Beal na Blaith when a messenger came in great haste with information that the party had returned + were held up on the road by our Barricade.

5. Fortunately 6 of our men had not left their position and three more managed to get back. Fire was immediately opened on the enemy by this section. The rest tried to get back to assist their comrades but were never in a position during the engagement to render any real assistance.

6. The firing was terrific the enemy relied chiefly on his machine guns. Now and again you could hear the crack of a rifle from our little party, who never budged an inch from their position.

7. The engagement lasted one hour. The enemy managed to remove the barricade, our men were to[o] far away to cover this part with their fire. They beat a retreat, leaving the motor cycle behind, towards Cork, our men continuing to fire on them.

8. I have since learned that Ml. Collins was shot dead during the engagement. Our casualties were nil.

9. The greatest praise is due to the 9 men who stuck to their positions under such a heavy fire. They claimed to have wounded at least three more of the enemy.

10. The enemy used explosive bullets in what ever little rifle firing they indulged in.

11. During the journey Ml. Collins travelled in the touring car and made himself very prominent.

There are a few inaccuracies here. The size of the escort is overestimated, and explosive bullets were not used. (Similar accusations were made against the IRA with as little truth.) By all accounts, Collins was hit while standing, firing a rifle – making himself a little too prominent, in other words. This may have been owing to drink taken (he had visited several pubs and hotels during the day) or to inexperience in combat, or both.

Despite the banality of his death, numerous writers have inevitably suggested a conspiracy lay behind it. Was it the British secret service? A republican double agent within the escort? Was it all arranged by de Valera, as was repeatedly charged by his enemies throughout his political career? Was it Collins's own cabinet, who feared his radical intentions? All such charges are ridiculously unsubstantiated by any credible evidence, although that has done little to diminish their popularity.

The guerrillas were not trying to kill Collins in particular, and many of those involved were sorry to have done so. Except for the outcome, it was just another ambush of opportunity in a war that would last another eight months, and consume the lives of Sean Hales, Rory O'Connor, Liam Lynch, Liam Mellows, Erskine Childers and hundreds of others. In personal terms, there is no reason to see Collins's death as any more tragic than any of the others that took place during the Civil War. If anything, as Collins was one of those responsible for starting the war and ordering men into combat, his killing was more justified than most, according to his own understanding of violence.

Collins's death was a lot cleaner and made a lot more sense than many of those that followed. Among the first killed were four young republicans – including Alfred Colley, the vice-commandant of the Dublin Brigade – picked up by gunmen four days after Beal na Blath, driven to the suburbs, and murdered. A drunken revenge for Collins by former Squad men out on a Saturday night? It was as much part of his legacy as the Irish Free State that came into being two months later.

HANNIE COLLINS, the person Michael was closest to in all the world, was stricken when the news of his death was delivered to her in the Savings Bank by a keen reporter looking – in time-honoured fashion – for the relative's reaction: 'Miss Collins, in a most-distressed condition, left the building, and went to the house of Sir John and Lady Lavery in Cromwell Place. Sir John had often entertained Mr Collins during his visits to London. Unfortunately Sir John and Lady Lavery are out of town, and Miss Collins left in tears.' The reporter kept on her trail and got the interview at home in her flat. 'I have always looked on him as mine, and the rest of the family have, I think, always recognized the fact ... There are lonely years ahead of me.'

Conclusion: The Making of Michael Collins

THE STORY OF MICHAEL COLLINS is also the story of a movement. The IRB and Sinn Fein were at best marginal players in Irish politics in 1910, and the separatist Irish Volunteers weren't much more important before 1916. Yet these were the central institutions of the revolution to come. Each would be transformed, acquiring vast new memberships and unprecedented money and power. Rapid expansion meant the sudden creation of many new jobs and responsibilities. Anyone in on the ground floor would almost certainly rise as a result, drawn upward by new hierarchies and pushed upward by new arrivals.

Michael Collins was therefore in the right place at the right time, although that would hardly have been obvious before 1916. He joined the IRB, Sinn Fein and the Volunteers in time to achieve a solid position within each – but not so soon or so prominently that it got him executed in 1916, imprisoned for long periods afterwards, or pushed upward and outward by the arrival of new blood. Taking part in the Rising – and he was in the GPO to boot – was an essential precondition for future success on the Dublin scene, as was his time in Frongoch. The few hundred men who shared these trials and joys would go on to dominate the movement at its centre.

His personal history in many ways makes Collins typical. The revolution produced hundreds of Michael Collinses up and down the country – unknown young men of no importance who suddenly took hold of their country's history: men who went from offices, shops or farms to battlefields and parliaments, who grabbed the reins of power in their own town, district or county, just as Collins did in Dublin. Hundreds of men led battalions, brigades or columns, organized clubs, constituencies, and campaigns, ran local boards and councils, collected the Dail loan, and sat as judges in rebel courtrooms – just as Collins split his time between army, secret society, party and ministerial duties. Most of them had grown up in the countryside, mostly on their parents' farms; a great many had had secondary schooling and had left home to get ahead, usually in a low-paying white collar job – teaching, shop work, the civil service. Even the absent father was a feature of many of their lives.

Collins was a little bit older, with a wider view of life than most, but he shared his basic pre-revolutionary origins and expectations with hundreds of other young men, all of whom also shared the liberating effects of the revolution, which transformed not just their nation but their obstructed lives. At last they had opportunity, power, a chance to find out who they were and what they could do, and to make that mean something glorious. The revolution released a vast reservoir of talent and ambition into Irish politics, so Collins's rise was also a collective one – part of the phenomenon looked back upon as 'four glorious years'.

Nevertheless, some swam and some sank. In the end there was only one Michael Collins. What was it that brought him and no one else to the summit of the revolution? Part of the answer lies in the character of the movement. Its history is not just one of collective advancement, but also of internal struggle, with winners and losers. In the end, a minority of radicals seized direction from within, thanks in no small part to Collins. His progress meant progress for those who thought like him, and vice versa. This created a different kind of opportunity even before the movement took off: advancement through one faction displacing another.

So it was in the Gaelic Athletic Association, both on and off the field, and in the Gaelic League and in Sinn Fein. So too with the Volunteer split and after, as even within Eoin MacNeill's Volunteers and the Irish Republican Brotherhood there existed a divide between those for and against a rising. This made Collins part of an even smaller and more militant minority, which got him promoted to captain by the conspirators, although not his longed-for command. (He had to make do with badgering the refugees at Kimmage and everyone else in the GPO.) Frongoch saw the same scenario played out again: Collins rose once the first cohort of leaders were taken away, and as part of an activist ginger group.

Post-Frongoch there was a leadership vacuum: some had died, others were still in prison in England, and others were discredited by their inaction. Collins made sure he was present in Dublin and at the early by-elections, and used his radical credentials to become the

Rising veterans' representative in the National Aid and in the early political deliberations. The proposed radical vehicle, the Liberty League, went nowhere, but the threat of another split made now-buoyant Sinn Fein buy off the League's activists by giving them, including Collins, a place in its leadership. Collins and the other 'young men' took over the Volunteers lock, stock and barrel by the simple expedient of declaring themselves the provisional leadership. Behind the scenes, in the ravaged IRB itself, the transfusion of new blood practically amounted to a transplant.

It was the conscription crisis of 1918 that gave the final boost to the revolutionaries' fortunes. Not only did the situation favour their ideas, it once again removed much of the existing – and moderate – political leadership, creating another power vacuum for Collins and his allies to fill. Doing so put him in charge of the Volunteer organization, and ensured his and other comrades' election in 1918. The situation took him to London at Christmas, allowed for a republican Dail, and guaranteed him office in its government. It also accelerated the shift in power from Sinn Fein to what was becoming the Irish Republican Army. Collins's takeover of Intelligence allowed him to start his war against the police without having to seek permission, and thereby helped launch the guerrilla war as a whole.

In the context of war – and in the crucial absence of de Valera – Collins became the single most powerful man in Ireland. His rise created enemies, however, and Dev's return put him back in second place. It took a final split over the Treaty to clear the way for his assumption of leadership of the new state. Collins never met a split he didn't exploit, but this one was different. According to the standard rules governing such matters, he actually lost the battle. His opponents maintained the ideological upper hand by refusing to agree to his compromises, and they also retained control of the disputed organizations, the IRA and Sinn Fein. Moreover, in the process, the previously decisive IRB was broken and its still-potent role as guardian of the republic was effectively taken over by the IRA.

Collins did not give these things up without a fight, but he was willing to sacrifice them to gain larger victories. He was now playing in the wider arena of public opinion, democratic politics and state power, so the old rules no longer applied. In fact he had been moving in this direction since late 1920. Riding an unrepresentative faction to power had taken Collins a long way, but it could not take him all the way. After pushing war in 1918, 1919 and most of 1920, he began to move towards a tactical advocacy of peace. This required very careful handling, as he did not want to lose his militant following or credibility. The enormous achievement of being the guerrilla warrior who made peace – while de Valera was away – must have beckoned in December 1920. His deep disappointment when the indirect talks fell through and his desire to avoid any hint of compromise, war-weariness or naivety made him very wary of such approaches again, and helped ensure he kept up a hard line in public for the next year.

What Collins seems to have been developing from late 1920 onward was a new strategy of triangulation. That is, he was manoeuvring to position himself at a politically optimal distance from both moderates and extremists, so as to maintain support from both quarters and from the general public – who might love a hero but who were looking for a peacemaker. Not coincidentally, this had been de Valera's policy within the movement: placing himself above factions, and manoeuvring to make a settlement fit for republicans.

This was not necessarily a matter of rivalry. Collins could just as easily have been adjusting himself to what he accurately saw as the new political reality, to be a player in the new game with de Valera still in charge. Nor was he confident about what the correct moves should be, as shown by his anxiety, ambivalence and passivity during the whole peace process. But when de Valera's external-association solution proved unworkable in the cauldron of negotiations, and de Valera failed to seize the moment by going in himself, Collins was able – or was forced – to impose a solution of his own (or at least make one his own). As a stroke of political ju-jitsu – unplanned, perhaps, but exploited none the less – it was a masterpiece, forcing de Valera back into Collins's old position of radical leader in 1922, only without the personal authority over the IRA or much public support.

Not that Collins's strategy worked all that well in many respects, as he was unable to retain much guerrilla or hardline support. This failure would lead to civil war and his own death. He did, however, retain enough of his old image and following to give him a decisive advantage over his opponents, and to make him the untouchable leader of his own side. In this sense he was able to triangulate all over again within the pro-Treaty camp, between the familiar poles of republicans and Griffithites and soldiers and civilians, even after his hand was forced again in starting the Civil War.

This, indeed, was the classic formula for gaining and holding power in Irish politics, as exemplified by Parnell: rise from the left, rule from the centre. Throughout the nineteenth and twentieth centuries, a radical background was essential to fill the role of the leader as fighter, together with demonstrated self-sacrifice shown by breaking the law, evading the police, and doing time in prison. Even John Redmond had been a Parnellite and had been in jail, while James Craig made his name with the Ulster Volunteer Force. But all parties and movements were coalitions, and debilitating splits were forever on the horizon. So, while it was necessary to retain a radical image and support, what separated winners from losers was building and maintaining alliances – and delivering results through some combination of threat, direct action, manoeuvre and negotiation.

No one had a perfect record in this regard – all coalitions eventually fail – but Parnell was the master, and de Valera would do the trick again with Fianna Fail in the 1920s, '30s and '40s. It was Collins who beat de Valera in one-on-one parliamentary combat in December 1921 and January 1922, and he maintained his advantage thereafter, forcing de Valera into outright political humiliation after civil war broke out. It is interesting to speculate how Irish politics would have gone if Collins had lived through the succeeding decades, as no one else on his side had nearly the same touch or popularity after he was gone.

MICHAEL COLLINS was a creature of opportunity and an astute and lucky political strategist, but there was still more to him than that. Opportunities are necessary, but they have to be made – or, when they appear, exploited to maximum advantage. And strategies have to be correctly implemented to be successful. The timing has to be right; allies have to be in place; friends have to help; opponents have to be circumvented, turned or beaten; rules have to be changed, broken or upheld; crises have to be engineered or defused – all the friction of political warfare has to be overcome. All this requires hard work, organizational ability, tactical skill, personal persuasiveness. This is the stuff of political mastery, and Collins possessed it all.

Collins had certain methods and techniques that worked for him, and he stuck with them throughout his career. These were not necessarily conscious or thought-out, but he used them over and over again with repeated success. The first of these was playing the protégé. In London and Dublin, Collins attached himself to a series of more senior men, who looked out for him and guided his way in the movement. In London there were Pat Belton, P. S. O'Hegarty and Sam Maguire, and perhaps his older-brother-like cousin Jack Hurley as well. Under their tutelage he learned to work committees, fight and win battles, and run organizations. In Dublin Belton helped again, but Collins was also taken up by Sean MacDermott and Joe Plunkett, who got him into the IRB inner circle. In 1917 Belton continued to help with the National Aid, joined by Kitty and Seamus O'Doherty along with Kathleen Clarke and Count Plunkett. Thomas Ashe was next, and once he died Collins seems not to have needed a successor. There was still a bit of the mentor–protégé dynamic in his relationships with de Valera and Griffith in 1921, however.

His series of mentors was a variation on a wider theme in Collins's rise – the theme of partnership. Collins always joined or formed small, friendly groups wherever he went: his hurling pals in London, the Kimmagers in 1916, the 44 Mountjoy Street crowd, the Keating-branch fellows, the people who gathered at the republican hut in Cullenswood House, and the Vaughan's Hotel circle.

Within these groups there was often one distinct partner he worked or spent time with. The most famous of these was Harry Boland, but he was just one among many. Others included Michael Staines, Gearoid O'Sullivan, Richard Mulcahy, Dick McKee, Sean O Murthuile, Robert Barton, Joe McGrath, Ned Broy, Austin Stack, Art O'Brien (although this was mostly a long-distance relationship) and, perhaps evolving out of mentor status, Eamon de Valera and Arthur Griffith as well. Liam Tobin and Frank Thornton could be described as his co-partners in intelligence and insurance. In almost every case these pairings worked well, and to mutual advantage. As Collins rose, so did his friends – and he rarely left any behind, as the Provisional Government cabinet and the National Army headquarters staff show.

These groups and partnerships were, in turn, part of the wider web of Collins's networking, which was a phenomenon unto itself. Like any successful politician, the mature Collins could always remember names and faces, kept a notebook to keep track of what was said, made people feel wanted and included, and kept in touch with a huge range of acquaintances through visits or by letter. If people were in trouble he looked after them, as any number of prisoners and ex-prisoners found out and were grateful for. This last constituency alone would have made an enviable political base.

He knew the invaluable trick of making people feel special and noticed, so people often wanted to like him back. A good example of this is the way he would include a personal word or a bit of gossip or information in an otherwise routine letter. He also had the ability to work with and befriend people others couldn't stand, like P. S. O'Hegarty, Sean O Murthuile, Gearoid O'Sullivan, James O'Mara, Art O'Brien and Eoin O'Duffy.

One key to this networking effort was retaining old friends when he moved on. London; Kimmage; Craig, Gardner; Frongoch; the National Aid; the Longford circuit; Organization; Intelligence – he took people with him when he left. Also unique was his reach across organizations and regions. Sinn Fein was undoubtedly his weak point, but his eventual influence within the IRB, the IRA and the Dail administration (at least while de Valera was away) was individually and collectively unparalleled. He knew the Dublin scene, the all-important Munster guerrillas, the key people in Longford and Roscommon, and also those within easy reach in Leinster. He was the only leader to keep in touch with activists in Britain. They were important for guns, money and communications, and became by default his own private fiefdom – and thus the target of Cathal Brugha's most damaging attacks. It may be noted that Parnell had made effective use of otherwise neglected British-based support in his own bid for leadership in the 1870s.

Collins hadn't always had these skills, and it is obvious from his ever-lengthening list of enemies that he didn't always exercise them. He had to work on them, and acquired only them through his time at the National Aid and as Director of Organization. But he had the discipline and memory (and typists) to develop them to a very high level indeed. No one could match the awesome list of contacts and clients he had assembled by 1920.

As with other powerful and successful men in business, politics or sport, Collins's loyalty and friendship often didn't outlive their utility. He rarely just discarded people, but emotional factors alone had little force in his political relationships. The list of people who were friends and allies and then opponents is remarkably long: de

Valera, Boland (although they retained some of their old bond), Liam Lynch, Florence O'Donoghue, Tom Hales, Austin Stack, Cathal Brugha, Rory O'Connor, Art O'Brien, Sean McGrath, Count Plunkett, Erskine Childers and Robert Barton. He also reversed this process, and turned Arthur Griffith, Darrell Figgis, Eoin MacNeill and J. J. O'Connell into comrades when necessary.

His lack of sentimentality was evident in the way he treated his intelligence men in 1922, once he felt they were no longer useful and more trouble than they were worth. He mostly ignored them, but also contemplated sending them to the United States. They were saved by the Civil War but, once they were back in harness he made sure someone else was in charge. Still, while some of these people felt betrayed and bitter, most retained affection and admiration for Collins. Lesser figures on either side of the Treaty split, like Richard Mulcahy, William Cosgrave, Mary MacSwiney or de Valera himself, did not inspire any such residual good feeling – even after death in Cathal Brugha's case.

ONCE HE HAD GAINED enough experience, Collins can undoubtedly be described as a formidable leader. But what kind of leader was he? He wasn't at all charismatic before he became important. As is so often the case, his personal authority was the product of fame and authority, not the other way around. But he did work harder than anyone else, and thereby set an example of dedication and efficiency that he insisted everyone else follow. And, despite his mastery of (or obsession with) detail, he knew how to delegate to people who could do the job: Joe McGrath, Michael Staines, Liam Tobin and Frank Thornton, Mick McDonnell and Paddy Daly, Joseph Brennan, Dan McCarthy and Eoin O'Duffy were good examples of this. These qualities enabled him to run several organizations at once, whether the National Aid and the Department of Organization; Organization and Finance; Finance and Intelligence; these two and the Treaty negotiations; and then the Provisional Government, two finance departments, the Northern Ireland portfolio and an election campaign.

So he was an effective manager of formal organizations and, informally, a genius at bringing people together via his personal connections. In these various ways he could get the most out of people. His profile first within the movement and then in newspapers made him a symbol of survival and resistance, which gave him a mantle of heroism – a huge source of political and moral capital. He also acquired a devoted personal following unlike that of any other leader except de Valera, and unmatched even by him. No one ever said, 'If it's good enough for Dev, it's good enough for me.'

Beyond all this, however, a leader is surely defined by the decisions that he or she makes, and so it was with Collins. Here we find another regular pattern to his career: whenever he had to make a big decision, he would deliberate and keep all possible options open until the last possible moment. But once the choice had to be made he made it decisively and determinedly, so as to make the most of whatever possibilities it presented. It was this combination that made him so successful.

So it was with his decision to leave London and his job with Guaranty Trust – to go not to Chicago, but instead to Dublin, to take part in the rebellion. So it was, arguably, with his decision to go to London as a plenipotentiary, which he was very reluctant to do but then followed through to its logical conclusion. So it was with his signing of the Treaty, keeping everyone guessing until the last possible moment and then defending it and using it to the utmost. And so it was with his agreeing to an attack on the Four Courts. He had been twisting and turning, trying every available avenue to avoid it until he had secured every benefit from the situation and there was, in hard political terms, simply no other choice. And then, once it started, he threw himself into the war, made himself Commander-in-Chief, and sought to bring about the quickest victory possible.

Here is another parallel with Parnell, who was nothing if not enigmatic and deliberative in his decision-making. His stringing along of his own militants in 1880 and 1881 before calling a rent strike, and then waiting out his time in jail before agreeing to the Kilmainham Treaty in 1882, seems a fair comparison, as do his manoeuvres in 1884 and 1885 before and during the general election in order to get a Home Rule bill. De Valera is another who would learn to let a situation mature and wait for his opportunities, as in his discarding of Sinn Fein and creation of Fianna Fail in the 1920s, or his dealings with Britain in the 1930s.

Collins could also recognize poor choices and the limits of successful ones. He wanted a war in 1919, but seems to have thought it had achieved its purpose by the end of 1920. When the British government took Sinn Fein's openness to negotiation as a sign of weakness, however, he moved swiftly away from a peace strategy until it was almost entirely risk-free. In 1922 he was obviously eager to make good his errors over Northern Ireland, but he was too clever to push aggression too far in a losing direction. Nor, despite his many protestations or insinuations otherwise, was he willing to seriously endanger the Treaty settlement by defying the British government. Not only would it have been terribly destructive, it would have wiped out his whole political position.

The bottom line for any leader must be success – always its own justification. Collins almost always made the right decision, judging by the goals and consequences. Armed violence, whatever the horrendous and unanticipated costs, did make Lloyd George, his cabinet, every political party and British public opinion concede Irish sovereignty. At the same time, carrying on the guerrilla war would not have ended partition or gained an outright republic – not without some freak occurrence. Collins was absolutely right that the Treaty he signed was about as much as could be got without another war. And he was right that the British government would fight to win, and that the IRA would lose in the face of public disappointment and disapproval. It is unclear if he realized – as de Valera did – that this would risk civil war with the IRA, but the decision was still the correct one given the more certain and immediate threat of renewed war with Britain.

And he was right again, after the election of June 1922, when he saw that a coalition with the republican party was now impossible and unnecessary, and that some major military action was inevitable given the IRA's and Britain's growing restiveness with the status quo. He did misjudge the republicans' unity and will to fight – he should have known better, knowing them and the movement as he did – but he was right that rapid action would force them out of the territory they controlled.

What he did not fully realize before either war was the uncontrollability of violence and its transformative power. Leaving aside the thousands of deaths, the IRA he worked to build nearly destroyed his vision of an independent state, while the men most identified with his war effort – the Squad and then the Dublin Guard – would go on to terrorize the guerrillas in turn when they were set loose on their former comrades. By 1922 he may have realized how dangerous and unstable they had become, but it was way too late then and he still used them in Oriel House and in the south. The Squad and the Intelligence Department have often been lionized as Collins's men in the triumphant struggle against British intelligence, but any real accounting of their history – and his – must include their murderous campaign against republicanism in 1922–3.

By comparison with Collins's record of decision-making, de Valera erred in spending so long in the United States, and was often clumsy in his handling of the political situation while there. He committed another great error in not going to London after July 1921, and an even worse one in refusing to recognize the legitimacy of the Dail vote on the Treaty in January 1922. This was after he had mishandled the whole debate. Parnell made a similar mistake in 1890, when he forced his party to choose between himself and the Liberal alliance over a supposed issue of principle, destroying the trust between the leader and the main body of his supporters. And he too misjudged his tactics and thereby made a bad situation worse.

DID ALL THIS make Collins irreplaceable? Not before 1919, when he was just one of the bright young things emerging as the next generation of leaders. Gearoid O'Sullivan did an adequate job in Organization once Collins handed it over to him in 1920, and Provisional Government intelligence worked well in other hands in 1922 and 1923. But in 1919, 1920 and 1921 what would have happened to the departments of Finance and Intelligence without him, both being so crucial to the revolutionary effort?

Once Collins had his departments up and running in 1920, they would probably have survived without him. He had set up their various successful systems, had found the people, and, to run much of the day-to-day business, had put in place middle managers who were in fact better experts in both fields. Collins was very bad at spotting spies, and had to be rescued from several near-misses. Nor was he a financial wizard like George McGrath – and it must be remembered that most of his money came from the US, not from the loan his department raised.

But as an architect or builder of organizations, Collins was the best. Tobin, Thornton and the others might never have gone into intelligence work without Collins, and his networking was the heart of the counter-espionage effort. It took his presence and clandestine skills to plan the money-raising and -hiding campaign for the Dail loan, as well as to drive it as hard as he did, and his budget sense was needed to plan expenditures and keep the revolution solvent. It would never have been audited without Collins's inner accountant on watch. By 1921, however, de Valera was right in thinking he could be replaced.

Moving forward in time, the same could be said of the Treaty vote and after. Without Collins's cadre of IRA and IRB supporters and his personal authority, the Treaty would surely never have passed. His presence and obvious reluctance no doubt made the Civil War more palatable to the public and to the pro-Treaty IRA, even if it was definitely not what voters had had in mind when they had backed Pact Sinn Fein or the Labour Party in the June election. But he *was* replaced in 1922, by Mulcahy and Cosgrave, who won the war and established the Free State, and governed it for the next ten years. It isn't at all clear that government policies in that period would have been any different either, although possibly his leadership would have added a few votes at election time. There is nothing to suggest he was the Lost Leader who would have made everything better.

Thus it would be wrong to see Collins's concentration of power in the movement, and then in the Provisional Government, as something necessary. It was impressive, as was his ability to carry the load, but it would actually have made more sense to redistribute it. After all, his capture or death would have meant creating gaps in several key departments instead of one.

COLLINS'S CONSISTENTLY opportunistic and utilitarian viewpoint raises the question of just how cynical and manipulative he was. Is this the story of a power-hungry and self-promoting man? He obviously sought power, but did he do so for its own sake? No, it would seem not. He used power to further his political goals, which were – like his ideas – those of the separatist movement. The way he used his power, however, by concentrating it and acting unilaterally, did increase it enormously. Collins's cabinet-making and leadership were far more dictatorial than de Valera's, for example. De Valera was also much less ruthless, and more willing to sacrifice power and take risks for principle. He was also much more honest about what he was doing in 1921 and 1922 than Collins ever was. De Valera would change, but at the time these qualities make him an admirable, if doomed, figure. Michael Collins was not a megalomaniac, but he did apparently come to believe that he had been the key to victory in the revolution, and that he alone was competent, or at least best equipped, to lead Ireland.

Collins took great personal risks from 1916 through 1922, as his death proved, and he retained his poise and effectiveness in the face of danger and while carrying tremendous burdens. There was no one else in the movement who could have pulled it off. But it must be remembered that thousands of men and women performed just as well and just as bravely in the face of the same dangers, even if they did not achieve so much. It was collective courage and collective heroism – a band of brothers and sisters who would later look back with nostalgia and even longing to when they had belonged to something nobler and greater than themselves. It is wrong to pick out Collins as someone apart or superior in his daring or courage: he was nothing special in this regard.

Was Michael Collins a hero? He was no warrior in the way he is usually understood – as a man of the gun and the uniform, uncomfortable with politics. The idea is laughable. De Valera was more of a soldier – he at least had held a combat command and had led men in battle. Nor was Collins a thinker or visionary, although he had read widely and was easily engaged by ideas. He was certainly a man of many parts and many roles, but he was a politician – albeit a revolutionary politician for most of his career, since it was cut short by his early death. He used the IRA to achieve his desired political effect, but when the ratification of the Treaty ended the war of independence he left it immediately, even though he continued to emphasize military aspects of his past to good political effect.

He did not care about his country any more than anyone else in the movement. He was not interested in sacrificing himself for others or in upholding any sacred principle so it would live on after him. He was willing to have people killed to achieve his goals, but he was not bloodthirsty – he clearly wanted to limit the killing as much as possible, and stopped quite a few deadly schemes. He tried to bring about a truce in December 1920, which would have saved many lives, but he was not willing to take political risks to make it work. None of what he did seems to have bothered his sense of morality overmuch (not that that made him different from any other active member of the IRA), although he did feel the loss of dead comrades like Ashe and McKee as badly as anyone.

Does this add up to being a hero? He must have been a wonderful person to have a drink with, and one of the most exciting friends you could ever imagine having. He loved children and small dogs. He was a genuinely tolerant and open-minded person. But true greatness surely requires the moral stature of a Daniel O'Connell, a Martin Luther King or a Nelson Mandela, and Michael Collins definitely didn't have that. Nor was he combating a great evil such as Franklin Roosevelt and Winston Churchill faced with Nazi Germany, or Paul Kagame with Hutu power in Rwanda. But, in the time allotted to him, he became the most ruthless, the most powerful, the most calculating and the most successful politician in modern Irish history, and his triple legacy of independence, partition and the IRA have challenged his legatees ever since.

Notes

Abbreviations

ORGANIZATIONS

DMP	Dublin Metropolitan Police
GHQ	General Headquarters
INA	Irish National Aid and Volunteers Dependants Fund
IRA	Irish Republican Army
IRB	Irish Republican Brotherhood
PG	Provisional Government
RIC	Royal Irish Constabulary

TITLES

A/G	Adjutant General
C.-in-C.	Commander-in-Chief
C/S	Chief of Staff
D/I	Director of Intelligence
MHA	Minister of Home Affairs
O/C	Officer Commanding
QMG	Quartermaster General

ARCHIVES

CAI	Cork Archives Institute
HLRO	House of Lords Record Office
IWM	Imperial War Museum
LHCMA	Liddell Hart Centre for Military Archives
MA	Military Archives of Ireland
NA	National Archives of Ireland
NLI	National Library of Ireland
POST	Post Office Archives

PRO	Public Record Office (now National Archives), London
TCD	Trinity College Dublin Archives
UCD	University College Dublin Archives
YULMC	Yale University Library Manuscript Collections

RECORD ORIGINS

BMH	Bureau of Military History
CAB	Cabinet Office
CO	Colonial Office
CSC	Civil Service Commission
DE	Dail Eireann
HO	Home Office
S	Taoiseach's Office
WO	War Office
WS	BMH Witness Statement

Introduction

page

xii 'I would not matter': Collins to George Gavan Duffy, 17 May 1921, George Gavan Duffy Papers, NA, 1125/20.

xiii 'one man': Collins to Art O'Brien, 31 May 1921, Art O'Brien Papers, NLI, MS 8430.

Advance of $25,000: John Tuohy to MC, 8 Jan. 1922, Piaras Beaslai Papers, NLI, MS 33,916(1).

'the Secret History': *World's Pictorial News*, 9, 16, 23 Sept. 1922; Beaslai Papers, NLI, MS 33,915(3).

Talbot and Beaslai: NLI, MS 33,915(7).

xiv Beaslai's own work: Much of this can be gleaned from his papers in the National Library of Ireland. See also Deirdre McMahon, '"A Worthy Monument to a Great Man": Piaras Beaslai's Life of Michael Collins', *Bullan*, winter/spring 1996, and her 'Michael Collins – His Biographers Piaras Beaslai and Rex Taylor', in Gabriel Doherty and Dermot Keogh (eds.), *Michael Collins and the Making of the Irish State* (Cork: Mercier, 1998).

O'Faolain's serial biography: This ('Michael Collins: The True Story of a Great Irishman') appeared in the *Sunday Chronicle*, beginning on 15 May 1932; the paper quickly denounced him (Beaslai Papers, NLI, MS 33,937).

Frank O'Connor's work: James Matthews, *Voices: A Life of Frank O'Connor* (New York: Atheneum, 1983), pp. 117–23.

Rex Taylor: McMahon, 'Michael Collins – His Biographers'.

xv 'Collins was virtually airbrushed': Tim Pat Coogan in *Cork Examiner* Supplement, 26 Feb. 1997.

xvi *In Great Haste*: This book was first published in 1983 (Dublin: Gill & Macmillan), but a second, expanded, edition appeared in 1996, edited by Cian O Heigeartaigh.

'As always': Margery Forester, *Michael Collins: The Lost Leader* (London, Sidgwick & Jackson, 1971), p. 238.

1: FAMILY

page

3 'He belongs': A. T. Q. Stewart, *Michael Collins: The Secret File* (Belfast: Blackstaff, 1997), p. 41.

Collins insists on Paulveug: Hayden Talbot, *Michael Collins' Own Story* (London: Hutchinson, 1922), p. 22. This was Collins's own spelling.

'My mother': Mary Collins Powell memoir, UCD, P151/1851. Unless otherwise specified, all statements by Mary Collins Powell are from this memoir.

4 Attempted reconstruction of MC's 'relations and supporters': 'Castle File No. 10', PRO, WO 35/206. For his actual family tree, see the Michael Collins Papers (belonging to his nephew Michael), NLI, MS 40,430/17.

'His uncles': *Free State*, 30 Aug. 1922.

'on my father's side': Talbot, *Michael Collins' Own Story*, p. 23.

Their parents used Irish: Sister Celestine Collins ('Auntie Lena') to John Pierse, 4 Sept. 1970, Collins Papers, NLI, MS 40,426/2.

5 'Mama called us': Ibid. A different deathbed statement is recorded in Forester, *Lost Leader*, p. 11. Michael junior also has several different sets of last words attributed to him.

'Oh! We have much to be grateful': *Irish Independent*, 25 Aug. 1922.

'Thank God': Sister Celestine to Pierse, NLI, MS 40,426/2.

'The Loose Box': Seamus Heaney, *Electric Light* (London: Faber, 2001).

6 'I was out in the fields': Talbot, *Michael Collins' Own Story*, p. 22.

7 Civil-service application: PRO, CSC 11/63 113356.

Parnell etc.: Conor Cruise O'Brien, *Parnell and His Party 1880–1890* (Oxford: Oxford University Press, 1957); L. P. Curtis, *Coercion and Conciliation in Ireland 1880–1892* (Princeton: Princeton University Press, 1963); Joseph Lee, *The Modernisation of Irish Society 1848–1918* (Dublin: Gill & Macmillan, 1973); Paul Bew, *C. S. Parnell* (Dublin: Gill & Macmillan, 1980); R. F. Foster, *Modern Ireland 1600–1972* (London: Allen Lane, 1988).

10 Michael Collins senior: Collins Powell memoir, UCD, P151/1851.

12 'a Cork man': Earl of Birkenhead, *Frederick Edwin Earl of Birkenhead: The Last Phase* (London, Thornton Butterworth, 1935), p. 150.

Woodfield: Census of Ireland reports, 1881, 1891, 1901, 1911.

Collins farms: Irish Valuation Office, Coolcraheen Electoral District revision book, 1859–1933, and household and townland manuscript census returns for 1901, NA.

13 Mike's property: On his death in 1897, his effects were valued at £266 (NA, Wills and Admons Book 1897).

Marianne's will: NA, Probate Grant.

'Very primitive': Sister Celestine to Pierse, NLI, MS 40,426/2.

14 Marianne's abilities: When she died, ten years after her husband, her effects were worth £474 – an increase of £200 over Michael senior's worth (NA, Wills and Admon Book 1907). Michael junior would leave nearly £2,000 when he died.

15 'to say that we loved this baby': Collins Powell memoir, UCD, P151/1851.

'the closest of chums': *Westminster Gazette*, 25 Aug. 1922.

'was convinced that Michael Collins': John McCaffrey, 'Collins and the Clerk: A Memory of 1910', *Irish Independent*, 21 April 1965.

'we were much more like': Hannie Collins to Piaras Beaslai, Beaslai Papers, NLI, MS 33,929(19).

16 'the only one': Geraldine Plunkett Dillon memoir, Geraldine Plunkett Dillon Papers, NLI, MS 33,731. In the manuscript, Dillon amended this to read 'the one he respected most', but her first phrasing is the one she used in her statement to the Bureau of Military History: WS 358. Duplicate copies of these statements can be found, identically catalogued, in both the Irish Military Archives and the National Archives.

'Do not blame me': Collins to Sister Mary Celestine ('Lena'), 21 Feb. 1918, NLI, Pos. 4548.

'You know I do not often address nuns': Ibid., 13 Apr. 1919.

'My brother Miceal': O'Brien to Collins, 30 June 1920, Art O'Brien Papers, NLI, MS 8461.

17 Last letter to Helena: Collins to Sister Mary Celestine, 5 Mar. 1921, NLI, Pos. 4548.

'People tell me': Collins to Kitty Kiernan, 14 Mar. 1922, in Leon O Broin and Cian O Heigheartaigh (eds.), *In Great Haste: The Letters of Michael Collins and Kitty Kiernan* (Dublin: Gill & Macmillan, 1996).

'did not recognize me': Iosold O Deirg (ed.), 'Oh! Lord the Unrest of the Soul: The Jail Journal of Michael Collins', *Studia Hibernica*, 1994, pp. 14–15.

Patrick Collins's fond memories: *Irish Independent*, 24 Aug. 1922.

'I am sorry': Collins to Boland, 14 Aug. 1920, Eamon de Valera Papers, UCD, P150/1665.

18 'As for my brother Patrick': Talbot, *Michael Collins' Own Story*, p. 27.

Patrick Collins interview: *New York Times*, 24 Aug. 1922.

Collins's and Jack Hurley's promise: Collins Powell memoir, UCD, P151/1851.

19 'Bridget Brown' account: Report on Clifden Convent Case, Dail Eireann records, NA, DE 5/68.

Attempted burning of Collins Powell's house: *Cork Examiner*, 9 Mar. 1923.

Collins's correspondence files: PRO, CO 904/24/3.

'Shafter': Patrick O'Brien statement, WS 812.

'I was proud': 'The Secret Diary of Michael Collins', *Irish Independent*, 3 May 1964.

'Peggy [. . .] was a child': Michael Lynch statement, WS 511.

20 'She is a loss': Collins to Sister Mary Celestine, 5 March 1921, NLI, Pos. 4548.

'when he is . . . moved': George Boyce, 'An Encounter with Michael Collins, 1921', *Journal of the Cork Historical and Archaeological Society*, July–Dec. 1975, p. 57.

'He had always been an advanced Irishman': Collins to Donal Hales, 1 Aug. 1921, NA, DE 5/56.

Johnny Collins's political career 1910–21: *Cork Accent*, 18 June 1910; *Southern Star*, 23 Feb. 1918; 7 Jan. 1922.

Johnny's pony cart: *Cork Examiner*, 4 Feb. 1921.

'The Enemy force': Collins to Hales, 1 Aug. 1921, NA, DE 5/56.

21 Johnny's arrest: *Cork Examiner*, 19 April 1921.

Johnny as intelligence agent etc.; kidnapped: Ibid., 25 Aug. 1922.

Johnny as administrator of Michael Collins's estate: Dept of Finance records, NA, FIN 1/3497.

Collins's memorial cross: Beaslai Papers, NLI, MS 33,966; Anne Dolan, *Commemorating the Irish Civil War* (Cambridge: Cambridge University Press, 2003), pp. 57–99.

22 The Collins and related families' electoral fortunes; These can be traced in outline in Brian Walker (ed.), *Parliamentary Election Results in Ireland, 1918–92* (Dublin, Royal Irish Academy 1992).

2: CLERK

page

23 'What always impressed me': *Westminster Gazette*, 25 Aug. 1922.

The Savings Bank: C. R. Perry, *The Victorian Post Office: The Growth of a Bureaucracy* (Woodbridge: Boydell, 1992), Appendix Table 6.

Number of boy clerks: Revisions of Regulations on Boy Clerks, J. LeB. Hammond to Sec., Treasury, 15 June 1908, PRO, CSC 5/4.

Boy cops: Short for copyists, an earlier designation; Mrs Michael Cremin (Cis Sheehan) statement, WS 924.

24 Exams: This description is based on the Notice of Regulations, 28 Mar. 1905, PRO, CSC 6/11/94, and on an examination of exam results published in 1905–1908, PRO, CSC files 10/2435, 2477, 2535, 2564, 2593, 2633, 2662, 2712.

'wanted to live in': Talbot, *Michael Collins' Own Story*, p. 25.

Lisavaird school: MS census returns for 1901.

Illiteracy figures: 1901 census report.

24 Denis Lyons: Beaslai, *Michael Collins and the Making of a New Ireland*, vol. 1 (Dublin, Phoenix, 1926), pp. 5–6.

Clonakilty classes: Beaslai, *Michael Collins*, vol. 1, p. 12, and Collins's civil-service application, PRO, CSC 11/63 113356.

25 No exams in Clonakilty: Report of Intermediate Education Board for Ireland, 1904 (House of Commons reports, vol. 28, 1905).

'the smaller farmers': Report on Intermediate Education, 1904, p. 5 (House of Commons reports, vol. 28, 1905).

Conditions of Marianne's will: NA, Probate Grant.

'In the matter of schooling': Talbot, *Michael Collins' Own Story*, p. 23.

26 Exam results: Collins's are in his civil-service file, PRO, CSC 11/63 113356. Everyone else's can be found in PRO, CSC 10/2564.

The Savings Bank: The physical description is based on my own visit. Its procedures are described in Appendices I and VI to the statement of evidence of Miss Cale to the Select Cttee of House of Commons to Enquire into the Wages and other Conditions of Post Office Staff, PRO, NSC 38/1. The number of boy clerks is given in the GPO Establishment Book 1906, p. 222, POST. The women's establishment is given in *The Post*, 7 June 1912.

27 The Writing Room: *Westminster Gazette*, 30 Aug. 1922; McCaffrey, 'Collins and the Clerk'.

28 'one day': McCaffrey, 'Collins and the Clerk'.

'remembered by his colleagues': *The Key* (Post Office Savings Bank Journal), Sept. 1961, p. 14.

'his marked characteristics': *Westminster Gazette*, 30 Aug. 1922.

Rated by superiors: Collins's civil-service file, PRO, CSC 11/63 113356.

29 'Most of the chaps': P. S. O'Hegarty statement, WS 840.

'The work Assistant Clerks perform': 'Assistant Clerks: History of Class', 28 Jan. 1910, POST 122/470.

Collins helped organize a deputation: *Freeman's Journal*, 29 Aug. 1922.

MacVeagh asked a question about Assistant Clerks on 16 Apr. 1907.

30 King's College classes: F. J. C. Hearnshaw, *The Centenary History of King's College London 1828–1928* (London: Harrap, 1929), pp. 308, 370, 421–2. Details of classes can be found in the King's College Calendar for 1906–7 and for following years, King's College Archives. I have checked the student register for evening classes and occasional students (as British policemen did in 1921), but there is no mention of Michael Collins.

J. J. Walsh and P. S. O'Hegarty go to Braginton's: J. J. Walsh, *Recollections of a Rebel* (Tralee: Kerryman, 1944), p. 11.

Bragington boys' success rate: King's College Calendar, 1906–7.

'A cyclist leaves London at 2': This and the other exercises quoted are taken from the King's College Civil Service Series: *Digesting Returns into Summaries* (1904); *Materials for French Composition* (1905); *Mathematical Papers* (1909).

Collins keeps a notebook: Michael Collins Papers, UCD, P123/14.

Surviving compositions: NLI, MS 13,329.

31 'I must congratulate you': J. L. O'Sullivan to Collins, 28 Aug. 1909, P123/32.

Wasn't a civil-service exam: There is no mention of such in his file, and no mention of Collins in various clerkship exam results of the period. It probably wasn't the Gaelic League either, although this organization was also fond of tests, which were much easier to pass.

1910 exam results: Collins's civil-service file, PRO, CSC 11/63 113356.

32 A later job application: Collins to Donal O'Connor, 10 Feb. 1917, INA Exec. Cttee Papers, NLI, MS 24,384.

Most boys had moved on: Figures for 1908 can be found in Hammond to Sec., Treasury, PRO, CSC 5/4.

Better jobs given to senior boys: Sec., Savings Bank Dept, Report on Changing Boy Clerk Regs., n.d., POST 30/1843A.

Later in life: Talbot, *Michael Collins' Own Story*, p. 25.

'He [Collins] was a very nice fellow': *West London Observer*, 25 Aug. 1922.

Minford Gardens, Coleherne Terrace and Netherwood Road: Post Office London Directory 1906 and 1914; 1901 British census returns, PRO.

33 'some fine political arguments': *West London Observer*, 25 Aug. 1922.

'Lots of young people': *Westminster Gazette*, 24 Aug. 1922.

Collecting at Brompton Oratory: C. O'C., 'Late M. Collins. An Appreciation', *Southern Star*, 22 Aug. 1922.

34 'He was well-read': P. S. O'Hegarty, *The Victory of Sinn Fein* (Dublin: Talbot, 1924), p. 24.

'How we discussed literature': Hannie Collins memoir, NLI, MS 33,929(19).

Collins 'hooted' *Patriots*: Frank O'Connor, *The Big Fellow* (London, Nelson, 1937), p. 19. This was zealotry even by Dublin standards, as audiences in the Abbey Theatre had taken it to be genuinely patriotic: Ben Levitas, *The Theatre of Nation: Irish Drama and Cultural Nationalism 1890–1916* (Oxford: Oxford University Press, 2002), pp. 195–7.

'I must be worrying you': 'William Field' to 'James Woods' [Collins to Boland], 5 Mar. 1920, UCD, P150/1665.

35 'Have you been reading Omar?': MC to Kitty Kiernan, 15 Feb. 1922, O Broin and O Heigheartaigh (eds.), *In Great Haste*, p. 127. See also Collins to the Governor HM Prison Lewes, 18 May 1917, Irish National Aid Letter Book, NLI, MS 23,465.

A house in 'the Bush': P. S. O'Hegarty, 'Personal Recollections', *Sunday Independent*, 26 Aug. 1945.

'when he came to London': O'Hegarty, *The Victory of Sinn Fein*, p. 24.

Collins's swearing: Warmly attested to by – among many others – Florence O'Donoghue in his memoir: O'Donoghue Papers, NLI, MS 31,124, pp. 59–60.

35 Asked to leave a boarding house: Interview with Alfie White, Ernie O'Malley Papers, UCD, P17b/110.

36 'There were many': Seamus de Burca, *The Soldier's Song: The Story of Peadar O Cearnaigh* (Dublin: P. J. Bourke, 1957), p. 65.

'In after life': Beaslai, *Michael Collins*, vol. 1, p. 22.

'Old London': Ibid.

3: ATHLETE

37 'He was gruff': P. Brennan, 'Micheal O'Coileain in London', *Free State*, 30 Aug. 1922.

Geraldine Athletic Club: The name was taken from a league of rebels in sixteenth-century Ireland.

'his particular chums': Hannie Collins memoir, NLI, MS 33,929(19). See also Edward McCarthy statement, NLI, MS 22,246.

38 'old Geraldines': Collins to Barney Harrison (a former 'Ger'), 2 Sept. 1921, Barney Harrison Papers, UCD, P132/1.

39 'It was evident': De Burca, *The Soldier's Song*, p. 65.

Maguire is often portrayed: See Margaret Walsh's interesting biography (the first to appear) *Sam Maguire* (Ballineen: Kenneigh Tower, 2003). After 1916 Maguire became an important agent in Collins's smuggling and intelligence schemes, but it was Art O'Brien (not a GAA man) who was Collins's main contact in London during the revolution.

'it was Michael Collins': Interview with Dinny Daly, UCD, P17b/102.

40 'exercised a sort of fatherly supervision': O'Hegarty, 'Personal Recollections'. Thomas Davis was the inspirational leader of Young Ireland in the 1840s.

'He means very well': Collins to Stack, 4 Nov. 1918, NLI, MS 5848.

'steady deterioration': Minute book of Geraldine Athletic Club, 14 July 1906, NLI, MS 13,329.

Collins a 'useful' and 'strenuous' hurler: GAA Notes, *Irishman*, Oct. 1912.

41 'the five best hurlers here': *Irishman*, July 1913. Collins is listed as the reserve in the June 1913 issue.

'On resuming': *Irishman*, Oct. 1913.

'It is as a hurler': Brennan, 'Micheal O'Coileain'.

42 'Mick was running a race': Joe Good, *Enchanted by Dreams: The Journal of a Revolutionary* (Dingle: Brandon, 1996), p. 8.

'I met Michael Collins': Daly interview.

'it was all mock-serious': Brennan, 'Micheal O'Coilean'.

'You see, the sort he was': Seamus (James) Kavanagh statement, WS 889, p. 73.

43 'Once at Frongoch': Good, *Enchanted*, p. 93.

Medals and cups prominently displayed: *Southern Star*, 2 Sept. 1922.

'In a word': *Irishman*, Dec. 1911.

'Tim Collins of "Davis"': Ibid., May 1912.

'Collins and Dunne': Ibid., June 1912.

44 'that was the proudest day': Sam Maguire statement, NLI, MS 33,929(14).

Collins's first reported individual triumph: The following results are found in the *Irishman*, Oct. 1911; July, Sept, Oct. 1912; June, Sept. 1913.

45 'An eventful half year' etc.: Geraldine G. A. Club Report for half-year ending December 1909, NLI, MS 13,329(4).

'the secretary's report': This and the following quotes are from the Geraldine club minute book.

'fall in and follow Mick': *Irishman*, Sept. 1912.

46 Collins pursued O'Sullivan: See Geraldine club minutes for 1910 and 1911.

'the most disastrous year': *Inis Fail*, Jan. 1908.

47 'No Irish boy': Ibid., Aug. 1908.

Collins's letter of protest: Ibid., Aug. 1909.

'I think that the new departure': Collins to unknown recipient, 8 Jan. 1911, NLI, MS 15,723.

48 'when the Brians and Cusacks left': *Irishman*, July 1913.

'after the defection': Ibid., April 1913.

49 His absence from the lists of firsts etc.: see *Inis Fail*, July, Sept. 1907; Sept. 1909; June 1910; *Irishman*, Aug. 1910. The programme for Feis Lonndan 1907 shows a M. Collins entered in many events and failing to win, place or show except for a second-place finish in the 120 yards race (UCD, P123/20).

4: Young Republican

page

51 'Collins instinctively impressed': *Daily Sketch*, 30 Nov. 1920. This article recalls Collins at a 1908 Sinn Fein meeting.

52 'this welter of meetings': O'Hegarty, 'Personal Recollections'.

53 Mainstream Irish nationalism etc.: Patrick Maume, *The Long Gestation: Irish Nationalist Life 1891–1918* (Dublin: Gill & Macmillan, 1999); John Hutchinson, *The Dynamics of Cultural Nationalism: The Gaelic Revival and the Creation of the Irish Nation State* (London: Allen & Unwin, 1987); Harrington Benjamin, 'The London Irish: A Study in Political Activism, 1870–1910', Ph.D. thesis, Princeton University, 1976.

55 'Why do those': *Inis Fail*, Jan. 1910.

'The average Irish working man': Ibid., Mar. 1910.

'almost on the first day': Maguire statement, NLI, MS 33,929(14).

56 Hannie and the landlord on Collins's studies: Hannie Collins memoir, NLI, MS 33,929(19); *West London Observer*, 25 Aug. 1922.

'traipsing surreptitiously in': *Inis Fail*, Jan. 1910.

'Indeed the prospects': *Irishman*, March 1911.

56 Irish-language exams: Annual Examination Report in *Irishman* Aug. 1912; a
    League certificate from 1912 shows a mark of 84.5% on an exam (UCD,
    P123/25).
    language fund: *Irishman*, Aug., Oct. 1912; Apr. 1913.
    'Tomas O Donncada': Ibid., May 1913.

57 Collins at 1913 Gaelic League convention: Ibid., July 1913.
    Collins wanted to be treasurer: Michael Crummin [Cremin?] interview,
        UCD, P17b/98. He wasn't elected to any positions in 1913, although it is
        unknown whether he ran or not. A voting paper for the 1915 annual
        election for positions lists Collins as running for a place on the local
        executive, but it is unknown whether he was elected (Art O'Brien Papers,
        NLI, MS 8434).

58 'into our Sinn Fein meetings': Margaret Gavan Duffy, 'Mick', *Free State*, 30
    Aug. 1922.

59 'twelve years ago': *Daily Sketch*, 30 Nov. 1920.
    'would get up': O'Hegarty, 'Personal Recollections'.
    'quite possibly the article': Collins to O'Brien, 1 Dec. 1920, NLI, MS 8426.
    'I do not defend': Draft notes, n.d., NLI, MS 13,329.
    'the absolute necessity': *Sinn Fein*, 26 Mar. 1910. Beetroots: ibid., 8 Feb.
        1908; poultry: ibid., 7 Nov. 1908.

60 'Do you remember': UCD, P123/41.

61 'the trend is downward': UCD, P123/42.

62 'free from all physical defect': Collins's civil-service file, PRO, CSC 11/63
    113356. On his teeth being noticed, see Senior, 'An Encounter with
    Michael Collins'.
    'I have spoken to my employers': Collins's civil-service file, PRO, CSC 11/
        63 113356.
    Horne & Co.: Stock Exchange List of Members 1913–14 and Applications
        for Admission to the Stock Market, Guildhall Library Manuscript
        Department; *The Stock Exchange Memorial of Those who Fell in the Great
        War MCMXIV–MCMXIX* (1920) has a page on Lamaison.
    'I took charge': Collins to Donal O'Connor, 10 Feb. 1917, NLI, MS
        24,384.

63 'Most members': David Kynaston, 'The London Stock Exchange,
        1870–1914: An Institutional History', D.Phil., thesis, London School of
        Economics, 1983, p. 98.
    23 Moorgate Street: *Post Office Directory* 1914; Insurance Plan of the City of
        London, Guildhall Library.

64 'Wherever one looked': Thomas Burke, quoted in David Kynaston, *The City
        of London*, vol. 2: *Golden Years 1890–1912* (London: Pimlico, 1995),
        p. 247. This is a remarkable book.
    'The trade I know best': This quote appears as part of what I believe is a
        collection of Frank O'Connor's notes for his biography of Collins, NA,
        DE 2/530(11). The source of the information is unknown. According to
        the otherwise accurate note, Collins did work at a labour exchange from

Sept. 1914 to April 1915, but there is no evidence for this: his civil-service file, his 1917 job application to the National Aid Association and Talbot's book do not mention it. The last two are unreliable, but there is no reason to think the official records are.

65 'the Executive ruled': P. S. O'Hegarty letter to the *Irish Statesman*, 8 Jan. 1927. O'Hegarty was very critical of Piaras Beaslai's book in a review on 27 Nov. 1926, which launched a long and informative exchange of letters between the two men, much of it concerned with Collins's career in the London IRB.

Joe Furlong's recollections: Joe Furlong statement, WS 335.

'the very worst period': Collins to Art O'Brien, 21 March 1921, NLI, MS 8430.

67 'Nice work that': Mary Powell to Michael Collins, 29 July 1914, UCD, P123/44.

68 'bayonet exercises': *Irish Volunteer*, 30 Jan. 1915. For the London Volunteers, see 'An Rathach', 'London Volunteers', *Irish Democrat*, Apr. 1948; Ernie Nunan, 'The Irish Volunteers in London', *An tOglach*, autumn 1966.

'found an active Company': *Irish Volunteer*, 16 Oct. 1915.

Volunteer convention: List of delegates, Michael Collins Papers, MA, A/0776.

'When I joined': Joseph Good statement, WS 388.

69 'Mick promptly choked me': Good, *Enchanted*, pp. 9–10.

'leading light': Maguire statement, NLI, MS 33,929(14).

'the interminable arguments': 'A Friend', 'The Late Michael Collins. A Retrospect', *Southern Star*, 26 Aug. 1922.

'Micheal O'Coileain': Brennan, 'Micheal O'Coileain'.

'awkward squad': McGrath to Art O'Brien, 22 Mar. 1935, NLI, MS 8461.

70 'the never-ceasing talk': Talbot, *Michael Collins' Own Story*, p. 24.

71 'I was resting': Good statement, WS 388.

'violent attack': Beaslai, *Michael Collins*, vol. 1, p. 19. For the talk by O Siothchain, see *Sinn Fein*, 25 April 1908.

'a passing phase': Beaslai, *Michael Collins*, vol. 1, p. 19.

72 'For the past few years': UCD, P123/42.

'May not we also': Collins draft notes, n.d., NLI, MS 13,329.

Geraldine Plunkett's recollections: Geraldine Plunkett, 'Irish Volunteers', p. 226, MA, CD 5/6/8.

'as far as he': Roddy Connolly, 'A Glimpse of Collins', *Michael Collins Memorial Foundation Supplement*, 20 Aug. 1966.

5: Rising

74 'When I first met him': Plunkett Dillon memoir, NLI, MS 33,731.

The Exchange had closed: Ranald Michie, *The London Stock Exchange: A History* (Oxford: Oxford University Press, 1999), pp. 143–9.

74 Guaranty Trust: Charles Short, *Morgan Guaranty's London Heritage* (1986). I am grateful as well to Shelley Diamond of the JP Morgan Chase Archives for sending me copies of *Guaranty News* for 1922. A photograph of the London head office can be found in the Oct. 1922 issue. Also useful were the *Post Office Directory* and the Insurance Plan of the City of London.

75 'My duties there': Collins to Donal O'Connor, 10 Feb. 1917, NLI, MS 24,384.

'very hostile to us': Collins to George McGrath, 8 Sept. 1921, NA, DE 5/62/2.

'Only on very rare occasions': Beaslai, *Michael Collins*, vol. 1, pp. 25–6. MacVey's name is here misspelled.

76 'I know very well': *Official Report: Debate on the Treaty Between Great Britain and Ireland* (Dublin, n.d.), p. 394.

'I often hit one of them': Ibid., p. 404.

Insisted on using Guaranty Trust: Collins to James O'Mara, 25 Sept. 1920, NA, DE 5/57/14.

'a very good clerk': *New York Times*, 24 Aug. 1922.

77 'none . . . satisfied my ideas': Talbot, *Michael Collins' Own Story*, p. 25.

78 Yeats's tales and gibes: 'Easter 1916'.

79 'so far as I know': This and the following quotes can be found in *Debate on the Treaty*, pp. 291, 309.

Collins apparently told Hayden Talbot: Talbot, *Michael Collins' Own Story*, p. 26.

80 'Mick Collins was present': McGrath to Art O'Brien, 22 Mar. 1935, NLI, MS 8461.

Sam Maguire: Maguire statement, NLI, MS 33,929(14).

Collins told his boss: Various versions of this story exist – see Beaslai, *Michael Collins*, vol. 1, pp. 70–71. For his feeling ashamed, see Geraldine Plunkett Dillon's memoir, NLI, MS 33,731.

'Now Michael': Patrick Collins to Michael Collins, 3 Aug. 1915, NLI, MS 13,329.

81 'At the end of 1915': Beaslai, *Michael Collins*, vol. 1, p. 70. Again, there are other versions of this discussion.

Geraldine asked for a bookkeeper etc. and following quotes: Plunkett Dillon memoir, NLI, MS 33,731.

82 'I was accepted': Collins to Donal O'Connor, 10 Feb. 1917, NLI, MS 24,384.

'too quiet': Plunkett Dillon memoir, NLI, MS 33,731.

83 'like a picnic': Grace Plunkett statement, WS 257.

84 'From what I have seen': 'A Friend', 'The Late Michael Collins'.

'After a week or so': Plunkett Dillon memoir, NLI, MS 33,731.

'He was crude socially': Plunkett, 'Irish Volunteers', p. 226, MA, CD 5/6/8.

'He was completely honest': Plunkett Dillon memoir, NLI, MS 33,731.

85 'you would not know': Ibid. See Ernie Nunan, 'The Kimmage Garrison',
    An tOglach, Easter 1967.
  'In that place': Collins to Donal O'Connor, 10 Feb. 1917, NLI, MS 24,384.
    On Craig, Gardiner, see H. W. Robinson, *A History of Accountants in
    Ireland* (Dublin: Institute of Chartered Accountants in Ireland, 1964).
  'I have looked up': G. H. Tulloch to F. O'Connor, 21 July 1936, NA, DE
    2/530.
86 'After a little training': Collins to Donal O'Connor, 10 Feb. 1917, NLI, MS
    24,384.
  'It was 99.9% audits': Derek Matthews and Jim Prie, *The Auditors Talk:
    An Oral History of a Profession from the 1920s to the Present Day* (London:
    Garland, 2000), p. 118.
87 '[Collins] was in my office': Frank Henderson interview, UCD, P17b/99.
88 'On one occasion': Charles MacAuley statement, WS 735.
  Collins joins Fintan Lalor circle: Eamon Dore statement, WS 392. Joe
    Furlong also mentions joining a circle of which Collins was centre, but
    this may have been after the Rising.
  'very thin and high strung': MacAuley statement, WS 735.
  'He was throwing': Furlong statement, WS 335.
  'Michael Collins sometimes visited': Good statement, WS 388.
  'when a good deal of fun': Good, *Enchanted*, pp. 18–19.
  'hurried and unusually discourteous': Ibid., p. 18.
  'during the last few days': Beaslai, 'The Big Man', *Freeman's Journal*,
    26 Aug. 1922.
90 'That night': Liam Archer statement, WS 819.
91 'He was in a state of great excitement': MacAuley statement, WS 735.
  'On Holy Saturday morning': Grace Plunkett statement, WS 257.
  'A tall, pale-faced man': W. J. Brennan-Whitmore, *Dublin Burning:
    The Easter Rising from Behind the Barricades* (Dublin: Gill &
    Macmillan,1996), pp. 32–3.
  Easter Rising: Desmond Ryan, *The Rising* (Dublin, Golden Eagle, 1957);
    Brian Barton and Michael Foy, *The Easter Rising* (Stroud: Sutton, 1999).
    Charles Townshend's forthcoming book on the Rising is eagerly awaited.
93 'there appeared to be a superabundance of officers': 'A Capt of Head-
    Quarters Bn of the Dublin Bde, Ir Repub Army', 'A Brief Personal
    Narrative of the 6 Days Defence of the Irish Republic', Joseph McGarrity
    Papers, NLI, MS 17,510.
  Collins's damaged hand: Maire Comerford, 'The Dangerous Ground',
    UCD, LA18.
  Collins on the roof: William O'Brien, *Forth the Banners Go: Reminiscences of
    William O'Brien as Told to Edward MacLysaght* (Dublin: Three Candles,
    1969), p. 136.
  'A great many of the men': Desmond Fitzgerald, *Memoirs of Desmond
    Fitzgerald* 1913–1916 (London: Routledge, 1968), p. 144.

94 'It was a post of little honour': Good, *Enchanted*, p. 46. See also Denis Daly statement, WS 291.

'We held the fire': John T. (Blimey) O'Connor, 'Some Have Come from a Land Beyond the Sea', *An tOglach*, autumn 1966.

Collins's breeches: Joe O'Reilly statement, NLI, MS 33,929(14).

W. J. Flynn: *Cork Examiner*, 12 Sept. 1922.

95 Collins argued strenuously: Good, *Enchanted*, pp. 67–8.

6: PRISONER

page
96 'A frenzied mass': Desmond Ryan, *Remembering Sion: A Chronicle of Storm and Quiet* (London: Arthur Barker, 1934), p. 215.

97 'When he was jailed': Plunkett Dillon memoir, NLI, MS 33,731.

'asked the man': *Catholic Bulletin*, Aug. 1916, p. 463. See also Mrs Martin Conlon statement, WS 419.

98 'heaped together': Ryan, *Remembering Sion*, p. 208.

'In Stafford': Ibid., p. 215.

'Mick Collins': Kavanagh statement, WS 889, p. 73.

100 'Let us be judged': William O'Brien autograph book, NLI, MS 15,662.

Frongoch: Sean McConville, *Irish Political Prisoners 1848–1922: Theatres of War* (London: Routledge, 2003); Sean O Mahony, *Frongoch: University of Revolution* (Killiney: FDR Teoranta, 1987); W. J. Brennan-Whitmore, *With the Irish in Frongoch* (Dublin: Talbot, 1917).

101 'Submit recommendations': Irish Prisoners of War Minute Book, NLI, Pos.1638.

102 'What Sandhurst was doing': Brennan-Whitmore, *With the Irish*, p. 30.

'About eight men': Tomas MacCurtain diary, MA, CD 24.

103 'he looked around': O'Brien, *Forth the Banners Go*, p. 136.

104 'Possibly you have heard': Collins to Ryan, 23 Aug. 1916, James Ryan Papers, UCD, P88/34.

105 'first got to know Michael Collins': Batt O'Connor statement, NLI, MS 33,929(14).

'quiet and unobtrusive': Richard Mulcahy, 'Talk on Michael Collins Given to Donegalman's Association', Mulcahy Papers, UCD, P7b/180.

'Michael Collins burst in': O'Reilly statement, NLI, MS 33,929(14).

106 'as Neeson is gone': Collins to Art O'Brien, 3 Nov. 1916, Art O'Brien Papers, NLI, MS 8429.

'For some time': Ibid., 13 Oct. 1916.

'You know what little value': Ibid.

107 'I have written to you': Ibid., 16 Nov. 1916.

'What is before us': NLI, MS 8429.

'sincere regrets': Collins to George Gavan Duffy, 14 Dec. 1916, MA, CD 45/4/3.

108 'I knew him in Frongoch': Frank Henderson interview, UCD, P17b/99.

'was a braggart': Robert Brennan, *Allegiance* (Dublin: Browne & Nolan, 1950), p. 153.

'Although prison conditions': 'Gerry Boland's Story', *Irish Times*, 9 Oct. 1968.

'Collins was called on': Dore statement, WS 392.

109 'I sat with you': Dail Eireann Debates, 16 Oct. 1931.

110 'a brilliant and daring individual': Brennan-Whitmore, *With the Irish*, pp. 90–91.

'as strong, forceful and pushful': 'Memoirs of Sean T.', *Irish Press*, 20 July 1961.

7: MANAGER

page

112 'Shortly after our release': R.H., 'Forgive Them The Dying Heros' Last Words', unknown newspaper clipping, NLI, MS 498.

'lived what may be': Report Suspect Michael Collins, Clonakilty, 22 May 1917, Stewart, *Michael Collins*, pp. 46–7.

'he boasts to his friends': Report on Collins, 31 Dec. 1916, ibid., p. 40.

113 Miracle of the Rising: 'Report of the Irish National Aid and Volunteer Dependants Fund', *Catholic Bulletin*, August 1919, pp. 419–20.

'experience in administrative work': Collins to Donal O'Connor, 20 Jan. 1917, NLI, MS 24,384.

Donal O'Connor: Robinson, *Accountants in Ireland*, p. 402.

114 'Mr Collins': O'Connor to INA Exec. Cttee, 6 Feb. 1917, NLI, MS 24,384.

'I was unaware': Collins to Donal O'Connor, 10 Feb. 1917, NLI, MS 24,384.

'Miss [Anna] O'Rahilly': Batt O'Connor statement, NLI, MS 33,929(14).

115 'The place was packed': Ibid.

Collins's meeting with Kathleen Clarke: 'Notes on Talk with Mrs Tom Clarke 6 July 1963', Mulcahy Papers, UCD, P7/D/1; Kathleen Clarke, *Revolutionary Woman: My Fight for Ireland's Freedom* (Dublin: O'Brien, 1991), pp. 137–8.

'On the way': William O'Brien statement, WS 1766.

116 Kitty O'Doherty's account: Her statement, WS 355.

'Finding the work': Collins to Donal O'Connor, 10 Feb. 1917, NLI, MS 24,384.

117 'The little knot': *Irish Times*, 14 May 1921.

118 'The work of the Association': Donal O'Connor to INA Exec. Cttee, 1 Jan. 1917, NLI, MS 24,384.

Collins's duties: Hon. Sec. to Collins, 17 Feb. 1917, NLI, MS 24,384. For a summary of the work of the organization, see 'Report of the Irish National Aid and Volunteer Dependants Fund'. The Irish administration

118 carried out a revealing forensic examination of the books in 1919–20: 'Report on the Results of an Investigation into the Accounts of the INA and VDF', PRO, CO 904/180/4.

J. J. O'Kelly: 'Sceilg', 'Michael Collins: An Effort to Appreciate his Complex Personality', *Catholic Bulletin*, 1922–3, p. 627.

'I suppose': Collins to O'Brien, 23 Feb. 1917, Art O'Brien Papers, NLI, MS 8435. It is unclear if this is false modesty or a reference to his previous complaints about the National Aid.

Collins's first office report: Office Report, n.d., NLI, MS 24,384.

119 The Sheridan case: INA Employment Cttee Minute Book 1916–17, NLI, MS 23,475.

'She went out to see Collins': Michael Hayes's comments on a talk by Richard Mulcahy, 29 Oct. 1963, UCD, P7/D/66.

120 Collins grant: INA American Grants Cttee, Civil Service Cases, NLI, MS 24,330. According to Patrick Belton, writing in a letter refuting O'Kelly's claims, Collins was offered a payment worth a year's salary and refused (although this might have been a separate matter): *Irish Independent*, 3 Nov. 1924.

'Michael, while in receipt': Sceilg, 'Michael Collins', p. 629.

'complete control of my finances': Grace Plunkett to Mrs [Kitty] O'Doherty, n.d., NLI, MS 24,357. Her threat to go into the workhouse: Plunkett to Donal O'Connor, 7 May 1917 (INA Letter Book, NLI, MS 23,465); see also Collins to Plunkett, 29 Jan. 1918 (INA Letter Book, NLI, MS 23,466); Hon. Sec. to Plunkett, 29 Mar, 30 May 1919 (INA Letter Book, NLI, MS 23,467).

121 'Nor do I expect one': Collins to Tadg O'Shea, 31 July 1917, NLI, MS 23,465. See also Collins to Tadg O'Shea, 24 May, 22 June; to N. M. Stack, 22 June; to Rev. Dr Kelly, 18 July – all NLI, MS 23,465. Police reports on INA funds can be found in PRO, CO 904/23 and esp. the detailed report in CO 904/180/4.

122 'We cannot thank you': McGarry to Collins, 25 June 1917, NLI, MS 24,357. On de Valera's income, see the report on the INA and VDF, PRO, CO 904/180/4.

8: Insider

page
123 'The next thing': Kenneth Griffith and Timothy O'Grady, *Curious Journey: An Oral History of Ireland's Unfinished Revolution* (London: Hutchinson, 1982), p. 108.

125 North Roscommon by-election: Michael O'Callaghan, *For Ireland and Freedom: Roscommon's Contribution to the Fight for Independence* (Boyle: Roscommon Herald, 1964), pp. 4–15. Geraldine Plunkett Dillon, 'The North Roscommon Election', *Catholic Bulletin*, 1967; Denis Carroll, *They*

Have Fooled You Again: Michael O'Flanagan (1876–1942) Priest, Republican, Social Critic (Blackrock: Columba, 1993), pp. 53–9.

126 'Mick was in our house': Kitty O'Doherty statement, WS 355.

'Some people thought': O'Brien, *Forth the Banners Go*, p. 144.

'Michael Collins took a leading part': Ibid.

'The first time': Michael Staines statement, WS 944.

127 'I was, therefore, rather uneasy': Michael O'Flanagan, 'We had been Waiting for This Chance' in O'Callaghan, *For Ireland*, p. 14.

'accompanied by Miss Plunkett': *Freeman's Journal*, 7 Feb. 1917.

128 Meetings at Plunkett's house: William O'Brien diary, 14 and 15 Feb. entries, William O'Brien Papers, NLI, MS 15,705; O'Brien, *Forth the Banners Go*, pp. 146–7.

'Count Plunkett, if elected': Staines statement, WS 944. On Plunkett and the politics of 1917, see Michael Laffan, *The Resurrection of Ireland: The Sinn Fein Party, 1916–1923* (Cambridge: Cambridge University Press, 1999), pp. 77–122.

129 'It was outrageous': O'Brien, *Forth the Banners Go*, p. 148.

130 'call a new Ireland': *Irish Times*, 26 Mar. 1917.

Collins saddled with tickets: Count Plunkett Papers, NLI, MS 11,383.

131 Plunkett convention: *Freeman's Journal*, 19, 20 Apr. 1917; *Irish Times*, 20 Apr. 1917; William O'Brien statement, WS 1766; Carroll, *They Have Fooled You*, pp. 64–7; Brian Murphy, *Patrick Pearse and the Lost Republican Ideal* (Dublin: James Duffy, 1991), pp. 79–84.

'Suddenly the door was thrown open': Michael Lennon, 'Looking backward. Glimpses into Later History', J. J. O'Connell Papers, NLI, MS 22,117(1).

132 'the men at present': Ibid.

'pretty rotten': Collins to Ashe, 2 May 1917, in Sean O Luing, *I Die in a Good Cause* (Tralee: Anvil, 1970), p. 122.

133 'when I was busily engaged': Dan McCarthy statement, WS 722.

'You can tell Con Collins': O Luing, *I Die*, p. 122.

134 Collins's wire to Lewes: Collins to Rev. Fr O'Loughlin, 14 May 1917, NLI, MS 23,465.

Joe McGrath saves the day: *Freeman's Journal*, 11 May 1917; Dan McCarthy statement, WS 722.

'Plunkett is certainly gaining ground': Gavan Duffy to O'Hegarty, 29 May 1917, Gavan Duffy Papers, NLI, MS 5581.

9: PLAYER

page

136 'I used to see': Michael Noyk statement, NLI, MS 18,975, p. 12.

137 Collins as assistant adjutant: Archer statement, WS 819.

138 May 22 Volunteer manifesto: MA, A/0777. This appears to be a proof corrected by Collins.

139 'He [Collins] had been in London': Alfie White interview, UCD, P17b/110.
Fintan Lalor circle: Dore statement, WS 392.
'Two or three of the men': Joseph O'Rourke statement, WS 1244.

141 Collins as conscientious attender: IRB Circles Attendance Record 1920, Martin Conlon Papers, UCD, P97/15.
new Supreme Council: Diarmuid Lynch statement, WS 4.
Collins's Belfast schemes: Michael Lynch statement, WS 511.

142 IRB unit in Cork: Peter Hart, *The IRA and Its Enemies: Violence and Community in Cork* (Oxford: Oxford University Press, 1998), pp. 240–41.
'I had eighteen hoops': Sean MacEoin, 'Memories of General Michael Collins' (1967), MacEoin Papers, UCD, P151/1865.

143 'Collins, who at the time': Valentine Jackson statement, WS 409.
'We walked along': Michael Lynch statement, WS 511.

144 Rumours of embezzlement: these persisted after his death: Sean McGrath to Art O'Brien, 20 Sept. 1922, Art O'Brien Papers, NLI, MS 8442.
'about fellows being entertained': Leo Henderson interview, UCD, P17b/105.
'I was that ignorant': Ibid.
'I was centre': Eamon Martin interview, UCD, P17b/105.

145 'Collins was a bully': Leo Henderson interview, UCD, P17b/105.

10: POLITICIAN

page

146 'Now when the meeting was over': MacEoin, 'Memories'.
'it was the men': Collins to N. M. Stack, 16 June 1917, INA Letter Book, NLI, MS 23,465.
'wonderful scenes': Collins to ? Haydon, 19 June 1917, NLI, MS 23,465.
'Republican flags still fly': Collins to Alec McCabe, 20 June 1917, NLI, MS 23,465.

147 'I quite agree': Collins to Ashe, 26 June 1917, NLI, MS 23,465.
'must receive their death blow': *Irish Times*, 14 July 1917.
Collins on Kilkenny election cttee: Minute Book of Kilkenny Election Cttee, NLI, MS 10,494(6).
Sinn Fein's most requested speakers: Sinn Fein Correspondence Precis, NLI, MS 10,494(1).

148 'if he saw his chance again': Police report on Ballinalee meeting, 25 July 1917, PRO, CO 904 23/3B.
'had not forgotten': *Irish Times*, 21 Aug. 1917.
'The speech was very moderate': Police report, Carrick-on-Shannon, 21 Aug. 1917, Stewart, *Michael Collins*, p. 62.
'We are not pro-Germans': Police report on Ballymahon meeting, 9 Sept. 1917, PRO, CO 904 23/3B. He had used this line in his Carrick-on-Shannon speech as well.
'M. J. Collens of Woodfield': *Cork Examiner*, 27 June 1917.

'The first time': Ernest Blythe statement, WS 939, p. 79.

149 'It is, I think': Collins to Madge Daly, 31 July 1917, NLI, MS 23,465.

'At last he could bear': Nora Ashe statement, WS 645.

Collins not seen as significant: In 1916 and 1917 the Irish police divided political suspects by dangerousness into 'A', 'B' and 'C' categories. Collins was a 'C' – not worth arresting or keeping in jail. RIC/DMP special war 'B' list of suspects, Dec. 1917, UCD, P16.

'a beautiful man': Mrs Batt O'Connor statement, WS 330.

'The whole business': Collins to Miss Nora Ashe, 3 Sept. 1917, Nora Ashe Papers, NLI, Pos. 5482.

150 'A huge mob': Good statement, WS 388.

'The death of poor Tom Ashe': Collins to Lynch (?), 28 (?) Sept. 1917, NLI, MS 23,466.

151 'Dublin is in the hands of the Volunteers': Collins to Gearoid O'Sullivan, 28 Sept. 1917, NLI, MS 23,466.

'Mr Michael Collins': *Irish Times*, 1 Oct. 1917.

152 'As a matter of fact': Mulcahy, 'Talk on Michael Collins', UCD, P7b/180.

'How Mr Collins': 'Sceilg', 'Michael Collins', p. 629. This could also be interpreted as meaning Collins was not allowed to give a longer speech unless it was in Irish, but this seems unlikely. See also UCD, P7b/134.

'At any rate': Mulcahy, 'Talk on Michael Collins', UCD, P7/D/66.

'Thomas Ashe is not dead': Police report on Ballinalee meeting, 8 Oct. 1917, Stewart, *Michael Collins*, p. 78. He recycled this line about the bullock's tail many times, as in a speech in Tipperary on 19 Sept. 1917, police report, PRO, CO 904 23/3B.

153 'Distant, strange, stand offish': Collins to Ashe, 2 May 1917, O Luing, *I Die*, p. 122.

'the Volunteer organization': De Roiste diary, 18 Oct. 1917, O'Donoghue Papers, NLI, MS 31,146.

46 Parnell Square: Diarmuid Lynch statement, WS 4.

154 Collins . . . almost walked out: Ibid.

'still doubtful': Ibid.

Sinn Fein convention: *Report of the Proceedings of the Sinn Fein Convention*, 25–26 Oct. 1917, PRO, CO 904/23.

155 'at all costs': Collins to Ashe, 28 May 1917, NLI, Pos. 5482.

'Mr Collins briskly suggested': *Proceedings*, PRO, CO 904/23, p. 36.

Brugha's organization scheme: Ibid., p. 37.

156 'the Volunteers have so far': Ibid., p. 16.

Volunteer convention: Richard Mulcahy, 'The Irish Volunteer Convention 27 October, 1917', *Capuchin Annual*, 1967; Frank Henderson statement, WS 821; Comdt P. Colgan's recollections, MA, A/0891; UCD, P7b/134, 198.

11: A Day in Court

page
159 Arrest warrant: Stewart, *Michael Collins*, p. 145.
  'a big blow out': *Longford Leader*, 6 Apr. 1918.
160 Collins's Legga speech: Report of Constable Hugh Maguire, 4 Mar. 1918, in Stewart, *Michael Collins*, p. 97.
161 'brought a crowd around': *Irish Times*, 3 April 1918.
  'a number of men': *Freeman's Journal*, 3 April 1918.
162 'The detectives who seized me': This and all other first-person statements by Collins about his arrest come from a diary he kept in prison (although he may have written at least some of it up after the fact): Iosold O'Deirg (ed.), 'Oh! Lord the Unrest of the Soul: The Jail Journal of Michael Collins', *Studia Hibernica*, 1994.
164 'What my name is': This and all other published quotes can be found in the *Freeman's Journal*, 4 Apr. 1918, and the *Longford Leader*, 6 Apr. 1918.
165 Attack on McNabola: Francis Davis statement, WS 496.

12: Director

page
171 'Collins, [Tomas] MacCurtain and I': O'Donoghue memoir, NLI, MS 31,124, p. 61.
  'The most effective means': This and the following quote are from Dorothy Macardle, *The Irish Republic* (London: Gollancz, 1937), pp. 233–4.
172 Conscription crisis: Adrian Gregory, '"You Might as Well Recruit Germans": British Public Opinion and the Decision to Conscript the Irish in 1918', in Gregory and Senia Paseta (eds.), *Ireland and the Great War: 'A War to Unite Us All'?* (Manchester: Manchester University Press, 2002).
  Volunteer general staff: Richard Mulcahy's notes, UCD, P7/D/3; Richard Walsh statement, WS 400; Mulcahy, 'Conscription and the General Headquarters Staff', *Capuchin Annual*, 1968.
  Collins as commandant-general: Letter to Collins, 26 Sept. 1918, Charles Howard Foulkes Papers, LHCMA, Epitome No. G/3547.
173 'somewhat incomprehensibly': Sceilg, 'Michael Collins', p. 628.
  'rushed the change': Belton letter, *Irish Independent*, 3 Nov. 1924.
  Volunteer documents captured: Sinn Fein Correspondence Precis, NLI, MS 10,494(6).
  Collins vs. National Aid board: INA Exec. Cttee Agenda, 14, 21 June; 1 July 1918, NLI, MS 23,472.
174 'I found Michael Collins': Ernie O'Malley, *On Another Man's Wound* (Dublin, Anvil, 1936), p. 76.
  Volunteer reorganization: The Sinn Fein Correspondence Precis (NLI, MS

10,494(6)) contains much of this paperwork, as do the Michael Collins papers in the Military Archives: see, for example, MA, A/778.

'Collins was working': O'Malley, *On Another Man's Wound*, p. 88.

175 Collins rewriting O'Hegarty: O'Hegarty to Florence O'Donoghue, 21 Jan. 1952, O'Donoghue Papers, NLI, MS 31,333.

'We are not establishing': 'Organization Notes', *An tOglach*, 14 Sept. 1918.

176 'Captain Collins': Police report, Ballinamuck, 17 Feb. 1918, Stewart, *Michael Collins*, pp. 92–3.

Tullyvrane court-martial: Police report, Lanesboro, 3 Mar. 1918, ibid., p. 88.

177 Letters from Collins captured: See the description sheets of 1918 deportees in PRO, CO 904/24/1.

Nov.–Dec. 1919: Armagh, MA, A/0314; Offaly, MA, A/0332; Carlow, MA, A/0335; Galtee Regiment and East Limerick, MA, A/0345; Leitrim, MA, A/0353.

178 'this is quite out of the question': Collins to Comdt, Cavan Bde, 11 Nov. 1919, MA, A/0316.

'You know Mick': McGuill to Collins, 7 Aug. 1919, MA, A/0324.

'The ready comradeship': Liam Deasy, *Towards Ireland Free* (Cork: Mercier, 1973), p. 81.

GHQ plans: *Irish Times*, 2 Jan., 2 Apr. 1919; Michael Lynch statement, WS 511, pp. 102–5.

179 Volunteer communications: See 'Communications Notes', *An tOglach*, August 1918 and subsequent issues.

'There was no time sheet': Collins to de Lacy, 18 Aug. 1918, UCD, P150/461.

'That's about the limit': Ibid., 30 Aug. 1918.

180 'A man named Jack Good': Edward O'Neill statement, WS 203.

181 'a not very impressive gathering': Collins to Stack, 21 Aug. 1918, NLI, MS 5848.

Collins rarely went to meetings: Sinn Fein standing cttee minutes, 1918–19, UCD, P7/D/39. He did not attend any meetings between May and November 1918.

Collins and Boland on the Supreme Council: Sean O Muirthile memoir, p. 69, Mulcahy Papers, UCD, P7a/209. See also David Fitzpatrick, *Harry Boland's Irish Revolution* (Cork: Cork University Press, 2003), p. 98.

182 'there are certain resolutions': Collins to Stack, 21 Aug. 1918, NLI, MS 5848.

'men whom warrants': *New Ireland*, 9 Nov. 1918.

Collins did better: *Irish Independent*, 30 Oct. 1918.

183 'Harry Boland rose': *New Ireland*, 9 Nov. 1918.

Collins blamed for no nominations: Richard Mucahy, talk with Paddy O'Keefe, 25 Sept. 1964, UCD, P7/D/5.

Boland and nominations: Boland to Austin Stack, 18, 20 Sept. 1918

183 (Kilmainham Gaol Archives, 18 L2 1D44 O4), 11 Oct. 1918 (18 LR 1D44 O5).

184 1919 Ard Fheis: see Collins to Stack, 17 May 1919, NLI, MS 5848, in which he refers to 'a Standing Committee of malcontents'.

'You are requested': 'To the Electors of South Cork', Michael Collins Papers, NLI, MS 40,422/5.

Deal with the Irish Party in Ulster: Sinn Fein standing cttee minutes, 28 Nov., 4 Dec. 1918, UCD, P7/D/39.

13: MINISTER

page

186 'Looking back': J. Anthony Gaughan (ed.), *Memoirs of Constable Jeremiah Mee, RIC* (Dublin: Anvil, 1975), p. 134.

Collins as whip etc.: Sinn Fein standing cttee minutes, 19 Dec. 1918; 16 Jan, 6 Feb. 1919, UCD, P7/D/39.

187 'We never got any nearer': Robert Barton statement, WS 979, p. 12. See also Sean T. O'Kelly statement, WS 1765, pp. 262–3.

Collins as Home Affairs minister: *Dail Eireann Minutes of Proceedings*, 22 Jan. 1919, p. 26. No whips were appointed, so Collins presumably lost that job.

Collins and Brugha: Collins and Brugha to Lynch, 15 Feb, 6 March 1919, O'Donoghue Papers, NLI, MS 31,416(1) and (2).

Lincoln jail escape: The best account is in Fitzpatrick, *Boland's Irish Revolution*, pp. 114–16.

188 De Valera's cabinet: *Dail Eireann Minutes of Proceedings*, 2 April 1919, p. 36.

Collins signing as Minister of Finance: Brugha and Collins to Lynch, 6 Mar. 1919, NLI, MS 31,416(2).

189 Collins inherited money: Francis M. Carroll, *Money for Ireland: Finance, Diplomacy, Politics and the First Dail Eireann Loans, 1919–1936* (Westport: Praeger, 2002), pp. 3–4. For the loan and the Department of Finance in general, see Carroll, pp. 4–29; Michael Hopkinson, *The Irish War of Independence* (Dublin: Gill & Macmillan, 2002), pp. 165–76; Ronan Fanning, *The Irish Department of Finance 1922–58* (Dublin: Institute on Public Administration, 1978), pp. 13–29.

190 'the power of energetic clergy': Collins to James O'Mara, 25 Sept. 1920, NA, DE 5/57/14.

191 'You misled us': Collins to Boland, 14 Aug. 1920, UCD, P150/165.

'our chief way': Ibid., 15 Oct. 1920.

Henry Mangan: Dathai O'Donoghue statement, WS 548.

192 'The organizers': Collins speech to Sinn Fein Ard Comhairle, 23 Aug. 1921, UCD, P150/579.

'You will understand': Collins to de Valera, 15 Nov. 1919, UCD, P150/726.

'Unfortunately the work': Collins to Boland, 18 Jan. 1920, UCD, P150/165.

193 'what work and energy': Collins to MacSwiney, 19 Dec. 1919, Terence MacSwiney Papers, CAI, PR/4/3.

'deliberately slow': Liam de Roiste diary, 3 Jan. 1920, de Roiste Papers, CAI, U271.

'were it not for that': Collins to MacSwiney, 29 May 1920, NA, DE 2/530.

'There are people': Ibid., 26 July 1920.

'after a pretty hard year': Collins to Boland, 19 Apr. 1920, UCD, P150/165.

'I am about to wind up': Collins to Sean Nunan, 29 Apr. 1920, NA, DE 2/292.

194 'I am anxious': Collins memo, 16 Jan. 1920, NA, DE 5/124.

Dail expenditures: Carroll, *Money for Ireland*, pp. 10–11. Various figures exist, but these seem the most complete.

195 'in favour of certain names': Collins to O'Mara, 16 Nov. 1921, NA, DE 5/57/14. See also Dathai O'Donoghue statement, WS 548.

Collins's buried treasure: Dathai O'Donoghue statement, WS 548.

196 'owing to a certain Banking Inquiry': Collins to O'Mara, 20 Apr. 1920, NA, DE 5/57/14.

Munster & Leinster account: NA, DE 5/64/2.

'we must reduce': Collins to George McGrath, 11 June 1921, NA, DE 5/15.

197 'We must somehow': Ibid., 8 Nov. 1921.

'I can see my reputation': Collins to Fintan Murphy and Dan Donovan, 16 Nov. 1919, NA, DE 5/124.

14: WAR

page

199 'Collins is the son': *Weekly Summary*, 12 Oct. 1920.

200 'strong fighting ideas': Collins to Stack, 17 May 1919, NLI, MS 5848.

Approval of Phoenix Park killings: Draft notes, n.d., NLI, MS 13,329.

'I listened': Dore statement, WS 392.

201 'You heard England': *Irish Times*, 18 July 1918.

Collins and killing the British cabinet: Walsh statement, WS 400; de Valera statement, 13 Mar. 1964 (including another account by Dick Walsh), UCD, P150/609.

202 'No soldier was shot': Collins to Stack, 28 Nov. 1918, NLI, MS 5848.

203 West Cork meeting: Deasy, *Towards Ireland Free*, p. 57.

Collins appoints himself D/I: Walsh statement, WS 400.

Duggan's files: Duggan to Collins, n.d., Foulkes Papers, LHCMA, Epitome No. 53/4435, p. 20.

204 New Ireland Assurance: Collins's work on this venture can be traced in the INA Letter Books, Collins to M. W. O'Reilly, 30 May; 14, 25 June; 21 Aug.; 17 Sept.; 20 Dec. 1917; 2 Jan. 1918 – NLI, MS 23,465–6. See also *New Ireland Comes of Age* (Dublin: New Ireland Assurance, 1939), pp. 7–11; William Acheson, *Achievement: The 28 Year's Story of New Ireland* (Dublin: New Ireland Assurance, 1946), pp. 3–7.

204 Liam Tobin and Frank Thornton: Tobin statement, WS 1753; Thornton statement, WS 615.

206 'Naturally I was at a loss': Thomas Gay statement, WS 780.

207 'I was filled': Eamon Broy statement, WS 1280, p. 75–6.

208 David Neligan: David Neligan, *The Spy in the Castle* (London: MacGibbon & Kee, 1999); Neligan statement, WS 380.

Lily Mernin: Mernin statement, WS 441.

209 *An tOglach*: 31 Jan. 1919.

Dick McKee's efforts: Bernard Byrne statement, WS 631; Frank Henderson, 'Richard McKee', *An Cosantoir*, June 1945, p. 309.

210 'From an early stage': Michael McDonnell statement, WS 225.

'I received instructions': James Slattery statement, WS 445.

211 'cold blooded serpentine organization': Broy statement, WS 1280, p. 76.

British intelligence: Eunan O'Halpin, 'British Intelligence in Ireland', in Christopher Andrew and David Dilks (eds.), *The Missing Dimension: Governments and Intelligence Communities in the Twentieth Century* (London: Macmillan, 1984); Christopher Andrew, *Secret Service: The Making of the British Intelligence Community* (London: Allen Lane, 1985); Peter Hart, *British Intelligence in Ireland* (Cork: Cork University Press, 2002).

212 'We had .38 guns': Slattery statement, WS 445.

Collins asking for .45 weapons: Collins to Joe Vize (in Glasgow), 15 May 1919, UCD, P7/A/11.

'asked me': Slattery statement, WS 445.

213 Hoey killed: *Irish Times*, 13 Sept. 1919.

Mick Dowling killed: Ibid., 20 Oct. 1919.

Wharton and Barton: Ibid., 30 Nov. 1919; 7 Feb. 1920.

Walshe and Redmond: Ibid., 22 Jan. 1920.

Walsh and Dunleavy: Ibid., 20 Feb. 1920.

Kells and Dalton: Ibid., 15, 21 Apr. 1920.

214 'never lifted a finger': Neligan, *Spy*, p. 68.

Revell: *Irish Times*, 10 May 1920.

'organized and bold': Michael Collins, *The Path to Freedom* (Cork: Mercier, 1968), p. 69. This is a collection of newspaper articles originally published in 1922.

215 'Well your letter': Collins to Stack, 26 Mar. 1919, NLI, MS 17,090.

216 'He spoke': Darrell Figgis, *Recollections of the Irish War* (London, E. Benn, 1927), p. 243.

'Things that way': Collins to Stack, 18 May 1919, NLI, MS 5848.

217 'Yet our hope': Ibid., 20 July 1919.

'after all': Ibid., 11 Aug. 1919.

'Collins was waiting': Seamus Robinson statement, NLI, MS 21,265, pp. 29–30. I am grateful to Liam Kennedy for giving me this reference.

219 'if any of us': Robinson statement, NLI, MS 21,265, pp. 46–7.

Detective O'Brien: Broy statement, WS 1280.

220 assassination plans: Peter Hart, *The IRA at War 1916–1923* (Oxford: Oxford University Press, 2003), pp. 198–9.

'would arouse': Dan Breen, *My Fight for Irish Freedom* (Dublin: Anvil, 1964), p. 81.

plans to kill Lord French: Ibid., pp. 81–95; Robinson statement, NLI, MS 21,265.

221 'They are bad shots': Charles Townshend, *The British Campaign in Ireland 1919–1921: The Development of Political and Military Policies* (Oxford: Oxford University Press, 1975), p. 49.

'The first time': Robinson statement, NLI, MS 21,265, pp. 47–8.

Collins boasting of ambushes: *Debate on the Treaty*, 3 Jan, 1922, p. 172.

222 'it was the first time': Sean McGrath interview, UCD, P17b/100. See also Hart, *IRA at War*, pp. 148–9.

'Michael Collins was more for': Denis Kelleher interview, UCD, P17b/107.

Frank Brooke: Neligan statement, WS 380; Patrick Daly statement, NLI, Pos. 4548.

15: SPY

page
224 'Height about 5' 8''': PRO, CO 904/196/65, description *c.* Oct. 1920.

'quiet, secluded district': *Freeman's Journal*, 3 Mar. 1920.

To the hotel staff: Ibid., 4 Mar. 1920.

'in some quarters': Ibid.

225 Mrs Byrnes: Ibid., 5 Mar. 1920.

Resurrected by biographers: Beaslai, *Michael Collins*, vol. 1, pp. 405–9; O'Connor, *Big Fellow*, pp. 84–91; Tim Pat Coogan, *Michael Collins: A Biography* (London: Hutchinson, 1990), pp. 127–31.

Isham: David Buchanan, *The Treasure of Auchinleck: The Story of the Boswell Papers* (New York: McGraw-Hill, 1974), pp. 55–7; *Monthly Army List*, Jan. 1920; *Who's Who 1941* (Britain); *Who's Who in America 1952–53*; *New York Times* obituary, 15 June 1955.

'wonderful gift': General C. F. Romer to Isham, 6 Jan. 1942, YULMC, Ralph Isham Papers, Group no.1455, Box 1.

226 J. C. Byrnes: Julian Putkowski, 'A2 and the "Reds in Khaki"', *Lobster 94: Journal of Parapolitics*, no. 27; 'The Best Secret Service Man We Had – Jack Byrnes, A2 and the IRA', ibid., no. 28. (This is the magazine edited by Stephen Dorrill, not to be confused with the ongoing *Lobster* magazine edited by Robin Ramsay.) Byrnes's many reports can be found in the Isham Papers at Yale. Julian Putkowski and I both worked on the fascinating story of Byrnes and Isham in the 1980s and '90s unbeknown to each other – I was the first to see the Isham papers, as I happened to be at Yale at the time, but he was the first to publish his results, and his is the definitive work on Byrnes and A2 in Britain. I am grateful for his generosity in sharing his knowledge, and to Paul Kennedy for telling me about the papers in the first place.

'a certain Irish soldier': Basil Thomson, *The Scene Changes* (London: Collins, 1939), p. 388.

'my man': Ibid.

'the best secret service man': Thomas Jones, *Whitehall Diary*, vol. 3: *Ireland 1918–1925*, ed. Keith Middlemass (Oxford: Oxford University Press, 1971), p. 19. This was the opinion of Walter Long at a cabinet conference, 31 May 1920.

227 ISDL radicalism: See, for example, Art O'Brien to William McMahon, 4 July 1919, Art O'Brien Papers, NLI, MS 8433; Agenda for ISDL standing cttee, Dec. 1919, NLI, MS 8435.

228 Misses Mooney, Rose etc.: Agent No. 8 (Byrnes) reports, 26 May, 8, 16, 21 June 1919, YULMC, Isham Papers, Series I, Box 1, File 7.

Byrnes and Art O'Brien: 'Notes on Interview with No. 8, 28 July 1919; No. 8 report, 25 Aug., 11, 29 Sept., 13 Nov. 1919 – YULMC, Isham Papers, Series I, Box 1, File 8; O'Brien to Collins, 3, 10, 12, 18 June 1919, NLI, MS 8430.

Byrnes and Collins: Collins to O'Brien, 6 June, 22 Nov. 1919, NLI, MS 8430. When they met in Dublin, Collins spoke of 'their recent meeting in London': 'Notes on No. 8's visit to Ireland, December 1919', YULMC, Isham Papers, Series I, Box 1, File 7. Collins may have been using the name 'Fergus Casey'. It is also possible they met in October, as Putkowski suggests ('The Best Secret Service Man', p. 22), as Collins was in England then to aid in another prison rescue: Collins to O'Brien, 23, 24, 31 Oct. 1919, NLI, MS 8426.

Isham seconded: Gen. C. F. Romer memo, 6 Jan. 1942, YULMC, Isham Papers, Box I, File 1.

Irish intelligence overhauled: O'Halpin, 'British Intelligence in Ireland'; for the military campaign in early 1920, see Hart, *British Intelligence*, pp. 19–20.

229 'practically the whole': 'Interview with No. 8', 13 Nov. 1919, YULMC, Isham Papers, Series I, Box 1, File 8.

'he should not expect': Collins to O'Brien, 15 Nov. 1919, NLI, MS 8426.

'Will you kindly': Ibid., 22 Nov. 1919.

'In addition': O'Brien to Collins, 3 Dec. 1919, NLI, MS 8426.

Composed by Thomson: Thomson, *The Scene Changes*, p. 391.

'I shall be': Collins to O'Brien, 4 Dec. 1919, NLI, MS 8426.

'He was met': 'Notes on No. 8's visit to Ireland', YULMC, Isham Papers, Series I, Box 1, File 7.

230 'expressed great surprise': Ibid.

231 'has duly arrived': Collins to O'Brien, 8 Dec. 1919, NLI, MS 8426.

'twice seen the leader': No. 8 Report, 2 Jan. 1921, YULMC, Isham Papers, Series I, Box 1, File 8.

'You kept him': O'Brien to Collins, 17 Dec. 1919, NLI, MS 8426.

'There has been': Collins to O'Brien, 19 Dec. 1919, NLI, MS 8430.

Isham at the Shelbourne: Receipts for Dec. and Jan. can be found in Box I, File 20 of the Isham Papers at YULMC.

'He has paid' and following exchange: Collins to O'Brien, 2, 6, 12, 13 Jan. 1920 (NLI, MS 8430); O'Brien to Collins, 15 Jan. 1920 (NLI, MS 8426); Collins to O'Brien, 16, 20 Jan. 1920 (NLI, MS 8430).

233 How Byrnes was caught: Thornton statement, WS 615, pp. 38–40; Batt O'Connor, *With Michael Collins in the Fight for Irish Independence* (Millstreet: Aubane, 2004), pp. 112–13.

'What I have to say': Collins to O'Brien, 20 Jan. 1920, NLI, MS 8430.

'I am not quite certain': Ibid.

'James. My opinion.': Ibid., 22 Jan. 1920.

'astonished': Ibid., 23 Jan. 1920.

234 'Unfortunately': McGrath to Collins, 23 Jan. 1920, NLI, MS 8426.

'I am most awfully sorry': Collins to McGrath, 24 Jan. 1920, NLI, MS 8426.

'disappointed': O'Brien to Collins, 28 Jan. 1920, NLI, MS 8426.

'The idea was agreed to': 'Notes on No. 8's visit to Wales', 30 Jan. 1920, YULMC, Isham Papers, Series I, Box 1, File 7.

235 'Jameson – reply favourably': Collins to McGrath, 28 Jan. 1920, NLI, MS 8426.

'There is little doubt': Collins to O'Brien, 2 Feb. 1920, NLI, MS 8426.

'I shall only': Ibid., 10 Feb. 1920.

'*Corry*': McGrath to Collins, 9 Feb. 1920, NLI, MS 8426.

'to allow him': Ibid., 17 Feb. 1920.

236 'Total ignorance': Collins to O'Brien, 18 Feb. 1920, NLI, MS 8426.

'I may have': Ibid., 20 Feb. 1920.

'if Sam can': Collins to McGrath, 28 Feb. 1920, NLI, MS 8426.

Killing of Byrnes: Joe Dolan statement, WS 663; Patrick O'Daly statement, NLI, Pos. 4548, pp. 31–2; Thornton statement, WS 615, p. 40.

237 'Yes indeed': Collins to O'Brien, 4 Feb. 1920, NLI, MS 8426.

'By the way': Ibid.

'I wonder': O'Brien to Collins, 28 Jan. 1920, NLI, MS 8426.

'What he was delaying about': Conversation with Vincent Byrne, UCD, P7/ D/3.

Quinlisk: *Cork Examiner*, 24 Feb. 1920; Walsh statement, WS 400; O'Connor, *With Michael Collins*, p. 113.

238 'and said that': Walsh statement, WS 400.

'the scoundrel': Beaslai, *Michael Collins*, vol. 1, p. 393.

Quinlisk caught: Walsh and Archer statements, WS 400 and WS 819; Beaslai, *Michael Collins*, vol. 1, pp. 393–402.

Quinlisk killed: *Cork Examiner*, 20, 23 Feb. 1920.

'tracked down': *Irish Times*, 25 Mar. 1920; Slattery and Dolan statements (WS 445, WS 663).

239 According to IRA memoirs: O'Connor, *With Michael Collins*, pp. 112–13; Thornton statement, WS 615.

'Sold again!': Batt O'Connor statement, NLI, MS 33,929(14).

'The second round': Hart, *British Intelligence*.

240 'hush-hush men': As they called themselves according to Caroline Woodcock in 'Experiences of an Officer's Wife in Ireland', *Blackwood's Magazine*, May 1921, p. 556.

Lynch murder: *Irish Independent*, 24–8 Sept. 1920. Neligan's first account of his findings is in his BMH statement (WS 380), but a different and less detailed version can be found in *Spy in the Castle*, p. 106. I have relied on the former, but it should be noted that the truth of the affair remains very uncertain.

241 Bloody Sunday: Charles Townshend, 'Bloody Sunday – Michael Collins Speaks', *European Studies Review* (1979), pp. 377–85; James Gleeson, *Bloody Sunday* (London: Peter Davies, 1962).

Cross-channel spectacular: Ernie O'Malley diary, 1 Nov. 1920, LHCMA, Epitome No. G/3547/I.662.

Other targets: Townshend, 'Bloody Sunday'.

Frank Thornton claims: Thornton statement, WS 615, p. 24.

242 'The arrest of Dick and Peadar': Liam Tobin interview, UCD, P7b/100.

Post-Bloody Sunday backlash: Townshend, *British Campaign*, pp. 141–60.

'the man who won the war': *Debate on the Treaty*, 19 Dec. 1921, p. 20.

'the founder': Tim Pat Coogan, 'Michael Collins', in Peter Collins (ed.), *Nationalism and Unionism: Conflict in Ireland, 1885–1921* (Belfast: Institute of Irish Studies, 1994), p. 155.

16: A Day in the Office

244 'I remember': Eamon Broy statement, WS 1285.

'crowded into every day': O'Higgins, 'Michael Collins', newspaper cuttings file, NLI, MS 498.

245 'read practically all night': Collins to Stack, 8 Aug. 1918, NLI, MS 5848.

'to prove my scorn': Collins to Kiernan, 29 Sept. 1921, O Broin and O Heigheartaigh (eds.), *In Great Haste*, p. 20.

'He slept': Sean MacEoin interview with Brian Farrell, 24 Aug. 1962, UCD, P151/1852.

'He duly pulled': Broy statement, WS 1280, p. 145.

short sleepers: Ernest Hartmann, *The Functions of Sleep* (New Haven: Yale University Press, 1973), pp. 53–70.

246 'My work': Collins to Art O'Brien, 17 May 1921, NLI, MS 8430.

Collins's offices: Mulcahy notes on talk to Central Branch, UCD, P7/D/3; anon. notes (Alice Lyons?), NA, DE 2/530; statements by Charles Dalton (WS 434), pp. 7–8, Sean Saunders (WS 817); Bridie O'Reilly (WS 454).

247 Collins's day at the office: Anon. notes, NA, DE 2/530; statements by Sean Saunders and Evelyn Lawless (WS 817, WS 414).

248 Cabinet agendas: Dail Eireann Ministry and Cabinet Minutes, 1919–22, NA, DE 1/1, 2, 3, 4.

'it is practical work that counts': Collins to de Valera, 15 Oct. 1921, UCD, P150/1377.

249 'One night': Julia O'Donovan statement, WS 475.

'First to arrive': A. K. Wordsworth statement, WS 1242.

250 'Michael Collins territory': Comerford, 'Dangerous Ground'.

'When you opened': Kevin O'Shiel statement, WS 1770, pp. 718–19.

252 'I found him frightening': Molly Ryan statement, WS 403.

'a kind natured man': Comerford, 'Dangerous Ground'.

253 'I have been looking': Collins to MacDonagh, 9 July 1921, NA, DE 5/17.

'Sorry No': Collins note on George McGrath memo, 19 Sept. 1921, NA, DE 5/17.

'good appearance': McGrath to Collins, 6 Oct. 1921, NA, DE 5/17. McCanna was also a contemporary of Collins's in London, who had left in 1916.

'I shall eternally': Collins to Cosgrave, 15 Oct. 1921; George McGrath to Collins, 6 Oct. 1921 and accompanying notes – NA, DE 5/129.

'"Houses"': Comerford, 'Dangerous Ground'.

254 44 Mountjoy Street: Fionan Lynch statement, WS 192; Walsh statement, WS 400, pp. 101–2; O'Shiel statement, WS 1770, pp. 731–2.

255 'I used to stay': Mary Woods statement, WS 624.

'One night': Mrs Woods statement, O'Malley Papers, UCD, P17a/150.

'it was settled': Ibid.

'Mother was impressed': Comerford, 'Dangerous Ground'.

'was distressed': Ibid.

'could not help': Mary Woods statement, WS 624.

256 'Mick had his arm': Mrs Batt O'Connor statement, WS 330.

'Mick Collins': Ibid.

'He was a rough type': Risteard Mulcahy, *Richard Mulcahy (1886–1971): A Family Memoir* (Dublin: Aurelian, 1999), p. 95.

Collins had a problem with women: De Valera to Joseph McGarrity, 21 Dec. 1921, Sean Cronin, *The McGarrity Papers* (Tralee: Anvil, 1972), p. 111.

Collins didn't seek comforts: Collins to Kiernan, 1 Dec. 1921, O Broin and O Heigheartaigh (eds.), *In Great Haste*, p. 78.

258 'disgraceful': Collins to de Valera, 28 Jan. 1921, UCD, P150/1377.

'I still remember': Maureen McGavock statement, WS 385.

'Things were getting': Kavanagh statement, WS 889.

O'Higgins's attempted resignation: LHCMA, Epitome No. 53/4435, p. 47.

'I don't want': Collins to de Valera, 17 June 1921, Epitome of Documents Captured 22 June 1921, PRO, CO 904/23.

'I am not at all': Ibid., 7 June 1921.

Austin Stack: J. Anthony Gaughan, *Austin Stack: Portrait of a Separatist*
(Mount Merrion: Kingdom, 1977), pp. 102–50.

259 'aware of the inner': Collins to Stack, 30 May 1921, NA, DE 2/509.
'May I however': Ibid., 31 May 1921.
'I know you': Stack to Collins, 1 June 1921, NA, DE 2/509.
'I am afraid': Collins to Stack, 3 June 1921, NA, DE 2/509.

261 'little man': See, for example, Collins to Paddy Daly, 8 Mar. 1921, Mulcahy
Papers, UCD, P17/A/4.
'I could forward': Ibid., 9 Mar. 1921.
'Cathal would sit': Mrs Woods statement, UCD, P17a/150.
'He said': Ibid.

262 'I am just as sorry': Brugha to Collins, 23 Sept. 1919, Foulkes Papers,
LHCMA, Epitome No.53/2567.
'With great respect': Ibid., 5 May 1920.
Brugha out of the loop: Tom McMahon interview, UCD, P17b/86.

263 'I was taken': Collins to McGrath, 25 Jan. 1921, NA, DE 5/7.
'The thing': Ibid., 17 Feb. 1921, NA, DE 5/15.
'Now as a specimen': Collins to de Valera, 10 Feb. 1921, UCD, P150/1377.
Reconciliation meeting: Sean Dowling in Uinseann MacEoin, *Survivors*
(Dublin: Argenta, 1987), quoted in Coogan, *Michael Collins*, p. 176. For
a different version of this encounter session, see Richard Mulcahy, 'The
Chapter on the New Army', UCD, P7/D/1.

264 De Valera's attempted removal: De Valera to Collins, 18 Jan. 1921, PRO,
CO 904/23.
Collins's health problems: Such complaints are scattered through his
correspondence from 1918 to 1922. See Jones, *Whitehall Diary*, vol. 3,
p. 218.
'Must have been': PRO, CO 904/196/65, description *c*. Oct. 1920.
'Are you free': De Valera to Collins, 10 Feb. 1921, Epitome of captured
documents, PRO, CO 904/24/3.
'I would be sorry': De Valera to Collins, 6 Jan. 1921, UCD, P150/1377.

265 'it is damnable': Ibid., 10 Feb. 1921.
'The Almighty': Ibid.
'your fundamental': Ibid., 18 Jan. 1921, PRO, CO 904/23.

266 'for at no time': J. J. O'Kelly statement, WS 384.
'That was another': Ibid.
'he was hardly': Ibid.
Collins horrified: Collins to Boland, 15 Oct. 1920, UCD, P150/1665.

17: PEACE

page

267 'There's a man': *Daily Mail*, 19 Aug. 1921.

268 Lloyd George's possible collusion: Townshend, *British Campaign*,
pp. 100–101.

268 'We have murder': Macardle, *The Irish Republic*, p. 369.

Patrick Moylett's efforts: Moylett statement, WS 767, pp. 49–81; memoir, UCD, P0078.

Archbishop Clune: Hopkinson, *Irish War of Independence*, pp. 177–91.

269 'apparently wants peace': Griffith to Collins, 13 Dec. 1920, NA, DE 2/234A.

Scotland Yard: Report on Revolutionary Organizations, 23 June, 7 July 1921, PRO, CAB 24/125, 126; Irish Intelligence Summary, Special Supplementary Report 259, 1 July 1921, Lloyd George Papers, HLRO, F/46/9/25.

Collins kidnapped or killed: John Ramsden (ed.), *Real Old Tory Politics: The Political Diaries of Sir Robert Saunders, Lord Bayford, 1910–35* (London: Historians' Press, 1985), p. 162.

'There is far': Collins to O'Brien, 15 Dec. 1920, NA, DE 2/234B.

270 'Nobody can tell': Collins to O'Brien, 15 Dec. 1920, NLI, MS 8426.

'a truce': Collins to Griffith, 16 Dec. 1921, NLI, MS 8426.

'I have a distinct': O'Donovan statement, WS 475.

'upon *Mick C's* authority': Sean MacEntee statement, WS 322.

'pointed out': Collins to Griffith, 26 Jan. 1921, NA, DE 2/242.

'No person': *Irish Independent*, 7 Dec. 1920.

'get on with the work': Collins to editor, *Irish Independent*, 7 Dec. 1920, NA, DE 2/234A.

271 'You will understand': Collins to Griffith, 14 Dec. 1920, NA, DE 2/234B.

'Events': Collins to McDonagh, 16 Dec. 1920, NA, DE 2/234B.

'Personally I am': Collins to Griffith, 16 Dec. 1920, NA, DE 2/234B.

'He agrees': Ibid.

'If the English government': Arthur Griffith to Diarmuid O'Hegarty, n.d., NA, DE 2/234A.

272 'of course nobody': Collins to O'Brien, 21 Dec. 1920, NA, DE 2/234B.

273 'Notwithstanding everything': Collins to Eamon Bulfin, 5 Feb. 1921, NA, DE 5/21.

'The work seems': Collins to Michael Staines, 8 Mar. 1921, NA, DE 2/500.

'We have been': Collins to O'Brien, 19 Apr. 1921, NLI, MS 8430.

'They ran me': Collins to Staines, 21 Apr. 1921, NA, DE 2/500.

'Myself': Collins to O'Brien, 4 May 1921, NLI, MS 8430.

'I am somewhat': Ibid., 28 May 1921.

'They have kept up': Ibid., 31 May 1921.

'I believe': Ibid., 28 May 1921.

'Some times': Collins to Harry Boland, 29 June 1921, UCD, P150/1665.

274 'Real progress': Collins to Gavan Duffy, 18 June 1921, NA, 1125/20.

'A statement': Collins to O'Brien, 6 July 1921, NLI, MS 8430.

275 'in a veritable panic': Collins to de Valera, 16 June 1921, PRO, CO 904/23.

'My chief desire': Ibid., 27 June 1921, UCD, P150/1377.

'They [the critics]': *Private Sessions of Second Dail*, 26 Aug. 1921, p. 65.

18: Negotiator

page
277 'Collins turned up': Trevor Wilson (ed.), *The Political Diaries of C. P. Scott 1911–1928* (London: Collins, 1970), p. 404.

278 'His letter': Collins to Boland, 29 June, 6 July 1921, UCD, P150/1665.
     'the country': Blythe statement, WS 939, p. 130.
     'The truth was': Ibid.
     Truce signed: O'Connell Diary 1921, Kathleen O'Connell Papers, UCD, P155/138.

279 'apart from': Collins to de Valera, 16 July 1921, NA, DE 2/244.
     Collins's piece of advice: Ibid., 11 July 1921.
     'their [the British] civilian': Ibid., 16 July 1921.
     'The car': Ibid., 20 July 1921.

280 'I am not dissatisfied': De Valera to Collins, 15 July 1921, UCD, P150/151.
     'You confirm': Collins to de Valera, 16 July 1921, NA, DE 2/244.
     'things "smelt"': Ibid., 20 July 1921.
     'Whilst everyone': Austin Stack memoir in Mrs Austin Stack statement, WS 418.

281 'dead against it': Ibid.
     'You all know': Sceilg, *Stepping-Stones* (Dublin: Irish Book Bureau, n.d.).
     '*Mick* Step on road': De Valera notes, 24 July 1921, in Ronan Fanning, Michael Kennedy, Dermot Keogh and Eunan O'Halpin (eds.), *Documents on Irish Foreign Policy*, vol. 1: *1919–1922* (Dublin: Royal Irish Academy, 1998), pp. 247–8.

282 'from my own': De Valera to McGarrity, 21 Dec. 1921, Cronin, *McGarrity Papers*, p. 110.

283 'to ascertain': *Private Sessions*, 14 Sept. 1921, pp. 87–8.
     'We can only': Ibid.

284 'seeing that': Ibid., 23 Aug. 1921, p. 59.

285 'I do not want': Ibid.
     'I know fairly well': Ibid., 14 Sept. 1921, p. 95.

286 'Having decided': De Valera to McGarrity, 21 Dec. 1921.

287 'he felt': *Private Sessions*, 14 Sept. 1921, p. 96.
     'it would be hard': John Murdoch, 'How Lloyd George Split the Irish Delegation', *Sunday Press*, 19 Sept. 1971.
     IRB Supreme Councillors: Sean O Murthuile memoir, p. 160, UCD, P7a/209.
     'I had to talk': Collins to Kiernan, 31 Aug. 1921, O Broin and O Heigheartaigh (eds.), *In Great Haste*, p. 15.
     'long sitting': Fitzpatrick, *Boland's Irish Revolution*, p. 228.
     'I will never': Batt O'Connor statement, NLI, MS 33,929(14).

288 'I'll never go': Richard Mulcahy, interview with Padraig O'Keefe, 25 Sept. 1964, UCD, P7/D/5.
     'became somewhat annoyed': O Murthuile memoir, p. 177 UCD, P7a/209.

289 'putting our Department': Minister of Defence [Brugha] to Adjutant
General [O'Sullivan], 30 July 1921, UCD, P7a/1.
'Before you are': Min. of Def. to C/S, 6 Sept. 1921, UCD, P7a/1.
Recommissioning the IRA: Maryann Gialanella Valiulis, *Portrait of a
Revolutionary: General Richard Mulcahy and the Founding of the Irish Free
State* (Dublin: Gill & Macmillan, 1992), pp. 104–9.

290 'to put the Army': Min. of Def. to C/S, 16 Nov. 1921, UCD, P7a/2.
'This place bloody limit': Collins to de Valera, 12 Oct. 1921, UCD, P150/
1377.

291 'The whole set-up': Barton to Margaret Forester, 2 Nov. 1964, Robert
Barton Papers, TCD, 1093/12.
'M.C. furious': Childers Diary, TCD, 7814/34.

292 'Liqs Miceal's Mixture': Allen Library, Dublin, Michael Collins Collection,
Box 188, Folder 9.
'He had evidently': A. J. K. Greenway (governor) memo, 20 Oct. 1921,
Lloyd George Papers, HLRO, F/45/6/37.

293 'the same effort': Basil Thomson to (Joseph?) Davies, 26 Aug. 1920, Lloyd
George Papers, HLRO, F/46/9/8; Carl Ackerman, 'Ireland from a
Scotland Yard Notebook', *Atlantic Monthly*, Apr. 1922, p. 440.
Second interview: Collins to Ackerman, 6 Apr. 1921, Lloyd George Papers,
HLRO, F19/3/19; Ackerman, 'The Irish Education of Mr Lloyd
George', *Atlantic Monthly*, May 1922, pp. 610–12.

295 'quick thinker': Birkenhead, *Birkenhead: The Last Phase*, p. 150.
'Collins seems': Ramsden, *Tory Politics*, p. 162.
'He had his own': Sir Charles Petrie, *The Life and Letters of the Right Hon.
Sir Austen Chamberlain* (London: Cassell, 1940), p. 162.
'Collins was undoubtedly': J. M. McEwan (ed.), *The Riddell Diaries
1908–1923* (London: Athlone, 1986), p. 354.
'an uneducated . . . man': *Political Diaries of C. P. Scott*, p. 405.
'he was such': Deborah Lavin, *From Empire to International Commonwealth:
A Biography of Lionel Curtis* (Oxford: Oxford University Press, 1995),
p. 203.
'That swine': Jones, *Whitehall Diary*, vol. 3, p. 186.
'Why did they': Ibid., p. 173.
'atmosphere of London': *Debate on the Treaty*, 19 Dec. 1921, p. 31.

296 'plain Irish way': *Private Sessions*, 16 Dec. 1921, p. 260.
'befogged': Ibid., 15 Dec. 1921, p. 172.
The talks: The only book-length account of the Treaty negotiations is Frank
Pakenham (Lord Longford), *Peace By Ordeal* (London: Cape, 1935;
Geoffrey Chapman, 1962) but it is now obsolete. The best detailed
account to date is in Joseph Curran, *The Birth of the Irish Free State
1921–1923* (University: University of Alabama Press, 1980), pp. 64–146.
Beaslai largely omits the negotiations, but Coogan has a fascinating
account (*Michael Collins*, pp. 236–76). Many of the Treaty documents
have been published in Fanning, Kennedy, Keogh and O'Halpin (eds.),

Documents, vol. 1, pp. 216–370. The British cabinet office also compiled an official Record of the Negotiations, PRO, CAB 43/4. I have particularly relied on Curran and on the document collections in the Public Record Office and the Irish National Archives for my own account.

297 'I would certainly': Irish Peace Conference, Third Session, 13 Oct. 1921, NA, DE 2/304.

'not because Ulster': Ibid., Fourth Session, 14 Oct. 1921.

'we don't even know': Ibid., Fifth Session, 17 Oct. 1921.

'Lloyd George described': *Political Diaries of C. P. Scott*, p. 405.

'There will be': Conference, Fourth Session, 14 Oct. 1921, NA, DE 2/304.

298 'very able': Cttee on Defence, 18 Oct. 1921, NA, DE 2/304.

'formidable': Conference, Sixth Session, 21 Oct. 1921, NA, DE 2/304.

'Good feelings': Cttee on Defence, 17 Oct. 1921, NA, DE 2/304.

'You know something': Ibid., 18 Oct. 1921.

299 'it would look': Ibid.

'two hours': Childers to de Valera, 18 Oct. 1921, UCD, P150/1503.

300 'Let us treat': Proceedings of Cttee on Financial Relations, 19 Oct. 1921, NA, DE 2/304.

'the stage is critical': Conference, Seventh Session, 24 Oct. 1921, NA, DE 2/304.

302 'Conditional': Griffith to Lloyd George, 2 Nov. 1921; Robert Barton's notes on the letter, NA, DE 2/304.

303 Collins and Griffith on unity: Jones, *Whitehall Diary*, vol. 3, pp. 155–6.

'Queer his [Lloyd George's] position': Ibid., p. 157.

304 'new world order': Memorandum by M.C., 23 Nov. ('Personal and Unofficial'), NA, DE 2/304. See also Barton's attached notes: 'The style precludes the possibility of Collins being the real author.'

'This is . . . interesting': Birkenhead, *Birkenhead: The Last Phase*, p. 157.

305 Collins claimed authorship: See *Private Sessions*, 14 Dec. 1921, p. 114.

'was sketched roughly': Collins to de Valera, 19 Nov. 1921, UCD, P150/1377.

Chartres: Brian P. Murphy, *John Chartres: Mystery Man of the Treaty* (Dublin: Irish Academic Press, 1995), pp. 51–87.

306 'This means war': Jones, *Whitehall Diary*, vol. 3, p. 176.

19: TREATY

page

307 'No one could': 'Mr Lloyd George Tells First Story From Within', NLI, MS 498.

308 Collins as a life-saver: *Cork Examiner*, 5 Dec. 1921. In fact Collins did nothing (there was nothing he could do), but his role was puffed up anyway.

'hand to Ulster': Dail cabinet minutes, 3 Dec. 1921, NA, DE 1/3.

309 'AG said': Childers Diary, 3 Dec. 1921, TCD, 7814(5).

310 'Collins did not': Mrs Stack statement, WS 418.

Collins's annotations: MS Notes by Mr Michael Collins re. 2nd Revise of Treaty Proposals, 2 Dec. 1921, NA, DE 2/304.

311 'people of Ireland': *Private Sessions*, 23 Aug. 1921, p. 57.

Agreement on the oath: Dail cabinet minutes, 3 Dec. 1921, NA, DE 1/3.

312 'When our meeting': O Murthuile memoir, p. 166, UCD, P7a/209.

'more sneers': Childers Diary, 4 Dec. 1921, TCD, 7814(5).

313 'I had': Collins memo on interview with Lloyd George, 5 Dec. 1921, NA, DE 2/304.

Griffith arranges meeting: Jones, *Whitehall Diary*, vol. 3, pp. 180–81; Collins memo on interview with Lloyd George, 5 Dec. 1921, NA, DE 2/304.

314 'said I wished': Collins memo on interview with Lloyd George, 5 Dec. 1921, NA, DE 2/304.

'things were so strenuous': Griffith's Memo on Two Sub-Conferences, 5, 6 Dec. 1921, NA, DE 2/304.

315 'the power of conviction': *Debate on the Treaty*, 19 Dec. 1921, p. 49.

'It was well understood': Ibid., p. 30.

At the start: This account of the two final subconferences of 5/6 Dec. is based on Griffith's and Barton's notes, NA, DE 2/304; Jones, *Whitehall Diary*, vol. 3, p. 182; Record of the Negotiations, PRO, CAB 43/4.

316 'cold and dreamy': *Irish Independent*, 6 Dec. 1921.

'could never give up': Ibid., 5 Dec. 1921.

'Never': Ibid., 6 Dec. 1921.

317 'there was much': *New York Times*, 6 Dec. 1921.

Kathleen McKenna: 'In London with the Treaty Delegates', *Capuchin Annual*, 1971, p. 329.

'as if he was going': Winston Churchill, *The World Crisis: The Aftermath* (London: Thornton Butterworth, 1929), p. 306.

'I don't know': *Irish Independent*, 6 Dec. 1921.

Barton amazed: Barton draft lecture, TCD, 1093/10.

'Home to drama': Childers Diary, 5 Dec. 1921, TCD, 7814(5).

318 'We agreed': Ibid., 6 Dec. 1921.

'First of all': Barton statement, WS 979.

'that he would feel': *Sunday Press*, 3 Oct. 1971.

'he stood': Ibid.

319 'He stated': Ibid., 26 Sept. 1971.

'Our opposition': Ibid., 3 Oct. 1971.

Dan McCarthy: McCarthy statement, WS 722.

320 Dirty work and stabbed in the back: O Murthuile memoir, pp. 161–7, UCD, P7a/209; Barton lecture, TCD, MS 1093/12.

322 Collins to Art O'Brien: Sadly, Collins's letter of 7 Dec. 1921 seems to have disappeared, but O'Brien's detailed reply of the 8th – from which much of Collins's argument can be reconstructed – can be found in the Art O'Brien Papers, NLI, MS 8425.

20: The Speech

page

323 'Michael Collins' appearance': *Irish Times*, 17 Aug. 1921.
    'I expect trouble': *New York Times*, 9 Dec. 1921.

324 'Dev head on hands': Childers Diary, 8 Dec. 1921, TCD, 7814(6).

325 'Strangely enough': Mrs Stack statement, WS 418.
    'it was not': Childers Diary, 8 Dec. 1921, TCD, 7814(6).
    'intimidated': Ibid.
    'if there was': Mrs Stack statement, WS 418.
    'strongly reproached': Childers Diary, 8 Dec. 1921, TCD, 7814(6).
    'to come into line': Ibid.

326 'He had worked': Ibid.
    'In a contest': Ibid.

328 'I think nobody': *Debate on the Treaty*, 4 Jan. 1922, p. 246.
    'The question': Ibid., 14 Dec. 1921, p. 6.

329 'I as a public representative': Ibid., 19 Dec. 1921, p. 20.
    'it is only': *Private Sessions*, 14 Dec. 1921, p. 125.
    'plain soldiers': Ibid., 17 Dec. 1921, p. 225.
    'the man': Ibid., p. 226.
    'a stepping stone only': Ibid., p. 242.

330 'a jumping off point': Ibid., p. 263.
    'The whole object': Ibid., p. 272.
    'the Gaelic civilization': Griffith's speech, *Debate on the Treaty*, 19 Dec. 1921, pp. 20–23. At the battle of Kinsale (Cork) in 1601, English forces effectively defeated those of the Earl of Tyrone, Hugh O'Neill, and his Spanish allies.
    'to the world': Ibid., p. 23.
    'I am against': De Valera's speech, ibid., pp. 24–7.

331 'a good speech': *New York Times*, 20 Dec. 1921.

332 'He looked': *Freeman's Journal*, 20 Dec. 1921.
    'he finished': *New York Times*, 20 Dec. 1921.
    'a torrent': *Freeman's Journal*, 20 Dec. 1921.
    'A dark December': *Irish Independent*, 20 Dec. 1921.
    'The answer': Collins's speech, *Debate on the Treaty*, 19 Dec. 1921, pp. 30–36.

336 'a most able': Ibid., p. 36.
    'He spoke passionately': *Irish Independent*, 20 Dec. 1921.
    'Michael Collins': *New York Times*, 20 Dec. 1921.

337 Frank Drohan etc.: *Freeman's Journal*, 6–7 Jan. 1922.
    'the man who made the army': *Private Sessions*, 17 Dec. 1921, p. 267.

338 'trying to tell': *Debate on the Treaty*, 20 Dec. 1921, p. 57.

338 'What is good enough': Ibid., 20 Dec. 1921, p. 81. This phrase may first
have been used by an anonymous member of a crowd outside the
Mansion House on 8 Dec.
'Michael Collins': Ibid., 21 Dec. 1921, p. 114.
'But suppose': Ibid., 6 Jan. 1922, p. 290.
'He is merely': Ibid., 7 Jan. 1922, p. 326.

339 'Except for war': Ibid., 21 Dec. 1921, p. 108.
Childers as chief adviser to de Valera: *New York Times*, 11 Jan. 1922.
Collins defended free speech: Ibid., 5 Jan. 1922, p. 265.
'Mr M. Collins': Ibid., p. 410. The exact wording of the exchange varies in
different accounts.

340 'Traitors and cowards!': *Freeman's Journal*, 11 Jan. 1922.
'redoubtable': *New York Times*, 11 Jan. 1922.
'I am reported': *Freeman's Journal*, 11 Jan. 1922. See also Piaras Beaslai,
Michael Collins: Soldier and Statesman (Dublin, Talbot, 1937), 423–4.
This is a condensed and slightly amended version of the earlier
biography.
'damned Englishman': *Debate on the Treaty*, 10 Jan. 1922, p. 416.

21: LOVING MICHAEL COLLINS

page

341 'A delightful dinner': Juliet Duff to Leonie Leslie, 23 Jan. 1922,
Georgetown University Archives, Shane Leslie Papers, Box 11, Folder
17.
'There is a suggestion': *Debate on the Treaty*, 3 Jan. 1922, p. 184.
'Some time': Ibid., p. 190.

342 'Hazel had': Elizabeth, Countess of Fingall, *Seventy Years Young* (Dublin:
Lilliput, 1937, 1991), p. 403.

343 'I don't think': Collins to O'Brien, 24 June 1920, NLI, MS 8426.
'I note': Ibid., 26 Feb. 1921.
'the abominations': Ibid., 4 June 1921, NLI, MS 8430.
'Shrewd': O'Connor, *Big Fellow*, p. 19.

344 'an admirer': General Nevil Macready, *Annals of an Active Life* (London:
Hutchinson, 1924), vol. 2, p. 603.
'No restrictions': G. Coffey to Collins, 24 July 1914, UCD, P123/43.
'Met Miss C': Draft letter, n.d., UCD, P123/29.
Susan Killeen: Coogan, *Michael Collins*, pp. 20–21.
'I succeeded': O'Deirg (ed.), 'Oh! Lord the Unrest of the Soul', pp. 21–2.
'had great hopes': Collins to Stack, 19 Sept. 1918, Kilmainham Gaol
Archives, 18 LR 1B 13 04.
'the lady': Collins to Stack, 7 Oct. 1918, NLI, MS 17,090.

345 'Is Mickel': Fitzpatrick, *Boland's Irish Revolution*, p. 148.
'I often think': Helen (surname not given, but addressed from Granard) to
Collins, n.d., LHCMA, Epitome No. 53/2567. The sentence is

345 underlined, but it is unknown if this is owing to Helen adding steamy
   significance to her words or to a titillated epitomizer.
'give you that chance': Collins to Kiernan, 21 Aug. 1921, O Broin and O
   Heigheartaigh (eds.), *In Great Haste*, p. 14. The best account of the
   Collins–Kiernan–Boland triangle is in Fitzpatrick, *Boland's Irish
   Revolution*, pp. 251–5.
'I told M': Fitzpatrick, *Boland's Irish Revolution*, p. 236.
'Why not marry': Kiernan to Collins, 1 Dec. 1921, O Broin and O
   Heigheartaigh (eds.), *In Great Haste*, p. 80.
346 'I am not': Collins to Kiernan, 30 Nov. 1921, ibid., p. 77.
'At times': Kiernan to Collins, 10 Feb. 1922, ibid., p. 122.
347 'Why is he afraid': Kiernan to Collins, 28 June, ibid., p. 196.
'Well, lovie': Kiernan to Collins, received 26 June 1922, ibid., p. 195.
348 'all very nice': Collins to Kiernan, 26 June, ibid.
'there was keen': *Irish Independent*, 10 Oct. 1921.
'Shouted out': Ibid., 12 Oct. 1921. The young women in the front row are
   shown in a photograph in the next day's issue.
'girls . . . pursued him': Tom Jones, *Lloyd George* (London: Oxford
   University Press, 1951), p. 191. Robert Barton describes girls kissing him
   in Murdoch's 'How Lloyd George'. One can imagine what other 'favours'
   may have been sought, but as to this our witnesses are silent.
349 'The Irish leaders': *Irish Independent*, 8 Dec. 1921.
'When the speakers': Ibid., 6 Mar. 1922.
350 'obviously a leader': J. M. Barrie to Mrs Hardy, 12 Jan. 1922, http://
   www.jmbarrie.co.uk, JMB/L146.
'not at all': Fingall, *Seventy Years Young*, p. 409.
'The Mahatma': O'Shiel statement, WS 1770.
351 Hazel Lavery: Sinead McCoole, *Hazel: A Life of Hazel Lavery 1880–1935*
   (Dublin: Lilliput, 1996), pp. 63–107. Tim Pat Coogan has much of
   interest to say: *Michael Collins*, pp. 288–91.
Lavery's political role: John Lavery, *The Life of a Painter* (London: Cassell,
   1940), pp. 213–14.
352 Collins reassured Kitty: O Broin and O Heigheartaigh (eds.), *In Great
   Haste*, p. 88, and Collins to Kiernan, 28 May 1922, ibid., p. 176.
'the most devoted couple': Margaret Gavan Duffy statement, WS 712.
Moya's first impressions: Forester, *Lost Leader*, p. 101; MacEoin, *Survivors*,
   pp. 405–6.
'As she was not well': Robert Brennan statement, WS 779.
353 Regular correspondents: Collins Letter Book 1919, NLI, MS 8426. This
   mentions letters to both Moya and Crompton. Also, among the captured
   correspondence epitomized in PRO, CO 904/24/3, were private letters
   from Moya.
'He never stayed': Brennan statement, WS 779.
'Her talk': Margaret Gavan Duffy statement, WS 712.
Crompton on the payroll: NLI, MS 31,703.

353 'She had lived': Nancy Wyse-Power statement, WS 732.
'The lieutenants': Brennan statement, WS 779.

354 Moya claimed they were lovers: Lis Phil, *Signe Toksvig's Irish Diaries 1926–1937* (Dublin: Lilliput, 1994), pp. 303, 317.

22: CEO

page

355 'Among the various': Macready, *Annals*, p. 603.
'broadly and agreeably': *Irish Independent*, 17 Jan. 1922.
'Surrender': PG minutes, 16 Jan. 1922, NA, G1/1.

356 'abject humiliation': *Freeman's Journal*, 17 Jan. 1922.
'Mr Collins indicated': PG minutes, 16 Jan. 1922, NA, G1/1.

357 'my government': See, for example, *Irish Independent*, 29 June 1922.
City Hall offices: *Irish Independent*, 24 Jan. 1922.
Collins's timetable: Conference on Ireland with Irish Ministers, 5 Feb. 1922, p. 1, PRO, CAB 43/6.

358 'We want': *Irish Independent*, 18 Apr. 1922, reprinted in Collins, *The Path to Freedom*.

359 'the absence': Collins to O'Brien, 12 Jan. 1921, NLI, MS 8426.
'we shall be': Memo General Situation, 26 July 1922, UCD, P7/B/28.

360 'If we were in charge': Proceedings of Cttee on Financial Relations, 19 Oct. 1921, NA, DE 2/304.

361 'try to put': Proceedings of Extraordinary Ard Fheis, UCD, P150/580, p. 47.
'I am in favour': Ibid., p. 108.

362 'if they did not have': Conference on Ireland, 5 Feb. 1922, p. 17, PRO, CAB 43/6.
Collins's motion: Ard Fheis agenda, *Irish Independent*, 2 Feb. 1922.

363 'true democratic constitution': D. H. Akenson and J. F. Fallin, 'The Irish Civil War and the Drafting of the Free State Constitution', part 1, *Eire–Ireland*, spring 1970, p. 23. See also J. Anthony Gaughan (ed.), *Memoirs of Senator James G. Douglas (1887–1954) Concerned Citizen* (Dublin: UCD, 1998), which includes notes written by Collins: pp. 85–6.

364 Oriel House: Testimony to Army Inquiry by Charles Russell (UCD, P7/A/C/28), David Neligan (UCD, P7/A/C29), Eamon Broy (ibid.); Eunan O'Halpin, *Defending Ireland: The Irish State and Its Enemies Since 1922* (Oxford: Oxford University Press, 1999), pp. 11–15. For examples of their activities, see *Irish Independent*, 5, 25 June 1922.
New police force: Liam McNiffe, *A History of Garda Siochana* (Dublin: Wolfhound, 1997), pp. 11–30; O'Halpin, *Defending Ireland*, pp. 4–8.
Collins promised no purges: *Irish Independent*, 16 Jan. 1922.
Finance a superministry: Fanning, *Department of Finance*, pp. 30–51.

366 'Protestant proletariat': 'The so-called Ulster "Question"', UCD, P7/B/28.
'Capitalism has come': Collins, *The Path to Freedom*, pp. 78–9.

366 'our people': For example, in Collins's memo on the 'Partition Act', 15 Jan. 1921, NA, DE 2/266.

Collins in Armagh: *Irish Times*, 5 Sept. 1921.

367 'freedom of choice': Conference, Fifth Session, 17 Oct. 1921, NA, DE 2/304.

'any kind': Collins to Louis Walsh, 7 Feb. 1922, NLI, MS 3486.

'English interference': *Irish Independent*, 6 Jan. 1922.

'in good will': Ibid., 26 Jan. 1922.

368 'they would give way': Ibid., 2 Feb. 1922.

'strained and anxious': Ibid., 3 Feb. 1922.

'we are giving': Ibid.

'a policy': PG minutes, 30 Jan. 1922, NA, G1/1.

369 Collins's photo opportunities: See, for example, the *Cork Examiner*, 14 Mar. 1922, which includes photos of Collins coming from mass and sitting on a new tractor at the Ford factory. Such posed pictures would be repeated frequently in various newspapers in the coming months.

370 'It is all over': *Irish Independent*, 15 Apr. 1922.

'We did nothing': Collins to Kiernan, 14 Apr. 1922, O Broin and O Heigheartaigh (eds.), *In Great Haste*, p. 159. This may be misdated.

'burst of confidence': Kiernan to Collins, 26 Apr. 1922, ibid., p. 167.

'I have known it': Collins to Kiernan, 26 Apr. 1922, ibid., p. 168.

'stone age plebiscite': *Irish Independent*, 1 May 1922.

'We opened': Notes of Meeting at University College, 18 and 19 May 1922, UCD, P7b/28.

372 'We had pleasant': *Dail Eireann Official Report*, 19 May 1922, p. 478.

'deep earnestness': Sean O'Kelly memoirs, NLI, MS 27,707, p. 336.

'I should like': Collins to O'Kelly, 2 May 1922, NA, DE 2/574.

'We haven't got': O'Kelly memoirs, NLI, MS 27,707, p. 337.

'There was heated argument': Ibid., p. 338.

373 'He seemed to me': Blythe statement, WS 939.

'it seems certain': Collins to Chartres, 5 May 1922, NA, S9242.

'a triumph': *Freeman's Journal*, 24 May 1922.

23: PROMISES

page

375 'Meeting him': Mark Sturgis [Assistant Under-Secretary of Ireland] Diary, vol. 5, 13 Nov. 1922, PRO 30/59.

'They were not': PG minutes, 25 May 1922, NA, G1/2.

376 'Asked whether': *Freeman's Journal*, 18 Apr. 1922.

Post-Treaty IRA: Florence O'Donoghue, *No Other Law* (Dublin: Anvil, 1954), pp. 208–46; Michael Hopkinson's invaluable *Green vs. Green* (Dublin: Gill & Macmillan, 1988), pp. 58–76; Hart, *IRA and Its Enemies*, pp. 112–17, 262–9.

378 'a mental reserve': J. J. O'Connell memoir, NLI, MS 22,126.

378 Jobs for the boys: See Fearghal McGarry's superb biography, *Eoin O'Duffy: Self-Made Hero* (Oxford: Oxford University Press, 2005).

Two jobs for Boland: Fitzpatrick, *Boland's Irish Revolution*, p. 302.

379 'lukewarm way': Hopkinson, *Green vs. Green*, p. 64; Blythe statement, WS 939, pp. 138–9.

'present': *Irish Independent*, 27 Apr. 1922.

'when he entered': O'Connell memoir, NLI, MS 22,126.

380 'God help them!': Collins to Kiernan, 14 Apr. 1922, O Broin and O Heigheartaigh (eds.), *In Great Haste*, p. 159.

381 'certain details': Anon. memo, n.d., Desmond Fitzgerald Papers, UCD, P80. This memo outlines pro-Treaty forces' actions in Northern Ireland in 1922. Much has been written on Collins's northern policies – see Eamon Phoenix, *Northern Nationalism: Nationalist Politics, Partition and the Catholic Minority in Northern Ireland 1890–1940* (Belfast: Ulster Historical Foundation, 1994), pp. 167–251, and his 'Michael Collins – The Northern Question 1916–1922', in Doherty and Keogh (eds.), *Michael Collins*; Hopkinson, *Green vs. Green*, pp. 77–88; Coogan, *Michael Collins*, pp. 333–85; McGarry, *Eoin O'Duffy*. To be clear, they have reached different conclusions from mine as to Collins's involvement in decision-making and violence.

'We will do': C/S to O/C Midland, 11 Feb. 1922, quoted in anon. memo, n.d., UCD, P80.

'They were not . . . official': Peter Woods, quoted in McGarry, *Eoin O'Duffy*.

Sligo kidnappings: Michael Farry, *The Aftermath of Revolution* (Dublin: UCD, 2000), p. 191.

382 'Collins has had': Cope to Tom Jones, 8 Feb. 1922, PRO, CAB 21/254.

'I had to hustle': Padraic O'Farrell, *The Sean MacEoin Story* (Cork: Mercier, 1981), p. 78. For the other releases, Collins to Cope, 19 July 1922, UCD, P7/B/27.

'there would be': McGarry, *Eoin O'Duffy*.

383 'Peace is today declared': *Irish Independent*, 1 Apr. 1922.

'It seems to us': Northern Advisory Cttee meeting in Dublin, 11 Apr. 1922, NA, S1011.

384 'as an alternative policy': Dail cabinet minutes, 21 Mar. 1922, NA, DE1/4.

Mulcahy's arms deal: see the discussion in the Dail on 8 Mar. 1928 regarding the legal responsibility of the Army Finance Officer.

'carrying out a campaign': Transcript of Ulster Advisory Cttee meeting, 15 May 1922, NA, S1011.

'a staggering blow': Deputation memorial, UCD, P7a/145; *Irish Independent*, 19 May 1922.

385 'the army for long': O'Shiel memo, 6 Oct. 1922, UCD, P7/B/287.

Final IRB meeting: First-hand accounts can be found in the O'Donoghue Papers, NLI, MS 31,333; 31,421(2).

'could not announce': Minutes of adjourned meeting of Supreme Council

385 and County and Division Centres, 19 Apr. 1922, O'Donoghue Papers, NLI, MS 31,250.

386 'deal with outside areas': Cabinet minutes, 16 May 1922, Martin S. Gilbert (ed.), *Winston S. Churchill: Companion*, vol. 5 (Boston: Houghton Mifflin, 1978), p. 1892.

'a case may perhaps': Memo to each member of the Defence Council, 21 Apr. 1922, UCD, P7/D/28.

387 1922 election: *Irish Independent*, 3, 7, 8 June 1922; Michael Gallagher, 'The Pact General Election of 1922', *Irish Historical Studies*, 1979.

388 'spirit of the agreement': *Irish Independent*, 9, 10 Jun 1922.

389 'I am not hampered': Ibid., 15 June 1922.

'support the agreement': Ibid., 16 June 1922.

'a political manifestation': Ibid., 26 June 1922.

'I have a pretty bad week': Collins to Kiernan, 12 June 1922, O Broin and O Heigheartaigh (eds.), *In Great Haste*, p. 187.

390 'Outrage': Gilbert, *Churchill: Companion*, vol. 5, pp. 1892–3. See Thomas Towey, 'The Reaction of the British Government to the 1922 Collins–de Valera Pact', *Irish Historical Studies*, 1980.

'the Ministers': Gilbert, *Churchill: Companion*, vol. 5, p. 1891.

'Your absence': Churchill to Collins, 22 May 1922, ibid., p. 1898.

'the Hamlet': 'Our London Letter', *Irish Independent*, 27 May 1922.

Collins in the House of Commons: Ibid., 1 June 1922.

391 'Insolent': Notes attached to Memo General Situation, 26 July 1922, UCD, P7/B/28.

Constitutional negotiations: The Draft Irish Constitution: Record of the Negotiations Between British and Irish Ministers, PRO, CAB 43/7; Curran, *Birth of the Irish Free State*, pp. 200–218.

'Things are serious': Collins to Kiernan, 28 (?) May 1922, O Broin and O Heigheartaigh (eds.), *In Great Haste*, p. 175.

'bad beyond words'; 'awful' and 'ghastly': Collins to Kiernan, 30, 31 May; 1 June 1922 – ibid., pp. 176, 178, 183.

'pugnacious' etc.: Jones, *Whitehall Diary*, vol. 3, p. 203.

'wild animal' etc.: Ibid., p. 206.

'"All over the shop"': John Vincent (ed.), *The Crawford Papers: The Journals of David Lindsay Twenty-seventh Earl of Crawford* (Manchester: Manchester University Press, 1981), pp. 422–3.

392 'very highly strung': Jones, *Whitehall Diary*, vol. 3, p. 204.

'no troops': PG minutes, 3 June 1922, NA, G1/2.

393 vote transfers: Gallagher, 'The Pact General Election'.

'We are hopelessly beaten': Fitzpatrick, *Boland's Irish Revolution*, p. 301.

24: COMMANDER-IN-CHIEF

395 'Lady Lavery': Trevor West, *Horace Plunkett, Co-operation and Politics* (Gerrards Cross: Colin Smythe, 1986), p. 198.

According to Sean T. O'Kelly: O'Kelly memoirs, NLI, MS 27,707, p. 343.

MacEoin wedding: *Irish Independent*, 22 June 1922.

396 'the first real sleep': Collins to Kiernan, 26 June 1922, O Broin and O Heigheartaigh (eds.), *In Great Haste*, p. 195.

Cabinet meeting: PG minutes, 26 June 1922, NA, G1/2.

IRA proposals: Report, n.d., O'Donoghue Papers, NLI, MS 31,249; O'Donoghue, *No Other Law*, pp. 245–6.

'causing uneasiness': *Irish Independent*, 22 June 1922.

Wilson killing: Hart, *IRA at War*, pp. 194–220.

397 Henderson's raid: *Irish Independent*, 27 June 1922.

Ex-soldier killed: Ibid., 23–4 June 1922.

398 'necessary military action': Ibid., 28 June 1922.

'replied fiercely': *Voice of Labour*, 19 Aug. 1922.

399 Collins's warning: Blythe statement, WS 939, p. 144.

Collins's letter on Northern Ireland: Collins to Churchill, 28 June 1922, Gilbert, *Churchill: Companion*, vol. 5, p. 1923.

'It is one of': Collins to Kiernan, 23 July, O Broin and O Heigheartaigh (eds.), *In Great Haste*, p. 211.

400 Gearoid O'Sullivan: Blythe statement, WS 939, p. 144.

'behave decently': Collins memo, 2 July 1922, UCD, P7/B/28.

Collins as Minister of Defence: PG minutes, 1 July 1922, NA, G1/2.

401 Collins as Commander-in-Chief: Ibid., 12 July 1922.

'It would be well': Collins to Griffith, 14 Aug. 1922, UCD, P7/B/30.

The cabinet had to ask him: PG minutes, 14, 26 July 1922.

402 Mulcahy could not handle O'Duffy: McGarry, *Eoin O'Duffy*.

403 'some avenue': Collins memo, 2 July 1922, UCD, P7/B/28.

'Let them': C.-in-C. to Govt, 30 July 1922, UCD, P7/B/28.

'I myself think': Ibid., 25 July 1922.

'Much of the criticism': C.-in-C. to Acting Chairman, 25 July 1922, UCD, P7/B/28.

'I may say': C.-in-C. to Govt, 29 July 1922, UCD, P7/B/28.

National Army and IRA records: Hart, *IRA and its Enemies*, pp. 119–23.

404 'it was decided': PG minutes, 27 Aug. 1922, NA, G1/2.

Army control of censorship: Ibid., 28 July 1922; Cosgrave to Collins, 28 July, UCD, P7/B/1.

Control of Oriel House: C.-in-C. to D/I, 10 Aug. 1922, UCD, P7/B/4.

'subject to': PG minutes, 19 Aug. 1922, NA, G1/2.

405 'it is physically impossible': C.-in-C. to D/I, 5 Aug. 1922, UCD, P7/B/4.

'It should be done': C.-in-C. to Minister of Home Affairs, 13 July 1922, UCD, P7/B/30.

405 'My own opinion': Ibid., 15 July 1922.

'It is never sufficient': C.-in-C. to Staines, 19 July 1922, UCD, P7/B/38.

'The Intelligence Officer is wrong': C.-in-C. to C/S, 7 Aug. 1922, UCD, P7/B/1.

'There is undoubted': Ibid., 8 Aug. 1922.

406 'in going on inspections': C.-in-C. to QMG, 1 Aug. 1922, UCD, P7/B/1.

'Practically speaking': Ibid., 17 Aug. 1922 (3–5 p.m.), UCD, P7/B/3.

'On Thursday 15th August': Ibid., 17 Aug. 1922 (4 p.m.).

407 'one tin of meat': C.-in-C. to Gen. O'Duffy, 14 Aug. 1922, UCD, P7/B/40.

408 Illness denied: In the spring and summer of 1922 there were a large number of very deliberate reports in pro-Treaty papers such as the *Irish Independent* asserting Collins's energy, work rate and good health.

409 'One rumour': *New York Times*, 23 Aug. 1922.

'The choice': Ibid., 6 Aug. 1922.

410 'issue an immediate statement': PG minutes, 28 July 1922, NA, G1/2.

Collins's itinerary: Meda Ryan, *The Day Michael Collins Was Shot* (Swords: Poolbeg, 1989).

Ambush report: A/G, 1st Southern Div. to C/S, 24 Aug. 1922, Moss Twomey Papers, UCD, P69/93 (177). I am grateful to Brian Hanley for giving me a copy of this document.

411 Explanations for Collins's death: John Feehan, *The Shooting of Michael Collins: Murder or Accident?* (Cork: Mercier, 1981); Ryan, *The Day*; Coogan, *Michael Collins*, pp. 408–27; Edward O'Mahony, 'The Death of Michael Collins', *Magill*, May 1989; P. J. Twohig, *The Dark Secret of BealnaBlath* (Cork: Tower, 1991); Michael O Cuinneagain, *On the Arm of Time: Ireland 1916–22* (Donegal: 1992), pp. 79–105.

412 Four republicans killed: *Irish Times*, 28 Aug. 1922. See O'Halpin, *Defending Ireland*, pp. 35–6.

'Miss Collins': *Southern Star*, 2 Sept. 1922.

Conclusion

page

414 Absent fathers: Hart, *IRA and Its Enemies*, pp. 174–6.

Index